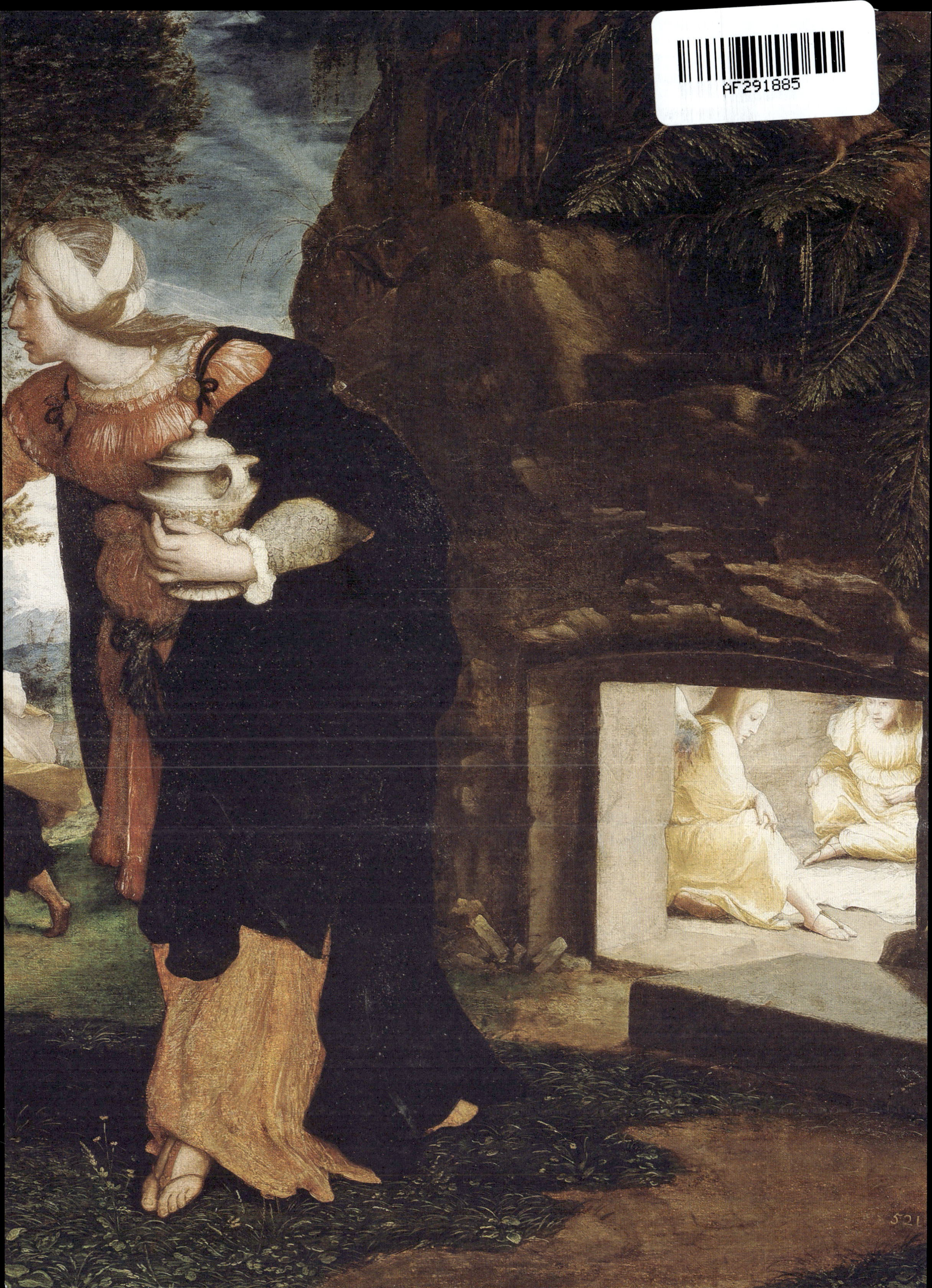

HOLBEIN

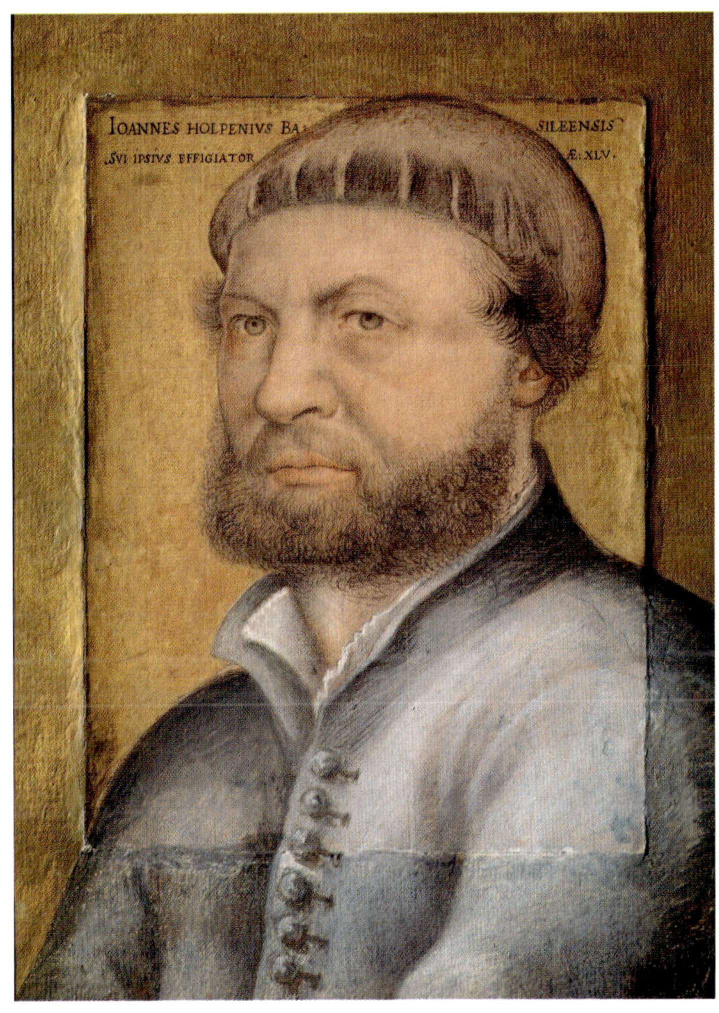

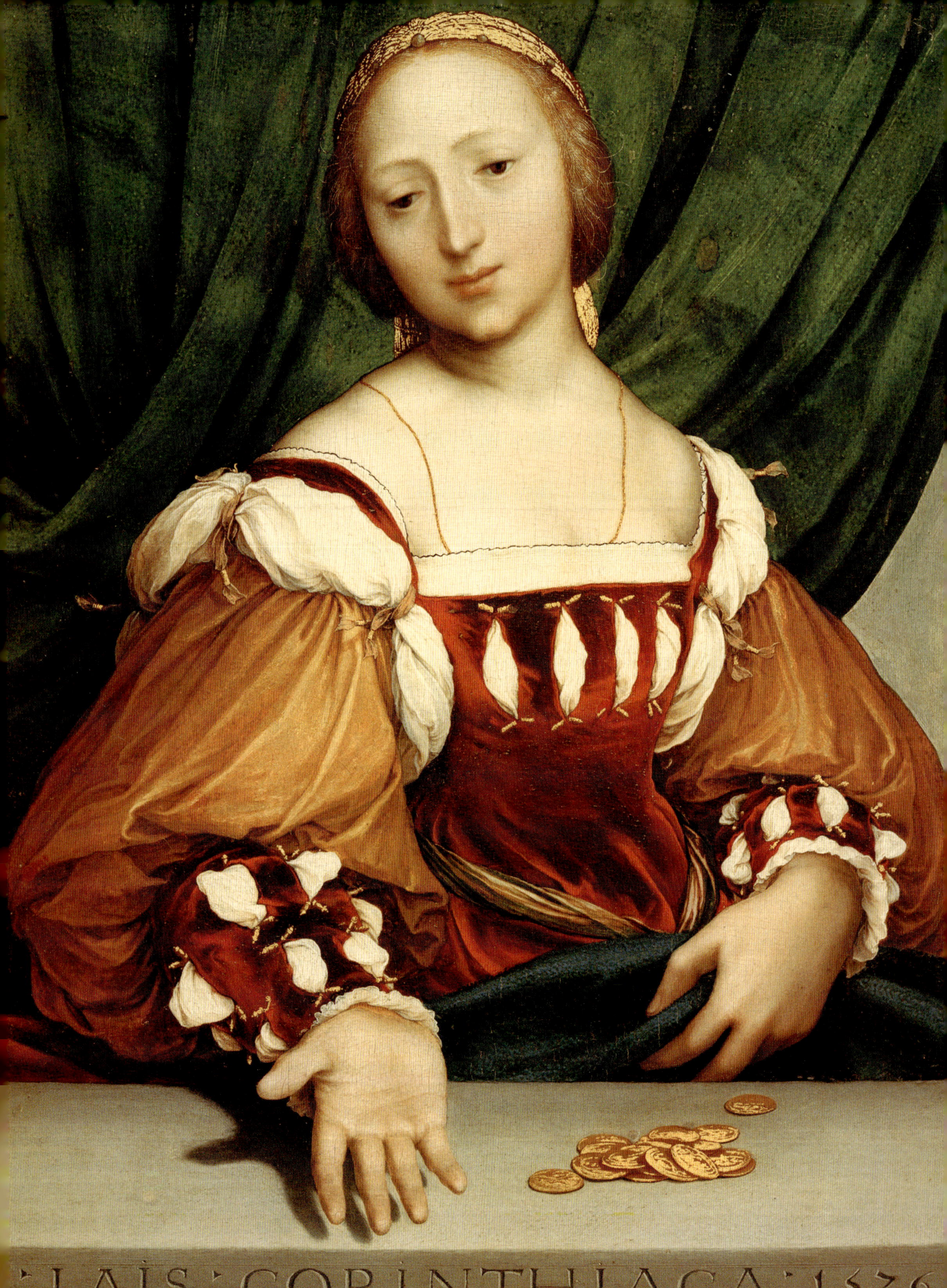
LAIS · CORINTHIACA · 1526

HOLBEIN

HIS LIFE AND WORKS IN 500 IMAGES

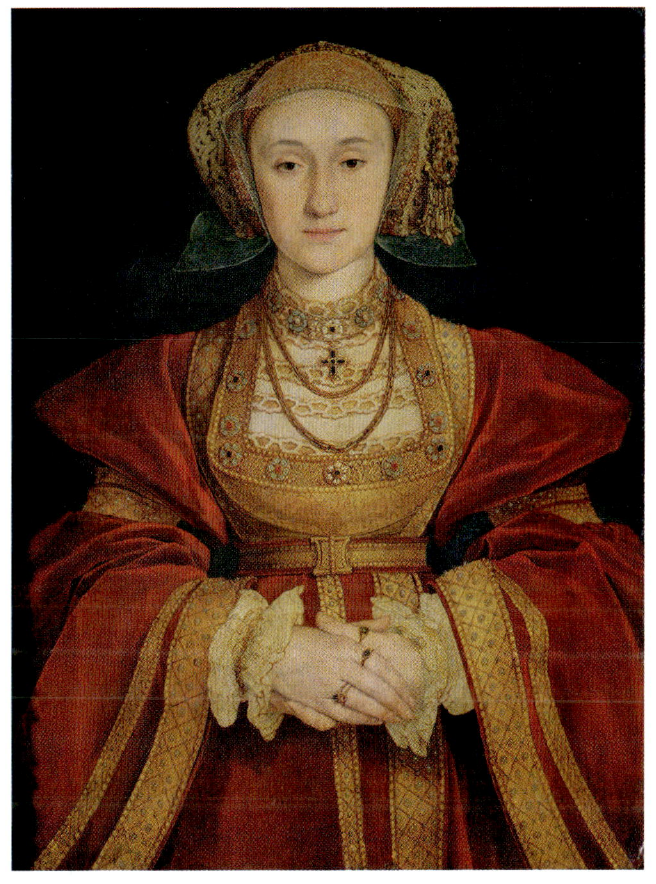

AN ILLUSTRATED EXPLORATION OF THE ARTIST IN CONTEXT,
WITH A GALLERY OF 300 PAINTINGS AND DRAWINGS

ROSALIND ORMISTON

LORENZ BOOKS

This edition is published by Lorenz Books,
an imprint of Anness Publishing Ltd

www.lorenzbooks.com; www.annesspublishing.com
info@anness.com

© Anness Publishing Ltd 2021

A CIP catalogue record for this book
is available from the British Library.

Publisher: Joanna Lorenzr
Designer: Nigel Partridge
Index: Elizabeth Wise
Production: Ben Worley

PUBLISHER'S NOTE
Although the information in this book is believed to
be accurate and true at the time of going to press,
neither the authors nor the publisher can accept any
legal responsibility or liability for any errors
or omissions that may have been made.

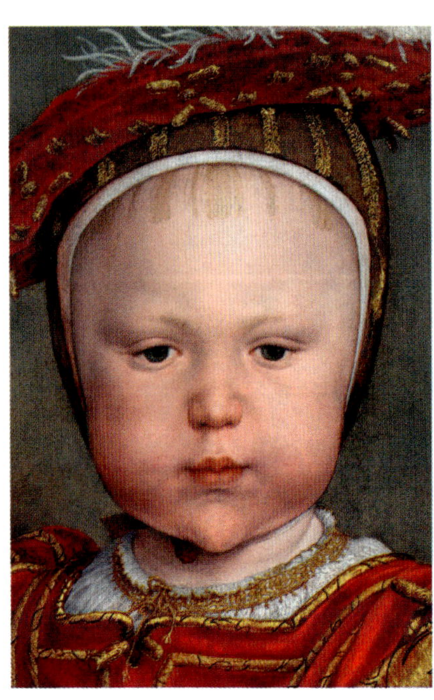

PRELIM IMAGES
Front endpaper: *Noli me Tangere*, see p.150; page 1: *Self-portrait*, see p.151; page 2: *Laïs Corinthiaca*, see p.140; page 3: *Anne of Cleves*, see p.235; page 4: *Edward VI, as Prince of Wales (detail)*, see p.233; page 5 top left: *Study of Sir Thomas More*, see p.155; page 5 top centre: *Drawing studies of Erasmus's hands*, see p.134; page 5 top right: *Study of Anna Meyer*, see p.145; back endpaper: *Sir Thomas More and his household, and his descendants*, see p.156–7.

ADDITIONAL PICTURE NOTES
[Display details where known are given in the Gallery section captions; the following notes supplement some of the History section captions. Key to abbreviations after the page number: t = top; b = bottom; c = centre; tl = top left, etc.]
13tl *The Goldsmith in his Shop*, Metropolitan Museum of Art, New York, USA; 13tr *Arnolfini Portrait*, National Portrait Gallery, London, UK; 13br *Self-portrait, aged twenty-eight*, Alte Pinakothek, Munich, Germany; 14 Augsburger Monatsbilder, Deutsches Historisches Museum, Berlin, Germany; 16tr *Self-portrait, Holbein the Elder*, Musee Conde, Chantilly, France; 16bl and 16br *Portrait of a Man, and Portrait of a Woman*, Thyssen-Bornemisza Museum, Madrid, Spain; 18 *Martyrdom of St. Sebastian*, Alte Pinakothek, Munich, Germany; 19tr *Sketch of Ambrosius and Hans*, Kupferstichkabinett, Berlin, Germany; 20 *Fountain of Life*, Museu Nacional de Arte Antiga, Lisbon, Portugal; 21t *The Martyrdom of the Apostle Bartholomew*, Old Masters Picture Gallery, Dresden, Germany; 21br *Studies of Four Heads*, University College London Art Museum, London, UK; 22t *Portrait of Jorg Schweiger*, Kunstmuseum, Basel, Switzerland; 22bl *Map of Basel*, Buyenlarge Archive; 25br *Crown of Thorns*, Stadeleches Kunstinstitut, Frankfurt am Main, Germany; 26b *Double Portrait of Hans and Barbara Schellenberger*, Wallraf-Richartz Museum, Cologne, Germany; 27t *Diptych of Maarten van Nieuwenhove, and Madonna and Child*, Memling Museum, St Johns Hospital, Bruges, Belgium; 27b *Portrait of a Young Man*, State Hermitage Museum, St. Petersburg, Russia; 28bl *The Creation*, Bible Society, London, UK; 29br *Portrait of Martin Luther*, Scholssmuseum, Weimar, Germany; 35tr *Virgin and Child with Pomegranate*, Kunsthistoriches Museum, Vienna, Austria; 36b *Lamentation of Christ*, Pinacoteca di Brera, Milan, Italy; 37t *The Deposition*, Galleria Borghese, Rome, Italy; 37b *The Crucifixion*, from Isenheim altarpiece, Musee d'Unterlinden, Colmar, France; 39b *The Seven Deadly Sins and the Four Last Things*, Museo del Prado, Madrid, Spain; 40b *Portrait of Erasmus of Rotterdam*, Palazzo Barberini, Rome, Italy; 41t *Statue of Desiderius Erasmus*, Rijkmuseum, Amsterdam, Netherlands; 45tl *Isabelle d'Este, Duchess of Mantua*, Musee de Louvre, Paris, France; 41b *The Presentation of Christ*, Hessisches Landesmuseum, Darmstadt, Germany; 47b *The Madonna of The Rocks*, Musee de Louvre, Paris, France; 49b *Henry VIII*, National Portrait Gallery, London, UK; 50b *Portrait of Sir Thomas More*, Private Collection; 50bl *Sir Thomas More*, Rubens, Private Collection; 51t *Portrait of Pieter Gillis*, Koninklijk Museum voor Schone Kunsten, Antwerp, Belgium; 53t *The Field of the Cloth of Gold*, Friedrich Bouterwek after Holbein the Elder, Château de Versailles, France; 53b *Greenwich Palace from the North Bank of the Thames*, Ashmolean Museum, University of Oxford, UK; 56 *Lady with an Ermine*, National Museum, Krakow, Poland; 57tl *Portrait of a Musician*, Pinacoteca Ambrosiana, Milan, Italy; 57bl *Mary Magdalene, detail from the Virgin and Child with St. Catherine and Mary Magdalene*, Giovanni Bellini, Gallerie dell'Accademia, Venice, Italy; 59b *Allegory of the Law and the Gospel*, Germanisches Nationalmuseum, Nuremberg, Germany; 63t *Portrait of a Merchant*, National Gallery of Art, Washington DC, USA; 66bl *Portrait of Jean de Dinteville*, Denver Art Museum, USA; 67tr *Moses and Aaron before Pharaoh*, Metropolitan Museum of Art, New York, USA; 67br *Portrait of Francis I*, Hôtel Carnavalet (Art Museum), Paris, France; 68t *Whitehall Palace*, Private Collection; 68b *Apelles*, Private Collection; 70b *Sketch of Queen Anne Boleyn under a canopy*, British Library, London, UK; 71t *Hever Castle*, Private Collection; 74tr *The Palace of Whitehall*, Stapleton Collection; 75bl *Henry VIII*, Denver Art Museum, USA; 79br *Drawing of Henry VIII in his privy chamber*, Private Collection; 80tr *Henry VIII, Metsys*, Metropolitan Museum of Art, New York, USA;

80bl *Henry VIII*, van Cleve, Royal Collection Trust, UK; 81bl *Francis I*, Musee du Louvre, Paris, France; 81br *Charles VII*, Musee du Louvre, Paris, France; 82tr *Edward VI, Duke of Cornwall*, Metropolitan Museum of Art, New York, USA; 83tr *Edward VI, King of England*, Musee du Louvre, Paris, France; 83bl *Edward VI as Prince of Wales, after Holbein*, The Wallace Collection, London, UK; 85tr *King Louis XII*, Welbeck Estate, Nottinghamshire, UK; 85bc *King Henry VII*, Welbeck Estate, Nottinghamshire, UK; 86br *Sir Philip Hoby*, Private Collection; 87tl *The Children of Christian II, King of Denmark*, Collection of the Earl of Pembroke, Wilton House, Wiltshire, UK; 87br *Portrait of Christina of Denmark*, Allen Memorial Art Museum, Oberlin College, Ohio, USA; 88tr *Chart of the North Sea and Zuyder Zee*, British Library, London, UK; 89tl *King Henry VII sees Anne of Cleves*, Private Collection; 89tr *Anne of Cleves*, Musee du Louvre, Paris, France; 90br *Guild Book of the Barber-Surgeons of York*, British Library, London, UK; 91tc *Barber Surgeon's Hall*, Private Collection; 91tr *The Barber-Surgeon*, Granger Collection; 91b *Satire of Barber-Surgeons*, Bibliotheque Nationale, Paris, France; 92t *newspaper*, British Library, London, UK; 92b *Map of Aldgate Ward*, London Metropolitan Archives, UK; 94 *The Family of Henry VIII*, Royal Collection Trust, Hampton Court Palace, UK; 95tl *Elizabeth I (possibly)*, Royal Collection Trust, UK; 95tr *Edward, Prince of Wales*, Royal Collection Trust, UK; 95br *Master Crewe as Henry VIII*, Private Collection; 97 *Sir Thomas More, his family, and descendants*, Victoria & Albert Museum, London, UK.

AKG
2/42l/140, 5c/134tr, 8/62/178, 12bl, 13br, 15tl 16bl, 16br, 17b, 18, 19t, 20, 22t, 23t/103, 26t/111t, 26b, 27t, 34t/107b, 33br/117t, 36t/122t, 36b, 37t, 38t, 38b, 39b, 43tl/137b, 44, 45tl, 46/166, 47, 52br/161b, 55tr/165, 55b/163t, 58t/119b, 58b/168t, 60/74, 63t, 64bl/162, 64br/185c, 67br, 69t/219, 69br/205t, 71bl, 73tl/220t, 73tc/224tl, 73br/207, 80tr, 80bl, 81bl, 81br, 82tr, 83tr, 91br, 92b, 95br, 106, 107t, 109t, 110t, 110b, 114tl, 117b, 118l, 118r, 119t, 128bl, 129, 133cr, 133tr, 136tl, 136tc, 136tr, 136cr, 136br, 137t, 137c, 138, 139l, 139r, 141, 167, 168b, 169t, 174c, 174b, 177t, 196tl, 205b, 206, 215bl, 216tr, 218b, 220t, 227t, 232c, 232b, 237br, 239b, 240, 241b, 242, 243, 249b

ALAMY
5r/45tr/98bl/145t, 6tl/121b, 6tr/246c, 7tr/19b, 12t, 21bl, 23c, 24bl, 24br, 25tr, 33tl, 33tr, 40tr/104–05(all), 43br, 49b, 50tr/154, 51b, 53c, 54, 55tl, 56, 57tl, 57br/99b/153/164, 63b, 66t, 66b, 67bl, 70t, 72, 76br, 77br, 78, 79bl/99t/230l, 85tl, 85tc, 85br, 90t, 91tr, 94, 97, 108(all), 111b, 114bl, 114br, 120, 132tl, 132br, 136bl, 136cl, 142, 143t, 143b, 144t, 145b, 146–49(all), 151, 153, 159b, 161t, 173, 175t, 176b, 179, 184b, 187t, 188t, 188c, 188b, 189t, 189b, 192b, 194t, 196tr, 201tl, 204t, 208t, 208c, 208b, 209b, 210bl, 213t, 213bl, 213br, 215tr, 217, 221, 223bl, 227c, 231, 237tl

BRIDGEMAN
1/93/251, 3/88/235, 5l/155t, 10/134l, 13tl, 13tr, 14, 15tr, 15br, 16tr, 17t, 21t, 21br, 22b, 24t, 25tl, 25br, 27b, 28bl, 28br, 29t, 29b, 30t, 30b, 31l, 31r, 34b, 35t, 37b, 40bl, 41br/135, 43bl/116, 45br, 48t, 48b, 49t, 50bl, 51t, 52br/152/160tl, 53t, 53b, 57bl, 59t/170, 65/182/185/186, 67t, 68tl, 68br, 69bl/223tr, 69bc/190tr, 70b, 71t, 71bl/209t, 74tr, 75tr/230, 75bl, 76bl/228l, 79t, 79br, 81tr/172/246tl, 83bl, 84, 85tr, 85bc, 85bl, 86tl/234, 86br, 87tl, 87br, 88tr, 89tl, 89tr, 90bl, 91tl, 92t, 95tl, 95tr, 98br/163b, 102, 109b, 115br, 122bl, 123bl, 123br, 144b, 150, 155c, 155b, 156, 158b, 159t, 159c, 160b, 169b, 174t, 176t, 177b, 181t, 184t, 190t, 190b, 191, 192t, 193t, 193b, 194b, 196br, 197t, 197bl, 198t, 198c, 198b, 199t, 199c, 199b, 200t, 200b, 201bl, 201br, 210tl, 210tr, 212, 213br, 214tr, 214bl, 216bl, 218t, 220b, 222tl, 222br, 223br, 226, 228tr, 228br, 229, 236t, 236c, 236b, 238t, 238b, 239t, 241t, 244, 247, 248t, 248b, 249t, 250c

With additional thanks to the museums and galleries who loaned images.

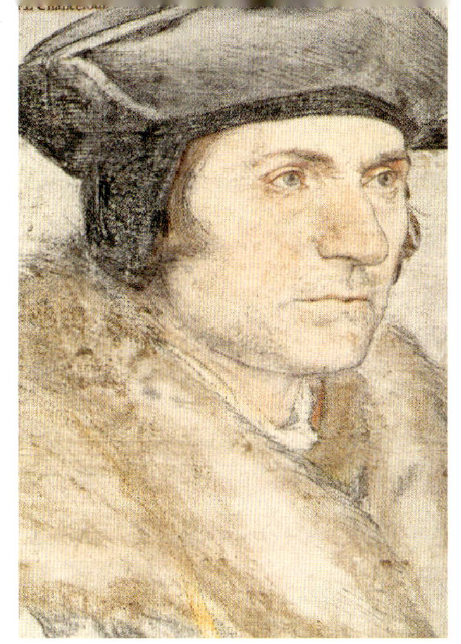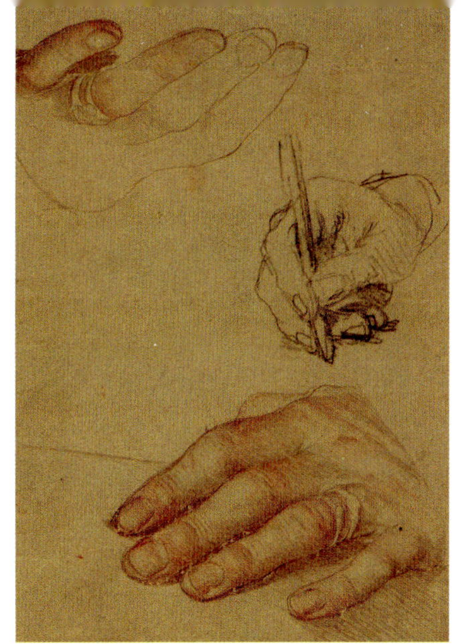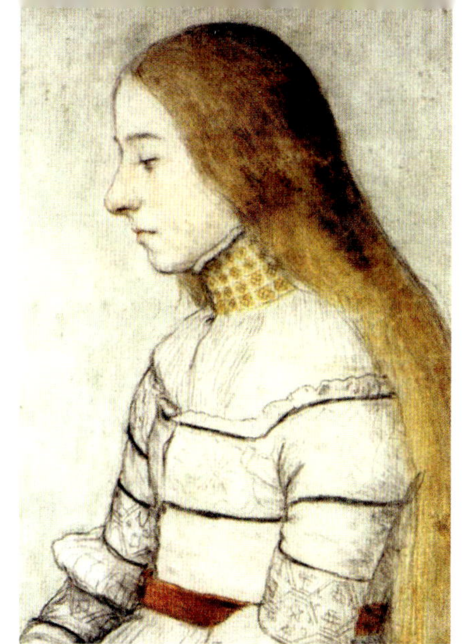

CONTENTS

Introduction   6

HOLBEIN: PAINTER   **8**

A LIFE IN ART   10

KING'S PAINTER   60

THE GALLERY   **100**

BASEL 1515–1526   102

LONDON 1526–28   152

BASEL 1528–32   166

LONDON 1532–43   172

Bibliography   252

Index   253

INTRODUCTION

Hans Holbein the Younger learned his craft from his father, a distinguished painter of religious art. The younger Holbein would become celebrated first in Basel, as one of the four greatest artists in Germany, then in England. He was acknowledged as the 'Apelles' of his time for the superb realism of his portraiture.

In 1497–98 in Augsburg, Bavaria, Germany, to the artist Hans Holbein 'the Elder' (c.1460/65–1524), and his wife, Barbara Holbein, née Burgkmair (c.1460/70–97/98), daughter of a painter Thomas Burgkmair, a second son was born. He was named Hans (Johannes), after his father, and today is differentiated by name from his father as Hans Holbein the Younger. His brother Ambrosius (c.1493/4–c.1519) was three years older. Together the boys grew up, watching and learning from their father, a distinguished painter with a successful artisan workshop.

The two children feature in paintings by Holbein the Elder, notably the triptych altarpiece *S. Paolo fuori le Mura*, 1504, where they appear with their father at the bottom right of the left panel (see detail, opposite). They are tenderly drawn by him in

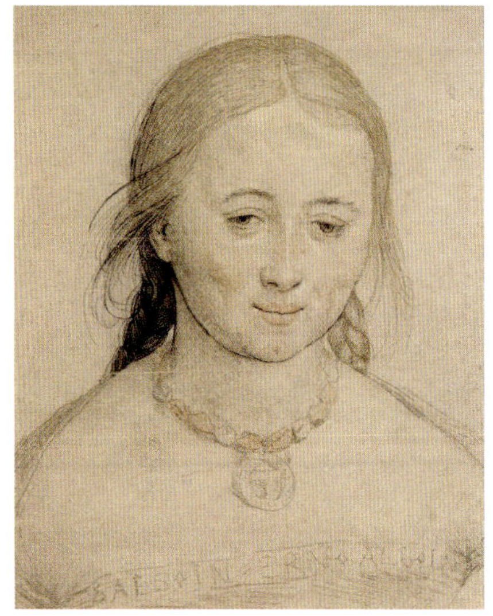

Ambrosius Holbein and Hans Holbein the Younger, 1511 (see page 19). The boys were destined to become painters in turn, working with their father on his commissions, carrying on a Holbein

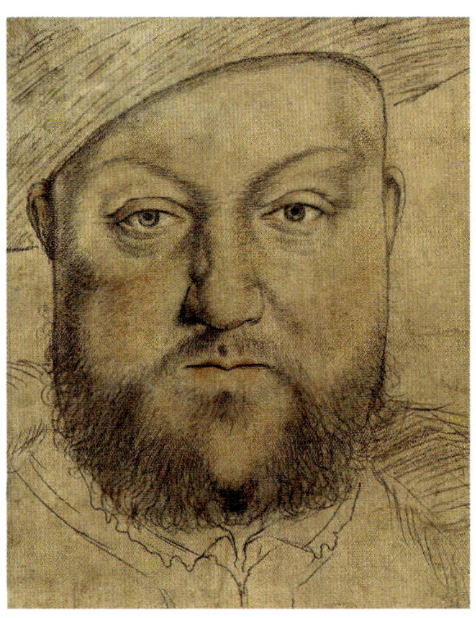

Above left and right: Holbein's skilled drawings captured each sitter's personality, from the shy gentle manner of the young woman, c.1520–22, to a character-revealing study of King Henry VIII, 1540.

TIMELINE

1497/8 Hans Holbein the Younger born in Augsburg, Bavaria, Germany.

1515 Travels as a journeyman to Basel, Switzerland, and probably enters the workshop of artist Hans Herbst.

1516 Hans Holbein the Elder leaves Augsburg, possibly travelling to Isenheim.

1517 Holbein the Younger travels to Lucerne.

1519 Holbein returns to Basel and is admitted to the Zunt zum Himmel (Basel Painters' Guild). He marries Elsbeth Binzenstock Schmidt. No records of Ambrosius Holbein after 1519.

1520 Holbein is elected Chamber-Master of the painters' guild. Obtains Swiss citizenship, aided by his marriage.

1523/4 Holbein travels to France, to seek commissions from the royal court of King Francis I. Hans Holbein the Elder dies.

1526 Via Antwerp, Holbein travels to England.

1528 Holbein returns to Basel in August, to maintain his citizenship.

1532 Holbein returns mid-year to London via Antwerp. He rents a house in Mayden Lane near St Paul's Cathedral.

1537 Holbein becomes court painter on an annual salary of £30.

1538 Holbein travels to paint Christina of Denmark, Louise of Guise and Anna of Lorraine as prospective brides for Henry VIII. He also visits Basel and returns to London via Paris, where he leaves his son Philipp apprenticed to goldsmith Jacob David.

1539 Holbein travels to Germany, to create a portrait of Anne of Cleves.

1540 Holbein's uncle Sigismund dies in Bern. The inheritance is accepted in Holbein's absence by his wife Elsbeth.

1541 Holbein becomes an English denizen.

1542/3 Holbein draws a self-portrait in chalks. He writes on it his age and that he is a burgher of Basel.

1543 Holbein designs his final work, a clocksalt to be presented to Henry VIII. He dies between the date of his Will (7 October) and its execution (29 November). He may have been buried in his parish church St Andrew Undershaft, or the church of St Katherine Cree, City of London.

tradition in the family-run workshop that included their uncle Sigismund Holbein (c.1470–1540).

It is presumed that the Holbein brothers undertook apprenticeships in their father's workshop in Augsburg. Holbein the Younger then travelled for work as a journeyman before settling in Basel, part of Switzerland, from 1515. He would ultimately divide his professional career between Basel and London, England. In Basel he became a member of the Painters' Guild on 25th September 1519. Established as a professional painter in the city, he set to work on a variety of commissions, which brought him recognition and respect. A few years later he travelled across Europe to further his career, residing in London from 1526–28, and returning in 1532.

During his time in England he became noted for realistic and intimate portraits, and drew the attention of Henry VIII's inner circle, resulting in prestigious commissions from influential

Right: A detail from the left wing of the altarpiece by Holbein the Elder for the church of S. Paolo fuori le Mura, shows the brothers Ambrosius and Hans in front of their father, observing Saul's baptism. (See also page 19.)

Below: A later etching of Hans Holbein the Younger, after a self-portrait by the artist.

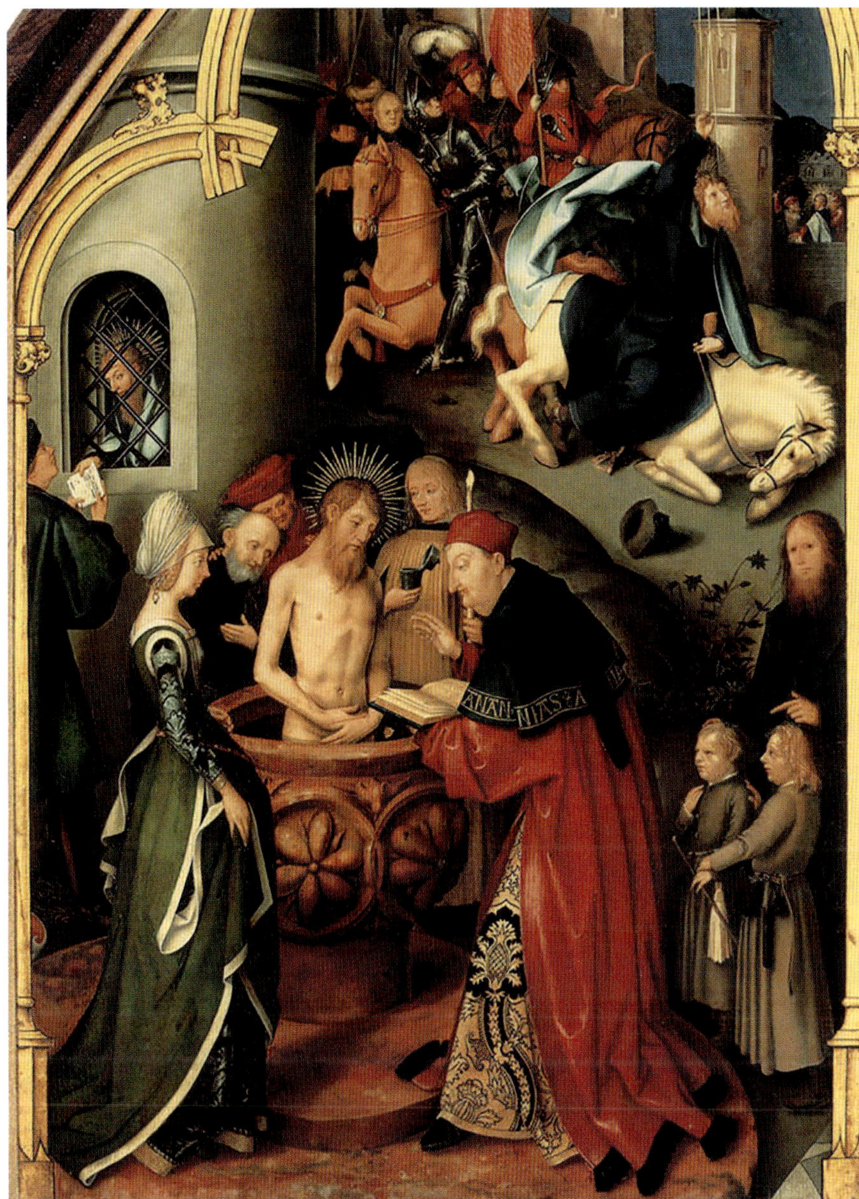

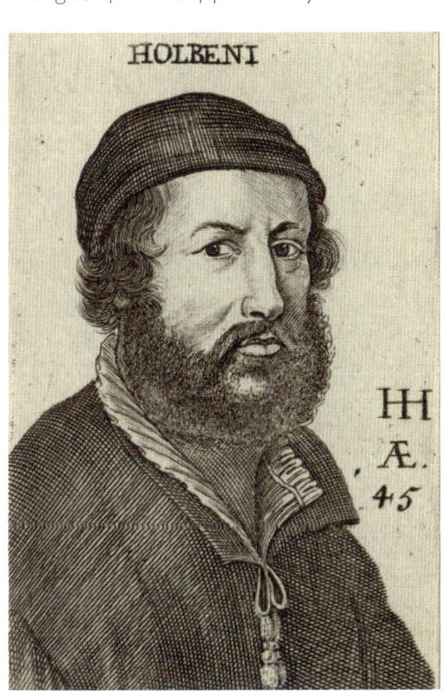

courtiers, and ultimately a salaried position as the King's Painter. Falling out of royal favour after the Anne of Cleves portrait debacle, he nonetheless kept working. He would die of illness in London in 1543, possibly from a widespread plague.

Hans Holbein the Younger lived through a traumatic period that saw the ruling Roman Catholic church split into Protestant Reformers and the Church of Rome. He witnessed the iconoclasm in Basel, which became a Protestant city in 1529. Holbein's clients were both of Protestant and Catholic disposition. He had to tread a delicate path, to please all, keep working and receiving commissions, and keep his head.

DISCOVERING HOLBEIN

Chronicling Holbein's life in detail is difficult as he documented very little himself, and what we know is pieced together from fragments – legal or financial records, letters and anecdotal references from friends and patrons, and of course what context can be ascertained from the works themselves. The difficulty of dating some works with accuracy is not confined to Holbein, but is typical of the period. There is additional complexity in attribution, where many works were copied by other artists, contemporary and later. Sometimes these copied works are our only representation of originals which have since been lost.

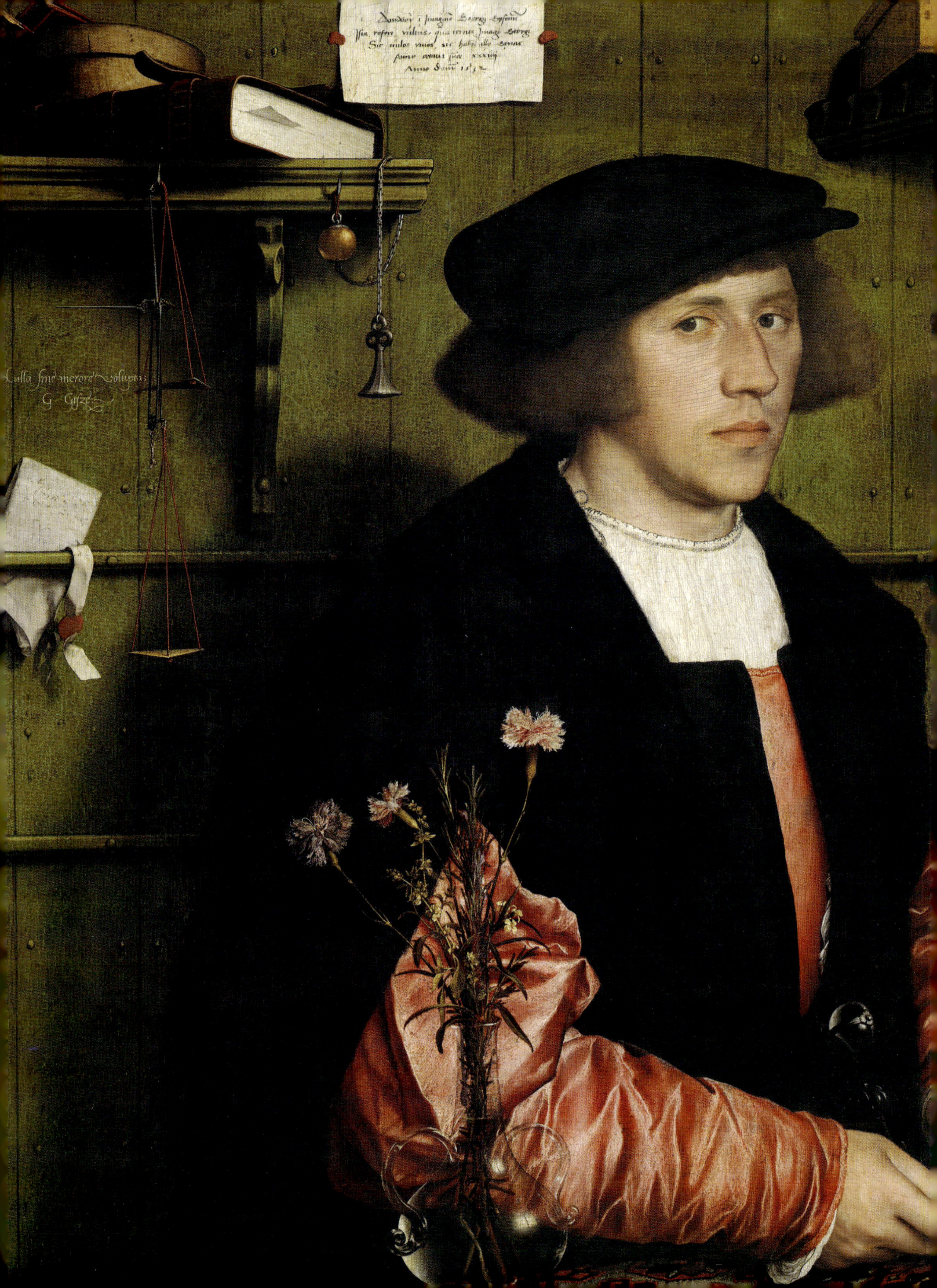

Distichon i[n] imaginem Georgy Gysenii
Ista refert vultus, quam cernis, Imago Georgi
Sic oculos vivos, sic habet ille genas
Anno ætatis suæ xxxiiij
Anno Dom. 1532
Nulla sine merore voluptas
G. Gisze

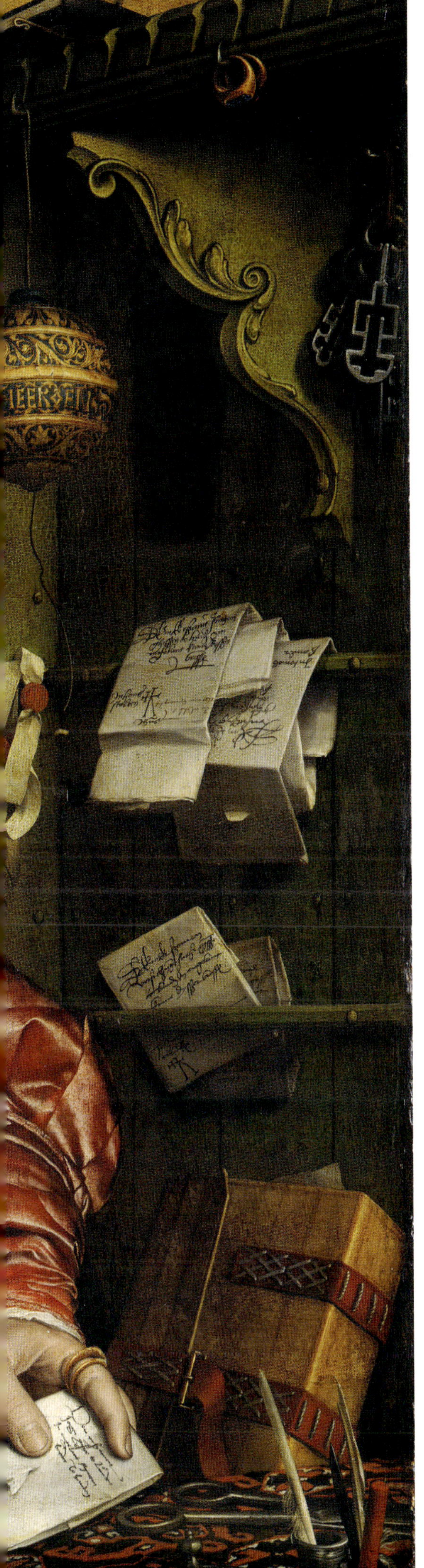

HOLBEIN: PAINTER

Hans Holbein the Younger's life is discovered through his artworks, his family, his patrons and the people who met him. Born into a family of talented artists, Holbein's future career was set at an early age. He learnt to be a draughtsman, a painter, a portraitist, and a designer for woodcuts. What could not be taught was his remarkable skill as a portrait painter that rose beyond that of his father and brother, uncle and cousins. From initiation in an Augsburg workshop as a youth, he would achieve high status as Painter to the King, at the English court of Henry VIII. Holbein had a talent to engage with his clients, proven by repeated commissions. He could capture a moment in time, from Erasmus sitting in his study in Basel, to rich Hanseatic merchants seated in their London offices. His gift as a painter was grounded in a sound knowledge of pigments, practical costings and time required to complete a work. In his lifetime he created a unique portfolio of groundbreaking work, predominantly in portraiture, that continues to astound today, near five centuries after his death.

Left: Portrait of the merchant Georg Gisze, 1532. Some of the notable commissions for Holbein when he arrived back in London were from the German Hanseatic League of merchants, based in Steelyard. This famous portrait shows Gisze in his office, surrounded by the trappings of his profession on the wall shelves — where his motto 'No joy without sorrow' hangs. In his hands he holds a letter.

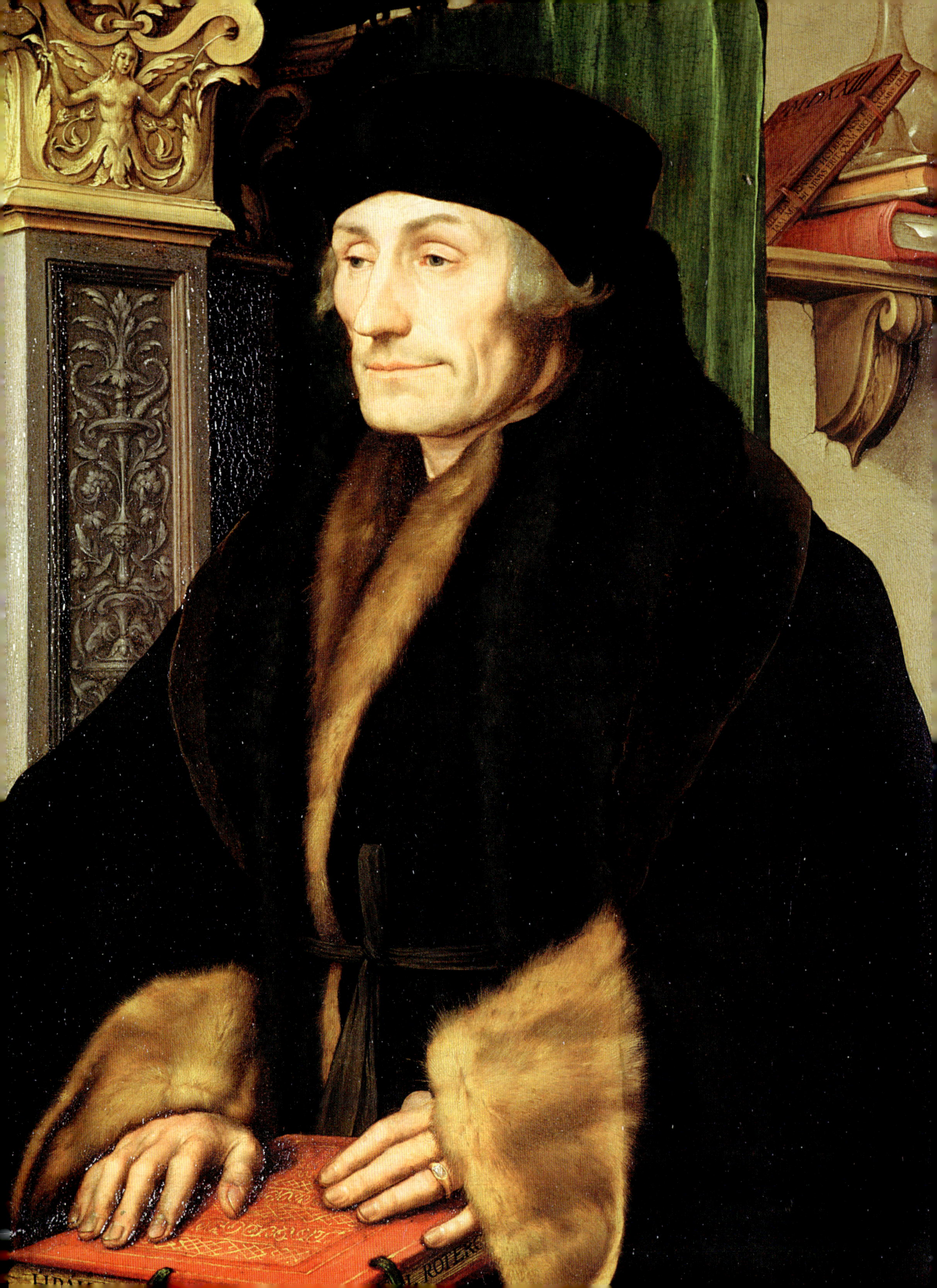

A LIFE IN ART

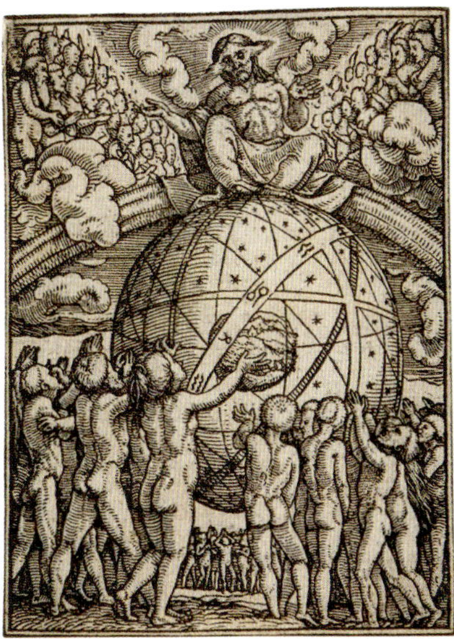

Hans Holbein the Younger was born surrounded by painters. His father Hans, his uncle Sigismund, uncle Hans Burgkmair, elder brother Ambrosius, and assistants in the Augsburg studio were his family unit. Here he learned to be a draughtsman and a painter. The city of his birth, Augsburg, was a wealthy commercial centre. Prestigious commissions for religious art, and a rising interest in portraiture, were directed at Holbein the Elder, a widely respected artist. At times, the family assisted in the completion of larger works, giving Ambrosius and the younger Hans time to discover which art forms suited them.

Holbein the Younger's move to Basel in 1515, centre of a prosperous print-publishing industry, broadened his knowledge and work in the field of illustration and woodcuts. He made useful contacts, establishing himself as 'a not unskilful painter', a dry understatement from the theologian Erasmus, whose portrait Holbein painted three times. From 1517, protests against the Roman Catholic church, led by protestant reformer Martin Luther, suppressed religious art in Basel. It was a difficult time for artists. After Holbein's non-productive work visit to France c.1523–24, and the death of his father in 1524, Holbein would leave his wife and young children in Basel and travel to England in 1526 to seek patronage from the English court and its king, Henry VIII.

Above: The Last Judgement, *the final scene in Holbein's 'Dance of Death' series of woodcuts, c.1523–26.*

Left: Portrait of Erasmus of Rotterdam, *1523, one of three portraits that Holbein painted of the Dutch philosopher, humanist scholar, and theologian Erasmus Desiderius Roterodamus (1466–1536).*

THE NORTHERN RENAISSANCE

A radical move toward narrative realism, described by art historians as a 'northern renaissance', emerged from the 1380s. The painting method was different to art evolving in southern Europe, but both were literary and artistic responses to the growing humanist movement and changing way of viewing the world.

The 'northern renaissance' refers to the emergence of naturalism in the art of northern Europe, instigated in the Netherlands and Germany. Moving away from the rigid traditions of medieval-era International Gothic, the new style of painting gradually spread through the rest of Europe. A cultural revolution was occurring, not only in literature but in the work of artists, goldsmiths, craftsmen, designers and decorators, builders and architects, printers and publishers. Holbein the Younger was in the second generation of painters to continue and develop in the new style.

NEW TECHNIQUES, NEW THEMES

A development in narrative realism can be seen in the first decades of 1300 in the work of Italian painters, an exemplar being the figurative naturalism of Giotto di Bondone's (1267–1337) frescoes in the Scrovegni chapel, Padua. The devastating spread of the 'Black Death' plague (1347–51) across Europe halted cultural patronage but when it returned, architects, artists and craftsmen were in demand. A strong economy in Germany provided ample funds for city

Below: The Iconoclasts, c.1530, print from a woodcut (coloured later), depicting the destruction of church art and objects during the Reformation.

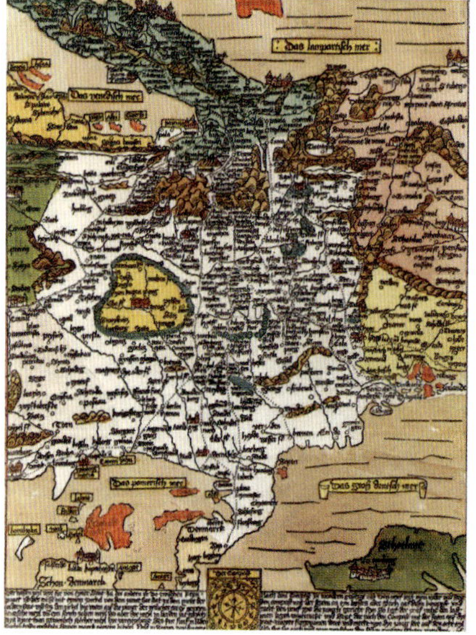

Above: Roadmap of central Europe c.1492, a woodcut by Erhard Etzlaub showing the network of trade routes at the time, linking Germany to southern Europe and to the north and west.

officials and patrons to commission new buildings and artworks, to enrich the communities.

Free movement allowed an exchange of knowledge in the creative arts, including paint practices. In Italy and southern European countries the most popular paint medium used by artists was the fast-drying egg tempera – paint pigments mixed with egg yolk – resulting in jewel-bright, colour-drenched works. In the northern Low Countries, painters changed to a different method using a slow-drying oil-based pigment thinly applied in layers, which allowed time to include microscopic detail.

The Reformation changed what writers could write, and what painters could paint; religious commissions dried up in Germany, the Netherlands and Belgium, due to Protestant reforms, but there was a surge in portraiture. The reduction in church work was why many left Germany, including Holbein, trying his luck in France and then England.

JAN VAN EYCK

The artist Jan van Eyck (active 1422; died 1441) was a key instigator of Early Netherlandish painting practice. His birthplace is unknown, possibly Maaseik, near Maastricht. He worked in Bruges and Lille under the patronage of Philip the Good, Duke of Burgundy. Other painters were Robert Campin (1378/79–1444), Rogier van der Weyden (1400–64), Petrus Christus (c.1410–73), Dieric Bouts (c.1415–75), Hugo van der Goes (1440–82), and the German painter Hans Memling (c.1440–94). They led the way toward a progressive realism in art through an innovative underdrawing paint technique, using monotone layers of a thin oil-based medium, allowing meticulously illustrated features. A build-up of translucent layers of thinly applied oil-based colour created the illusion of light and shadow, a luminosity reflected on faces, drapery, objects, walls, and landscape. Van Eyck worked quickly but the slow drying time allowed attention to detail. His masterpiece *Portrait of Giovanni Arnolfini and his Wife*, 1434, creates the illusion of real people in a solid space. Van Eyck autographed the work above the mirror 'Johannes de Eyck fuit hic' ('Jan van Eyck was here').

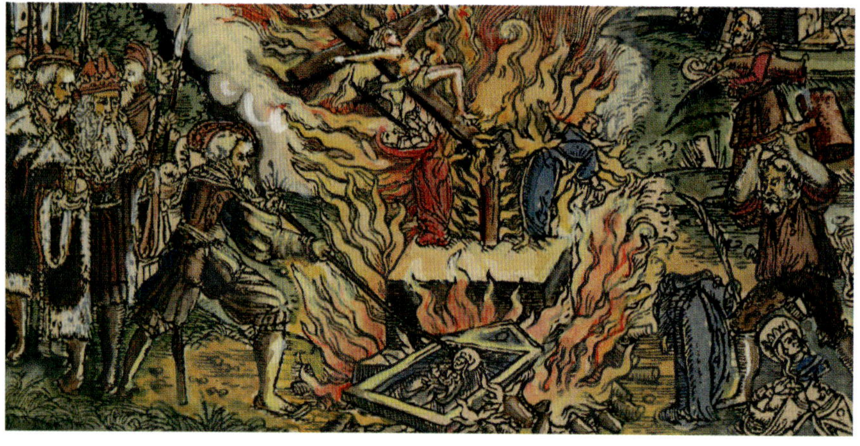

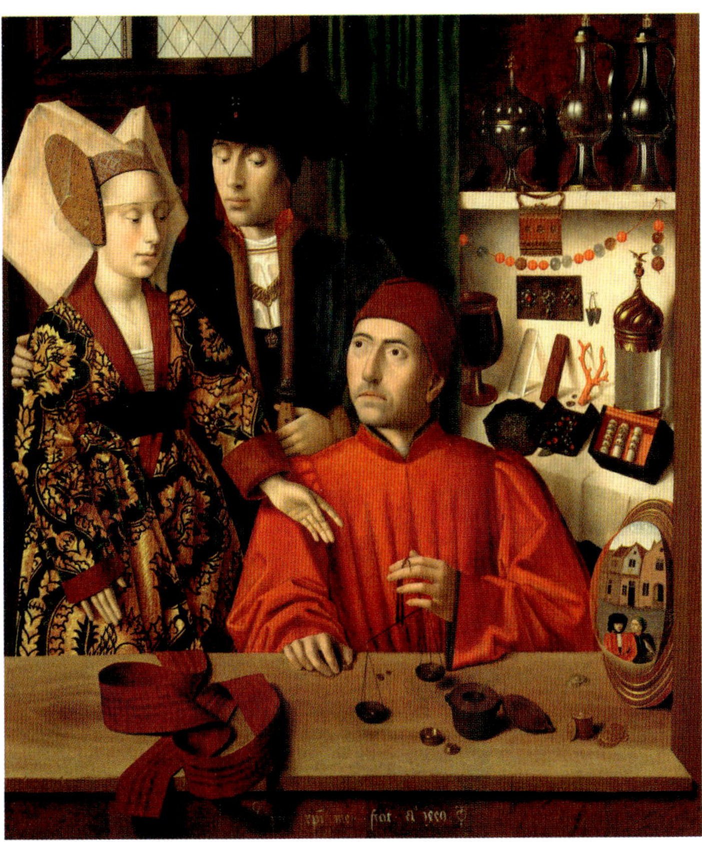

Above: The Goldsmith in his Shop, *1449, by Petrus Christus. Commissions for secular rather than religious works inspired artists to move away from the rigidity of static grouping and ornamentation.*

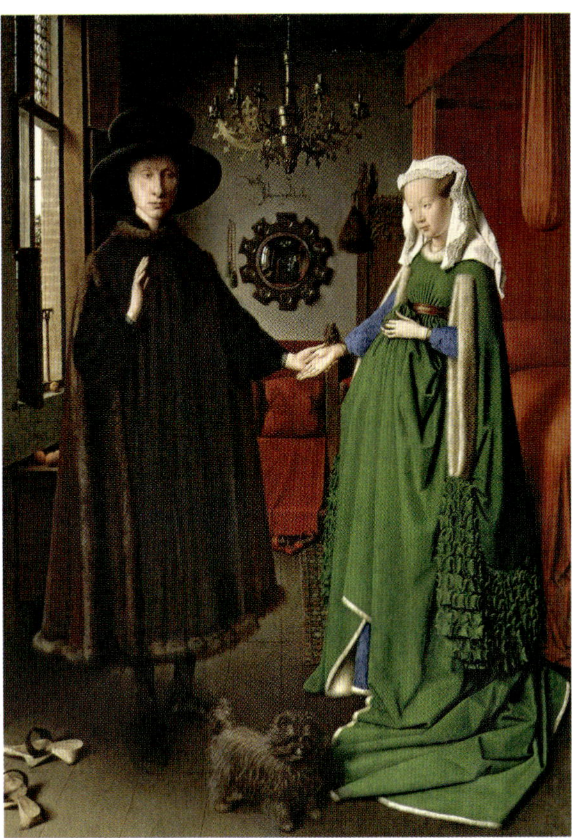

Above: Portrait of Giovanni (?) Arnolfini and his Wife (The Arnolfini Portrait), *by Jan van Eyck, 1434. The translucency, intricate detail and refracted light created a realism of photographic quality.*

A GERMAN RENEWAL

German painters, after apprenticeship, travelled as journeymen, not just for work but to learn from the skills of other artists. The painter Hans Memling spent 30 years of his professional life in the Hanseatic town of Bruges, gaining citizenship in 1465. Bruges, as the chief residence of the Dukes of Burgundy, was a wealthy city, flourishing as a centre of commercial trade and creative hub for artists. In Augsburg, Hans Holbein the Elder (c.1465–1524), although based in his native community, travelled for work. He adapted his style from the depictive International Gothic to the naturalism emanating from Italy and the painting methods of the Low Countries. Humanist realism is evident in other art of Germany at the time, including that of Martin Schongauer (c.1450/53–91) and Albrecht Dürer (1471–1528), as well as Hans and Ambrosius Holbein.

THE GOLDSMITH'S SHOP

An innovative painting by Petrus Christus in 1449 highlights the new painting method. The focal character is a goldsmith, serving a betrothed man and woman, who watch as he weighs gold wedding rings. The metal objects on the shelves gleam. The concave mirror in the forefront reflects two people in the street, bringing the outside world into the shop. Every detail, from the expressive facial features and the rich luminosity of the gold fabric of the woman's dress, created with oil and yellow pigment, to the shop's interior space and outside street-view, are carefully painted to create the illusion of reality. Hans Holbein the Younger would also use this compositional style, illustrating the tools of the sitter's profession, in his portraits of the Hanse merchants of London, for example *Portrait of Georg Gisze, 1532* (see pages 8 and 62).

Right: The Nuremberg-born painter *Albrecht Dürer created many portraits of himself, to advertise his skills, including the remarkable* Self-portrait aged twenty-eight, *1500.*

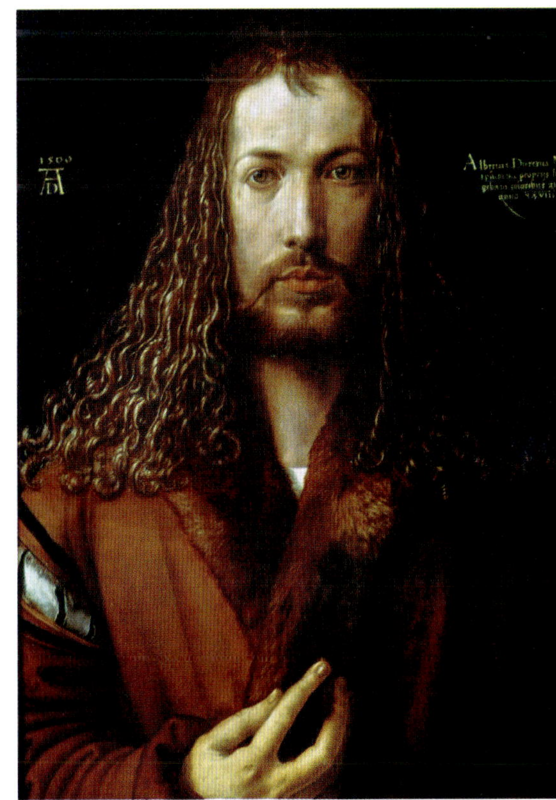

AUGSBURG

The city of Augsburg, in Bavaria, the home of the Holbein family, was founded in 15BC by the Romans who named it Augusta Vindelicorum after the Roman emperor Augustus (63BC–AD14). As an Imperial free city from the thirteenth century, it prospered through its valuable trade routes.

The Roman emperor Claudius (10BC–AD54) constructed a trade route through Augsburg to the north. After wars and changes of ownership, it became an Imperial free city in the thirteenth century under the auspices of the Holy Roman Emperor. Its geographic position, directly north of Venice, with roads to the Dutch and Scandinavian north, or west toward France and England, made it central to trade. In AD1500 Augsburg's population was about 45,000 to 50,000 inhabitants, though it declined to around 16,000 during the Thirty Years War, 1618–48.

Below: Augsburger Monatsbilder c.1531, by Jörg Breu is the first of four colourful depictions of the seasons in Augsburg, highlighting the beauty of the city.

A CITY OF TEXTILES AND PUBLISHING

In the era that the Holbein family lived in Augsburg it was an immensely wealthy city, built on its textiles and cloth trade and the publishing industry. Merchant families dominated city trade, particularly the capitalist merchant Fugger family, made rich from global commerce and trading, including copper and silver mining in Silesia, and monetary loans to kings – which would encompass King Henry VIII of England too. The Fugger family's close connections to the Vatican, and to the Royal courts, drew artists and craftsmen to the city. In addition, the banking dynasty of the Welser family shared in the domination of capitalist enterprises that made the city wealthy.

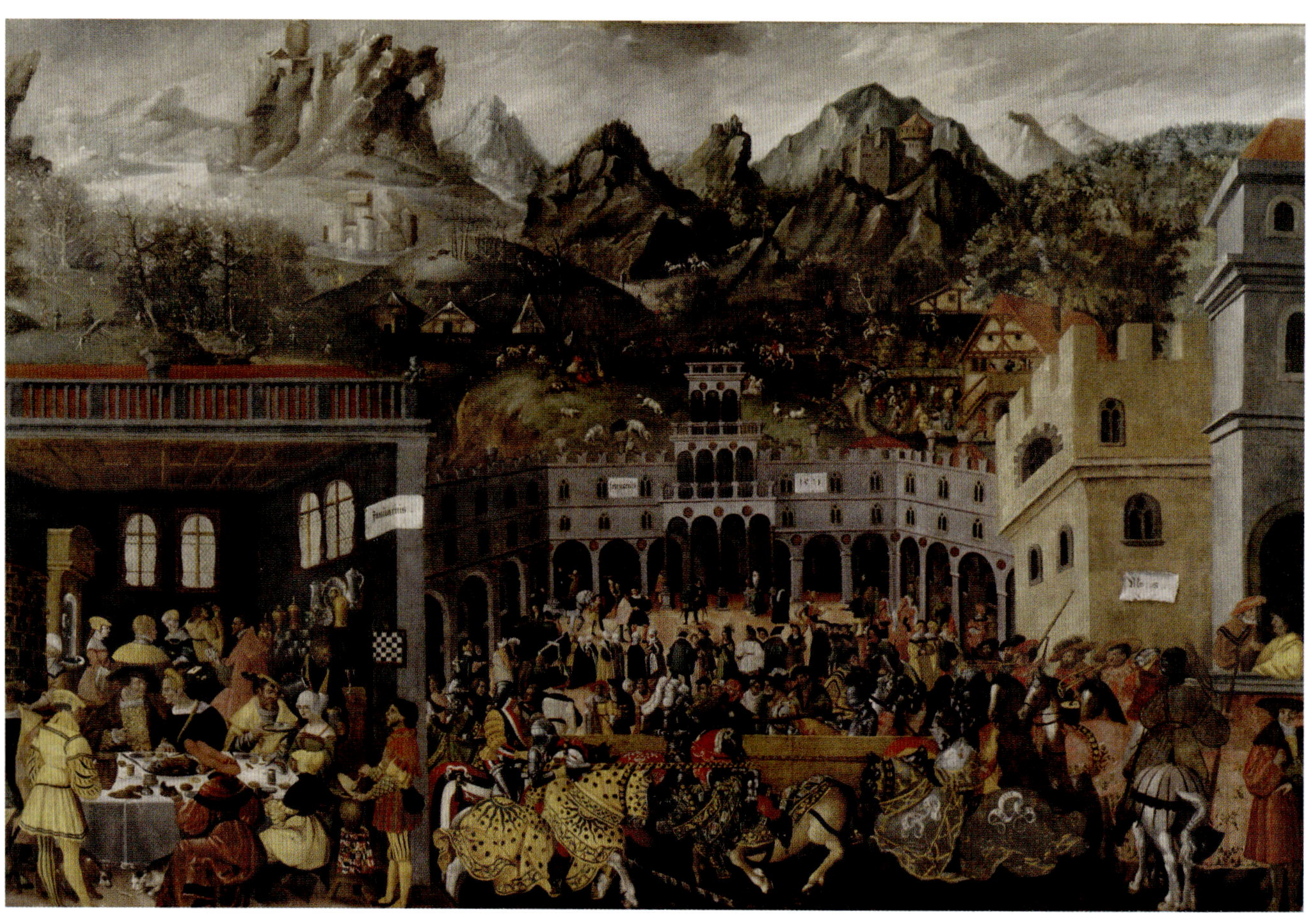

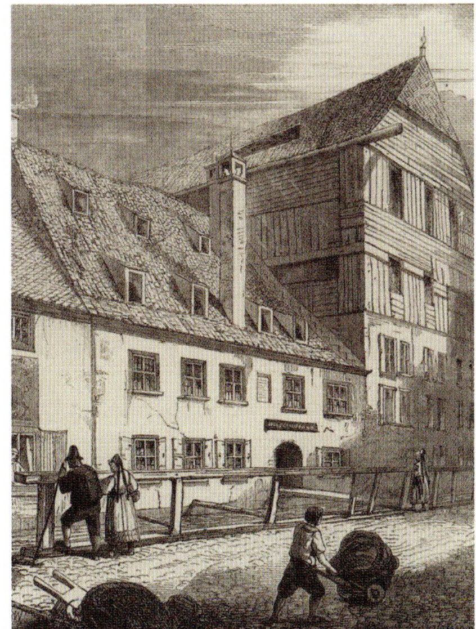

Above: A wood-engraving, dated 1859, of Hans Holbein the Elder's house in Augsburg, where it is said Holbein the Younger was born.

Augsburg was a city of cultural importance too. Much like the rich merchant-class Medici and Strozzi families in Florence with their close ties to banking, trade and the papal court, Augsburg reflected the significant rise of the merchant class, the development of the publishing print industry and the increasing status of the artist, in its buildings and works of art. The Holbein brothers grew up and worked surrounded by artisans, intellectuals, commercial entrepreneurs, and moneyed merchants.

JAKOB FUGGER

The Fugger family, rich merchants of the textile industry since the fourteenth century, was headed by Jakob Fugger II (1459–1525), who was drawn and painted by both Holbein the Elder and Younger. In monetary and power terms Jakob Fugger was considered the 'Cosimo de Medici' of Augsburg. At his death he had capital of two million gulden, a princely sum. (The archives in Augsburg hold letters from Fugger to Emperor Charles V – who was in his monetary debt – writing in 1523, 'It is also well known that Your Majesty without me might not have acquired the Imperial Crown, as I can attest with the written statement of all the

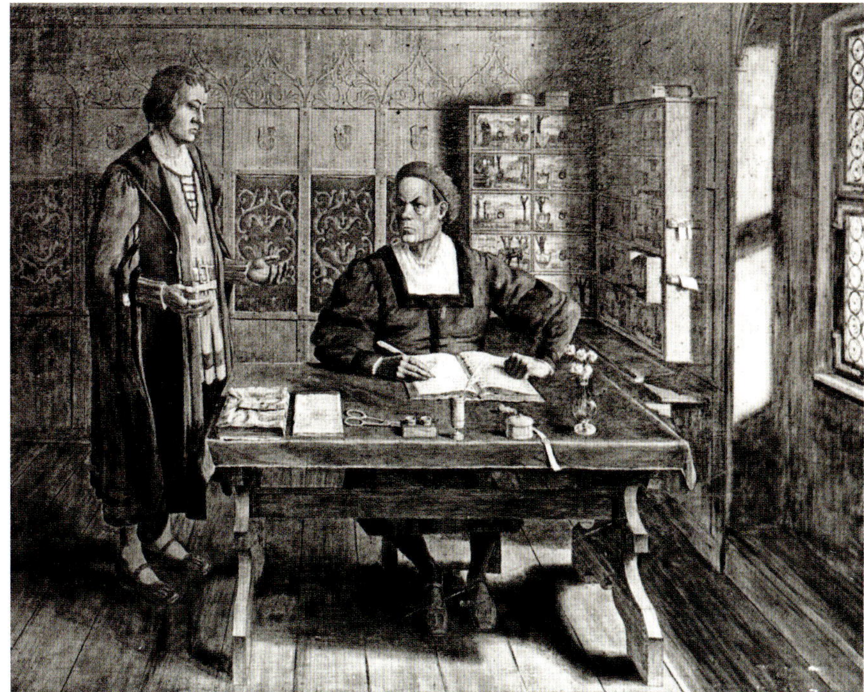

Above: Jakob Fugger and Matthäus Schwarz in the so-called Golden Orderly Room (Goldene Schreibstube) in Augsburg.

delegates of Your Imperial Majesty'.) The words reveal his powerful status, lending power to the nobility. Financially, the Fugger dynasty gave back to the city's community with the Fuggerei building development, a garden city of fifty cottages in Augsburg, which housed a hundred families, needy members of the community, at a low rent. These beautiful buildings are still used as social housing in the present day.

In Augsburg society one must include mention of Matthäus Schwartz (1497–1574), a well-dressed accountant working for Fugger, who kept a catalogue of everything he wore between 1520 and 1560, in *Klaidungsbüchlein* or *Trachtenbuch*, translated as 'Book of Clothes', the first fashion history book.

Below: A 1930 illustration of The Fuggerei, in Augsburg, which is the world's oldest housing complex. It is still in use. The charming 'garden city' of fifty cottages was established by the Fugger family.

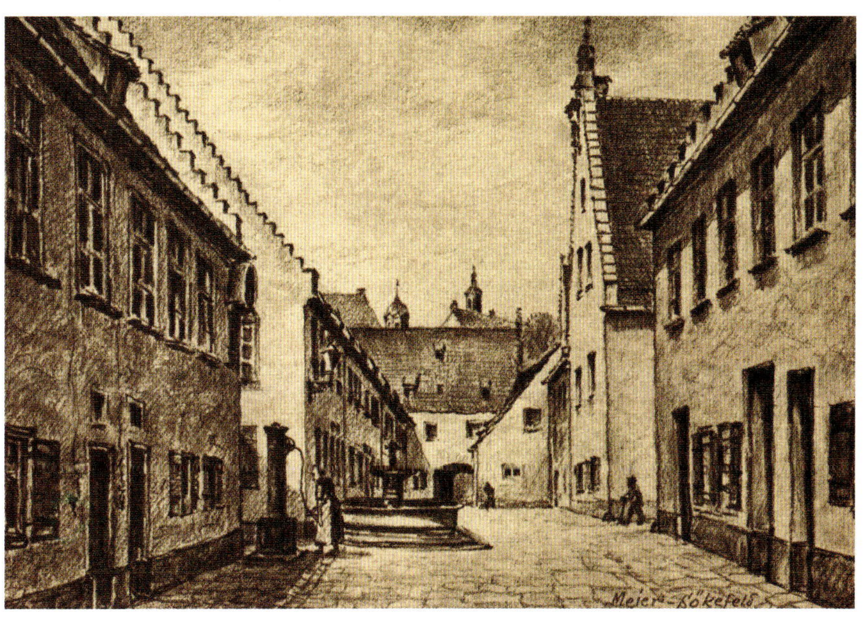

HANS HOLBEIN THE ELDER

The Elder Hans Holbein (1460/65–1524) was a highly distinguished painter, born and living in Augsburg. He ran a workshop of talented artists and apprentices, serving clients across Germany with commissions for altarpieces and singular religious works, occasionally portraits.

Hans Holbein the Elder was born in the free Imperial city of Augsburg, Swabia, in Bavarian Germany, in 1460/65, to Michael Holbein (1435–87), a prosperous leatherworker, and his wife Anna, née Mair. Hans was one of six children to the couple. His siblings were his younger brother Sigismund, also to become an artist, born c.1470, and sisters Mechthild (Matilda) born 1469, Ursula, born 1471, Anna, born 1473, and Marguerite (1475–1542).

Official papers record Holbein the Elder buying a house in Augsburg in 1493, possibly linked to his name in tax records the following year. The record refers to him as 'Hans Holbein the Painter, citizen of Ulm'. He was again recorded amongst the citizen population of Ulm in 1499, and Frankfurt in 1501, plus Basel and Alsace, and his native city of Augsburg. Through his mother Anna Mair, Holbein the Elder was related to noted artists and sculptors working in and near to Augsburg, including cousins Gregor Erhart, Paulus Erhart and Hans Daucher, all sculptors; and his painter-sculptor uncles, possibly Mair von

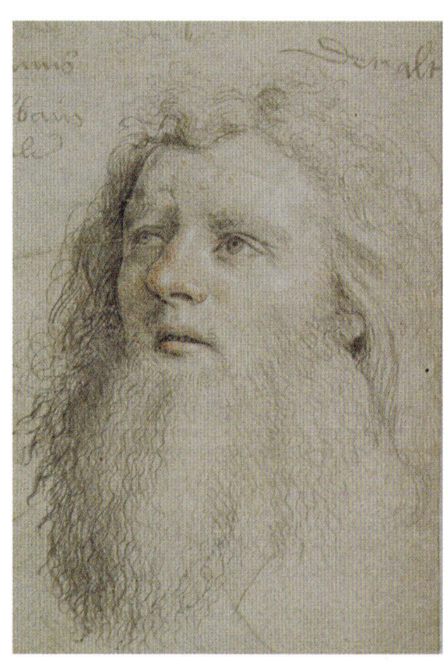

Below: These portraits of a woman and man by Holbein the Elder c.1518–20 are thought to have been a pair, with the woman placed on the left.

Right: This self-portrait drawing by Holbein the Elder c.1516 identifies the artist's strong facial features and clear eyes, with a full head of curly hair and lengthy beard.

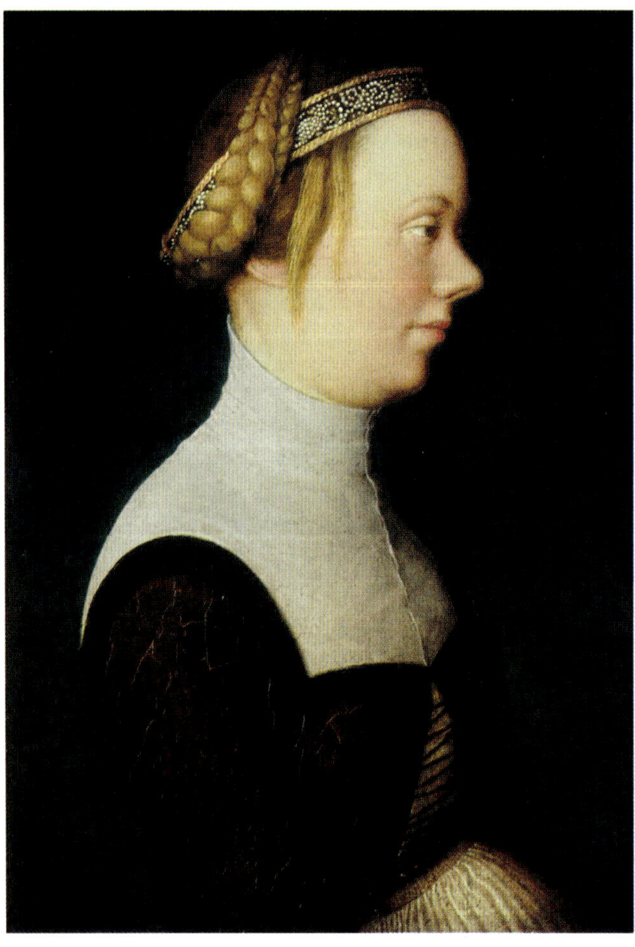

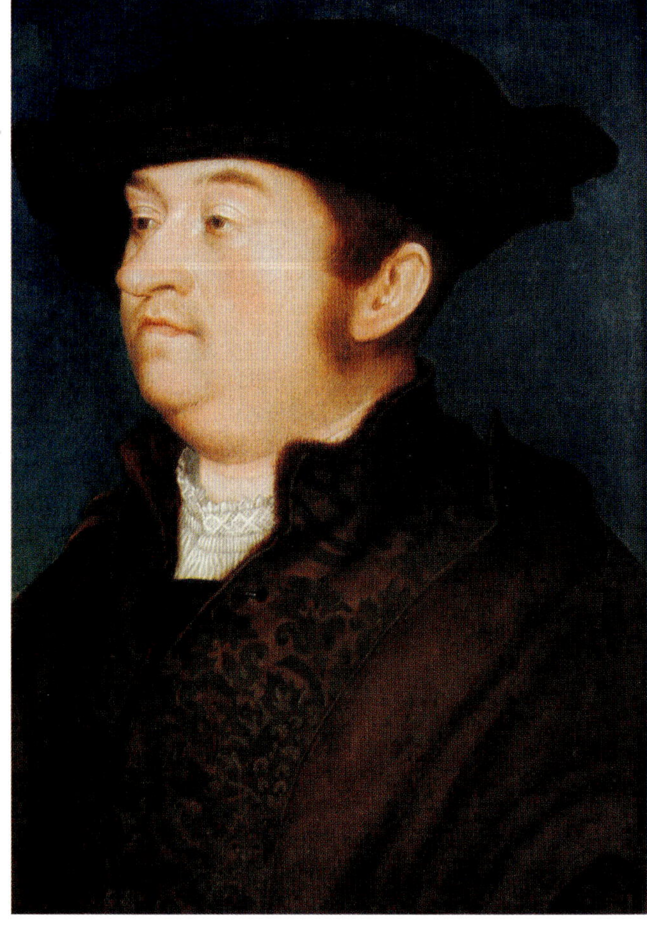

Landshut (c.1450–1504) also known as Mair, an artist from Freisling; and Michel Erhart (1440–1522), a gifted sculptor.

THE ARTIST-CRAFTSMAN

Holbein the Elder spent much of his adult life running a large workshop, which included family members. Little is known of its artistic foundation. Some historians state that he might have studied art in the studio of the Schongauer family of goldsmiths, engravers and painters, although documentation is scarce. His nomadic travels as a young journeyman – following a period of workshop practice – probably took him as far as Cologne, and perhaps further. He was sought after as an outstanding draughtsman, who produced delicately rendered

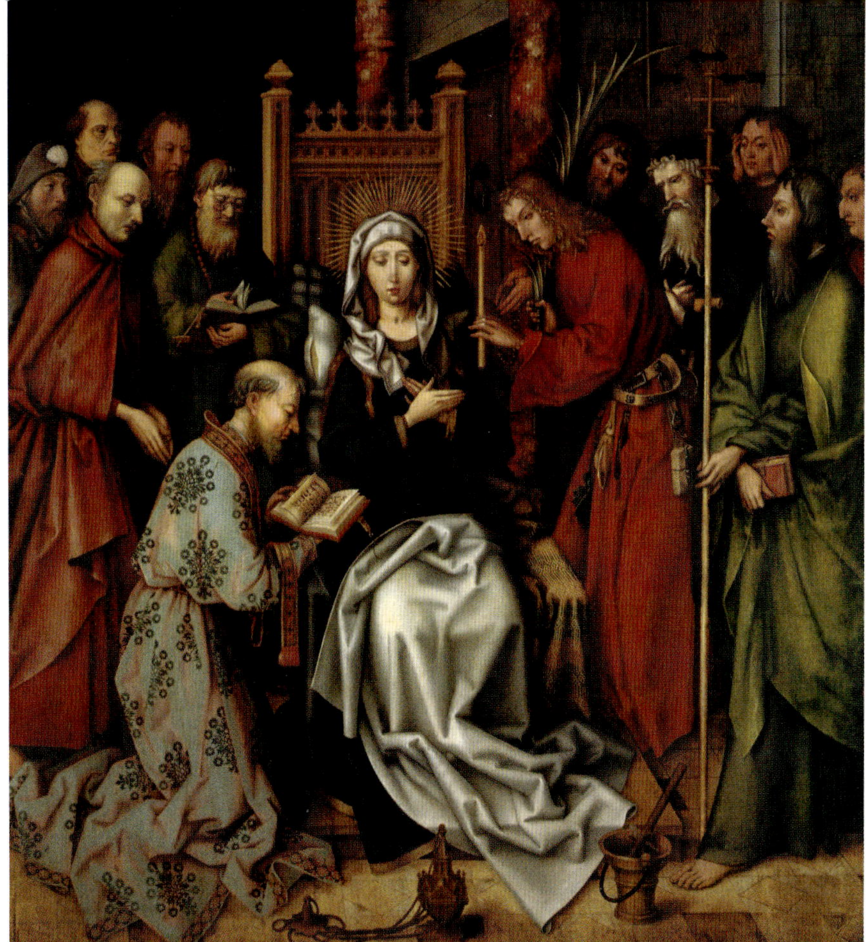

Above: Death of the Virgin, *1501, by Hans Holbein the Elder. Originally painted for the altarpiece of the Dominican Church in Frankfurt, now displayed in the Kunstmuseum, Basel.*

drawings, such as *Self-Portrait* (opposite top), and architectural interiors, as in the *Basilica of St Paul* (below right). As a superlative designer of woodcuts, stained glass and other decorative arts, including illuminated manuscripts, and possibly sculpture, his reputation was high. He had many patrons, and travelled in order to gain and carry out commissions in Frankfurt, Kaisheim, Isenheim and Alsace. He was the first artist in Augsburg to sign his artworks, which signals both that he was in demand, and that the status of the artist had risen enough to warrant the added value of a named work.

Holbein the Elder was one of the first painters to emancipate German art from the International Gothic style. He softened depictions of the Holy Family, placing them in naturalistic settings, and included architectural backgrounds, for example in *Death of the Virgin*, 1501 (see above). His aptitude for portraiture, must have also inspired Holbein the

Younger to take up the art form.

Holbein the Elder's exemplary technical skills were passed to his two sons. He favoured silverpoint, an exacting skill, and used coloured chalks for preparatory drawings. His sons were also adept at silverpoint, following his example. Comparing drawings by Hans Holbein the Elder with those of his sons, one can see how similar they are stylistically.

Below: Plan for the Basilica of St Paul, *c.1501–04, by Hans Holbein The Elder.*

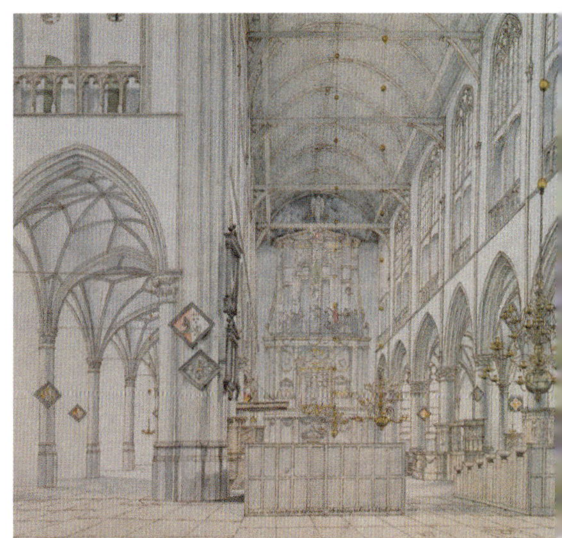

THE HOLBEIN WORKSHOP

Hans and his elder brother Ambrosius learned the skills of an artist from their father, as apprentices in what was considered to be the most talented workshop in Augsburg. As their skills progressed, they painted altarpieces with him. Also in the family workshop was their uncle, Sigismund Holbein (c.1470–1540).

APPRENTICESHIP

Both sons joined their father's workshop as apprentices. An apprenticeship would have followed traditional lines, from grinding and mixing paint pigments, to learning the arts of drawing and painting, and of gilding – which Holbein the Younger would use in his portraits – then on to complete the minor, peripheral characters in large artworks before progressing to single works. These were just a few of the stages of apprenticeship, usually experienced over a three-year period, before graduating to become a member of the Painters' Guild. Holbein the Younger with his brother is known to have painted altarpieces in their father's workshop.

FAMILY PORTRAYALS

Holbein the Elder used his family as models for paintings. A drawing dated to 1511 has an inscription indicating it is a double portrait of Ambrosius and Hans the Younger (opposite, above). The inscription with their ages is no longer legible but they are considered to be seventeen and fourteen respectively. Depicted in Holbein the Elder's 1504 triptych altarpiece *S. Paolo fuori le Mura* (opposite, below), the boys stand with their father in a scene witnessing the baptism of Saul. In it Holbein the Elder clearly depicts himself pointing with his left hand to his youngest son, as if to single him out for prominence.

ARTISTIC INFLUENCES

Any artist of talent borrows and adapts ideas from other artists. The work of Holbein the Elder, such as *The Mystic Marriage of St. Catherine*, 1519, was informed by the Netherlandish style of painters Rogier van der Weyden (1400–64), and Hans Memling (c.1440–94), renowned for magnificent altarpieces. Van der Weyden's three-panel

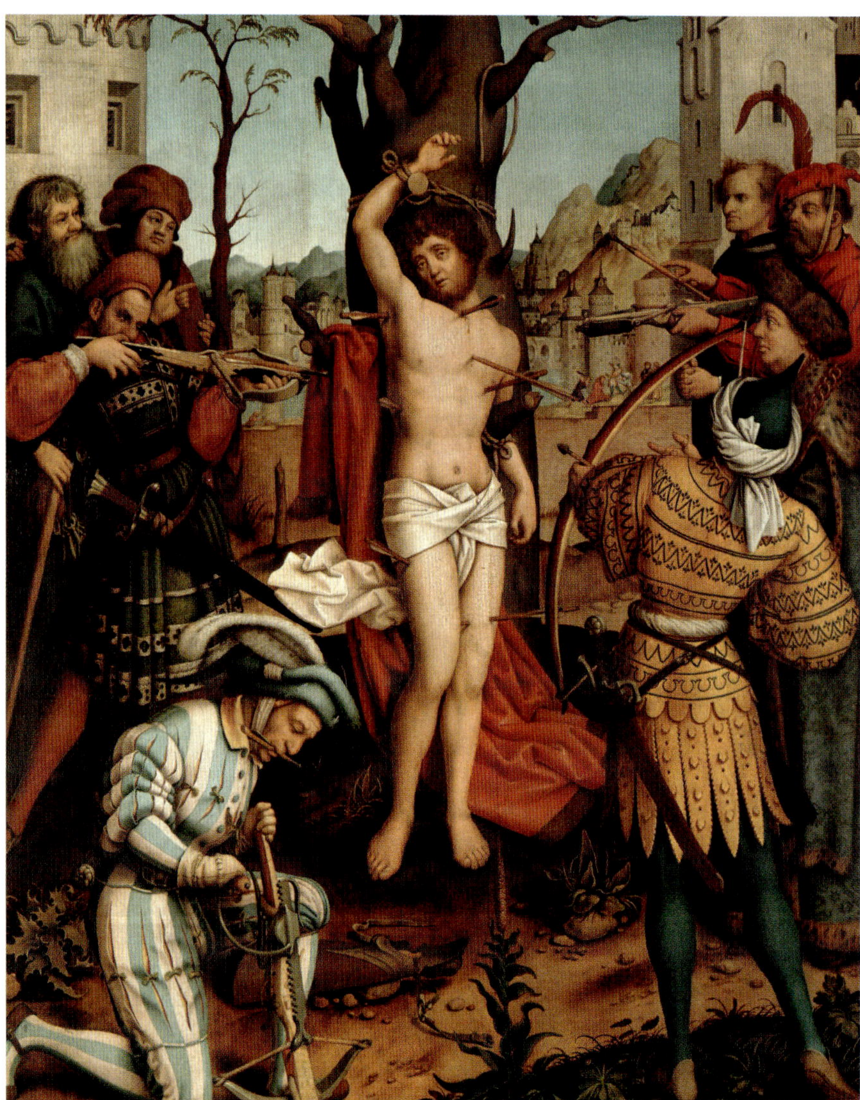

Above: Martyrdom of St. Sebastian, 1515–16, the central panel of the magnificent altarpiece triptych painted by Holbein the Elder, showing his dexterity for portraiture, and landscape painting.

altarpiece for St. Columba Cathedral, Cologne, *St Columba (Adoration of the Kings)*, c.1455, with its distinctive architectural backdrop, would have been known to him. Netherlandish contemporary art, including work by Hubert and Jan van Eyck, and artists of the Cologne School of Painting (1350–1550), may also have informed his style, such as in the altarpiece for Augsburg cathedral. These works would also be known to Holbein the Younger. The workshop would have sketches and drawings and layouts, and probably

relevant prints, of other artist's works from which he could study and learn.

The elder Holbein retained his interest in the late medieval style, but some historians consider him to be one of the pioneers in the transformation of German art from Late Gothic to the humanistic influence of the Renaissance.

In practice, he straddled both eras, possibly acknowledging the preference of the individual patron in the manner of style.

LATE GOTHIC OR RENAISSANCE?

The works of Hans Holbein the Elder, his style of draughtsmanship and painting, is a valuable insight into Holbein the Younger's early portfolio. Two notable masterpieces by Holbein the Elder dated to this period are the triptych for the St. Sebastian altarpiece (see opposite), and *The Fountain of*

Below: A triptych altarpiece for the Basilica of San Paolo fuori le Mura, 1504, was created by Hans Holbein the Elder. The Holbein brothers, Ambrosius and Hans, are depicted with their father bottom right in the left panel (See also page 7.)

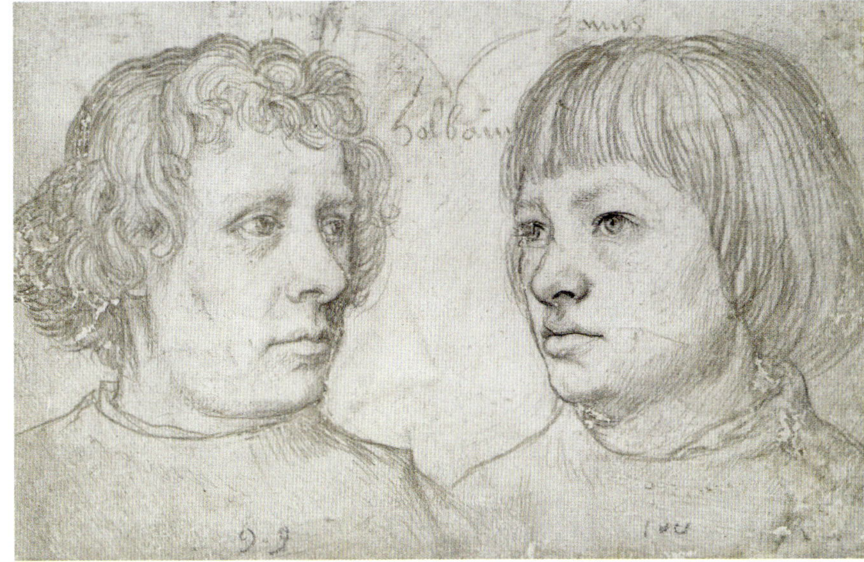

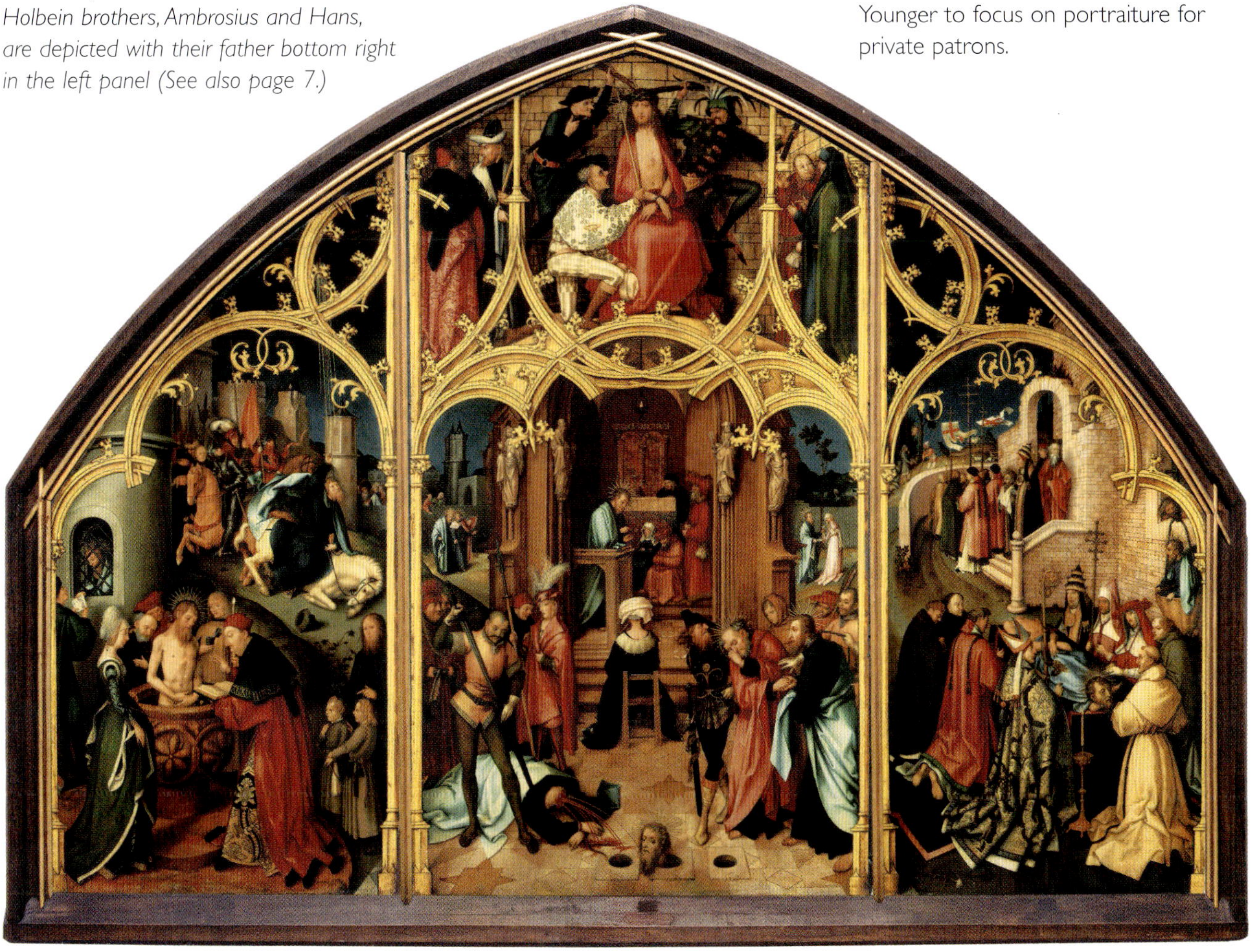

Life, 1519 (see detail, overleaf), which highlight his move away from the Late Gothic style toward a more natural form prevalent in the Renaissance. His sons, and possibly his brother, would have had aided him with these works. This naturalistic style is also intrinsically linked to Holbein the Younger's later altarpieces and religious works, such as the father and son(s) collaboration on *The Adoration of the Magi*, c.1520–22 (see page 118). It was perhaps the emergence of the Reformation, with fewer commissions available for religious works, that encouraged Holbein the Younger to focus on portraiture for private patrons.

FAMILY OF PAINTERS

Holbein father and sons, and their uncle Sigismund, collaborated on large works, such as altarpieces, which were widely praised and exposed the brothers to major patrons. However, at the height of the workshop's artistic creativity, Holbein the Elder was declared a tax defaulter and fled to Isenheim or Basel, Switzerland.

SIGISMUND HOLBEIN

Very little is known about the life of Sigismund Holbein (c.1470–1540), the younger brother of the elder Holbein. He is known to have collaborated on religious commissions with his brother. His name also appears in the tax register of Augsburg, from 1505–09. What scant history there is reveals that the brothers worked constantly, and were in demand as a highly skilled workshop team, although Sigismund may have first worked as Hans the Elder's assistant. Rare extant drawings by Sigismund reveal his vast skill in capturing character and expression.

It is thought, from documentation, that Sigismund moved to Bern, bought a house and became a citizen of the city. A falling-out between the brothers was the result of unpaid debts, for which Sigismund sued. He then worked on solo commissions, travelling widely in Europe. When Sigismund died in Bern, his nephew Holbein the Younger was 43 years old and a celebrated portrait painter. His uncle had made an official will in 1540, bequeathing his possessions, including his artist's tools, to his nephew, a confirmation of their close association and Sigismund's acknowledgement of and pride in Hans' phenomenal talent. It was a poignant gift that affirmed their bond, and a relevant fragment of Holbein's history that enlightens our understanding of his family relationships.

AMBROSIUS HOLBEIN

Ambrosius (c.1493/4–c.1519), the eldest son of Hans Holbein the Elder, and elder brother of Holbein the Younger, also trained to be an artist in his father's workshop. Along with his brother, his first extant works are humorous marginal drawings in Erasmus's book *Praise of Folly*, in a copy owned by the Protestant scholar Oswald Myconius. The career of Ambrosius Holbein as an independent artist began in 1514–15, possibly with an assisted commission for the main banqueting hall of the monastery of St. George's Abbey, Stein am Rhein, working with Thomas Schmid of Schaffhausen (active 1504–1550/60), to paint murals, although the evidence for this is circumstantial. It is known that he assisted on paintings in his father's workshop and his skills brought commissions. A woodcut dated to 1518 created for Sir Thomas More's book *Utopia* is thought to be his work.

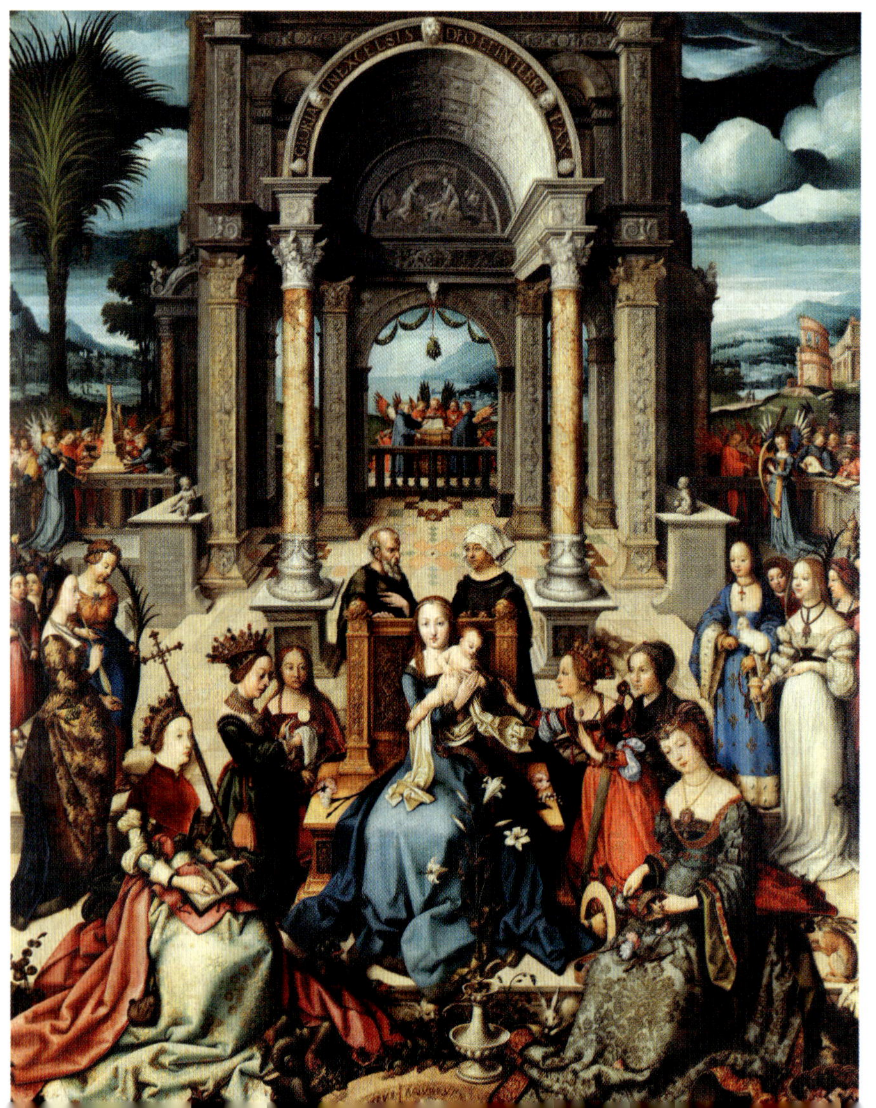

Left: Detail of The Fountain of Life, 1519, *by Hans Holbein the Elder, probably in collaboration with Holbein the Younger, centres on the Madonna and Child, placed in an architectural setting, with many in attendance. The use of perspective takes the eye beyond the Virgin Mary to a distant landscape.*

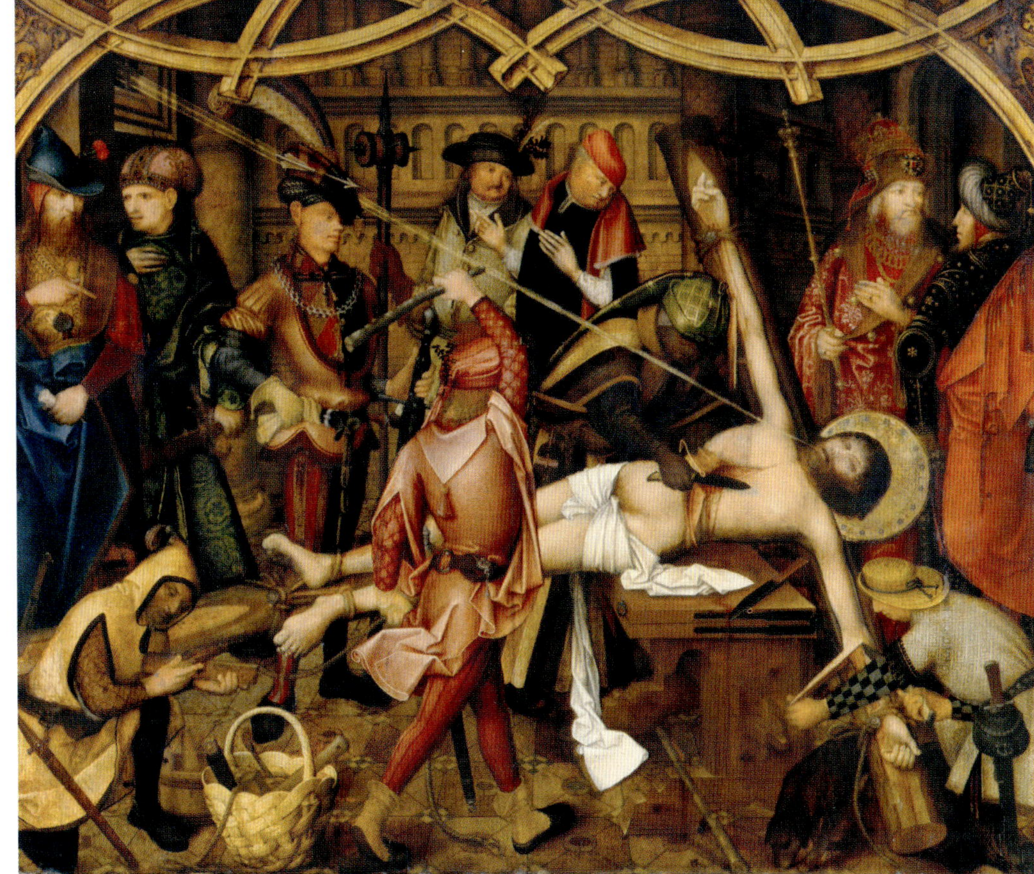

His presumed death in 1519 robbed the family of a wonderfully talented artist. Ambrosius' drawing style mirrored that of his father. Paintings such as *Portrait of Jörg Schweiger*, 1518 (see page 22), and his last work, *Portrait of a Young Man* (see page 27), prove that his artistic skills were comparable to those of his father and brother. In this

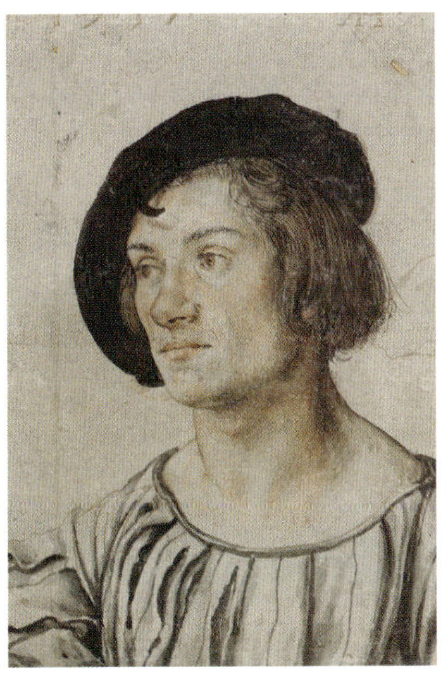

last work the background reveals his knowledge of classical architecture and possibly artists of the Italian Renaissance. Similar backdrops are in later paintings by Holbein the Younger.

THE LATER YEARS OF HANS HOLBEIN THE ELDER

Around 1514, in the middle of undertaking prestigious commissions, Holbein the Elder fled Augsburg due to his unpaid taxes, also falling out with his brother Sigismund for unpaid debts. After Holbein the Elder was declared a tax defaulter in Augsburg, he was forced to accept commissions further afield. At Isenheim in Alsace, where Matthias Grünewald was employed at the time, Holbein found other patrons and was contracted to complete an altarpiece.

Various accounts are written of Holbein the Elder as remaining poor and in debt in later life. After 1524 his name no longer appeared on the register of the Augsburg guild, and his last five years are unrecorded officially. Some sources say he fled Isenheim, when pursued there by his brother Sigismund and others for debt, abandoning his work and equipment. It is said by some that he ended his days in a monastery in Isenheim. Holbein the Elder's death was recorded in

Augsburg's *Malerbuch* (Book of Artists). Heinrich Meltinger, burgomaster of Basel, in a letter to Antoine Abbey, Isenheim, requested that two boxes of painting tools and materials of the late Holbein the Elder be returned to Holbein the Younger. Holbein was still trying to recover them in 1526.

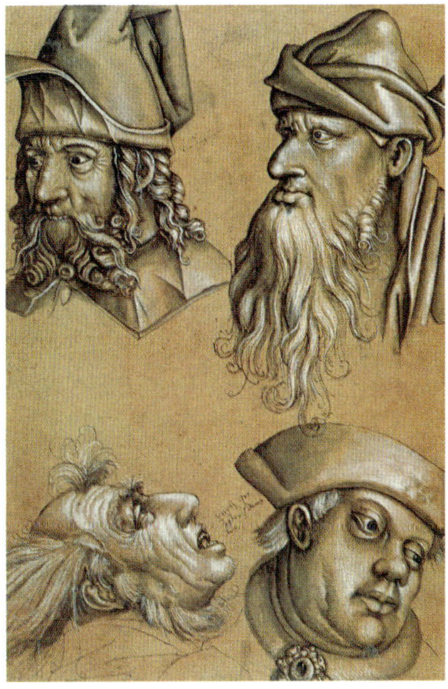

THE MOVE TO BASEL

Sued by many for payment defaults, the elder Holbein, despite his substantial career, died a poorer man in comparative obscurity. Hans and Ambrosius Holbein both travelled to Basel in about 1515–16, joining the workshop of Hans Herbst, and taking on new commissions.

Between 1515 and 1516 Hans and Ambrosius Holbein moved to Basel. It may have been their father's forced departure from Augsburg that prompted them also to leave. The elder Holbein knew the goldsmith Jörg Schweiger, who had become a guild member of Basel in 1507, and a citizen in 1508, and was a useful person to assist the Holbein brothers' introduction to art patrons in the city.

JOURNEYMEN FOR HERBST

Both brothers initially worked for the painter Johannes or Hans Herbst (see overleaf), a friend of their father, as journeymen before their acceptance into the Basel Painters' Guild. It was usual to work as a journeyman after finishing an apprenticeship. They had been taught the art of drawing, engraving and painting in their father's workshop; it would make sense for them to leave the family workshop and collaborate with another painter, to broaden their skills.

Ambrosius Holbein was accepted on the register of the Painters' Guild of Basel in 1517 and was made a citizen of the city on 6th June 1518; Jörg

Below: Map of Basel in the 1600s; founded in Roman times, a city on the Rhine, on the Swiss-German border.

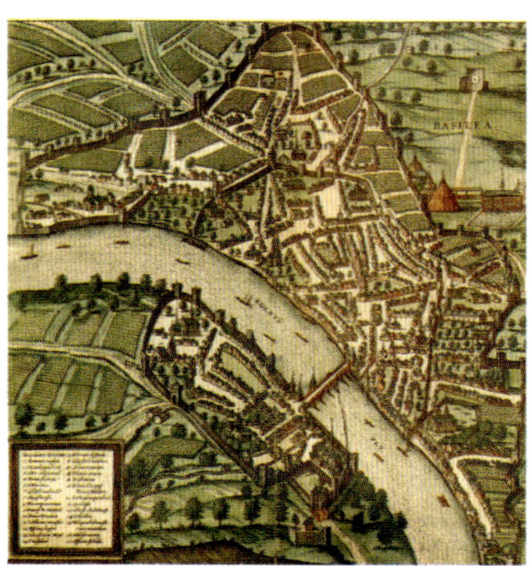

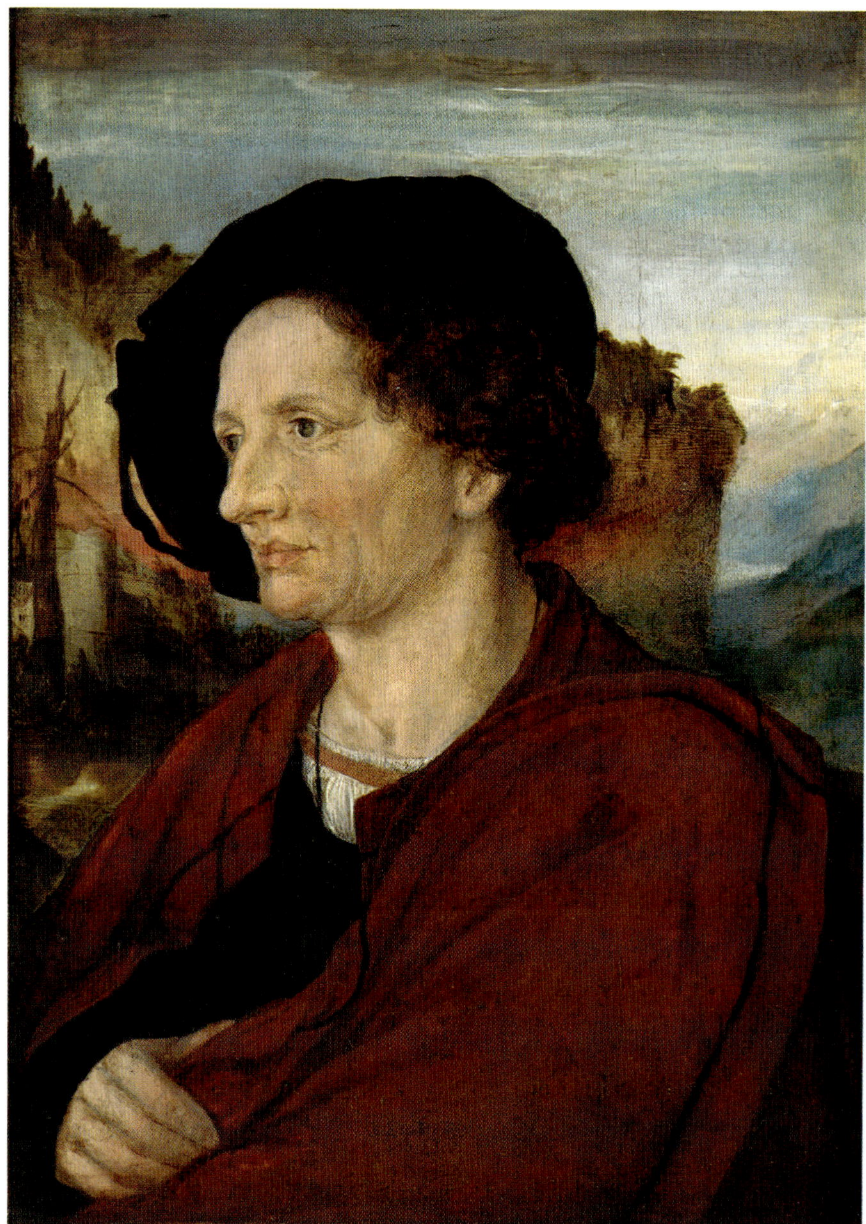

Above: Portrait of Jörg Schweiger, 1518, painted by Ambrosius Holbein, coincides in date with the artist's acceptance as a member of the Painter's Guild of Basel, and as a citizen of Basel on 6th June 1518. Schweiger had acted as his guarantor. Jörg Schweiger (c.1470/80–1533) was an Augsburg-born artist and goldsmith, resident in Basel, and a longstanding friend of Holbein the Elder.

Schweiger had acted as his guarantor, which may have instigated Ambrosius' portrait of him that year. It is difficult to compare fairly the work of the two Holbein brothers due to Ambrosius's death in 1519 (a presumed death, through absence of records after 1519). His work did not reach a pinnacle of maturity like his brother, but his paintings show his remarkable talent.

THE TRADE GUILDS

Guilds were initiated in the medieval era, to protect professions, choose members, fix fees, and define the terms of entrance to would-be members. Citizens of each city were intensely protective of their guilds, keeping a close-knit group of skilled professionals employed by refusing to allow non-members to work in the city. In Augsburg in 1468, soon after moveable type had been invented, the woodcutters insisted that only members of their guild, or the affiliated Carpenters' Guild, could cut decorative woodblocks for book illustration. In one recorded instance, a printer, Gunther Zainer from Strasbourg, wanted to make his own woodblocks but was unable to publish unless he used Augsburg woodcutter guild members.

As guild members became more reputed, they signed their work. Hans Lützelberger was the woodcutter in Basel who created the c.1526 series of woodblocks for Hans Holbein the Younger's 'Dance of Death' – 51 woodcuts, 41 of which were published in 1538 in book form (see pages 38–39 and 124–28). Lützelburger's signature can be found on the woodblock of 'The Duchess' in the series.

A VARIETY OF WORK

The print revolution happening in Basel at the time, and the university's commercial needs, in addition to local wealthy patrons, stimulated commissions. The brothers' work included woodcuts, engravings, portraits, and religious pieces for church interiors. Their work was varied, as can be seen from the two-sided *Signboard for a Schoolmaster* created to hang above the premises of the schoolmaster Oswald Myconius (1488–1522) ,the Protestant reformer, theologian and classical scholar (family name Geisshüsler).

IN PRAISE OF FOLLY

Erasmus's book *Praise of Folly* was published in 1511. Ambrosius and Hans drew 82 marginal drawings, many humorous, in a copy of the 1515 second edition owned by their schoolmaster friend Myconius. The

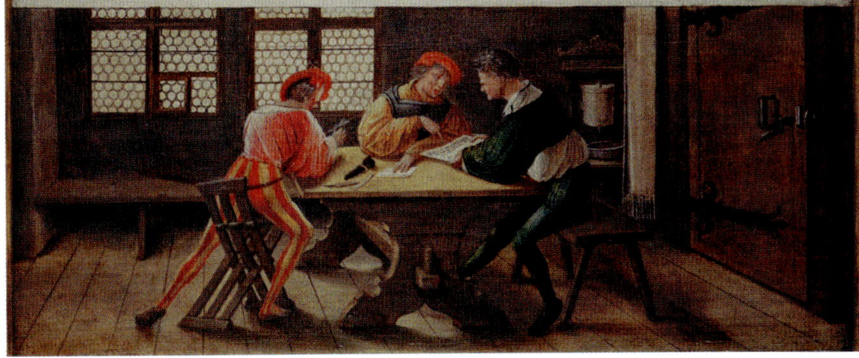

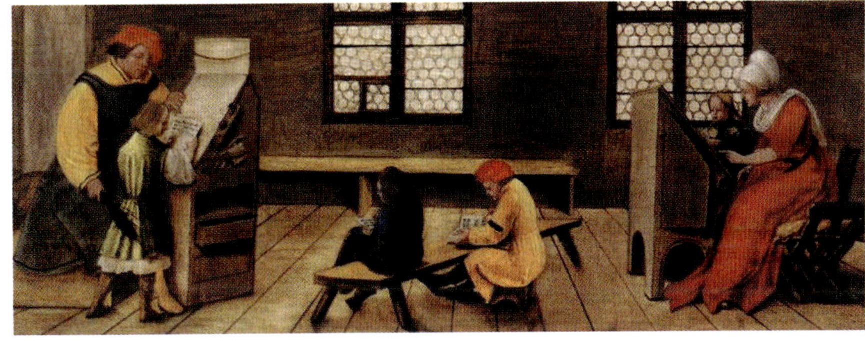

Above: Signboard for a Schoolmaster (A School Teacher Explaining the Meaning of a Letter to Illiterate Workers), c.1516, by Hans Holbein the Younger. The reverse side (also shown here) depicted a different scene, of a children's lesson in progress, which was painted by Ambrosius Holbein.

plan was for Myconius to show the illustrated work to his friend, the author. The marginal drawings are the first extant works by Ambrosius and Holbein the Younger, and highlights their perceptive knowledge of religious debate, as well as revealing the young men's social circle of learned associates even at a young age. (See also pages 40–1, and 104–5.)

Right: One of the many marginalia drawings by the Holbein brothers in a copy of Erasmus's Praise of Folly; their illustrations are light in touch, and sometimes with a gently mocking tone.

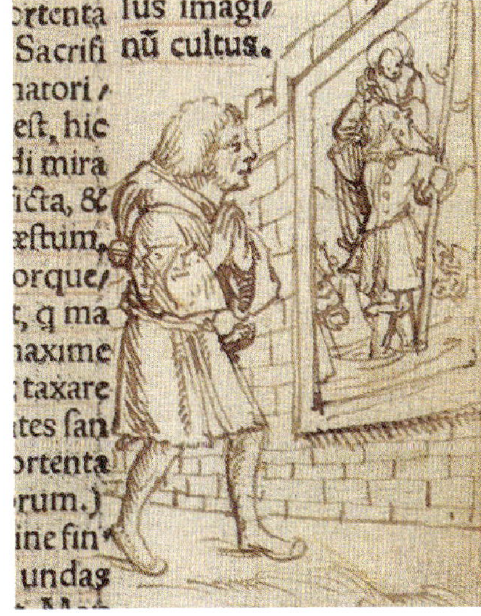

HANS HOLBEIN: JOURNEYMAN

After completing an apprenticeship, an artist or artisan wishing to become a Master of their trade, first travelled to seek work as a journeyman, a day's work for a day's pay, in different workshops. In Basel, the Holbein brothers joined the workshop of the painter Hans Herbst (1470–1552).

Until both brothers were members of the Painters' Guild, they could not work in Basel as independent artists, thus were attached to Herbst's workshop until Ambrosius was accepted in 1517, and Hans in 1519.

It is likely that Ambrosius Holbein, three years senior to his brother, spent time travelling as a journeyman c.1511–12 before the brothers worked for Hans Herbst in Basel. It is thought that in 1515 he was employed as painter under supervision of artist Thomas Schmid from Schaffhausen (active 1504–1550/60), in the mural decoration of the Great Hall of the Benedictine monastery of St George in Stein am Rhein, Switzerland.

HANS (JOHANNES) HERBST

Little is known of the Strasbourg-born painter Hans Herbst who is listed as a member of the Basel Guild of Painters in 1492. Herbst probably mentored

Below: Portrait of Johannes Herbster, 1516, by Ambrosius Holbein. Shown in three-quarter profile, the artist has framed the sitter with an architectural surround.

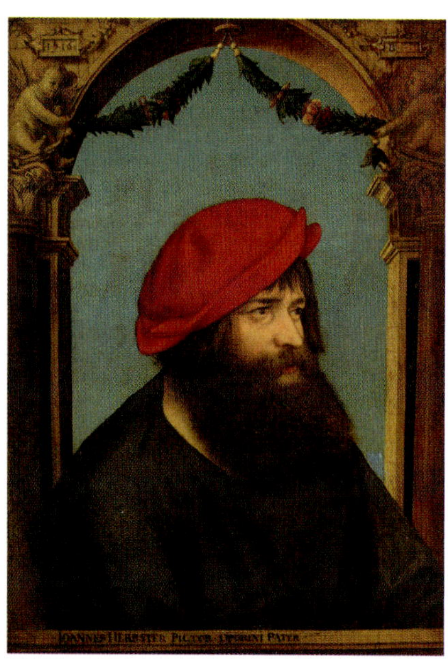

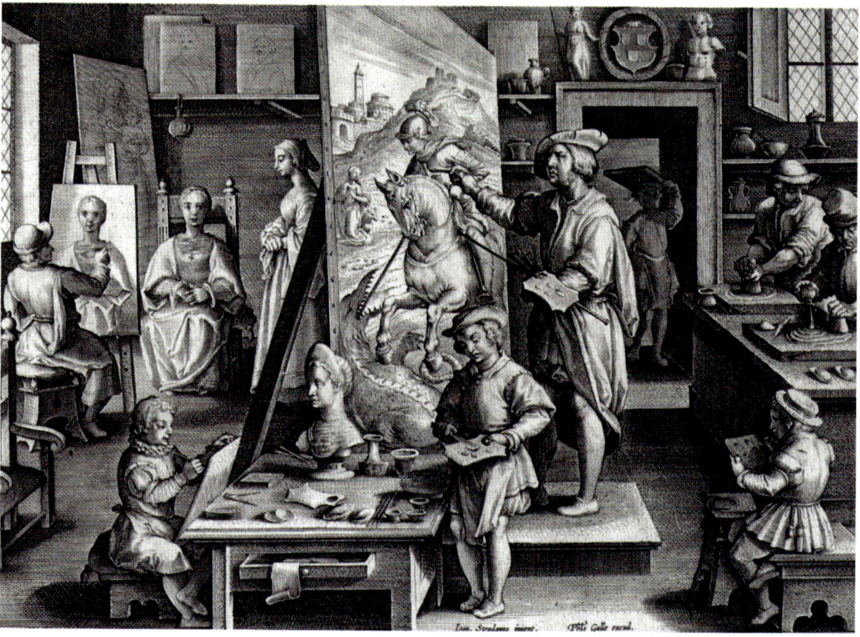

Above: Color Olivi (The Inside of a Painter's Studio) from the Nova Reperta c.1580–1605 published by Philip(s) Galle. An artist is shown painting a canvas of Saint George and the Dragon; next to him, an assistant prepares oil pigments and a young boy copies from a sculpture; to the left, a man paints from life a portrait of a lady; to the right, two men grind colours.

Journeymen apprentices did not sign their own names until they became a Master of their trade themselves, an official member of the Painters' Guild. Some paintings therefore, such as the Meyer double portraits which we consider to be by Hans Holbein the Younger, were signed 'HH by Holbein'. This is thought to signify both Holbein and his workshop Master, Hans Herbst (also known as Herbster), who is the one who had been commissioned. Holbein the Younger also collaborated with Hans Herbst on a sequence of altarpiece paintings of the Passion of Christ for St Peter's Church in Basel.

Right: Design for a Stained Glass Window with a Swineherd, c.1518–19, one of Holbein the Younger's earliest designs for stained glass. At this time he used a richly varied wash, rather than the unifying wash of his later style.

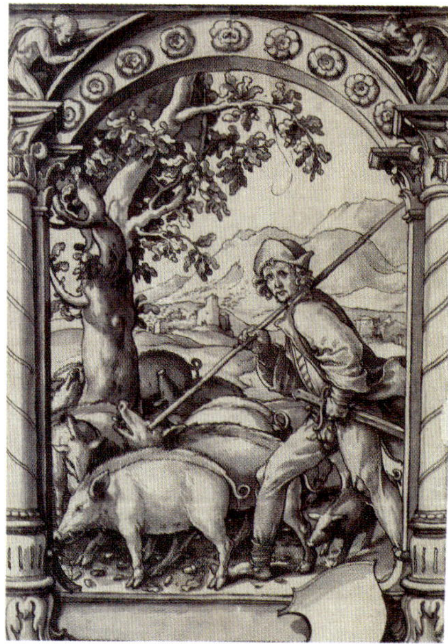

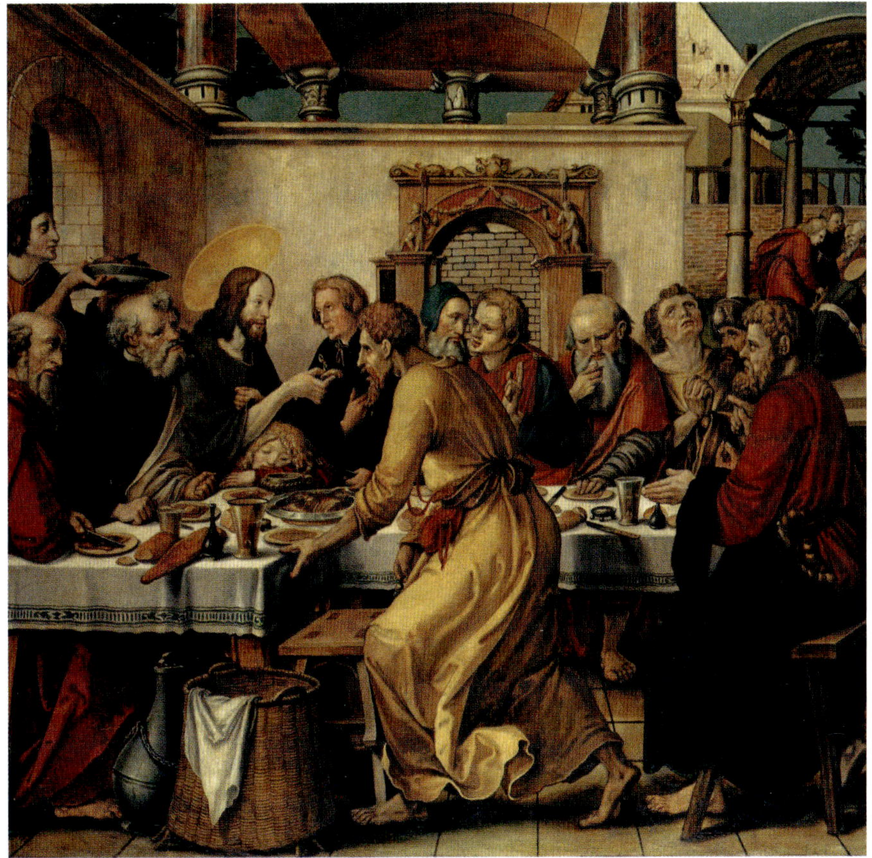

Above: Last Supper *was the first in the Passion series of paintings by Hans Herbst with Hans Holbein the Younger.*

A Passion cycle could begin with Christ's entry into Jerusalem and end with his entombment, 'Noli me Tangere' (Touch me Not), or the Resurrection. Holbein's later *Passion of Christ* altarpiece, *c.*1524 (see pages 138–9) depicts eight scenes, some set dramatically at night. His Passion series for stained glass windows, 1526–28, featured ten scenes (see pages 146–9).

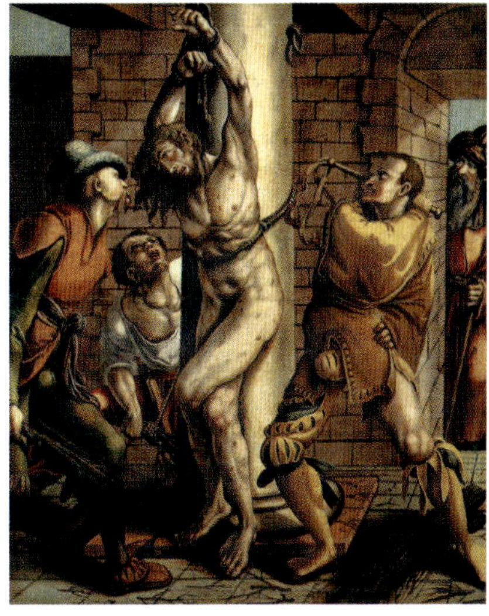

Above: The Flagellation *from the Passion series, painted by Hans Herbst with Holbein the Younger.*

Ambrosius Holbein; Ambrosius painted *Portrait of Johannes Herbster* in 1516. Herbst mentored Holbein the Younger too. It is thought that Herbst may have served with the Basel military in Italy for a period, and died in Basel in 1550–52 of the plague.

The absence of detail in our knowledge about Herbst's personal life is a reflection of how little the lives of lesser-known artists were accounted for in northern Europe in the fifteenth and sixteenth centuries. In Italy, the rise of status in the artist's profession was aided by the success of Giorgio Vasari's book *Lives of the Most Excellent Painters, Sculptors and Architects*, published in 1550, with a second edition in 1556.

PASSION OF CHRIST

A constant patron-request for artists in Europe was a depiction of the Passion of Christ. 'Passion' is taken from the Greek and Latin word 'to suffer'. The narrative was told in the New Testament Gospels: Matthew 26–27; Mark 14–15; Luke 22–23; and John 18–19. Artists visualised the arrest, trial, torture and crucifixion of Christ.

A remarkable 'Passion of Christ' series, *c.*1515–20, painted on canvas, was possibly destined to be hung on the rood screen separating the Choir from the Nave in the Church of St Peter's, Basel, where Holbein received Latin lessons. Commissioned by Basel master Hans Dyg (active 1503–26), it is considered to be the work of Hans Herbst and his assistants, including Holbein the Younger. Of the sixteen, five survive, including *Last Supper* (see above), *Christ on the Mount of Olives*, *The Taking of Christ*, *The Flagellation* (above right) and *Pilate washing his Hands*. Art collector Basilius Amerbach referred to the *Last Supper* and *The Flagellation* as Holbein's 'first works'. Christ in *The Flagellation* bears characteristics of Holbein's *Dead Christ in the Tomb*, 1521 (see pages 122–23). Amerbach later owned the *Sacrament* (now lost) and *Last Supper*, about which he wrote 'A great night meal, H. Holbein's first work, a vf cloth with oil coloured'.

Below: The Crown of Thorns *was part of the 'Grey Passion' series by Hans Holbein the Elder, painted between 1494 and 1500, when he lived in Augsbuurg, with twelve distinctive monochrome panels painted for the Altarpiece of the Dominican Church.*

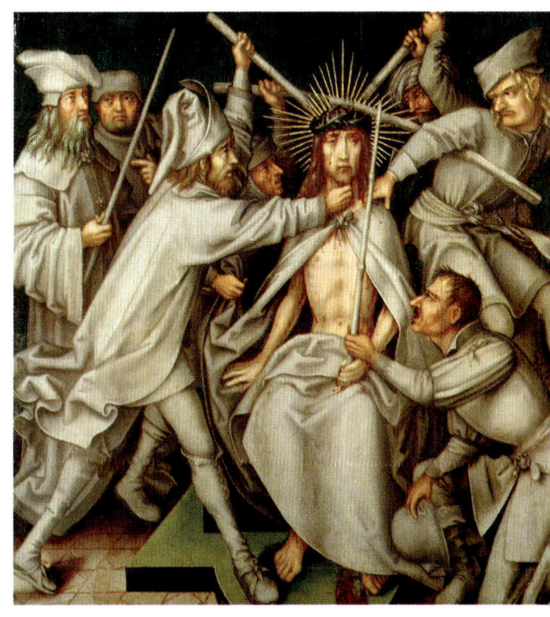

PORTRAITS IN CONTEXT

Ambrosius Holbein and the younger Hans Holbein, under the mentorship of Herbst, received commissions for secular portraits of Basel dignitaries. The content reflected a prevailing taste for architectural settings, an artistic device practised by their father.

PAIRED PORTRAITS

Holbein the Younger undertook the pendant works *Double Portrait of Mayor Jakob Meyer zum Hasen and his wife Dorothea Kannengiesser,* 1516, portraying the young mayor of Basel, Jakob Meyer zum Hasen (1482–1531), and his second wife Dorothea Kannengiesser. Holbein's preparatory underdrawings (see page 110) are informed by the method of his father, the elder Holbein, using silverpoint, red and black chalks on white ground.

Some factors in the representation of the sitters bear the influence of other high-calibre German painters such as Albrecht Dürer, and Augsburg-born Hans Burgkmair the Elder (1473–1531), Holbein's uncle; Burgkmair's painting *Double Portrait of Hans and Barbara Schellenburger,* 1505, possibly informed Holbein's similar composition in the Meyer work. However, the Meyer portrait is suffused with Holbein's own originality. His patron, Meyer, would also have voiced an opinion on how he wanted to be represented, being newly elected to his post as mayor. Meyer holds a newly-minted coin in one hand,

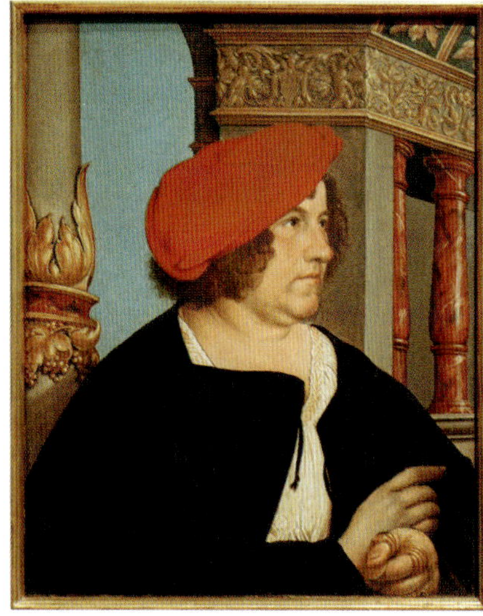

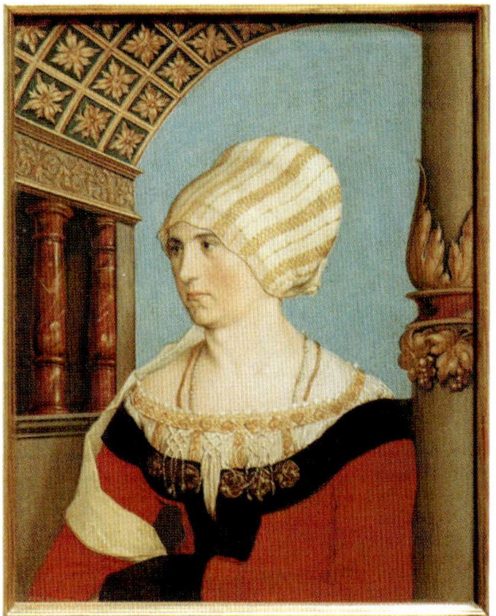

a possible reference to the honour bestowed on the city by the German emperor, Maximilian I, in 1516, to mint coins, as well as to Meyer's professional trade in finance.

Holbein paints the double portrait as one work, using a background of architecture continued across both works to join the two separate portraits. The diagonal placing of the buildings create spacial depth. This was not a new idea, it was used by

Above: Double Portrait of Mayor Jakob Meyer zum Hasen and his wife Dorothea Kannengiesser, *1516. The diptych shows Meyer and his wife facing each other in separate 'companion' portraits, intended to be hung together. The portrait was to celebrate Meyer's prestigious appointment. This was Hans Holbein the Younger's first independent commission.*

Hans Burgkmair and other painters, but Holbein's attention to detail is particularly meticulous, making the sitters look as though they are posing within the buildings. One sees this also in many of Holbein's later portraits, as well as in some of his sacred works such as the diptych *Christ as the Man of Sorrows with the Virgin Mary,* 1518–19 (see page 109).

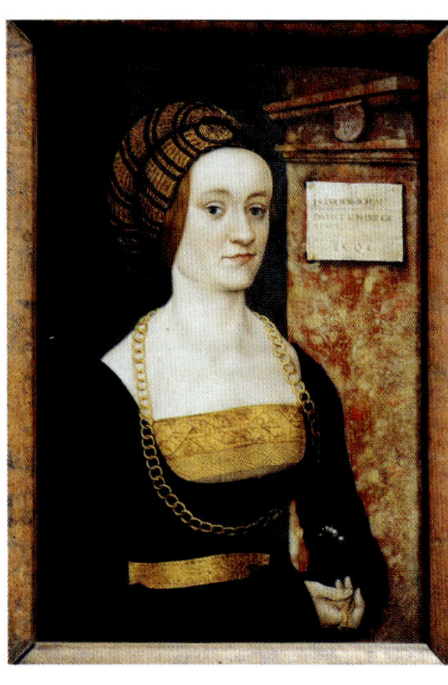

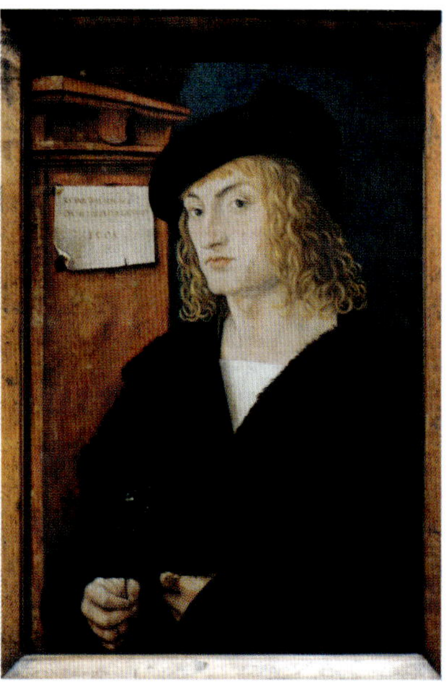

Left: Double Portrait of Hans and Barbara Schellenberger, 1505, *by Hans Burgkmair the Elder. The two portraits were clearly designed to be hung together, with their mirrored compositional elements. Hans Burgkmair was a painter and designer of woodcuts based in Augsburg. His own son, another Hans the Younger, became a painter as well.*

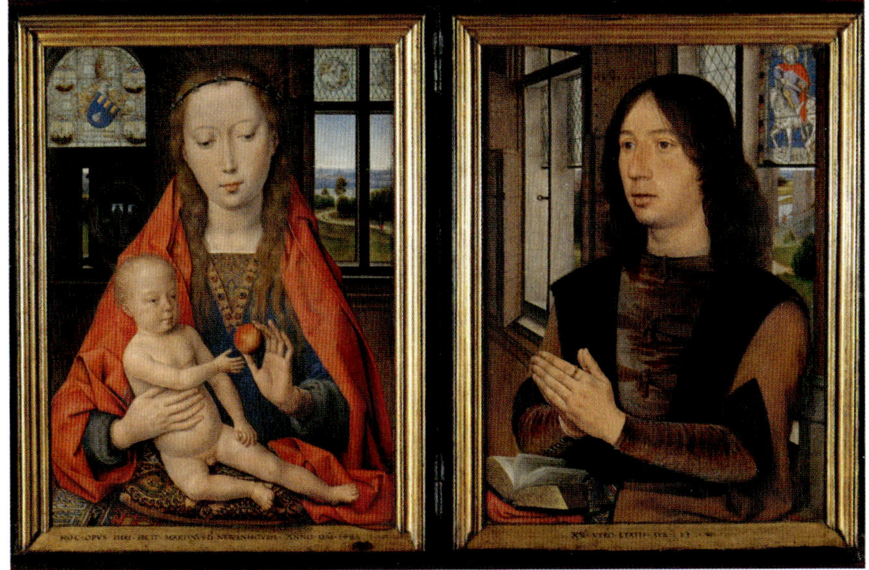

Right: Diptych of Maarten van Nieuwenhove, and Madonna and Child, *1487, by Hans Memling.*

THE RISE OF PORTRAITURE

Portraiture, emerging in Bohemia, France, and England around 1360, would become the status symbol of the rich throughout Europe during the 15th century, when van Eyck's new techniques (see page 12) produced a more realistic portrayal than portraits created in the quick-drying egg tempera method. There was a rise in commissions, indeed, Even Italian patrons would often commission a Netherlandish artist. Self-portraits advertised their artistic skills. Self-portraits of Hans Holbein in oils, if they existed, are not extant but his commissioned portraits are full of masterful realism.

MODERN SETTINGS

Hans Memling (*c.*1440–94), an influential artist in the emerging northern Renaissance, painted an earlier pendant-style portrait with realistic setting in a devotional diptych (see above). In the left-hand panel the Virgin and Child are seated in a room of the residence of the 23-year-old donor, Maarten van Nieuwenhove (1463–1500), shown at prayer in the right-hand panel. His coats of arms are illustrated in the stained glass of the window behind the Virgin. This double portrait places the Virgin in 15th-century Bruges. Placing the Holy Family within recognisable city landscapes would gain in popularity, and settings for biblical narratives were placed in German cities, showing Christ amongst the people; Hans Holbein placed a scene from Christ's Passion in Basel (see page 147).

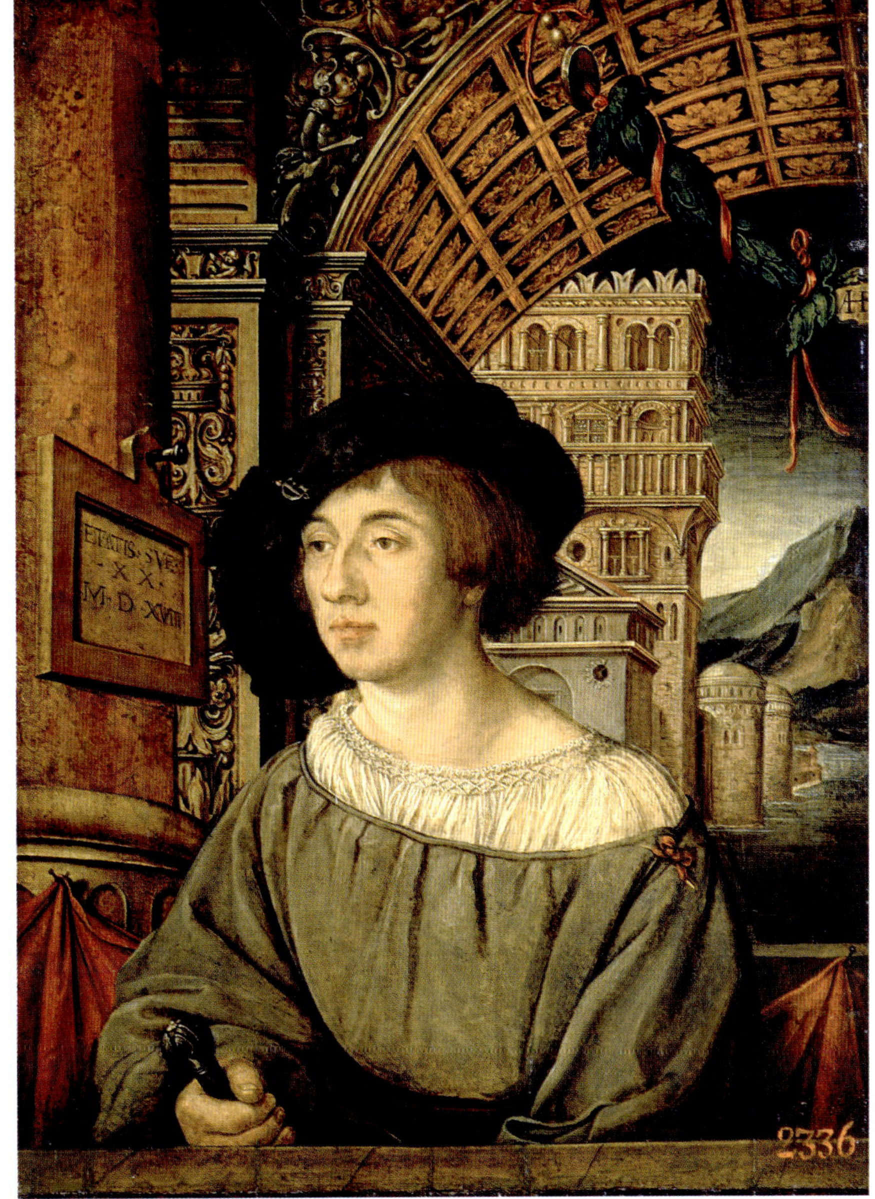

Right: Portrait of a Young Man, *1518, by Ambrosius Holbein. The superb architectural background behind the sitter demonstrates the artist's knowledge of Italian Renaissance architecture. It is close in figurative composition to* Portrait of Jörg Schweiger *(see page 22).*

ART AND RELIGIOUS REFORM

The Church of Rome's selling of 'indulgences', to forgive sins through monetary payment, sparked a reformative breakaway movement instigated by the German friar Martin Luther. For artists in Germany and the Low Countries it led to fewer religious commissions but an increase in demand for print illustrations.

'Indulgences' were a system of paying money to the church for the remission of sins for a living person, or to save the soul of a person in Purgatory after death. The practice of buying 'indulgences' spread throughout Roman Catholic congregations in Europe, and changed a spiritual aesthetic to one based on materialistic monetary acquisition. It was an ingenious plan to raise money to rebuild the Church of St Peter in Rome and aid the Vatican economy. Money was procured from the church's poorest to richest members, paying for redemption. The practice led a German theologian, the Augustinian friar Martin Luther (1483–1546) to condemn the Church as immoral, after his visit to the Holy City, Rome in 1510, seeing for himself lax behaviour and corrupt monetary practices within the Vatican. His condemnation of the Roman Catholic Church was printed in 95 theses that, it is said, he nailed to the door of the Castle Church in Wittenberg, and preached his beliefs in the Church of St Marien, Wittenberg.

LUTHER AND CRANACH

Lucas Cranach the Elder (1472–1553), a contemporary artist to Holbein the Elder, was integral to the promotion of Lutheranism across Europe. Engravings, etchings and portrait drawings by Cranach of his friend Martin Luther, the instigator of religious reform in the Catholic church and breakaway Protestant creed, were distributed via print publishing. They both lived in the small town of Wittenberg, which aided their plans for expansion of knowledge of Lutheranism. Images of Luther are invariably drawn from Cranach's portrayals, created by him and copied in his workshop for mass distribution.

Both men planned to spread the protest Reformant aesthetic via print publishing, which was considered integral to the success of widening knowledge and interest in the Reformers' beliefs, and arguments against the Catholic church. Luther employed Melchior Lotter the Elder (c.1470–1542/49), a skilled printer from Leipzig, who opened a new print shop in Wittenberg to facilitate the quality, speed and accuracy that Luther required. Run by Melchior's son, it was a superior workshop to that of the only other commercial print shop in Wittenberg, run by Johann Rhau-Grunenberg, who primarily published material for the university. Luther employed Cranach, the best woodcut illustrator, and Melchior, the printer, to market his message. To aid distribution, and reduce the costs, Cranach bought a paper mill, and joined forces with a local distribution company, owned by Christian Döring,

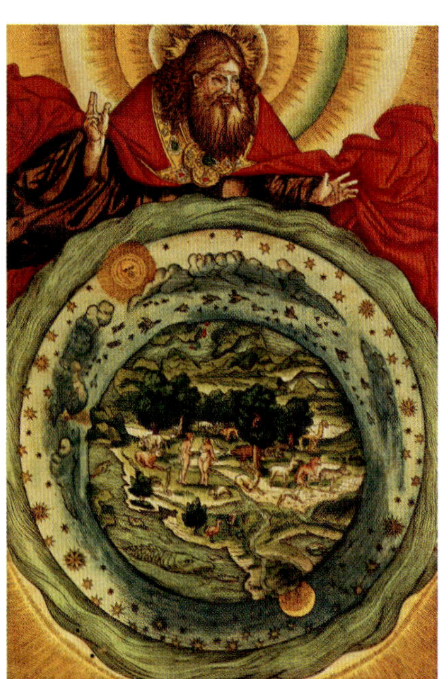

Below: The Creation, *a coloured woodcut by Lucas Cranach the Elder, c.1530, for the Luther Bible. Cranach was a close friend of Martin Luther.*

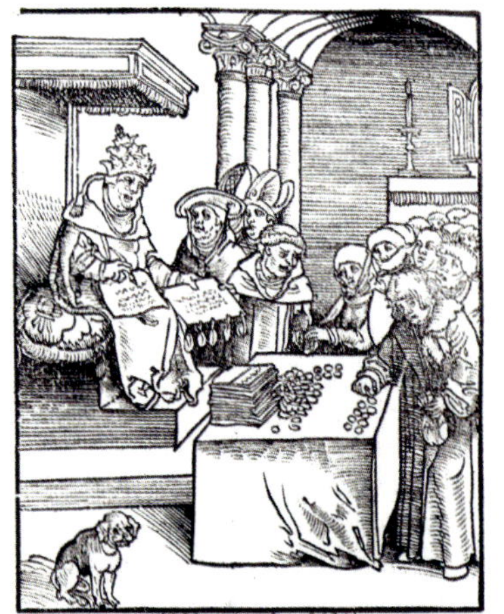

Hic sedet Antichristus in tēplo Dei, ostendens se tanquā sit Deus. Sicut Paulus p̄dixit.ij.ad Thessa.ij. Cōmutat & subuertit omes diuinas constitutiones, quēadmodū Daniel dicit, Opprimit sacram scripturam, vēdit dispensatioes, indulgentias, pallia, epatus, bñficia, tollit thesauros ſęculi, dissoluit matrimonia, grauat suis legibus cōscientias, sancit iura, & rursum eadē p pecunia rescindit, refert in nūerū diuorū sanctos, siue Canonizat, bñdicit & maledicit in quartā gñationē, & p̄cipit suā vocē audiri tāquā vocē dei. c. sic omis. dist. xix. Et nemini ē p̄missū de sedis Aplice iudicio iudicare vel retractare, xvij. dist. iiij.c, Nemini.

Below: The Pope selling Indulgences *from 'Passional Christi und Antichristi' by Philipp Melanchthon, published in 1521, woodcut, school of Cranach.*

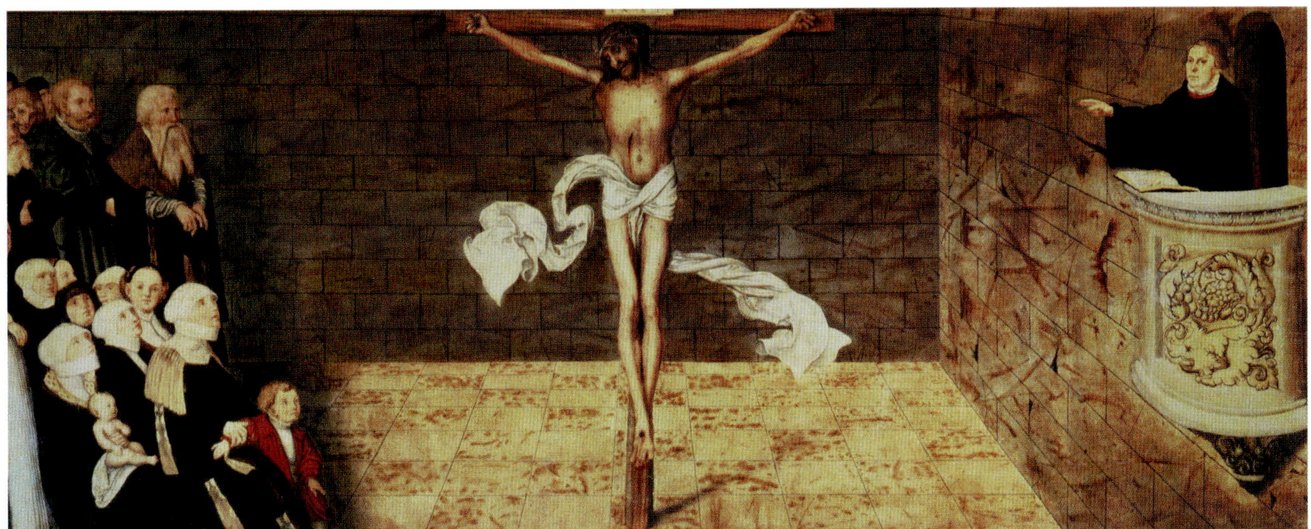

Above: Martin Luther's Sermon, *a detail from a triptych, 1547, by Lucas Cranach the Elder, depicting the preacher's 1510 oration to his congregation in the Church of St Marien, Wittenberg.*

MARTIN LUTHER IN AUGSBURG

Luther's reforms are synonymous with the city of Augsburg, Holbein's birthplace. After the 1517 Diet of Augsburg, Martin Luther paid two short visits to the city. His first was from October 12–18, 1518, to meet Cardinal Thomas Cajetan, to be questioned on his devout beliefs. The people of Augsburg, including the Holbein family, would no doubt have been aware of the meeting, although the unrest between the Catholic church and protesting Reformers had led to some uneasiness within the artist-craftsman community, as the religious fraternities were still a major source of income to them. In 1517 Holbein was beginning his professional career as an artist, after a move from Augsburg to Basel. Although he would have been aware of the momentous occasion – The Diet of Augsburg 1517 – he was set apart from it, and at the time of the second Diet of Augsburg in 1530, Holbein was settled in Basel.

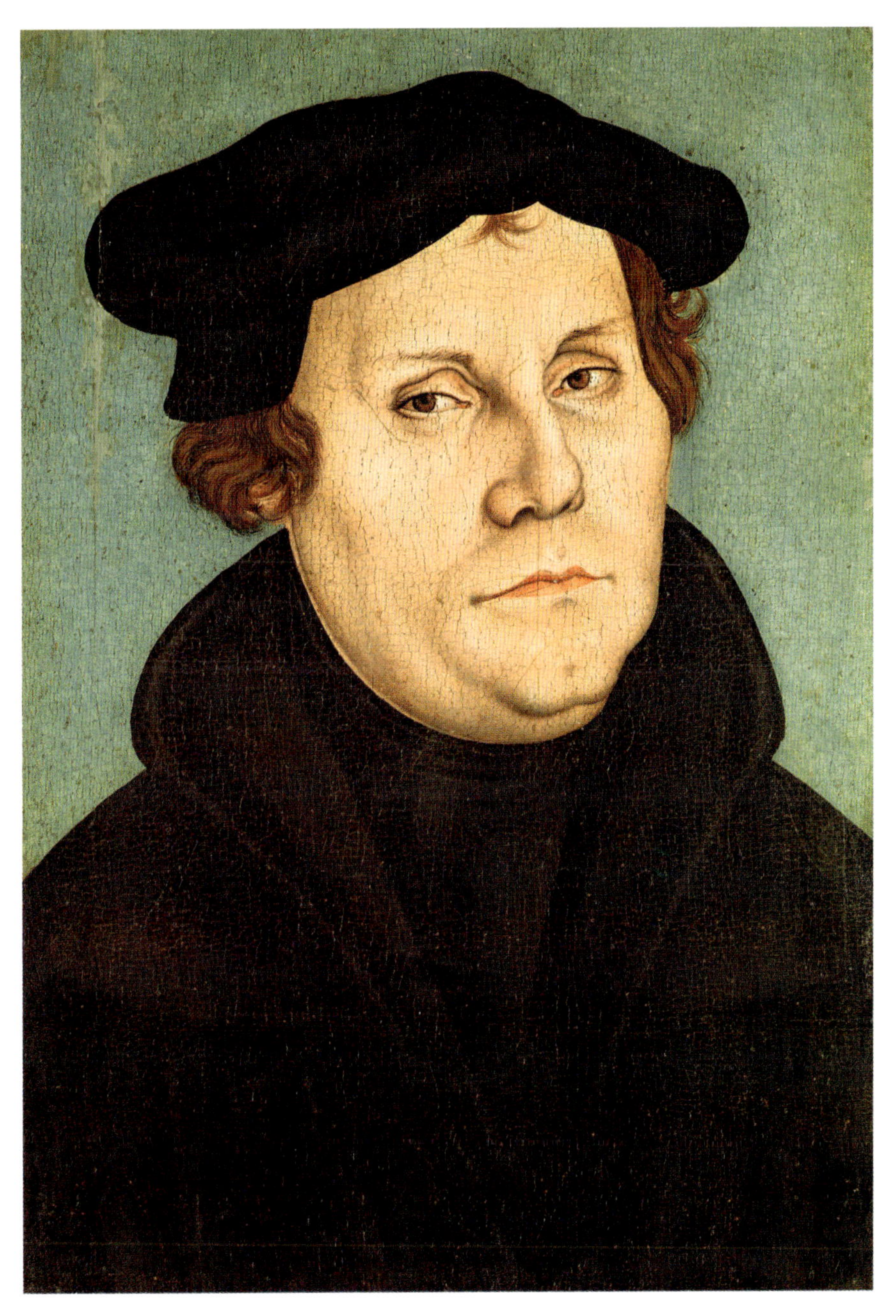

Right: Portrait of Martin Luther, *1529, by Lucas Cranach the Elder, presents the Reformant preacher aged forty-six. The left-hand panel of a diptych, it is a counterpart to Cranach's portrait of Katharina von Bora, Luther's wife.*

A PRINT REVOLUTION

At the time of Holbein the Younger's birth, Germany was experiencing an outstanding surge in print-publishing. Mainz and Augsburg in Germany and Basel in Switzerland were centres of publishing, art and commerce. Holbein became involved, creating woodcuts and illustrations for print.

GUTENBERG PRESS

In 1433 the Gutenberg press launched the first mechanical moveable type in Europe, instigated by the German goldsmith, engraver and printer Johannes Gutenberg (c.1400–68), born in Mainz. (The Chinese had invented moveable type four centuries earlier, but it was not available in the West.) Born into a prosperous merchant family, Gutenberg introduced a method of mass communication which, amongst other printed matter, allowed religious and secular texts with artists' illustrations, in pamphlets and books to be replicated and distributed to a wide audience. Gutenberg persuaded rich patrons to invest in his idea for

Right: A 15th-century German School engraving, Portrait of Johannes Gutenberg *depicts the man who launched the first mechanical-type printing press in Europe, thus widening knowledge through access to printed books.*

Below: The German engraving Printing Press 1498, *from a book published the same year, illustrates industrious printers at work in the print workshop.*

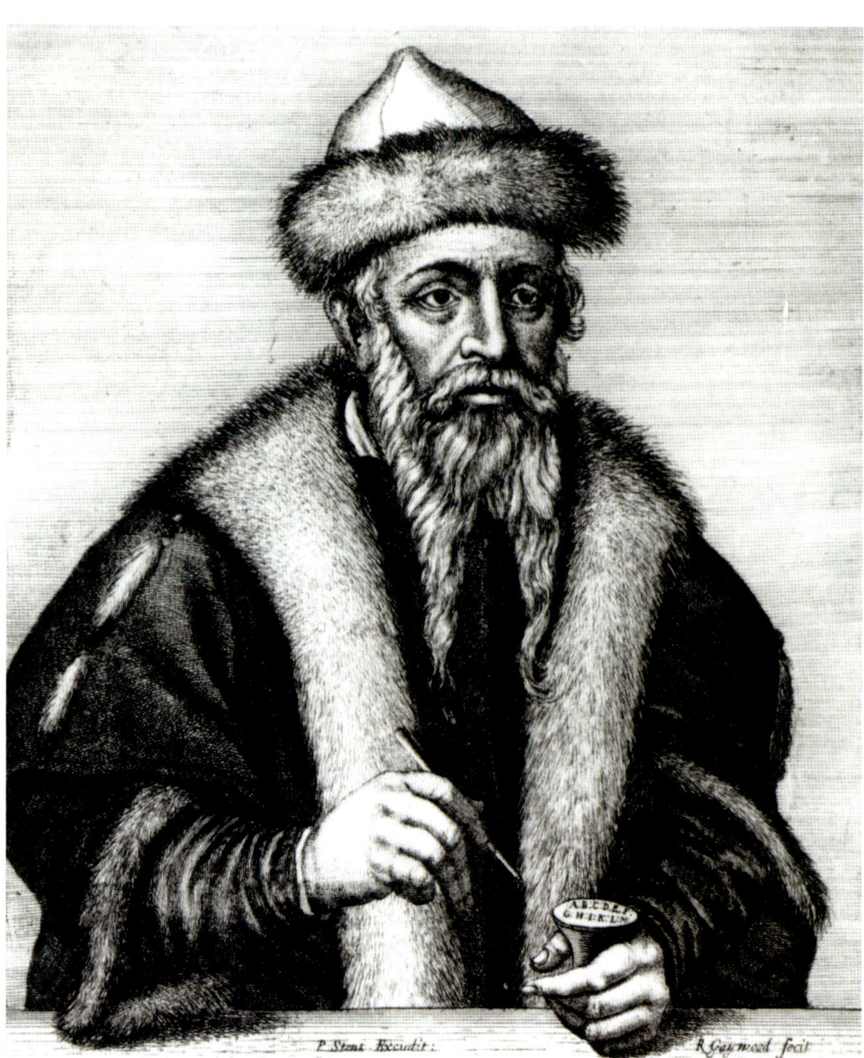

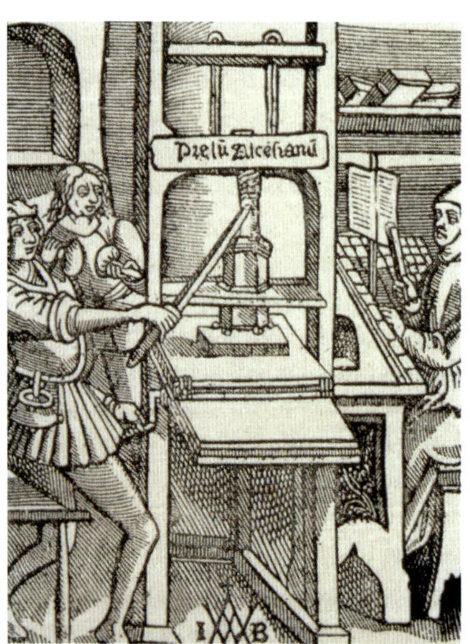

mechanical printing, and his experiments were carried out in secrecy to avoid theft of his concept and delivery. Gutenberg printed his first edition of the Bible in 1455, possibly begun around 1450, completed before 1456.

PUBLISHING REFORMATION

The invention of the mechanical printing press, a ground-breaking method of type-casting, aided the spread of the Reformation. Martin Luther's *Ninety-Five Theses* of 1517 were circulated via the new print method, allowing mass distribution and wider knowledge of

Luther's argument throughout Europe. Gutenberg's method of printing allowed a freer exchange of ideas, including Humanism and religious reform.

In Basel, where Holbein lived, Johann (Johannes) Froben (1460–1527), and Johann (Johannes) Amerbach (1440–1513), both successful, wealthy print-publishers, employed Holbein to paint their family portraits (see pages 116–7) and also woodcut illustration. Erasmus's printed works were often accompanied by illustrations, and a portrait of himself, which he sent to his noble friends in France and England.

THE WOODCUT AND THE REFORMATION

More than any other medium, the woodcut aided the spread of knowledge of Martin Luther and his protestant reforms. His sermons against the Roman Catholic Church's authority were illustrated primarily by Lucas Cranach the Elder (1472–1553) alongside Lutheran texts. Cranach decorated the frame of the title page with a single woodcut illustration, a radical innovation. The title page denoted the content through text, and bold illustrative borders. A portrait of Luther, strong in facial character, impassive, devout, looking outward to the future, was the heroic central motif. Luther's name would dominate the bold text, with Wittenberg given large lettering, to link the place of publication to the origin of the Reformation. Luther approved of Cranach's marketing tactic and is known to have signed copies of Cranach's engraved portrait of himself. Throughout Germany, print versions of text and woodcut were widely copied and redistributed in other towns, and on to other cities in Europe. In Mainz, Gutenberg's new printing press revolutionised printing. In Basel, Switzerland, the German-born publisher Johannes Froben commissioned his friends the Holbein brothers to create woodcut illustrations for his book publications. In Germany, art and literature were united in cultural and religious activity.

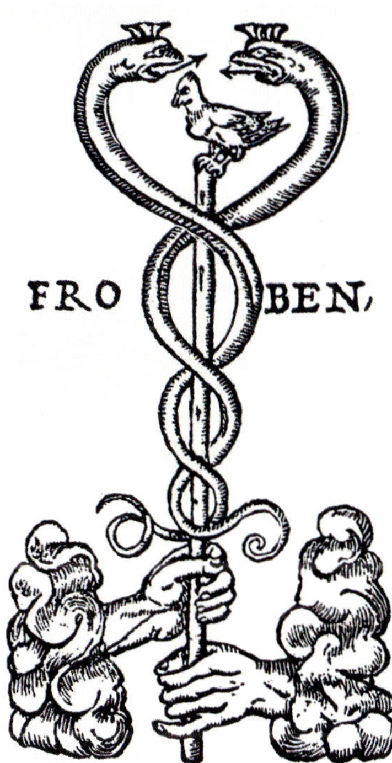

Above: The Trademark Printer's Device *1515, of the distinguished German-born publisher Johannes Froben, living in Basel. Froben was a friend to the Holbein brothers, commissioning them for woodcut book illustration.*

Right: In 1518 Froben published the first Basel edition of Sir Thomas More's book Utopia 1516, *with woodcut illustrations by the Holbein brothers. The title page depicted here,* The View of Utopia, *was probably created by Ambrosius Holbein. This edition was hand-tinted at a later date. It is thought that the island in the shape of a skull (with a ship of teeth) is a hidden memento mori.*

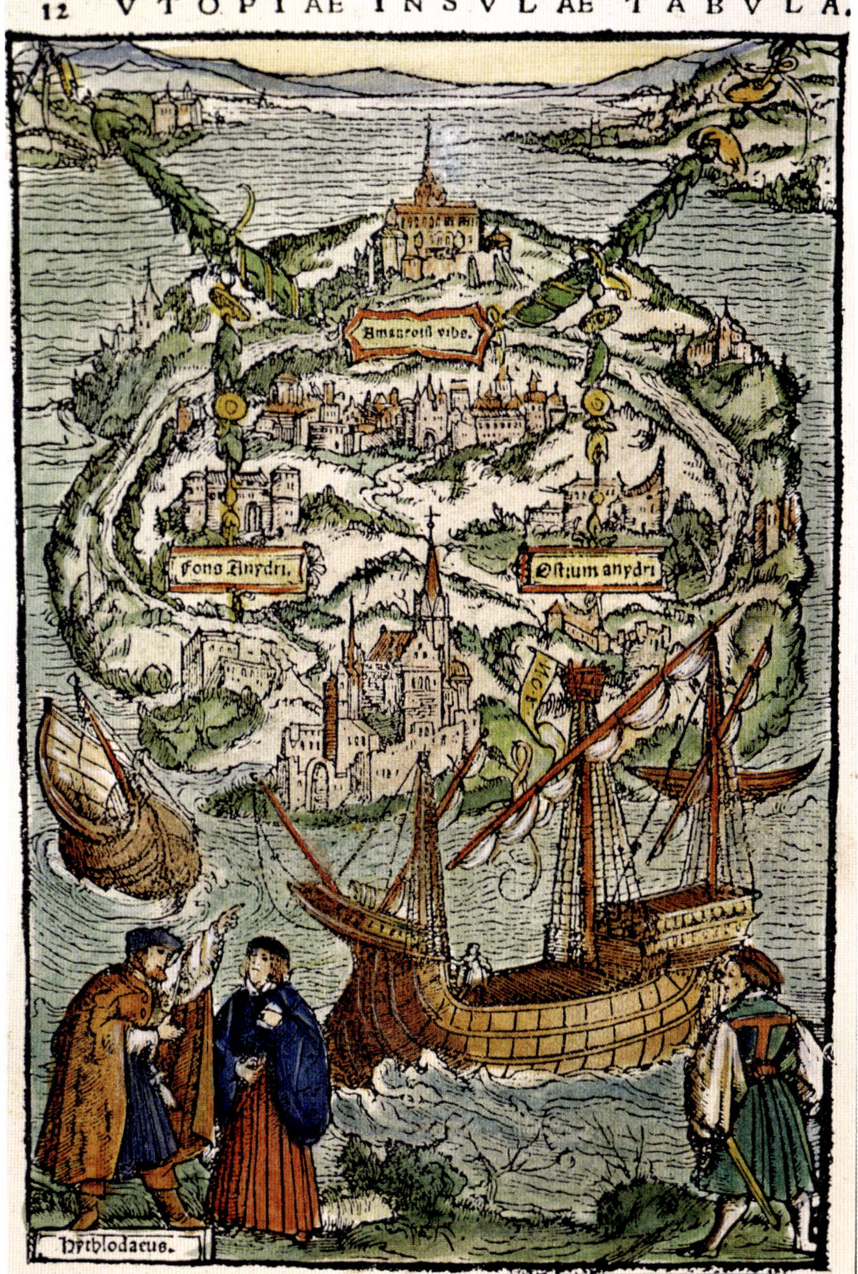

PEOPLE AND HOUSES

The Holbeins travelled to take up various commissions, and Holbein the Younger is recorded as working in nearby Lucerne as well as Basel. Architectural and portrait commissions from the prominent Hertenstein family further established his artistic reputation.

Holbein the Younger is first recorded as being in Lucerne by 28th October 1517, and it is thought that he lived there for two years. He and his father were commissioned to decorate the new house of the mayor Jakob von Hertenstein (c.1460–1527). The mayor also commissioned Holbein the Younger to paint a portrait of his eldest son, Benedikt von Hertenstein (c.1495–1522). In 1517 Benedikt von Hertenstein became a member of the Great Council of Lucerne, an event that may have prompted the portrait commission.

BENEDIKT VON HERTENSTEIN

It is interesting to note that Holbein, concurrently working on the frieze façade for Hertenstein senior and his son's portrait, also includes an illusionistic classical Roman sculptured frieze above the younger Hertenstein's head. Holbein painted it in oil and gold on paper, transferred and laid down on wood. This probably meant that he began the work as a drawing on paper and worked it up to a finished painting in oils. Benedikt, wearing a robe with voluminous sleeves, glances directly at the spectator, as if to speak the words that Holbein painted on the work. The sitter states: 'When I looked like this I was twenty-two years old'. The quote continues to inform us that 'HH' painted the work. The sitter looks out at us sideways, and one almost feels that it should be viewed standing at the right, looking to the left toward the shadowed corner niche.

BONIFACIUS AMERBACH

On his return from Lucerne to Basel, Holbein was commissioned to paint a portrait of Bonifacius Amerbach (1495–1562). Bonifacius was the third son of Johann (Johannes) Amerbach (1440–1513), a university master, and distinguished printer of Basel. Bonifacius was a humanist like his father, studying law and classical languages from 1512 at the University of Freiburg (Breisgau), followed by University of Avignon in 1520, earning a doctorate in 1524–25. His academic achievements led to a professorship in Civil and Roman law awarded at University of Basel in 1525.

A learned intellectual, the artist paints Bonifacius aged twenty-four, at the midway point of his university studies. The 1519 portrait is a composition in an

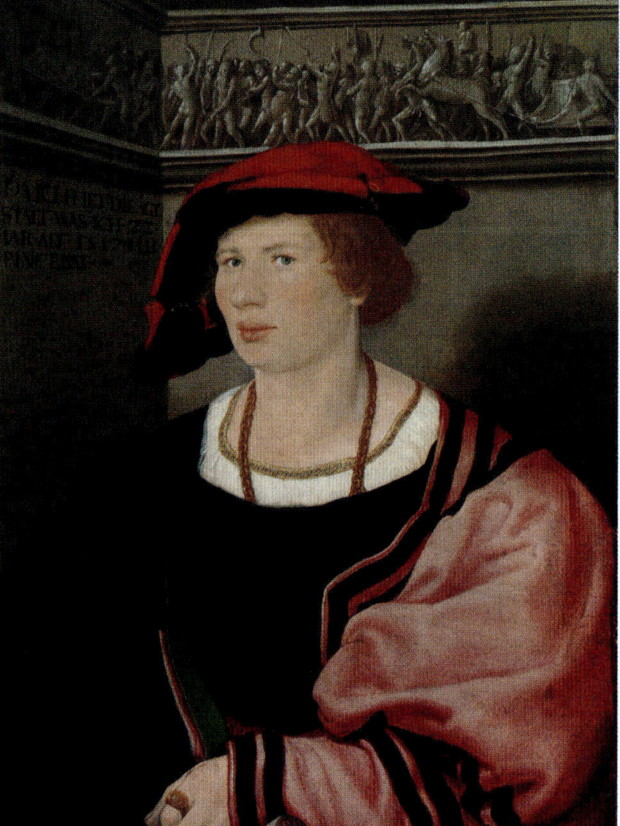

Left: A superb half-length Portrait of Benedikt von Hertenstein, *1517, by Holbein the Younger, depicts the sitter in his twenty-second year, as indicated by the script on the wall behind him. Benedikt, near in age to Holbein, lived only five years after this portrait was completed.*

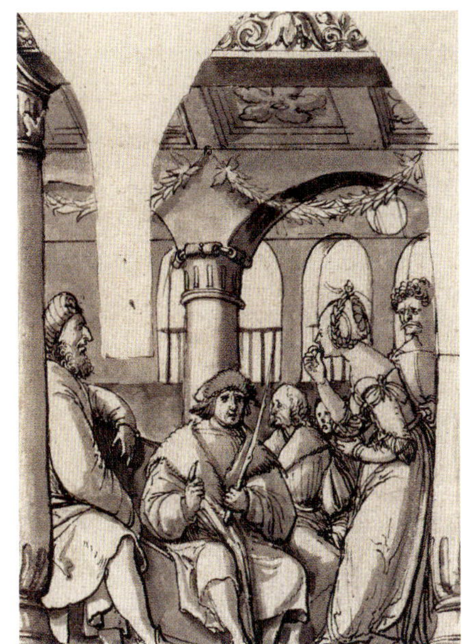

Above: Holbein's extant drawing for one of the Hertenstein murals, depicting Leaina, a legendary courtesan from ancient Athens. She bites off her tongue rather than testify to judges against her lover Aritogeiton, for tyrannicide.

outdoor setting. Holbein deftly captures his sitter's youthful visage, and the soft hair of the beard and moustache. He wears a large outdoor cap and fur-edged coat. Bonifacius stands in semi-profile, looking toward a wooden tablet affixed to a tree. The Latin inscription written on the wooden tablet, that hangs from a broken twig on a tree, is a self-portrait in metrical verse, composed by Bonifacius himself. It was fitting that the academic Bonifacius should compose a text to accompany the work. In the painting he turns his head half-right to face the verse, as if to speak the words. In translation it reads:

'Although only a painted likeness, I am not inferior to the living face; I am instead the counterpart of my master and distinguished by accurate lines. Just as he completes three intervals each lasting eight years, [which means Bonifacius is twenty-four years old] *this work of art diligently renders his true character. Jo* [Hannes] *Holbein painted Bon* [ifacius] *Amerbach on 14 October 1519.'*

The date in the inscription on the portrait, 14th October 1519, was Bonifacius' twenty-fourth birthday, not the date of the sitting, and it is thought

that another portrait had been planned, showing Bonifacius clean-shaven, possibly as a companion pair – not an unusual occurrence – but this did not materialise, possibly due to the death of Bonifacius' brother Bruno, on 22nd October, and the sorrow that had come suddenly upon the family.

THE ZUM TANZ HOUSE

After his work on the Hertenstein house exterior in Lucerne, in Basel, Holbein was commissioned in 1520 to decorate the façade of the 'Zum Tanz' house of a rich goldsmith, Balthaszar Angelroth (*c*.1480–1544). The gold merchant's house, on the corner of Eisengasse, had a history related to dance since 1401, and Angelroth wanted a design that incorporated this. Holbein created a frieze of dancing figures, crossing the house frontage. It was spectacular. The result created a sensation in Basel, and sealed Holbein's reputation as designer, decorator and painter. Two initial sketches survived (see page 115) but the house did not.

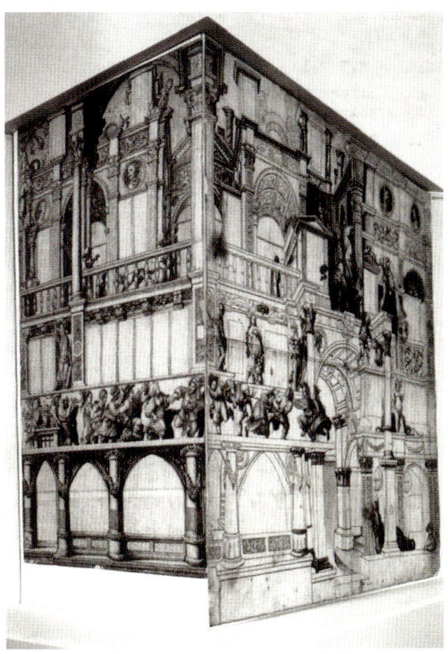

Above: The façade of the Zum Tanz house, or 'the House of the Dance' (shown in a reconstruction).

Below: Portrait of Bonifacius Amerbach, 1519, a humanist, and a friend of Erasmus of Rotterdam, was painted by Hans Holbein the Younger in Basel.

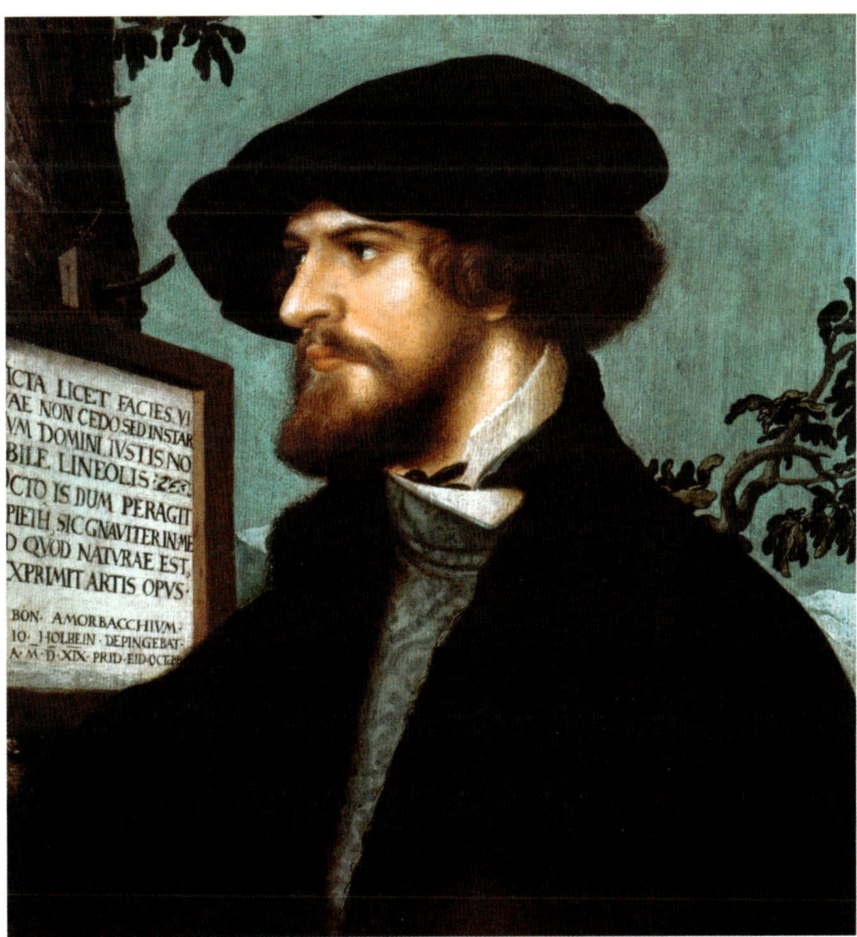

RELIGIOUS COMMISSIONS

Holbein's portraits reveal an exceptional skill for capturing likeness, and a sense of the temperament of the sitter. This ability carried through to his religious depictions of biblical characters, bringing naturalism to ancient faces. There were recurring religious themes for artists, but individual interpretations can be seen.

Holbein's earliest known religious artworks – he decreased this during the zealous fracas between Reformers and Catholics, particularly in Augsburg and Basel – were the beautiful pendants *Head of a Male Saint* and its companion piece *Head of a Female Saint, c.1515* (see pages 106–7) possibly part of a larger work, since destroyed.

ADAM AND EVE

The subject of Adam and Eve, and their Fall from the Grace of God, was a popular choice for patrons of visual art in monastic fraternities, in churches, private chapels, and devotional works for private homes. In the Christian world it was a perpetual reminder

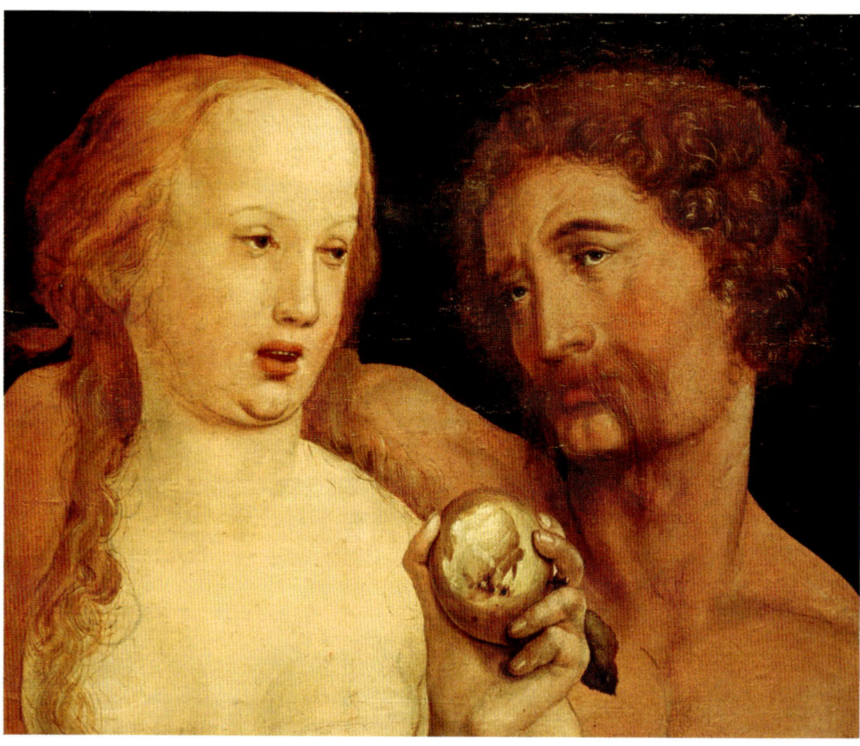

Above: Adam and Eve, 1517, by Holbein the Younger, is a perhaps curious depiction of the first man and woman. A moustachioed Adam drapes his arm around Eve's neck as she holds the apple, purveyor of carnal knowledge.

Right: Nearly a century before, Italian painter Tommaso Masaccio (1401–28) depicted a sorrowful, harrowing narrative of Adam and Eve banished from Paradise, c.1427 (detail of fresco in Santa Maria del Carmine, Florence).

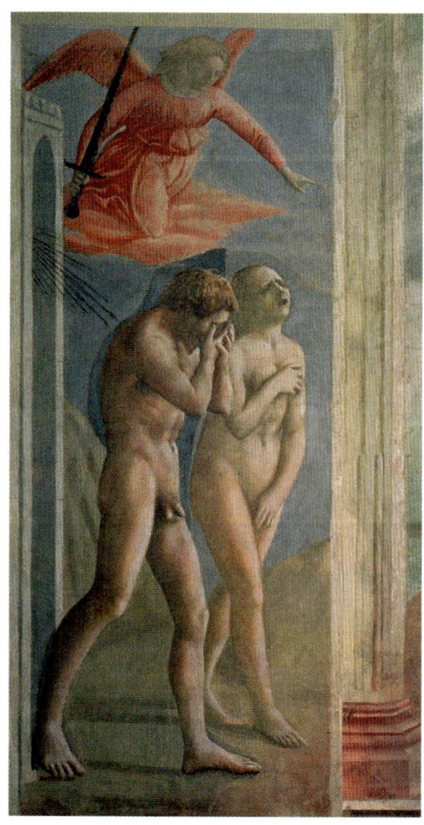

of the power and wrath of God in a period that fervently believed, whether a Catholic or Reformant, in an Almighty God and the Hereafter. Holbein's depiction of Earth's first man and woman, *Adam and Eve*, in 1517, reveals his talent for adding a touch of mortal reality. He portrayed Adam with an arm draped loosely around Eve's shoulder. She holds in her hand a worm-ridden half-eaten apple. Her skin is pale in contrast to the heavily tanned head and body of Adam. Her mouth is small, her chin double, her expression worried. Adam has grown a wispy, long moustache on his weathered, weary face. Holbein's face of Eve expresses an element of shock. She seems to comprehend the consequence of ignoring God's command not to eat the fruit. Holbein captures the tired resignation of Adam and Eve that pre-empts their expulsion from the Garden of Eden.

It was the profession of the artist to consider innovative ways to depict the life of Adam and Eve from the biblical account (Genesis 1:1–2:4). It is very different from the Italian early Renaissance artist, Tommaso Masaccio's depiction, created nearly one hundred years before for the Brancacci Chapel of Santa Maria del Carmine in Florence. In the fresco *Expulsion of Adam and Eve from Eden*, Masaccio movingly captured the emotional couple in physical pain, distraught in their suffering, and the naturalism of their weakness, the cause of the original sin of mankind.

DEPICTING THE MADONNA

Holbein painted images of the Madonna many times, from altarpieces to private, devotional paintings. In larger works, such as *The Solothurn Madonna* where the Madonna is the focal point, his idealised interpretation follows the style of Netherlandish and Italian art from the mid-1400s, but in an informal

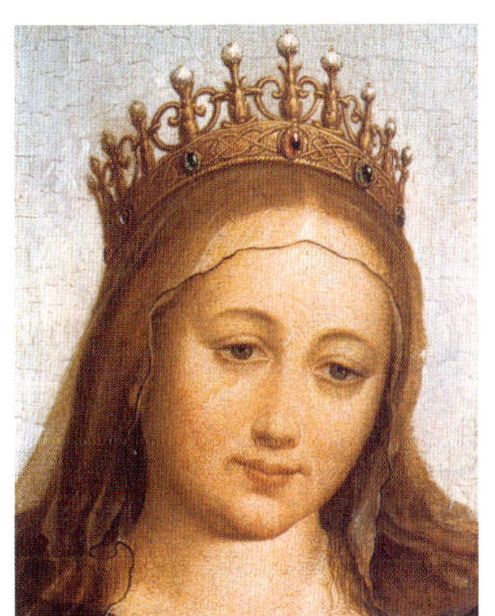

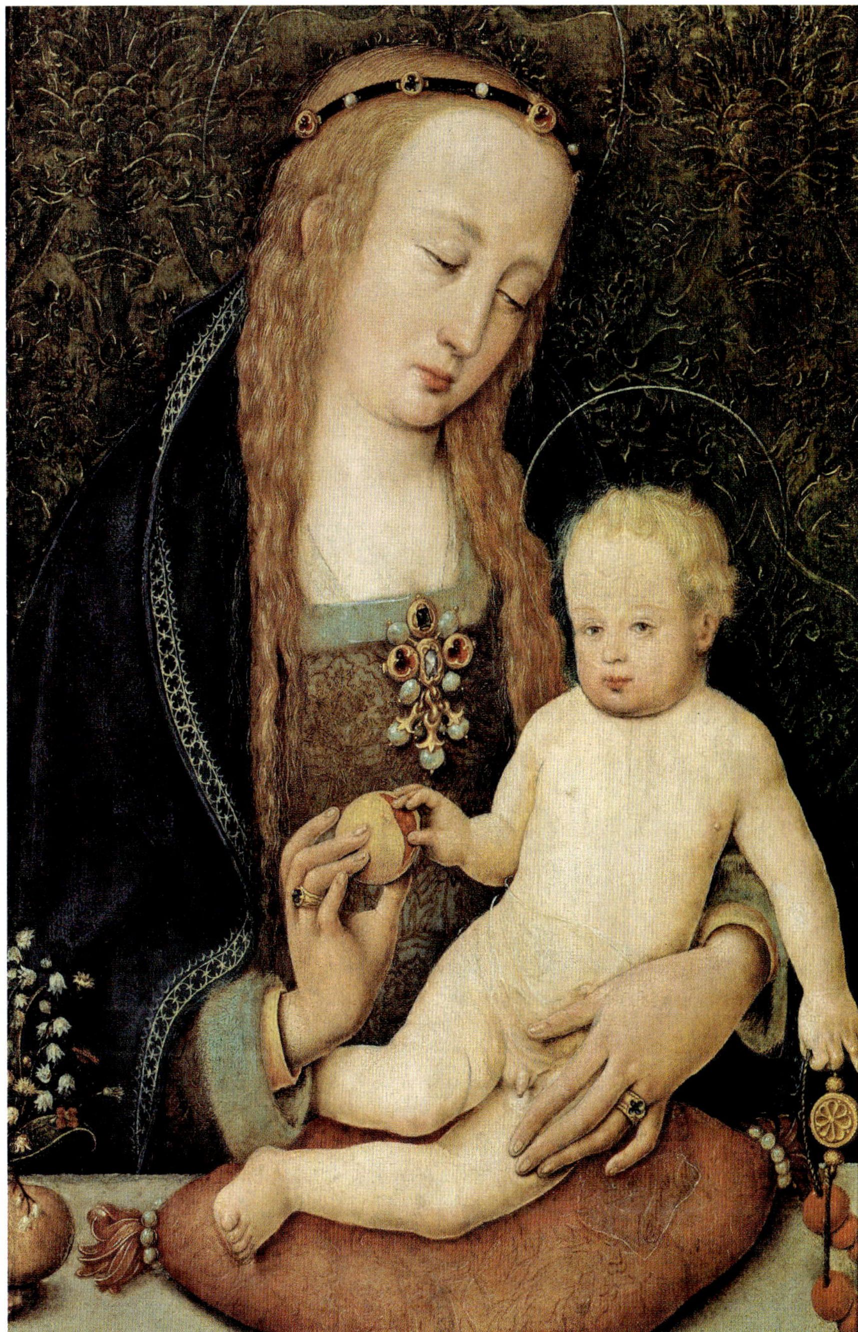

portrayal, a perception which unites the humanist earthly world with the eternal world. After Holbein's visit to France in 1523–24, where he was exposed to Italian and French art, possibly at the court of Francis I, his depictions of the Madonna and infant Christ became more humanist, as can be seen in *Darmstadt Madonna*, 1526–after 1528

Left: A detail from The Solothurn Madonna *(see pages 120–1), painted by Holbein the Younger in 1520–22, depicts the gentle mother of the infant Christ.*

Above: Holbein the Elder painted this beautiful depiction of Mary in Virgin and Child with Pomegranate, *1510–12.*

(see pages 44–45), where Mary, Queen of Heaven, Virgin of Pity, protector of the Meyer family, is visualised as a young mother. In this painting, commissioned by the deeply religious Meyer, the donor's family are depicted kneeling in the presence of the Virgin Mary, the infant cousins Christ and John the Baptist, and possibly the apostle James as a boy, kneeling.

DEPICTING THE DEAD CHRIST

Following decorative works in Basel, Holbein turned his attention to a religious portrayal, a remarkable visualisation of the dead Christ lying in his tomb, rightly considered to be one of his most groundbreaking works. Comparing the differing depiction of the Passion by other artists offers interesting contrast.

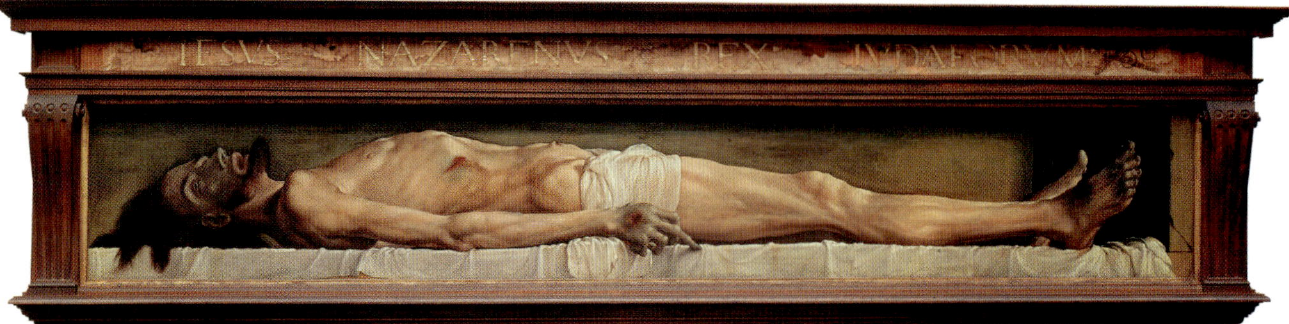

The large limewood panel work of 1521–22 portrays Christ after crucifixion, lying entombed after death, his eyes rolled back, and mouth open. The human realism is explicit. Holbein portrays the evidence of brutality. Christ's torture and death are laid before the viewer.

In the 1587 house inventory of its later owner Basilius Amerbach (1533–91) – son of lawyer and humanist Bonifacius Amerbach (1495–1562), a patron of Holbein – the work is simply described as 'An image of a corpse by HHolbein on wood in oils'. The horizontal landscape format adds to the claustrophobia the spectator experiences when viewing the work. Its narrow, rectangular life-size tomb shape has led historians to consider it

Below: Lamentation of Christ, c.1480 *by Italian painter Andrea Mantegna is an outstanding example of foreshortening.*

Above: Holbein the Younger's Dead Christ in the Tomb, *1521–22, is one of his first masterpieces. The realism of bruising on the body of Christ is remarkable. The composition connotes a burial chamber.*

to be a predella panel, the lower part of an altarpiece, but this would seem unlikely due to the painted inscription above it: 'IESUS NAZARENUSREX JIUDAEORUM' (Jesus of Nazareth, King of the Jews), held by angels carrying the instruments of the Passion. Another theory is that it was destined for the sepulchral chapel of Bonifacius Amerbach's family, possibly not realised due to iconoclastic tensions in Basel caused by the Reformation.

Holbein's command to portray a life in death, highlights how natural it was for him to signify a person and their life through expression, room setting, clothing, and gesture. If he could create the masterpiece *Dead Christ in the Tomb*, so early in his career, what would follow would be down to contacts, and introductions to the patrons who recognised his undoubted talent. Bonifacius was closely linked to Desiderius Erasmus, and he became executor and heir to his estates in 1536.

The painter's portrayal of *Dead Christ in the Tomb* reveals Christ the man, his body broken by a human, painful, agonisingly slow death. It is a painting that is poignant and terrible

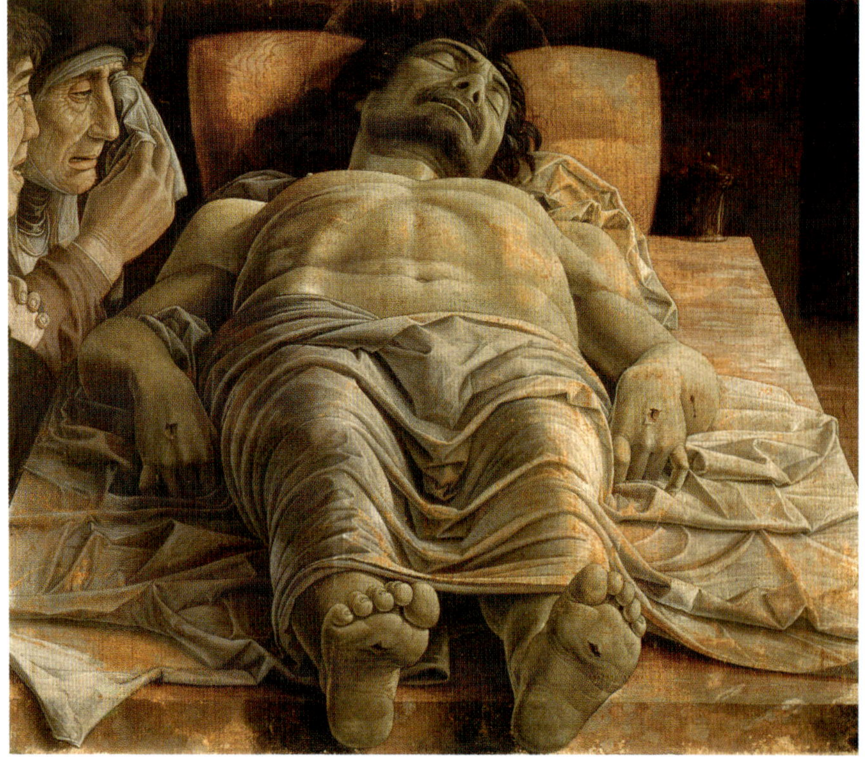

DOSTOYEVSKY AND HOLBEIN'S 'DEAD CHRIST'

In the novel *The Idiot*, 1868–69, by Russian writer Fyodor Dostoyevsky (1821–81) there is a text passage in which two fictional characters discuss a painting. This work is Holbein's *Dead Christ in the Tomb*, which Dostoyevsky had viewed in 1846–7. He was moved by Holbein's unflinching depiction of the life-size body with its battered flesh showing evidence of physical pain. In the text Dostoyevsky's character Prince Myshkin states that it had the power to make you lose one's faith. The writer discussed artists' representations of the dead Christ, and how different this depiction is [by Holbein], who shows Christ as a fragile human being, whose broken body has suffered torture and painful death. Dostoyevsky's character Hippolite Terentyev poses questions on faith. He asks what effect that sight of 'this face so mangled and bleeding and bruised' must have had on Christ's followers and family? Reading Dostoyevsky's analysis of the painting allows one to consider if Holbein also related the human suffering of Christ with the human suffering experienced in his time by Christian congregations, split as they were between Catholicism and Lutheran Protestantism.

in its realistic depiction of the suffering of one man who represents humanity. In 1847, when the Russian dissident, Fyodor Dostoyevsky stood in front of the work, he was visibly shaken, shocked to view the reality of Christ's death, to bear witness to the frailty of a young man, tortured and reduced to a sunken-flesh mortal frame. Is there a link between Holbein's portrayal and the radical religious reform that was slowly building momentum in Basel, where he was living and working? Holbein was a witness of the tremors resulting from Martin Luther's stand against the Catholic church. The humanists, who

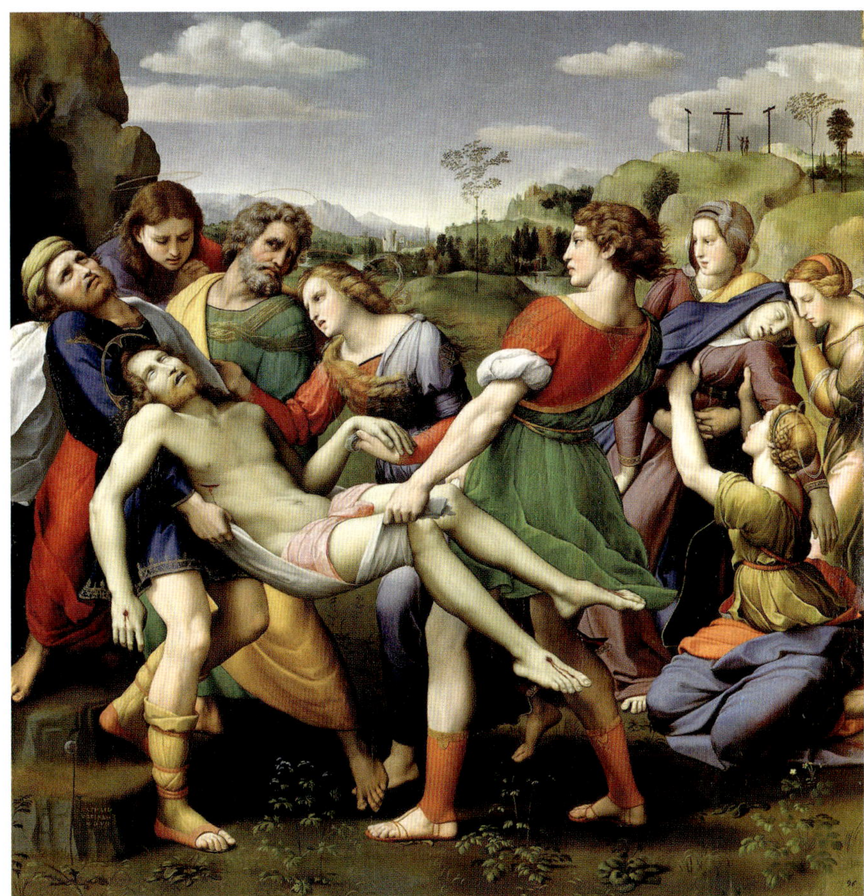

increasingly gained in influence and status from the mid-fourteenth century in Italy, acknowledged that Christ, son of God, was human and that Man was the mirror-image of God, and thus God was within all Mankind, and they equal to him.

Above: Italian Raphael Sanzio's (1485–1520) The Deposition (Pala Baglioni), 1507, is a more colourful visualisation.

Below: A detail from The Crucifixion on the Isenheim altarpiece c.1512–15 by Mathias Grunewald (c.1470–1528).

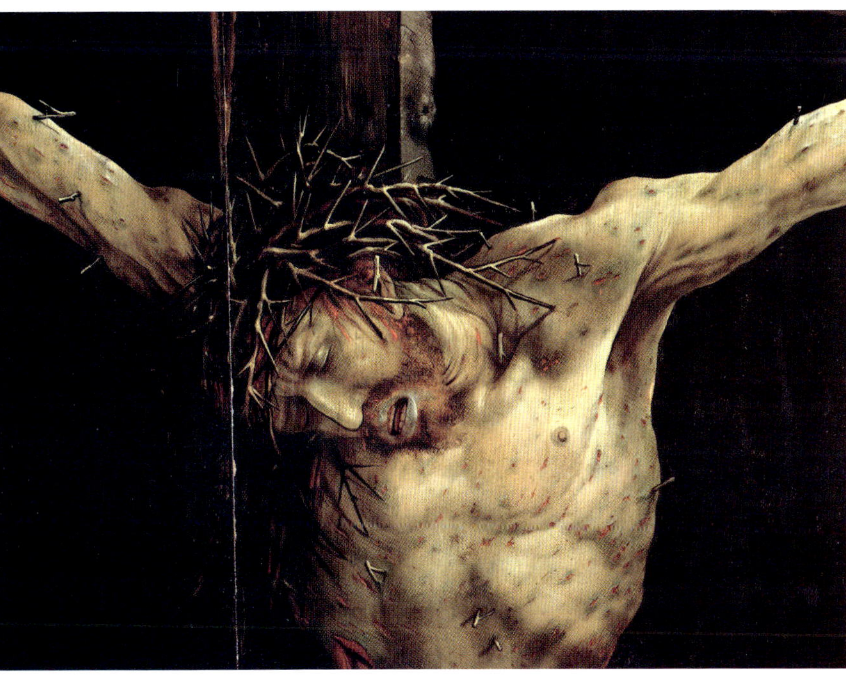

THE DANCE OF DEATH

A series of 51 woodblocks by Holbein, 41 of which were later published as *The Dance of Death*, was informed by a late-medieval allegory, popularised in woodcut prints and paintings, that visualised the moment where life meets death. Holbein created the series c.1523–26 but it was not published until 1538.

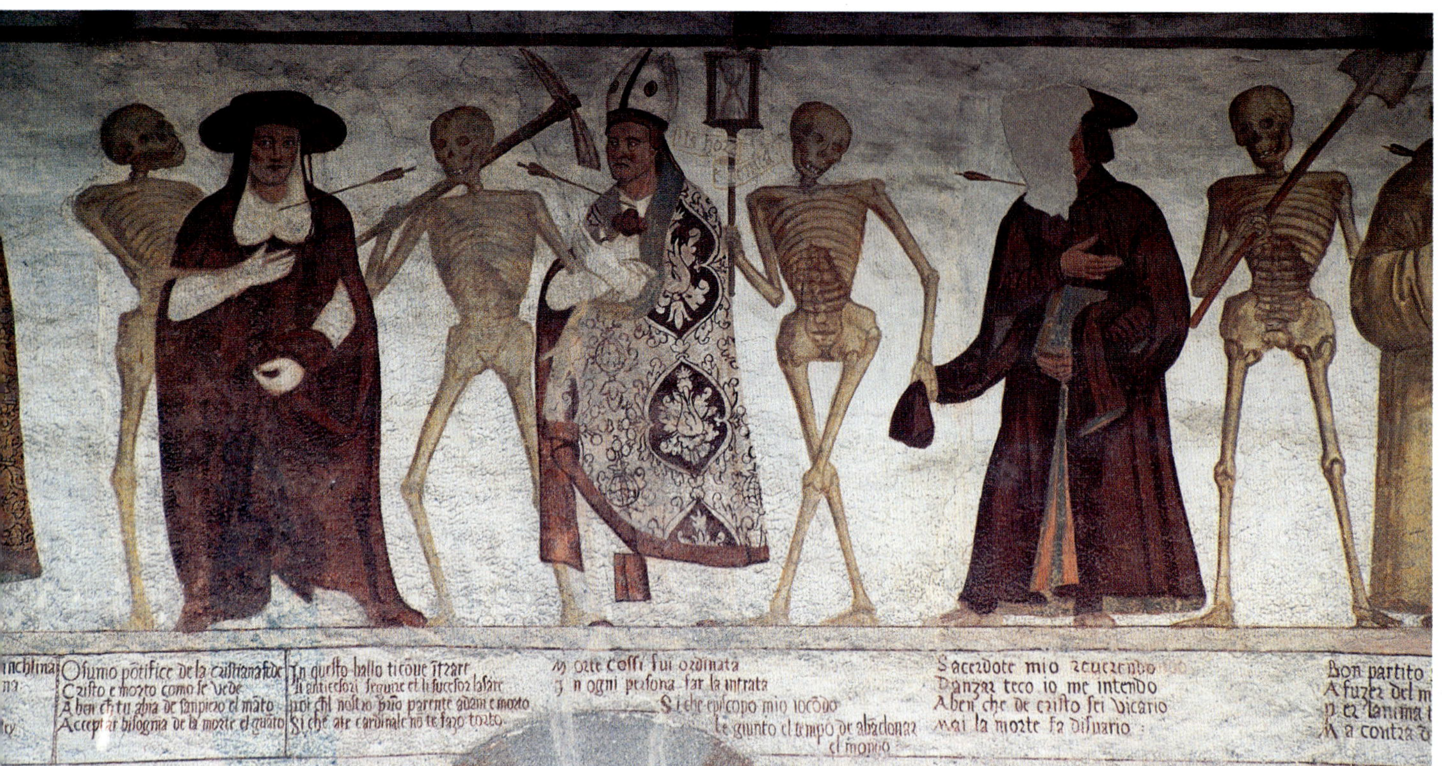

The 'Dance of Death' is a macabre visual reminder that life is brief, and death awaits all, however rich, titled, good or evil. It is thought to have originated in ancient times, and later brought to public display in religious or morality plays, and connected to funeral rites. Death is the embracing leveller: images of the Dance of Death show skeletal figures calling to many

Above: Danse Macabre, *where skeletal figures gaily accompany clerics and priests to their death, is a detail from a 16th-century fresco by Simone Baschenis (1519–1544), in the Church of St Vigilius, Pinzolo, Trentino, Italy.*

Right: Deceased, decaying bodies dance with lively skeletal figures in Dance of Death, *a late 15th-century engraving by German painter Michael Wolgemut (1434–1519) for* Liber Chronicarum (Nuremberg Chronicle), *1493.*

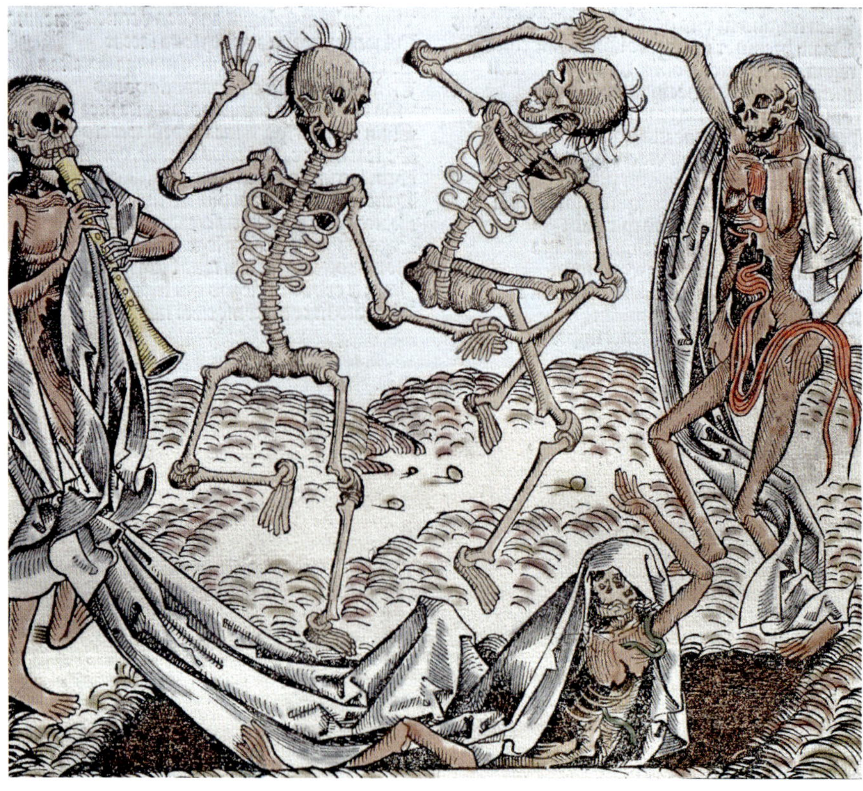

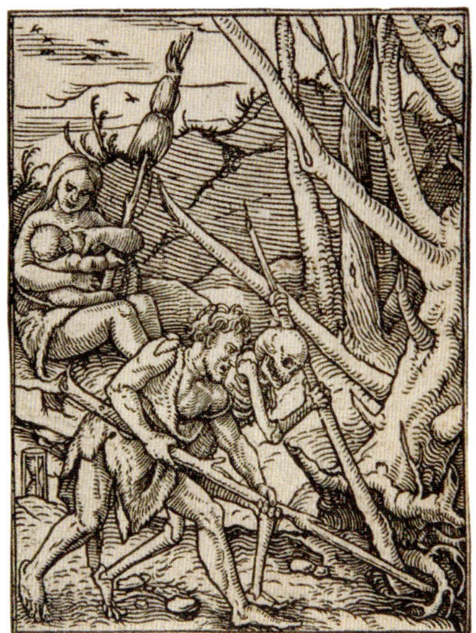

Above: Eve nurses her baby while Adam tills the soil, rooting up a tree. Skeletal Death accompanies Adam to his fate. From Holbein the Younger's woodcut series Dance of Death.

from all walks of life, from the highest rank to the lowest peasant; from the Pope and members of the clergy, the Duke and Nobleman, to the astrologer and the physician, and down to the more rudimentary ploughman, seaman, peddler, merchant and old woman. Death, in the form of dancing skeletons, calls upon them all to claim their lives.

IMAGES OF DEATH

The intricate woodblock series (later called Dances of Death, or Pictures of Death) was created early on in Holbein's career, c.1523–26, but published later in 1538 and 1545. He added to the series, and also created a number of decorative alphabets on the theme of Death, commissioned by woodcutter Hans Lützelburger, and used and printed in a number of publications.

The dance of death as a subject was popular in Germany and Switzerland during the fourteenth and fifteenth centuries. Before Holbein executed his series, at least two paintings of the subject were extant in Basel but not published, and may have been known to him, plus earlier woodcuts, such as *The Dance of Death* (1493) by the German Late Gothic painter and printmaker Michael Wolgemut, who

with his stepson Wilhelm Pleydenwurff, created hundreds of designs for the woodcuts of *Liber Chronicarum* (Nuremberg Chronicle), written by Hartmann Schedel. This book is the most extensively illustrated work of this period and would have been known in the art circles that Holbein frequented.

The dance of death was portrayed in many formats. Often it took the visual form of Death calling on the terminally ill. In a painting, thought to be by Hieronymus Bosch (c.1450–1516), *The Seven Deadly Sins and the Four Last Things*, c.1480, the first of the four last things (Death, Judgement, Hell, Paradise) is a smiling skeletal figure peeping from behind wood panelling, to view the near-dead man lying in bed, surrounded by family and clergy. Death waits for the body's life to cease; close by, an angel and satanic devil look on the death scene, waiting to see where the man's soul will go. In another Bosch painting, *Death and the Miser*, c.1500–10, an angel and a devil are in attendance, as Death appears from behind the door, pointing the arrow of death at the dying miser. The vision is macabre and humorous.

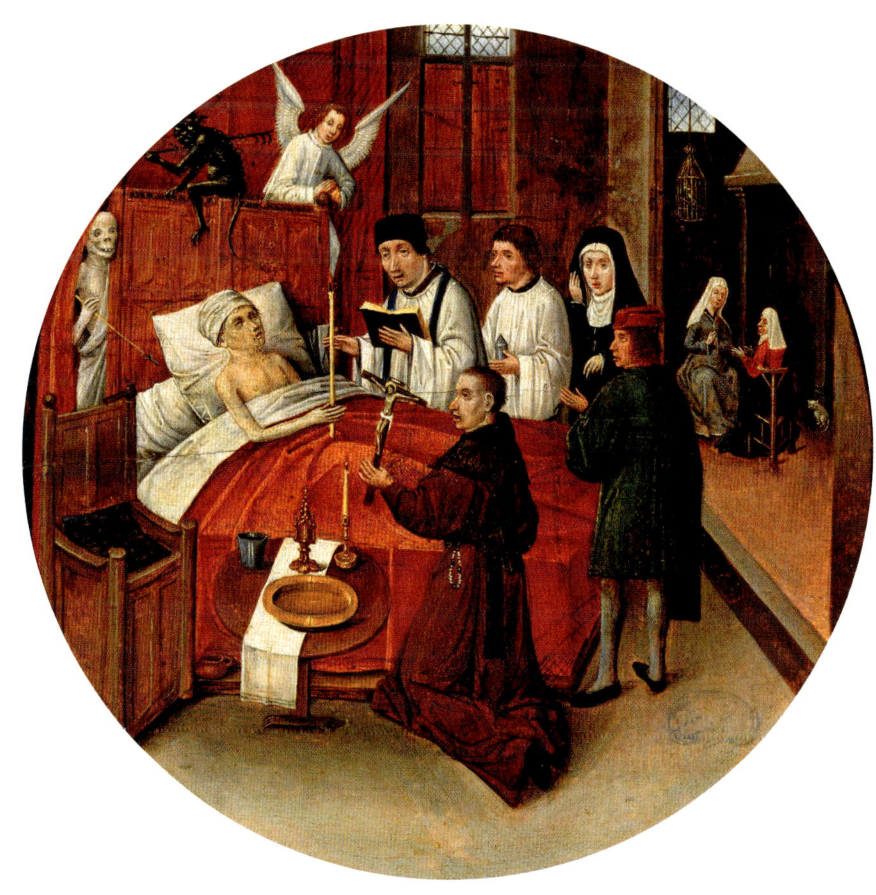

Below: In The Seven Deadly Sins and the Four Last Things, *c.1480, by Netherlandish painter Hieronymus Bosch, Death waits for his moment as a priest serves the Last Sacrament to an ailing, bedridden man.*

A PORTRAIT OF ERASMUS

An important patron of Hans Holbein in Basel was the scholarly priest and humanist Desiderius Erasmus (1466–1536), held in intellectual esteem throughout Europe. Erasmus was born illegitimate, in Gouda, near Rotterdam. From this inauspicious beginning he became the leading thinker of the day.

On October 27th 1466, to Margaret, daughter of a physician of Zevenbergen, in the northern province of Nord-Brabant, Netherlands, and a priest, Robert Gerard of Gouda, a baby was born, whom they named Gerard Gerardson. They called him Erasmus, meaning 'beloved'. In adulthood he would be the lynchpin to Holbein's distinguished career at the court of Henry VIII, king of England. Erasmus was educated from the age of four at a local school in Gouda, and from age nine was sent to a Latin school to further his education. In his late teens, in 1483, Erasmus's parents died of plague, and thence he was subjugated to parental control by guardians. It was their wish that Erasmus enter monastic life. As a monk, religious dogma forced him to weigh his staunch belief in Humanism alongside a dutiful, pious life of faithful

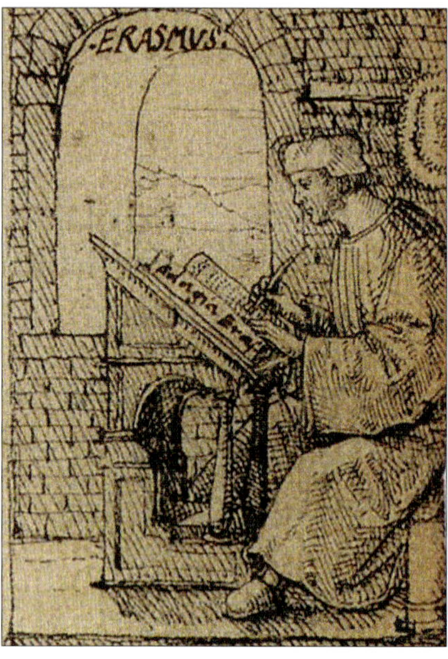

Above: A margin drawing of Erasmus, 1515, by Holbein the Younger. The Holbein brothers made many margin illustrations in schoolmaster Oswald Myconius' copy of Erasmus's book Praise of Folly.

servitude. He travelled through Europe and spent some years in England, staying with Thomas More (where he wrote *Praise of Folly*), and lecturing; an esteemed scholar, he was received in intellectual circles and courts, at one point tutoring the French king Francis I's sons.

MEETING HOLBEIN

When Erasmus journeyed to the city of Basel in 1513, he met and made friends with the jurist, professor of civil law and noted Basel-born scholar Bonifacius Amerbach (1495–1562). Educated in law at Avignon, Bonifacius was the son of publisher Johann Amerbach (1430–1513). It was possibly Amerbach

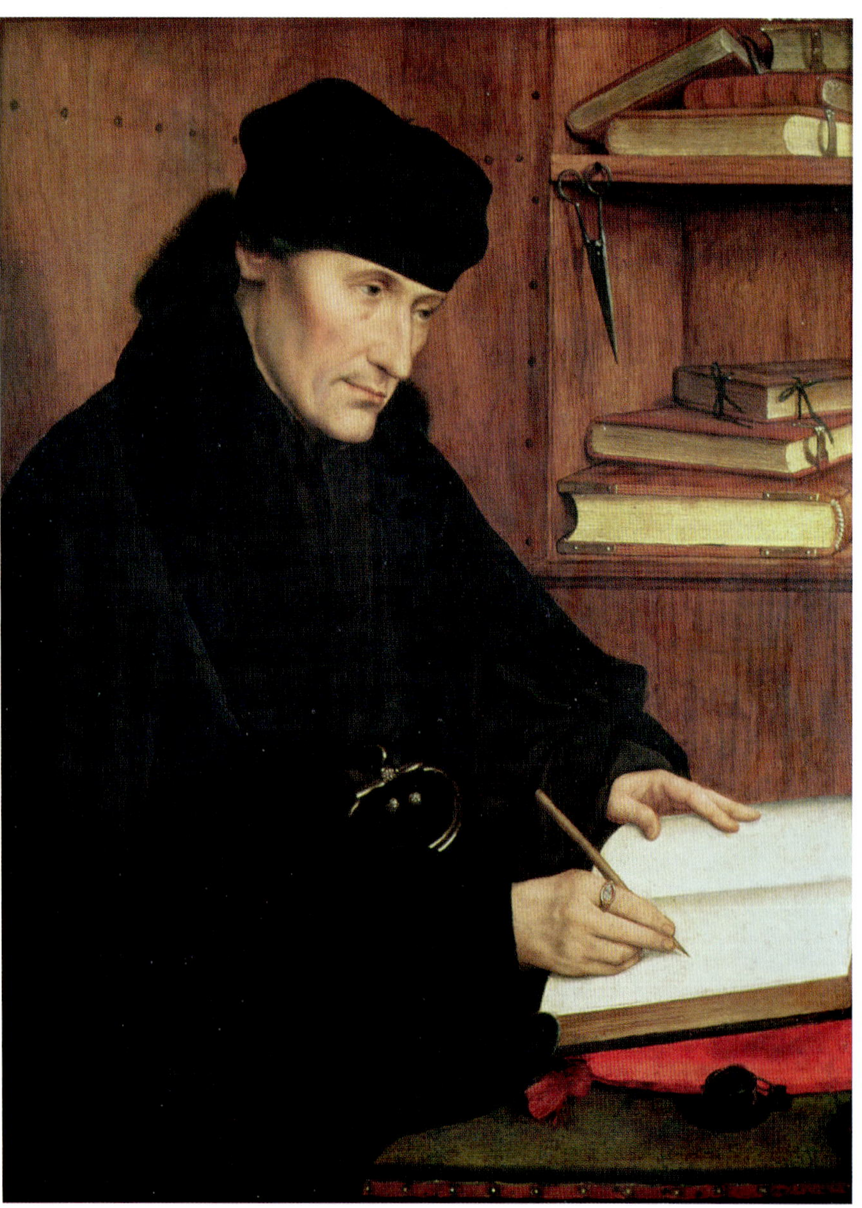

Left: Portrait of Erasmus of Rotterdam, *1517, superbly painted by the Flemish artist Quinten Massys/Metsys (c.1466–1530).*

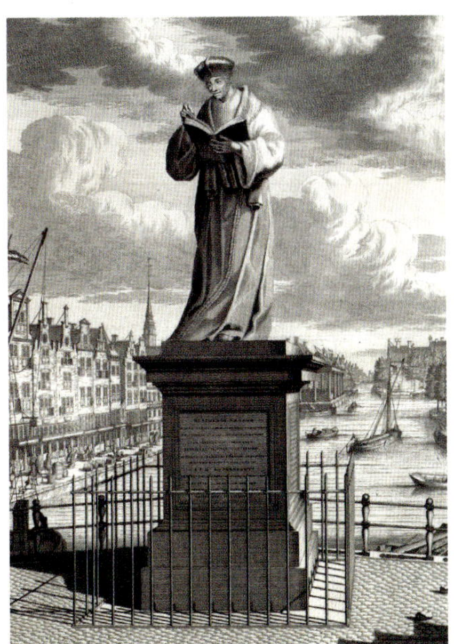

Above: The statue of Erasmus in Rotterdam, city of his birth. In 1622 the stone statue was replaced with a bronze.

that introduced Erasmus to Holbein the Younger. All three – Erasmus, Bonifacius and Holbein – became friends.

PAINTING ERASMUS

Holbein painted at least three portraits of Desiderius Erasmus (see also pages 134–35 and 169). One can see in his portrayals an artist bringing everything that he has learned and accomplished in portraiture over the previous ten years to fruition in *Portrait of Erasmus*

IN PRAISE OF FOLLY

Erasmus wrote many scholarly papers. One polemical work *Moriae Encomium: Stulticiae Laus*, 'Praise of Folly', written in Latin, first published in 1511 and then revised in 1515, is generally known by its shortened title *Moria*, the name given to the main character. It is within this text that Erasmus, whilst recognising the worthiness of his Roman Catholic faith, highlights under the guise of debate the arguments made by the protester Reformants breaking away from the Church of Rome. He, like Holbein the Younger, carefully walked a neutral 'tightrope' between two major religious factions.

of Rotterdam, 1523. This portrait (see page 10 and 134), now in England, is considered by some art historians to be the most important painting in the country. In it Holbein paints a realistic rendering of a remarkable man, a famous writer and respected humanist.

BASEL ICONOCLASM

Desiderius Erasmus moved from Basel to Freiburg in April 1529, a city he found to be calmer, following the iconoclastic violence that erupted in Basel in February against the city's Catholic clergy. Letters written by Erasmus at the time reflect the fear felt by many citizens of Strasbourg and Basel. Catholic churches were being ransacked and religious paintings and

icons destroyed. Erasmus missed his friends in Basel and was saddened by those who had turned against him for their differing opinions towards Luther's reformative programme. Erasmus was sympathetic to Luther's anti-corruption drive, but not to the extreme measures being taken. On his death in 1536 (on a visit to Basel) Erasmus left his Estate, including his collection of Holbein paintings, to his friend Bonifacius Amerbach.

Below: This half-length painting Portrait of Erasmus of Rotterdam, 1523, *by Holbein the Younger, now in the Louvre, compares in its realism and composition, clothing and action of writing, with Quentin Metsys' portrait of 1517 (opposite).*

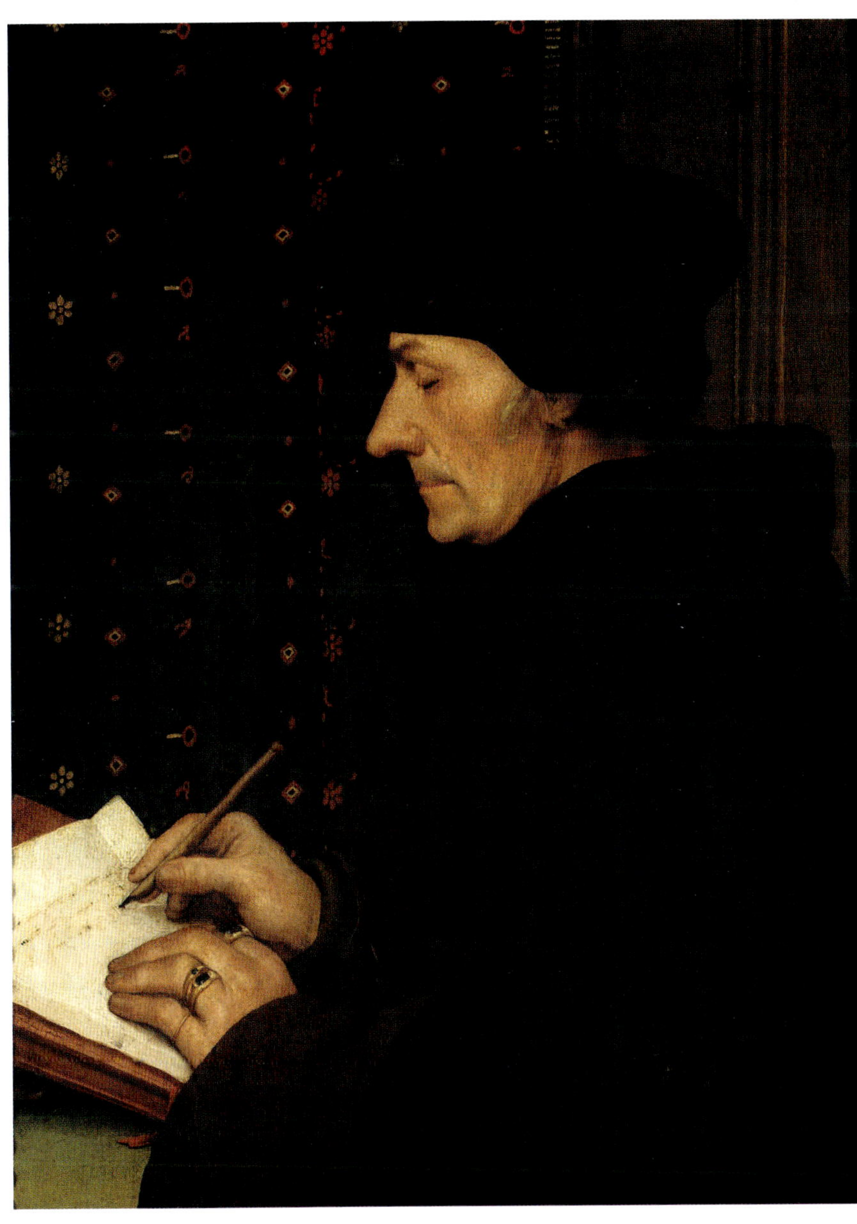

SUCCESS AND IDENTITY

Holbein the Younger was based in Basel from 1515–32, with an extended trip to England in 1526–28. In 1524 the renowned Alsace-born humanist Beatus Bild, living in Basel, placed Holbein alongside artists Albrecht Dürer, Lucas Cranach, and Hans Baldung as one of the four greatest German artists of the period.

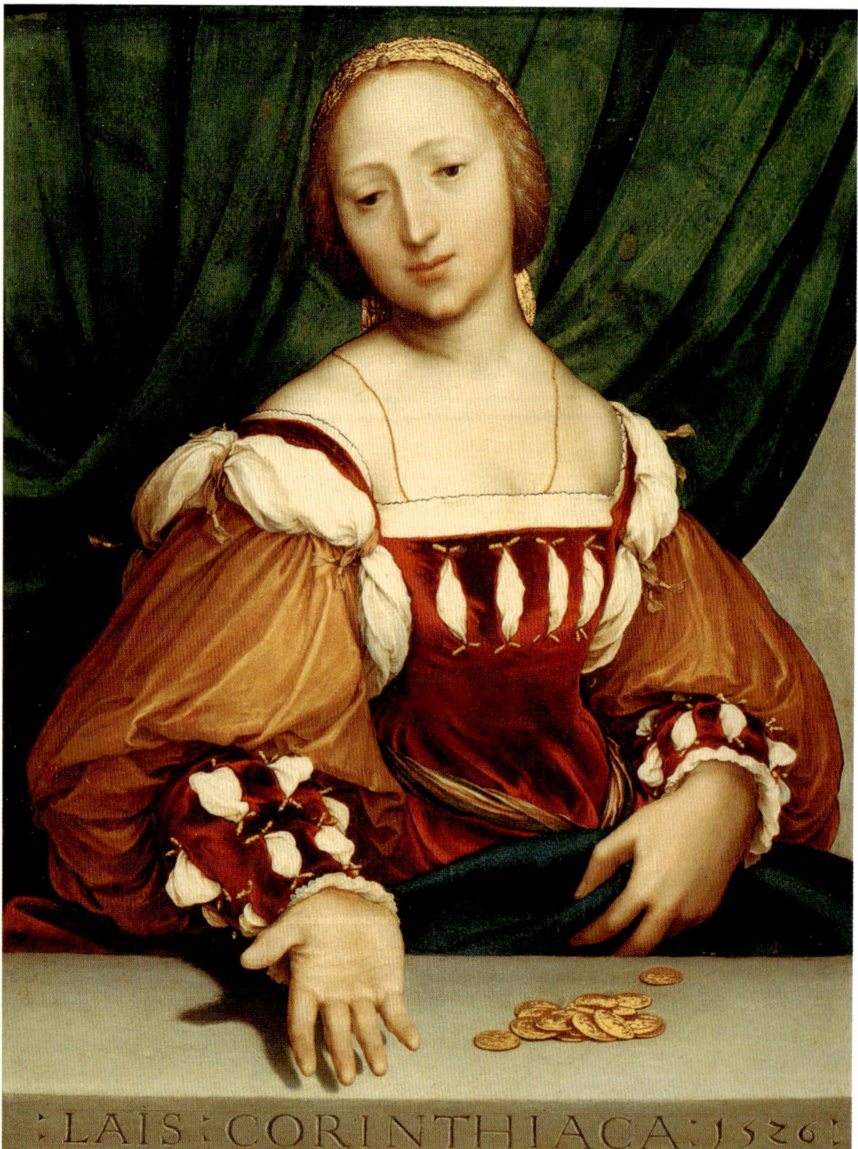

Above: A portrait of Magdalena Offenburg, posing as Holbein the Younger's Laïs Corinthiaca, 1526–28, possibly earlier and finished later. Laïs of Corinth was an hetaira, a high-class courtesan in Greek antiquity, who commanded huge fees for her services, the price of her great beauty, hence her hand outstretched for additional gold coins. Her name is 'carved' into the stone ledge.

In Basel, Holbein had set up a small personal workshop, lesser in size and ambition than his father's, for this was to be for Holbein's own commissions, not a school for apprentices. He accepted a wide variety of work, from prestigious wall designs to small portraits, as well as woodcuts for book illustration. Basel was the perfect city to hone an artistic talent that would ultimately attract royal patronage when he reached the court of Henry VIII.

'ONE OF THE GREATEST'

Prasied as 'one of the four greatest German artists.' by Beatus Bild (1485–1547), also known as Beatus Rhenanus, in 1524, was a considerable endorsement of Holbein's talent, as the artist had been working professionally for only eight years. Bild's statement reflected the opinion of art patrons; Hans Holbein was an exemplary painter.

From a Holbein drawing, it is thought that a highly-skilled assistant in his Basel workshop created, or helped to create, the mythological portrait *Venus and Cupid*, c.1526, depicting the Roman goddess and her infant son (see page 141). Holbein created the painting *Laïs Corinthiaca* in 1526–28. The model in both works is thought to be Magdalena Offenburg, a friend of Holbein's. In his work she poses as Laïs (c.425BC), coveted mistress of the revered painter Apelles (4th-century BC), court artist to Alexander the Great. Holbein, through this remarkable work, was consciously

Below: Beatus Bild, a 1567 printed engraving by Philip Galle, of the German humanist, religious reformer, classical scholar and book collector.

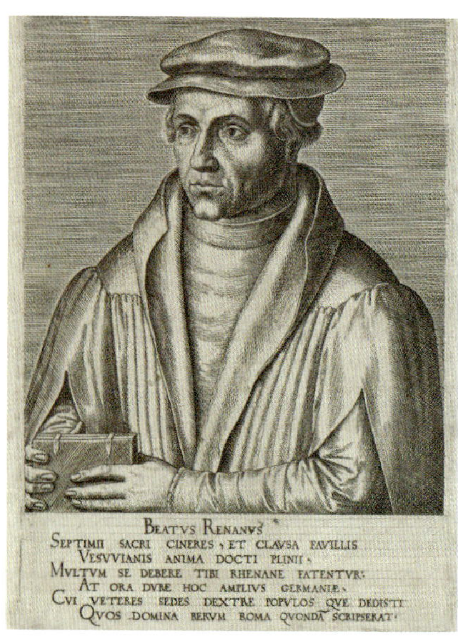

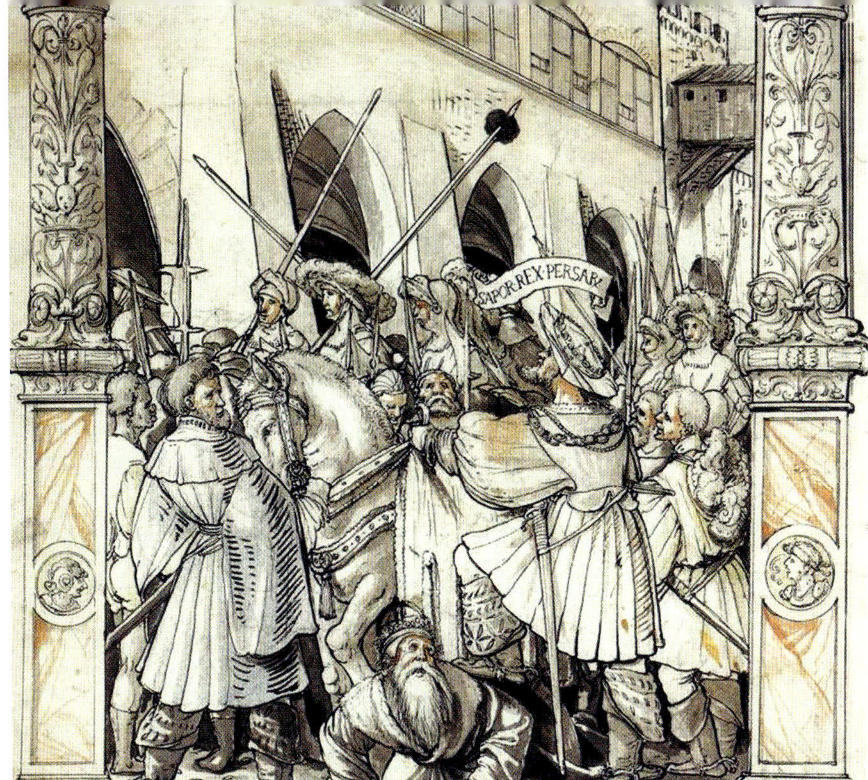

Above: A significant commission for Holbein the Younger was the decoration of Basel's Great Council Chamber. As part of a series he depicted Humiliation of Valerian by Shapur I, Edessa 259AD, *in a preparatory drawing of 1521.*

presenting himself as a German Apelles.

In 1521 the Basel town council commissioned Holbein to create a series of murals, allegories of Virtues and history scenes, for the Great Council Chamber, for which he was paid 120 gulden in instalments from June 1521 to November 1522. Other important work included organ-shutter designs for Basel Cathedral, c.1525.

JOHANNES FROBEN

For his friend Johannes Froben, the talented printer-publisher, Holbein designed a company sign (see page 114) and painted a portrait (see below). Froben, a cultured humanist, helped create Basel's reputation as a centre for printing. He printed the first translation of the Greek New Testament by his friend Erasmus, the humanist, theologian, and Catholic priest, who lived in Froben's house in Basel. When Froben had to make a choice between Erasmus or Martin Luther – both his clients – due to their difference of opinion on the doctrine of grace, Froben chose Erasmus.

FROBEN AND AMERBACH

In 1516, when Johann Froben (1460–1527), published Erasmus's new translation of the Greek New Testament, he was the major publisher in Basel, a city famed for print-publishing of the highest quality. Froben had moved to Basel in 1491 and trained to be a printer and academic editor in the workshop of the esteemed publisher Johann Amerbach (1440–1513), who had trained in Venice before setting up a large print publishing company. Amerbach's first publication had appeared in 1478. He was the first Basel printer to use Roman typeface in preference to Gothic or Italian.

Amerbach approached distinguished authors and owners of manuscripts, to ask to publish them, such as the Augustinian monk Augustinius Dodo, and the humanist Jacob Wimpfeling. Letters reveal him to be generally admired for his honesty and professional acumen. On the death of Amerbach, Froben set up independently in 1513, concentrating on religious publications. He commissioned the Holbein brothers, both accomplished draughtsmen, to design woodcuts for his books.

Below: Apelles painting Campaspe, the mistress of Alexander the Great, an etching by Francesco Fontebasso, c.1744.

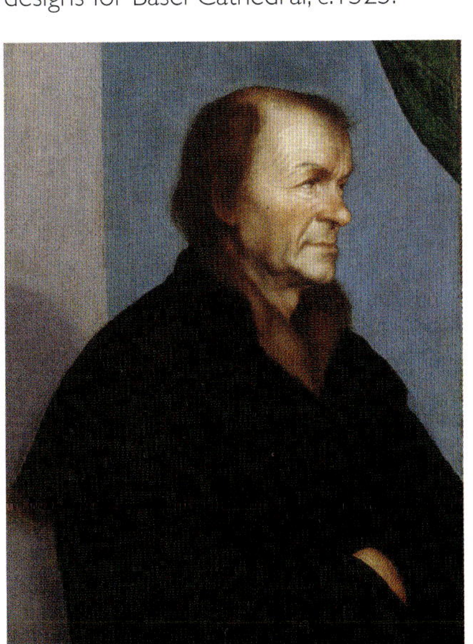

Left: Portrait of Johannes Froben, *c.1522–23 by Holbein the Younger. Froben was a highly successful printer in Basel, who worked closely with Holbein.*

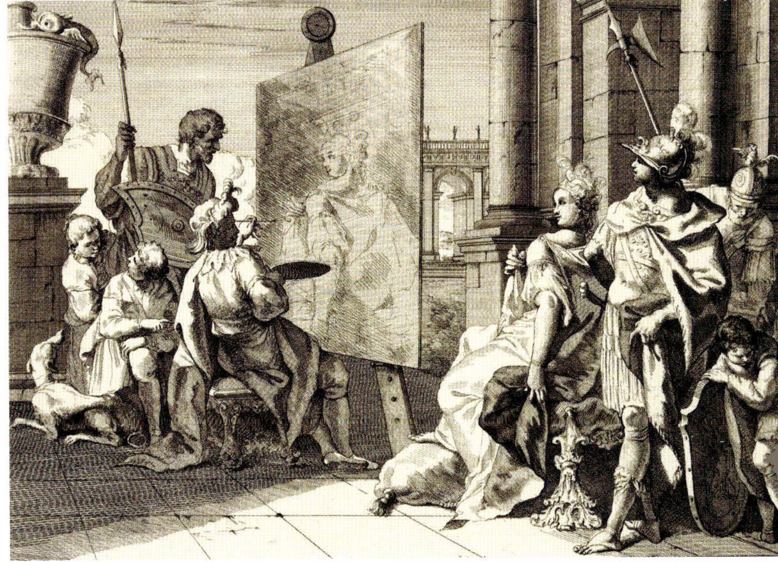

THE DARMSTADT MADONNA

One of the last religious works created by Hans Holbein before he focused on portraiture was *Darmstadt Madonna,* also known as *The Meyer Madonna* and *Madonna of the Burgermeister Meyer.* It was commissioned by the former Mayor of Basel, Jakob Meyer, in 1526.

Painted in 1526–29, *Darmstadt Madonna* is a 'Virgin of Pity' composition, in the style of paintings such as *The Presentation of Christ in the Temple,* by Stefan Lochner, which also includes the donor and his family gathered around the Virgin Mary and the infant Christ. In it one can see influence from Italian art too, particularly religious paintings by

Leonardo da Vinci in the naturalism of the Holy Child. Christ is depicted as real baby, not a child dressed in finery. Jakob Meyer had visited Italy, most probably in his capacity as a military leader and a financier, and would have been aware of the humanistic development evident in Italian painting of the time.

Meyer, whom Holbein had portrayed ten years earlier in a pendant portrait (see page 111), had since fallen from grace. Elected in 1516 as the first non-patrician mayor of Basel, in 1521

he had been sacked due to financial discrepancies, resulting in political and financial humiliation. His new position as leader of the Catholic faction in Basel during a fraught period of the Reformation is noted in the Darmstadt painting by the inclusion of an imperial crown on the Madonna's head. This is a symbolic reference to Meyer not wishing for the state and church to be separated.

A MEYER FAMILY PORTRAIT

The style and composition of the Darmstadt painting bears some resemblance to paintings by Raphael and Leonardo da Vinci. Surrounding

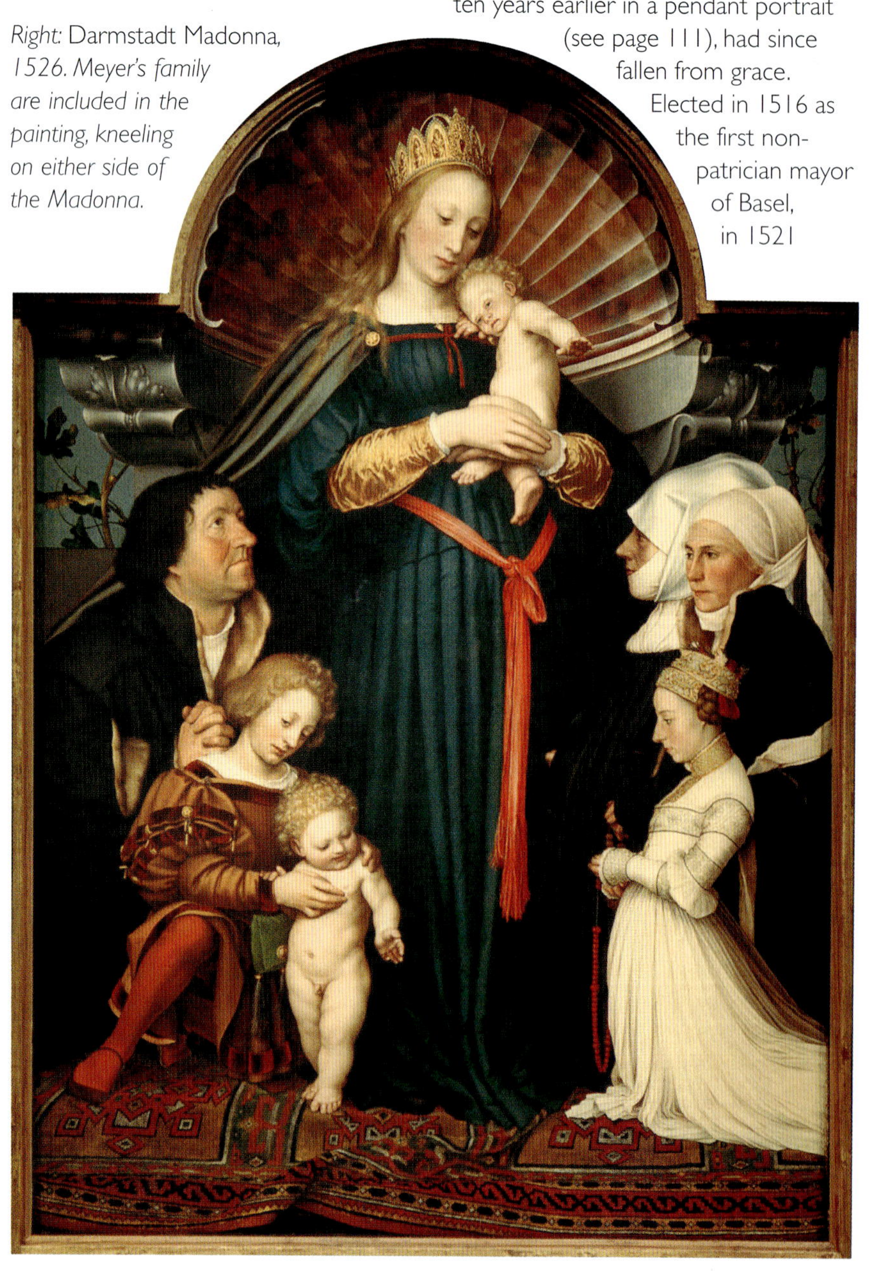

Right: Darmstadt Madonna, *1526. Meyer's family are included in the painting, kneeling on either side of the Madonna.*

ANALYSING A HOLBEIN

Holbein the Younger created portrait drawings of his sitters first in red or black chalk and silverpoint, later to transfer the likeness to a prepared painted panel. He first used coloured chalks in 1523–24 in drawings for polychrome sculptures of Jean de Berry and Jeanne de Boulogne in Bourges, France. His first recorded use of black with coloured chalks was for *Portrait of Anna Meyer* in 1526 (see opposite). Here he used a pale green tint as background, which highlighted the yellow-gold chalk depicting her hair and dress collar. Her face is tinted pale pink, and details of her dress are picked out in black chalk on the white background. This portrait reveals Holbein's knowledge of Jean Perréal and Leonardo da Vinci's techniques using coloured chalks, which he copies and masters. The approach is evident too in his preparatory drawing for his *Portrait of Dorothea Kannengiesser* in 1526 (see page 110).

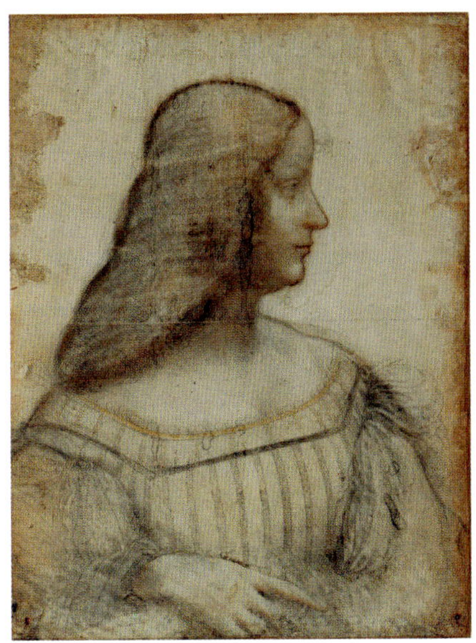

Above: Leonardo da Vinci's drawing in black, red and yellow chalk for Portrait of Isabella d'Este, Duchess of Mantua, *1499–1500.*

the Madonna and Child is the Meyer family. Kneeling at her feet to her right are Jakob Meyer, with an unidentified young boy – possibly the apostle James the Great (Jakob in German) as a child – and a naked infant, credibly Christ's young cousin John the Baptist. To her left are two women, Meyer's late wife Magdalena Baer, who had died in 1511, and his second wife, Dorothea Kannengiesser, with their daughter Anna. It was thought that the inclusion of Meyer's late wife Magdalena was a later addition, but infrared research of the painting proves that it was Meyer's and Holbein's intention to include her from the outset. The artist would repeat this stratagem later in a portrait of the family of Henry VIII.

Holbein's depiction of the Christ child's outstretched hand mirrors that of the Madonna's hand in Leonardo's *Madonna of the Rocks*, 1483–86 (see page 47), with which Holbein may have been familiar. The painting was acquired by Louis XII between 1499 and 1508; Holbein may have had access to it when in France, or to copies of it.

ANNA MEYER IN DA VINCI STYLE
Holbein created a preparatory drawing of Anna for the larger-scale painting *Darmstadt Madonna*. In *Portrait of Anna Meyer*, c.1526, Holbein captures Jakob and Dorothea Meyer's daughter's youth and timidity. In this half-length portrait she sits in profile, her long golden hair, beyond waist-length, flowing freely down her back (in the finished painting, opposite, her hair is tightly plaited and fixed under a head-cap). Historians draw attention to the similarities between Holbein's coloured chalks and Leonardo's drawing *Portrait of Isabella d'Este*. The d'Este cartoon (left) was a preliminary sketch of Isabella d'Este, Marchioness of Mantua (1474–1539), in preparation for a portrait, which Leonardo never painted. Although it was not the first time that Holbein used coloured chalks, his portrait of Anna Meyer is the first time in which he experiments with black and coloured chalks following the French style, initiated by the sought-after French-born artist Jean Perréal (1450–1530), a favourite of royalty at the French court. In fact it was Perréal who was originally meant to paint Isabella d'Este.

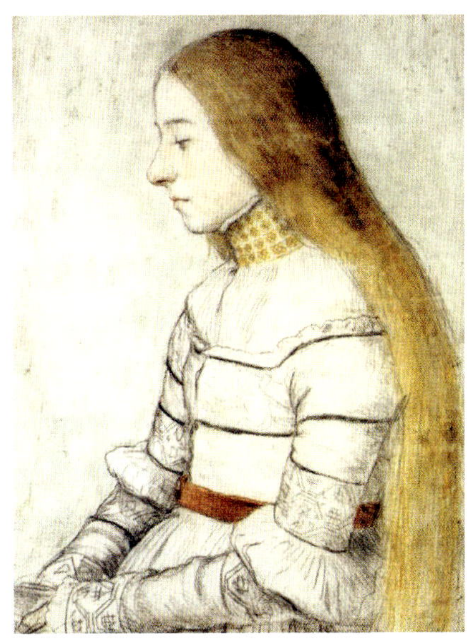

Above: Portrait of Anna Meyer, c.1526, is a preparatory detail for Darmstadt Madonna.

Below: Another 'Virgin of Pity' composition, where the patrons appear in the painting, The Presentation of Christ in the Temple *by Stefan Lochner, 1445–47.*

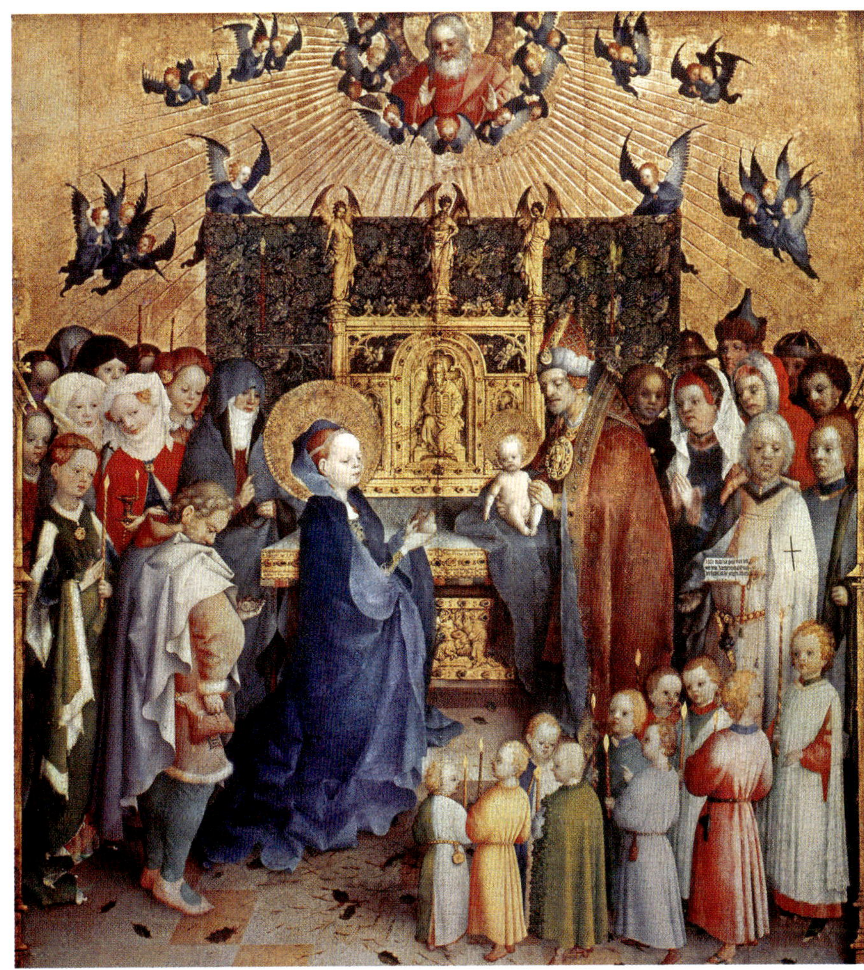

FAMILY IN BASEL

Ambrosius and Holbein the Younger worked alongside in Basel, and both careers developed. Within a few short years Ambrosius had possibly died, about 1519. In the same year Holbein married a widow with a young son. They were to have four children but much of their marriage was spent apart.

Unlike his Italian near-contemporaries Michelangelo Buonarotti (1475–1564), and Leonardo da Vinci (1452–1519), or his German contemporary Albrecht Dürer (1471–1528), Holbein the Younger left no written records of his private life, just a few public statements on matters relating to his paintings, and his religious belief of the Mass. Thus historians know little about the marriage of Holbein to a widow, Elsbeth Binzenstock, slightly older than Holbein, who lived in Basel. His marriage to Elsbeth was a quiet affair. It was a marriage made harder by long periods of separation during Holbein's years in England. There is no record of her travelling to England during the two longer periods of his absence from Basel, 1526–28 and from 1532.

ELSBETH BINZENSTOCK HOLBEIN

Elsbeth Holbein (1495–1549), née Binzenstock, had been married previously to a tanner Ulrich Schmid (died 1517), with one son Franz Schmid. Holbein and Elsbeth probably married in 1519. An oil on paper portrait by Holbein of his wife and two of his four children was painted around ten years after their marriage. The painting was originally dated in the bottom right-

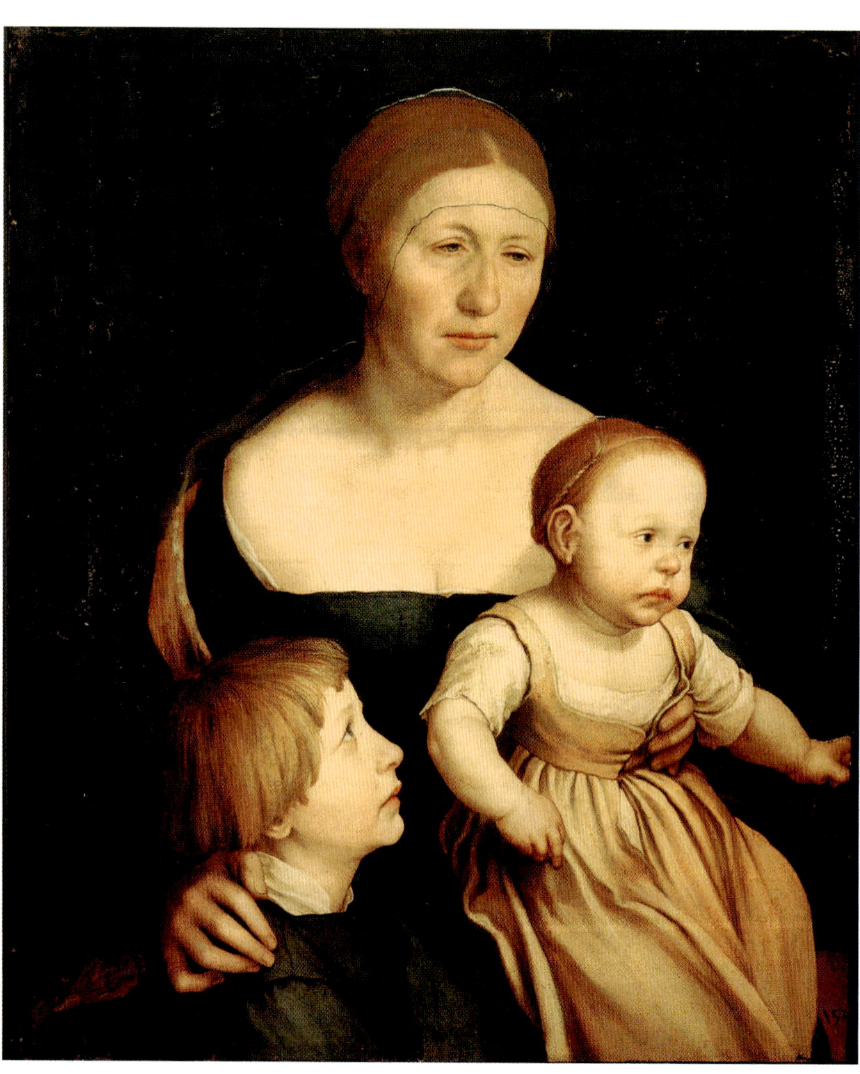

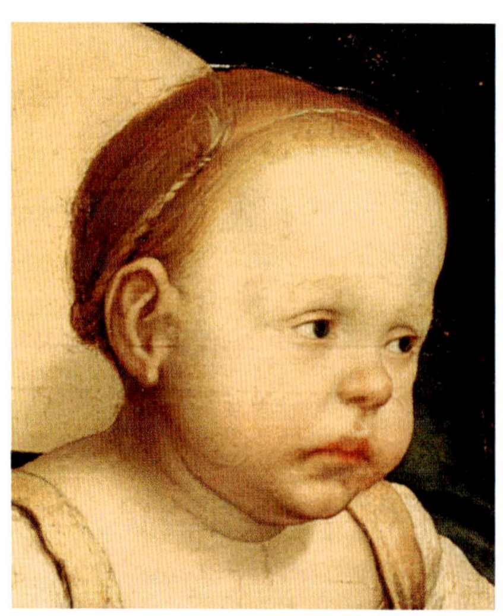

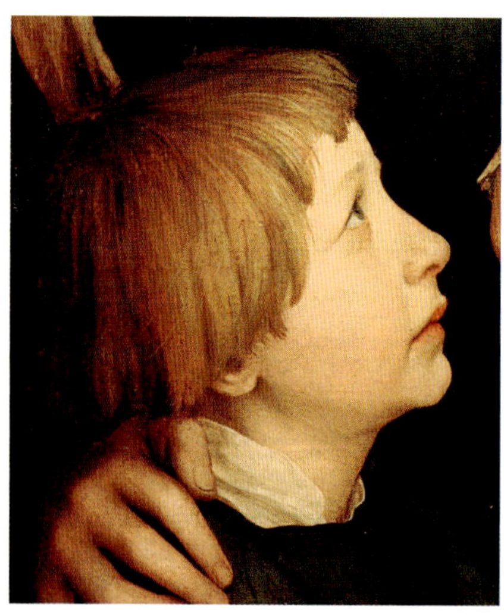

Above: Portrait of the Artist's Wife with the Two Elder Children (*Elsbeth Binzenstock Holbein with her children Philipp and Katharina*) *was painted on paper by Holbein the Younger c.1528–29. They reveal similar characteristics of auburn hair and fair skin.*

Left: Detail of the face of Katharina. It is thought that she would be two years old when the portrait was created.

Right: A detail of the beautiful head and face of Philipp, the eldest son of Holbein the Younger, in profile, aged six or seven.

hand corner, but its removal has led historians to speculate on its date. It is a contemplative depiction. The figurative composition of Elsbeth is reminiscent of Holbein's *Laïs Corinthiaca*, 1526 (see page 42), itself informed by the Venetian style of Giorgione (1470–1510). In the family portrait, Holbein's son Philipp (c.1522–1602) looks about six or seven years of age, and daughter Katharina, born c.1526, possibly two years old. It is possible that Holbein painted this work on his return to Basel in 1528.

During his adult life, and after death, rumours circulated that Holbein had badly neglected his wife and children. He had spent years away from the Basel, in spite of pleas from the city authorities to stay, with an annuity 'So that you may remain at home and feed your wife and child'. (Document dated 2 September, 1532.) But Basel did not have enough work for an artist of his calibre, and he needed to make a good income, hence working abroad.

PORTRAIT OF A FAMILY

The painting remained in the family home. Two further children, Jakob, born circa 1529, and Küngold, in 1530, were not born when the work was made, thus dating it to c.1528. For a

portraitist who could make courtiers look like kings, the portrayal of his own family was a depiction full of quite brutal realism – their faces are etched with uncertainty. His wife, son Philipp, and his infant daughter look in different directions, perhaps to capture a moment from the portrait sitting. The work might have been planned as a companion painting to one of Holbein at his easel, in the act of painting them, the children watching him. It has been noted that the protective hand of Elsbeth on the shoulder of Philipp bears similarity to the hand of the Virgin in Leonardo da Vinci's *The Virgin (or Madonna) of the Rocks*, which has a triangulated composition with the figures looking in different directions. Holbein may have seen print copies of this work.

Holbein's Will, made in London on October 7th, 1543, leaves money for the care of two nursing infants, which reveals acknowledgement of illegitimate children born later in England.

Below: Madonna of the Rocks, *1483–99, (detail), by Leonardo da Vinci. Holbein used a similar composition for his family portrait.*

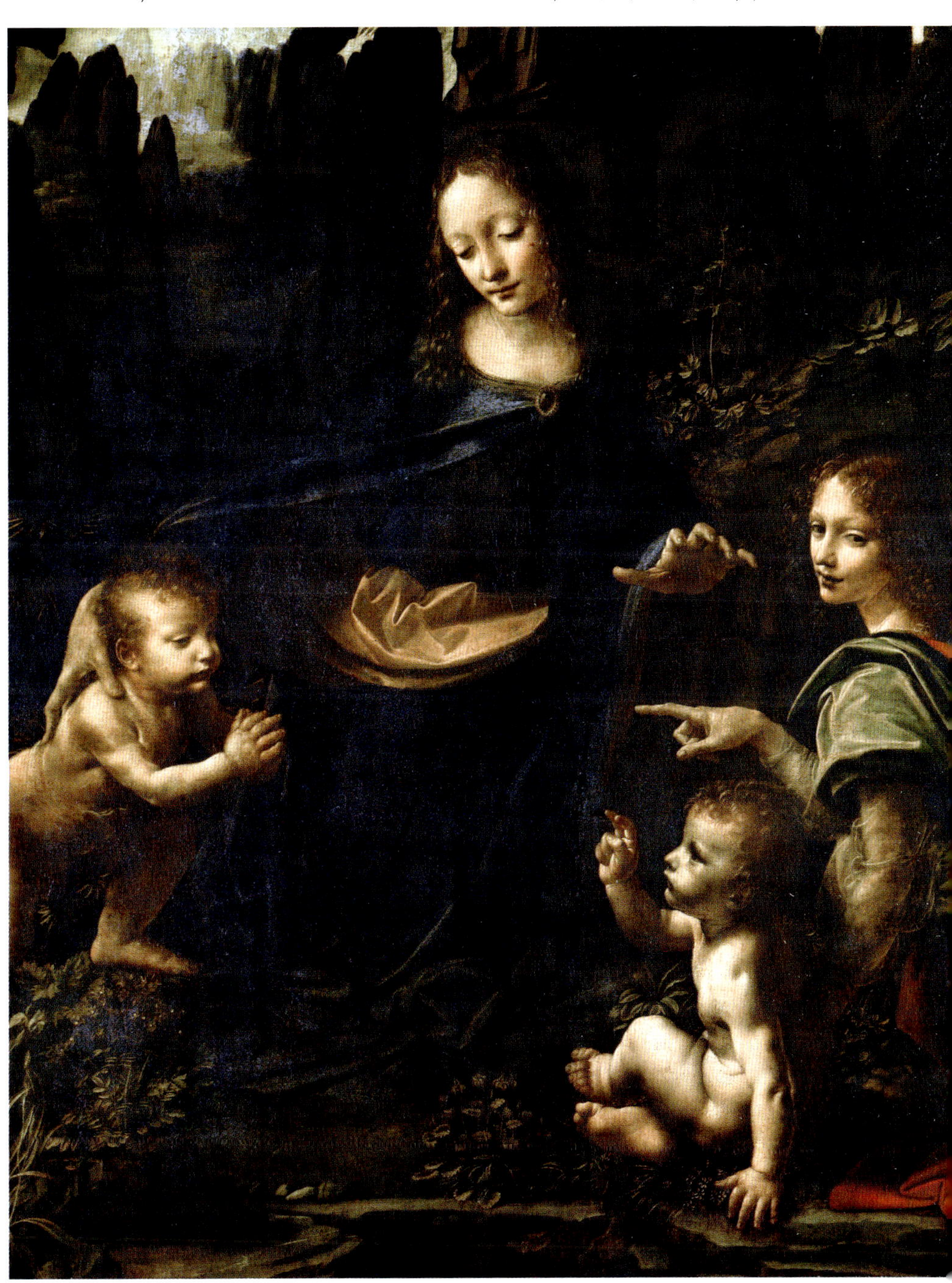

A JOURNEY TO ENGLAND

Holbein the Younger paid two visits to England. On the first in 1526, his intention was to become a court painter to the nobility. An introduction to Thomas More, through Erasmus, gave Holbein the right credentials. During Holbein's second stay in England from 1532, he would become the king's painter.

EARLIER TRAVELS TO FRANCE AND THE NETHERLANDS

As a citizen of Basel, Holbein was allowed a two-year absence before his citizenship would be revoked. Permanent residence in another city would rescind his rights. Before his journey to England in 1526 he had left Basel from 1523–24, to travel through France, and then to the Netherlands, seeking commissions, and patronage. In France, it is thought he may have visited the royal residence of king Francis I, the Château d'Amboise, in the Loire Valley. Holbein may have tried to gain patronage of the king, a humanist and patron of the arts, and the nobles of the French royal court, but without success. Ongoing territorial disagreements with Emperor Charles V (1500–58), the Holy Roman Emperor, king of Spain and Archduke of Austria, with an extensive empire in Europe including the Netherlands and the kingdom of Naples, had occupied Francis I since Charles V became emperor in 1519 with his sights on French territories. In addition, Francis I embraced the Italian Renaissance, its art and architecture, already employing Italian artists and architects, including Leonardo da Vinci, who resided as a paid retainer in the king's Château de Clos Lucé in Amboise from 1516 until the artist's death in 1519. Holbein would have been introduced to Italian works but there is no evidence that he travelled further than France to Italy.

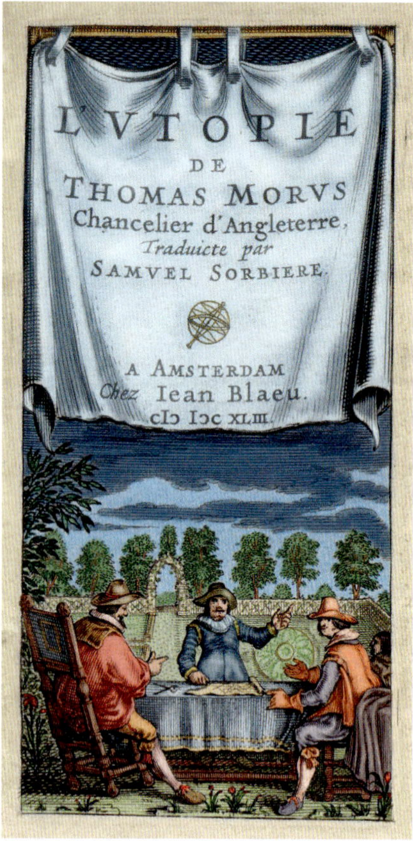

Above: The title page of the 1642 French edition of the popular novel Utopia 1516, *by More; a narrative of religious, political and social customs on a fictional island.*

ERASMUS' LETTER TO SIR THOMAS MORE

It was Erasmus who furnished Holbein with a letter of introduction to Sir Thomas More, King Henry VIII's privy councillor, a man of great prominence and importance in the Royal Court, and a formidable statesman. In the letter, Erasmus wrote, in part, '*Here the arts are shivering with cold; he [Holbein] is going to England to pick up a few angels [coins].*'

Holbein entered More's elite circle on arrival, possibly staying in More's own household in Chelsea. England was about to become deeply divided over the king's decision to divorce his wife Katherine of Aragon, a staunch Catholic, in order to marry his younger mistress Anne Boleyn. It would lead to an irrevocable break from the Catholic church, and Rome. Holbein arrived at the beginning of this upheaval. One can understand that Holbein, wishing to keep away from religious politics, would choose to concentrate on secular portrait painting, the interior decoration of buildings, and on the decorative programmes for festivities.

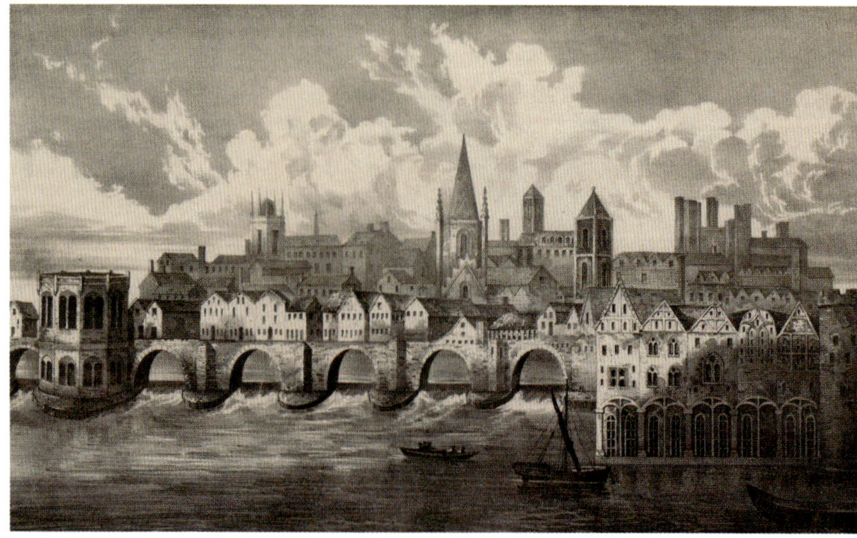

Below: A 19th-century view of Old London Bridge, visualised in the reign of Henry VII. Henry VIII became king in 1509; Holbein travelled to England for work in 1526.

TO LONDON VIA ANTWERP

Holbein left Basel again toward the end of August 1526, travelling to Antwerp. This is known from a letter written by Erasmus to his friend Pieter Gillis, the Antwerp town clerk, and delivered by Holbein. In the content of one letter Erasmus describes the artist in Latin as *insignis artifex*, a distinguished, or noted artist. He requested that Holbein meet the renowned Leuven-born Flemish painter Quinten Massys/Metsys (1466–1530) who lived and worked in Antwerp. The reason for this was Massys' 1517 commission to paint pendant portraits of Erasmus and Gillis, that were sent as a gift that year to their friend Sir Thomas More (1478–1535) in London. There are no records of their meeting, but one can surmise it was for Holbein to learn of Massys' method of pendant portraiture, and perhaps insight into the clients he might secure in England.

ERASMUS RECOMMENDS HOLBEIN

Holbein arrived in London in December 1526 and met Sir Thomas More, to deliver letters from Erasmus, one of which contained an introduction. Erasmus' letter cited the difficult climate for artists in Basel. Holbein's skill as a portraitist was exemplary – he had painted a magnificent portrait of Erasmus – but he needed More's influence to work for the nobility, landed gentry and hopefully, royalty. A requirement to be a member of the English Guild of Painters & Stainers was exempt to notable painters, particularly of German origin for they were considered amongst the finest, and so Holbein could begin work immediately. He planned to paint portraits rather than the iconography of Christian art.

Above right: A 19th-century English School view of Thomas More's house in Chelsea, London. Erasmus introduced Holbein to More, by letter, recommending him as a painter. Holbein may have resided in the house while working on More's portrait commission.

Right: King Henry VIII, c.1520, painted by an unknown Anglo-Netherlandish artist.

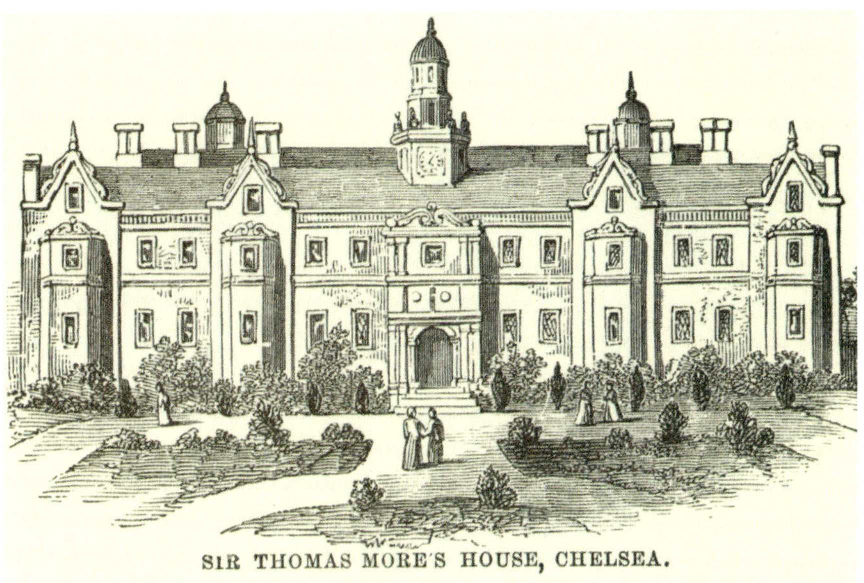

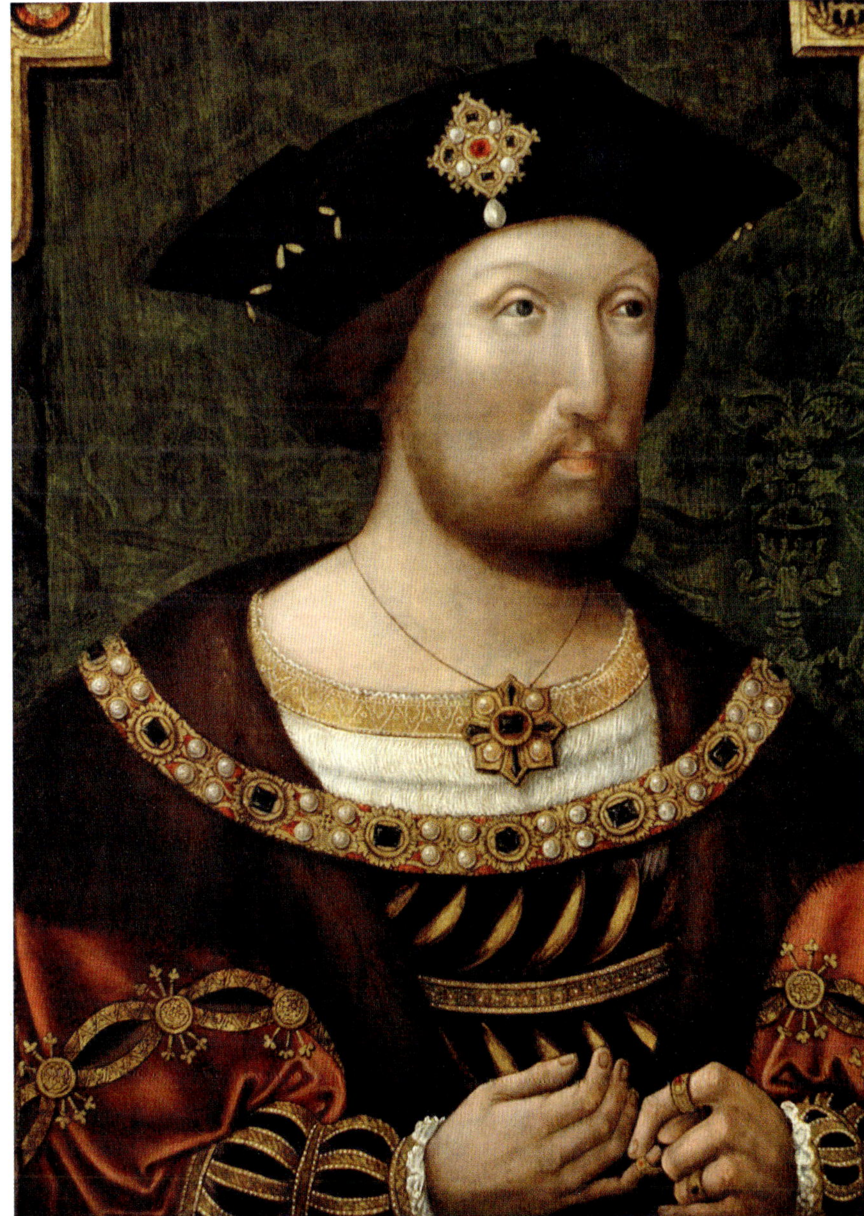

SIR THOMAS MORE

'Your painter, my dear Erasmus, is a wonderful artist but I am afraid that he may not find England as fruitful and profitable as he hopes. However, I will try to do my best to ensure that he shall not find it completely arid.' These were the words written to Erasmus, by Thomas More, promising to try to find work for Holbein.

While he was still in favour with the king, Henry VIII, Thomas More (1478–1535) was the most influential person in the English court. In 1527 Holbein painted *Portrait of Thomas More* (right, and on page 154). It was a significant work, and one that led to further commissions from More and his circle. In this portrait, using complementary colours, including rich green for the silk drape, and red for More's sleeves, the colour juxtaposition makes the viewer aware of space between background and foreground, and the bold presence of the sitter. In Holbein's work, More wears the heavy, link S-S gold chain of office, signifying service to the king, with a Tudor Rose medallion at its centre. ('S-S' stands for *Souvent me souvien* -Think of me often.)

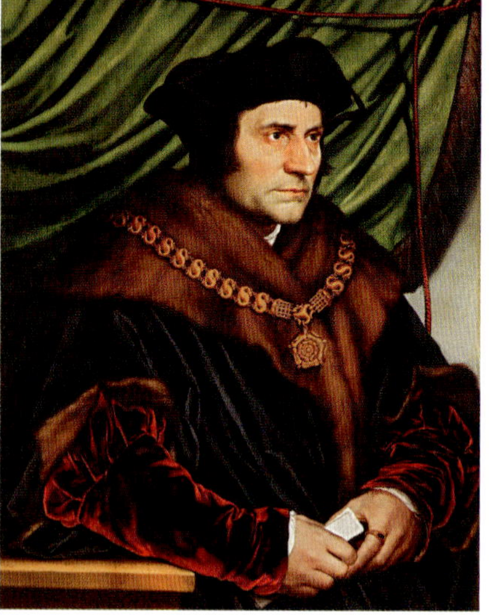

Above: Portrait of Sir Thomas More, 1527, by Holbein the Younger.

In style, one can see similarities between the finished painting and two paintings by the renowned Antwerp painter Quinten Massys/ Metsys (1466–1530), whom Holbein had met before travelling to London. These are the pendant portraits of More's friends, *Portrait of Pieter Gillis* (opposite), and *Portrait of Erasmus of Rotterdam* (see page 40). The paintings were commissioned by the sitters as a personal gift for More.

A PORTRAIT OF MORE'S FAMILY

More was pleased with Holbein's portrait of him, and wrote to his friend Erasmus that Holbein was 'a wonderful artist'. However, he expressed doubt that he would be inundated with work. Following the successful portrait, Sir Thomas More commissioned a

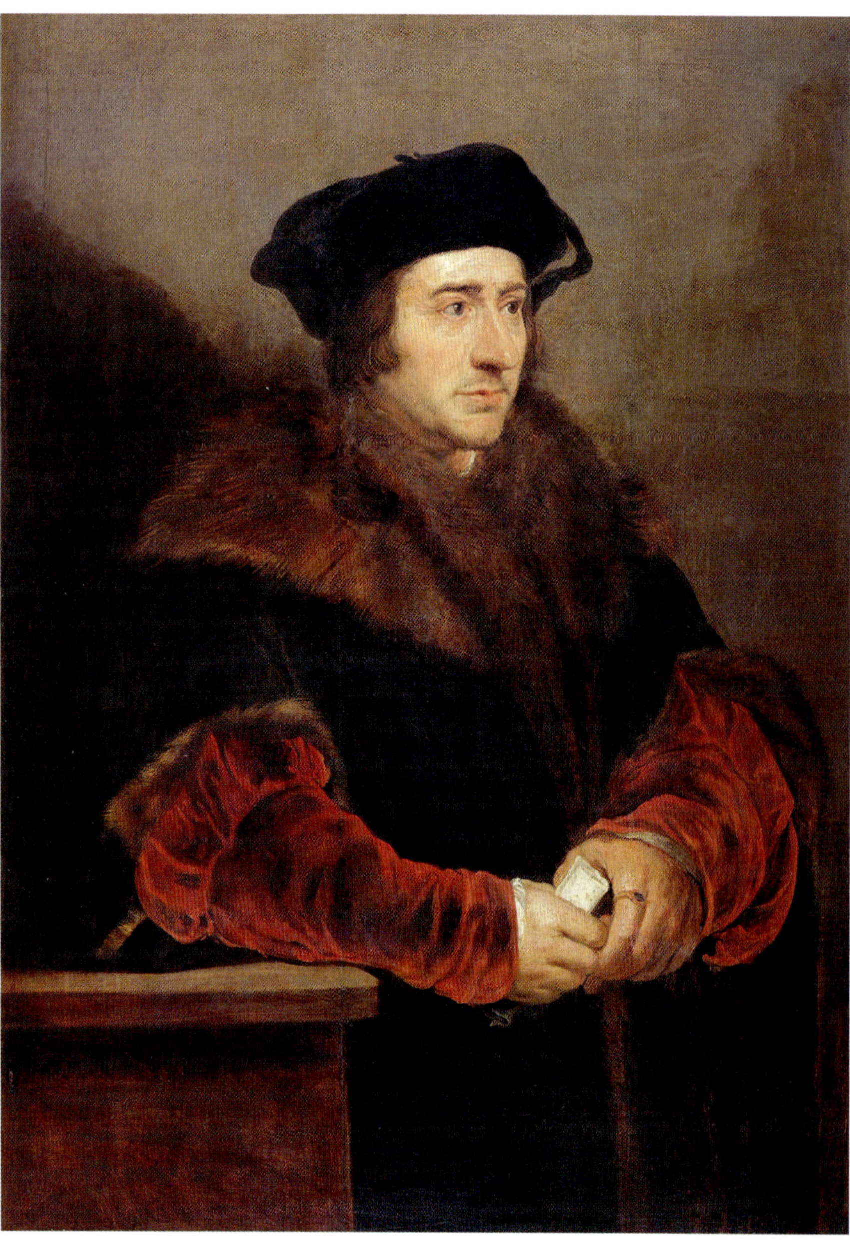

Left: Portrait of Sir Thomas More, 1625–30, by Peter Paul Rubens (1577–1640), after Holbein the Younger's earlier portrait of More. It was considered complimentary to acknowledge works of revered artists by copying or reinterpreting them..

MORE'S RISE AND FALL

At the time of Holbein's first visit to London, Thomas More was one of the king's right-hand men. The situation was very different when Holbein returned in 1532. More's later dismissal from office and loss of his close relationship with King Henry was perhaps inevitable. More viewed marriage as a sacred vow and did not approve of the king seeking a divorce from Katherine of Aragon. More refused to acknowledge King Henry's 'Act of Supremacy' that placed the king as Supreme Head of the Church of England, thus allowing proceedings for divorce to be instigated. The king was embittered at More's refusal to concede, subsequently leading to More's conviction for high treason. He was beheaded on July 6th, 1535.

domestic group portrait of himself with his family and household set in his mansion in Chelsea, London, a vast *Portrait of the Family of Sir Thomas More*, 1527–28. The original work was destroyed in a fire in 1752; today it is known through painted copies by Rowland Lockey. A preparatory drawing by Holbein in pen and black ink (see page 158) shows ten people gathered in a room of More's home. Nikolaus Kratzer, the astronomer Royal, made a note of the name of each person on the drawing. In 1528, when Holbein returned to Basel, he gave the drawing as a gift to Erasmus. It was one that Erasmus treasured; he stated that he immediately felt himself to be in the More household.

Above right: Portrait of Pieter Gillis, 1515–7, by Quinten Massys (or Metsys), is a pendant to the artist's portrait of Erasmus (see page 40). Its content reveals a contemporary prevalence for learned, scholarly context.

Right: Portrait of Sir Thomas More and his Family, c.1593, by Rowland Lockey, one of the copies of the original painting by Holbein the Younger, dated 1527.

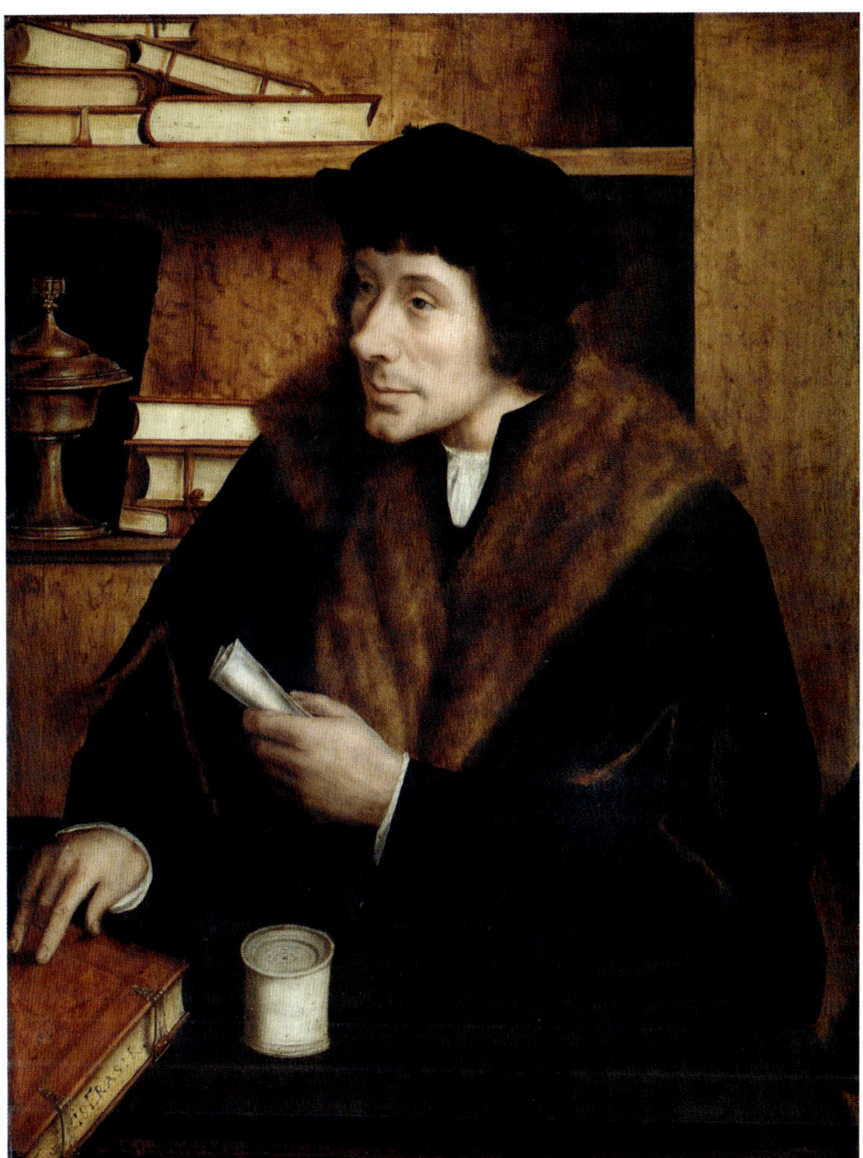

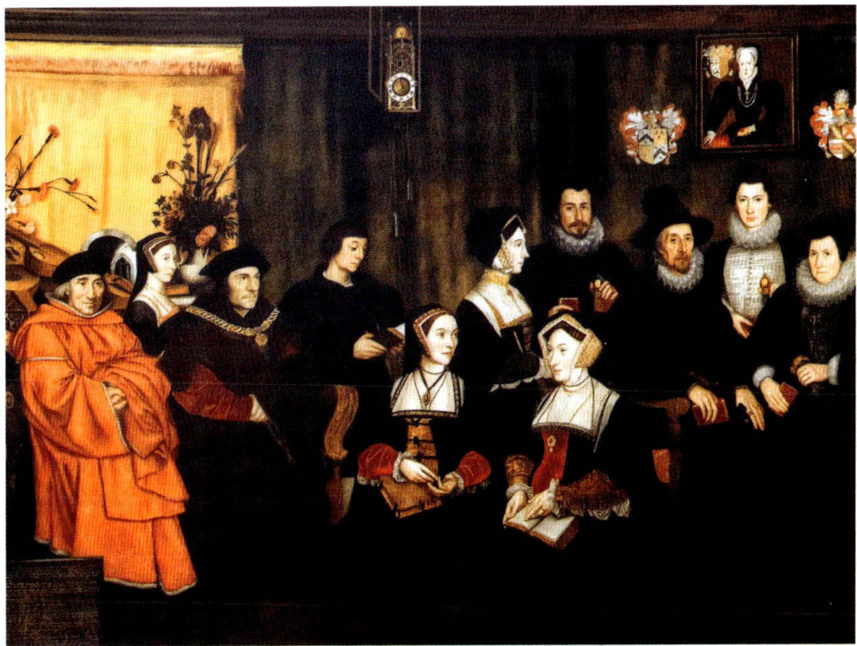

PORTRAITS AND PEACE REVELS

An influential introduction for Holbein was to Sir Henry Guildford (1489–1532). One of the commissions achieved by Holbein during his first visit to England were two half-length pendant portraits, of Sir Henry Guildford and his second wife, Mary Wotton, Lady Guildford, and decorations for the 1527 Peace Revels.

Holbein's introduction to Sir Henry Guildford was probably facilitated by Erasmus, via Thomas More. Guildford and Holbein, both Humanists, worked together on the revels for the 1527 Peace Accord between France and England. Holbein designed and painted decorative elements of the festivities at Greenwich, and in the same year painted companion portraits of Sir Henry, and his wife, to commemorate the historic occasion.

Sir Henry was one of King Henry VIII's firmest friends, holding prominent positions until his death in 1532. In 1509, when Henry, Prince of Wales acceded the throne as King Henry VIII of England (1491–1547), Henry Guildford was employed in the privileged position of Esquire of the Body, a personal attendant to the king. Other prestigious duties included Master of the Revels, Master of the Horse, and Comptroller of the Household. In his Holbein portrait, Sir Henry holds the Comptroller of the Household's white staff of office. His hat bears a badge with a clock and geometrical instruments. The Guildford portrait commission reveals that Holbein had gained immediate access to the king's inner circle.

PENDANT PORTRAITS

Pendant paintings were created as companion works, intended to be displayed together, usually in the home. Artists often created double works, in landscape, still life, or portraiture, usually thematically or compositionally related. Stemming from a Dutch tradition, it was particularly popular type of art for an engagement or marriage, or for official commemorations (see also pages 26–7). Pendant portraits of a couple, such as Holbein's portraits of Sir Henry and Lady Guildford, would have been placed together. It was tradition that the portrait of the woman would hang to the left of the man portrayed, thus hanging to the right when viewed. To add liveliness, the couple often proffered a gift, or object, to link the compositions. After marriage, a couple's children might be included.

SIR HENRY AND LADY GUILDFORD

The paintings of Sir Henry and Lady Guildford are considered two of Holbein's finest works. The preliminary drawings (see pages 160–61) show Holbein's finesse in capturing likeness and personality. The daughter of Sir Robert Wotton of Boughton Malherbe, Mary Wotton was twenty-seven years of age at the time of her marriage to Sir Henry Guildford. He was forty-nine years old. After Sir Henry's death in 1532, Lady Guildford married again, as second wife of Sir Gawain Carew of Devon. She is known to have sat for

twenty-five portraits in her lifetime.

In her painted portrait Holbein depicts Lady Guildford as a pleasant but serious young woman. However, his preparatory drawing, in black and coloured chalk on white paper (see page 161) reveals a prettier, happier person, with beautiful eyes, looking away from the spectator. The date, ANNO MDXXVII. AETATIS SUAE XXVII is painted on the architrave, above Lady Guildford's head, in the finished work.

In the companion paintings of the married couple, their bodies quarter-turn toward each other, with Lady Guildford looking toward the spectator, a typical feature of the popular pendant form of portrait. This pendant pair bear similarities with Holbein's first double portraits ten years earlier of Jakob Meyer and his wife Dorothea Kannengiesser (see page 111). In the Guildford companion paintings, Holbein has articulated the difference in the couple's physical and symbolic stature. Sir Henry is a bold giant-of-a-man with strong facial characteristics. His wife is more diminutive and reserved. Their fine clothing, symbols of wealth and courtly status, is richly painted, their garments' fabrics complementing each other.

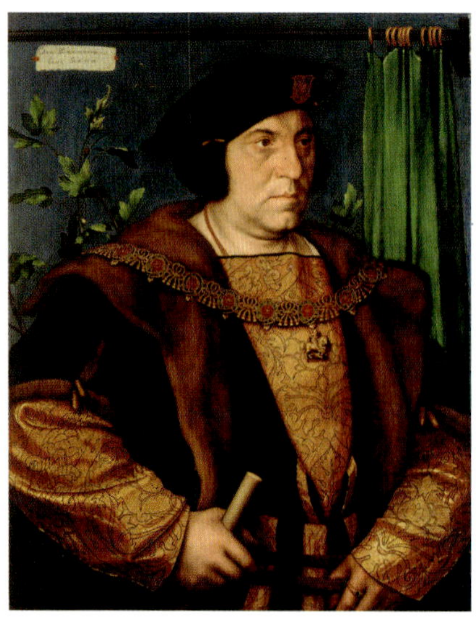

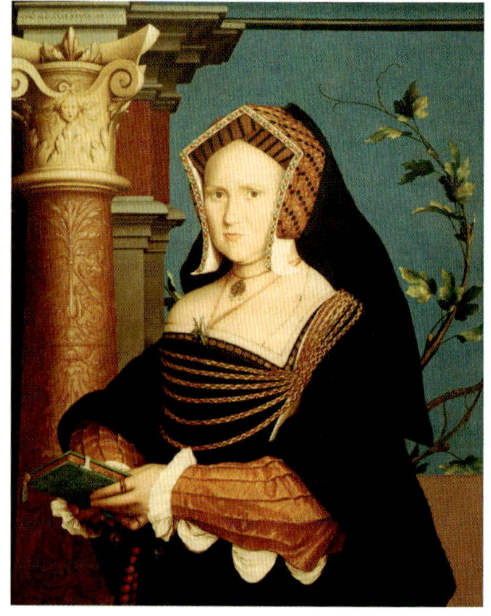

Left and Right: Companion portraits of Sir Henry Guildford, royal courtier to King Henry VIII, and his wife, Lady Guildford, by Hans Holbein the Younger, 1527.

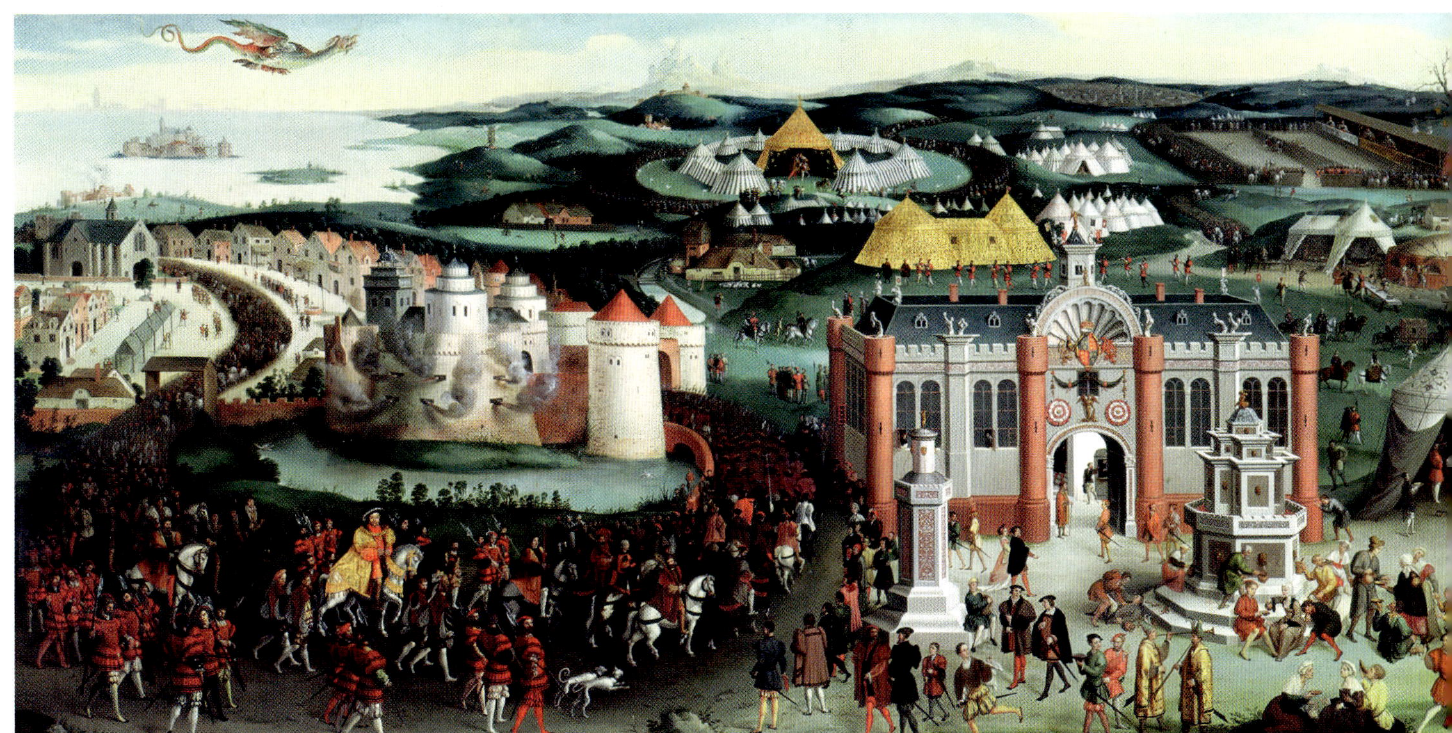

THE 1527 PEACE REVELS

The occasion for the pendant portraits is the role that Sir Henry played in organising the lavish revels, with masked balls and royal banquets at Greenwich, taking place in honour of the peace accord in 1527 between King Henry VIII of England, and King Francis I of France.

On Holbein's arrival in England his first task was to design and paint festive accompaniments for the 1527 Peace Accord. He was well-rehearsed in this type of commission. In Greenwich, under the auspices of Sir Henry Guildford, Holbein was part of a team of nineteen painters. It is known that eight of the group were members of the London Company of Painters-Stainers. Holbein, like the rest of the group, was paid daily, but at a much higher rate (of four shillings, or 48 pence) than senior-ranked English painter Robert Wrythoke, who was paid 12 pence per day, followed by painter Richard Rippingall at ten pence per day. Others got less.

Right: Pen and ink drawing of the Royal Greenwich Palace from the north bank of the Thames, c.1544, by Netherlandish artist Anthonis van den Wyngaerde (1525–71/72). The palace was significantly rebuilt by Henry VII c.1500.

Above: A 16th-century painting of The Field of Cloth of Gold, *a location near Calais, in Balinghem, France that hosted a ceremonial meeting 7–24th June 1520, intended to create a bond of friendship between King Henry VIII of England and King Francis I of France.*

Below: This bas-relief of the Field of Cloth of Gold *captures the pageantry of the 1520 meeting between England and France. Later, in 1527 at Greenwich, Holbein created artworks for Peace Revels held in honour of Francis I.*

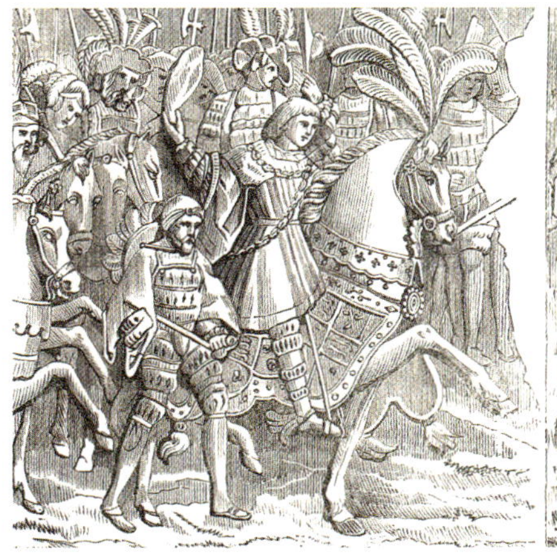

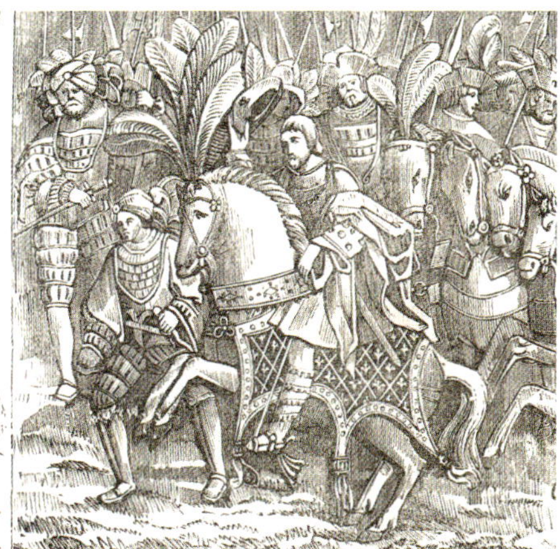

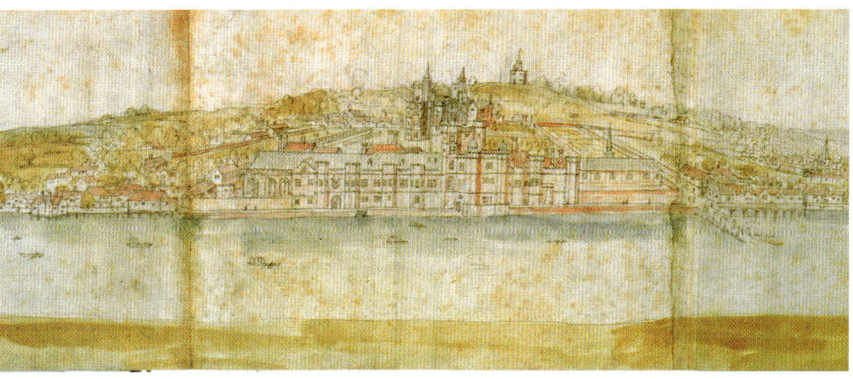

THE ENGLISH COURT 1526

Portrait commissions in the English court relied on the right patronage. Sir Thomas More, Sir Henry and Lady Guildford, and society's wealthy, kickstarted Holbein's English career in London during his first visit in 1526. He soon obtained another useful patron, Sir William Warham, the Archbishop of Canterbury.

LUCAS HORENBOUT

Around the period of Holbein's first visit to England in 1526, Lucas Horenbout (1490/95–1544) was favoured as portrait painter in the service of the royal court. His notable works include *Portrait of Katherine of Aragon c.*1525, holding her pet monkey, and the miniature *Portrait of King Henry VIII, c.*1525–26. Horenbout travelled to England in the mid-1520s, becoming the 'King's Painter' to Henry VIII from 1525.

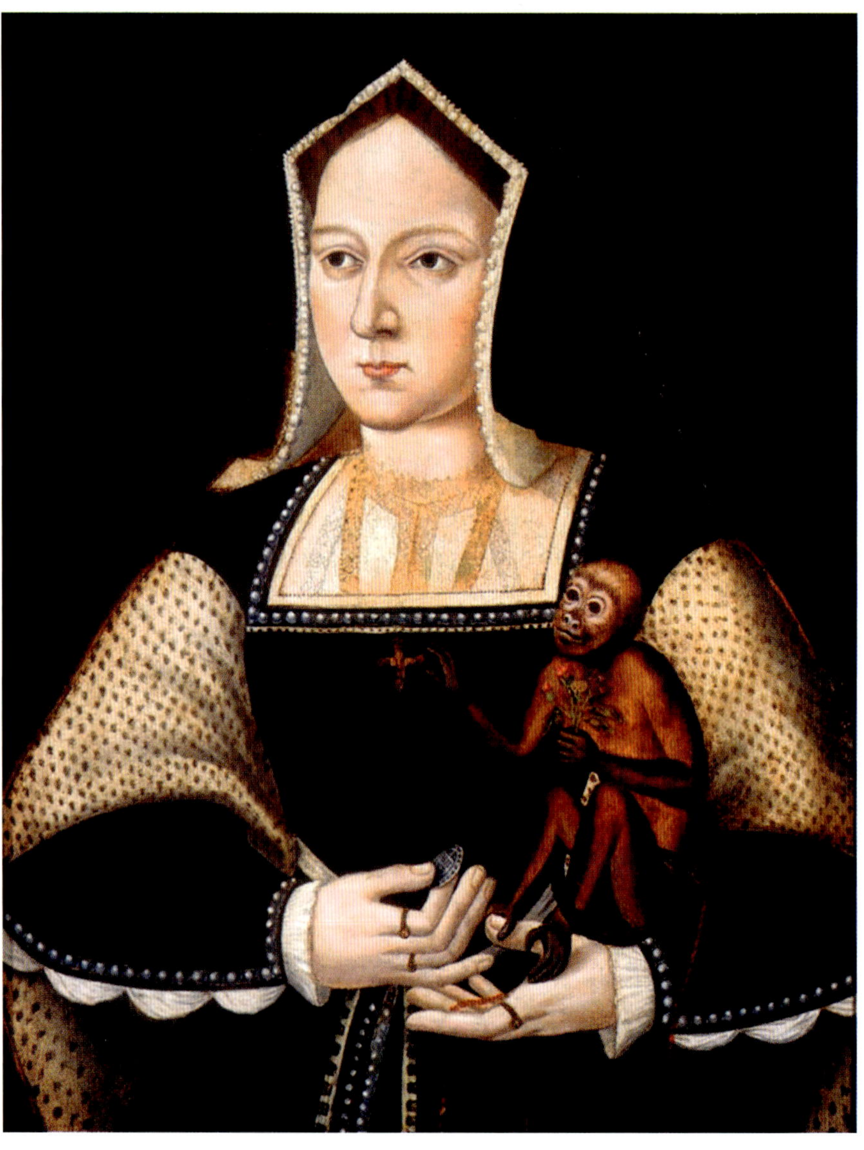

Above: Portrait of Katherine of Aragon, holding a Monkey, *c.*1525, was painted by Belgian-born Lucas Horenbout.

HOLBEIN'S EARLY COMMISSIONS

During Holbein's first stay in London he was initally introduced to prestigious clients through his fortunate association with Erasmus in Basel. The significant recommendation from Erasmus, and his subsequent participation in the decoration of Greenwich Palace and Theatre, led to portrait commissions from England's nobility and high society.

One can see from Holbein's portfolio of portraits, beginning with Sir Thomas More, councillor to Henry VIII, that he chose notable patrons and clients in order to gain access to the inner circle of courtiers. One of the first was a friend of Erasmus, the Archbishop of Canterbury, William Warham (1450–1532), archbishop from 1503 until his death in 1532. In 1509 Warham had the duty of marrying Henry VIII to Katherine of Aragon and presiding over their

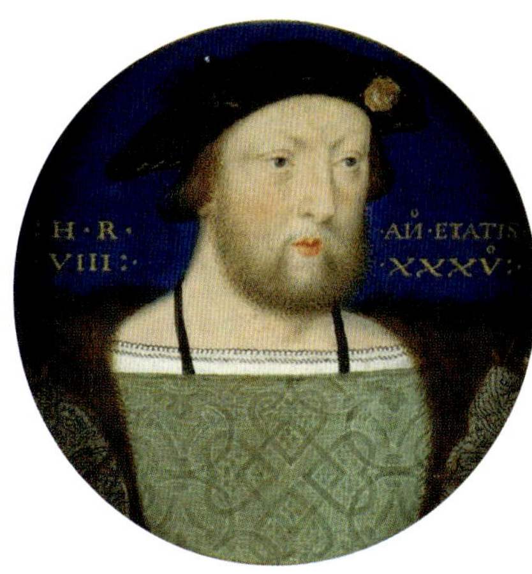

Above: Portrait of King Henry VIII of England, c. *1525–26, one of a number of miniatures of the royal court painted by Lucas Horenbout.*

Coronation a few weeks later. Warham commissioned two identical portraits from Holbein. One was to be sent as a gift to Erasmus, in return for a portrait of Erasmus sent to Warham. The other was to hang in the Archbishop's palace. There are obvious similarities between the composition of the Erasmus portrait that Holbein painted in 1523 (see page 134) and that of the Archbishop. They may have been hung as companion portraits in Erasmus's home. (The preparatory drawing of Warham in chalks is shown on page 163.)

Before his compulsory return to Basel in 1528, in order to maintain his citizenship there, Holbein completed a double portrait *Thomas Godsalve and his Son, John.* Thomas Godsalve (*c.*1481–1545) of Norwich, England, was a wealthy landowner and registrar of the consistory court at Norwich. His association with Thomas Cromwell allowed his son John Godsalve (*c.*1506–1558) to become Clerk of the Signet and Clerk of the Mint, with access to the royal circle. The portrayal of father and son relates in style and composition to another of Holbein's earlier portraits of Erasmus (see page 135), in the facial expressions, particularly of the older man, who is also writing, and in the half-length, three-quarter poses. The pair,

Right: Portrait of William Warham, Archbishop of Canterbury, c.*1527, by Holbein the Younger.*

each facing toward their left, mirror each other in tilt of the head and solemn, thoughtful expression. They are similarly dressed, although Godsalve senior wears a hat. In contrast to the Erasmus composition, however, this work has a plain background. There are no shelves of books, stone columns, or cultural attributes on display. Instead, Godsalve senior is portrayed writing. At upper left, above the son's head, is a strip of parchment, on which the handwritten words state 'Anno D[o]m[ini] MD XXVIII' ('The year 1528'). Other parchment paper, in front of Godsalve senior, and on which he writes, contains the handwritten missive 'Thomas Godsalve de Norwico Etatis sue Anno/ quadragesimo septo'. Godsalve writes on the paper in front of him that in this year (1528) he is 47 years old.

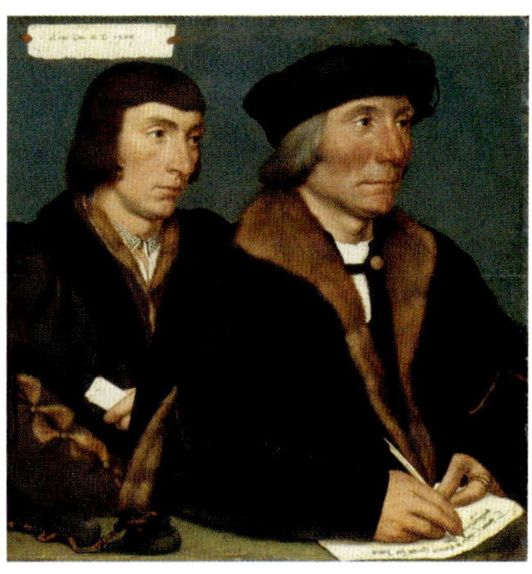

Above: A double portrait of merchants Thomas Godsalve and his Son, John, *c.1528, painted by Holbein the Younger, probably one of the last commissions before leaving for Basel. Both were wealthy and influential; Sir John was a secretary of Sir Thomas Cromwell.*

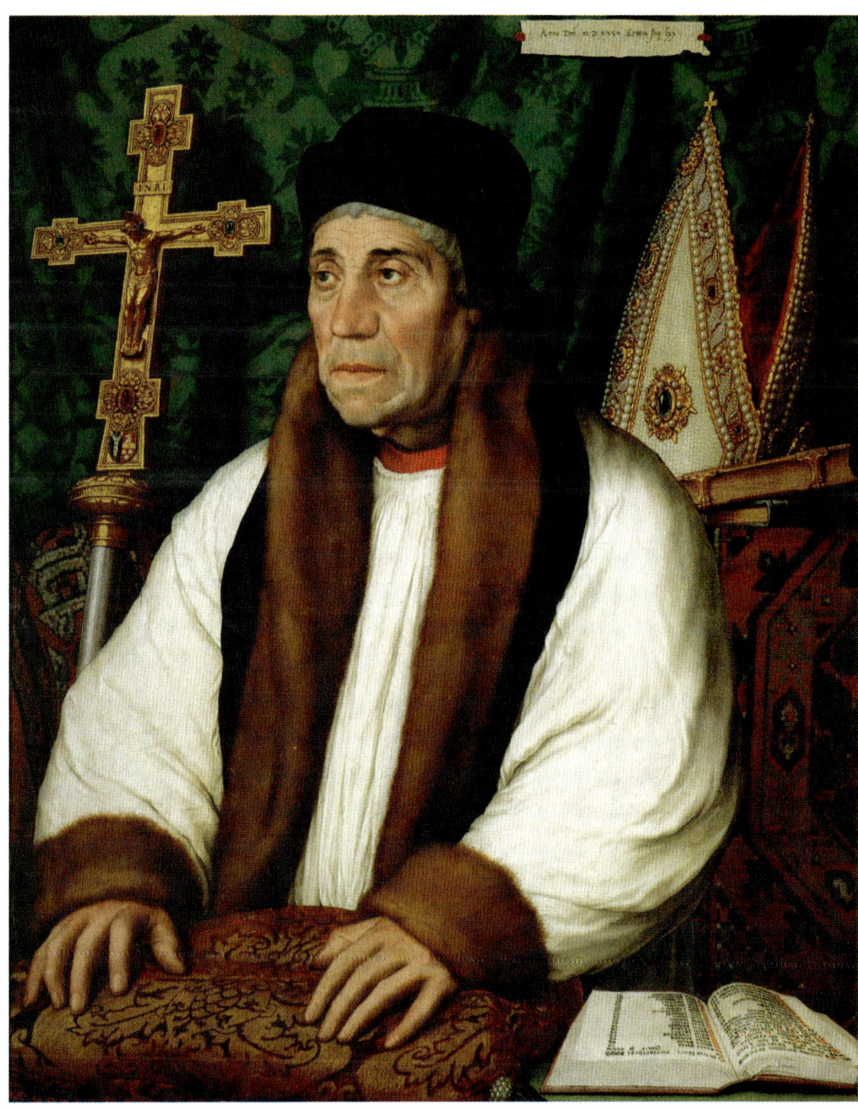

HOLBEIN AND DA VINCI

A focus on two portraits of young women reveal the masterful techniques employed by Florentine painter Leonardo da Vinci, and Hans Holbein the Younger. In Europe, an increasing availability of engravings and etchings of Renaissance artists' work widened awareness of a new natural realism in portraiture.

LADY WITH AN ERMINE

Painted in Milan in c.1489–90, *Lady with an Ermine* is a portrait of a young Italian noblewoman, Cecilia Gallerani, the fashionable mistress of Ludovico Sforza, the regent of Milan, as depicted by Florentine artist, Leonardo da Vinci (1452–1519). In his portrayal Leonardo depicted the essence of the person, the natural movement of her body, her head turning to the left with body twisting to the right, capturing a brief moment in time. The pet ermine's head

THE FINEST PORTRAITISTS IN EUROPE

By the time of Holbein's arrival in England, some of the most noted portrait artists in Europe were dead. Urbino-born Raphael Sanzio (1483–1520) died at the height of his career, aged thirty-seven in 1520. Venetian master Giovanni Bellini (c.1430–1516) had died, and the Florentine Leonardo da Vinci three years later, in France in 1519, when Holbein was twenty-two. Bellini's *Mary Magdalene*, c.1500, and *Doge Leonardo Loredan*, 1501–02, reveal the Venetian's gift for realism in portraiture; the great German artist Albrecht Dürer defined Bellini as 'The best painter of all'. Dürer was himself one of the most respected northern European artists, with examples of his skilful portraiture including *Self-portrait*, 1500 (see page 13), and his picture of his sister-in-law, *Portrait of Katharina Frey*, in 1497. The death of Dürer in 1528, who was revered as 'the German Apelles' for his outstanding portraiture and engravings, gave an opportunity for a new 'German Apelles' to come forward, Hans Holbein the Younger.

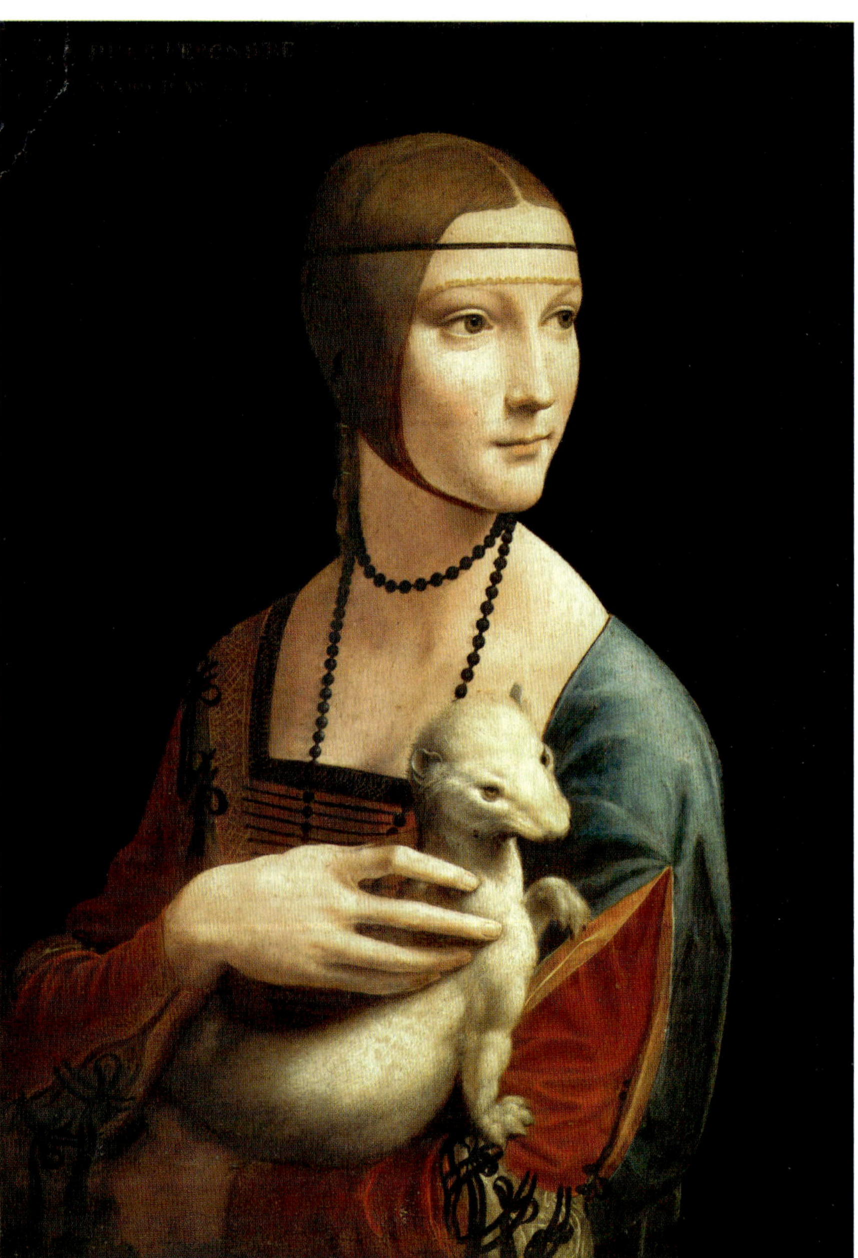

mirrors that of the lady. Both figures are realistic, and Leonardo captures Gallerani's youth, beauty and vitality. It can be compared in many aspects to a work by Hans Holbein the Younger, *A Lady with a Squirrel and a Starling*, painted thirty years later during Holbein's first period of living and working in England.

Above: Lady with an Ermine (Portrait of Cecilia Gallerani), *painted c.1489–90 by Leonardo da Vinci, illustrates the new naturalism in Italian portraiture, and the capturing of a moment in time.*

Right: Mary Magdalene *(a detail from a larger painting), c.1500, by Giovanni Bellini, is comparative in style.*

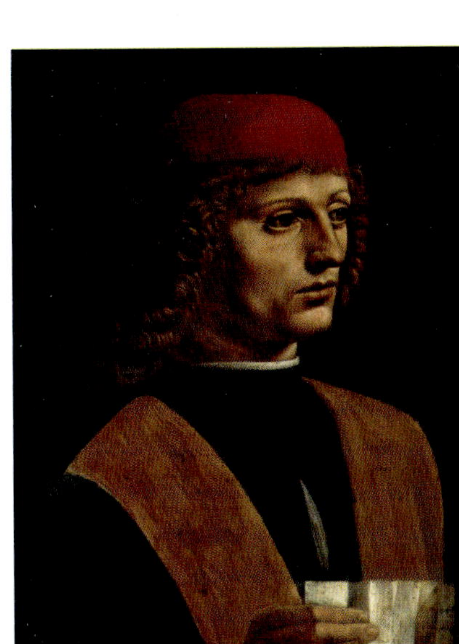

A LADY WITH A SQUIRREL AND A STARLING

Painted during Holbein's first short visit to England, 1526–28, this half-length portrait is unusual in English portraiture for its additional content of a starling, and a red squirrel with collar and lead, possibly the young woman's pet. The blue-green background strewn with vine leaves is a distinguishing feature in Holbein's work, appearing in other portraits. The pose of the young woman is also typical of Holbein's style; he realistically captures her characteristics, her plain features, the steadfast gaze of her dark eyes, and her plain mode of dress, effecting heightened realism and naturalism but noticeably without the seductive charm of Leonardo's *Lady*

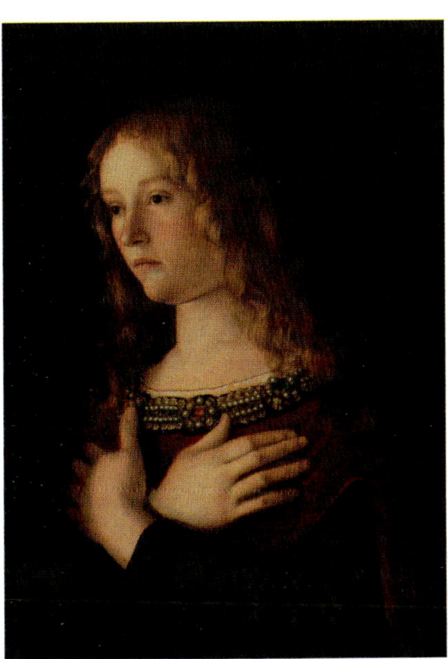

Left: The earlier Portrait of a Musician, *c.1485, by Leonardo da Vinci, is similar in its composition to Holbein's* A Lady with a Squirrel and a Starling.

with an Ermine. The patron of each would have influenced the content of the portrait, Leonardo's possibly allowing more animation, depicting the teenage mistress of Milan's regent.

Although the name of the sitter of Holbein's work is lost, it is now thought to depict Anne Lovell. Its anonymity lends one to think it was meant to be hung in a private residence. The composition of the lady in three-quarter profile looking to her left suggests that it may have been one half of a pendant portrait of husband and wife. Holbein simplifies strong tonal colours, using a bright blue-green background for contrast. X-radiography of the work reveals the squirrel was not in the original design but added at a later stage of the painting's creation.

Below: Holbein's A Lady with a Squirrel and a Starling, *dated 1526–28, is thought to have been Anne Lovell because the Lovell family of Norfolk included squirrels on their Coat of Arms, and the lady holds a tame pet squirrel on a chain, in her lap.*

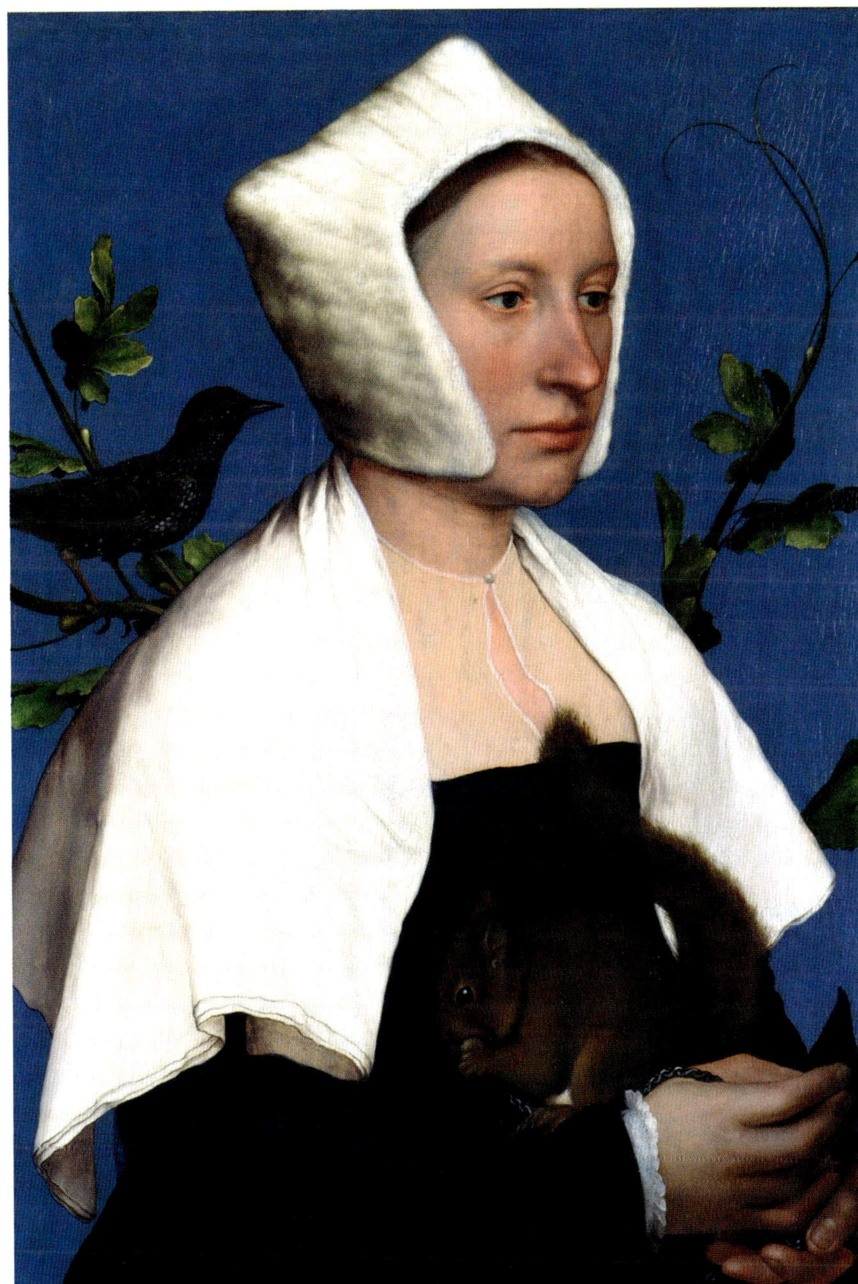

A RETURN TO BASEL

In 1528 Hans Holbein returned to Basel, a prosperous man with a celebrated reputation. He was able now to complete his unfinished commission for the Town Hall Council Chamber. On his departure in 1532 the city council would offer him an income to try to persuade him to stay permanently, as a resident artist.

It was a regular practice for artists in Europe to travel to other cities and countries, wherever work was available and services required. However in Basel, to maintain citizenship, inhabitants were not allowed to be away for more than two years at a time, hence Holbein's return to the city, one that recognised him as a celebrated resident.

THE GREAT COUNCIL CHAMBER,

In 1520–21 Holbein had embarked on murals in the Great Council Chamber of the new Basel Town Hall. One wall had been left blank because the council had agreed that it would be painted at a later stage. On Holbein's return to the city they commissioned him

Below: Rehoboam rejecting the advice of the Elders, *1530, Holbein's preparatory design for the wall painting to decorate the Great Council Chamber.*

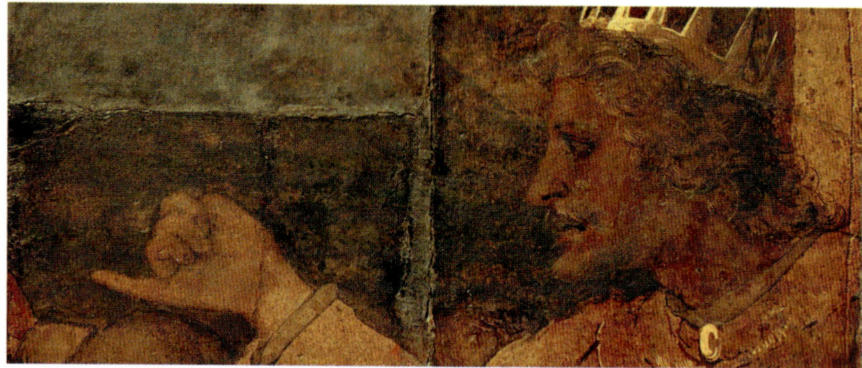

Above: King Rehoboam, *a fragment of Holbein's original wall painting for the Great Council Chamber in 1520–21. On Holbein's return to Basel, he completed the murals for the Great Council Chamber.*

to complete the decoration of the chamber. For this work Holbein was paid 60 gulden. Holbein's method was to paint *al secco* on to plaster. Humidity destroyed the surface of the plaster, and

the murals were replaced around fifty years later in 1579 by the French-born and highly respected artist Hans Bock the Elder (1550–1624) who lived and worked in Basel, and who was awarded citizenship in 1572. During subsequent restoration works in 1817 and 1825, fragments of Holbein's original works were found and copied. Their exact sequence and subject matter is unclear, but Holbein's drawings and remaining

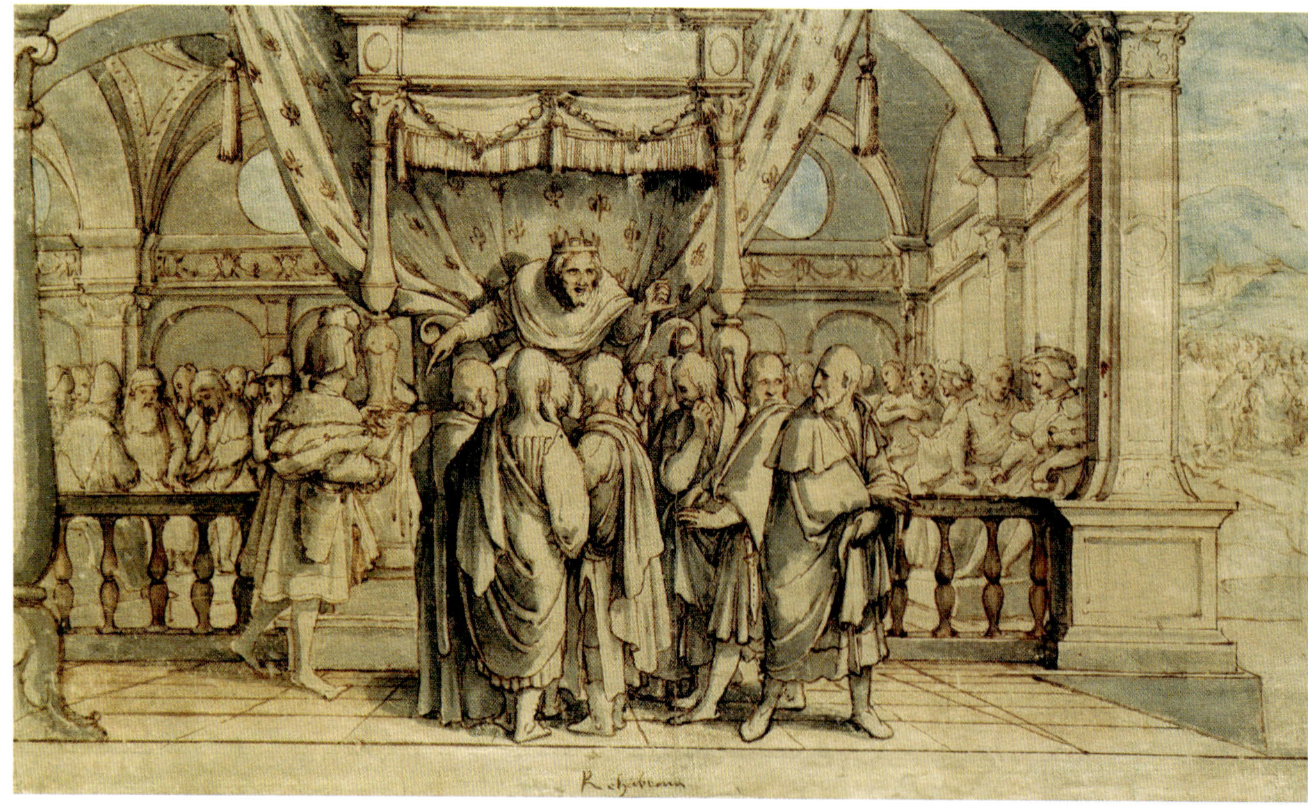

Right: The superb religious work Allegory of the Old and New Testaments *was painted in the early 1530s by Holbein.*

fragments include scenes of Saul and Samuel, and Rehoboam, three of the Kings of Israel.

ALLEGORIES OF THE REFORMATION

A painting, *Allegory of the Old and New Testaments*, is dated to the early 1530s. In 1529 in Basel, Protestantism became the official religion. Did this prompt Holbein to paint the work? There are versions by other artists with similar visual content, and the painting *Allegory of the Law and the Gospel*, 1529, by Lucas Cranach the Elder, a friend of the reformist Martin Luther, is said to have informed Holbein's work. It is possible that the environment of religious conversion in Germany and Switzerland spurred Holbein to return to religious artworks, particularly if patrons commissioned them.

HOLBEIN'S FAMILY

From 1528 until 1532 Hans Holbein stayed in Basel to maintain his citizenship, and he had been given

Below: Lucas Cranach's Allegory of the Law and the Gospel, 1529, *possibly influenced the content of Holbein's painting on a similar theme.*

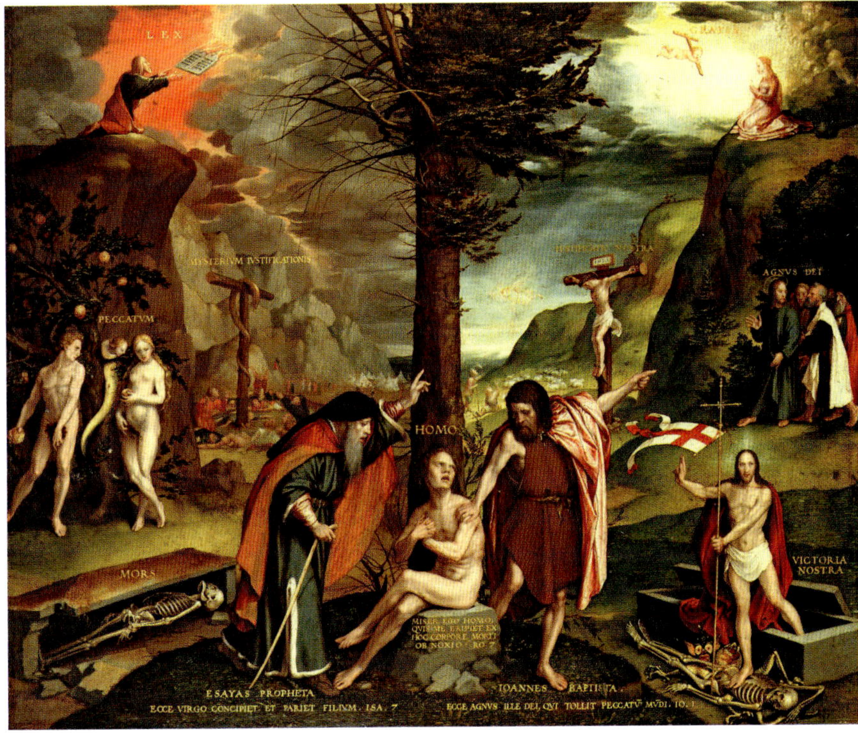

dispensation from King Henry VIII to return. One can imagine the reception Holbein received, fêted by dignitaries of the city, and a reunion with his wife and young children. He stayed in Basel for four years. City officials wanted him, a famous artist, to live and work permanently in Basel. But commissions for an artist of his ability were gone, and Basel officially had become a Protestant city in 1529, lessening the staple of religious commissions. Hans Herbst, Holbein's mentor, had closed his

workshop in 1529. Holbein needed a good income, to be found in London.

There is no record of the family visiting Holbein in England between 1532 and his death in 1543. Holbein returned briefly to Basel in the autumn of 1538. The council once more offered him an annual pension, at an increased rate, and offers of commissions, but he returned to London. This time he travelled via Paris with his eldest son Philipp, who would be apprenticed as a goldsmith under the mentorship of the Basel-born goldsmith Jacob David (died 1564). Philipp would stay in Paris until the death of Holbein in 1543. It is thought he then moved to Augsburg. It is recorded that Holbein's other son Jakob (1529–52) also trained as a goldsmith, and worked in Basel. He died in his early twenties. Holbein officially became a denizen – a permanent resident – of London in 1541.

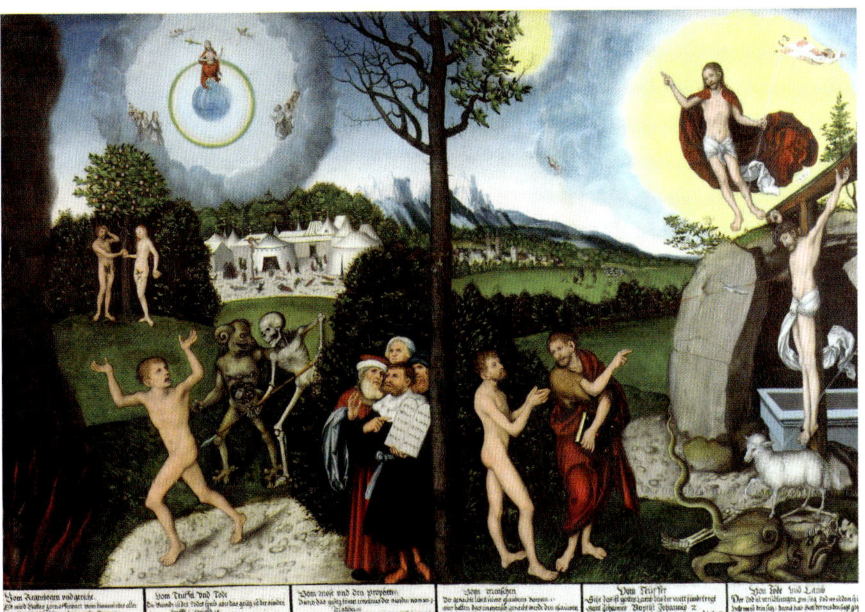

FAMILY PORTRAIT

It was during Holbein's residence in Basel c.1528–29 that he probably painted the portrait of his family (see page 46). Before 1542, Elsbeth sold the work to Hans Asper, a painter from Zurich.

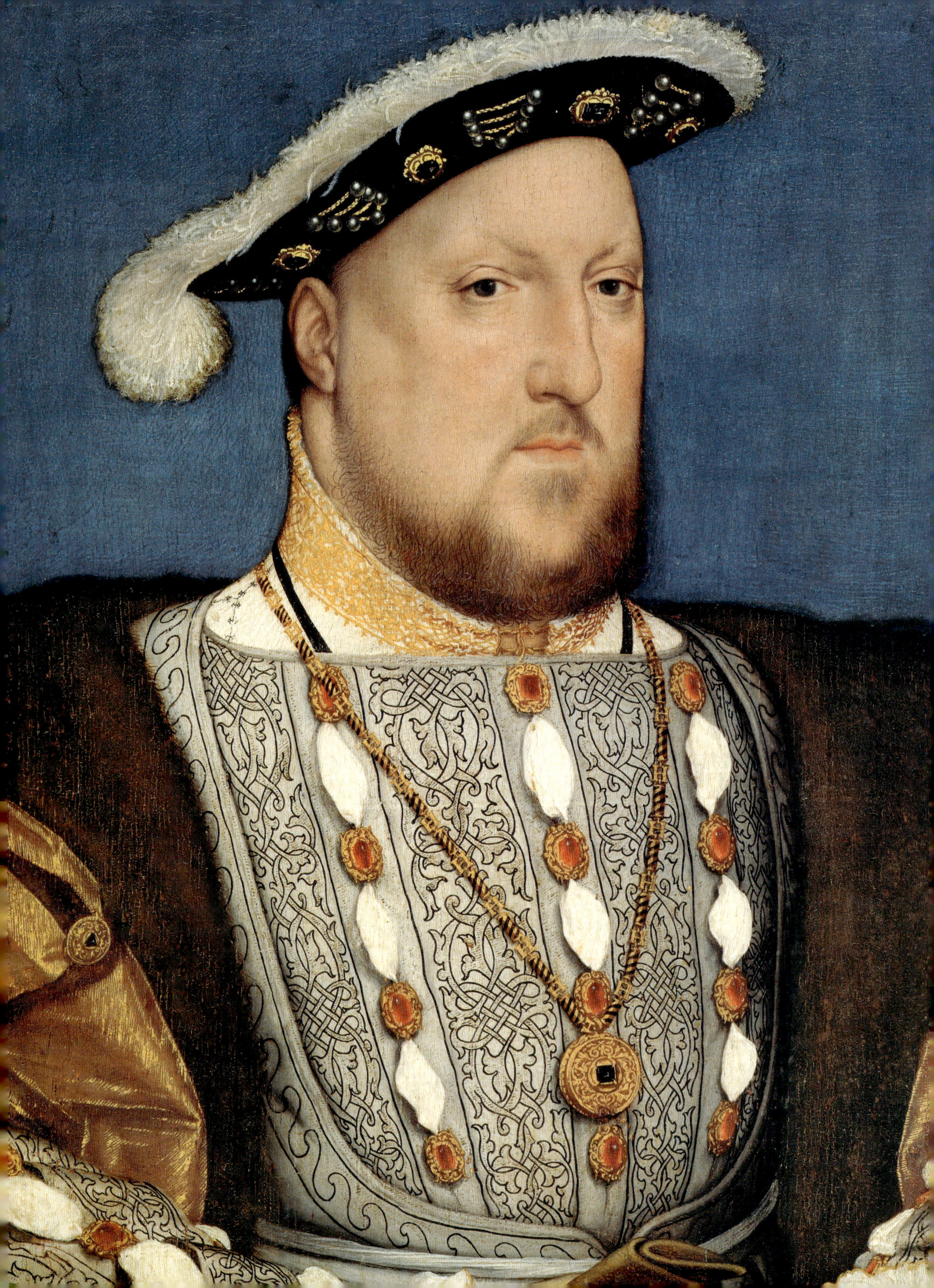

KING'S PAINTER

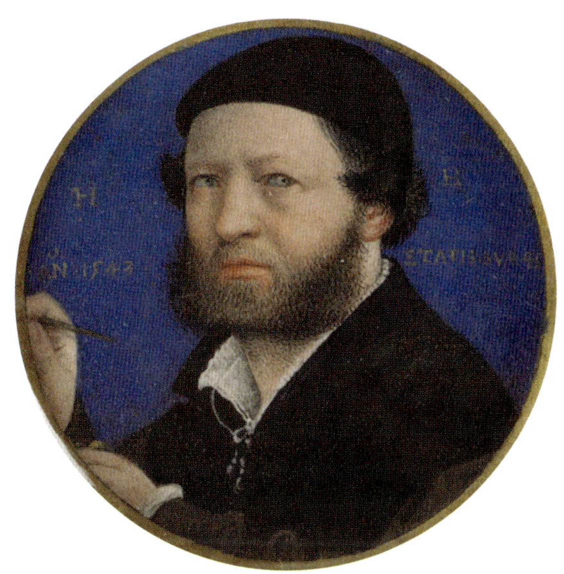

An English School portrait in oils of Henry VIII, dated c.1509 (see page 75) depicts a youthful boy, barely seventeen. It was painted in the year that he ascended the English throne and married Katherine of Aragon, the widow of his late brother Arthur. On the new king's shoulders was laid the future of England.

A little over twenty years later Holbein became part of Henry's court. The exact start date of his employment is unknown due to the household accounts of 1533–37 being lost, but his works date from 1533. He joined the Royal court at a critical time. Not only was Martin Luther's reformation in Germany spreading through Holbein's native city, but was now spreading toward England. Henry revised his plan to support the Catholic Church when he decided to divorce Katherine of Aragon to marry Anne Boleyn. Holbein captured in his drawings and paintings the changing faces of the Royal court, always treading a light path between royalty, politics and religion.

Above: A portrait miniature of Hans Holbein the Younger, c.1532–43, attributed to Dutch painter Lucas Horenbout (1490/95–1544), and thought to be based on a self-portrait by Holbein, now in the Wallace Collection, London, UK.

Left: Portrait of Henry VIII, King of England, c.1536–7, by Hans Holbein the Younger, tempera on wood, 26 x 19cm (10.2 x 7.5in), Thyssen-Bornemisza Museum, Madrid, Spain.

THE HANSEATIC LEAGUE

Holbein's clients in England included the German-born Hanseatic group of merchants, rich traders resident in the Styllyarde (Steelyard), City of London. Holbein rented a house close by in Mayden Lane. His superb portraits, full of character and realism, often were commissioned to send home to the merchants' families.

European trade had existed since seafaring allowed merchants to establish colonies, to export and import goods to foreign shores. The Hanseatic League of north Germany traded from the Baltic shores with England, establishing a base in London in the medieval era. In the mid-1300s, due to the increased success of English maritime trade in the Baltic region, trade relations soured, and charter privileges, such as reduced customs fees, were removed from the Hanse by the English parliament in 1377. Reciprocal trading rights were however then agreed between Germany and England in 1380, and thereafter the Hanse merchants were again embedded in London and, like other foreign traders, given special privileges from the English parliament. This included a waiving of trade taxes such as port and wharf fees. The advantages were many, including freedom from arrest and corporate denizenship – the rights of a foreign-born alien to permanent residence.

Below: On Holbein's return to London he undertook many portrait commissions from members of the German Hanseatic League, including Portrait of Georg Gisze, 1532. *The house he rented in Mayden Lane, south of St Paul's Cathedral, was close to the Steelyard headquarters.*

These were plentiful privileges and economically beneficial to the Hanse. Hans Holbein would have been familiar with the prosperous mercantile families of Germany. In London, he would have been an agreeable choice of artist to create portraits for the group.

THE STEELYARD

The Hanseatic establishment is documented from the early fourteenth century. It was listed at Steelyard, in Thames Street, as the 'chief executive authority of the Hanse'. By the end of the century, twenty-eight Hanseatic merchants lived and worked in Steelyard. Around seventy Hanse towns in Germany were represented here, divided between four regional centres: Cologne, Danzig, Brunswick and Lubeck, with other towns under their jurisdiction.

In the Steelyard, security rules governed, to keep strangers out and avoid theft from the warehouses. No English merchants were allowed for fear

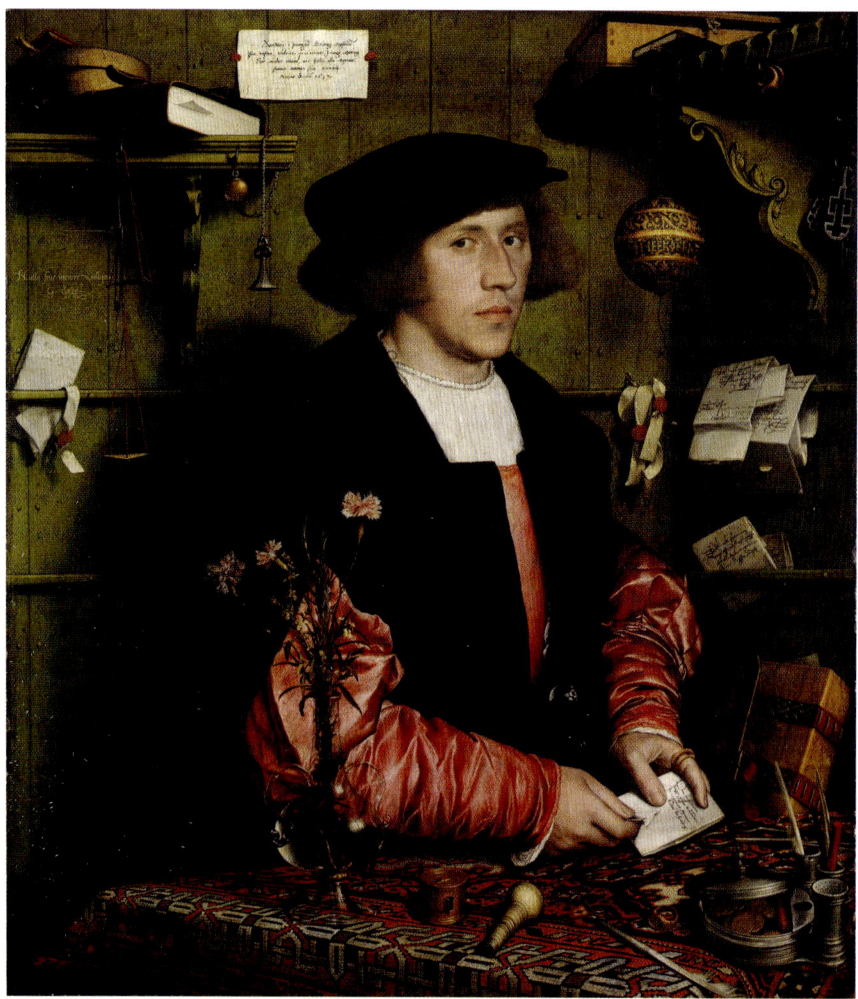

HOLBEIN IN MAYDEN LANE

The location of the German-owned Steelyard complex on the north bank of the Thames river, south of London Bridge (in close proximity to present-day Cannon Street) was a bare half-mile walking distance from Holbein's lodgings in Mayden Lane, where he rented a house. To prepare a portrait it is most probable that he first made sketches at the merchant's office, to create background context, as well as preliminary studies of a patron's features. The painting would then be created in Holbein's studio with perhaps one or two further sittings to complete the work.

of trade secrets being revealed. It was like an embassy, a part of Germany with a foreign community exempted from City of London laws.

CONTEMPORARY PORTRAITS

Holbein was commissioned to paint portraits of Hanse merchants (see also pages 176–181). As a fellow German, and a celebrated painter from Basel, Holbein would have had access to the Steelyard on trust. This allowed some portraits to be created in their working environment, in the private offices where business was transacted. Holbein focused attention on details that highlighted elements of their profession. The visible ledgers, letters, documents and small weighing scales all give context to the sitters' mercantile existence in London. Holbein captures a specific moment in time, an historical record full of realism and intimacy.

HOLBEIN AND GOSSAERT

A depiction by Holbein of one of the Hanseatic merchants, *Portrait of Georg Gisze*, 1532 (opposite), has been noted for its similarity of composition to one painted a year or two earlier by renowned Netherlandish artist Jan Gossaert, a native of Flanders, and considered one of the founding fathers of the Northern Renaissance. Gossaert's crowded *Portrait of a Merchant* (right) is possibly a portrayal

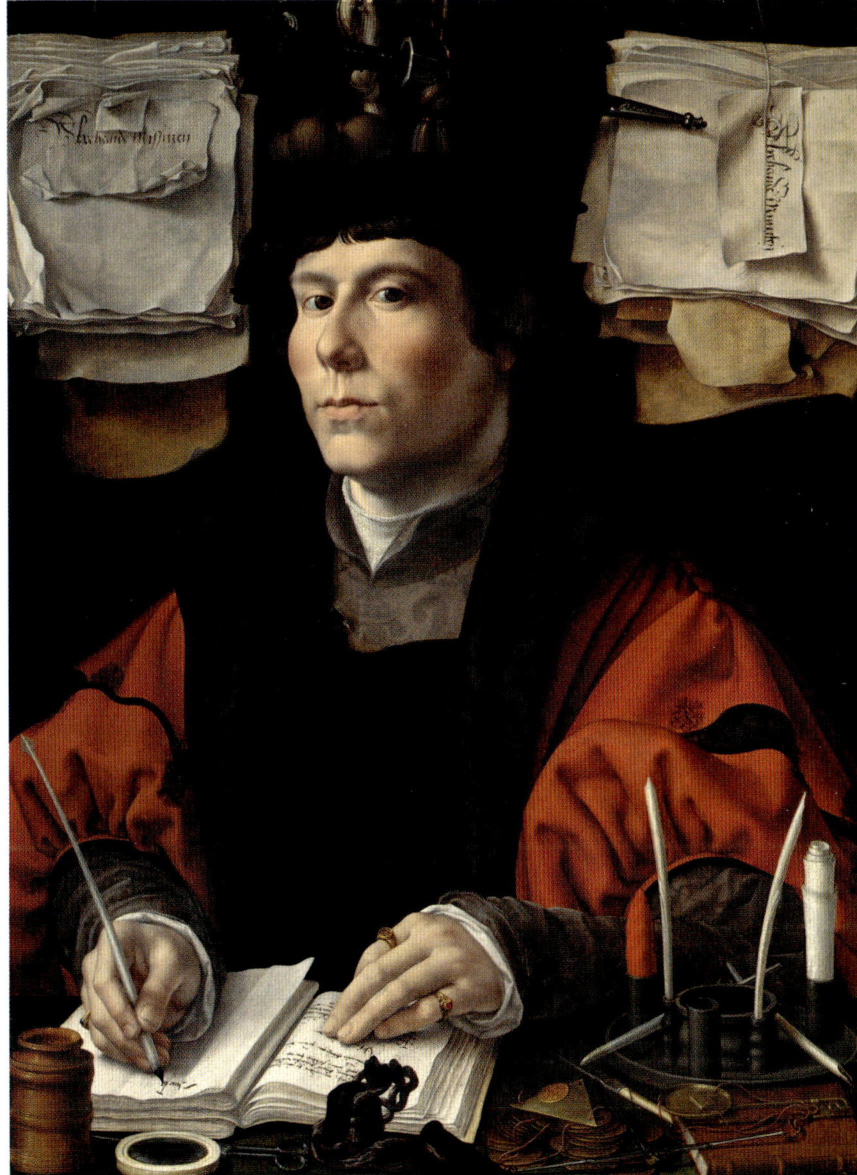

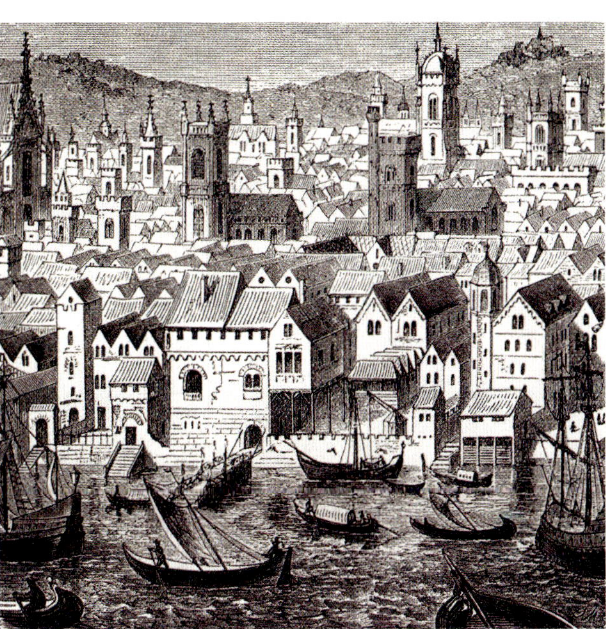

Above: Portrait of a Merchant, *1530, by French-born painter Jan Gossaert (c.1478–1532), aka Jean Gossaert, is similar to Holbein's* later *Portrait of Georg Gisze.*

Left: The Steelyard Depot of the Hanseatic Merchants, London, in the 15th Century, *engraving published in Ward and Lock's* Illustrated History of the World, *c.1882.*

of the merchant-banker Jan Jacobsz Snoeck (c.1510–85). Snoeck, if it is him, is writing in a ledger, quill pen poised. Gossaert portrays the sitter in three-quarter pose, his pale face set with a serious expression, with eyes cautiously fixed on the viewer. Around him are many objects: his writing equipment – pens, paper, sealing wax, an ink pot, and a talcum shaker for drying ink – and scales for weighing coins. The portrait bears similarities to Holbein's depiction of Gisze, which also highlighted the sitter's profession. It may have been seen by Holbein when he stayed in Antwerp in 1532 for a month (according to Erasmus) before returning to England, or it could have been seen by Georg Gisze.

THE AMBASSADORS 1533

The life-size double portrait of French ambassador Jean de Dinteville, Sieur de Polisy, and his friend, the priest Georges de Selve, Bishop of Lavaur, is a Holbein masterpiece. From their mode of dress to a distorted skull at their feet, Holbein presented two young French nobles amongst symbols of their lives.

A UNIQUE DOUBLE PORTRAIT

The content of *The Ambassadors* takes the spectator directly to the heart of French and English courtly life. The full-length painting was commissioned by Jean de Dinteville (1504–55) to be placed in his palatial, private château in Polisy, France. During de Dinteville's second stay in England, from February–November 1533, acting as French ambassador at Henry VIII's court, Holbein created a personal moment in time between de Dinteville and his friend and confident George de Selve (1508–41).

The life-size painting reveals a relaxed relationship with combined interests, in science, music, religion, poetry and prose. Holbein's composition and content in the painting references their earthly status, as well as their interest in the heavenly celestial sphere. The artist not only represented their physical features but spiritual and material lives. From sumptuous clothing, rendered in exquisite detail, to the celestial globe

Below: Detail of scientific instruments from Portrait of Nikolaus Kratzer, *1528 (see page 162); Kratzer, mathematician and astronomer at the court of Henry VIII, was a friend of Holbein.*

that accurately pinpoints 1,022 stars of Ptolemy's star catalogue (2nd-century AD), this was Holbein's masterpiece. He signed the large-scale panel painting in Latin '*Ioannes Holbein pingebat 1533*' ('Hans Holbein painted it, 1533').

No preparatory drawings survive. It is presumed that Holbein drew on to the prepared white ground panel surface before directly applying paint using linseed oil in two different formats: a plain linseed, and a heated-bodied linseed, mainly on de Dinteville's fur.

SYMBOLIC DETAIL

There is so much detail included within the large painting that it is hard for the eye to rest upon individual items (some are featured on pages 184–191). The most obvious is the placement of de Dinteville on the right side (to our left when looking at the painting). In a double portrait the stronger, usually male person, is placed to the right, recognised as the more powerful position. In addition, the viewer immediately notices the geometry and symmetry of the magnificent marble patterned floor of the room in which they stand. The floor was created by Odoricus, an artist from Rome, in 1268 for Westminster Abbey, London. This choice of floor symbolically places the men at the heart of Christianity in England. They are standing on *terra firma*, whilst the many objects and texts and books on the shelves allude to their celestial, literary, musical and spiritual interests. The cluttered shelves visually show de Dinteville and de Selve's wide range of pursuits, and allude to their undoubted intellectual capacity. Holbein may have borrowed the astronomical instruments from his friend, the mathematician, horologist and astronomer Nikolaus Kratzer. This conjecture is based on similar instruments, closely observed and

accurately portrayed, in Holbein's earlier work, *Portrait of Nikolaus Kratzer*, 1528.

ORDER OF ST MICHAEL

Holbein portrays the two young men, dressed to reflect their positions at court, with a degree of informality for this private meeting. Holbein pays great attention to the fur-lined robe and fine clothing that de Dinteville wears, a contrast to the informal daywear of the cleric de Selve. Attention is paid to the French Royal Order of St Michael, a pendant worn around de Dinteville's neck and permitted to be worn this way on a chain in private by the members of the Order. It was usually attached to a ceremonial collar.

A MUSICAL CONUNDRUM

The religious conciliations between Catholic and Protestant reformers that would have occupied de Selve's thoughts, and political conciliations sought by de Dinteville, may be alluded

Below: Detail of an anamorphic skull, used as a memento mori *illusion by Holbein in his painting* The Ambassadors. *When viewed from the front, the skull appears strangely distorted; viewed from a position on the right, it becomes clear, as below.*

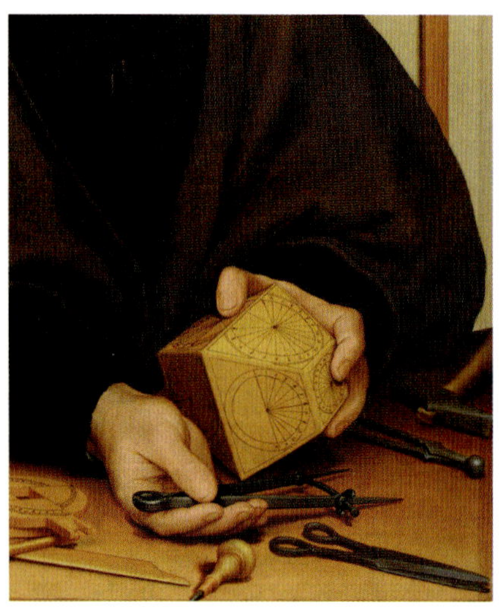

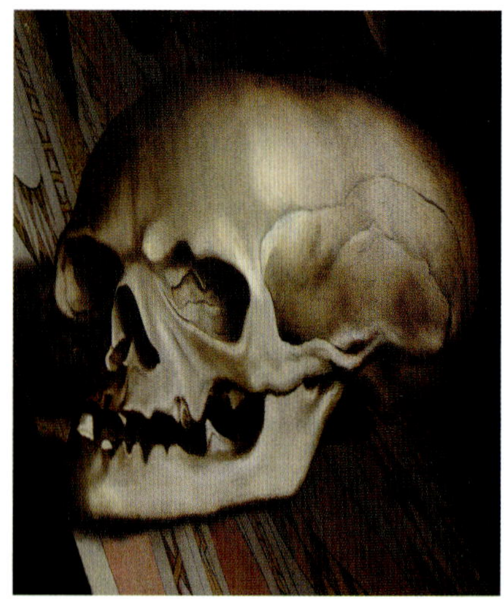

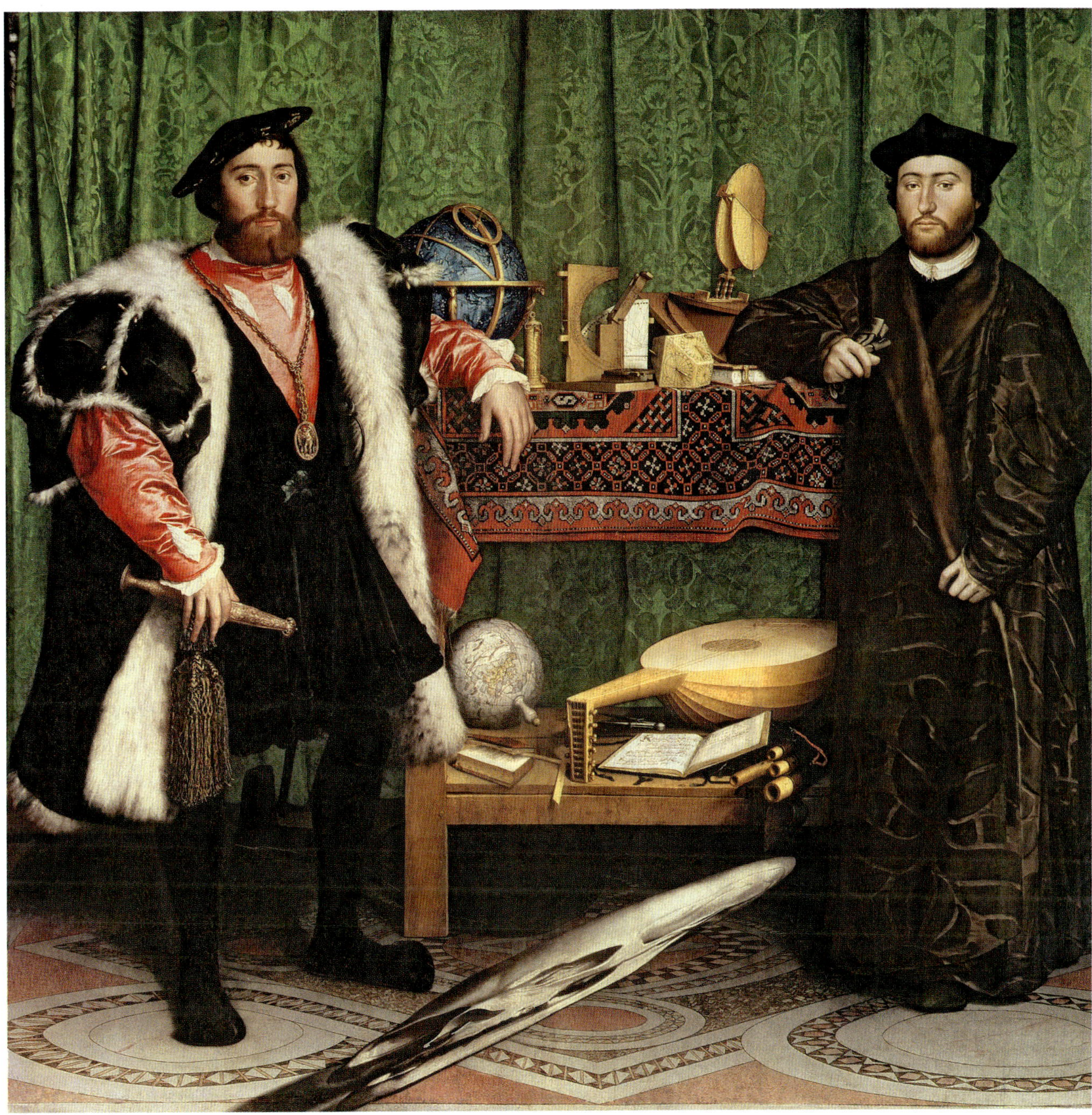

Above: The Ambassadors, *1533, a vast and magnificent painting by Holbein the Younger, was ground-breaking for its full-length double portrait depiction of Jean de Dinteville and George de Selve.*

to in the choice of music on display in the Lutheran hymn book, the tenor part of the 2nd edition of Johann Walther's spiritual vocal *Geistliches Gesangbiich lein*, published by Peter Schöffer in 1525. The open hymn book lies between the lute and flute case. The lute has its middle string broken, a symbol of discord, with the possibility

of future harmony when mended. The tenor part was the only book publication to include works recognised by Catholic and Reformant faiths. The second hymn is Walther's setting of *Veni sancte spiritus*, by Martin Luther, and number 19, the beginning of a short version of the Ten Commandments by Martin Luther, 'Mensch wiltu leben seliglich'. The inclusion of hymn music celebrating the descent of the Holy Ghost to the disciples at Pentecost was we assume agreed by de Dinteville and de Selve, symbolic of a coming-together of religious understanding.

A MEMENTO MORI

In the painting's foreground, the lower part of the panel, the strange shape is Holbein's distorted image of a skull, a *memento mori* of worldly, human life, a counterpoint to the celestial and spiritual worlds that surround de Selve and de Dinteville in the painting. The distorted skull appears correctly formed when viewed from the right-hand side of the painting (see left).

JEAN DE DINTEVILLE

The young French nobleman who commissioned *The Ambassadors* from Holbein in 1533 was a central figure in the French court, and the incredible detail in the background of the double portrait reflects the sitters' status and interests, and provides a fascinating insight into the preoccupations of the time.

THE FRENCH AMBASSADOR

De Dinteville had been sent to London to allay any concerns that Henry VIII may have had, following the announcement in 1533 of the French king of France, Francis I (1494–1547), that his second son Henry, duke of Orléans (the future Henry II of France) was to marry Catherine de' Medici, the daughter of Lorenzo de' Medici,

Below: Portrait of Jean de Dinteville, 1540, painted by Ambrosius Benson (1490–1550), an Italian-born painter working primarily in northern Europe.

Duke of Urbino. She was the niece of Pope Clement VII, Giulio di Giuliano de' Medici, pontiff from 1523–34, thus strengthening Italian-French family bonds, and papal ties between Italy and France. The marriage between Henry II and Catherine took place in Marseille on October 28th, 1533.

ART BEYOND BORDERS

Prior to journeying to London, Holbein had spent time in France, feasibly hoping for royal commissions from Francis I. This did not materialise, but it is possible that Holbein met Jean de

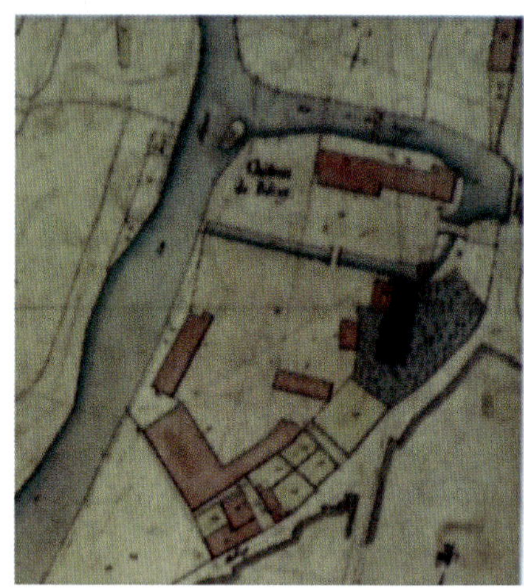

Above: Map of Château Polisy, the French home of Jean de Dinteville, the rich courtier of king Francis I, and Ambassador at the court of Henry VIII in England. It shows the chapel and church.

Dinteville through the French court, for the wealthy ambassador of noble heritage was widely and prestigiously connected.

A multicultural coming-together, *The Ambassadors* (see page 65) was painted by Holbein, a German artist, of two distinguished French men, and happened to be created in London where all three were staying. It was destined for the French château of Jean de Dinteville. The commission may indicate Holbein was in pursuit of work from French nobility and the royal family. For this majestic, yet relaxed portrayal of two friends, residing in London and attendant at the court of Henry VIII, the composition and content illustrates their wealth and status.

DE SELVE, CLERIC

At Easter in 1533 de Selve arrived in England, which helps to date the painting. He was a diplomat and courtier, acting as ambassador to the Emperor, to the Venetian Republic, and the Holy See, and was also Bishop of Lavaur in south-west France. De

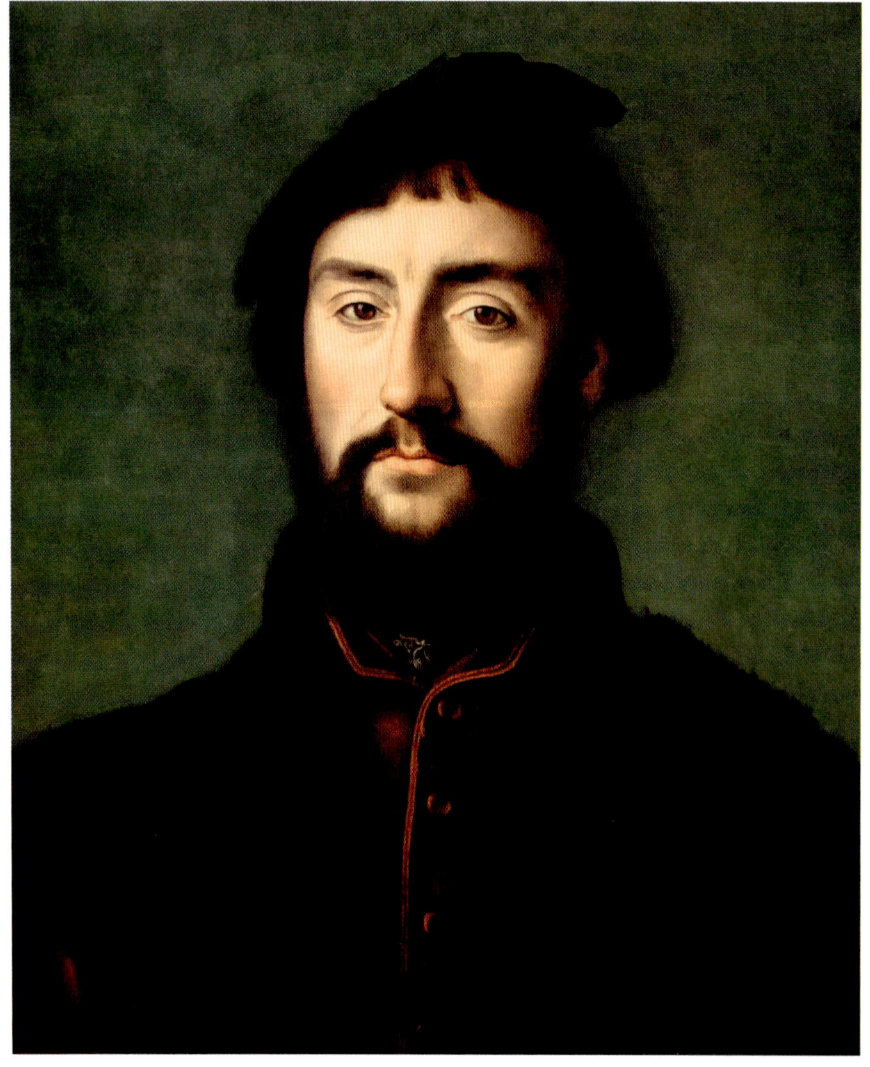

AN ALLEGORY OF DE DINTEVILLE FAMILY

In a large, allegorical painting of the de Dinteville family, *Moses and Aaron before Pharaoh*, 1537, painted soon after *The Ambassadors* by a Netherlandish or French artist, the de Dinteville brothers act out parts of Exodus 7:9. Jean de Dinteville played Moses, while François de Dinteville as Aaron begs Pharaoh to free the Israelites. He transforms a rod into a serpent to show that God is overseeing his actions. Gaucher and Guillaume de Dinteville stand behind Aaron and Jean. The painting was hung in the de Dinteville château at Polisy.

Selve was visiting de Dinteville at a sensitive time. Upheaval in the Catholic church, instigated by Lutheranism, and the reform of Christian belief toward the spiritual away from the material aesthetic, made it a dangerous time for clerics.

The age of the sitters at the time of Holbein's commission is included within the painting. De Dinteville's age

Below: Portrait of Jean de Dinteville, Sieur de Polisy, c.1533, *a chalk drawing by French artist Jean Clouet (c.1485– 1540/41), created about the same time as* The Ambassadors *by Hans Holbein the Younger.*

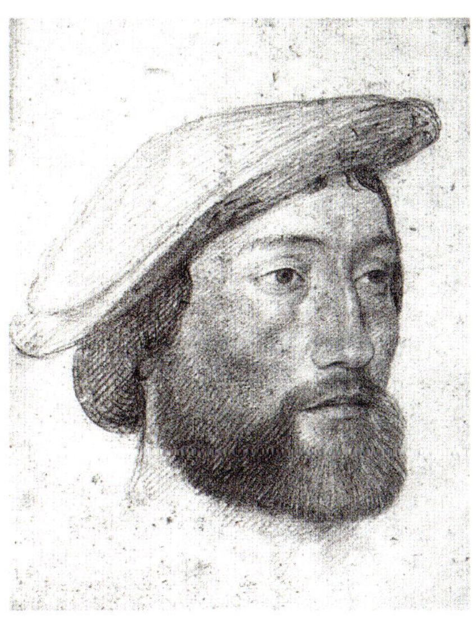

of twenty-nine is embossed on the magnificent dagger his right-hand rests upon. De Selve's age of twenty-five is inscribed on the book on which he rests his right arm.

Holbein includes many visual references in *The Ambassadors* that allude to the interests and relationship between the sitters, known to them but not necessarily to be shared with the onlooker. For example, the diamond rings they wear are symbolic of fidelity, their shared outlook, and bond of friendship. The success of the life-size portrait led to Holbein's commission from Henry VIII, c.1537, for a life-size mural depicting three generations of the king's family, for the wall of Privy Chamber in Whitehall Palace (see pages 78–79).

Right: A detail of Portrait of Francis I, *king of France from 1515–47, painted 1530– 35 by the renowned German-born painter Joos van Cleve (1485–1540).*

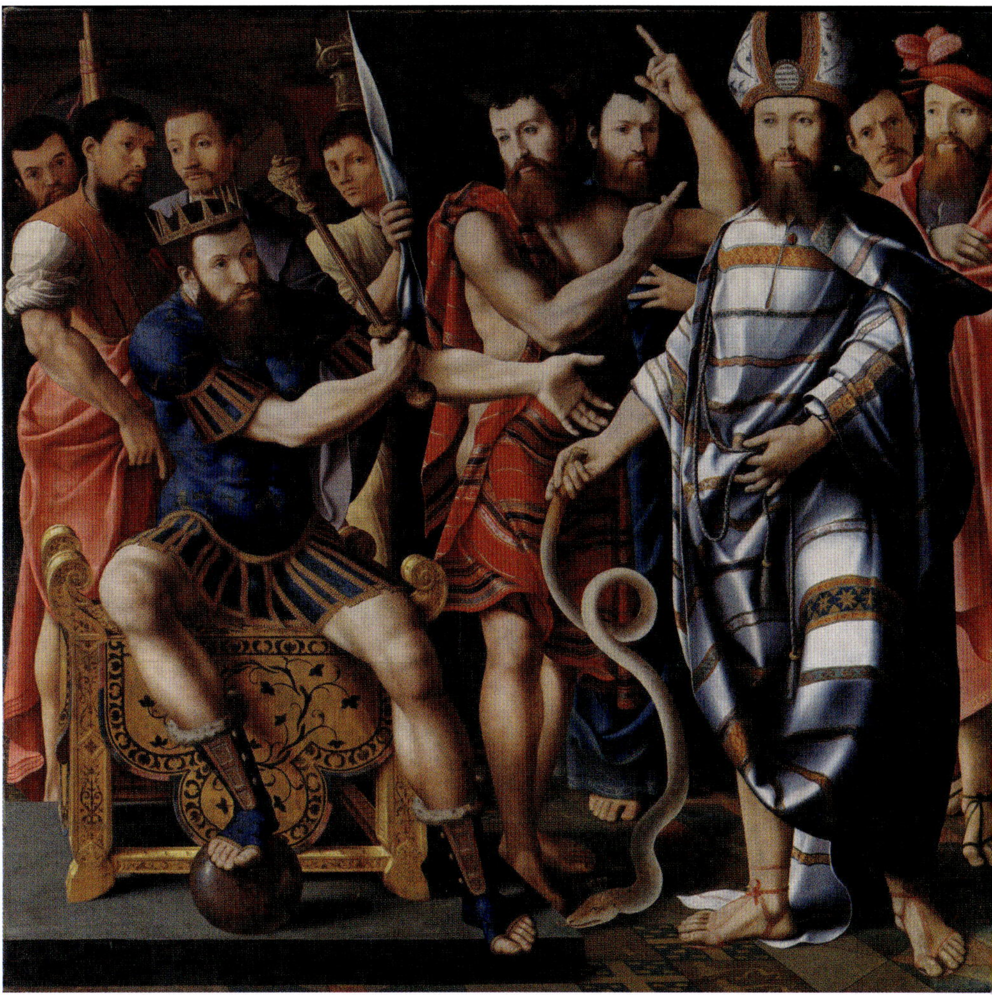

Above: This remarkable painting by an unidentified artist, Moses and Aaron before Pharaoh: An Allegory of the Dinteville Family, *1537, portrays Jean de Dinteville (as Moses), his brother François II de Dinteville (as Aaron) and King Francis I (as Pharaoh) in a recreation of Exodus 7:9.*

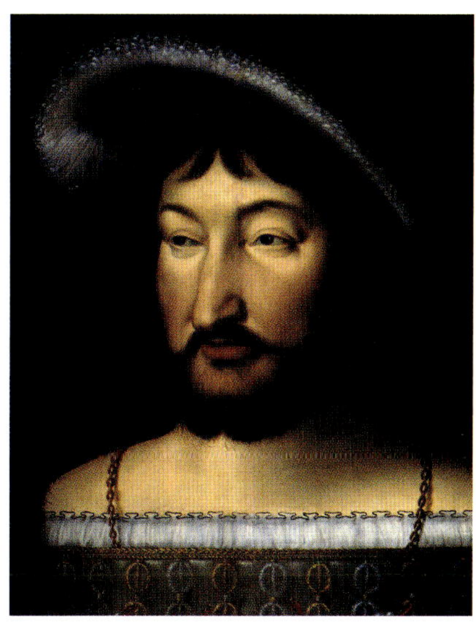

PAINTING THE NOBILITY

Having created superb portraits of the Hanseatic community of German merchants in London, Holbein's attention turned to the gentry and courtiers at Whitehall Palace, close to the king. Notable portraits of prominent nobleman – French and English – were commissioned.

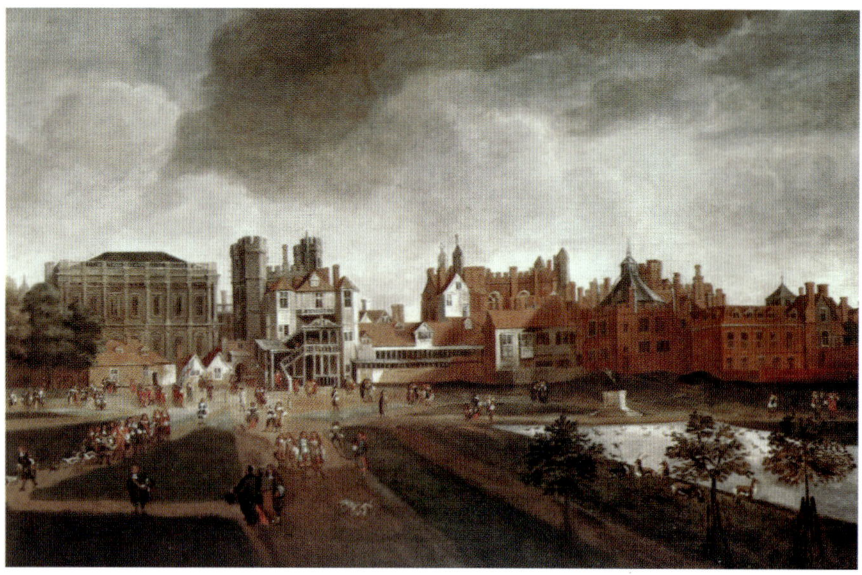

Above: A later view of Whitehall Palace and St. James's Park, *c.1675, attributed to Dutch artist Hendrick Danckerts (c.1625–80).*

NICHOLAS BOURBON

An exquisite profile drawing, *Portrait of Nicholas Bourbon*, 1535, in black and coloured chalks, pen and ink on pale pink prepared paper (see opposite), reveals a young man in left profile. His face, with reddish beard and chin-length straight hair, is in repose, a scholar in thought, seated at a writing desk in the act of writing. In the eighteenth century an inscription was added to the top left of the paper with handwritten appellation 'Nicholas Bourbonius Poeta'. The work portrays Holbein's acquaintance Nicholas Bourbon (c.1503–1549/50), a French poet and courtier, visiting the court of Henry VIII. Holbein made more than one portrait of Bourbon, although only a preparatory sketch survives, and likewise Bourbon mentioned Holbein in several writings. A letter from Bourbon to a friend, Thomas Solimar, c.1535, alludes to Holbein. It is the first document that records Holbein's presence at court in the employ of the King. Bourbon, on his way back to France, records the people he met: '*Mr. Cornelius Heyss, my host, the King's Goldsmith; Mr. Nikolaus Kratzer, the King's Astronomer, a man*

who is brimful of wit, jest, and humorous fancies; and Mr. Hans, the Royal Painter, the Apelles of our time. I wish them from my heart all joy and happiness.'

Bourbon, a recognised poet, was known for his many verses on Apelles, and it is fitting that he should recognise Holbein thus. The ancient Hellenistic Greek painter, active in the fourth century BC, was court painter to Philip of Macedon and his son Alexander III ('The Great'). Apelles was acknowledged as the most accomplished artist, recognised for centuries after as the supreme painter of the ancient era, although none of his work survives.

Bourbon had been imprisoned in France for suspected Humanist sympathies, and found a safer haven in England amongst the circle of Anne Boleyn, after the dishonouring 'Affaire des Placards', of 17–18th October 1534, when anti-Catholic posters were put up in Paris and in four major cities Rouen, Tours, Orléans, and Blois, which implicated Bourbon. His circle included Erasmus, who wrote, '*Farewell, my dear Bourbon, most honeyed poet, and see that those Muses who grant you such friendly favour are made to serve the glory of God rather than that of men.'* Bourbon returned to France in 1536.

WILLIAM RESKIMER

On his return to England in 1532, Holbein chose to use pink prepared paper for preparatory drawings, as used on the drawing for the portrait of William Reskimer. The hatched underdrawing and finished work (see pages 190–1) reveals that little changes were made, and the drawing outlines transferred to the portrait with a stylus. Holbein positions the sitter in profile facing right. In the half-length portrait Reskimer's face is composed, as if deliberating, with elegant, twisting hands, caught at a moment in time. His long beard, of deep red-gold, follows the silk strings hanging from his shirt, worn under a rich robe of fine fabric. Holbein

Below: An homage to Apelles, the ancient Greek artist, in an engraving by Joachim von Sandrart (1606–88).

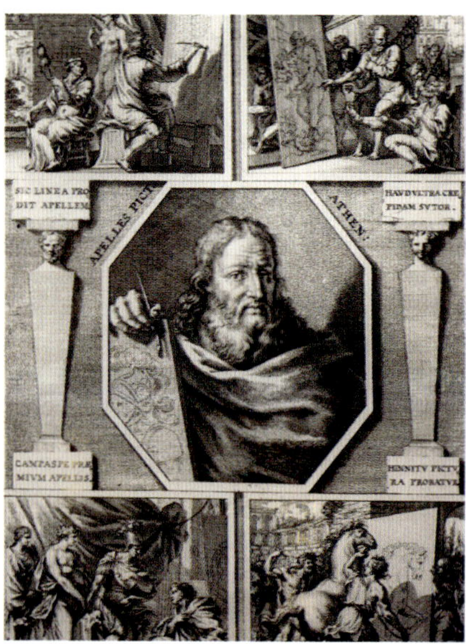

inscribes the work *Reskemeer, a Cornish Gent*. William Reskimer (1515–1552) had held several positions in court, from Page of the Chamber in 1526. On the dark green background of the finished portrait, Holbein includes vines and figs, a recognisable signature style of the artist. Later, the painting was presented to Charles I, by Sir Robert Killigrew, a direct descendent of Reskimer.

SIMON GEORGE

Another notable painting by Holbein of a Cornish nobleman can be seen in his portrait of Simon George of Quocote, 1535–40. A rectangular drawing in black and coloured chalks, pen and ink, and metalpoint on prepared paper (below right) was prepared in readiness to create a small circular painting (see page 205). The finished work reveals George wearing fine clothes and magnificent hat and holding a red carnation.

CHARLES DE SOLIER

A French ambassador to England, Charles de Solier (1480–1552), was portrayed in one of Holbein's most magnificent works. The artist paints Solier life-size, with a stern facial expression, connoting a strong-willed man, large in stature. He wears a sumptuous courtly costume and holding an exquisite ceremonial sword. The composition is similar to Holbein's later portraits of Henry VIII. The

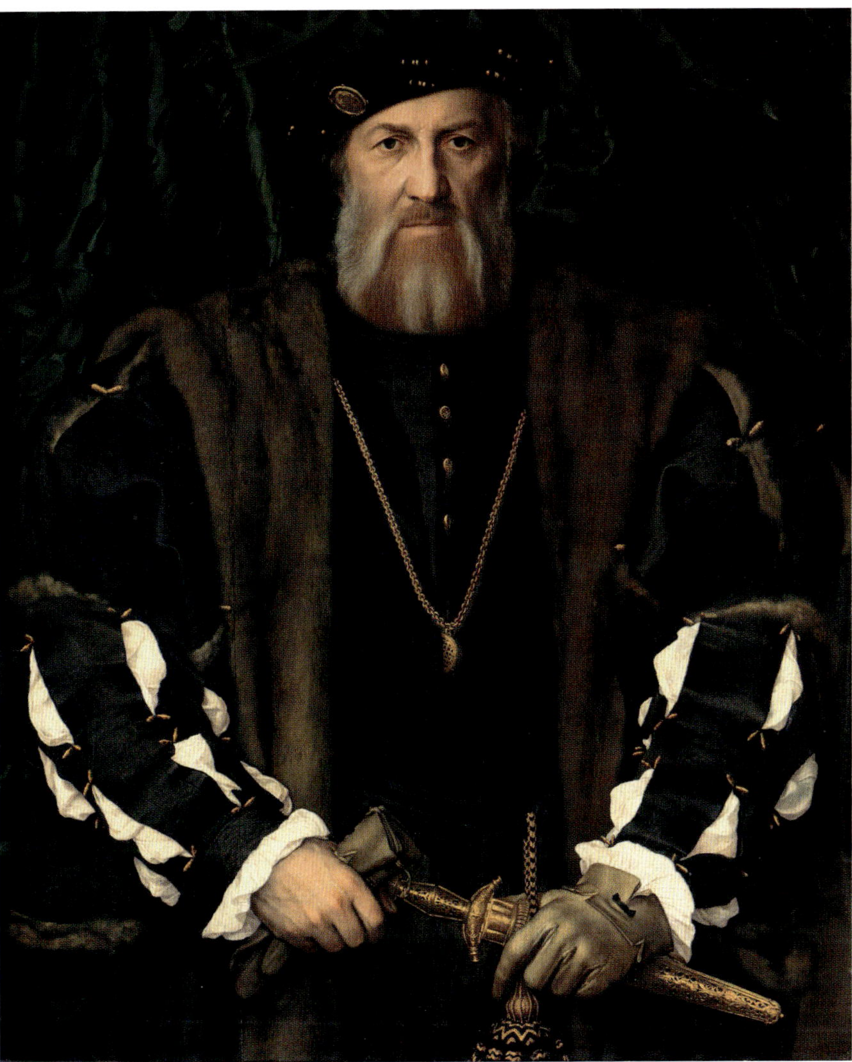

half-length composition that Holbein, or de Solier, chose for this work was more usually reserved for members of a royal family.

Below: A portrait drawing, c. 1532–34, of Cornish gentleman William Reskimer.

Above: Charles de Solier, Sieur de Morette, 1534–35, a sumptuous portrait of the French ambassador by Holbein.

Below: Holbein's preparatory drawing of Simon George, c. 1535–40.

Below: Nicholas Bourbon was a French scholar and poet. He arrived in England in 1535, becoming part of the inner circle of the royal court.

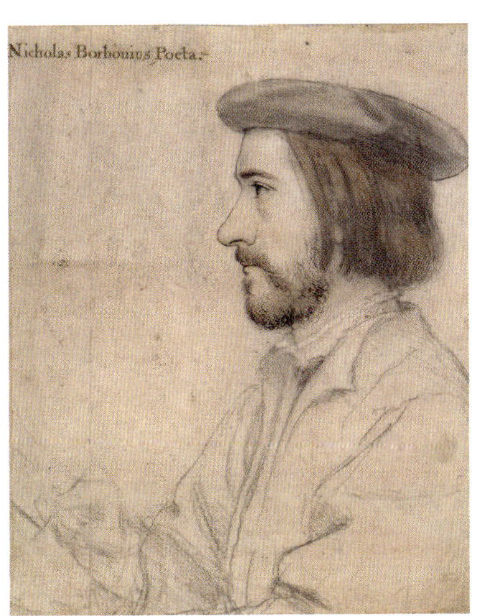

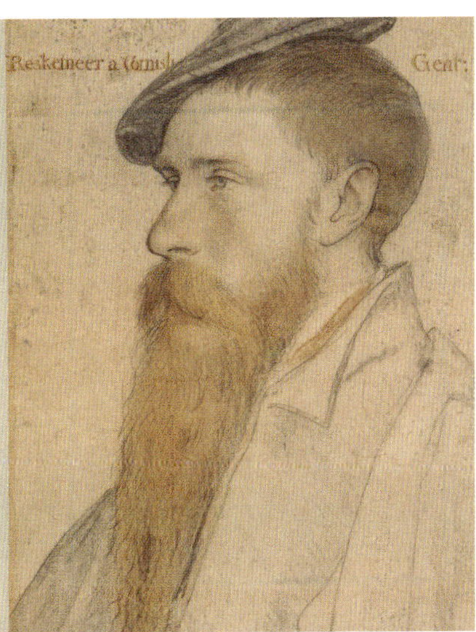

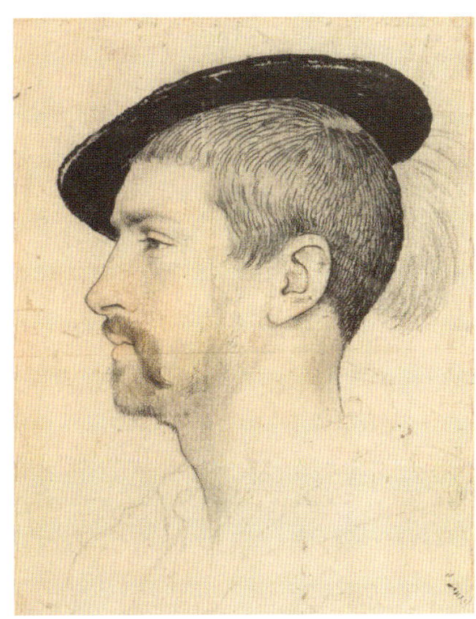

ANNE BOLEYN

Queen Anne Boleyn (1501–36) is thought to have been Hans Holbein's first protector at the Royal court and possibly introduced him to Henry VIII. Surprisingly, Holbein produced designs for festival decorations, silver, glass and jewellery for Anne, but if he painted her we have only sketch portraits extant.

FIRST ROYAL COMMISSION

Holbein's first royal commission was one relating to Queen Anne Boleyn. It was a festival decoration, created as part of the coronation programme of May 1533. Commissioned by the Hanse merchants of the Steelyard, the work is known today through a sketch *Apollo and the Muses on Mount Parnassus, 1533* (see page 197). It was to be displayed for the royal procession when the queen travelled from the Tower of London to Westminster, to be crowned Queen Consort on St Paul's Day, 25th January 1533. Official records are scant for Holbein's commissions from Anne Boleyn, but it is established that he designed jewellery for her, which would fit well with plans for her marriage, and the coronation year of 1533. Her commission for Holbein to create works for the coronation confirmed his royal credentials.

Below: Sketch of Queen Anne Boleyn seated unter a canopy, crowned, with sceptres in each hand. The Archbishop of Canterbury is on her right. Below is a plan for the queen's Coronation dinner.

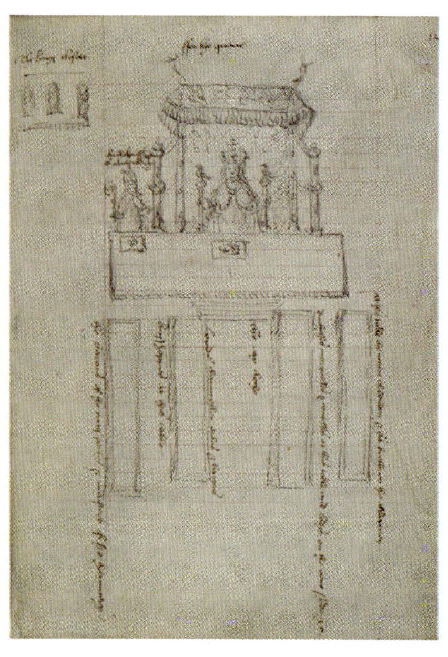

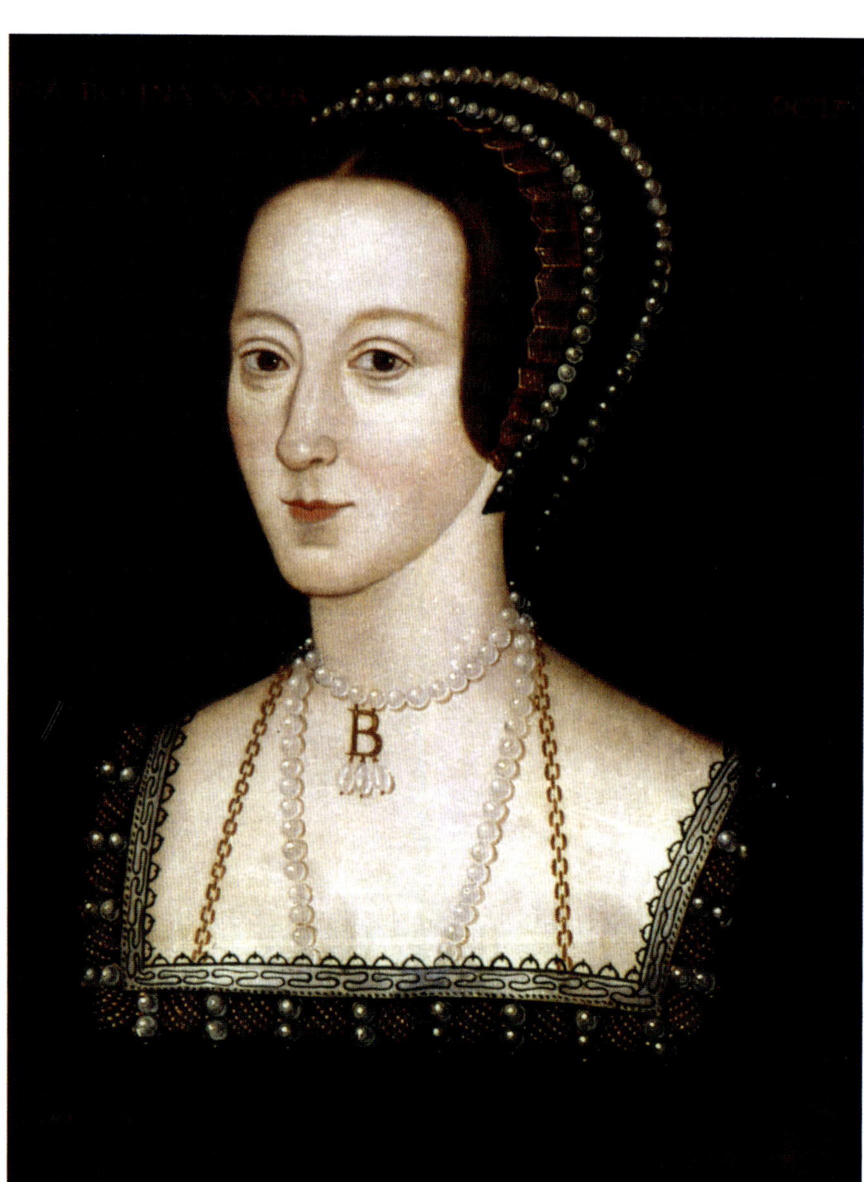

Above: A portrait of Anne Boleyn, second Queen of Henry VIII from 1533–36, painted by an unknown artist.

SIR THOMAS BOLEYN

Anne was the daughter of a favoured royal courtier Sir Thomas Boleyn (1477–1539), 1st Earl of Wiltshire, 1st Earl of Ormond, 1st Viscount Rochford KG KB; he was created a Knight of the Bath at Henry VIII's coronation in 1509. His wife, Lady Elizabeth Howard, spent her childhood years at the family home Blickling Hall, a Jacobean mansion, near the village of Blickling, Norfolk. Anne, or Nan as she was familiarly called, was one of three children, with an elder sister Mary, and younger brother George. Her family dynasty allowed her to argue that she was 'descent of right noble and high thorough regal blood'. When Boleyn's father was assigned for a year to the Archduchess Margaret, Regent of Netherlands' court in Brussels, as English ambassador in 1512, it led the way for Anne to attend the Archduchess as one of eighteen *fille d'honneur* (maid of honour) at court. There, known as Mademoiselle Boullan, she perfected speaking and writing in French. During this period until about 1521 when she returned to England, she cultivated friendships that would aid her status at European courts. Amongst her close acquaintances she befriended Margarite of Angoulême (1492–1549), who became the wife of Henry II of Navarre (1503–55) and was the older sister of the young French king, Francis I (1494–1547).

It is to the father of Anne Boleyn that one looks to understand how a young girl became the usurper of Katherine of Aragon's rightful place as Queen of England. Sir Thomas Boleyn, through his contacts, manoeuvred Anne into a high-profile position at the royal court, as a maid of honour to Katherine. By 1526 Henry VIII had fallen in love with Anne and made overtures to make her queen.

VISUALISING BOLEYN

Holbein portrayed Anne in a coloured chalk drawing, 1533–36, which dates it to the coronation year or near after.

Below: The Coronation Procession of Anne Boleyn to Westminster Abbey, 1st June 1533, *an engraving by an anonymous artist, printed in 'Old and New London', 1881.*

Here, a determined woman who had the skill and personality to capture the heart of a king, looks demure.

An attributed portrait, *Anne Boleyn,* by the English School (opposite), captures her beauty. Her long, ivory neck is highlighted by a pearl necklace with a 'B' pendant. This may have been copied from a lead medallion depicting Anne, with the words '*A.R. The Moost Happi Anno 1534*', thought to have been issued to celebrate the forthcoming birth of Anne and Henry's child, in the year after their coronation.

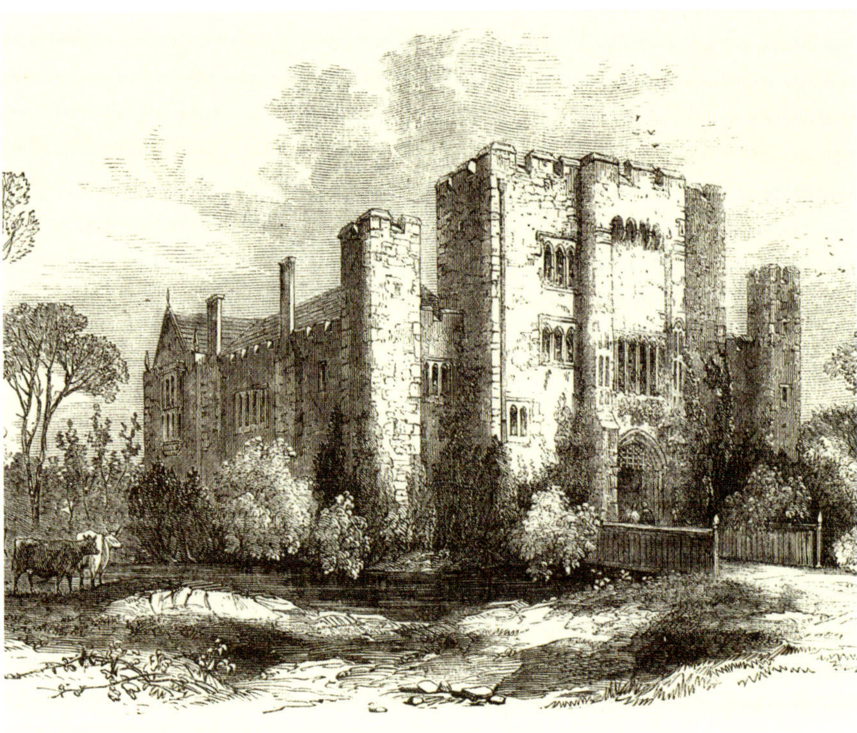

Above: An exterior view of Hever Castle, Kent, built in the early 12th century for the Bullen (Boleyn) family. Anne Boleyn and Henry VIII possibly met here.

Below: A chalk drawing by Holbein, 1533–36, inscribed at a later date 'Anna Bollein Queen'. Her fresh young face, shown in three-quarter profile, has a heavy chin, with hair hidden beneath a bonnet. It is thought this may show her clothes for the coronation. Reports (probably partisan) on the event state the high neck shirt was to cover a cyst and swollen throat glands.

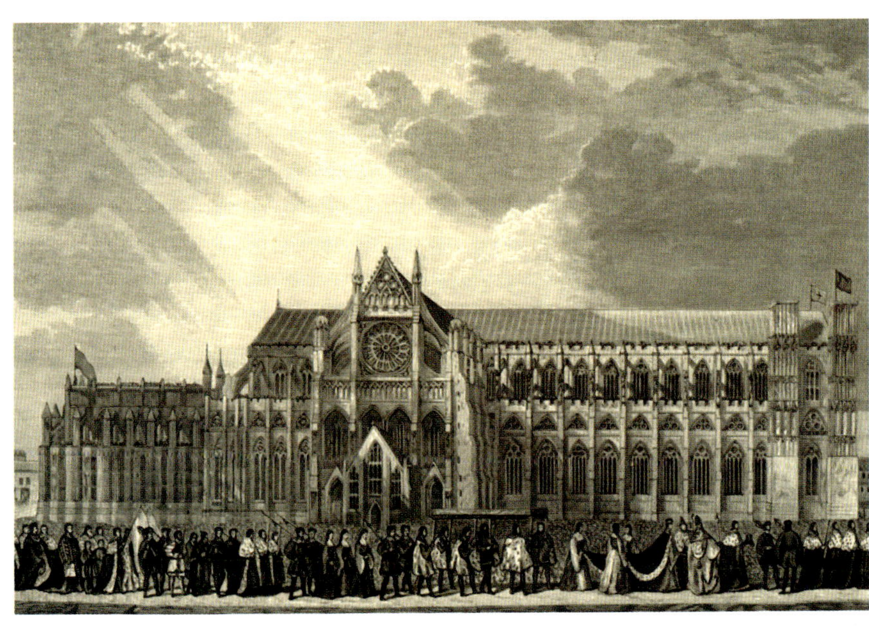

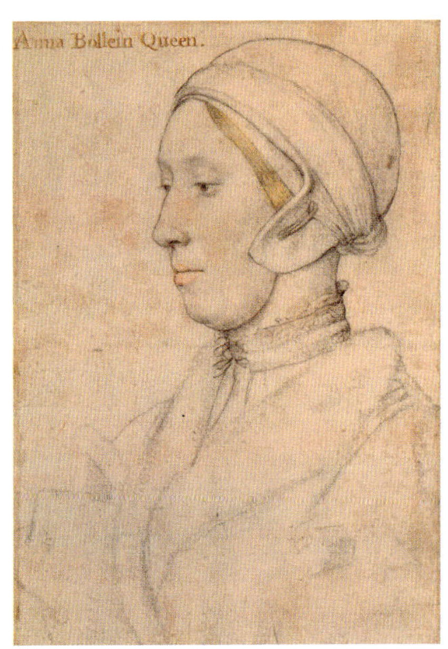

THE ROYAL COURT

The approval of Queen Anne Boleyn brought Holbein into direct contact with the inner circle of Henry VIII's court. As an outstanding painter of portraits, courtiers engaged Holbein to portray them in exquisite detail. Most prominent of all his new patrons was the 1st Earl of Essex, Thomas Cromwell.

THOMAS CROMWELL,

Until Thomas Cromwell's downfall, due to the disastrous outcome of the marriage of Henry VIII to his fourth wife, Anne of Cleves, which led to his execution, Cromwell was one of king's most important ministers. In the year of the Act of Supremacy in 1534, which divided Henry VIII from the Pope and the Church of Rome, Cromwell enjoyed near-royal status. There are at least twenty-five extant portraits of Thomas Cromwell by different artists, including three attributed to Holbein which are now known only through copies. Each

reveal an assured man. From a copy of one of Holbein's portraits dated to 1532–34, the content of the letter that Thomas Cromwell has laid out before him reads 'To our trusty and right well-beloved Councillor, Thomas Cromwell, Master of our Jewel House'. The date is determined to c.1532–34 when Cromwell was Master of the

Below: Thomas Cromwell, Earl of Essex, an early 17th-century copy after Hans Holbein the Younger's original of 1532–3 (see page 217). The banner 'Earl of Essex' was an addition.

Jewel House, a prestigious position. This appointment was probably the reason for Holbein's commission. In 1534 Cromwell was promoted again, to King's Secretary.

SIR RICHARD SOUTHWELL

The MP and diplomat Sir Richard Southwell (1503/4–1564) was, alongside Thomas Cromwell, involved with the legislation of the dissolution of the monasteries in 1536, from which time his portrait by Holbein is dated. Holbein's half-length painted portrait (opposite) and its accompanying preliminary drawing (see page 220), reveal his method of preparation, putting precise detail into a primary sketch before creating the painting in oils. The drawing, in chalks, pen and ink and metalpoint, is unique amongst extant works for its inclusion of the lettered inscription that also appears in the final work. In addition, a note by Holbein written on the drawing, read sideways, observes that Southwell's eyes were 'a little yellow'.

Southwell wears a hat with an emblem of a Moorish woman, and a collarless off-white shirt, laced at the neck. The buttons of his jacket stand out against the plain shirt. The finished painting does not show the sitter in the exact clothing of the sketch, but follow the shape of it, its line and folds, albeit in a different colour and now a rich silky satin. Holbein otherwise carefully follows his detailed drawing, with the sitter seated and facing left away from the viewer. The final work does include an adjustment to the shape of the back of Southwell's neck. There is close observation of Southwell, with his small mouth and dimpled chin, clearly defined eyebrows, and yellow-brown hazel-coloured eyes; the scars on his neck are reddened and there are visible reminders of tubercular disease.

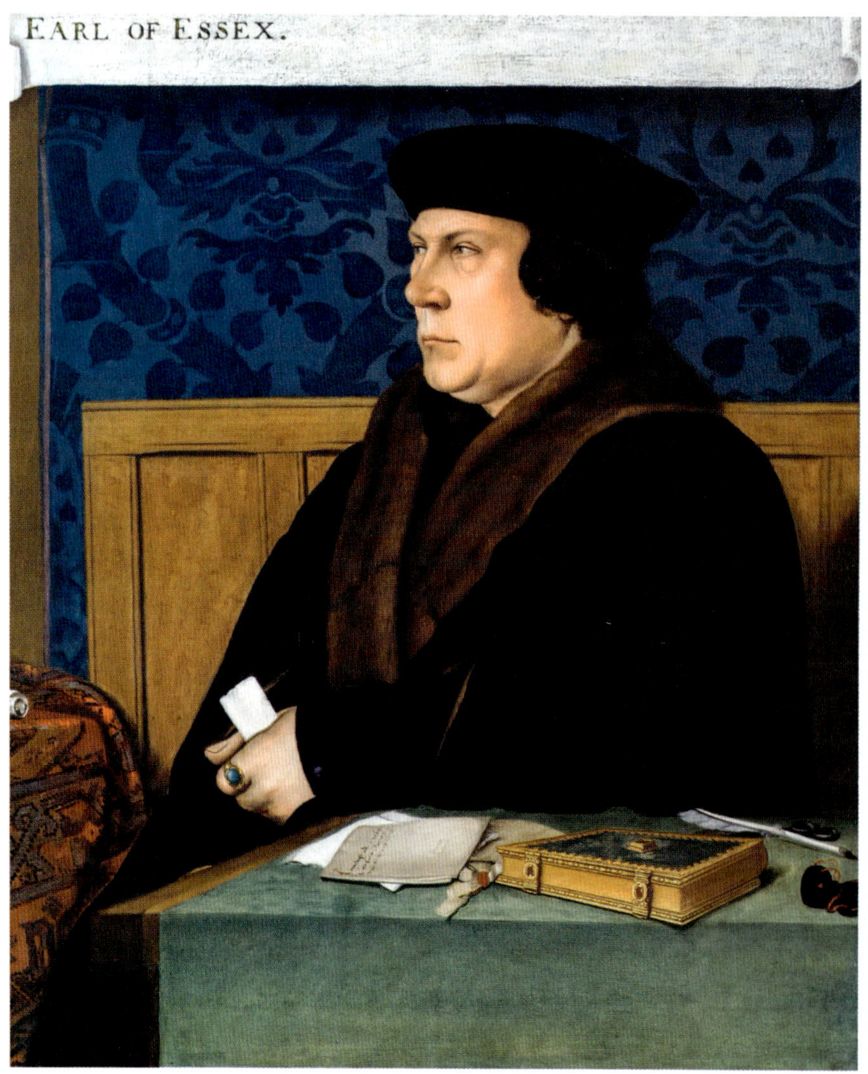

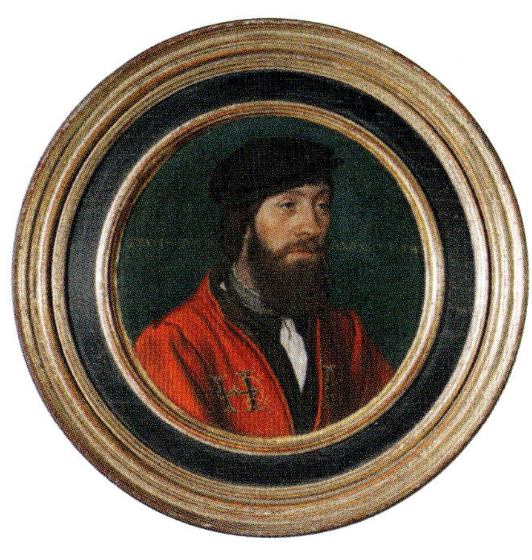

Above: A Courtier of Henry VIII, *1534, a portrait miniature, in a fashionably circular composition, of a now unknown courtier.*

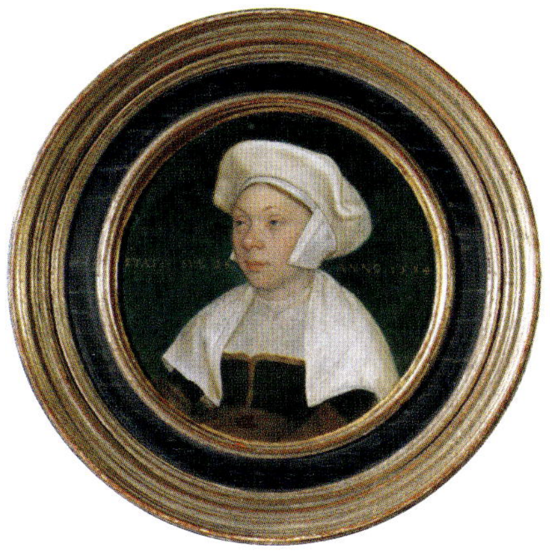

Above: Wife of Courtier of Henry VIII, *1534, is a companion pendant piece to the miniature above.*

Below: Portrait of Elizabeth Widmerpole *c.1536 by Hans Holbein the Younger.*

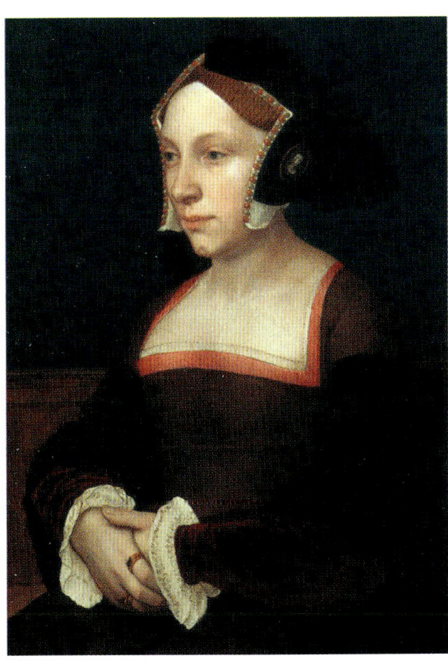

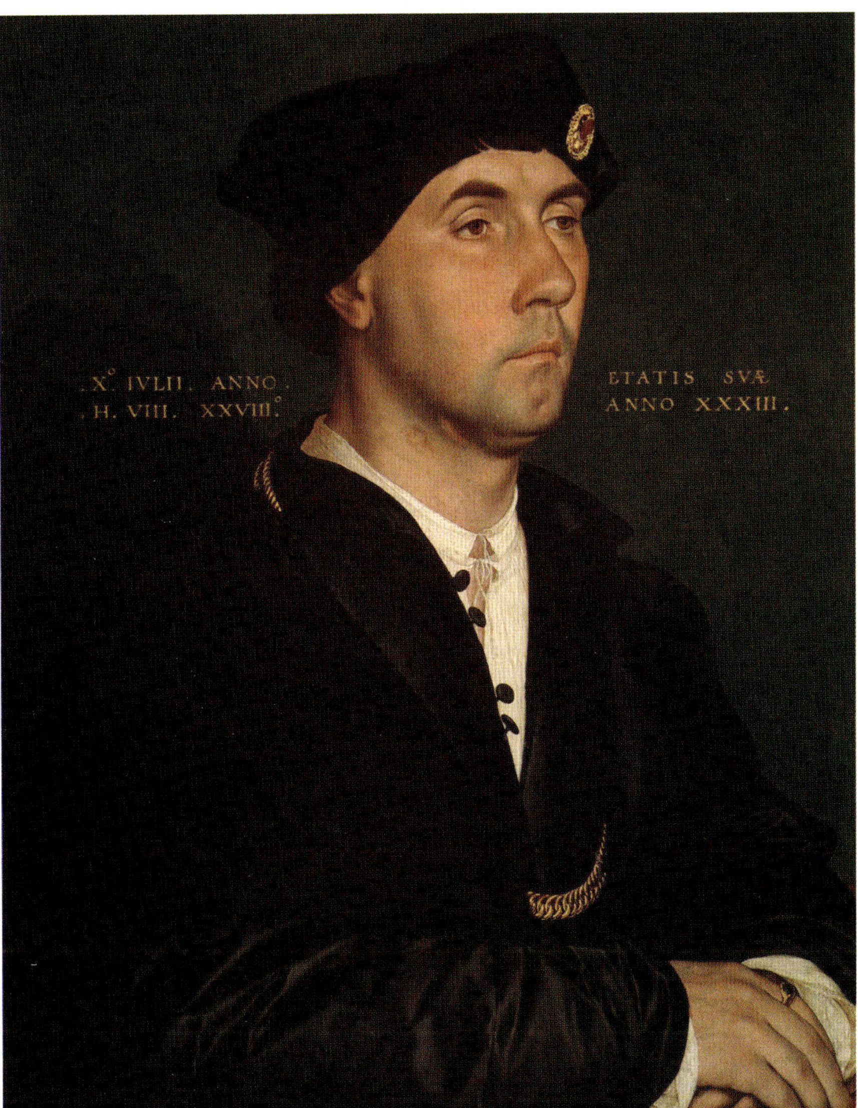

Above: Sir Richard Southwell, *1535–36. Grand and aloof, Holbein depicts Southwell's demeanour and physical details superbly, including the remains of scarring on his forehead and neck.*

COURTIER COMMMISISIONS

On Holbein's return from Basel in 1532, he was commissioned again by John Godsalve for a portrait. Only a preparatory drawing remains (see page 206) but we see Godsalve established in his role of courtier. Godsalve fills the half-length portrait frame. His body and head are turned but his eyes remain fixed on the viewer with a steadfast, serious expression. Godsalve also commissioned a small painting of his second wife, *Portrait of Elizabeth Widmerpole.* Other courtiers commissioned Holbein for single and pendant portraits, as in *A Courtier of Henry VIII,* and *Wife of Courtier of Henry VIII.* Some also commissioned other painters to copy Holbein's originals.

Right: Portrait of Lady Elisabeth Rich, *1540, wife of Lord Chancellor Richard Rich (1496/7–1567). A copy after the original work by Holbein the Younger.*

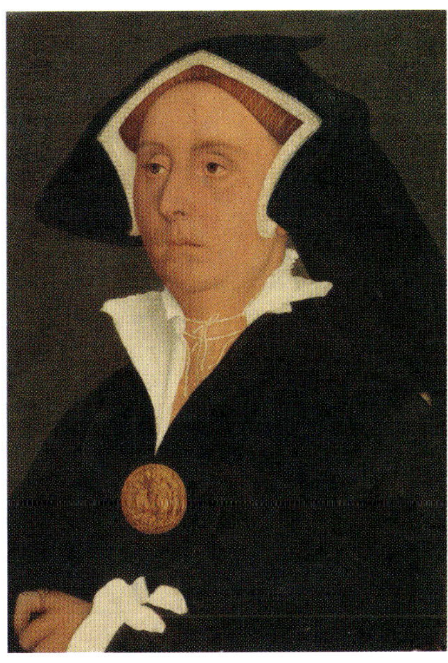

PAINTER TO HENRY VIII

From his first arrival in England in 1526, Holbein networked through his commissions to gain acceptance into the Royal household and then into Henry VIII's inner circle. His outstanding portraits of nobles and courtiers pushed him forward. By 1536 he was officially the 'King's Painter'.

King Henry VIII's household accounts for 1533–37 are lost, but there are references to Holbein. He is mentioned in 1536 within correspondence from Nicholas Bourbon (a French courtier at the court, a member of Anne Boleyn's circle, and a friend of Holbein), as the 'King's Painter', and naming him the 'Apelles of our time'. Accounts for 1537 show Holbein receiving £30 per year salary from the royal court, to paint whatever the king requested. Holbein was allowed to work for other clients too, thus making his skill as a portraitist and designer lucrative.

In 1534 King Henry had become, through The Act of Supremacy, head of the Church of England. The breakaway from the powerful Church of Rome shows his tenacity and determination. Perhaps through portraiture the king now wanted to communicate that message, and affirm his royal lineage.

Below: Portrait of Henry VIII, *King of England, c.1536–37 by Holbein the Younger, a small close-cropped painting, now displayed in the Thyssen-Bornemisza Museum in Madrid (see also page 60).*

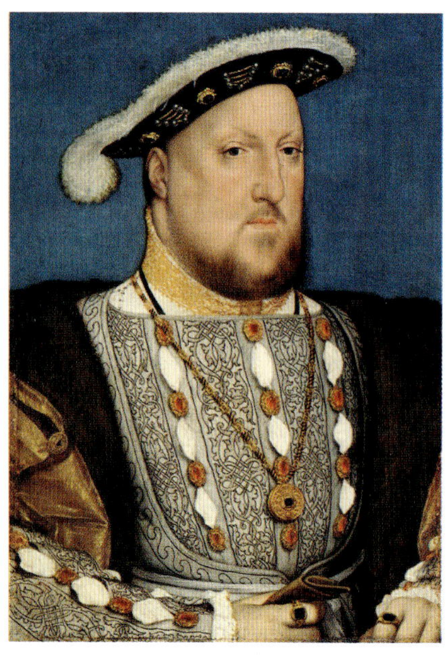

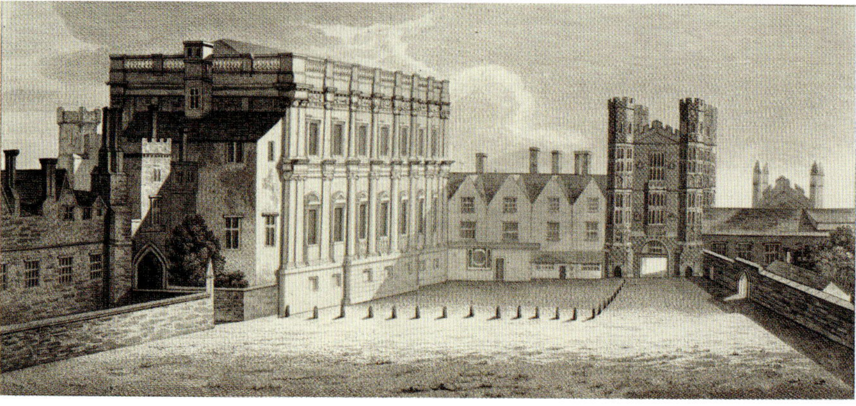

Above: The Palace of Whitehall, home to Henry VIII, from a drawing in the Pepysian Library, Cambridge, published 1809, an engraving after Wenceslaus Hollar (1607–77).

ANNE BOLEYN'S DEMISE

Henry, after years of being in love with Anne Boleyn, three years of marriage to her, the birth of their daughter Elizabeth – the future Queen Elizabeth I of England – but lacking a male heir, had tired of his second wife. Excuses were invented to have the queen dethroned and put to trial, accused of illicit affairs with men, including a young musician in her household and her brother. She was beheaded at the Tower of London, on May 19th, 1536, the same place from where she set out to her coronation three years before. Fortunately for Holbein, artists were recognised for their skills rather than associations with royal patrons, and his commissions continued.

The king was at a crucial moment in his life. Eleven days after Anne's execution, he married Jane Seymour. The same year the king had a major accident when jousting. His horse fell on him, crushing him and the armour he wore, and he was in a coma for two hours. He recovered, but his health would begin to fail.

PAINTING THE KING

When one visualises Henry VIII as a powerful, solidly built man, and a magnificently dressed king, it is most probable that a portrait by Holbein comes to mind. He painted the king as a masterful ruler in his prime of life, and divine representative of God on Earth (in England, at least).

The small portrait *King Henry VIII* (left) was painted by Holbein in around 1536–37. The king is portrayed half-length, to waist-level, his head and upper body filling the composition in a small work. Holbein's dark background of rich ultramarine blue throws attention onto the facial features of the king. As was traditional in royal portraiture, the subject is painted looking down at the viewer. Henry's small, dark eyes rest on observers of the work. His face is long, with small ears, and a long, straight nose. A lightweight dark-haired beard frames his chin, rising to his ear lobes with a wisp of moustache above the upper lip of his small mouth. He is resplendent in courtly clothes of silver and gold thread, painted in exacting detail. Henry's beringed hands, holding gloves, are visible at the front lower edge of the composition.

This is in fact the only remaining original portrait of the king by Holbein's hand; the others are known to us through copies. A later portrait of

THE PALACE OF WHITEHALL

In 1529, Henry VIII commandeered York Place, London, a 13th-century palatial building originally built for the Archbishops of York. It was requisitioned from Cardinal Thomas Wolsey, Archbishop of York, Lord Chancellor of England (1473–1530), and renamed White Hall. The Elizabethan playwrights William Shakespeare (1564–1616) and John Fletcher (1579–1625) included a stanza on its change of ownership, in their play *King Henry the Eighth* of 1613:

'You must no more call it York Place:
that is past.
For since the Cardinal fell that title's
lost.
'Tis now the King's and called
Whitehall'

In 1537 Holbein was commissioned by the king to create a painting of Henry VIII's Tudor dynasty, on a wall of the Privy Chamber of Whitehall Palace (see pages 78–9).

Below: An English School Portrait of Henry VIII, *c.1509, a portrait of the young king in the year of his accession, contrasts with Holbein's later depiction of the king.*

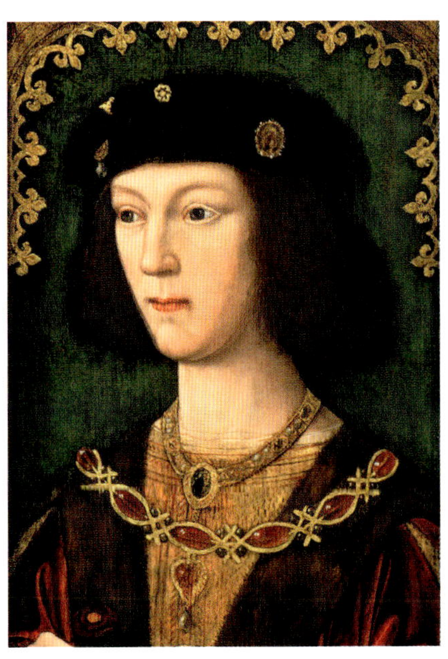

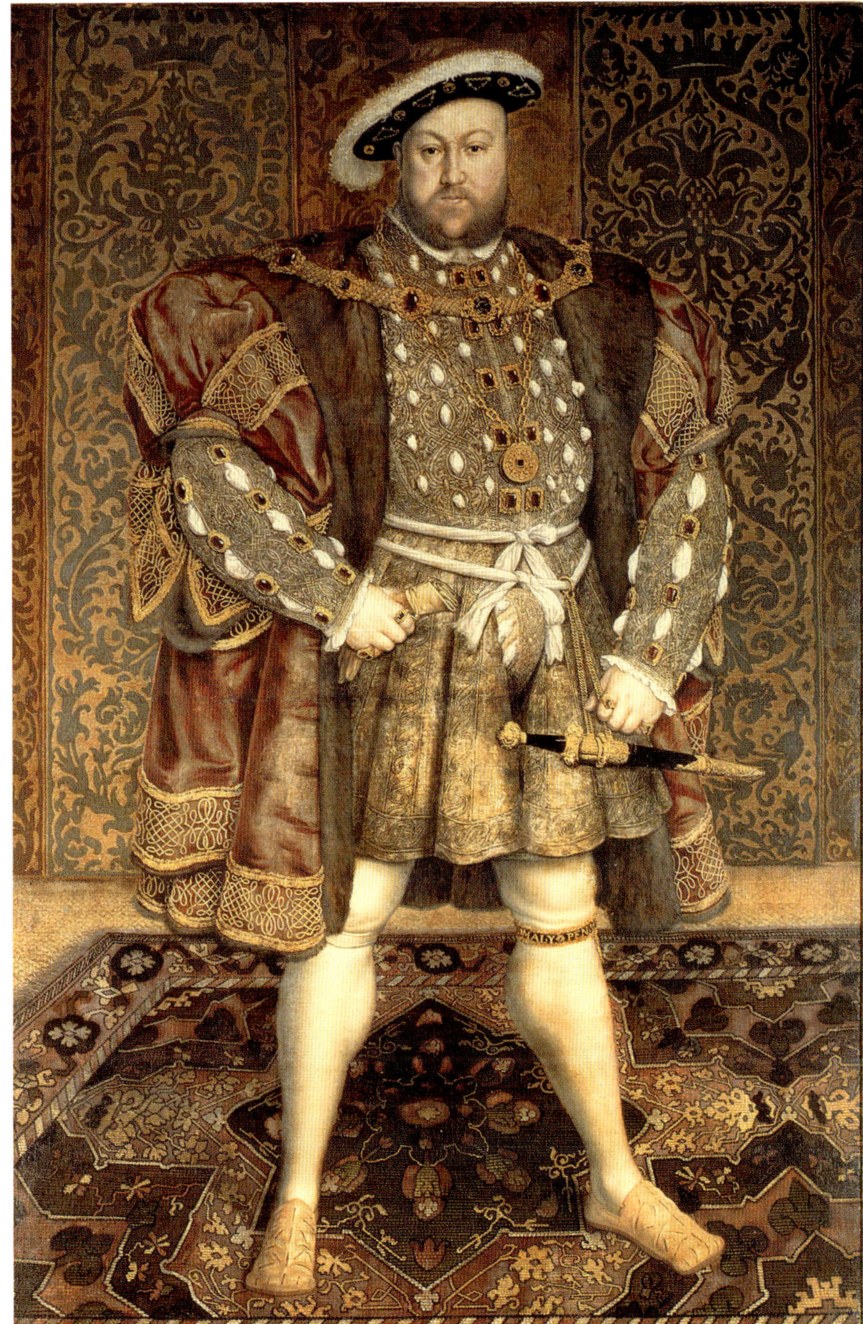

similar size, *Queen Jane Seymour,* may have been intended as a companion piece (see page 229). Jane Seymour was now Henry's third wife, the mother of his son, Edward. Both portraits appear similar in style and composition to Holbein's figures of the king and queen in the Privy Chamber Wall Painting (see pages 78–79). The composition is also similar in some aspects to another painting of the king, *Henry VIII, c.*1530–35 by the Netherlandish artist Joos van Cleve (*c.*1485–1540/1) of Antwerp (see page 80).

Above: Portait of Henry VIII, *a famous painting of the King, and popularly attributed to Holbein the Younger's own hand. Displayed at Belvoir Castle in England, it is a contemporary copy of Holbein's work, by an unknown artist, based on Holbein's original portrayal in the now-lost 1537 Privy Chamber Wall mural in Whitehall. (see pages 70–79). Many copies, all slightly different in execution, were made of this iconic portrait of the king.*

JANE SEYMOUR

Jane Seymour (*c.*1508/9–37), lady in waiting to Queen Katherine and to Queen Anne Boleyn, married Henry VIII on 30th May 1536, becoming his third wife. Seymour also became Holbein's patron, including a commission in 1536 for a silver cup inscribed with her and the king's initials and the motto 'Bound to obey'.

Jane Seymour was the daughter of John Seymour of Wolf Hall and, through her mother Margaret Wentworth, a direct royal descendant of Edward III (1312–77). Jane had already established a life at court through her positions as a lady in waiting to the king's first wife Katherine of Aragon, and then to his second wife, Anne Boleyn. The king lost no time in his betrothal to Jane Seymour, choosing the day following the public execution of his second wife Anne, on 19th May, 1536. The wedding took place on 30th May the same year. Holbein's 1536–37 individual portraits of Henry VIII and Queen Jane Seymour may be commissions related to the marriage. She was proclaimed Queen Consort on 4th June but due to plague that year and her early death was not crowned queen.

BIRTH AND DEATH

In 1537, the birth of Jane Seymour's son Edward, Prince of Wales, the future Edward VI, and Henry VIII's only legitimate male heir, deepened the king's

Below: Sir Edward Seymour, Jane Seymour's brother, later Duke of Somerset, attributed to Hans Holbein the Younger.

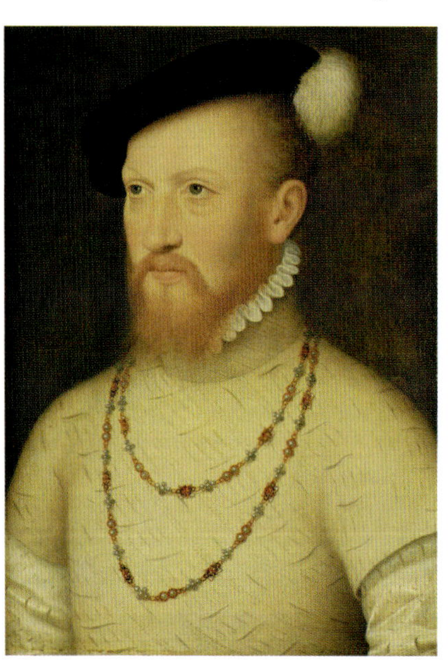

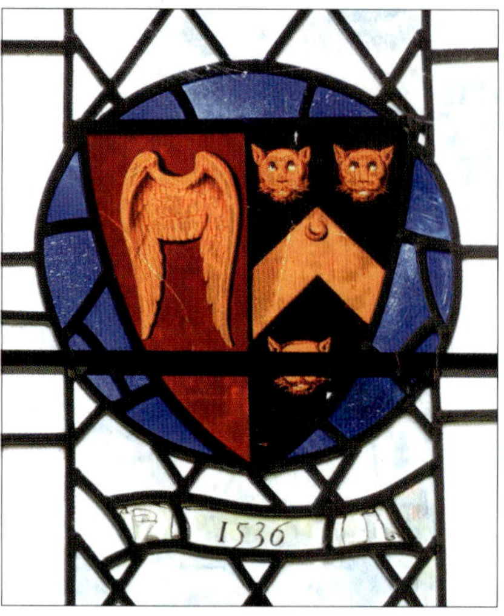

Above: The arms of Sir John Seymour of Wolf Hall, Wiltshire, 1536 (in stained glass), by English school artists.

devotion to her. The queen's untimely death on 24th October, just twelve days after giving birth to Edward, from complications after a Caesarian delivery, left Henry bereft. Although after her death he married a further three times, it was with Jane Seymour that Henry VIII chose to be buried, in the vault of St George's Chapel, Windsor.

HOLBEIN PORTRAYS THE QUEEN

Soon after, or possibly at the time of the marriage of Henry VIII to Jane Seymour, Holbein made drawings of the queen, in coloured chalks, pen and ink, on pink prepared paper. The preparatory drawing (opposite) of a half-length portrayal developed into the portrait *Queen Jane Seymour* (see page 229) with only minor adjustments to clothing and jewellery. In the three-quarter length portrait, the queen in three-quarter profile faces to her right. Holbein depicts her standing elegantly, as if waiting for someone. She clasps her beringed hands at waist level. The paleness of her skin is accentuated by the rich red velvet of her dress,

embroidered with silver and gold threads.

Eustace Chapuys (1490–1556), who served Charles V, Holy Roman Emperor, as his Imperial ambassador to England from 1529–45, in attendance at court, wrote to Antoine Perrenot, on 18th May 1536:

'*… I have no news to add to what I write to His Majesty, except to tell you something of the quality of the King's new lady, which the Emperor and Granvelle would perhaps like to hear. She is sister of one Edward Semel [Seymour]… of middle stature and no great beauty, so fair that one would call her rather pale than otherwise. She is over 25 years old.*'

Reading Chapuys' somewhat bland description, it would seem that Holbein created a perhaps flattering but essentially lifelike portrayal of Jane, yet the drawing in particular reveals a clear-eyed, thoughtful person. Looking closely at Holbein's preparatory work for the Seymour painting, one might suppose, through Holbein's eye, that he was also portraying what he thought the king wanted to see.

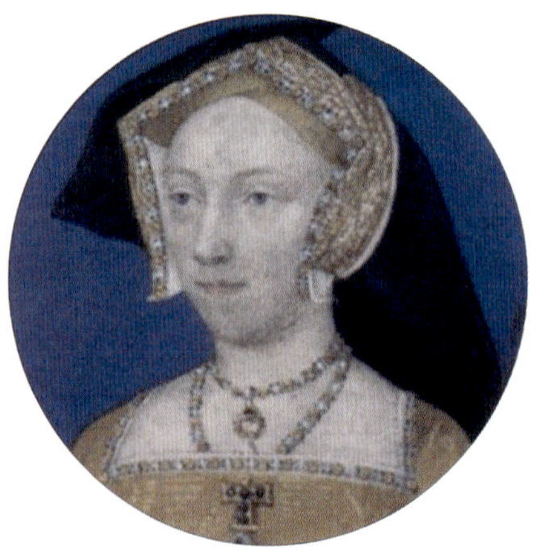

Above: A miniature of Queen Jane Seymour, c.1536–7, painted by Lucas Horenbout.

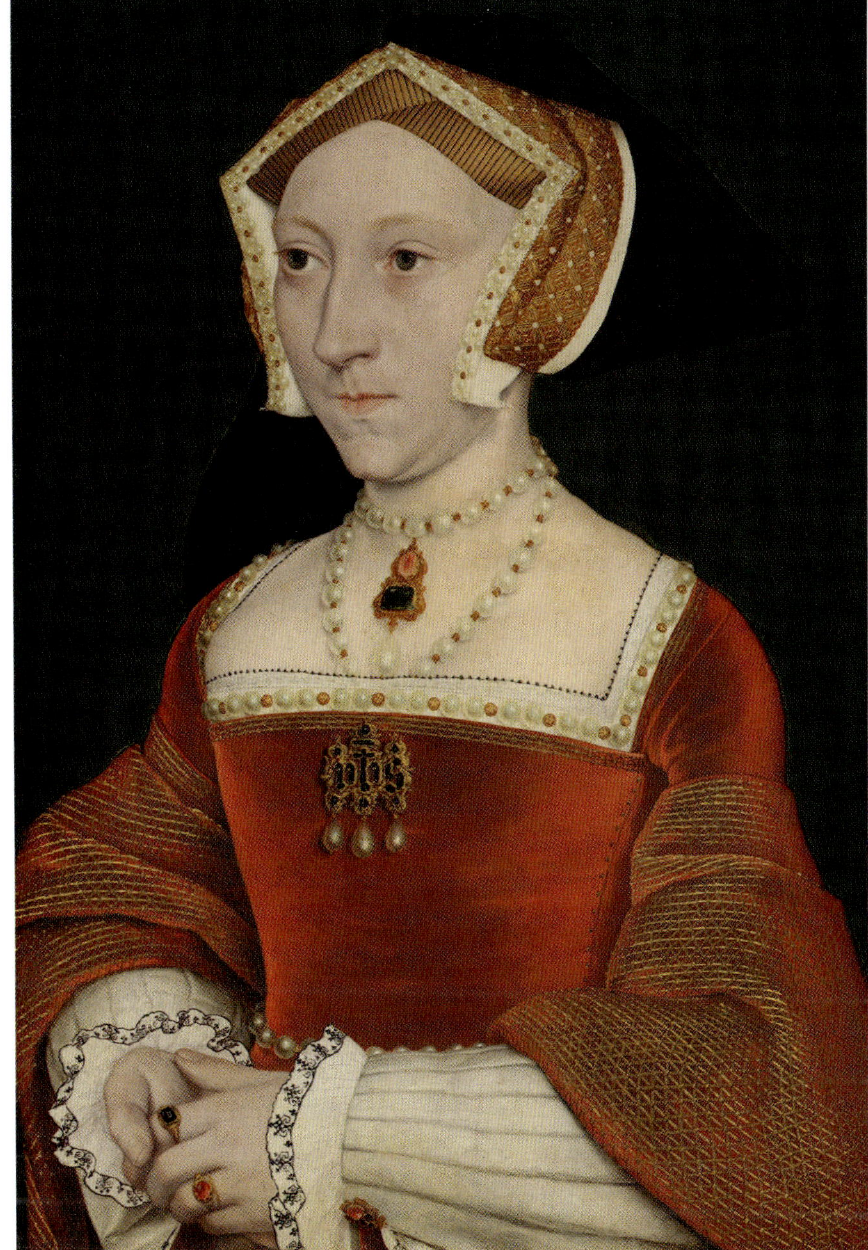

Below: Holbein's preparatory drawing for his painting of Queen Jane of 1536–37 (see page 229), completed not long before she died, following complications shortly after giving birth to her baby son, Edward.

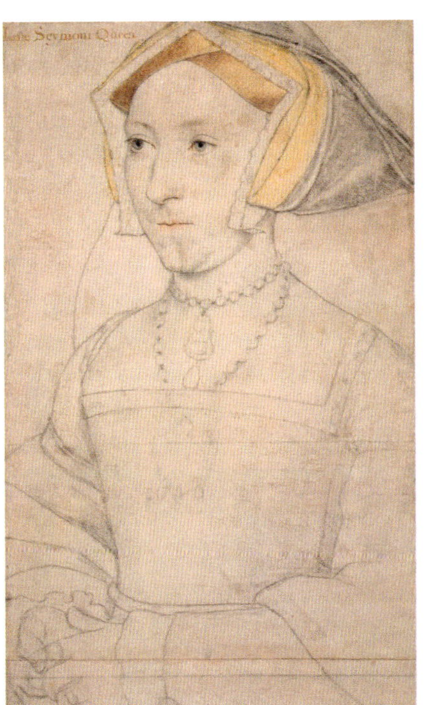

Above: Portrait of Jane Seymour, 1540, a later copy by the workshop of Holbein the Younger based on his 1536 portrait (see page 229).

Below: A letter from Queen Jane Seymour to Thomas Cromwell, Lord Privy Seal, announcing the birth of Prince Edward (Edward VI) on 12th October 1537.

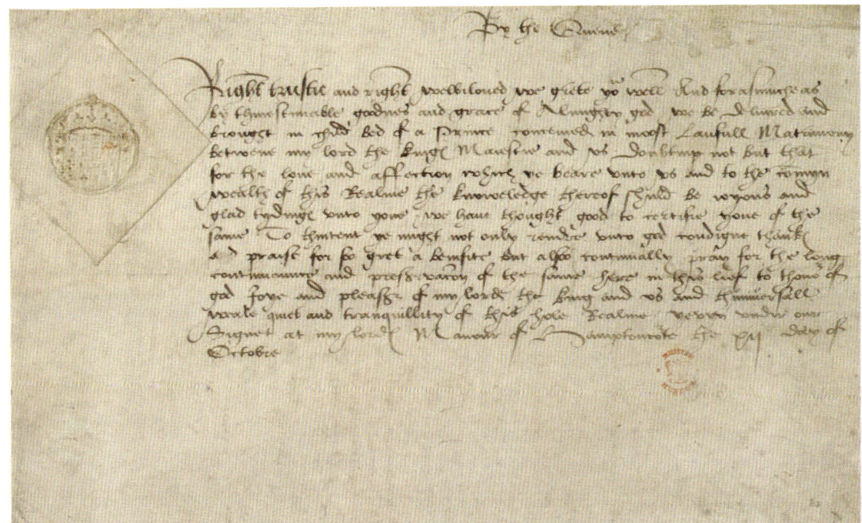

THE PRIVY CHAMBER WALL

A magnificent wall painting created circa 1537 by Hans Holbein for the Privy Chamber of Henry VIII's Palace of Whitehall, London, was later lost to a major fire that engulfed the building on January 4th, 1698. What we know about the painting comes from later copies, and written observations by visitors.

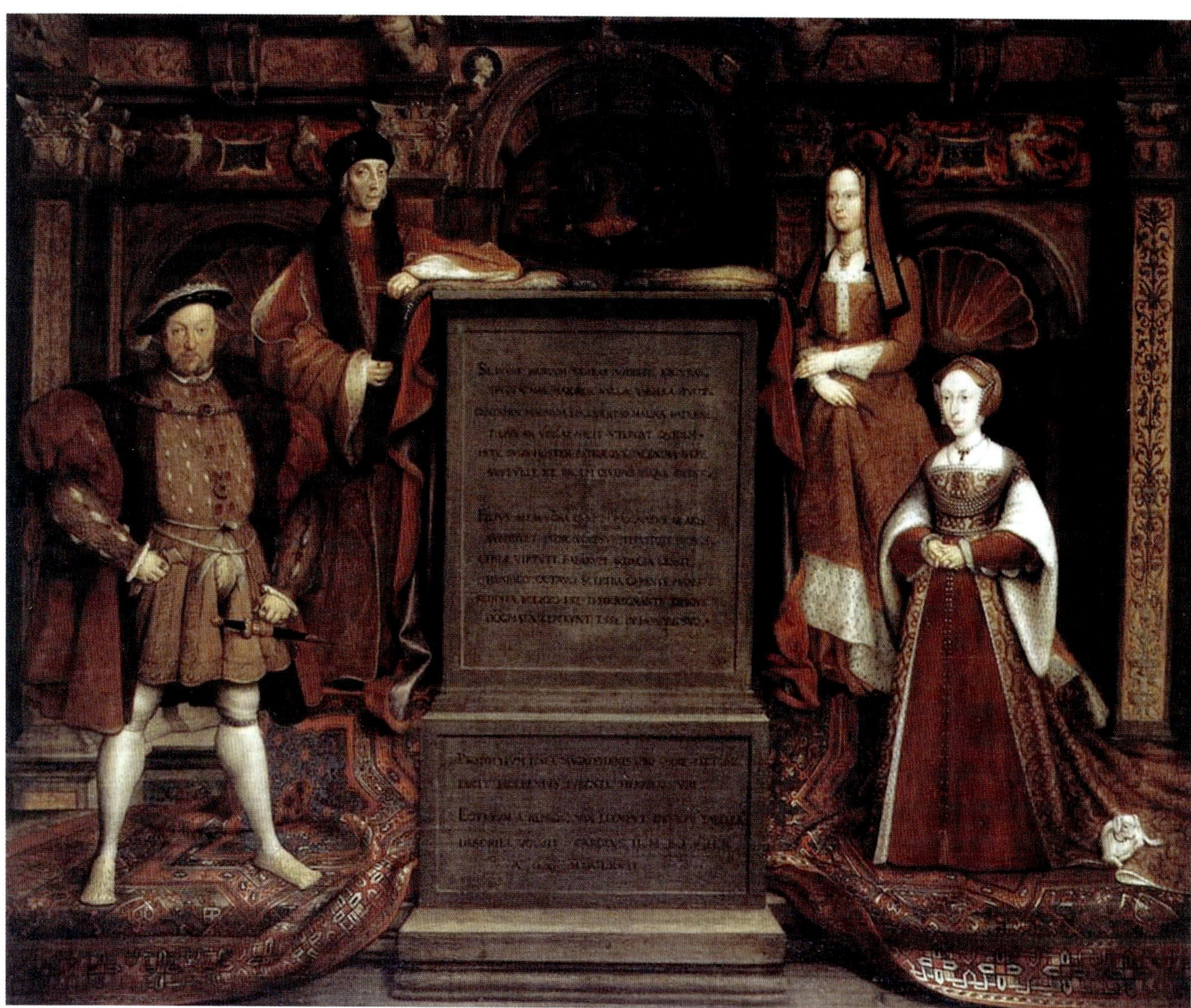

The origination of the painting, dating to 1537, sprang from Henry VIII's decision to portray three generations of the Tudor dynasty, in a group setting, brought on by the imminent birth of his hoped-for son, by his third queen, Jane Seymour. The birth of a legitimate male heir, the future Edward VI, added to the momentum of the painting's progress. In an architecturally-rich room setting with a centre arch flanked by two Renaissance-style shell-niches, the monumental wall painting portrays four members of the royal dynasty, all richly attired in magnificent clothes. They stand either side of a large stone pedestal, inscribed with Latin text. The inscription asks who the greater hero is.

A ROYAL DYNASTY

Arranged in two tiers, the life-size figures show King Henry VIII, to the right of the stone, standing with arms akimbo. He dominates the painting's composition. To his left on the other side of the stone monument is his queen, Jane Seymour. Behind him, raised up on a stepped platform, is the king's

Above: The 1667 copy by Remigius van Leemput was commissioned by Charles II, and is considered to be the closest to Holbein's original mural of 1537. Depicted are (left to right): Henry VIII, Henry VII, Elizabeth of York, and Jane Seymour.

father, Henry VII, who was triumphant in the War of the Roses. Opposite his father stands Elizabeth of York, his mother. Under their feet, a large and richly-coloured Turkish carpet covers the lower and upper steps, swathed around the base of marble stone at its back. The only other figure illustrated is Jane Seymour's pet dog, which lies at her feet on the train of her dress.

Holbein recreated his renditions of Henry VIII and his queen from earlier portraits of his. For Henry VII, and Elizabeth of York's facial features and clothing, Holbein referred to earlier portraits of them by other artists. Holbein's aim was to create a dynamic visual personality for Henry VIII. In the few portraits of his that are extant, most only known through copies, the king is magnificent, strong, powerful and full of confidence, at times even swagger. Holbein's *Henry VIII*, c.1536 (see page 74) is a half-length portrait where the king, sumptuously attired, looks down on the spectator, directly engaging the onlooker with his eyes. The king was pleased with this portrait, which led to Holbein's commission for the Whitehall Palace wall painting, depicting the dynasty of Henry VIII's family, and where one sees Holbein using a similar composition in the preparatory cartoon of Henry VIII

Below: Henry VIII and Henry VII, 1537, a detail from the preparatory cartoon of the mural for Whitehall Palace, by Hans Holbein the Younger.

for the mural, standing in front of his father Henry VII.

The life-size wall painting was placed in a raised position, in the King's antechamber, elevated above and behind Henry VIII's throne. From its position, all four royals looked down on those assembled below in the Privy Chamber. The gimlet-eyed Henry surveyed all. A remark, thought to be made by a visitor to the Privy Chamber – possibly Lucas de Heere in 1567 – observed that all who viewed the image of Henry were 'abashed and annihilated' by his aura, as if he was present' (as reported by Karel van Mander, in *Livre des Peintres*, 1604).

Below: Henry VIII in his privy chamber, sketched in pen and ink by Holbein.

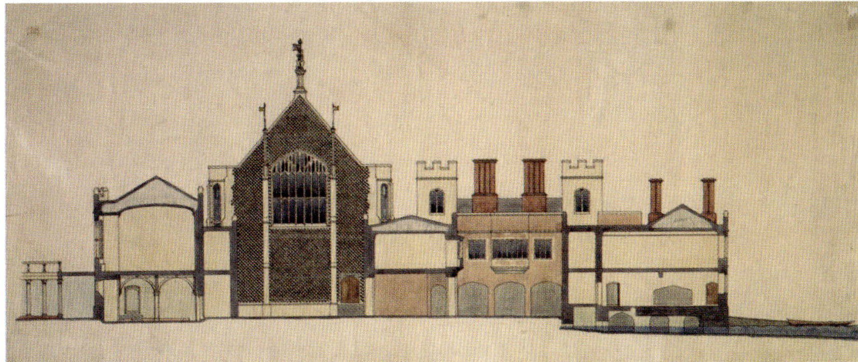

Above: Cross-section of Whitehall Palace in 1547, the London home of Henry VIII.

DESTROYED BY FIRE

Copies were made of Holbein's painting, both at the time and in succeeding years. Most of the copies isolated the figure of Henry VIII, becoming an iconic image of the king. In 1698, the original wall painting was destroyed. The fire was accidently started by a maidservant drying linen in a lodging house in Whitehall; the 'merciless and devouring flames' destroyed the king's palatial apartments, and about 150 residences nearby. In the aftermath of the fire efforts were made to move the wall painting; it was not possible. Only the Banqueting Hall escaped the blaze.

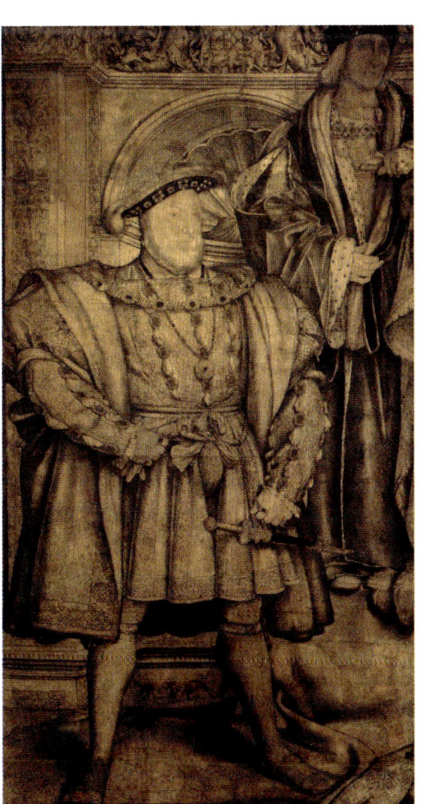

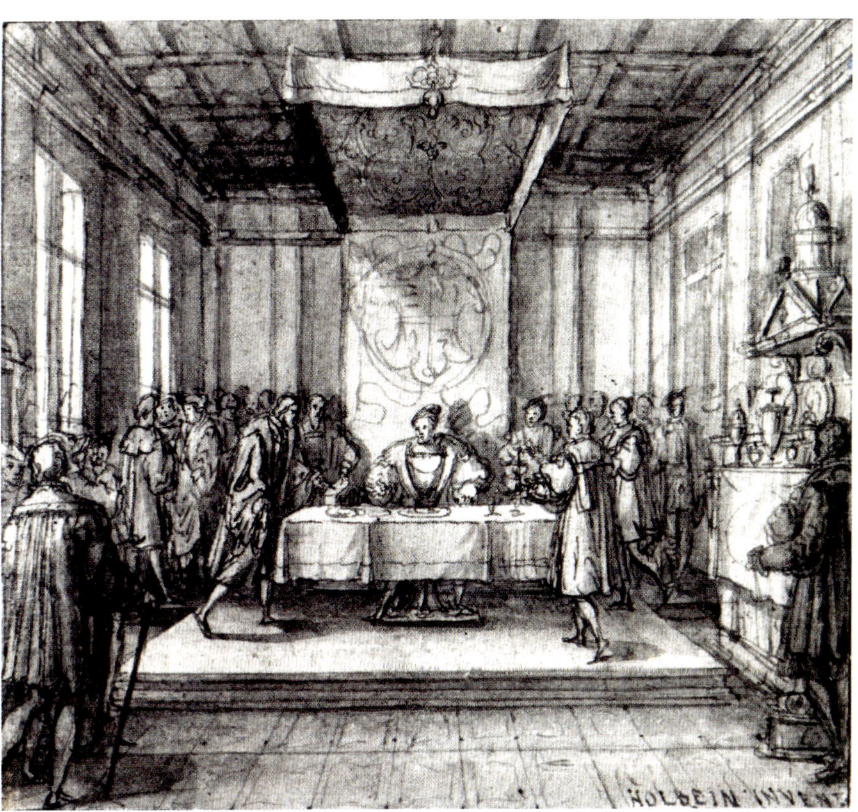

PAINTING KINGS

Holbein used portraiture to endorse Henry VIII as a powerful king. In reality, from 1537 the king's health was gradually deteriorating. He became obese, and leg ulcers led to painful incapacity. Hardly able to walk, the king was carried or wheeled in a chair (a tramme). Holbein chose to portray kingship, not physical weakness.

A ROYAL IMAGE

There are 98 portraits related to Henry VIII, by various artists. Early paintings, such as the half-length *King Henry VIII*, *c.*1520 (see page 49), by an unknown Anglo-Netherlandish artist, reveal a quite reticent man, hands clasped, body in three-quarter profile, with eyes turned away from the viewer. After the monarch's break with the Church of Rome in 1533, portraiture would become a useful utility to establish the monarch as all-powerful protector of England, the country and its people. Portraiture could re-emphasise the magnificence of the Tudor dynasty while asserting the king's position in Europe. The king, as head of the new Church of England, used portraiture to authenticate his role as secular and religious divine ruler.

At the time of Henry VIII's break from Rome, Holbein the Younger was edging his way into the king's favour through royal contacts, most notably Thomas More and Anne Boleyn. He would make

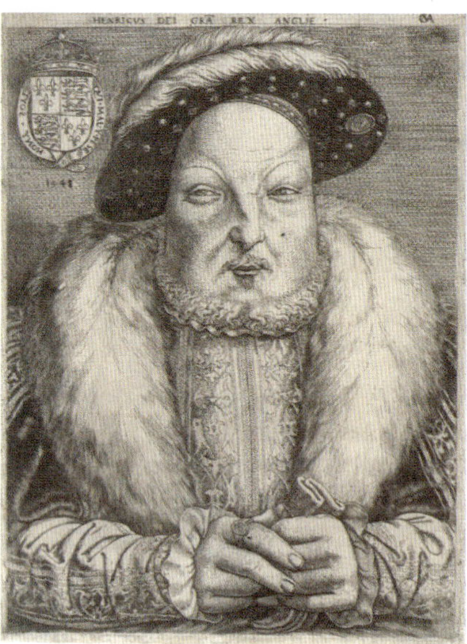

Above: Portrait of Henry VIII, c.1544, by Cornelis Metsys. Metsys worked at the court so we can presume Henry approved of the image; it includes all of the king's finery although depicts a bloated face.

the king look magnificent in his portraits, a mirror image of how the monarch perceived himself in life.

An impressive portrait by Holbein, clearly exuding all the power of monarchy, is *Portrait of Henry VIII aged 49*, 1540 (see right). Henry was in reality suffering much pain at this time; his body was obese, and his leg sores treated as open wounds. The king had to take less exercise after several hunting and jousting accidents. A head injury had caused headaches, and he was to suffer then-unknown type-2 diabetes. It was changing the king from an athletic man into a portly, corpulent figure. None of this could be imagined from viewing his portraits.

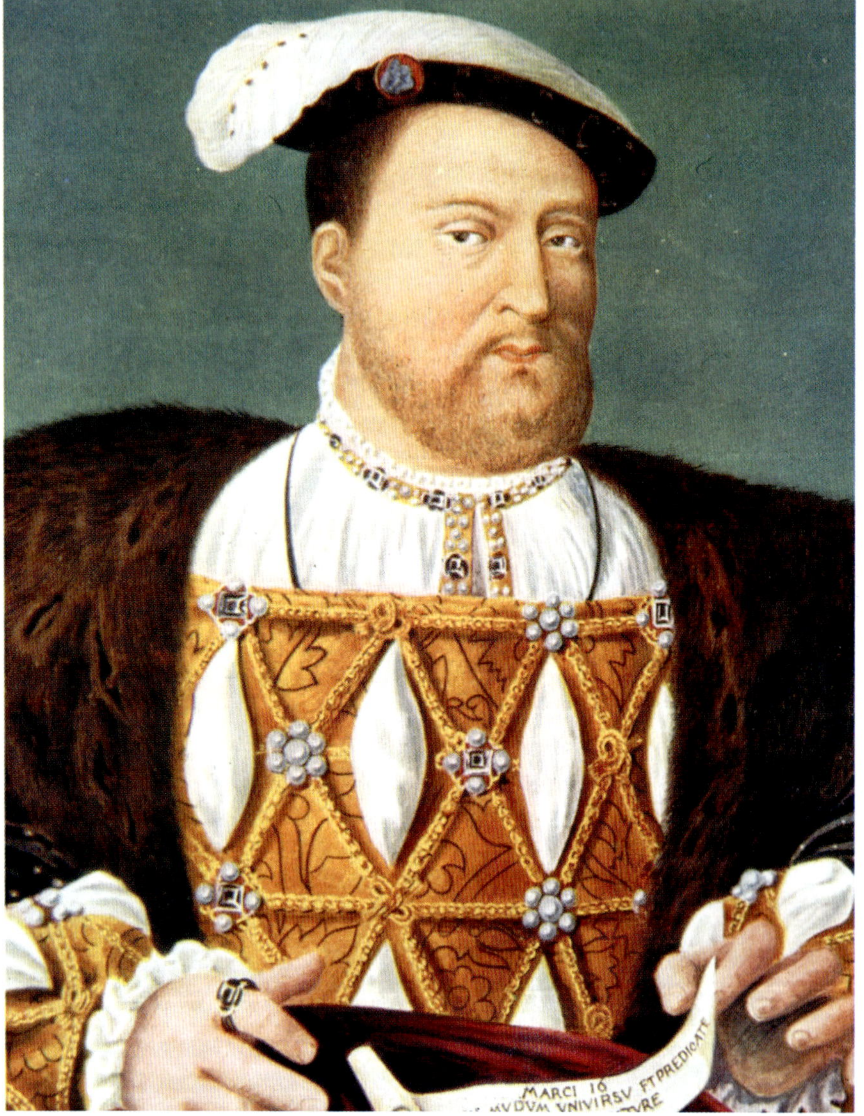

Left: Portrait of Henry VIII, king of England, c.1530–35, by Joos van Cleve (1485–1540/41), comparable by date to Clouet's commanding portrayal of Francis I (opposite). The portrayal is lively.

In 1544, the year following the death of Holbein, and three years before the king's death, Flemish artist Cornelis Metsys (1508–62), now court painter to Henry VIII, created a relatively realistic engraving of the king (see left, above). Here Henry has heavy jowls, a crooked nose and small mouth, and swivels beady eyes to the right, avoiding the viewer's gaze.

A COMPARISON OF STYLE

It is interesting to compare paintings by other artists and their depictions of monarchy. The French painter Jean Clouet (c.1485–1540/41) had presented a majestic Francis I, king of France, in the half-length *Portrait of Francis I, c.*1535 (below). Here the king is sumptuously attired in an Italian-style voluminous tunic; Clouet fills two-thirds of the picture plane with the costume's fashionably wide sleeves. The eye is led down to the exquisitely painted hands, the left one clasping a gold sword hilt. This kingly presence needs no crown to portray supreme status; the portrait connotes power and majesty. The concept of the work was informed by the Italian Renaissance portraiture of the period, notably that of one of Francis I's favourite painters, Leonardo da Vinci, and of Titian and Raphael. It also echoes an earlier portrait of another French King. An exceptional portrait of Charles VII (who reigned

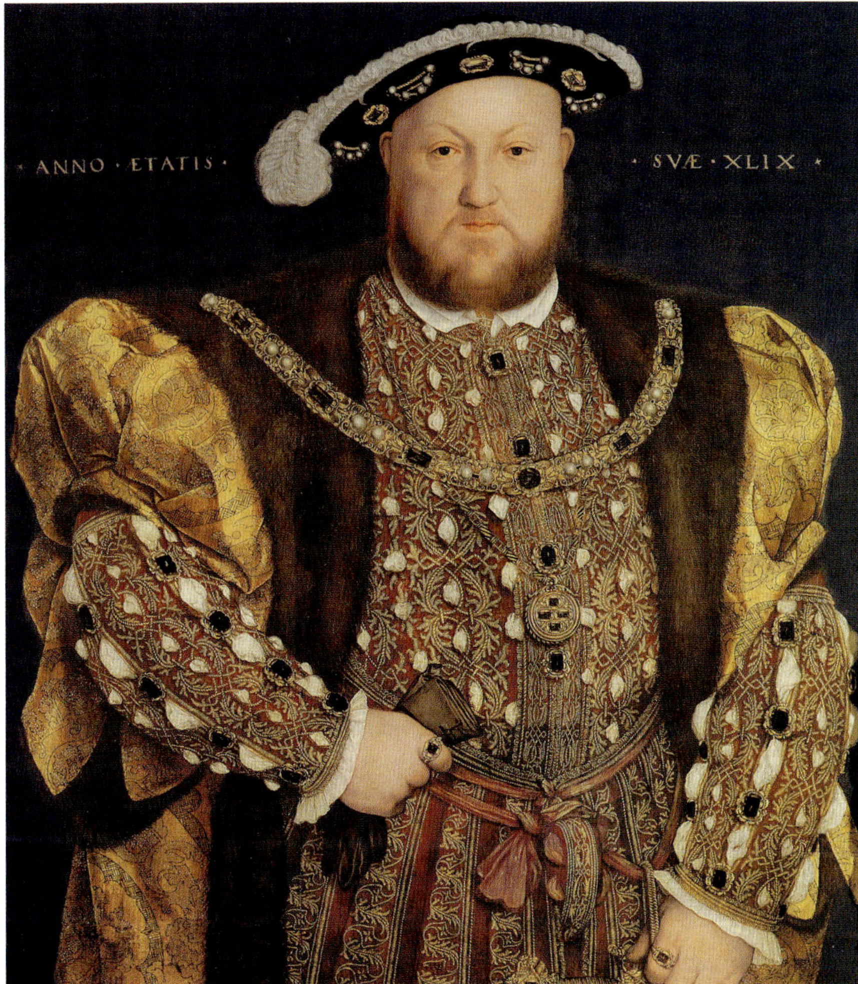

Above: Portrait of Henry VIII aged 49, *1540, by Hans Holbein the Younger, now displayed in the Barberini Gallery in Rome. The grandness of the portrayal disguises Henry's physical decline.*

Below: Charles VII, King of France *(detail), c.1445/50, by Jean Fouquet. Painted a century earlier, this influential painting established the compositional style of royal portraits for years to come.*

1422–61), by French painter Jean Fouquet (1420–81), is both intimate and realistic in the Flemish style of the Northern Renaissance. Fouquet's family were of Flemish origin. This painting is considered the prototype of official royal portraiture, later practised by Jean Clouet – compare Fouquet's portrait to Clouet's of Francis I (left) and Holbein's depiction of Henry VIII (page 74). Fouquet's portrait depicts the king facing front – a tradition – but to add realism, his body is slightly turned, and he looks to his left. Fouquet captures a moment in time.

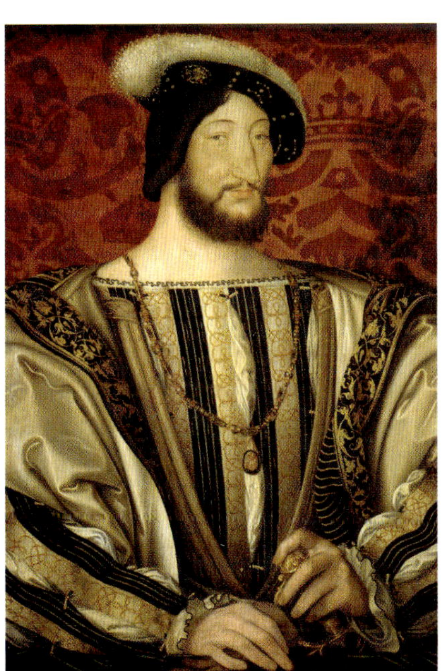

Left: Portrait of Francis I, c.*1525–30 by Jean Clouet, is a powerful image of the fashionable king of France.*

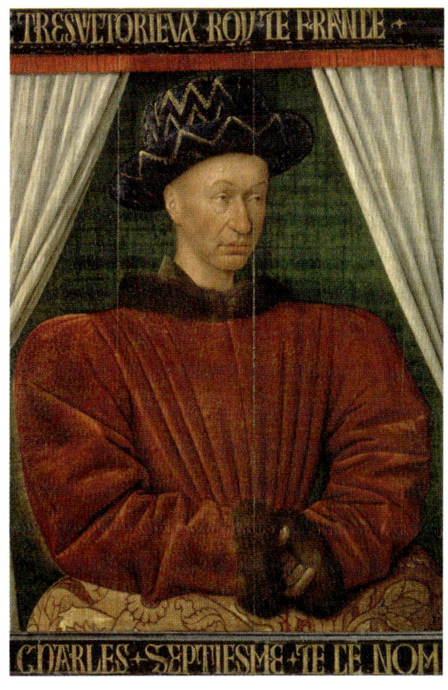

EDWARD, PRINCE OF WALES

In 1538 Holbein painted a special portrait of Henry VIII's only legitimate son, Edward, Prince of Wales (1537–1553), aged one. It was a New Year's Day gift from the painter to his patron, the king. He depicted the boy in a composition and costume reminiscent of his royal father.

A PRINCELY GIFT

The young prince, Edward of Wales, born at Hampton Court Palace on 12th October 1537, was Henry VIII's only legitimate son. He would become king at the age of nine in January 1547, and die aged fifteen, suffering from tuberculosis. As an infant he was painted by Holbein in 1538. The remarkable portrait *Edward VI, as a*

Below: Edward VI, as a Child, 1538–39, by Hans Holbein the Younger.

Child, was given as a gift to the king by Holbein on New Year's Day, 1539. It is the earliest-known painted portrait of the prince. Holbein depicted the infant as a mirror-image of his father, as a child. In the work the infant is dressed in regal, princely attire, and holds a golden rattle, connoting that he will later hold royal ceremonial objects – orb and sceptre – and the rule of England in his hands. His pose, with one arm leaning on a marble parapet, was one reserved for royalty (and occasionally

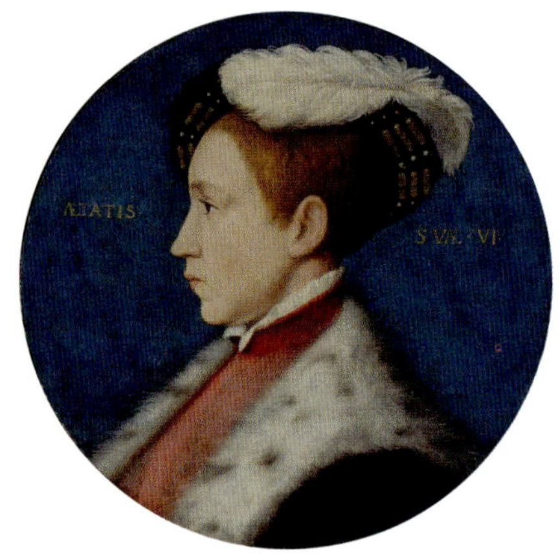

Above: Edward VI, Duke of Cornwall, painted c.1545 when he was six, then revised after 1547 to add coronation robes; a miniature based on a drawing by Holbein but painted after his death.

senior members of the church). He is ready to greet his people with a wave of his right hand, an infant blessing and salutation. The preparatory drawing is smaller in size than the finished painting, confirming that Holbein did not use his chalk outline method of transferring the outline to oak panel. The drawing captures the child's gentle gaze, the clear-set eyes, and expressive concentration.

A POEM FOR A PRINCE

Holbein's gift to Henry VIII of a portrait of the future Edward VI had a Latin text written on a 'stone parapet' on which the child leaned. This poem, created by the English poet Sir Richard Morison, a friend of Holbein's, praises the king, and emphasises the young prince's role in the royal succession. Translated into English it reads:

'Little one, emulate thy father and be the heir of his virtue; the world contains nothing greater. Heaven and Earth could scarcely produce a son whose glory would surpass that of such a father. Do thou but

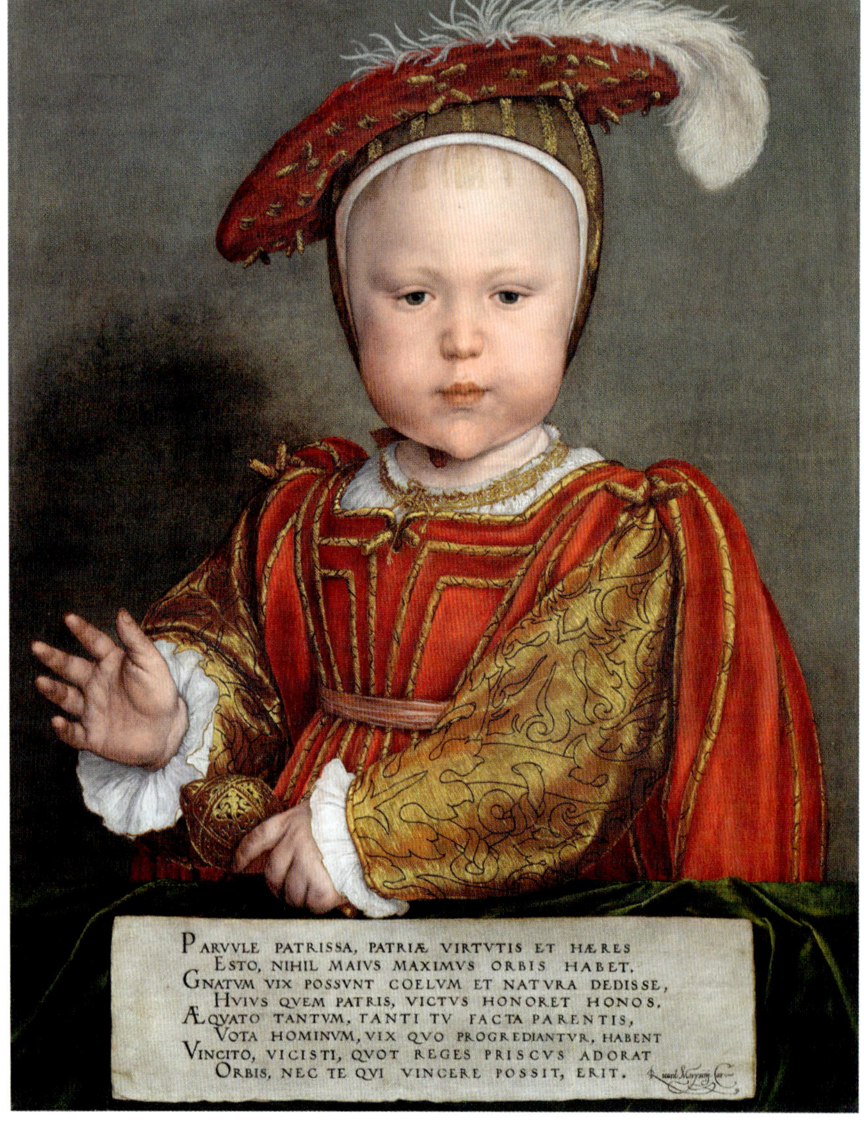

HENRY VIII'S SONS

Much has been written on Henry VIII's resolve to have a son to inherit the kingdom of England. His first son, Henry, Duke of Cornwall, born to first wife Katherine of Aragon (1485–1536), Queen of England 1509–33, was born on 1st January 1511 but died a few weeks later on 22nd February. Another son, Henry Fitzroy, 1st Duke of Richmond and Somerset, was born in June 1519, the illegitimate child of Henry VIII and his mistress Elizabeth Blount. The king acknowledged his son and the boy was brought up as a noble. At St James Palace, on 23rd July 1536, he died aged seventeen, possibly of tuberculosis or consumption. The following year on 12th October 1537, to Queen Jane Seymour, Henry's legitimate heir Edward VI was born.

equal the deeds of thy parent and men can ask no more. Shouldst thou surpass him, thou hast outstript all kings the world has revered in ages past.'

Below: Edward VI as Prince of Wales, after Hans Holbein the Younger. The painting is dated c.1795–1820 so is a much later work, perhaps based on the miniature above left.

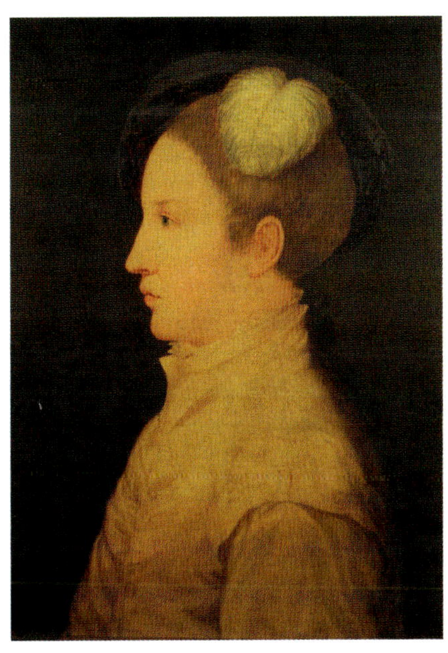

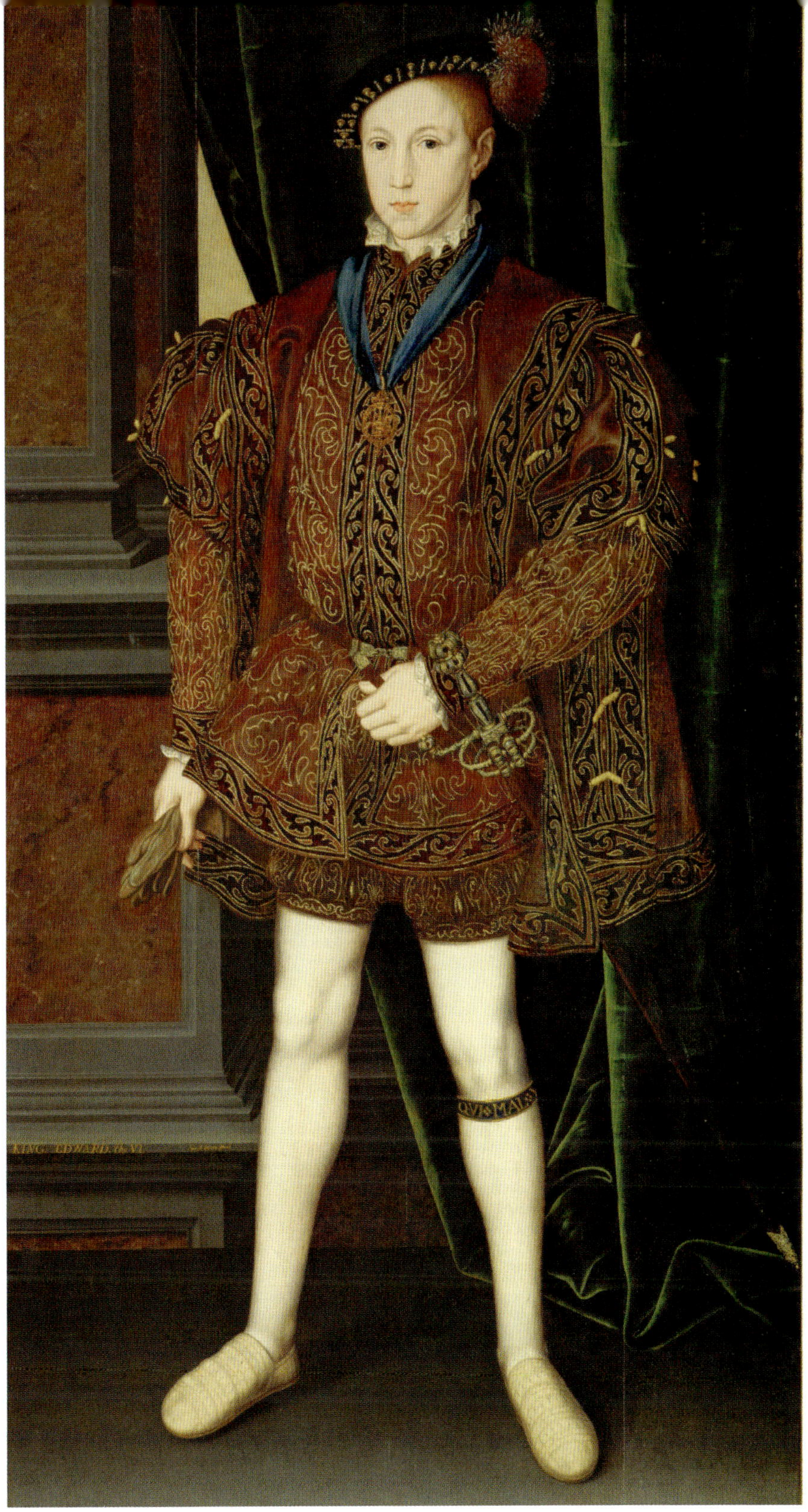

ANOTHER PORTRAIT?

A few years after his first portrait of the baby Edward, Holbein painted a young boy with his pet marmoset (see page 237). Previously assumed to be a portrait of Edward, the subject of the painting is now disputed, and seems more likely to be another young noble, though the characteristics are similar to those of Holbein's portraits of Edward as a baby and of Henry VIII.

Above: Edward VI, King of England, c.1551, by Guillaume Scrots (active 1537–53), who became King's Painter following Holbein's death The young king wears the symbol of the Order of the Garter beneath his left knee, to which he was elected on 6 February 1517, nine days after his accession.

PORTRAIT MINIATURES

Seen as a new art form, the earliest portrait miniatures in Europe were French, painted for Francis I, by Jean Clouet. In England, the first recorded miniature portraits were commissioned by Henry VIII from Lucas Horenbout (1490/95–1544), and later from Levina Teerlinc, both renowned Flemish painters at the royal court.

The fashion for portrait miniatures started in France, one notable example being the painting of King Louis XII from 1510–14 attributed to Jean Perréal. This specialised art form became a very popular commission at the court of Henry VIII in the 1520s and reached a zenith during the reigns of Elizabeth I and James I of England. Lucas Horenbout painted many miniatures, and Levina Teerlinc (1510s–76) was a renowned miniaturist, commissioned by Henry VIII, Edward VI, Mary I and Elizabeth I. Nicholas Hilliard (1547–1619), a noted English miniature portraitist during that period, believed the practice 'excelleth all other painting whatsoever in sundry'. Nicholas Hilliard wrote a theoretical text on this form of painting, in *A Treatise concerning The Art of Limning*, written around 1600 although not published in Hilliard's lifetime.

Miniature portraits were sometimes given by royalty as diplomatic gifts to

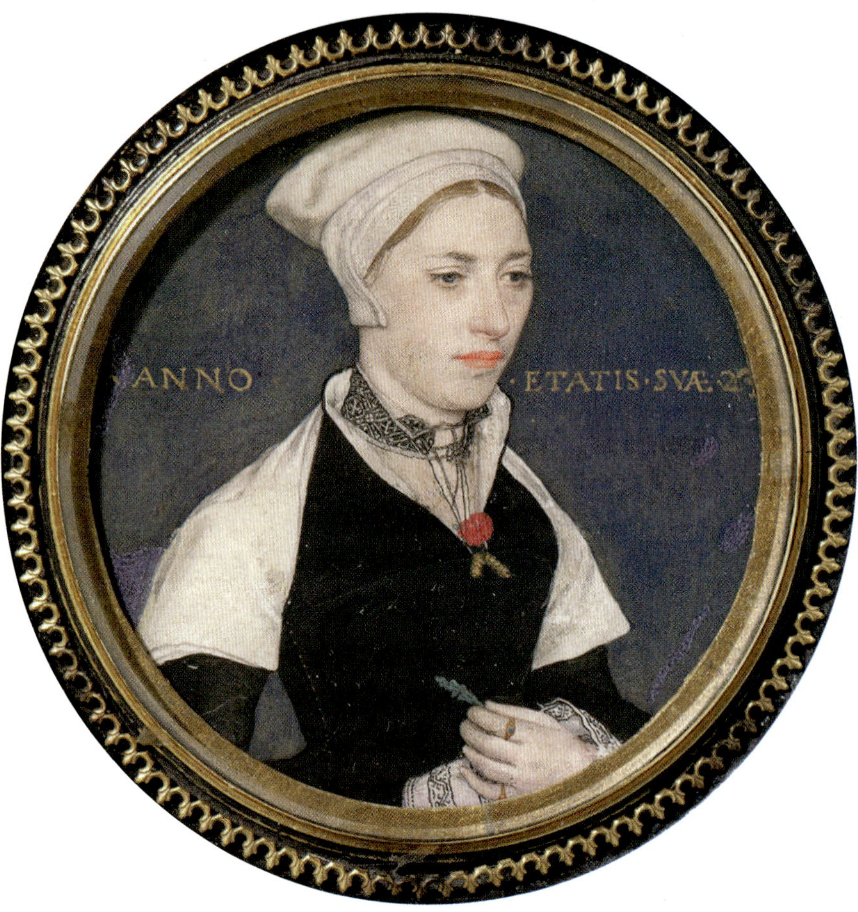

Above: Portrait Miniature of Jane Pemberton, c.1540, a watercolour painted on vellum laid down on card, by Hans Holbein the Younger.

ON MINIATURES

The term 'miniature' does not refer to a small size but to *miniare*, to use red lead, a technique employed by the illuminators of manuscripts, using watercolour and opaque bodycolour. In England miniature painting was called 'limning'. The portraits were painted on vellum, a thin, soft paper. To avoid shrinkage and puckering from the water-based paint, the vellum was glued on to a pasteboard. Playing cards were ideal 'ready-made' pasteboards because of the size and rigidity of the card, with one side being blank. In the 18th century bone ivory replaced card as a backing for some works. Miniatures often copied larger works, but not the other way around.

important visitors. Unframed copies might be given to loyal subjects, as framing a miniature was expensive. On occasion, portraits would be a gift between rulers as a means of conveying the likeness of proposed future spouses. When Henry VIII was considering Anne of Cleves as a possible fourth wife, his painter Hans Holbein the Younger was sent to paint miniatures of Anne and her sister. Henry VIII commissioned Holbein to paint a three-quarter length portrait of Anne of Cleves plus miniatures of Anne and her sister Amelia. The miniature of Anne of Cleves is similar to Holbein's larger painting of her (see pages 234 and 233). Holbein was commissioned to paint several miniatures. His biographer Karel van Mander had seen two of Holbein's

miniatures and commented on his craftsmanship and painting technique: *'I have also seen two of his own portraits made by himself; the one small and round, a miniature, very tiny but made very neatly and precisely and in the possession of the art-loving Jacques Razet; the other is a small face, perhaps about the size of the palm of a hand, excellently flesh-like in skin tones, subtly and precisely executed, that is in the possession of Bartholomeus Ferreris, who is most devoted to art.'*

Painting in the tradition of early Netherlandish meticulous detail, Holbein

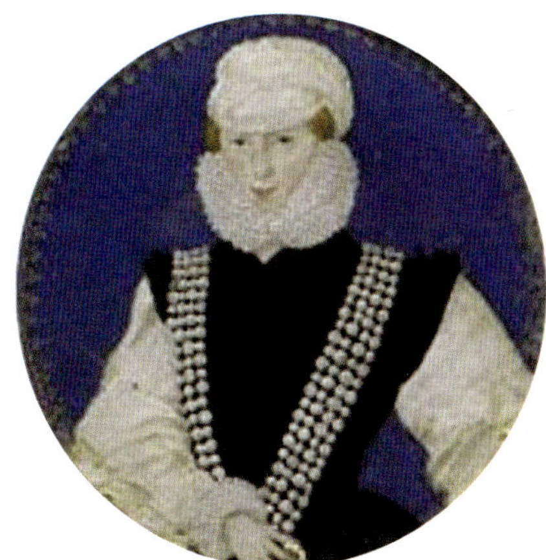

Above: Portrait Miniature of Mary Dudley, Lady Sidney (c.1531–1586), c.1575, by Levina Teerlinc, in watercolour on vellum, mounted on a playing card with 4 of Spades on the reverse.

Below: Portrait Miniature of Queen Katherine of Aragon (1485–1536), c.1525, in watercolour on vellum, attributed to Lucas Horenbout.

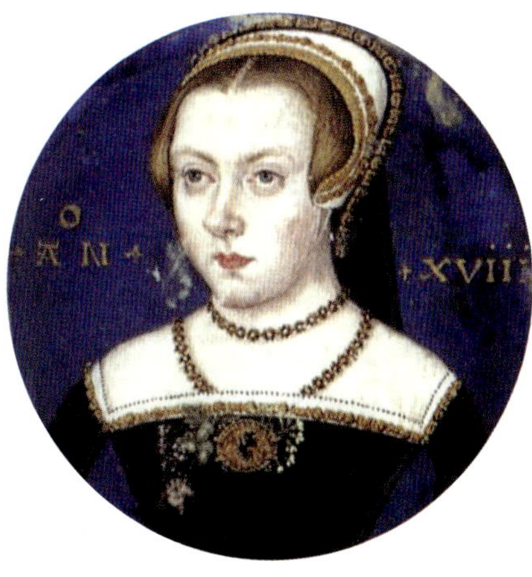

Above: Portrait of a Lady, *possibly Lady Jane Grey, c.1545–47, a miniature attributed to Flemish artist and miniaturist Levina Teerlinc.*

Below: Portrait of King Henry VIII, c.1534–44, in grey doublet and fur robe with jewelled collar, and black cap with white feather, by Lucas Horenbout.

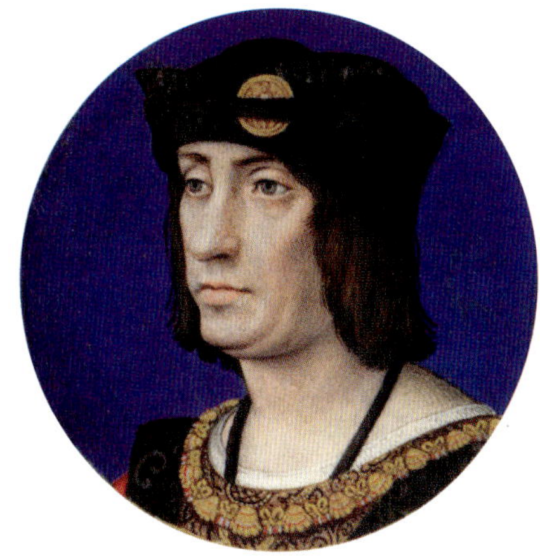

Above: Portrait Miniature of King Louis XII of France (1462–1515), painted c.1510–14 in watercolour on vellum, attributed to Jean Perréal (c.1460–1530). The king is wearing a gold collar of the Order of St Michael, and a black cap with gold badge.

Below: Portrait of Thomas Cromwell, c.1537, attributed to Holbein.

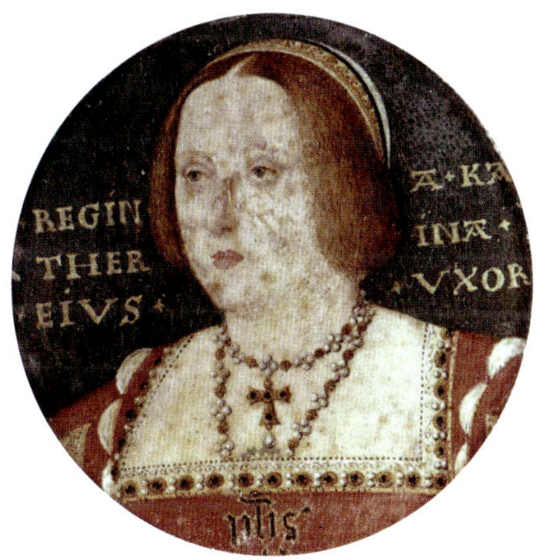

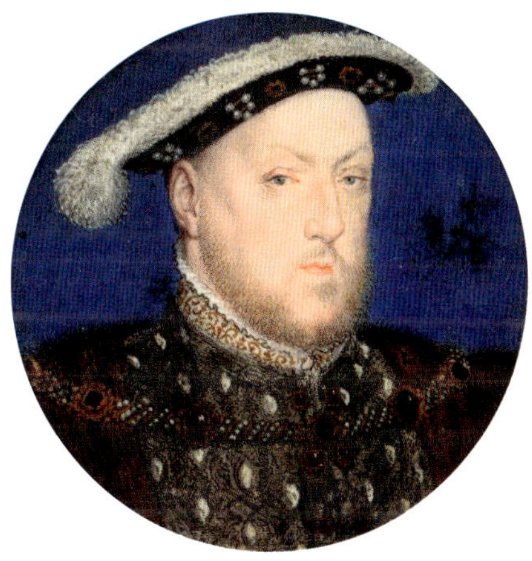

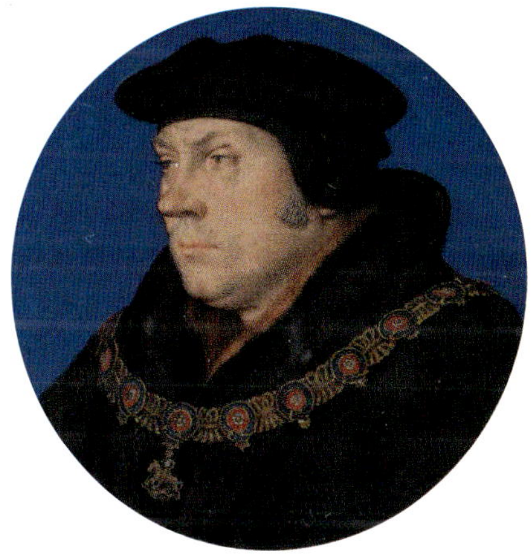

produced portrait miniatures that were reduced down from a standard-size portrait without loss of likeness, realism, or rich colour. It places him with elite specialists, like Clouet and Horenbout, that could transfer their technical skills of portraiture to any size, from life-size portrayals to the smallest work.

A MERCHANT COMMISSION

Miniatures were conventionally commissioned only by members of the nobility but Holbein notably painted an intimate portrait of Jane Pemberton (d.1602), wife of a London merchant Nicholas Small (d.1581), a well-connected, wealthy couple. One

of their leased properties was 'The Hand' near Hay Wharf in Thames Street, near to the Hanse Steelyard, and to Holbein's residence. Nicholas Small was trading with the Hanseatic ports, thus crossing paths with the Hanse, and Holbein. The miniature demonstrates Holbein's meticulous precision. A Coat of Arms painted on vellum, placed in the lid of the painting's case, identified the sitter. Close scrutiny shows that the signet ring on Jane Pemberton Small's finger is engraved with a four-quarter family Coat of Arms. Holbein, working in small-scale, paid attention to every detail. It is considered to be his finest portrait miniature.

THOMAS CROMWELL

There are two similar portrait miniatures of Cromwell, one painted in 1532–23 (see page 216), and a later one above: the difference between the two being the somewhat older appearance of the sitter, and the addition of the collar of the Greater George, a chain of office of the Knight of the Order of the Garter, which was conferred on Cromwell in August 1537. An entry in the financial accounts of Thomas Cromwell refers to a payment of 40 shillings to Hans Holbein on January 4th, 1538, linked to a portrait miniature of Cromwell painted around August–September 1537.

CHRISTINA OF DENMARK

The young widow, Christina of Denmark, Duchess of Milan (1522–90), was contemplated as a prospective bride for Henry VIII, so before a marriage could be considered Hans Holbein was sent to paint her portrait. The marriage was not to be, but the portrait was considered a success.

The portrait *Christina of Denmark*, 1538, commissioned by Henry VIII, is Holbein's only full-length portrait of a woman. His subject was the teenage Christina of Denmark, sister of Charles V, and youngest daughter of three children to King Christian II of Denmark (1481–1559) and Isabella of Austria. She is known today by two titles: Duchess of Milan, due to her 1533 marriage by proxy to Francesco II Sforza, Duke of Milan (1495–1535), and later, as the Duchess of Lorraine, from her 1541 marriage to Francis, Duc de Bar, later Duc de Lorraine. Prior to her second marriage the court of Henry VIII considered the widowed duchess as a possible choice of fourth wife for the king. His third wife, Jane Seymour, briefly queen 1536–37, had died from post-natal complications ten days after the birth of her son.

THE PORTRAIT SITTING

After the formalities of both parties agreeing to a portrait sitting, a meeting took place between Holbein and the duchess in Brussels, on March 12th, 1538. An English court envoy Philip Hoby travelled with Holbein. There would be one sitting only, lasting three hours. There is no record of what happened during the sitting, but it would have given enough time for Holbein to study the duchess's features, and make preliminary sketches to work from, possibly in chalks or watercolour. He made at least one studied drawing of her face. She would never see the finished work.

Holbein returned to England on 18th March. From the drawings, which pleased the king, he was commissioned to paint a full-length portrait. Those that were privileged to see the preliminary

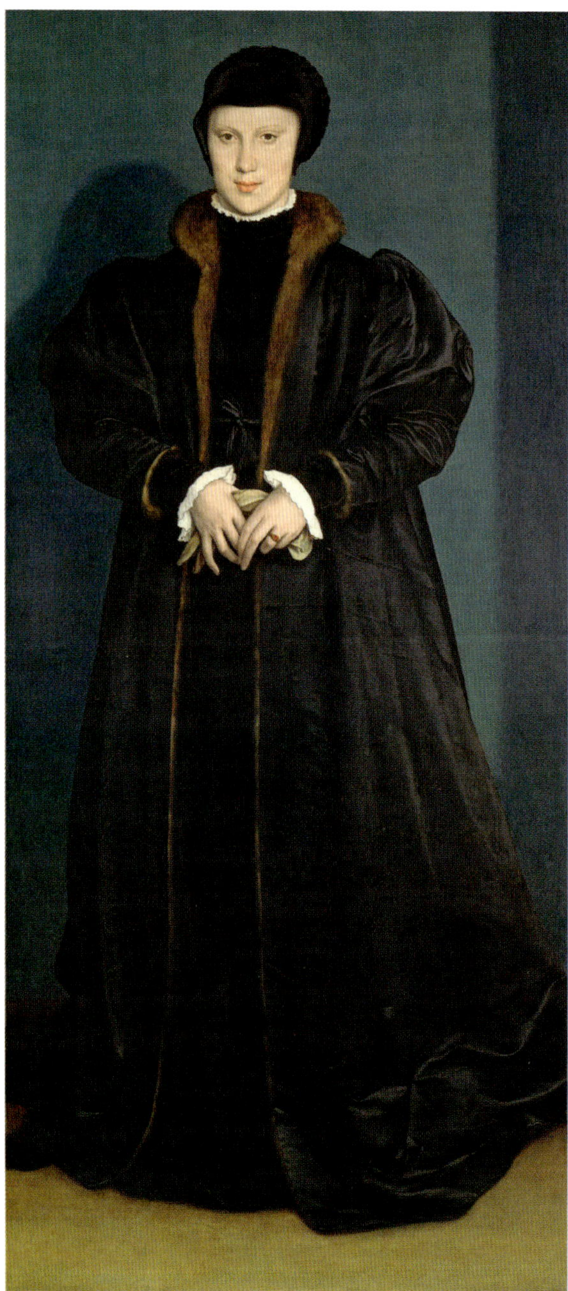

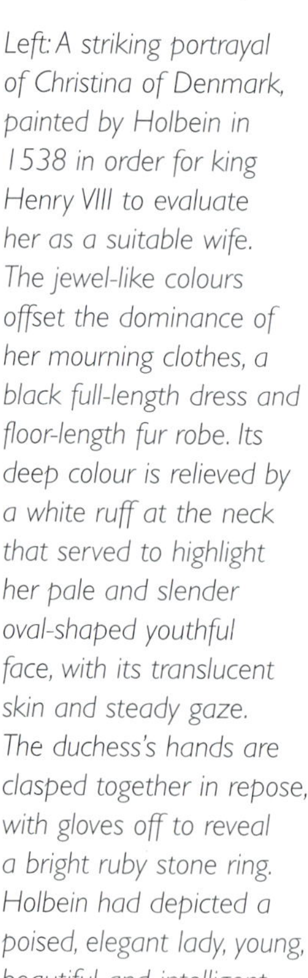

Left: A striking portrayal of Christina of Denmark, painted by Holbein in 1538 in order for king Henry VIII to evaluate her as a suitable wife. The jewel-like colours offset the dominance of her mourning clothes, a black full-length dress and floor-length fur robe. Its deep colour is relieved by a white ruff at the neck that served to highlight her pale and slender oval-shaped youthful face, with its translucent skin and steady gaze. The duchess's hands are clasped together in repose, with gloves off to reveal a bright ruby stone ring. Holbein had depicted a poised, elegant lady, young, beautiful and intelligent.

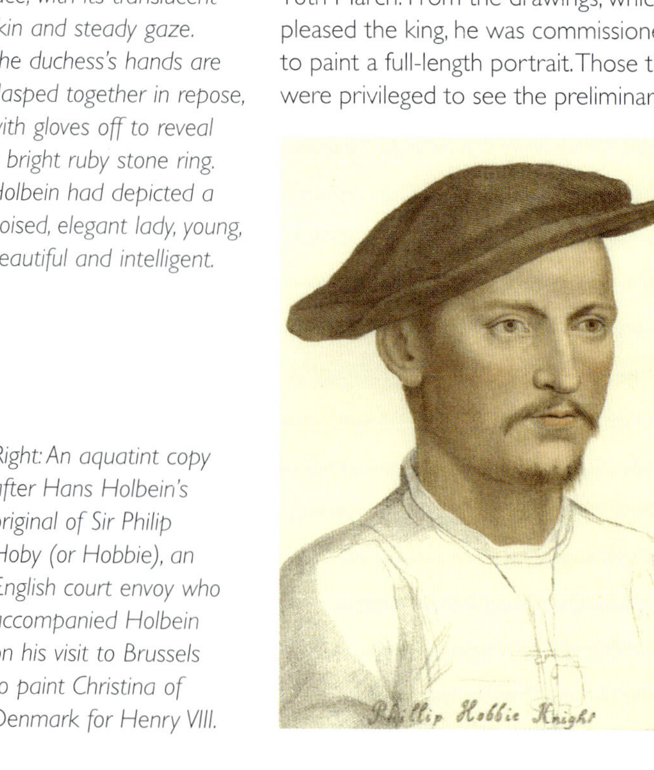

Right: An aquatint copy after Hans Holbein's original of Sir Philip Hoby (or Hobbie), an English court envoy who accompanied Holbein on his visit to Brussels to paint Christina of Denmark for Henry VIII.

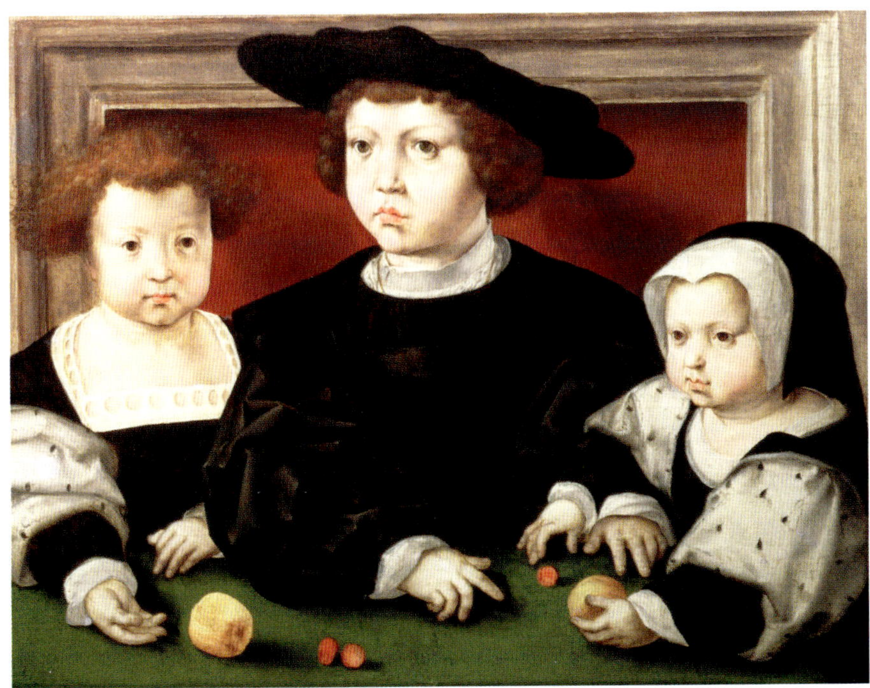

to be the king's wife. It was related that she had said she would have married the king 'had she got two heads'. A remark in jest, to show that she knew what her fate might be, if married to him. Henry held on to the portrait of her until his death; it was listed in the court inventories for 1542 and 1547.

OTHER PROSPECTIVE BRIDES

While negotiations with Denmark were underway, a French marriage was also mooted, and Holbein travelled, again with Philip Hoby, in early June to Le Havre, for a visual account of Louise de Guise; and again in August to the city of Nancy, to portray Louise's younger sister Renée, but she was destined to be Abbess of St Pierre, Reims, so the next choice was Francis I's cousin, Anna of Lorraine.

Above: The Children of Christian II, King of Denmark, *depicting John, Christina, and Dorothea, 1525/6, painted by French artist Jan Gossaert (c.1472–c.1533).*

Right: A half-length and contemplative Portrait of Christina of Denmark, *1545, by Flemish artist Michiel van Coxcie (1499–1592). There are stylistic elements of Holbein's portrait of Christina of Denmark in this work.*

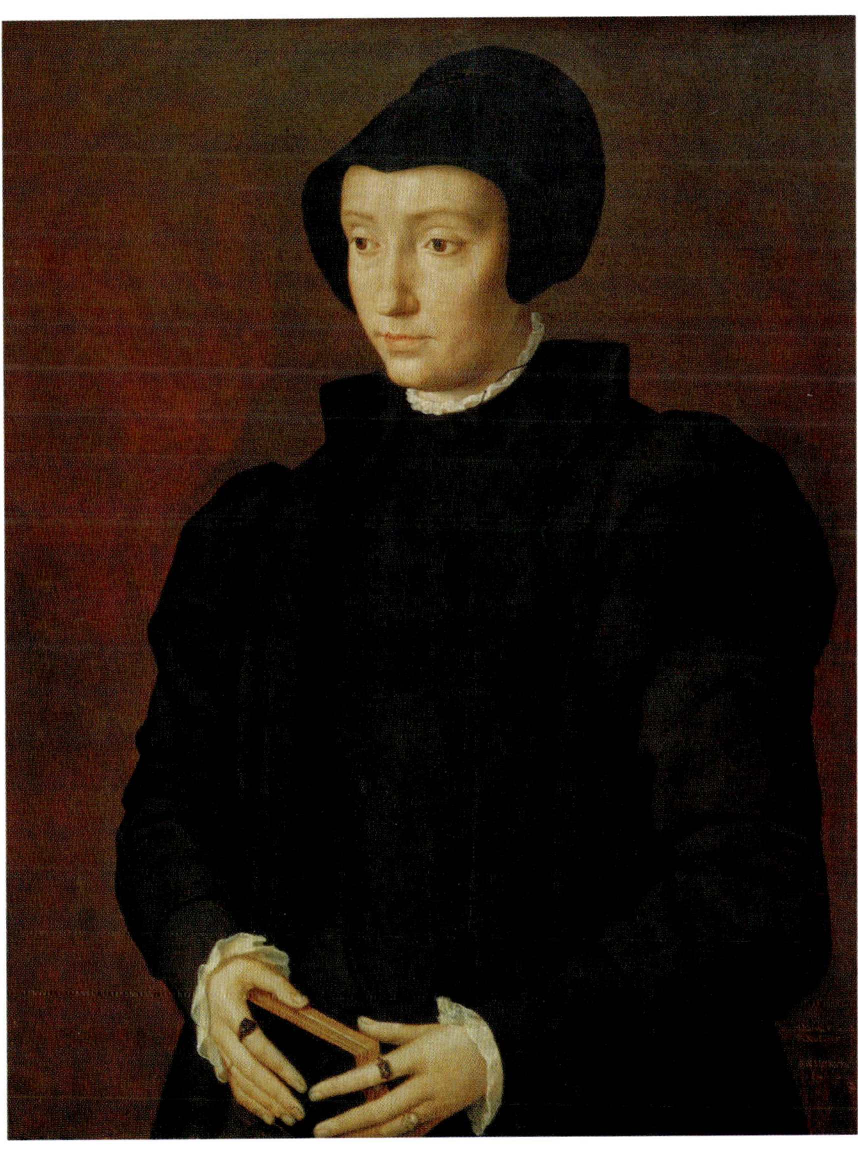

drawings included John Hutton, the English ambassador to the Flemish court in Brussels, who commented that Holbein was 'a master of that science, for it is very perfect', in likeness to her.

Holbein began work on the finished portrait soon after his return from Brussels. He chose to frame Christina of Denmark on a plain turquoise backdrop, with a pale gold-colour plain floor. Her body moves slightly toward the left, whilst her head is tilted down, facing the viewer. It is said that she had a 'wall-eye'; in the painting the left eye looks slightly away, whilst the right gazes steadily at the observer. Holbein creates a formality as though one was in the presence of the young duchess.

A REJECTED PROPOSAL

The proposed marriage alliance fell apart. Christina was probably reluctant

ANNE OF CLEVES

When negotiations opened in 1539 for Henry VIII to marry the German-born Anne of Cleves (1515–57), a Lutheran Protestant and second daughter of the Duke of Saxony, a portrait from Hans Holbein was commissioned so that Henry could judge her appearance before making a proposal of marriage.

English envoys had already been sent to the court of Saxony to meet Anne (Anna) von Kleve and her younger sister Amalia, but the courtiers were unable to fathom exactly what the young women looked like due to their 'monstrous habit and apparel'. The girls' father, Duke John III of Cleves, had reproached the courtiers, berating them sardonically 'would you see them naked?'. The answer to this reluctance to show the intended bride was to send Holbein on assignment to paint Anne. It would be his final mission to paint a potential bride for Henry VIII. He set out in early August 1539, his expenses of £13.6s.8d paid in advance for material necessities 'for the preparation of such things as he is appointed to carry with him'.

A 'LIVELY PORTRAYAL'

Holbein's superb three-quarter length portrait was to prove his near-undoing

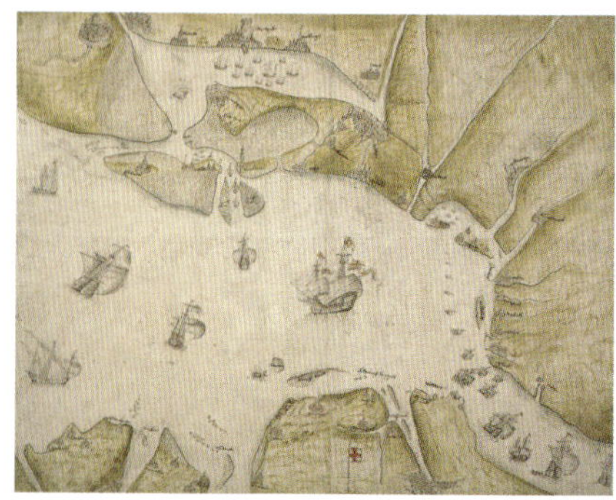

Above: Chart of the North Sea and Zuyder Zee, 1539, *showing the route taken by Lady Anne of Cleves across the sea to England.*

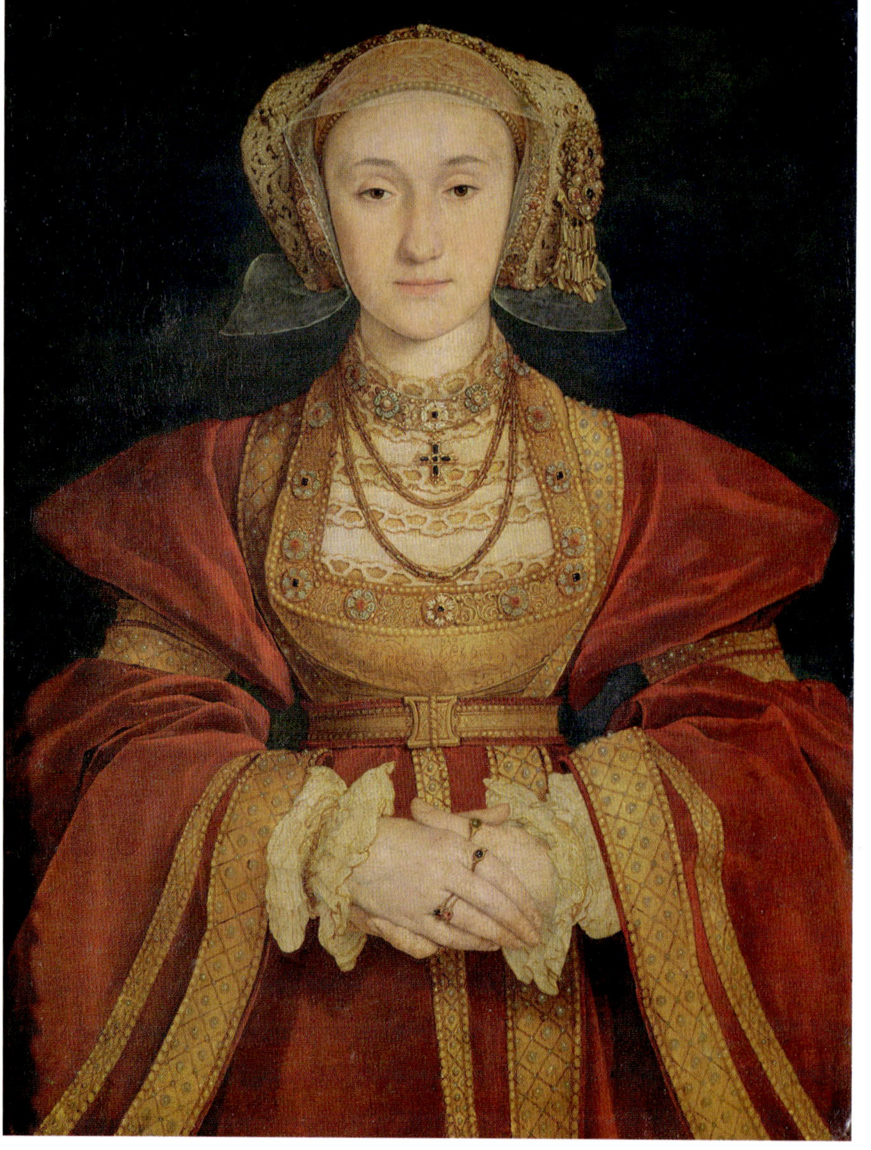

Left: Holbein's painting of Anne of Cleves pleased King Henry but the reality of meeting her in person led to bitter disappointment.

as portraitist to the king. Holbein was sent to Dùren, a town located between Aachen and Cologne, in North Rhine-Westphalia, Germany, where Anne and her sister resided, to draw an accurate portrayal of likeness, deportment and character. He was to portray Anne's younger sister, Amalia of Cleves too.

Holbein would have created drawings in rapid succession, in chalks, his usual method. Life-size watercolour drawings on parchment were easy to transport, and they would be transferred to canvas later. Holbein's painting shows Anne to be of calm, solemn demeanor, the symmetry of her facial features highlighting a pleasant disposition. Her clothes had been copied splendidly and in detail.

After Holbein completed his task, a comment from Nicholas Wotton, one of the English envoys, confirmed that Holbein had 'expressed their images very lively' and confirmed that Holbein had drawn or painted both sisters, Anne and Amalia, possibly to give Henry a choice. The location of the painting of

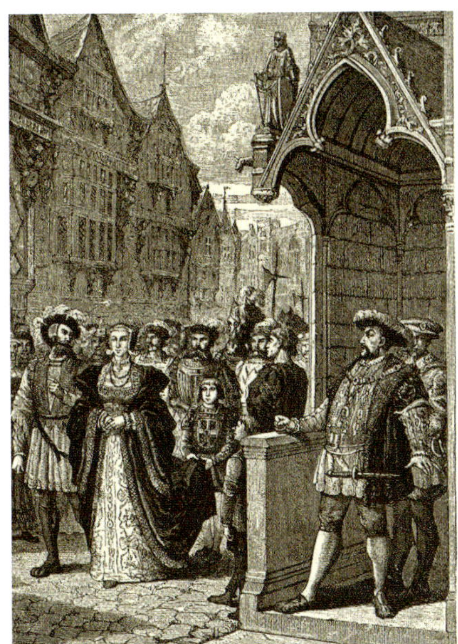

Above: The English School engraving King Henry VIII sees Anne of Cleves, c.1890, visualises Henry VIII surprising Lady Anne of Cleves unprepared at the Bishop's Palace, Rochester, with an early, unplanned meeting.

Right: This Portrait of Anne of Cleves, from the mid-16th century, offers a different portrayal of Henry VIII's fourth queen, attributed to German painter Bartholomaeus Bruyn the Elder (1493–1555).

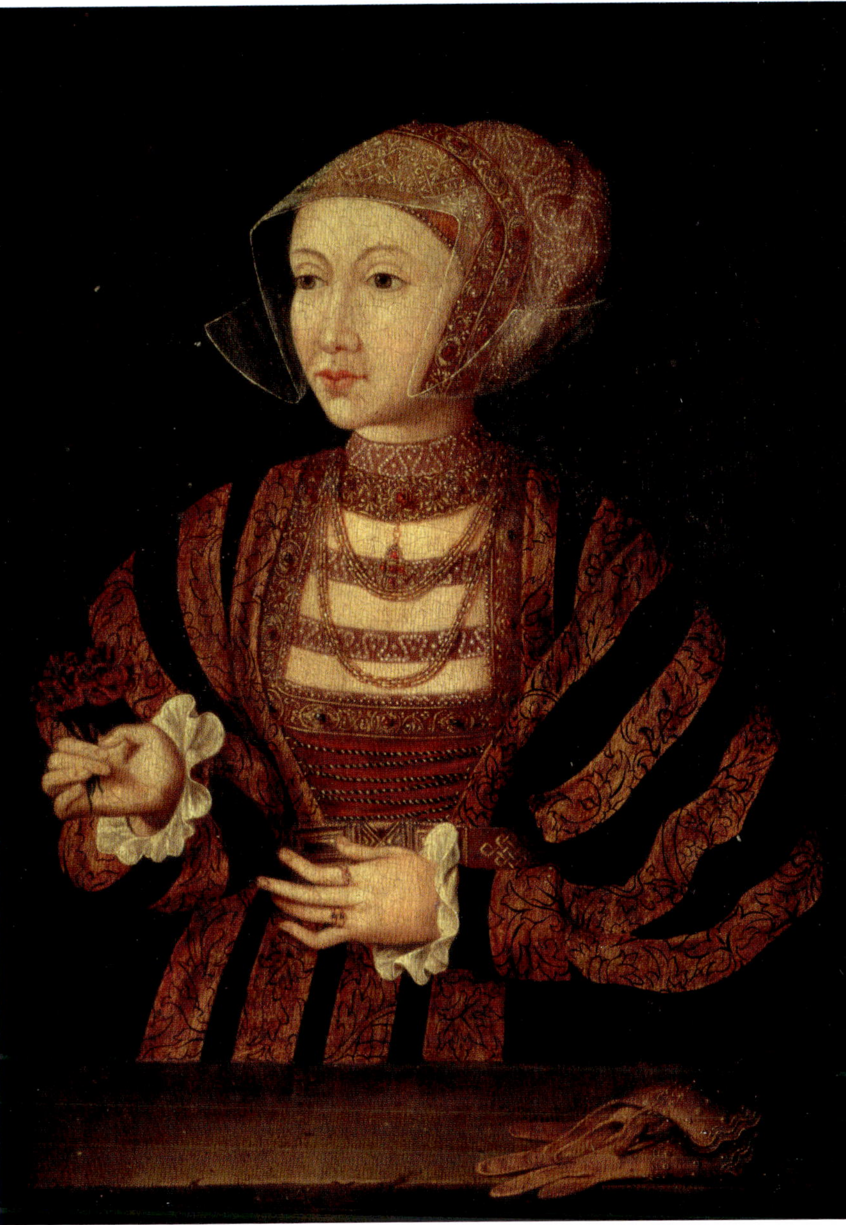

HOLBEIN FALLS FROM FAVOUR

Holbein had made a grave error depicting Anne of Cleves as pleasing to the eye. The king saw her 'nothing so fair as has been reported'. It would cost Holbein his status as the king's painter. It would cost Thomas Cromwell, the instigator of the marriage treaty, his life. Without court documents or Holbein's own account, the fall from favour of Holbein can be ascertained by the lack of royal portraits that followed the Anne of Cleves debacle. It did not curtail Holbein receiving further court commissions for paintings, however they were not of the same significance as his earlier works for Henry VIII.

Amalia is unknown. On Holbein's return to London at the end of August, the portraits were shown to the king. The picture of Anne persuaded Henry to make a proposal. The marriage contract between Henry and Anne was drawn up and signed on 4th October 1539.

'I LIKE HER NOT'

When Lady Anne of Cleves, aged 24, arrived in England in late December 1539, betrothed to Henry VIII, Holbein's portrayal of her 'did not mirror reality' according to the king. That Henry called her a 'fat Flanders mare', is apocryphal, an anecdote of the 17th century made by Gilbert Burnet (1643–1715), Bishop of Salisbury. Whatever may have

been said, Anne's demeanour was not pleasing to Henry. Thomas Cromwell stated that after meeting Anne in the Bishop's Palace in Rochester, Henry declared 'I like her not'. Courtiers reported the king's keen anticipation of meeting Anne turned to dismay on seeing and talking to her. She spoke no English and addressed the king in German. Queen Anne was stripped of her position as Henry's wife, on the grounds of non-consummation, barely six months after the marriage. Henry was then free to marry his latest love, Katherine Howard, one of Anne's ladies in waiting. As a footnote, Anne chose to remain in England and was comfortably settled.

A WORSHIPFUL COMPANY

In 1540 by Act of Parliament in England, members of the Company of Barbers joined forces with the Fellowship of Surgeons, to create a new body, The Worshipful Company of Barber-Surgeons. The union was recorded in a life-size painting of the company in 1541–43, by Hans Holbein the Younger.

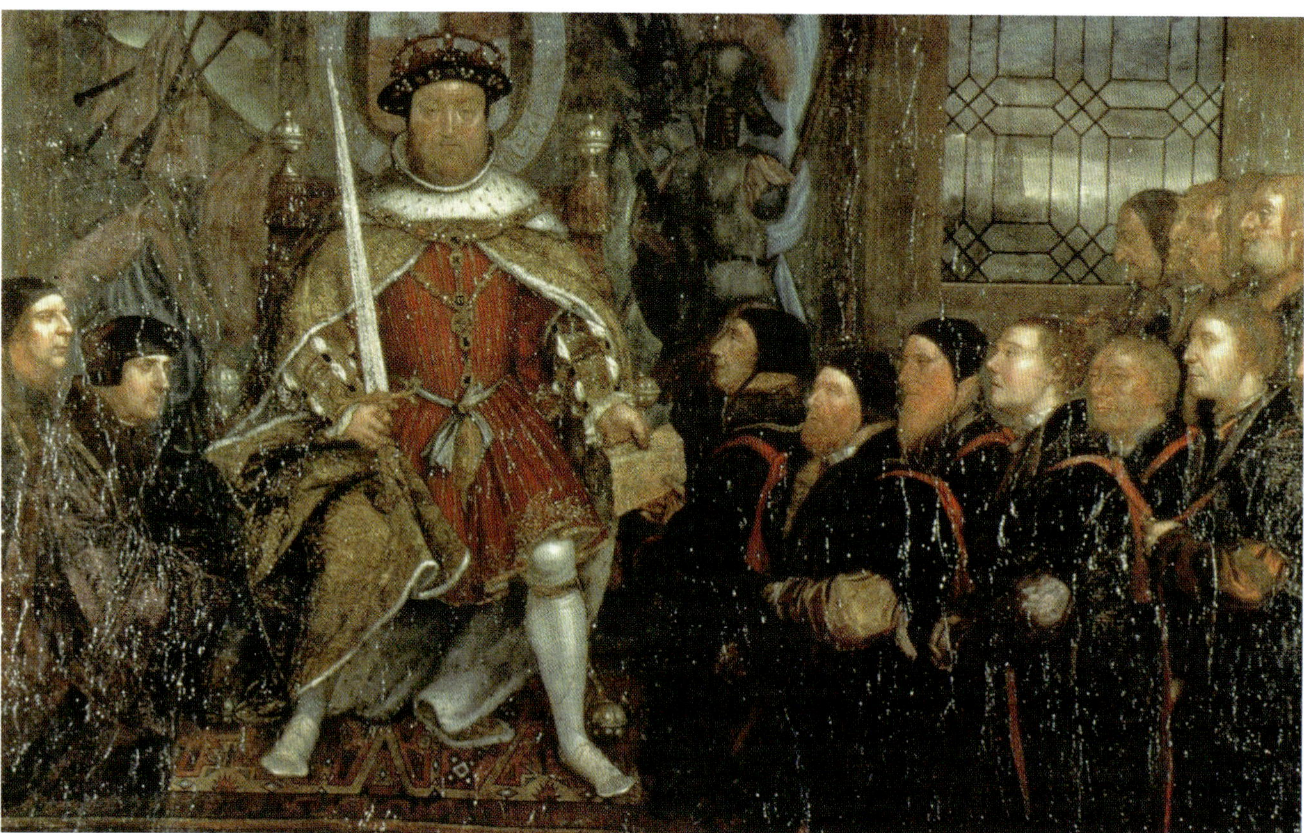

THE BARBER-SURGEONS

To recognise the Act of Union and merger of two companies in 1541, The Worshipful Company of Barbers, at the Barber-Surgeons' Hall, London, a life-size painting, *Henry VIII and the Barber-Surgeons*, 1541–43 was commissioned from Holbein, to depict Henry VIII with members of the amalgamated company. The cartouche in Latin on the background wall translates as:

'To Henry VIII, best and greatest King of England, France and Ireland, Defender of the Faith and Supreme Head of the English and Irish Church, the Company of Surgeons with vows in common consecrate these lines: Sadder than ever had the plague profaned the land of the English, harassing men's minds and besetting their bodies; God, from on high pitifully regarding so notable a mortality, bade thee undertake the office of a good Physician. 'The light of the Gospel flies round about thee on glowing wings; that will be a remedy for a mind diseased, and by thy counsel men study the monuments of Galen; and every disease is expelled by speedy aid. We, therefore, a suppliant band of thy Physicians, dedicate to thee with reverence this house; and mindful of the gift with which thou, O Henry, hast blest us, we wish the greatest blessings on thy rule also.'

FOCUS ON HENRY VIII

Holbein positioned the king to the left of centre. Henry VIII, wearing a crown, holds the mitre in his right hand and receives from Thomas Vicary, Master of the Barber-Surgeons, the official document, with his left hand. The Charter and Seal are Holbein's addition to the assembly painting, as the union was created by an Act of

Above: A later copy of The Barber-Surgeons' Picture, *Holbein's painting of 1541–43 (see 244–45), with variations.*

Below: Guild Book of the Barber-Surgeons of York, originating in 1486.

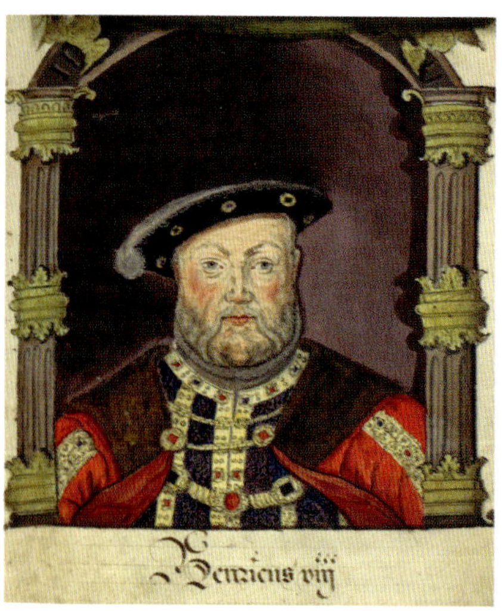

Parliament. The king sits facing the viewer, resplendent in a ceremonial ermine-lined robe, a 'cloth of gold of tissue'. His figure dominates the painting; much larger in size than the rest of the attending officials, he physically and symbolically towers over the newly formed assembly. Members and non-members are gathered to either side below him. Fifteen members to his left look toward him in reverence. The name of each person is painted in gold on their image. To the king's right (the viewer's left) are depicted the royal physicians Dr Butts and Dr Chambers. As they are not members of the company, they are separated from the main group. The painting is traditional in its group-portrait composition. There is no interaction, or communication, between the members.

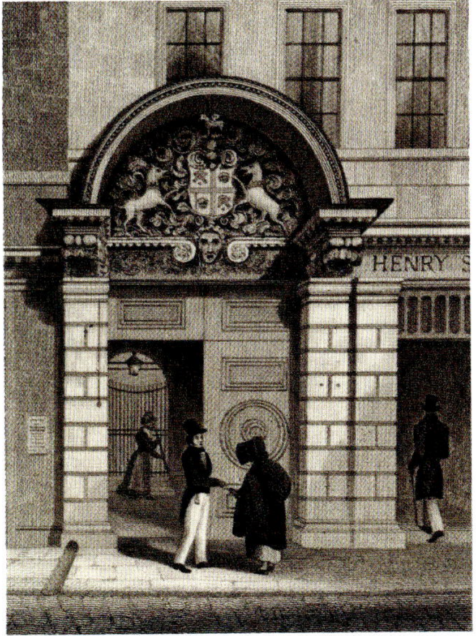

Above: The Barber-Surgeon's Hall, in Monkwell Street, London, 1830, an engraving by English artist Thomas Hosmer Shepherd (1793–1864).

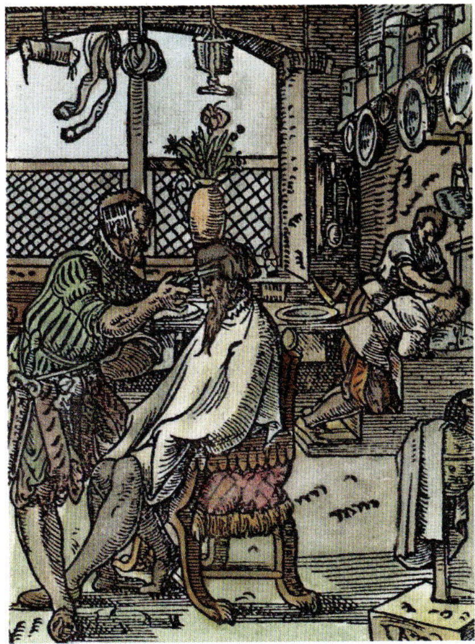

Above: The Barber-Surgeon, 1568, a colourised woodcut by Swiss-German artist Jost Amman (1539–91). It depicts a customer in the barber-surgeon's shop, where services might include hair-cutting, pulling teeth, treating wounds, broken bones, and syphilis.

SURGERY AND SHAVING

In Europe, and initially in the City of London, surgery and shaving could be carried out by the same person. In 1512 an Act was passed in England to prevent barbers without surgeon qualifications carrying out surgery within the City of London and seven miles beyond the city's perimeter, without formal agreement from the office of the Dean of St Paul's or the Bishop of London, to maintain the higher standing of the surgeon's profession. In 1540, the two companies of barbers and surgeons were amalgamated, with the condition that barbers did not carry out surgery except for blood-letting and teeth extraction. These two practices are said to be why the Barber's shop pole, displayed outside their premises, is blood-red and white. The conjoining of the two companies in 1540 was the reason for Holbein's commission. Many painters depicted the barber-surgeon at work, being a popular subject in northern European art, as the woodcut *The Barber-Surgeon 1568*, by Swiss-German artist Jost Amman shows.

AN UNFINISHED WORK

The Barber-Surgeons' painting is mentioned in Karel van Mander's Life of Holbein (published in his *Schilder-Boeck* in 1604). Van Mander pointed out that the work was completed by another artist, after the sudden death of Holbein. What Holbein conveys is the great honour that the king's presence bestows on the new confraternity. The larger figure of the king denotes his superiority. Further depictions of members were added later to the work, as new Masters or members joined the group, notably placed at the end of the first and second rows. The painting later received damage on its left side during the Great Fire of London in 1666.

Below: An engraving Satire of Barber-Surgeons, c.1570, by an unknown artist, depicts a team of barber-surgeon monkeys, attending to clients' many requests for blood-letting, treatment of wounds, pulling teeth and hair cutting.

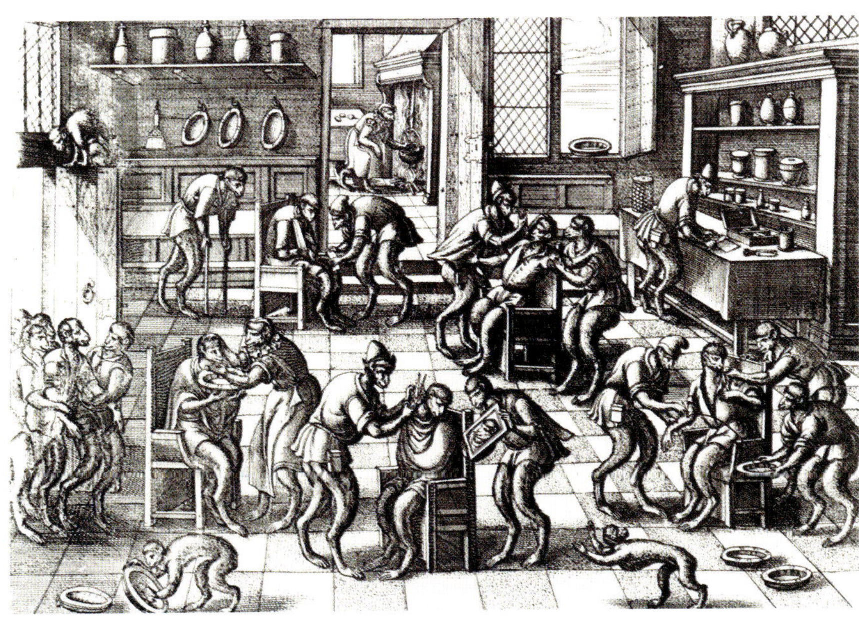

A SUDDEN DEATH

In 1543 a virulent plague spread throughout Europe. In England Henry VIII issued the first plague-order, a preventative practice with measures to contain and curtail the disease. Hans Holbein made a Will before his death this year. It is not known if he did definitely die of the plague, although it seems most likely.

LONDON 1543

England had previously experienced decimations of the population due to plague. Records of 1543 held by Henry VIII's Privy Council state that the plague began on May 21st and lasted through to the winter months. It records that there was 'a great death'. The king issued the first plague-order to control the virus. Inhabitants of houses with plague had to stay indoors and place a sign of a cross on their door for forty days, to highlight that the plague was within. Those with infection needing to go to work had to carry a white rod, two feet

Below: Map of Aldgate Ward, City of London, 1739, by R. W. Seale. It includes margin images of Aldgate and four ward churches: St James, Duke Street; St Katherine Cree; St Katherine Coleman; and St Andrew Undershaft, which was Holbein's local parish church.

long, with them, to alert other citizens. Holbein's Will, made not long before he died, may indicate that he was ill or preparing for possible death. There is no specific written evidence that he died of plague. He lived in the parish of St Andrew Undershaft and may have been buried in the church cemetery, or in the church of St Katherine Cree nearby, but no records survive. The *Dance of Death* frescoes from Basel macabrely remind that the plague took rich and poor alike. Holbein's woodcuts of 1523–26 highlight 'death calling suddenly'.

HANS HOLBEIN'S WILL

The Will of Hans Holbein the Younger, dated 7th October 1543, was discovered in the archives of St Paul's Cathedral in 1861. Possibly written in the knowledge that his death might be imminent or, to settle accounts officially before a return to Basel, Holbein

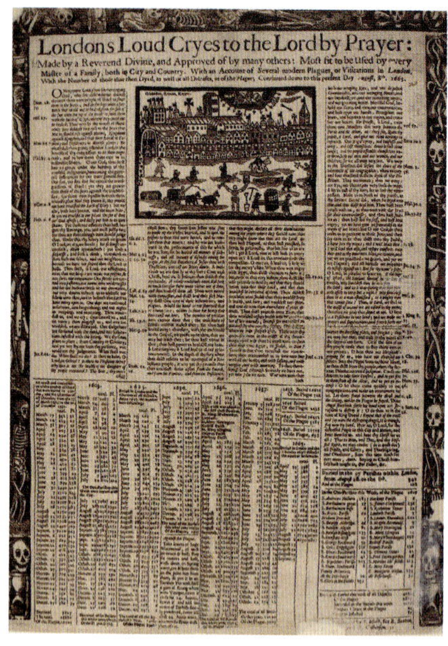

Above: A 17th-century newspaper account of plagues in London; there were many waves of plague through Europe over the centuries.

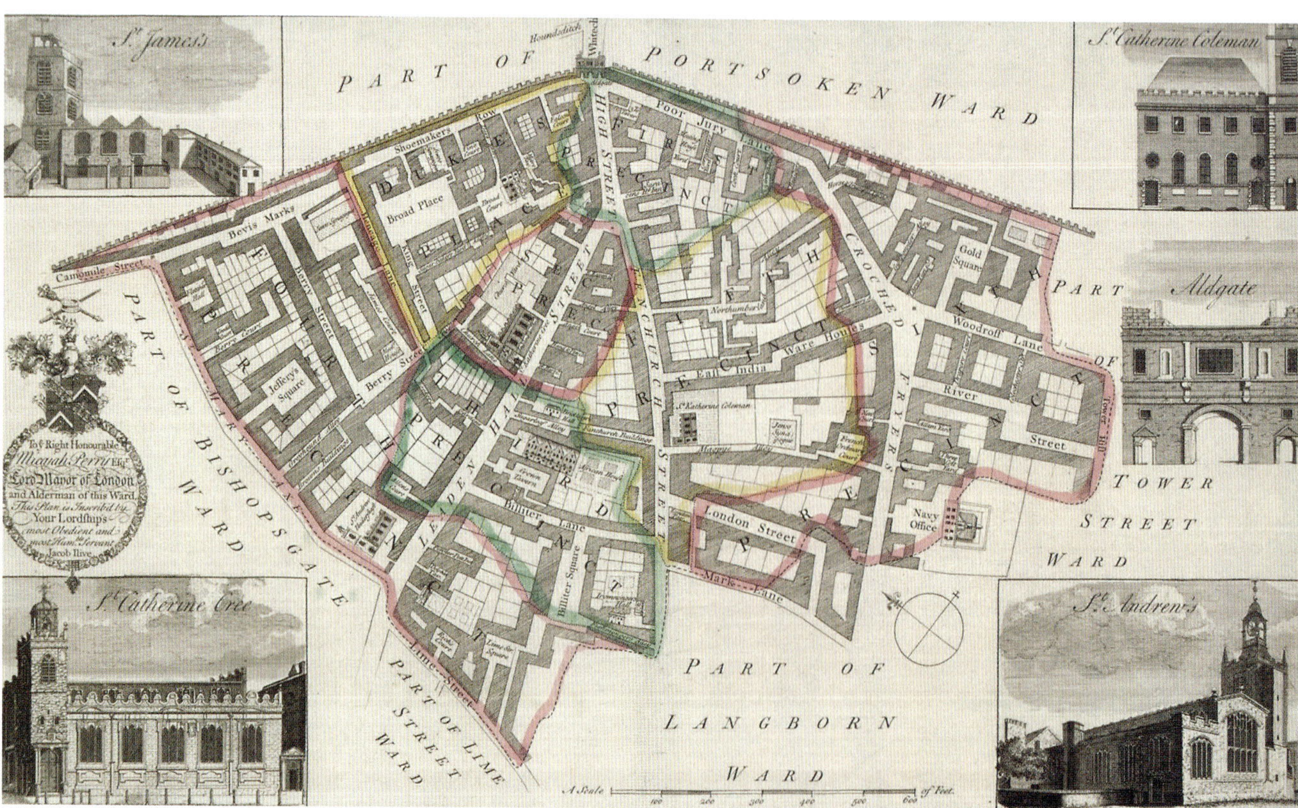

HOLBEIN'S LAST SELF-PORTRAIT

In the months before his unexpected death, Hans Holbein completed a self-portrait. It is a small work in coloured chalk, pen, and gold. No oil-painted portrait from this drawing exists. Holbein does not portray himself exactly as he portrayed the king, and nobles, but his signature style is there, depicting himself as a serious, sombre, plainly dressed, professional man. He is cropped closely in a head and shoulders composition, and a three-quarter pose, possibly using a mirror to achieve this angle. His hooded eyes, without expression, look directly at the viewer. Lettering reads 'Johannes Holbein of Basel at the age of 45', written on a gold background, which experts say was added later.

paid his debts and, according to his biographer Karel van Mander, settled money for his two illegitimate infant children in London. By 29th November 1543, he was spoken of as dead. He was 45 years old.

The text below is an extract from *Ancient, Curious and Famous Wills* by Virgil M. Harris (Little, Brown, 1911):

'In the name of God the Father, Sonne, and Holy Ghoste, I, Johan Holbeine, servante of the King's Majistie, make this my testamente and will, to wyt, that alle my goodes shall be sold, and also my horse; and I will that my debtes be payd to wyt: furste to Mr. Anthony the kynges servant of Greenwiche, ye summe of ten poundes thirtien shyllinges and sewyne pence sterlinge. And, moreover, I will that he shal be contented for all other thynges between him and me. Item: I do owe unto Mr. John of Anwarpe, Goldsmythe, saxe pounds sterling, which I will alsoe shalle be payde unto hyme with the fyrste. Item: I bequeathe for the kypyng of my two chylder, which be atte nurse, for every monthe, seyvene shellinges, and sexpence styrlynge. In wytnes I have sealed and sealed thys my testamente, thys sexthe daye of October, in the yeare of our Lorde

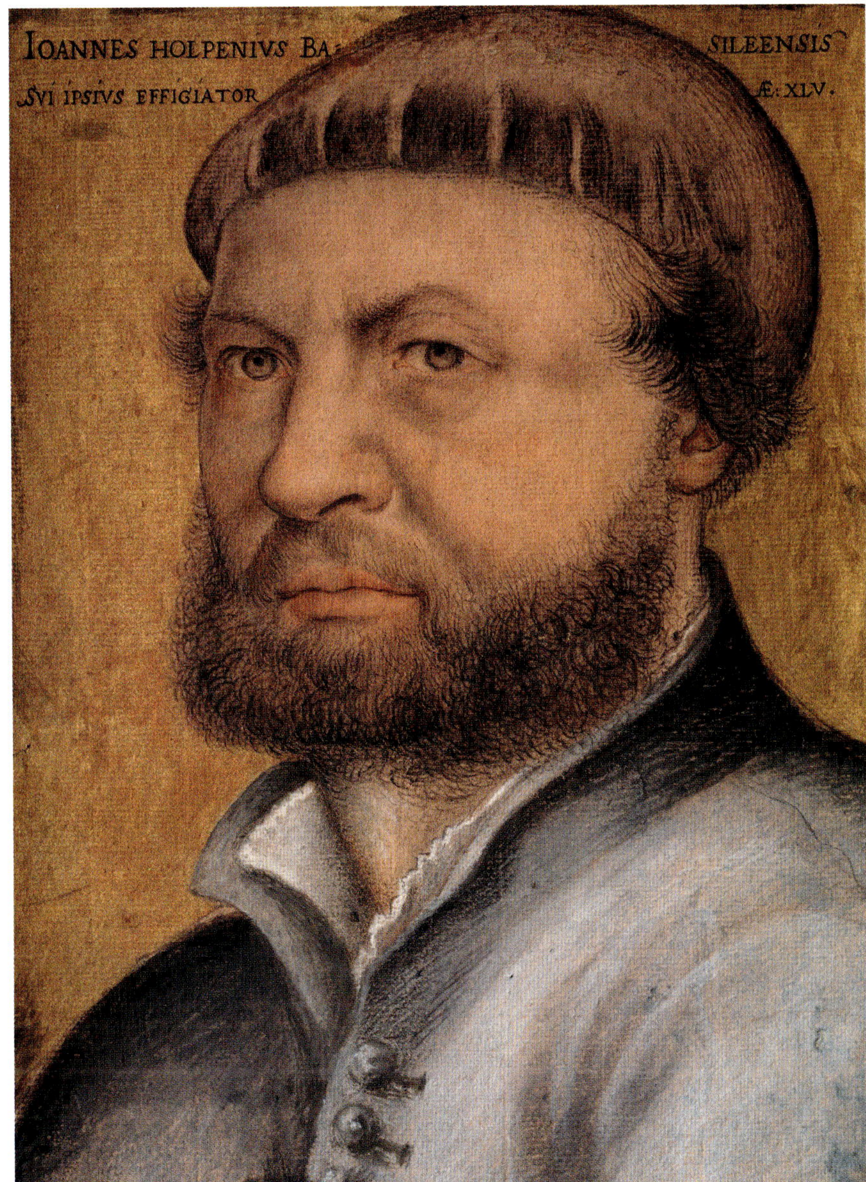

Above: Holbein's self-portrait in chalks, 1542–43. He writes on it his age and that he is a citizen of Basel: 'IONNES HOLPENIVS BASILEENSIS / SVI IPSIVS EFFIGIATOR Æ: XLV.'

MIVCXLIIJ. Wytnes, Anthony Snetcher, Armerer, Mr. John of Anwarpe, aforesaid, Goldsmythe, Obrycke Obynger, Merchante and Harry Maynaert, Paynter.'

The witnesses offer a small insight into Holbein's life in London. Money due to Mr Anthony Snetcher, the armourer, and the goldsmith Mr John of Antwerp, makes them work colleagues; Mr Harry Maynaert (Maynert) was a painter who may have been an assistant because Holbein could officially run a workshop after becoming a denizen of London in 1541. Obryche Obynger (Ulrich Obinger) was a merchant.

Right. From Holbein's Dance of Death alphabet, a woodcut created in Basel in the early 1520s.

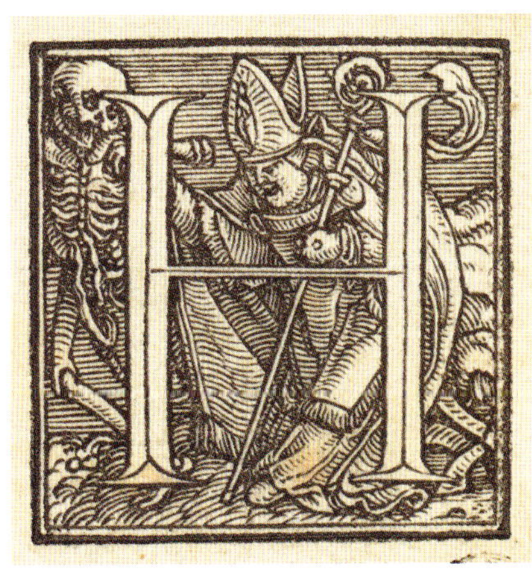

AFTER HOLBEIN

Thomas More wrote to Erasmus, '*Your painter, my dear Erasmus, is a wonderful artist*', thanking him for an introduction to Holbein. His subsequent impact on portraiture was undeniable. After Holbein's death in 1543 his influence on court paintings continued and many artists copied, or were inspired by, his works.

When Holbein arrived in England in 1526 there was comparatively little demand for portraiture. Thomas More explained this in a letter to Erasmus, regarding potential commissions for Holbein. Portraiture was not fashionable, possibly due to a lack of exceptional portraitists. The vacuum would soon be filled by Holbein, and the Flemish painter Lucas Horenbout, who settled in England in the mid-1520s and who was also employed as the King's Painter, from 1525. The deaths of Holbein in 1543 and Horenbout in 1544 found the English court seeking new painters. Guillaume Scrots and Levina Teerlinc were highly regarded artists at the time and both became king's painters to Henry VIII and the Royal court.

IN THE STYLE OF HOLBEIN

Copies were made of Holbein's paintings during his lifetime, varying in their closeness to the original, and continued to be made centuries after his death. His paintings inspired many adaptations in similar style. An impressive large-scale painting (see below) was commissioned by King Henry shortly after Holbein's death, which is similar to the painting made for the Privy Chamber Wall (see pages 78–79), depicting the wider royal family, and including the late Queen Jane. It was probably hung in the Presence Chamber at Whitehall.

GUILLAUME SCROTS

Portrait of Edward, Prince of Wales, c.1546 (opposite), was painted by Guillaume Scrots, a Flemish artist (active 1537–53) of notable talent. The painting is clearly in the style of Holbein, depicting realism, majesty and intimacy. Scrots became 'King's Painter' to Henry VIII in 1546, receiving an annual salary of £62.10 shillings. He maintained the position during the reign of Henry's son Edward VI, until the young monarch's death in 1553. Scrots also died that year.

LEVINA TEERLINC

Another Flemish artist, Levina (also known as Livinia, Lavinia, Levyn) Teerlinc (1510/20–1576) was born in Bruges, to the distinguished miniaturist and illuminator of manuscripts, Simon Benninck (also Bening). Teerlinc was invited to England by Henry VIII, arriving with her husband in November 1545. Two months later her name appeared

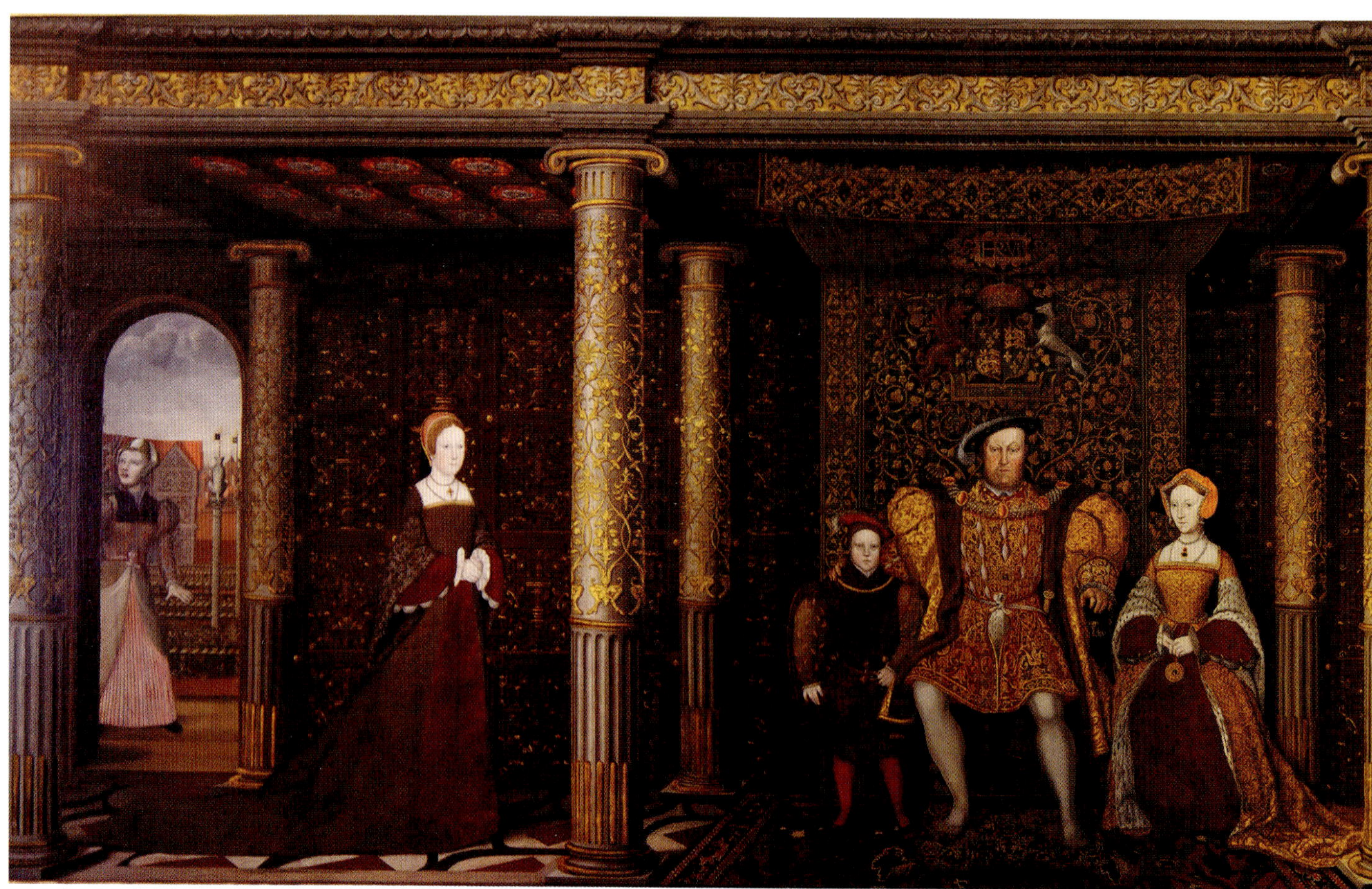

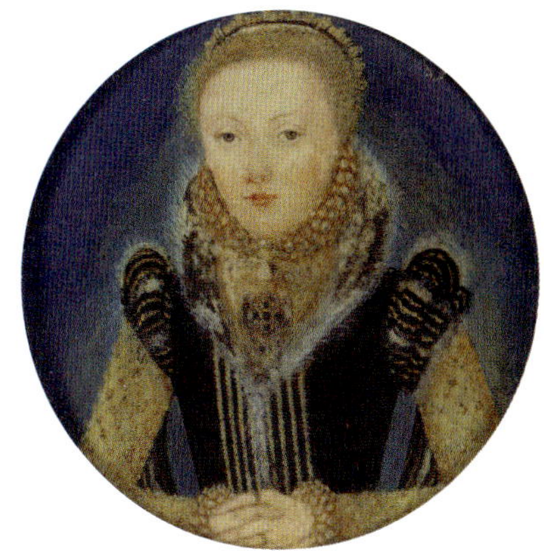

Above: Portrait miniature possibly depicting Elizabeth I, c.1565, watercolour on vellum laid on playing card, attributed to Levina Teerlinc (1510–1576).

in the court accounts as the 'King's Paintrix'. Her annual salary of £40 was above that paid to Holbein, although royal painters often received gifts, including money, on top of a salary. Teerlinc was in particular demand for her portrait miniatures (see pages 84–85) working for successive monarchs after Henry VIII: Edward VI, Mary I and Elizabeth I.

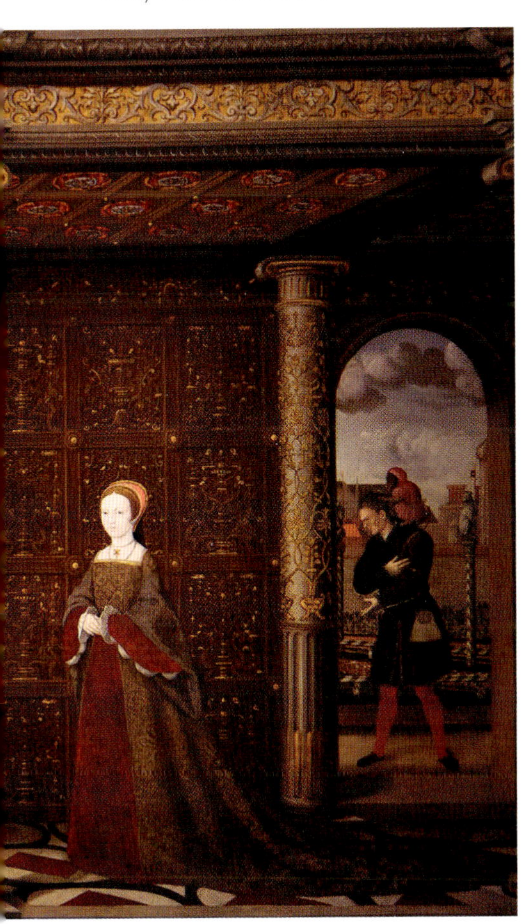

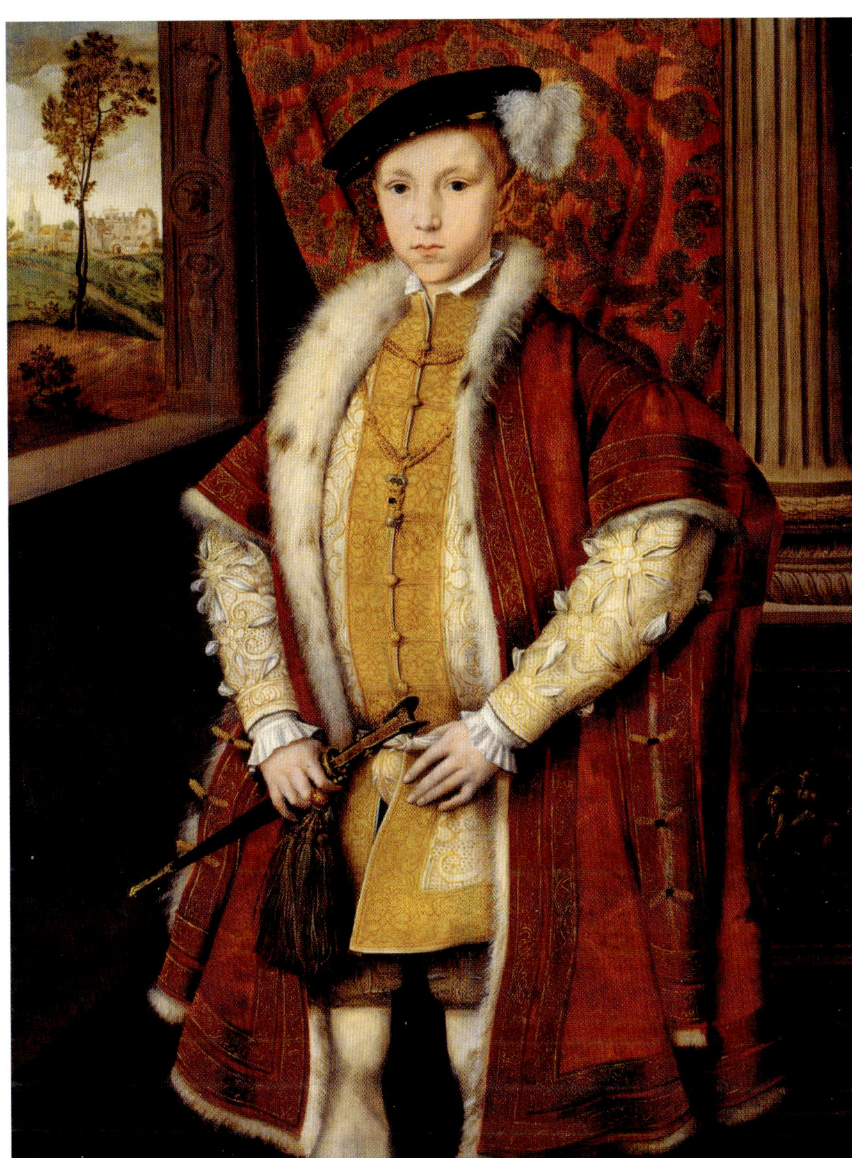

Above: Portrait of Edward, Prince of Wales, c.1546, a three-quarter length painting depicting the young king of England, attributed to Guillaume Scrots who became King's Painter after Holbein.

Left: The Family of Henry VIII, c.1545, by an unknown artist, is an imaginative collecting-together of personages from the Tudor dynasty, commissioned by Henry to display in Whitehall Palace (now on view at Hampton Court Palace). From left to right are Princess Mary, Prince Edward, Henry VIII, Queen Jane Seymour, and Princess Elizabeth. In the distance are members of the household, including the king's jester Will Somers. The figures are strongly influenced by and copied from Holbein's portraits, as well as the rich background and detailing.

Below: A light-hearted homage to Holbein two centuries later, in Master Crewe as Henry VIII, 1775, by Sir Joshua Reynolds. John Crewe was aged three.

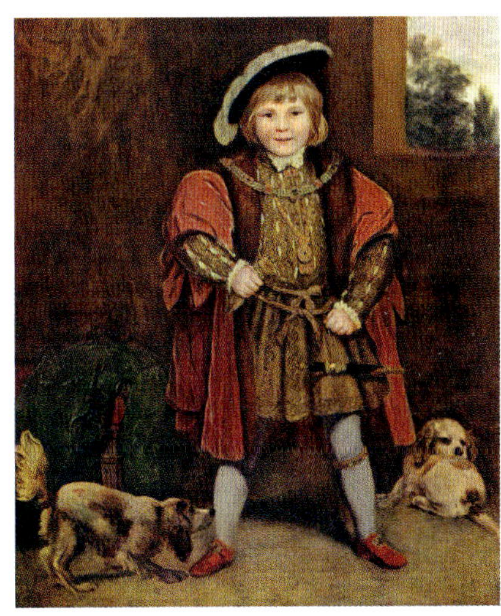

SOURCES ON HOLBEIN

There are very few primary sources on Holbein. Contemporary records exist but are fragmentary – only a few letters, notes and receipts for work are extant. Historians rely mainly on secondary sources, such as Holbein's brief biography in a work by the Flemish artist and writer Karel van Mander.

Chronicling Holbein's life through family and work is piecemeal because it relies on scarce documentation relating to commissions, letters of introduction, and recorded anecdotes by persons who knew him, and these are rarities. If Holbein kept a diary it is not extant. There are no records of his planning for works in progress, or notes on his methods. He left no accounts of his life, clients or art. He did not write theoretical texts on the art of painting. Unlike the Italian artist Leonardo da Vinci (1452–1519) and German artist Albrecht Dürer (1471–1528) of his peer generation, who both wrote copiously, it must have been an explicit decision not to communicate ideas and theory on art. Letters to his family in Basel must have been written by him during his nine-year residence in London (1532–43), but are not extant.

BASEL SOURCES

Swiss document records for Basel have references to Holbein and his family, including his membership of the painters' guild in 1519; the commission for the new Council chamber; the offer of an annuity in 1532, and again in 1538; and the two houses that he bought between 1528 and 1531. Basel records show that the council's 1528–32 negotiations with Holbein for him not to return to England but remain in the city, included an annuity of 30 gulden. When he left in 1532 the annuity was paid to Holbein's wife, Elsbeth, and continued during the years of his absence, on the understanding that he would return. In autumn 1538, Holbein briefly returned and the council raised their annuity offer from 30 to 50 gulden, with the promise that Holbein could sell his paintings across Europe if he stayed. Records show 40 gulden per annum, in four quarterly instalments, was paid to Elsbeth in his absence.

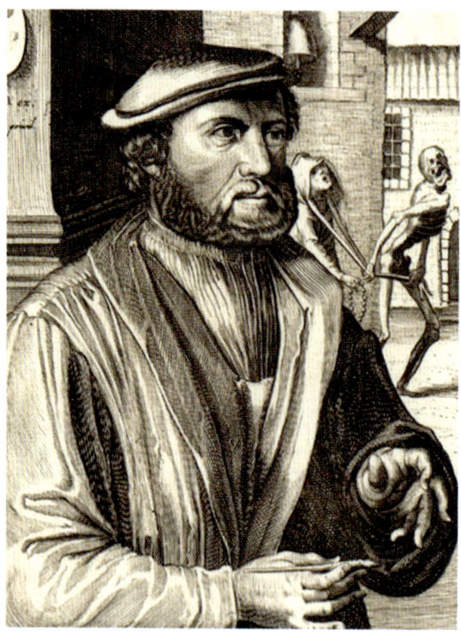

Above: A Portrait of Hans Holbein the Younger, *1497. A copper engraving from* Schilder-Boeck (The Book of Painters), *by Karel van Mander.*

FINANCIAL FRAGMENTS

The financial accounts of Henry VIII's courtiers Thomas Wyatt and Sir Henry Guildford dated 1527 relate to artists creating works for the king. They refer to payment to 'Master Hans for the plat of Tirwan', a reference to a battle scene Holbein painted, depicting the 1513 battle of Thérouanne, Artois, after the Battle of the Spurs, which resulted in victory for Henry VIII and Emperor Maximillian against the French. The scenery was commissioned for the temporary Banqueting House at Greenwich Palace and painted on the reverse wall of a temporary triumphal arch. Indirectly, through Guildford, Holbein was commissioned by the king soon after arrival in England to create paintings in cloth, for the temporary

Right: Karel van Mander, *the Flemish painter, author, writer, and biographer. A copper engraving from his* Schilder-Boeck *published in Amsterdam, 1604.*

buildings erected for the festivities to welcome the French king on 6th May. The Greenwich accounts list the paint supplies ordered for 'Master Hans' and the other painters employed. In addition, he was paid more than other painters, receiving 4 shillings (48 pence) per day, compared to the highest-paid English artist Robert Wrythoke, at one shilling (12 pence) per day.

MASTER HANS

Holbein liaised with the king's astronomer, a fellow German, Nikolaus Kratzer. He would design the object and Kratzer would help with technical parts of the design. One object created for Henry VIII was a gift of a clock from Sir Anthony Denny, presented to the king on New Year's Day 1544. It was a clocksalt, designed by Holbein and Kratzer in 1543 (see page 248). Two of the notes on Holbein's pen and ink and wash sketch on paper are in Kratzer's hand. In Greenwich 1526–27, for the Peace Revels (see page 53), they collaborated on a design for an astronomically correct depiction of the heavens, above a map of the world. In the accounts for it Holbein was

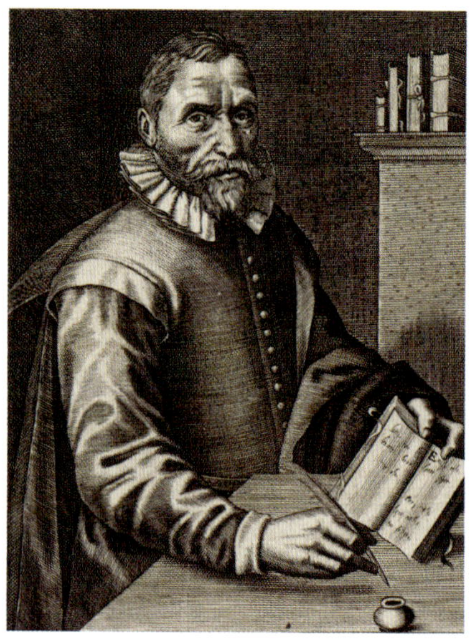

Right: Sir Thomas More, his father, his household and descendants, *1594, a copy after Holbein, by English painter Rowland Lockey. Lockey created copies of Holbein's original painting a number of times, based on the 1527 work. In this 1594 version (now displayed in the Victoria & Albert Museum, London) some non-bloodline people have been removed – Alice More, Henry Patenson, Margaret Clement – to make way for newer members of the More family, some not alive when Sir Thomas More commissioned Holbein, but Lockey captures the dynastic intention of the original work.*

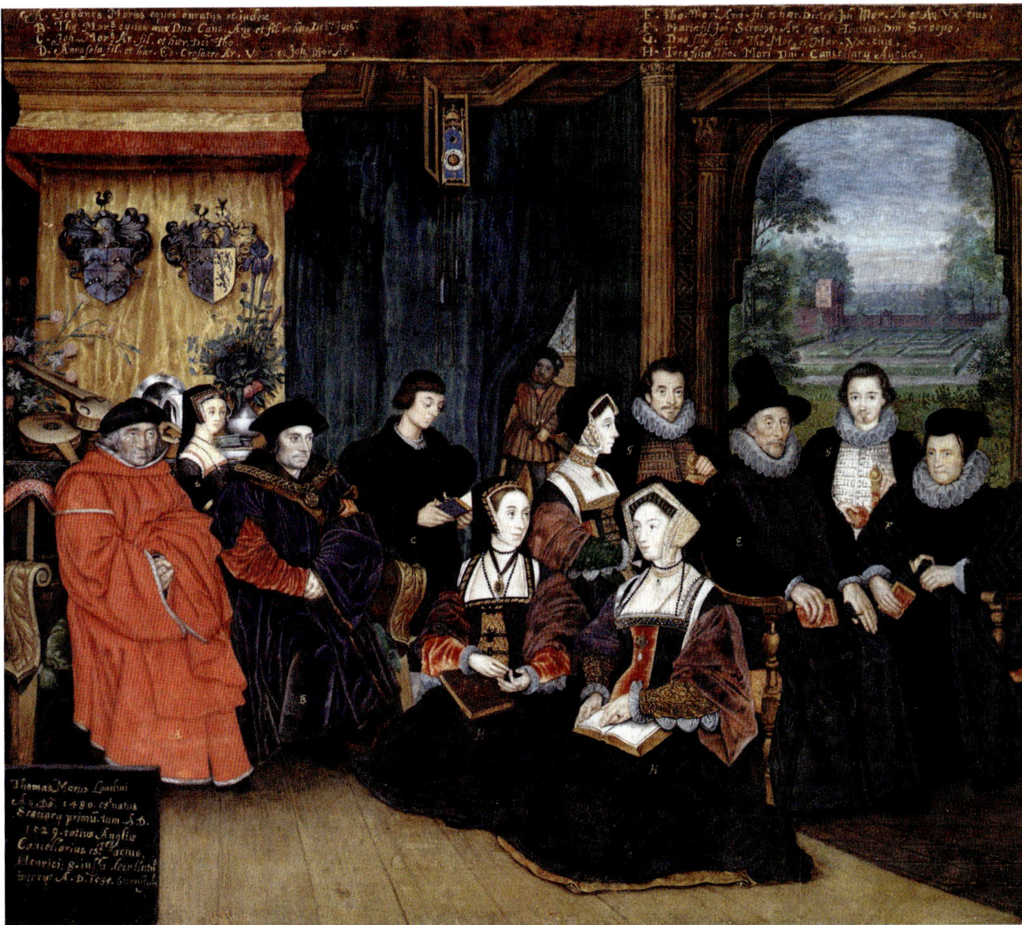

mentioned by name 'Master Hans and hys company' – nineteen painters are recorded for payment – from January. It has been suggested that Kratzer may have helped Holbein in technical discussions with painters, although we do not know how well Holbein spoke English when he arrived in 1526. Accounts refer to Holbein's work on 'ye rouf and 'works by him wrought' and 'ye iiii clothes'…'ye ii clothes'. On finishing, the king inspected the work. The painted ceiling cloths, sewn together, were hung up on April 10th, and removed on 7th May, after the festivities had concluded.

SCHILDER-BOECK (THE BOOK OF PAINTERS)

The Flemish artist, writer and biographer Karel van Mander (1548–1606) is noted for his ten-year study of the lives of Netherlandish and German artists, published in *Schilder-Boeck, The Lives of the Most Illustrious Netherlandish and German Painters* in 1603–04, which included etchings. The section on the lives of German painters included a short biography of Hans Holbein the Younger. This entry has been the one most sourced by art historians, due to so little being known about the artist. Van Mander used Holbein as an example of a painter who used illusion to great effect in his portraiture, complimenting the artist as a 'bold liar'.

Karel van Mander determined that Holbein had never visited Italy, to substantiate his own opinion that the painter was unaffected by Florentine or Venetian artists. Holbein in Italy (or not) remains unproven, however. There is a definite influence of Leonardo da Vinci in Holbein's religious depictions. He may have seen original works, or engravings and prints of Italian paintings in Basel, the heart of the German publishing business. In addition, he would have seen Italian paintings on his travels through France in 1523–24. One must also consider van Mander's objectivity, bearing in mind his preference for German and Netherlandish art over Italian Renaissance schools.

MULTIPLE HOLBEINS

Many of Holbein's original paintings and works no longer exist, but are known to us through copies. To analyse just one example, significant works by Holbein for the More family are now known through contemporary copies. Holbein's original painting *Family of Sir Thomas More,* 1527–28, was accidentally destroyed by fire in 1752. We know of its composition from Holbein's small sketch sent to Erasmus (see page 158) plus a remaining fragment of the original cartoon. The painted copies include a number of versions by English artist Rowland Lockey (c.1565–1616). Not all of his copies were true to the original however, as the sitters and background varied. *Sir Thomas More, his father, his household and descendants,* c.1593 (see pages 156–57), was probably commissioned by More's grandson, Thomas More II (1531–1606). Two other slightly different versions by Lockey were also painted in the 1590s – the painting shown above, and on page 51.

HOLBEIN'S TECHNIQUE

Even by the time Holbein the Younger graduated from workshop apprentice to journeyman, his skill as a draughtsman and portraitist was evident. His techniques were wide-ranging and flexible, to suit the brief, subject and the available materials, whether working with chalks, pen and ink, oils or mixed tempera.

HOLBEIN AS DRAUGHTSMAN

In the Augsburg workshop Holbein had gained advanced practical drawing skills, which makes some drawings hard to date due to the maturity of his draughtsmanship. There are just over 400 drawings existing today, around 130 dating from 1515–32 with nearly 100 preparatory drawings for portraits dating from 1526–28 and 1532–43, from Holbein's time in England. These are a small proportion of his preliminary works. The few notes Holbein made were handwritten on drawings. Exceptions were detailed drawings for house decorations such as the Hertenstein house in Lucerne *c*.1517 (see pages 32–33) and stained glass windows (see pages 136 and146–49), for the glass painter to reproduce, and designs for jewellery and ornaments, which needed precise detailing. The illustrations he created for book titles, page borders and woodblocks may have been the property of the print-publishers. It is thought that preliminary drawings for paintings of

Below: Anna Meyer's long, golden hair is not depicted in the final painting (page 145).

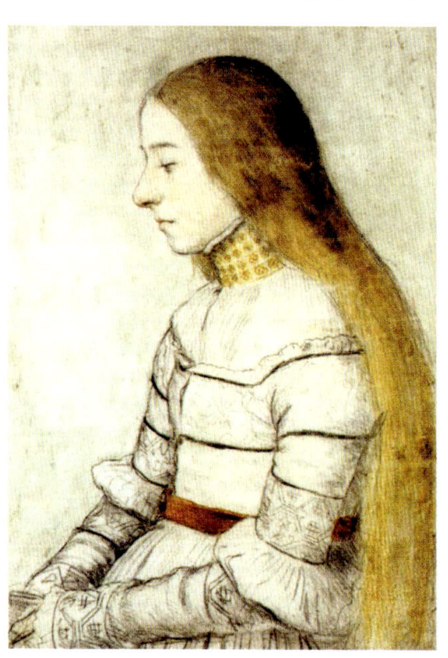

Henry VIII were the property of the king. Holbein may have kept sketchbooks, and accounts of his commissions, but no documentation has been found to date.

DRAWING METHODS

Holbein's early drawings used the method taught by his father, the highly skilled medium of silverpoint. Paper colour and size varied during his career. Early works such as *Portrait Drawing of Anna Meyer*, *c*.1526 (see left), used silverpoint, pen and ink, white heightening, and white and red chalk on a pink prepared paper. In France, Holbein used yellow chalk for the first time. The drawing *Jeanne de Boulogne, duchess of Berry*, 1523–24, is in black, yellow, and coloured chalk on paper (see page 132). In later drawings Holbein used many more colours, as in his preliminary sketch of *John Colet*, *c*.1535, employing black chalk, red chalk, brown chalk, white chalk, pen and ink, brush and ink, and metalpoint on pink-prepared paper (see page 201).

Other tools and mediums were used, depending on the subject, for example for altarpieces, Holbein favoured a reed pen and brush with a thin wash of black carbon ink, using cross-hatching for shading and detail. For the set of highly-finished drawings created for the Great Council Chamber in Basel, 1521–22, including The *Humiliation of Valerian by Shapur I, Edessa, 259*AD (see page 137), he used pen and ink over a preliminary chalk drawing, grey wash,

and watercolour. Holbein's dexterity in changing drawing mediums to suit individual works is revealed in the range of works that remain extant.

FROM DRAWING TO PORTRAIT

For portraiture, Holbein would make a preliminary drawing with the sitter present. He often favoured the sitter looking to their right, in a three-quarter profile, using a half-length composition. *Portrait of William Warham*, *c*.1527 (below), is typical. In the preliminary drawing, in coloured chalks on off-white paper, the size of Warham's head and shoulders matched the finished portrait (page 163). It was traced, probably using a carbon-coated paper between drawing and primed panel, to transfer the image.

Commissioned to portray Christina of Denmark in 1538 (see page 234), Holbein was recommended as 'a man very excellent in taking of physionamies' [sic]. The sitting took three hours. Many drawings would have been made for the near-lifesize portrait, including head,

Below: The preparatory head drawing of William Warham (see also page 163).

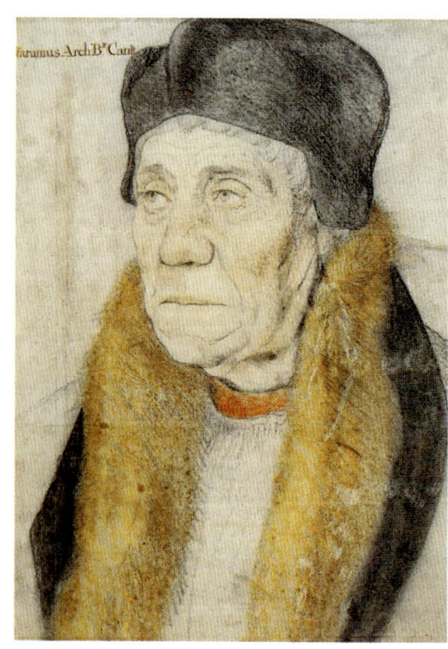

face, hands, and clothing. For full-length portraits, such as *The Ambassadors*, 1533 (see pages 182–83), individual sections were drawn on separate pieces of paper, then assembled and stuck onto a backing paper. This cartoon was pricked out – pounced – to transfer one image to another surface – that is, pinned to the primed panel, brushed over with charcoal dust or dark chalk, to leave an exact-size underdrawing imprint, then removed, to be ready for painting. Holbein's process then followed the Netherlandish technique, layering in oils.

Similarly, for the mural in the Privy Chamber at Whitehall in 1536–37, Holbein's preparatory cartoons (see right) were created in black ink and watercolour on several sheets of paper, and the cut-out faces and figures were then pasted on to a larger backing paper. The work was then pricked out, ready for transfer to the prepared wall. The cartoon is exactly the same size as the finished painting and was used to transfer Holbein's design to its intended position on the palace wall. During the painting process Holbein changed the direction of Henry VIII's face, from looking to the right in the preliminary sketch, to looking forward in the finished portrait. The cartoon for the right-hand side of the painting is lost.

EXPERIMENTAL TECHNIQUE

Holbein's method primarily followed Netherlandish practice (see pages 12–13). Usually painting onto a primed white ground, and following the outlines of the transferred drawing, features were added with minute precision, and miniscule details of clothing textures. The layers of transparent oil glazes allowed light to penetrate and reflect back through the paint colour, creating light and shadow, and a sense of realism. Holbein experimented, using oil and gold on paper, to great effect, as in the early *Portrait of Benedikt von Hertenstein*, 1517 (see page 102) and later *Self-Portrait* 1542/43 (see page 251), in coloured chalk, pen and gold.

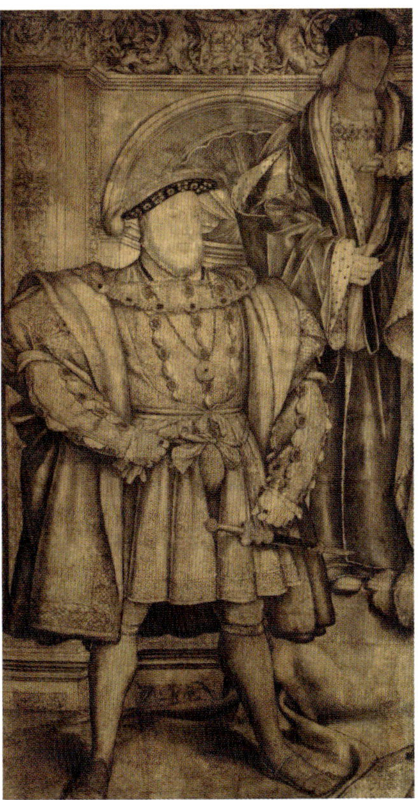

Above: The extant section of preparatory cartoon for the Whitehall mural.

UNDER THE SURFACE

To learn about Holbein's painting techniques, x-radiography – to reveal under-modelling of face and hands, lines and brushstrokes – and infrared reflectography – to detect underdrawings and compositional elements – are methods used. The National Gallery, London, keepers of *Portrait of a Lady with a Squirrel and a Starling*, 1526–28 (see right), revealed changes by Holbein's hand of several elements during the stages of this painting's creation. It included alteration to the sitter's hairline and the sides of the ermine cap she wears. Surprisingly, however, the squirrel she holds was not present in the initial pentimenti, the visible trace of the earlier painting under layers of paint.

PAINT AND PIGMENTS

Holbein mixed his ground pigments with oil, in the Netherlandish method, gradually building up thin layers of paint. It was a usual practice to paint on a primed white background for an effective refractive light through translucent glazes of oil-based ground colour pigments. The tonal layers of oil paint, rich in colour, create luminosity in refractive light. He experimented to achieve the right effect. Bright yellow was a difficult colour to achieve, and Holbein on occasion added powdered gold leaf to yellow ochre to achieve an intense yellow.

Holbein used blue azurite mineral mixed with lead white for the stunningly blue background of the portrait of a lady (below), painted on in two layers. Other paintings, such as his *Portrait of Henry VIII, c.*1537 (page 60), used lapis lazuli ultramarine, the most expensive mineral, from Afghanistan, which produced the richest blue.

In some older paintings the pentimenti underlayers now show through to the surface, altering the finishing layer of pigment, notably in background colours that have changed from rich blue to aquamarine, and with yellowing caused by some oils, such as linseed oil.

Holbein adapted his colour techniques to suit the work. This is evident in the grey flat tones he painted over white ground primer in *Dead Christ in the Tomb*, 1521–22 (see pages 122–23). The grey base was a deep tone on which to apply realistic flesh-coloured pigments for the body. Holbein's brushwork created lifelike textures for the skin, the beard, and bloodstained-red nail holes.

Below: Portrait of a Lady with a Squirrel and a Starling (see also page 164).

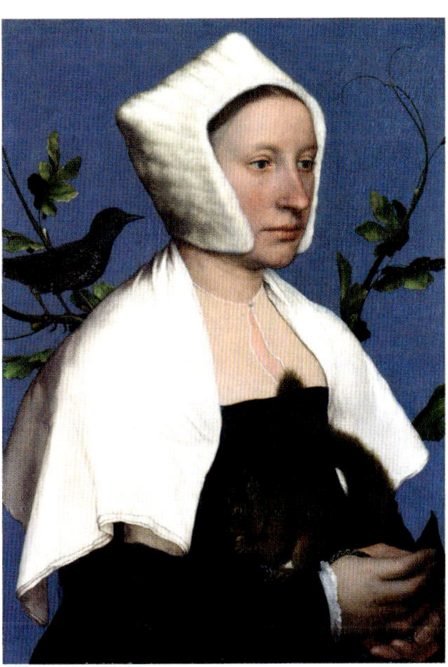

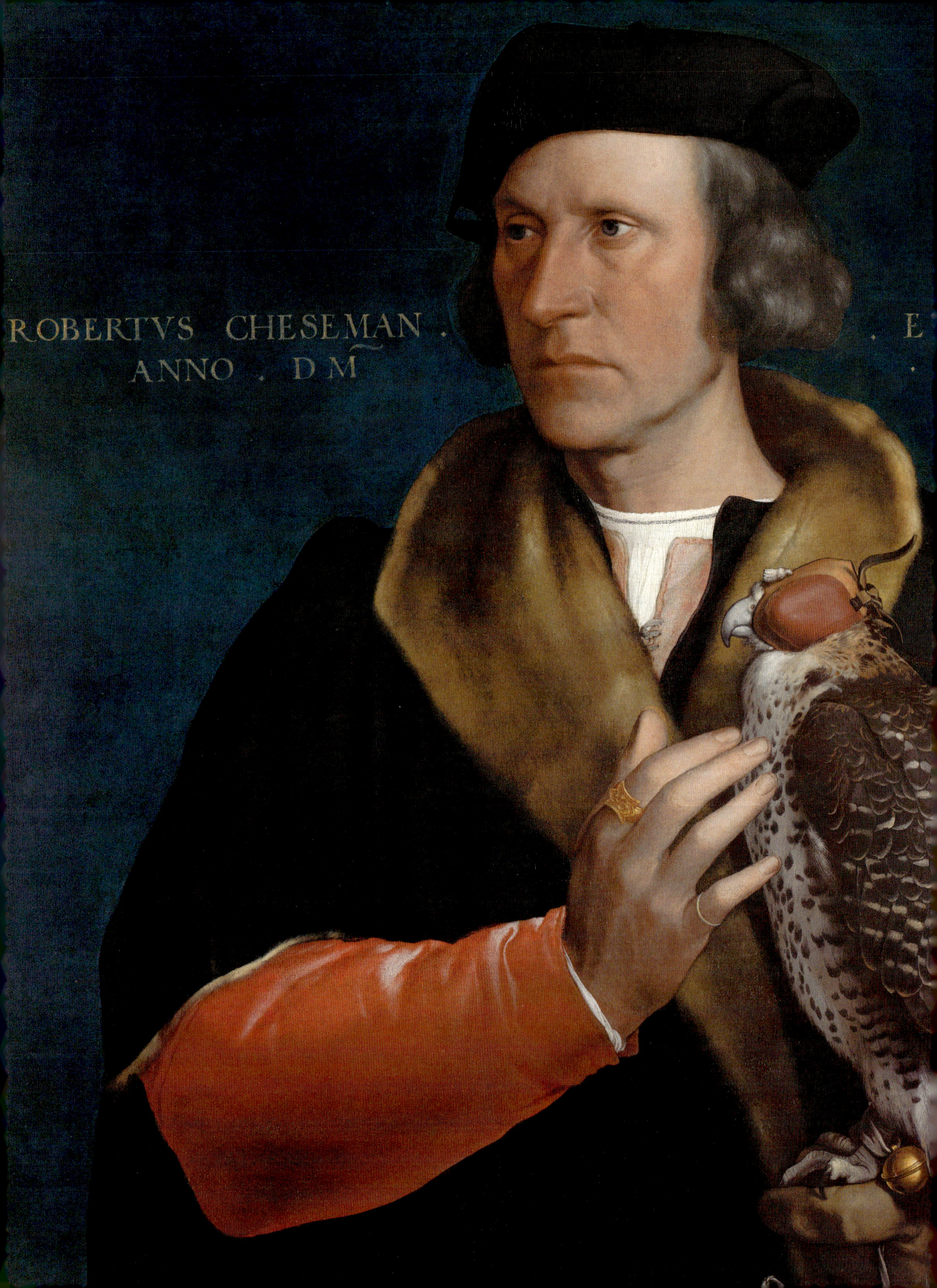

ROBERTVS CHESEMAN .
ANNO . DM̃
E

THE GALLERY

Superb portraiture and religious works, scene painting on a large scale, intricate designs for woodcuts, glass, silver and jewellery, all highlight how versatile the work of Hans Holbein the Younger was. Near-nothing is known of his character but he was clearly intuitive to the demands of his various patrons, in Germany, Switzerland and England. The solid foundation of early training with his father Hans Holbein the Elder in the Augsburg family workshop led him ultimately to the prestigious position of Painter to King Henry VIII.

Left: Portrait of Robert Cheseman holding a Falcon, *1533, by Holbein the Younger, oil on panel, 58.8 x 62.8cm (23.1 x 24.7in), Mauritshuis, The Hague, The Netherlands. The printed letters on the wall behind state: 'Cheseman, aged 48, chief falconer to Henry VIII' ('ROBERTVS CHESEMAN . ÆTATIS . SVUÆ . XLVIII . / ANNO . DM . M . D . XXXIII'.)

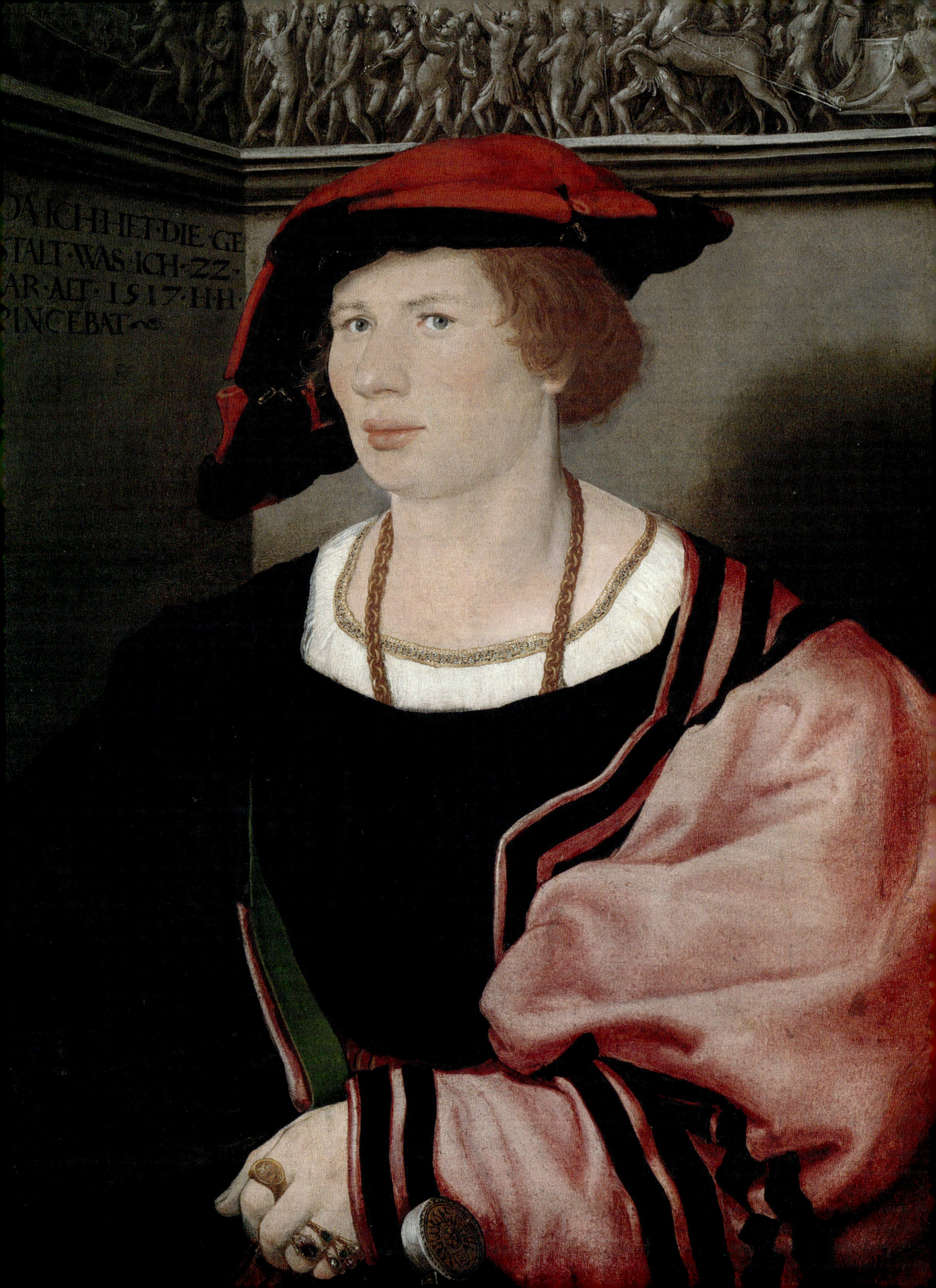

DA·ICH·HET·DIE·GE
STALT·WAS·ICH·ZZ·
AR·ALT·1517·HH·
PINGEBAT

BASEL
1515–1526

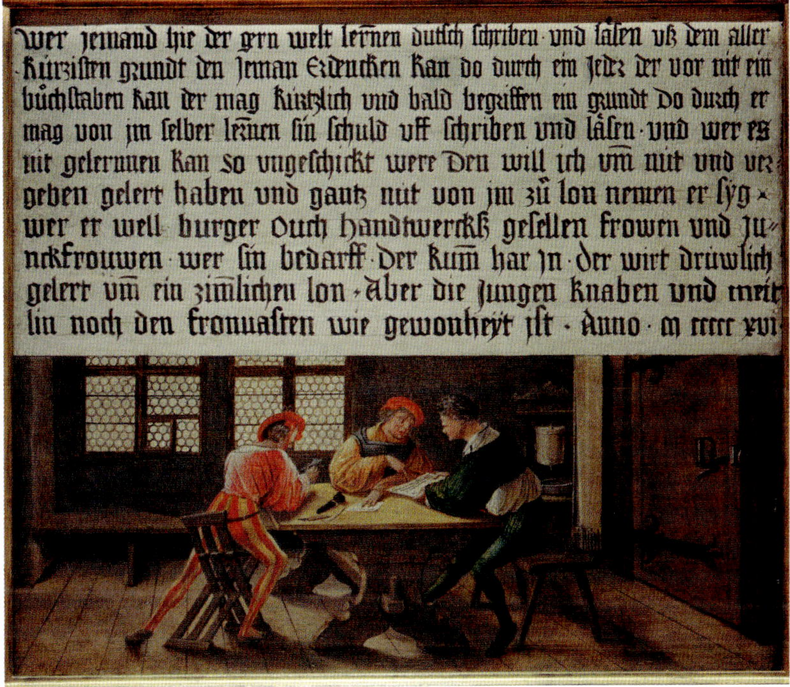

The initial period of Holbein's professional life in Basel included outstanding portraiture, such as *Portrait of Benedikt von Hertenstein*, 1517, and a remarkable portrayal of *Dead Christ in the Tomb*, 1521–22; a design for the façade decorations of the Zum Tanz house, and mural designs for the council chamber of the new town hall. He produced a huge number of woodcuts, including the *Dance of Death* series, and designs for stained glass windows, buildings and signs. In 1526 he left Basel to explore opportunities in London.

Above: Signboard for a Schoolmaster c.1516, oil on wood, 55.5 x 56.5cm (21.8 x 22.2in), Kunstmuseum, Basel. The signboard was created for a schoolmaster Oswald Myconius, a friend of Erasmus. The painted decoration of the other side of the board is attributed to Ambrosius Holbein.

Left: Portrait of Benedikt von Hertenstein, 1517, oil and gold on paper, laid down on wood, 52.4 x 38.1cm (20.6 x 15in), Metropolitan Museum of Art, New York, NY, USA. Benedikt von Hertenstein (c.1495–1522) was the eldest son of Jakob von Hertenstein, the mayor of Lucerne, and second wife, Anna Mangold. Benedikt studied at the University of Basel. In 1517 he became a member of the Great Council of Lucerne, which may have motivated this early commission for Holbein. Hertenstein died just five years later, at the battle of Bicocca in Lombardy on April 27th 1522 while serving with Swiss mercenaries.

Praise of Folly written by Desiderius Erasmus in 1509; margin drawings by Hans Holbein the Younger and Ambrosius Holbein in 1515, in pen and black ink, and black ink oxidised to brown, Kunstmuseum (excepting no.1), Basel, Switzerland

Erasmus wrote *Praise of Folly* in 1509 while in England staying with Thomas More, and it was first published in Paris in June 1511. Erasmus made changes to the second edition, printed by Froben in Basel in 1515. The Holbein brothers drew 82 marginal

sketches in a personal copy owned by classical scholar Oswald Myconius (1488–1552), a Swiss protestant theologian and friend of Erasmus. Myconius planned to show the result to the book's author. Many of the sketches are humorous, and

reveal decorative flair and quick wit. They are the first extant works by the two brothers. Of the examples shown here, all are identified as being by Hans except no. 43 and no.55 by Ambrosius.

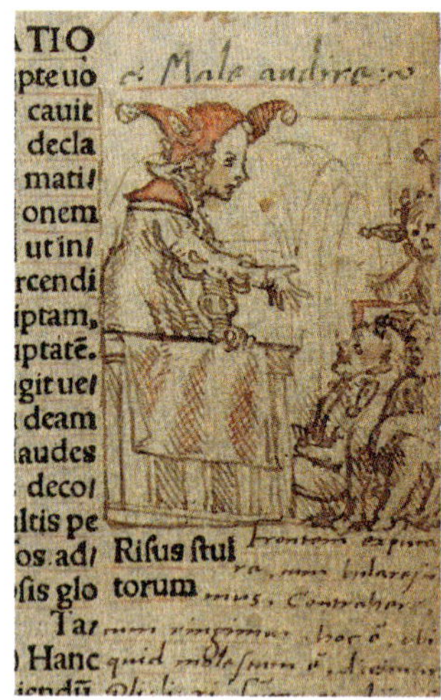

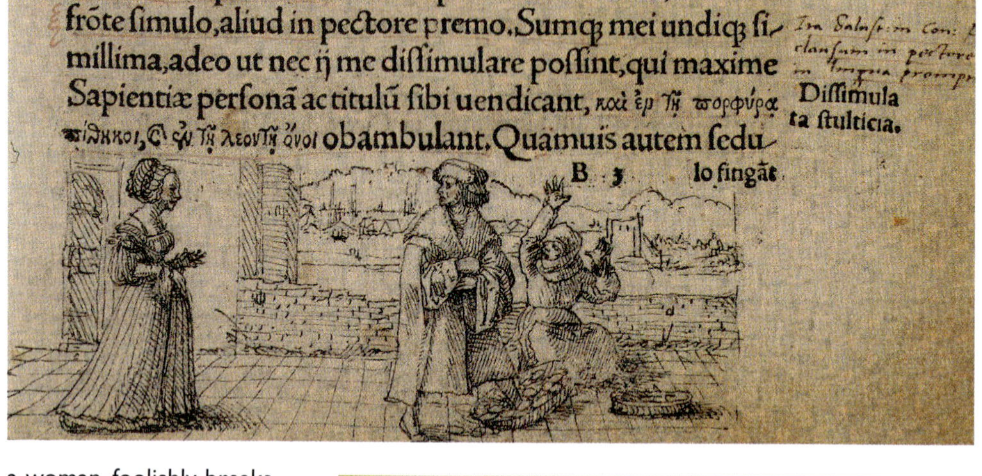

Above left: *Folly in the Pulpit* (no.1), Folly wears a 'fool's cap' to preach from the pulpit to a congregation, similarly attired. She gestures to the crowd with her right hand. Above right: *A Scholar Treads on a Basket of Eggs* (no.3), an educated man, his head turned by

a woman, foolishly breaks eggs. Right: *Sertorius and the Example of Horses* (no.15), demonstrates that strong enemies can be defeated, one by one, showing that you can pull hairs from a horse's tail singly but not the whole tail in one pull.

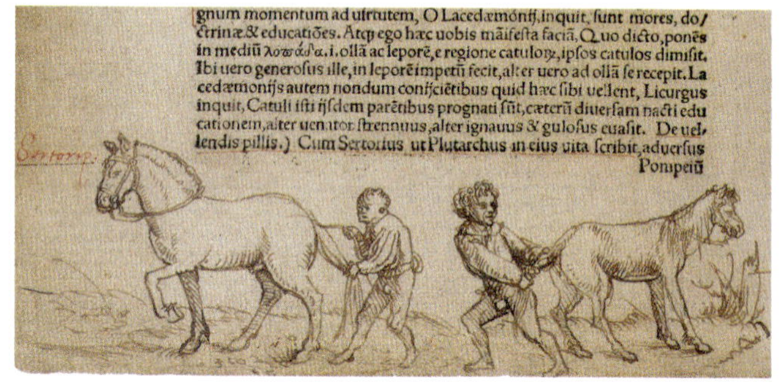

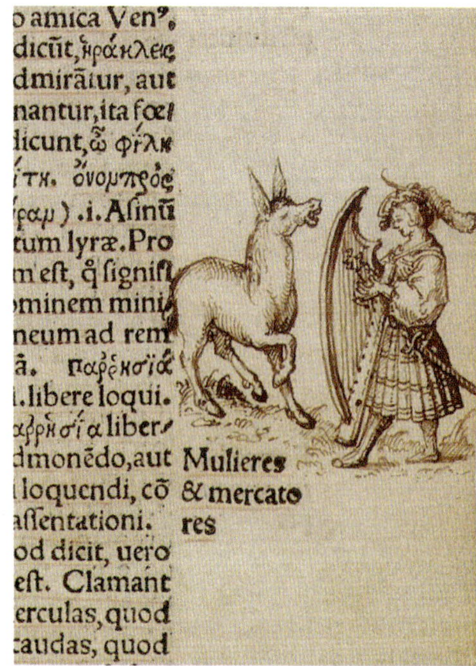

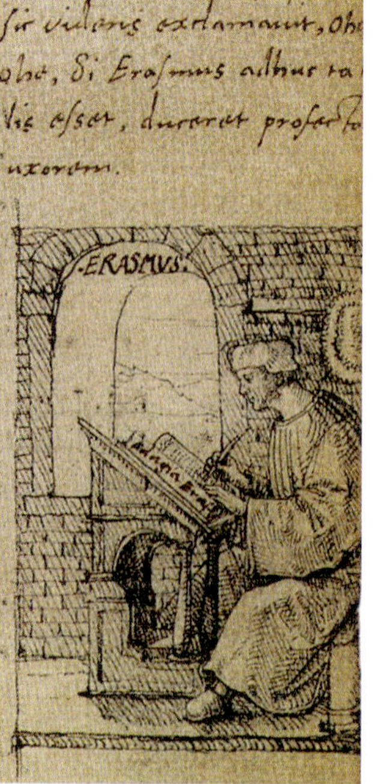

Far left: *A Mule Sings to the Accompaniment of a Harp* (no.55), referring to a Greek proverb of a donkey at the lyre, illustrating the folly of people working in a profession that is beyond them.

Left: *Erasmus in his Study* (no.64); the handwritten text above the illustration is thought to be by Myconius, '… Oh, if Erasmus still looked like that, he would certainly take a wife.'

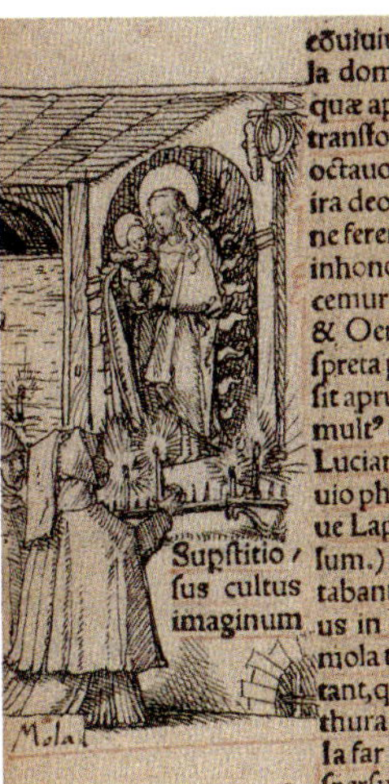
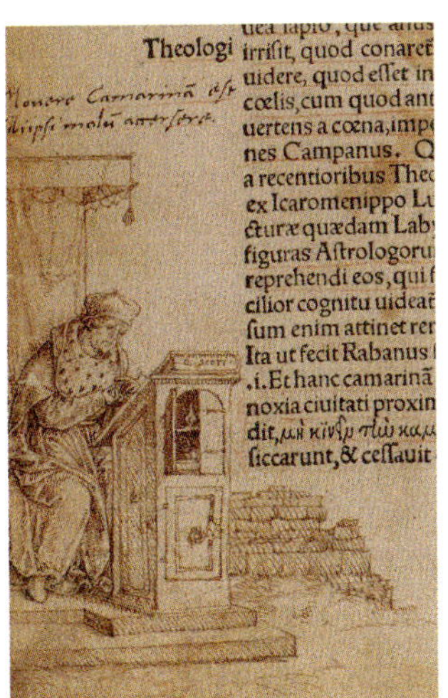
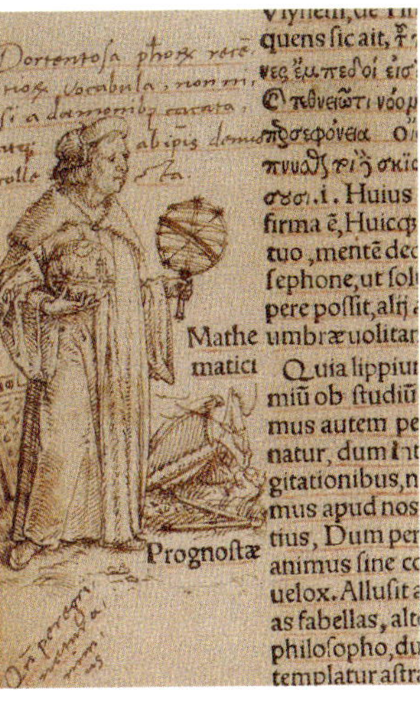
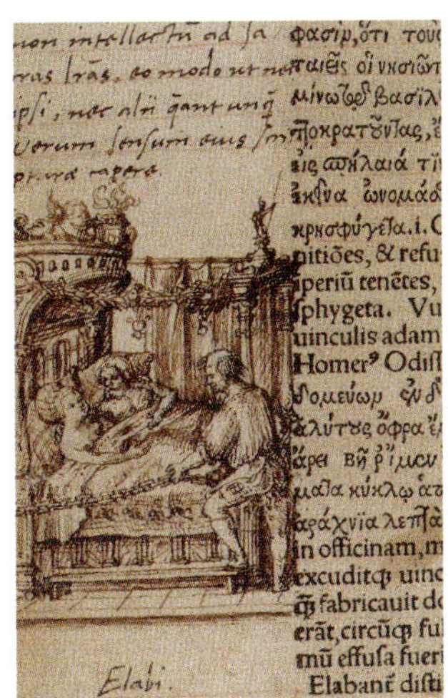

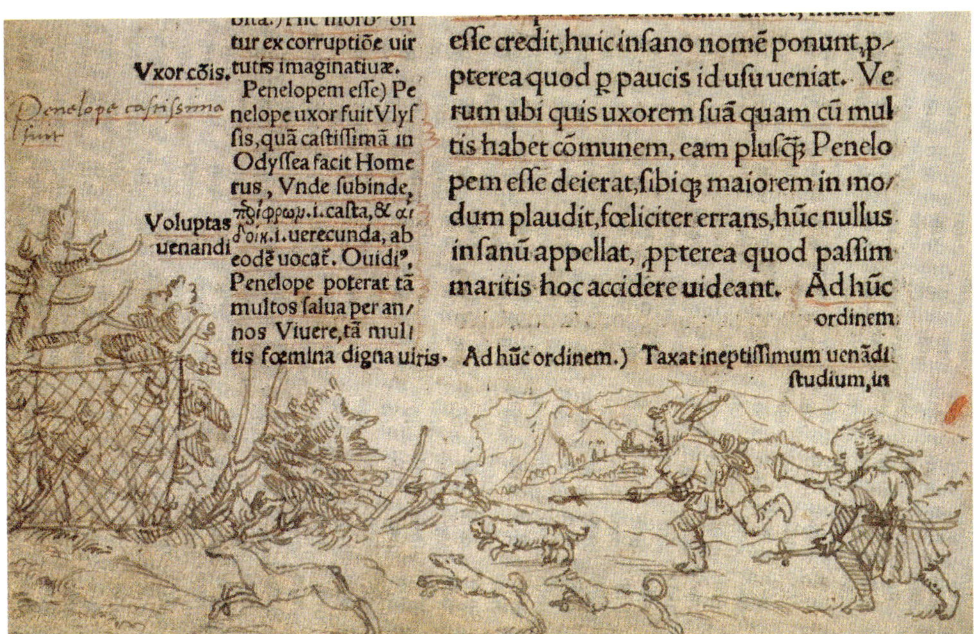

Above, left to right: *Two Women Dedicating Candles* (no.54), the implication that it is better to do good works than burn candles to an image. *A Mathematical Scholar* (no.41) who aims to baffle people with scientific phenomena. *A Theologian Reads…* (no.42) shows a cleric studying medieval philosopher John Duns Scotus 1266–1308). *Mars and Venus Caught in Bed by Vulcan* (no.43), who chains up the adulterers.

Above: *Deer Hunting* (no.24); the marginal note says 'Voluptas venandi' ('The joy of hunting'). Holbein depicts the hunters in fools' caps driving a deer toward a trap-net where a hunter lies in wait to kill.

Right: *Folly Steps Down From the Pulpit* (no.82). In the last sketch, Folly steps down from the pulpit (seen in no.1) and takes leave of her captivated audience: '…farewell, clap your hands, live and drink lustily, my most excellent disciples of Folly'.

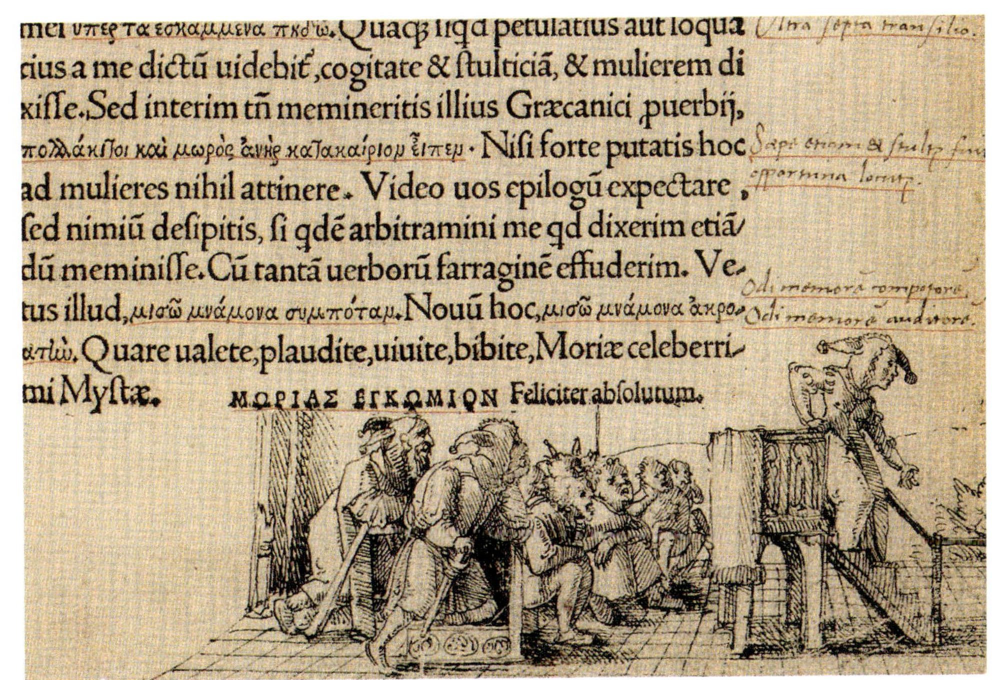

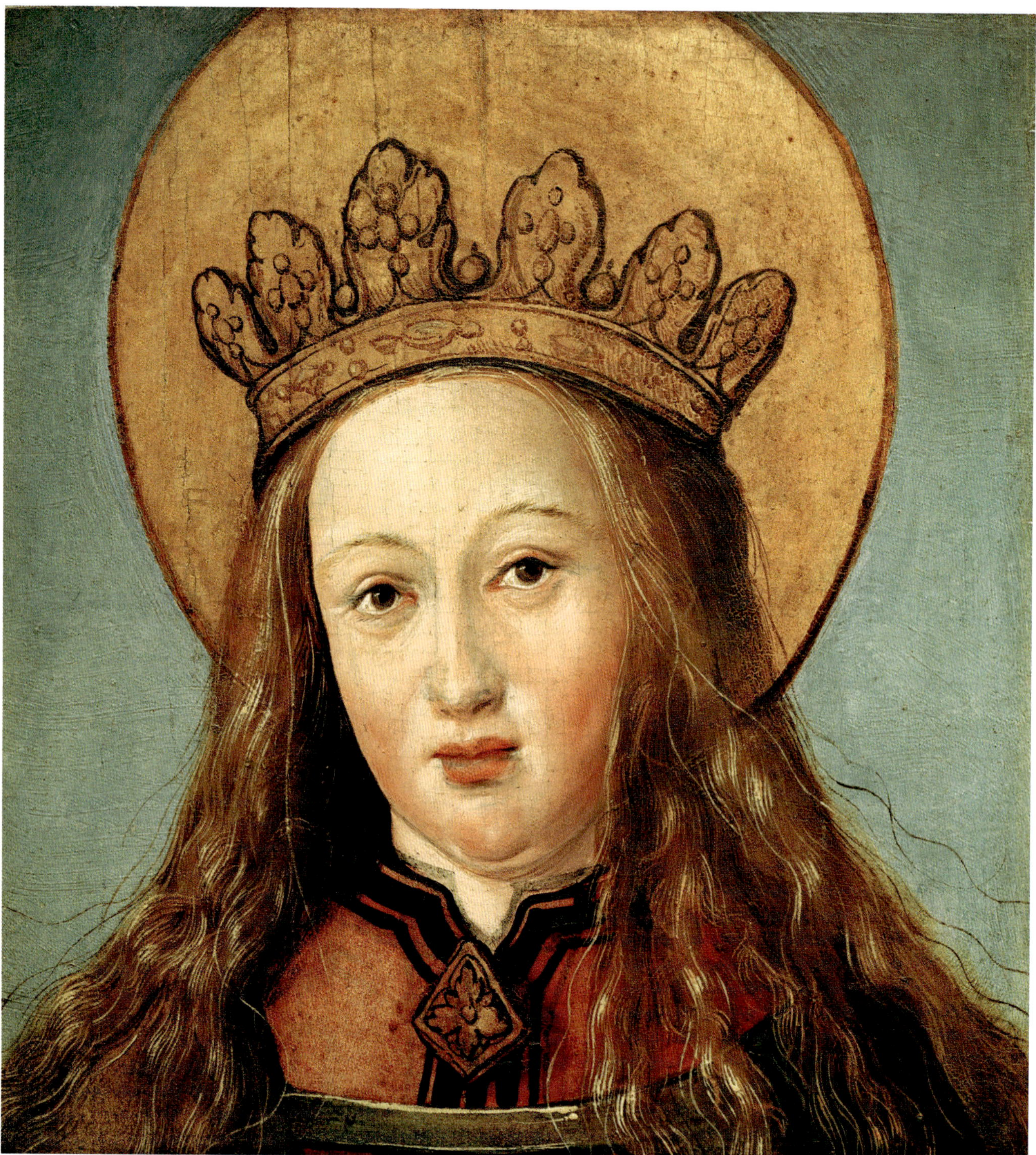

Head of a Female Saint, c.1515, oil on wood cut down, thinned and cradled, 23.5 x 22cm (9.25 x 8.6in), Kunstmuseum, Basel, Switzerland

This small-size work – cut out, or sawn from a larger panel – by Holbein the Younger was possibly painted in his father's workshop in Augsburg, noted for religious art. Its origin remains unknown. The vibrantly coloured head and shoulders of a female saint shares parallels with a male *Head of a Saint*, c.1515, opposite.

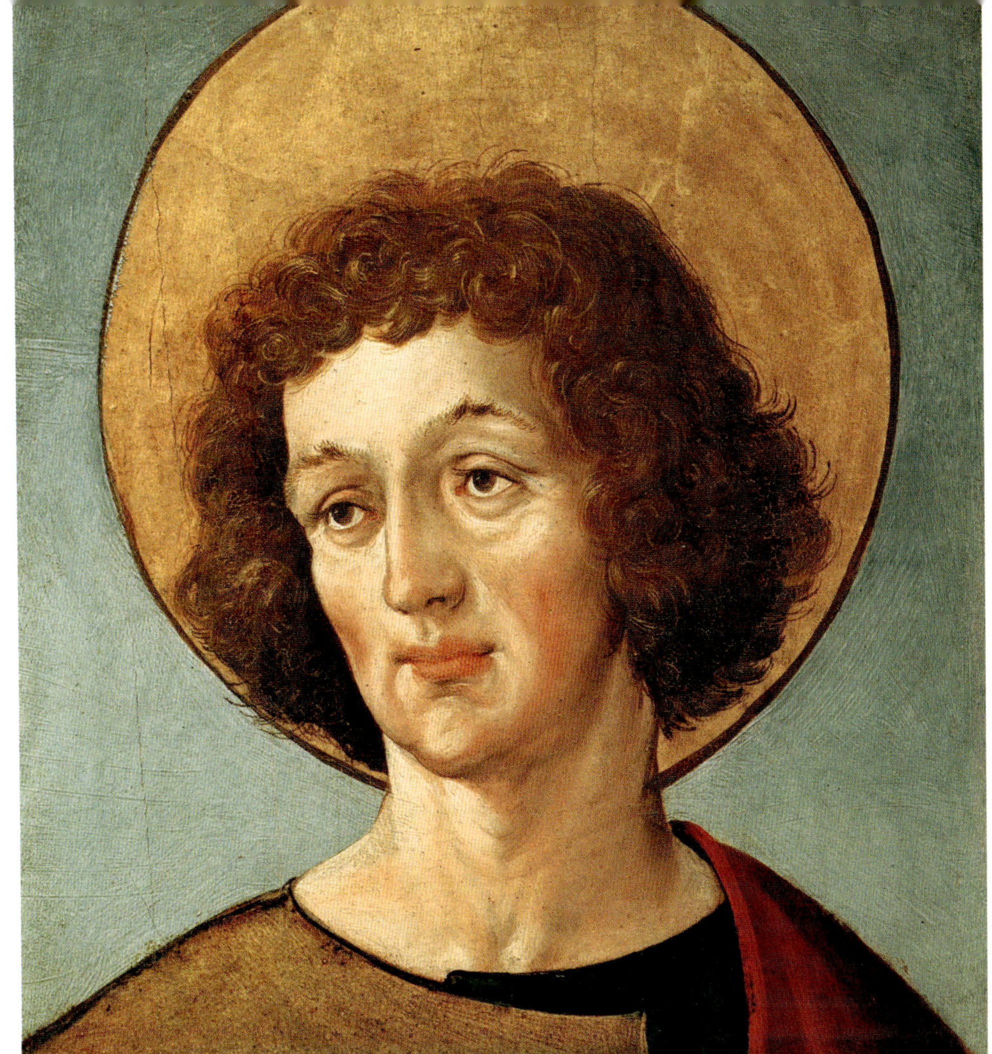

Head of a Male Saint, c.1515, oil on wood cut down, thinned and cradled, 23.5 x 22cm (9.25 x 8.6in), Kunstmuseum, Basel, Switzerland

This cut-down work from a larger painting, painted in oils on spruce wood, is a companion work to *Head of a Female Saint, c.1515* (opposite). Both works show Holbein's dexterity with colour, capturing human character in the similar panels.

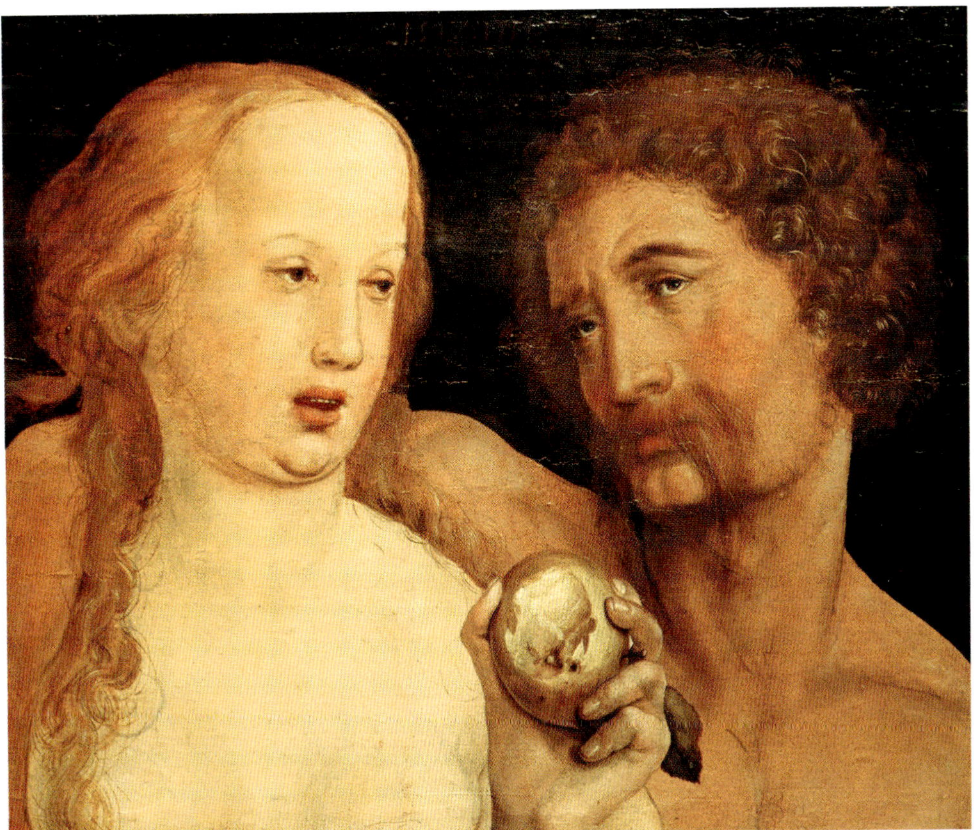

Adam and Eve, c. 1517, paper on wood panel (possibly cut down), 30 x 35.5cm (11.8 x 14in), Kunstmuseum, Basel, Switzerland

A head and shoulders portrayal of biblical Adam and Eve, Earth's first man and woman. Eve clutches an apple, the source of knowledge from the Tree of Good and Evil in the Garden of Eden. Holbein captures the moment that Eve tastes the forbidden fruit. The model for Eve is similar in facial character to *Head of a Female Saint* (opposite) This is also possibly part of a much larger work.

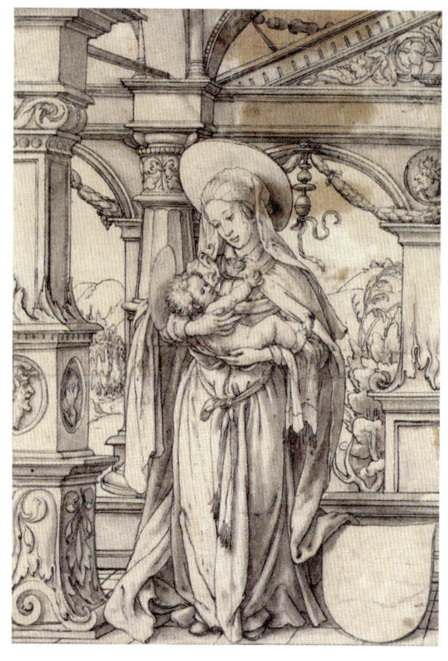 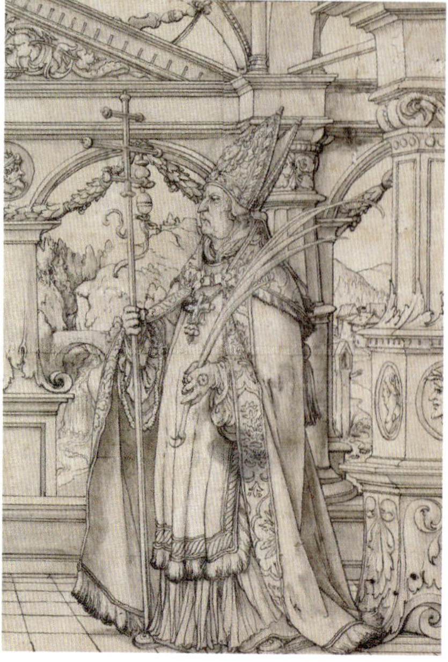 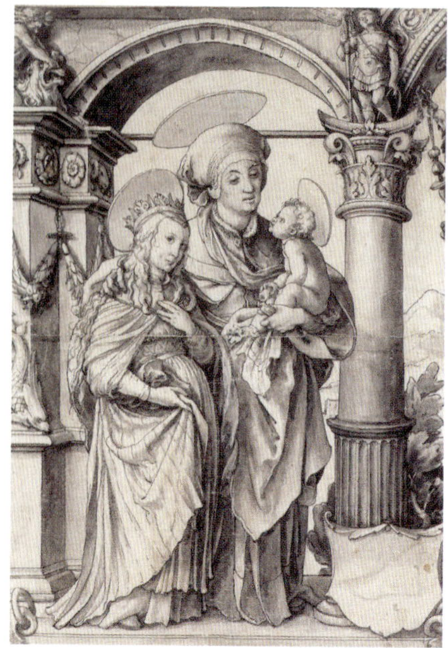

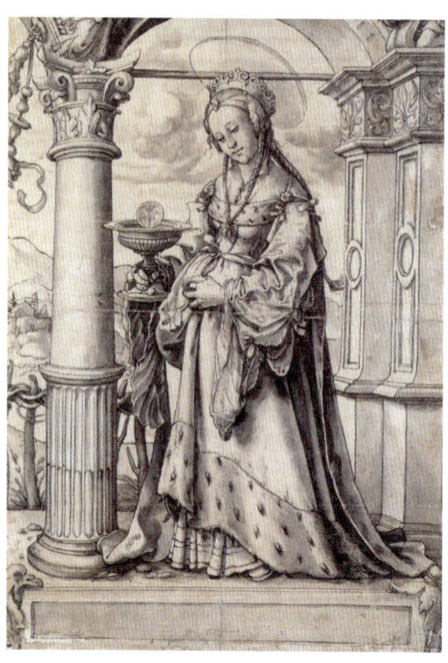 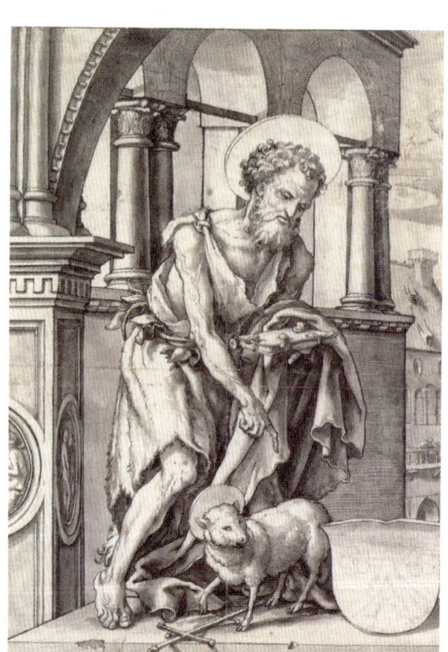 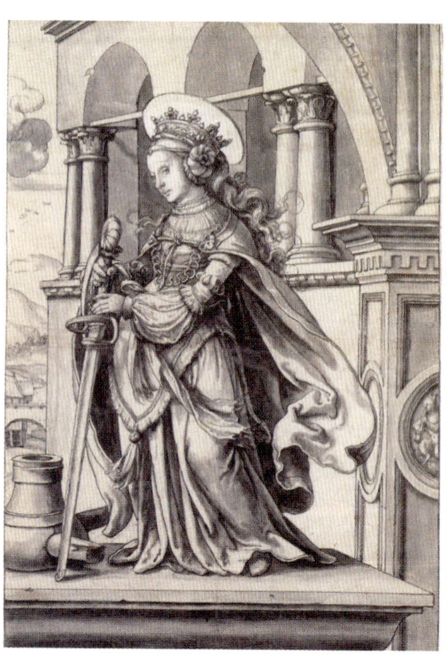

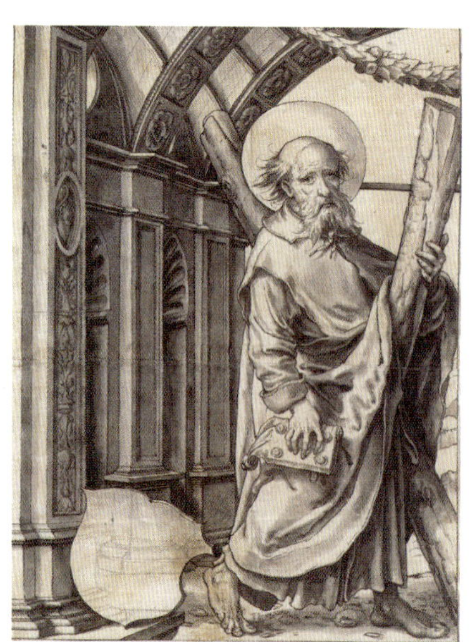 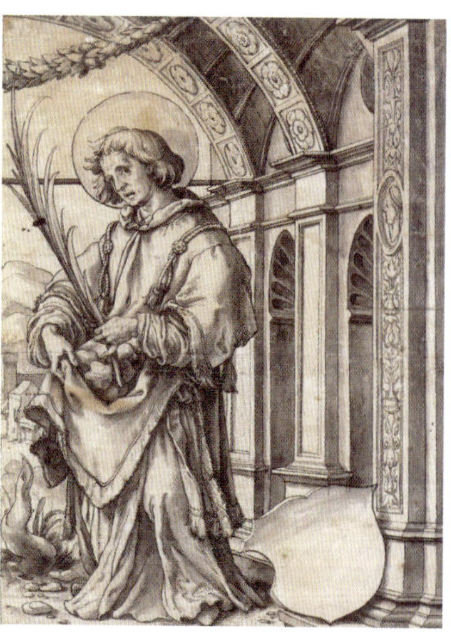

Designs for stained glass windows, depicting (from top left) *Virgin and Child; St Pantalus; St Anne with the Virgin and Child; St Barbara; St John the Baptist; St Catherine of Alexandria; St Andrew;* and *St Stephen. c.*1519–22, pen and black ink over chalk drawings, grey-brown wash, on paper with slight variations in size up to 60.5 x 37.3cm (23.8 x 14.68in), Kunstmuseum, Basel

This sequence illustrates Holbein's intention to unite four pairings of saints through their architectural portico settings, and mirror images, to complement their destined location (possibly a cloister of Basel cathedral).

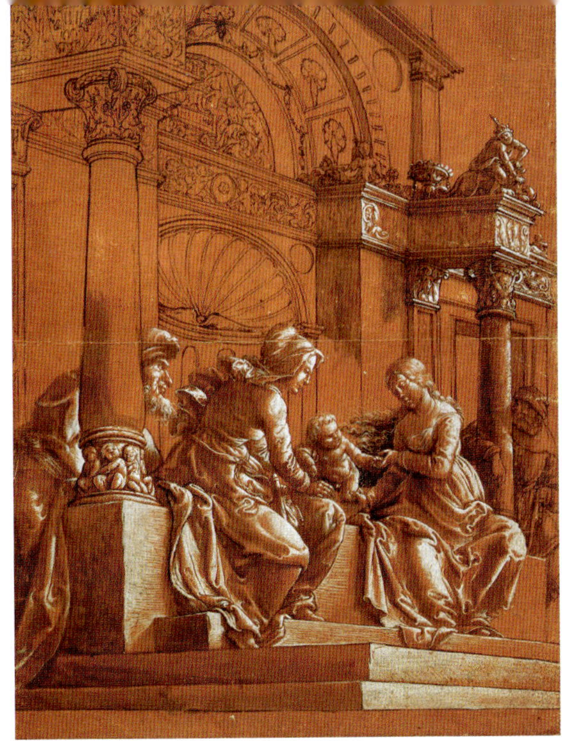

The Holy Family, 1519 pen and black ink on reddish-brown primed paper, grey washed and heightened with white, 42.7 x 30.8cm (16.8 x 12in) Kunstmuseum, Basel, Switzerland

Holbein places the observer at the lower edge of the steps, as if walking toward where Mary is seated, holding the Christ child. The figure of Joachim, at left on the upper level behind a column, leads the viewer toward the scene. Holbein displayed his name 'hans hol' on a small tablet in the tympanum (the vertical recessed triangular space forming the centre of a pediment).

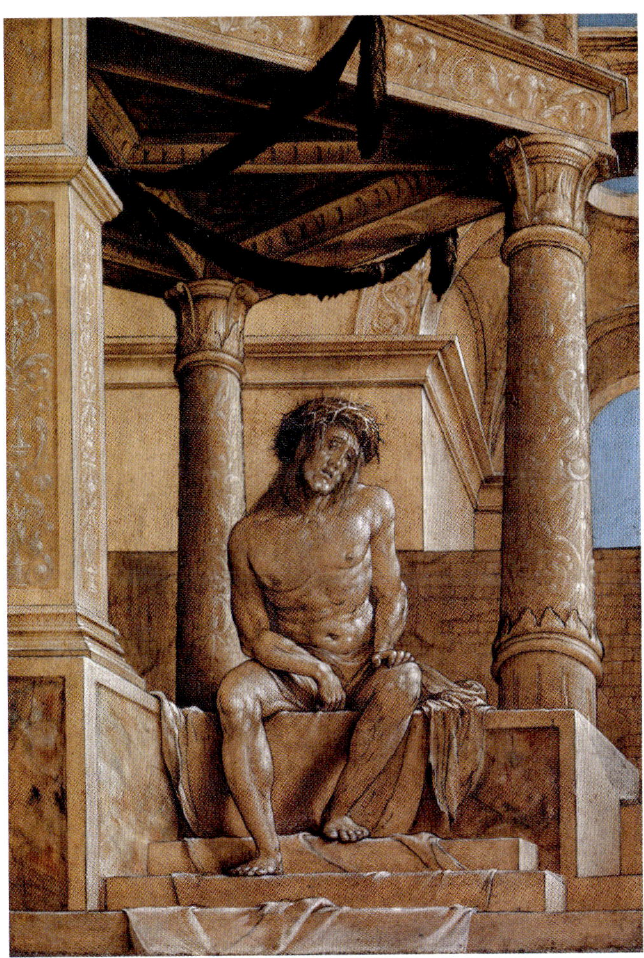

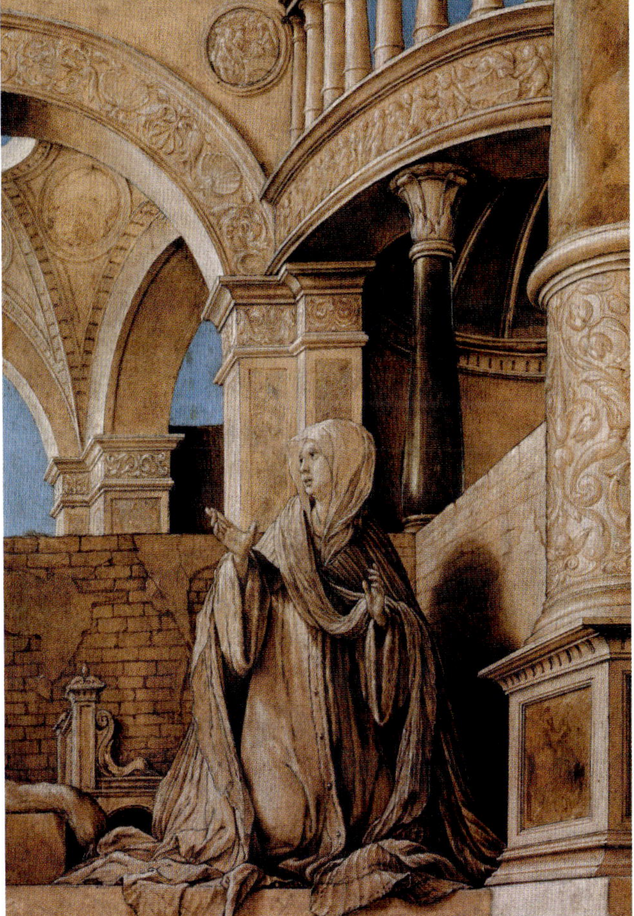

Above left and right: *Christ as the Man of Sorrows with the Virgin Mary*, 1518–19, oil on lime wood, two panels, each 29 x 19.5 x 0.4–0.6cm (11.4 x 7.6 x 0.15–0.2in), Kunstmuseum, Basel

In the left panel, the near-defeated figure of Jesus Christ is seated. In the right panel, the standing figure of the Virgin Mary, grieving, looks across to her son. Christ and the Virgin are placed within the same architectural setting and mirror imaging, which unites them in time and place. As the Man of Sorrows, Christ wears the Crown of Thorns, one of the instruments of the Passion, following his arrest after betrayal by Judas Iscariot.

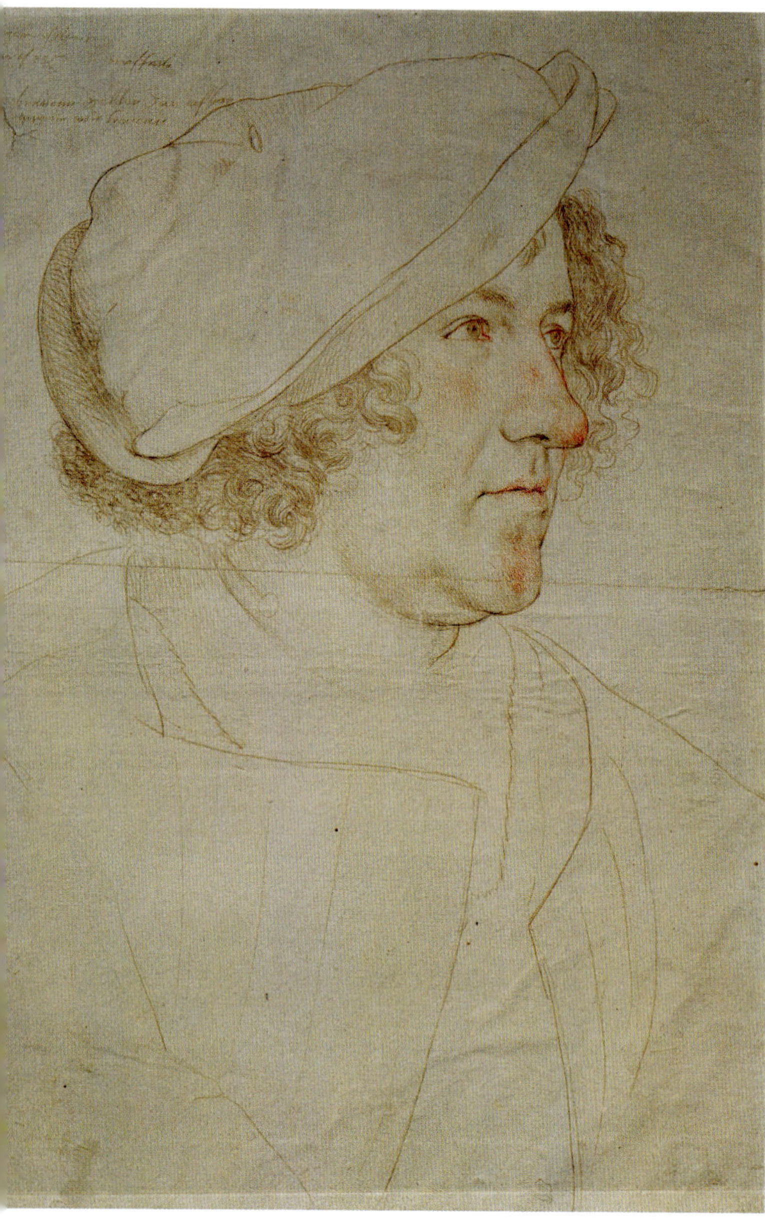

Portrait study of the Dorothea Kannengiesser c.1516, silverpoint, red chalk and black chalk on paper, 28.6 x 20.1cm (11.25 x 7.9in), Kunstmuseum, Basel, Switzerland

On paper, in silverpoint and red and black chalk, the delicate features of Dorothea, second wife of Jakob Meyer zum Hasen, are captured by Holbein in his preparatory study for the diptych painting.

Portrait study of Jakob Meyer zum Hasen, 1516, silverpoint and red chalk on paper with white, 28.1 x 19cm (11 x 7.5in), Kunstmuseum, Basel, Switzerland

A study for Holbein's diptych of Mayor Jakob Meyer zum Hasen. The newly appointed mayor of Basel commissioned a double portrait of himself and his wife, to celebrate his prestigious position as representative of the prosperous city of Basel. In Holbein's important first portrait commission, he carefully outlined Mayer's features. In the top left corner of the drawing he added notes about colours for the painting.

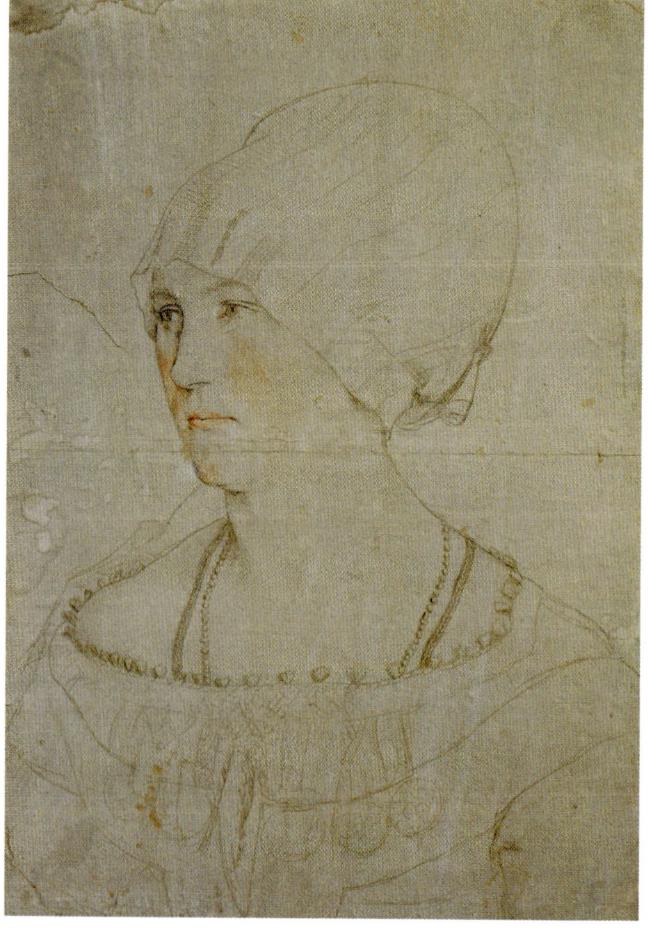

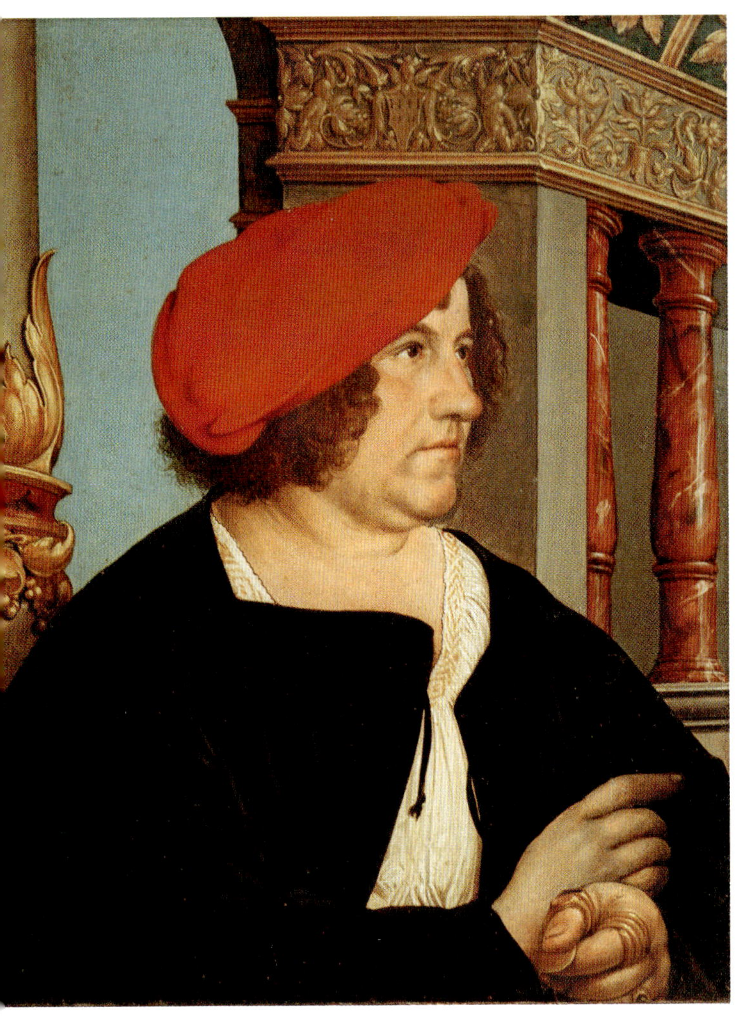

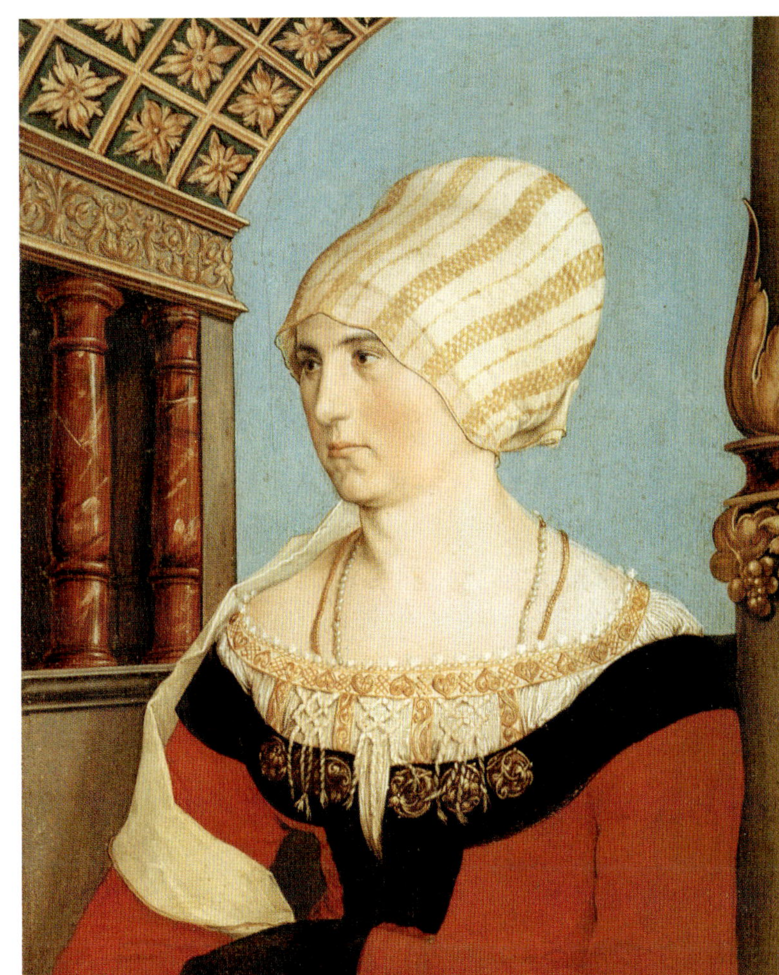

Portrait diptych of Jakob zum Hasen and his wife Dorothea Kannengiesser, 1516, tempera on panels, each 38.5 x 31cm (15.1 x 12.2in), Kunstmuseum, Basel

Mayor Meyer and his wife Dorothea face each other in separate 'companion' portraits, intended to be hung together as a diptych. The sitters, fresh-faced with reddish cheeks, look toward the space their spouse occupies, away from the spectator. One can see in this early work that Holbein had researched other pendant portraits created by high-calibre artists from Augsburg, like Hans Burgkmair the Elder. a contemporary to Holbein the Elder, and Quinten Massys, whom he met in Antwerp.

Meyer Family Coat of Arms, tempera on panel, 38.5 x 31cm (15.1 x 12.2in), Kunstmuseum, Basel, Switzerland

On reverse of the diptych, on the outer side of the portrait of Meyer, the Coat of Arms of the Meyer family is depicted. This is a later addition possibly not painted by Holbein.

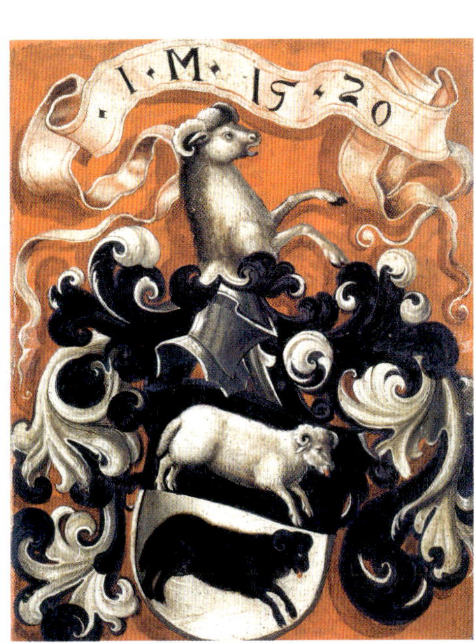

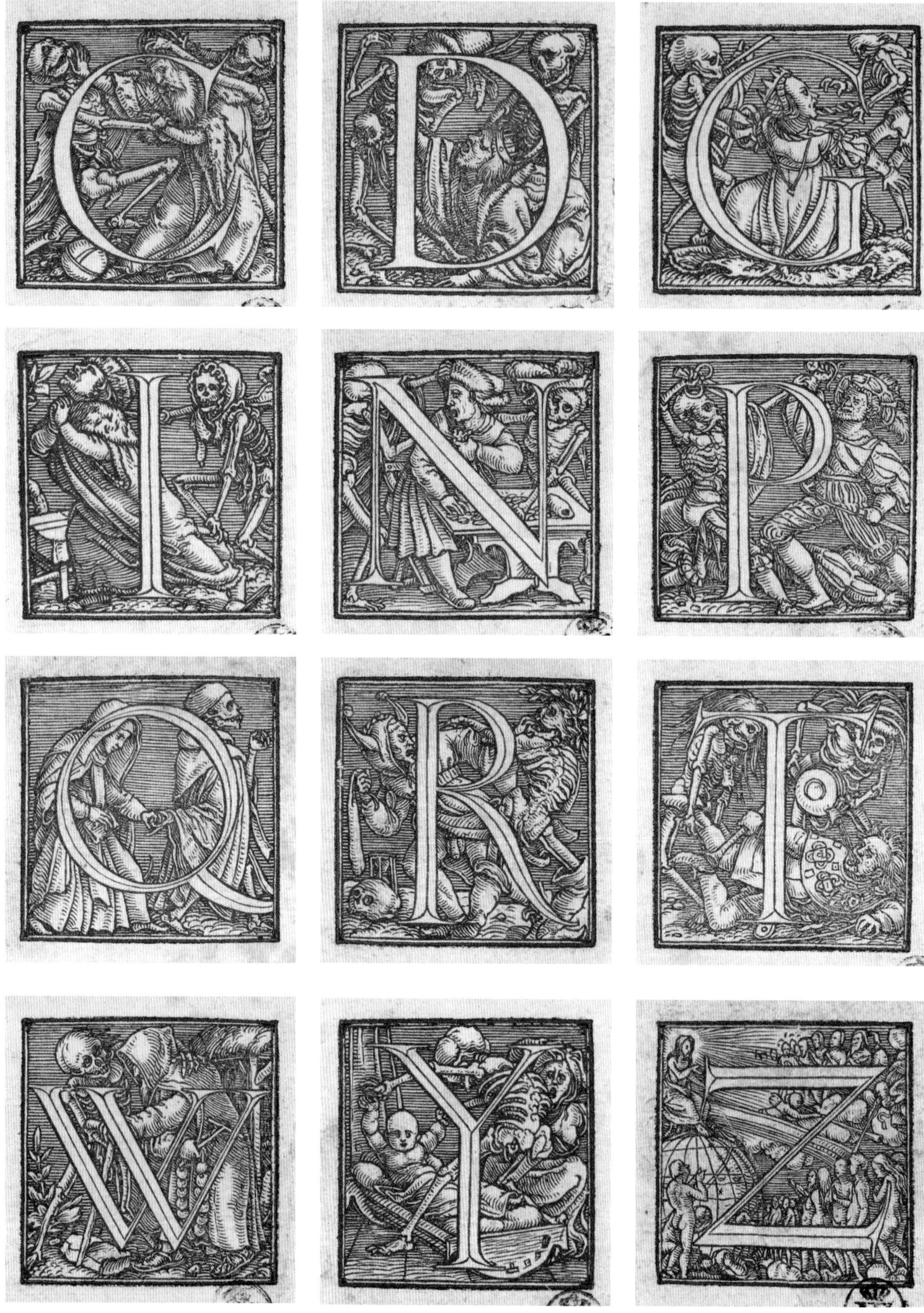

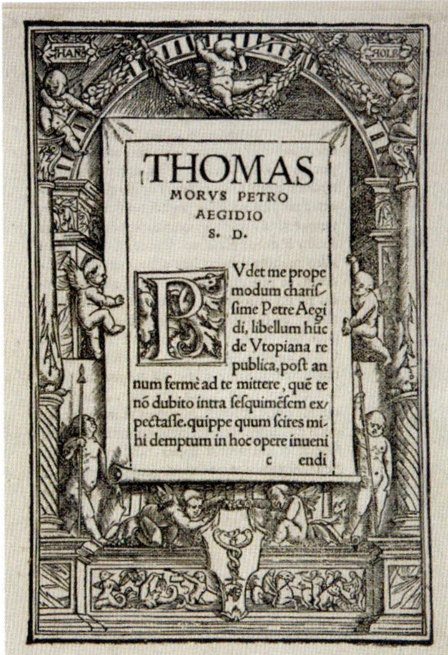

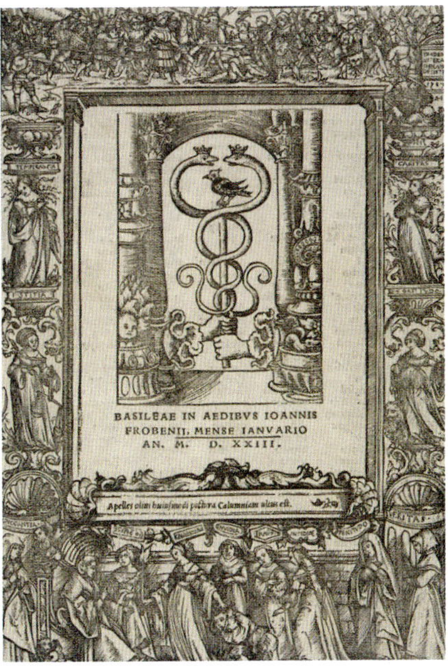

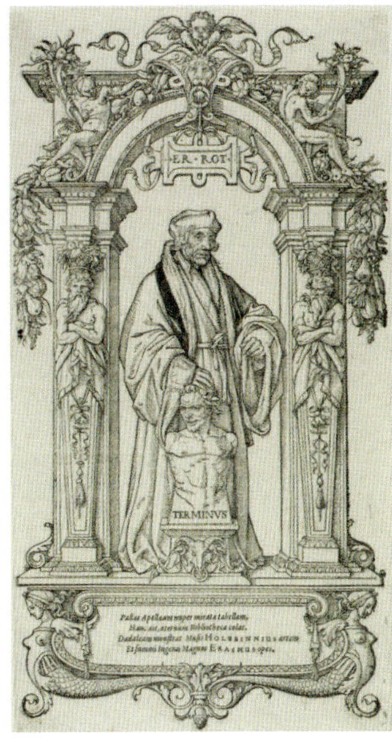

Above: The title page of *Utopia*, by Thomas More, woodcut by Holbein the Younger

Above: The printer's mark of Johann Froben, from the 1518 third edition of *Utopia* by Sir Thomas More, woodcut

Above: *Erasmus with the deity of the terminal, Terminus,* 1535, woodcut

Used for earlier Froben publications in 1516–7, and reused for the publication of this third edition of *Utopia*, Holbein's border is signed top left and right, 'HANS HOLB' in cartouches.

Holbein designed the printer's mark for publisher Johann Froben, showing two hands holding the caduceus – a symbolic staff entwined by two serpents with a bird perched on top.

Verses by Gilbertus Cognatus, secretary to Erasmus: 'Corporis effigiem si quis non uidit Erasmi, Hanc scite ad uiuum picta tabella dabit.' ('If anyone has not seen the shape of the body of Erasmus, it is to be found in this skilfully portrayed panel.')

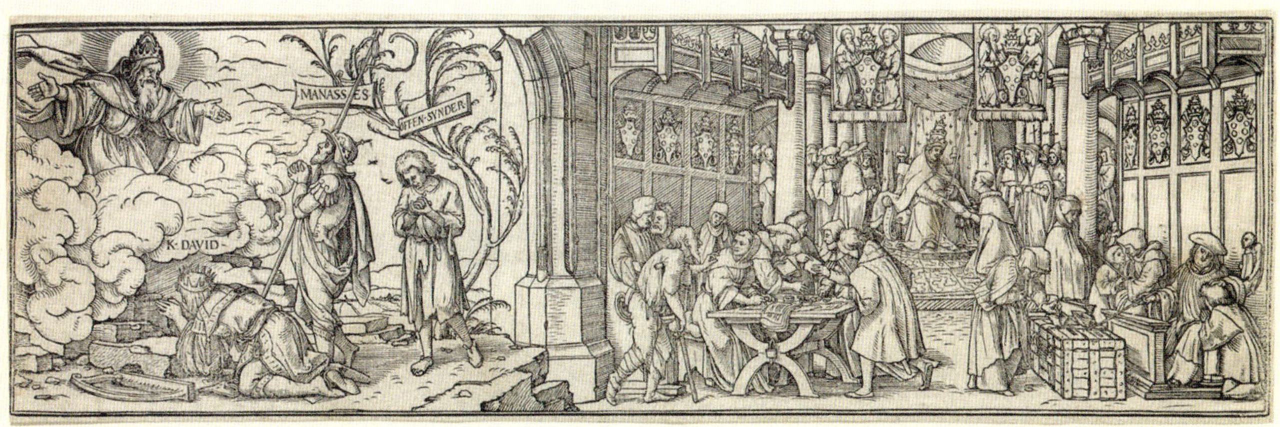

Left: *Dance of Death Alphabet*

Twelve letters from the 'Dance of Death' series of twenty-four woodcuts. Holbein created a number of similar alphabets on the theme. It is thought that he drew his final designs directly on to each small woodblock. The woodcutting was undertaken by Hans Lützelburger, the finest craftsman of block-cutting at this time. It is likely that he and Holbein created the alphabet with the idea of selling them as illustrations; the publisher Froben chose the alphabet to illustrate More's Basel editions of *Utopia*.

Above: *Selling of Indulgence, c.*1524, attributed to Hans Holbein the Younger

A woodcut with a Reformation message, depicting Pope Clement VII as a seller of indulgences.

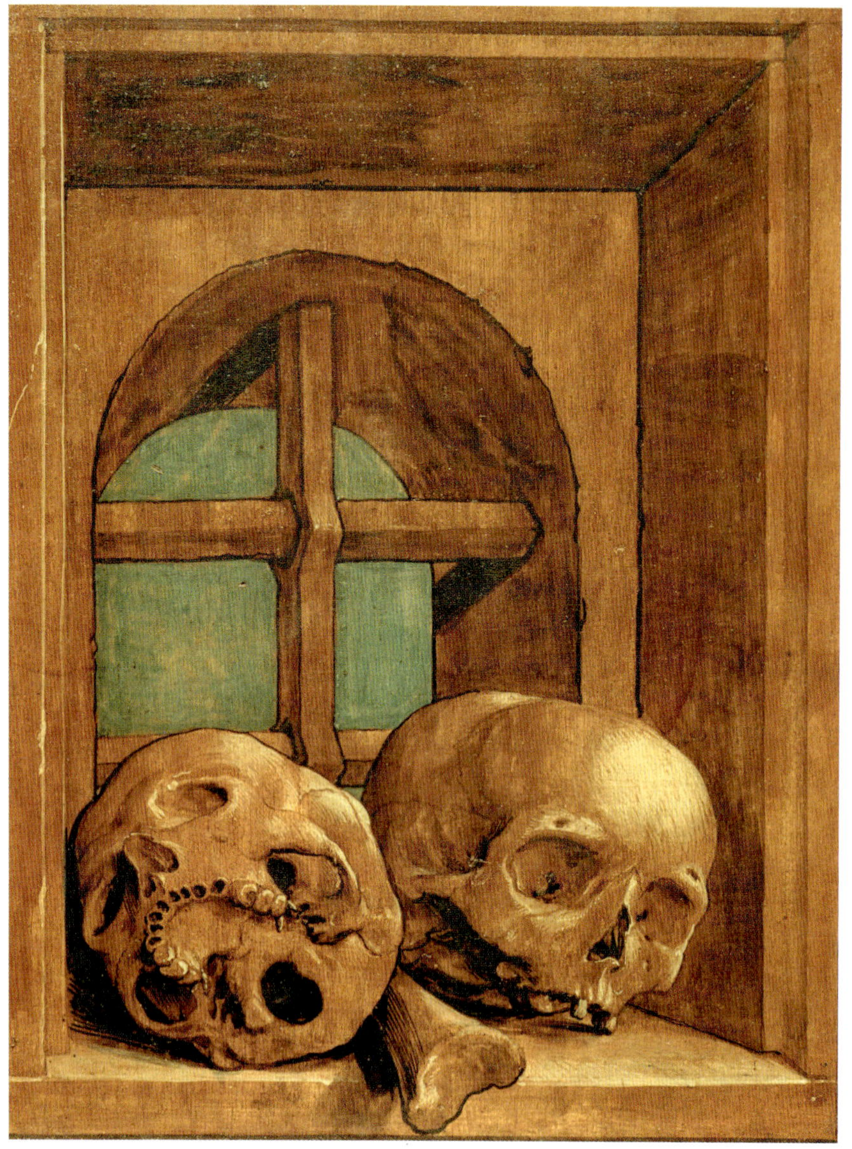

Left: *Portrait of Two Skulls in a Window Niche*, c.1520, tempera on panel, 33 x 25cm (12.9 x 9.84in), Kunstmuseum, Basel, Switzerland

The purpose of this portrait of skulls is unknown. It is an illusional work, two skeletal heads seemingly placed in the niche of a small, barred window with a large, human bone between them. The bone projects out toward the viewer, giving the illusion of reality.

Below: *Holbein's Coat of Arms,* 1519, wood, 18.5 x 14.3cm (7.2 x 5.6in), Historiche Museum, Basel, Switzerland

Holbein was accepted as a Master of the Basel Painter's Guild (Zum Himmel Zunft) on September 25th, 1519. 'De Maller' means Painter. The 'bull' was chosen for him by the guild, to associate him with St Luke's attribute, a bull (St Luke was the patron saint of artists). The ox head with star was the escutcheon of the Society of Zum Himmel in Basel.

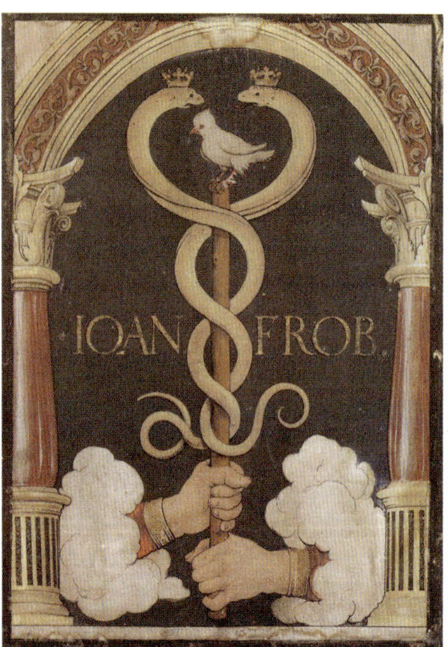

Left: *Printer's Device of Johannes Froben,.* tempera on canvas, heightened with gold, 44 x 31cm (17.3 x 12in), Kunstmuseum, Basel, Switzerland

Holbein probably painted the device to hang in Johannes Froben's printing shop; it survived because Froben's grandson gave it to the Holbein collector Basilius Amerbach in 1583.

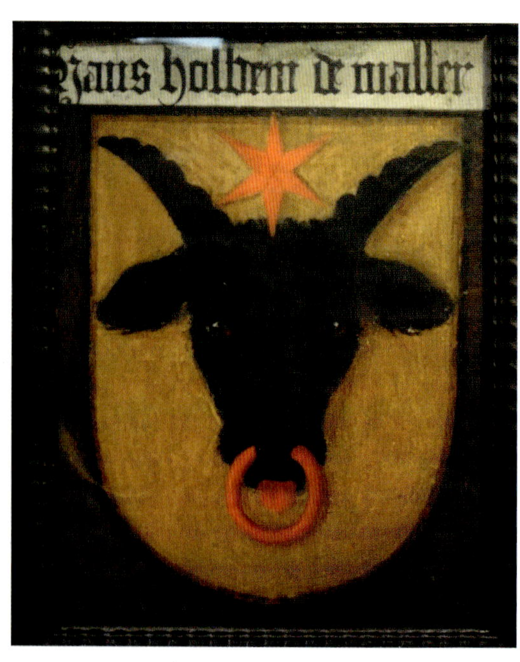

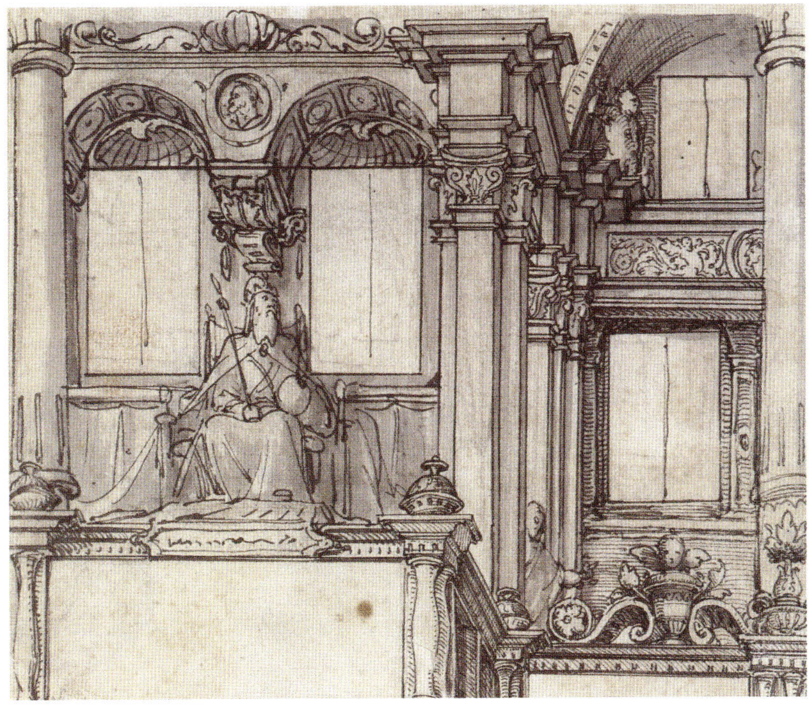

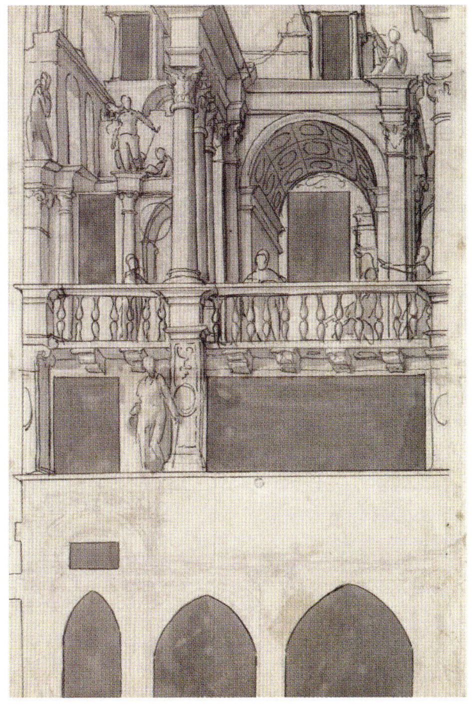

Above left and right (and below):
Design for façade paintings for the House of the Dance, c.1520, pen and ink over preliminary chalk drawing with grey wash, 53.3 x 36.8cm (21 x 14.5in), and 16.7 x 20cm (6.5 x 7.8in), Kunstmuseum, Basel, Switzerland

Sketches by Holbein the Younger of the proposed façade of the house Zum Tanz in Basel, on a two-sided sheet. One of Holbein's first commissions in Basel was to design a frieze for the façade of a house known as the Haus 'Zum Tanz'. These are significant as the only surviving designs by Holbein's hand. Other designs, for example the one shown below left, are workshop copies created prior to commencing work on the building. Holbein's practice was to draw increasingly detailed and finished designs; the loose style of these drawings therefore suggest they come from early in the design process. The wall paintings themselves no longer exist.

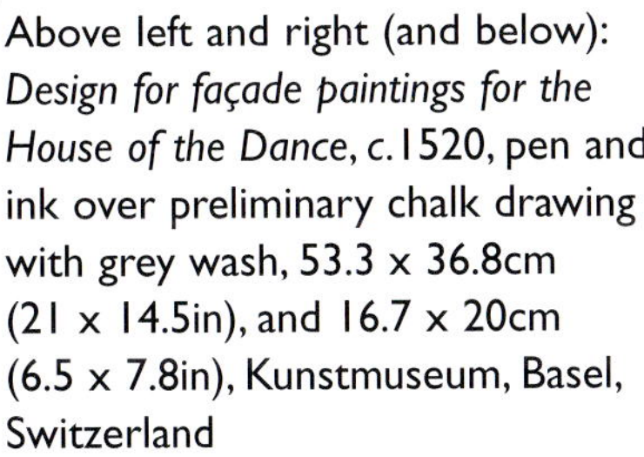

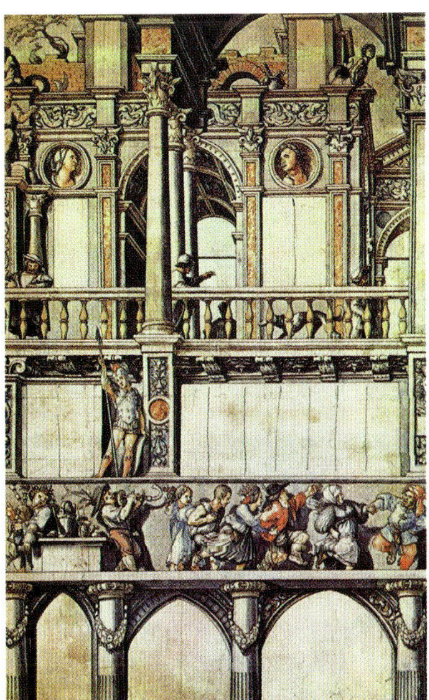

Right: *Proposal for the façade of a three-storey house and a gable*, 1520–21, pen and ink on paper, 58.2 x 26.8cm (22.9 x 10.5in), Musée de Louvre, Paris, France

A sketch by Holbein for the proposed decorative façade of another house. It is not known if the design went into construction.

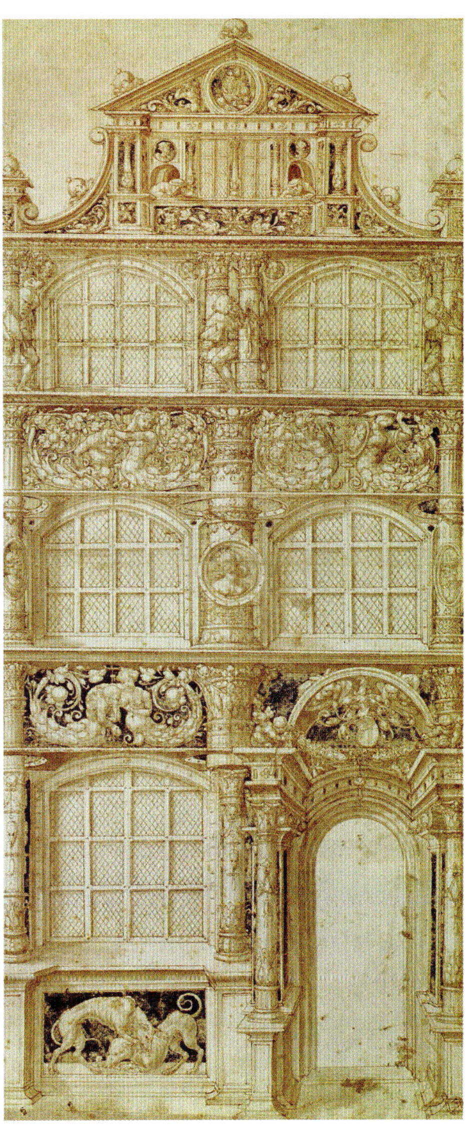

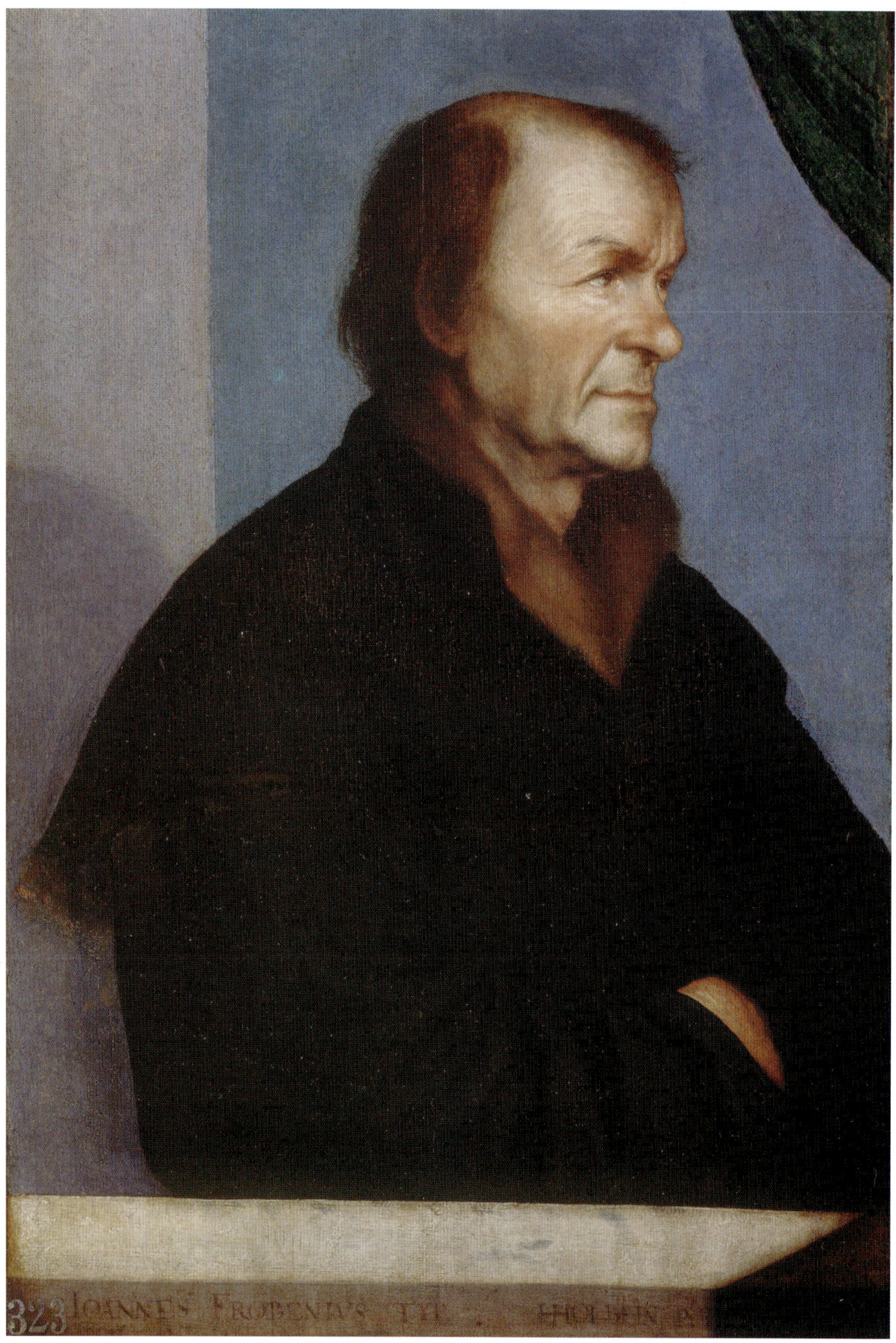

Portrait of Johannes Froben, c.1522–23, oil on panel, 48.8 x 32.4cm (19.2 x 12.75in), Royal Collection Trust, UK

Johannes Froben (1460–1527) was a highly successful printer in Basel, who worked closely with Holbein. In this portrait, Froben's age is reflected in the ageing skin texture and receding hair lines of a man in his fifth decade, carefully painted with remarkable skill. The Latin inscription on the stone ledge identifies the sitter and the artist.

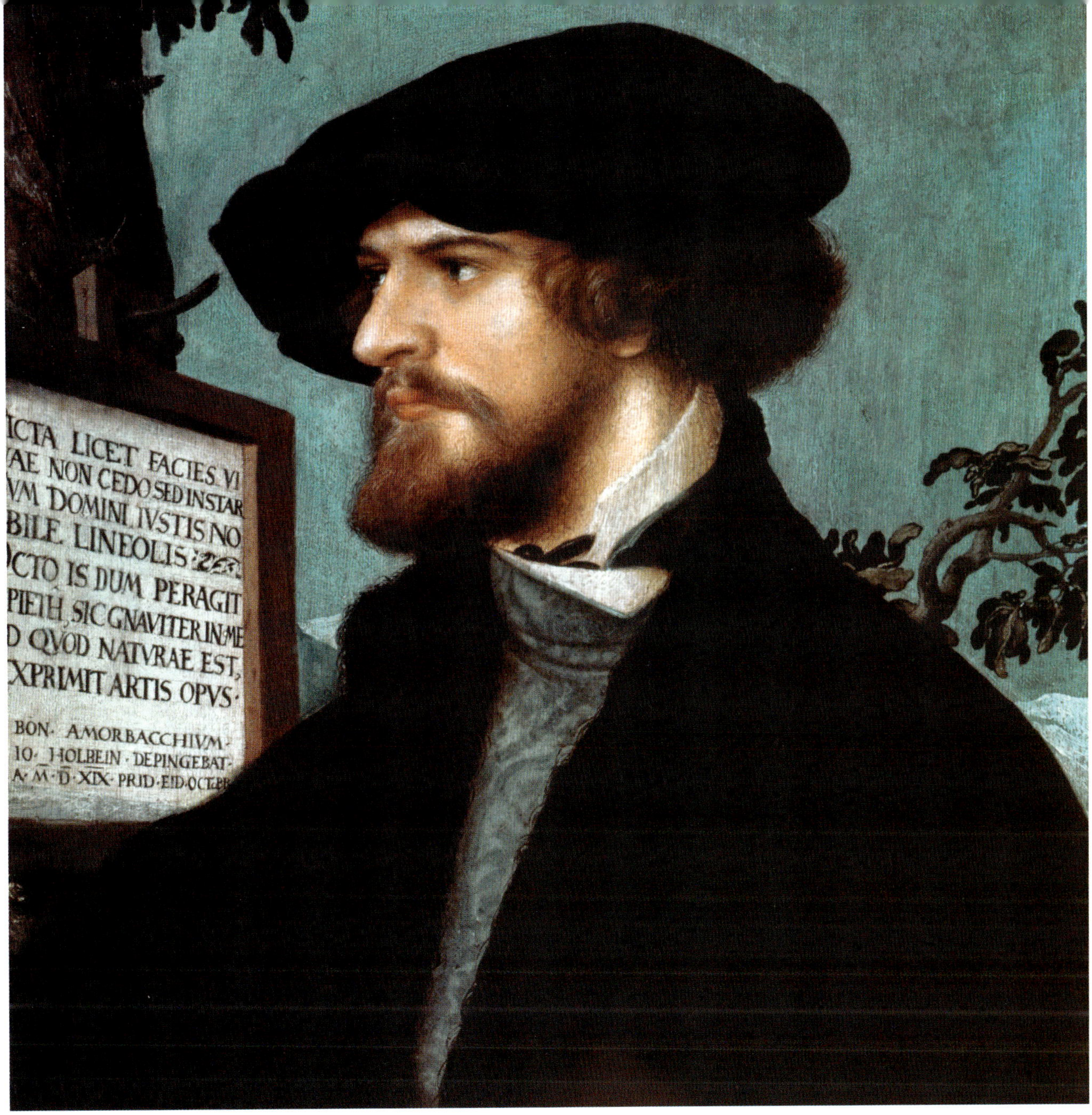

Above: *Portrait of Bonifacius Amerbach*, 1519, tempera on wood, 28.5 x 27.5cm (11.2 x 10.8in), Kunstmuseum, Basel, Switzerland

When Erasmus moved to Basel in 1513 he befriended Amerbach, thus possibly leading toward Holbein being commissioned to paint his portrait. Holbein's association with Bonifacius Amerbach was of benefit to him. Amerbach was a good patron, introducing the artist to friends and colleagues.

Right: *Portrait study of Bonifacius Amerbach*, c.1525, black and coloured chalk, lead pencil on hair and hat, 40 x 36.8cm (15.75 x 14in), Kunstmuseum, Basel, Switzerland

Bonifacius Amerbach (1495–1562) was a Swiss lawyer and jurist, a scholar, a humanist, and a friend to Erasmus. Holbein's drawing captured the facial characteristics of the sitter for this later portrait study.

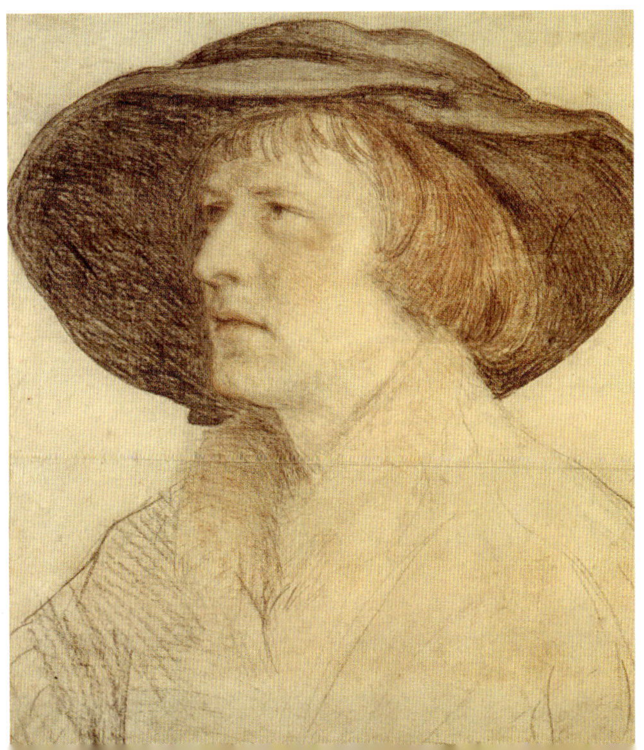

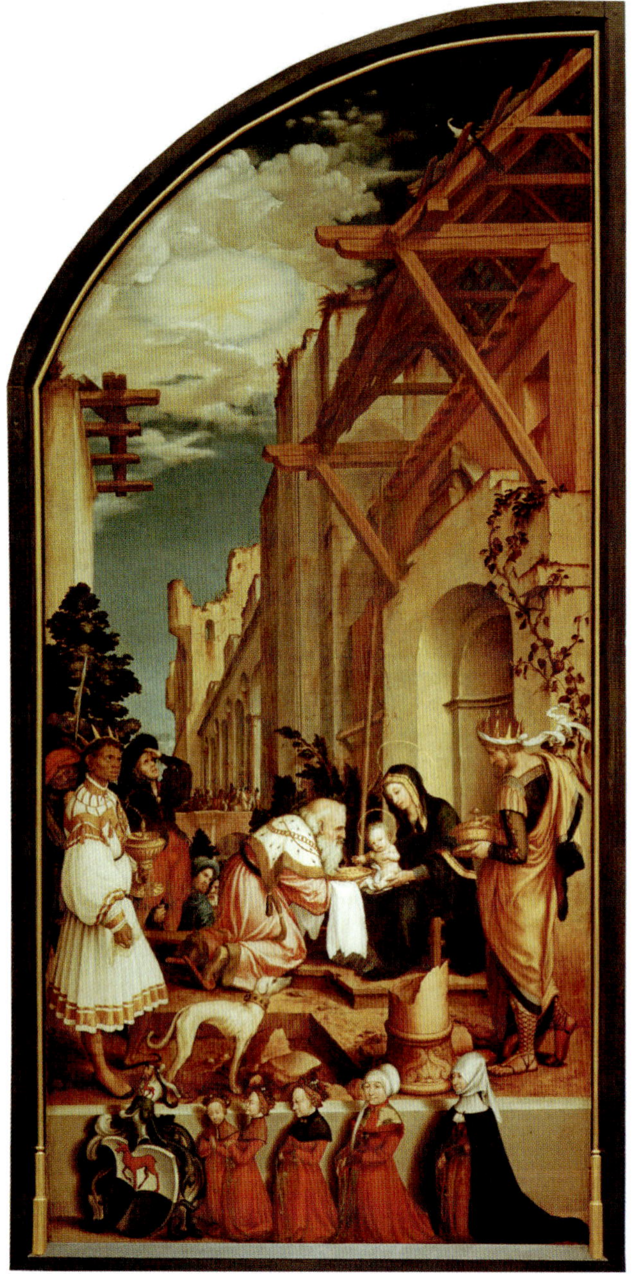 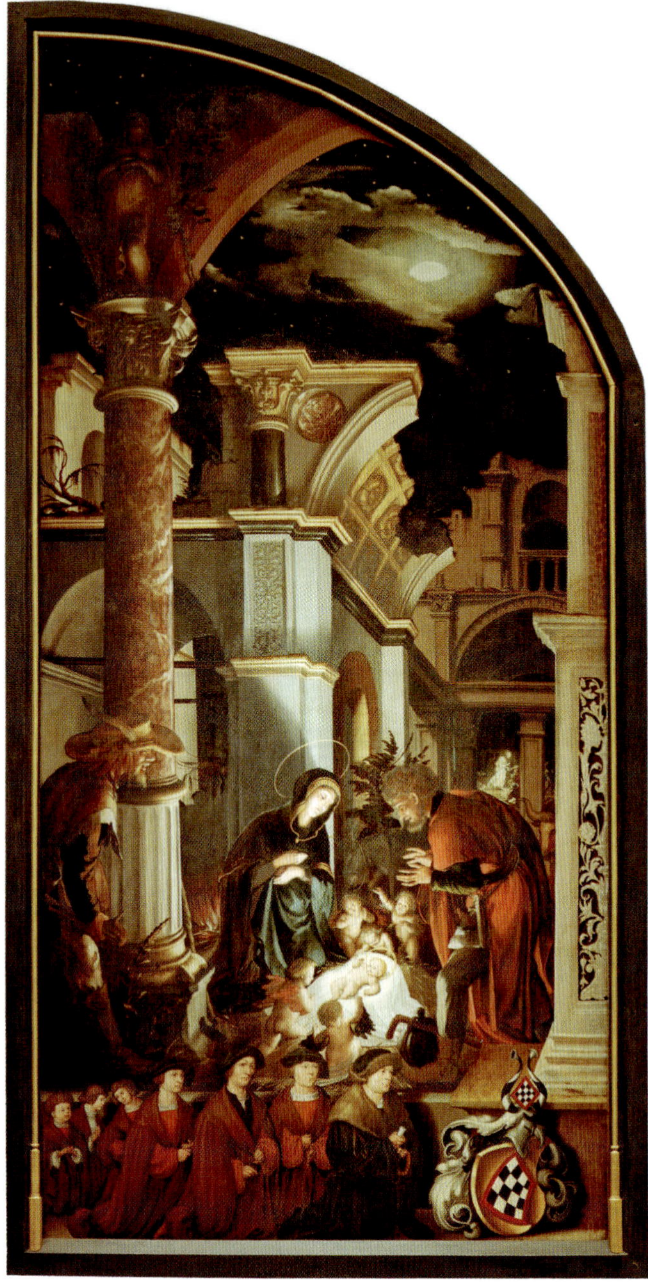

The Adoration of the Magi (left) and *Birth of Christ* (right), 1520–22, pine wood, two panels each 230 x 109cm (90.55 x 42.9in), 'Oberried Altar', University chapel, Freiburg im Breisgau, Germany

On the inside panels of the Oberried altarpiece, Holbein (working with his father, Holbein the Elder) depicts two scenes from the birth of Christ, both in an exterior architectural setting. In the left panel, the Magi gather around the Christ child as he is held by the Virgin Mary. The birth of Christ is depicted on the right companion panel, within the ruins of a grand building. A shepherd leans around a stone and marble column, to catch a glimpse of the newborn infant Jesus Christ. He and his fellow shepherds were told by an angel to follow the star to where Christ would be born in the city of David. Holbein captures a private moment in the look of surprise and delight on the man's face. A heavenly light shines down onto the newborn child.

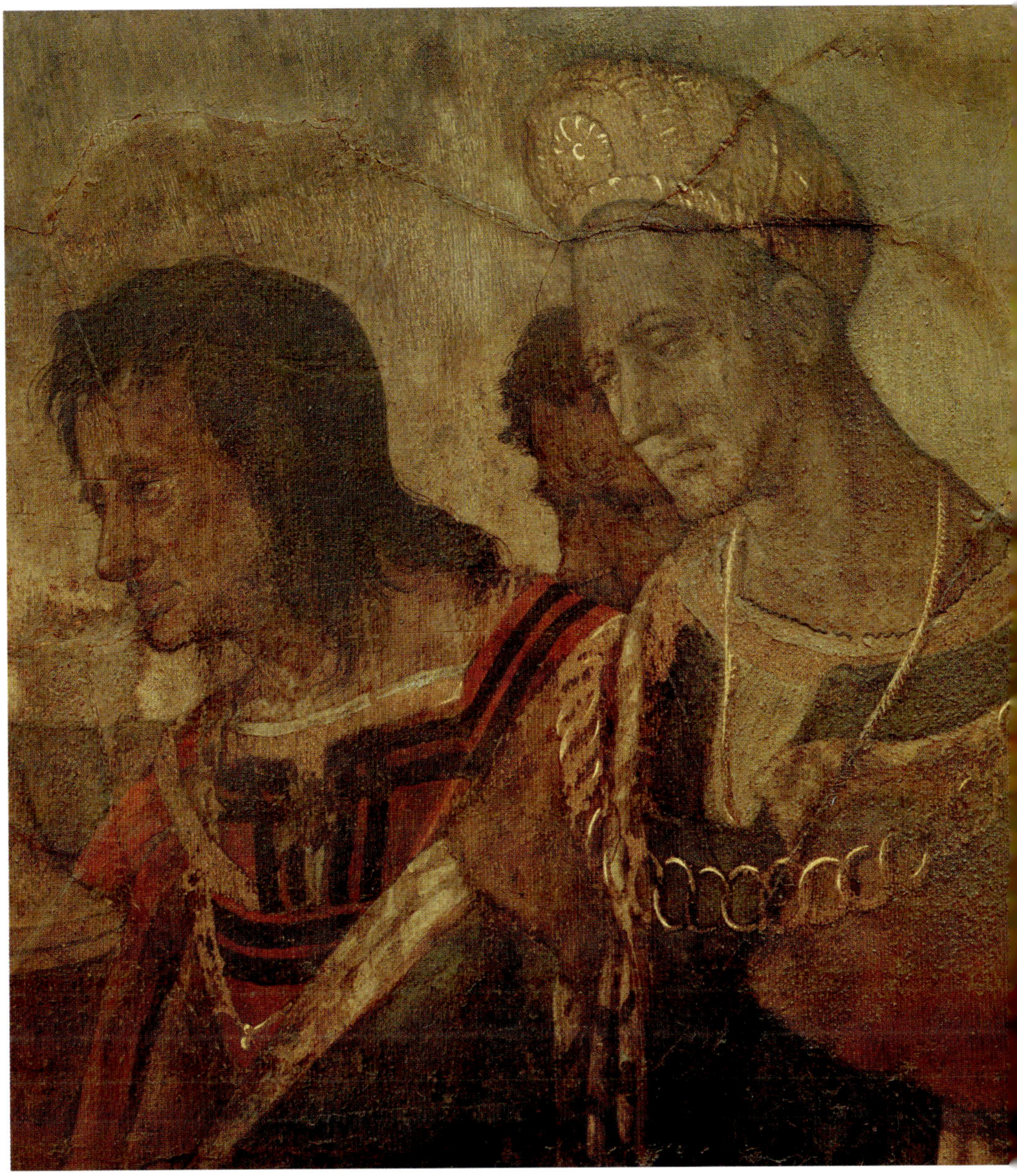

Manius Curius Dentatus rejects the gifts of the Samnites, c.1521–22, 'al secco' paint on plaster, 50 x 49.5cm (19.6 x 19.4in), Kunstmuseum, Basel, Switzerland

Manius Curius Dentatus (died 275BC) was the Roman commander noted for ending the Samnite War. This detail depicting the Samnite ambassadors was from the east wall of the Great Council Chamber, Basel; there are few remaining fragments of Holbein's original 1521–22 wall paintings of the Old Testament history of the Kings of Israel. One wall was left unpainted and then completed on Holbein's return to Basel in 1528–32 (see page 168).

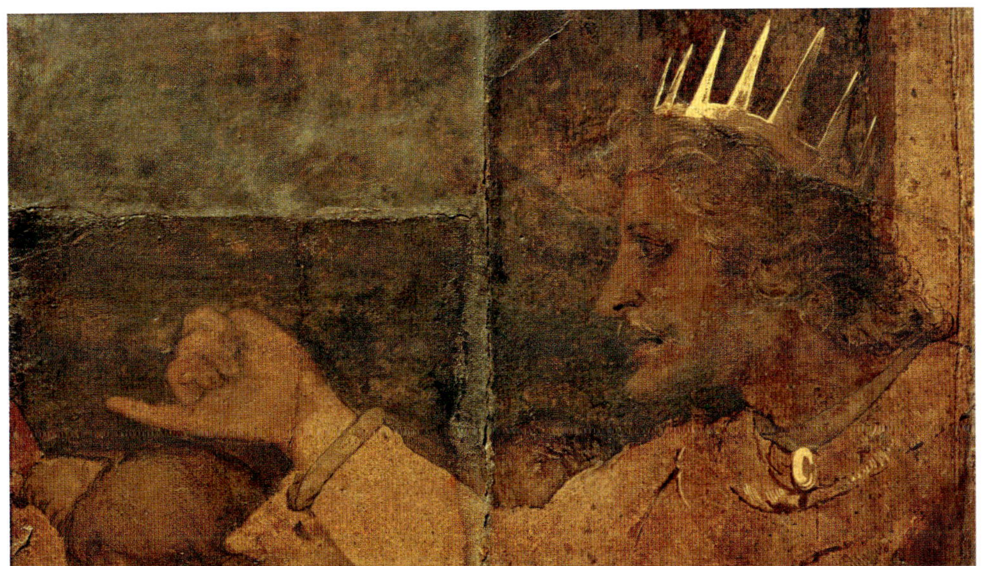

King Rehoboam, c.1521–22, 'al secco' paint on plaster, 50 x 49.5cm (19.6 x 19.4in)

This depiction of King Rehoboam (972–915BC), the first king of the Kingdom of Judah, is another fragment remaining of the original wall painting in the Great Council Chamber, Basel.

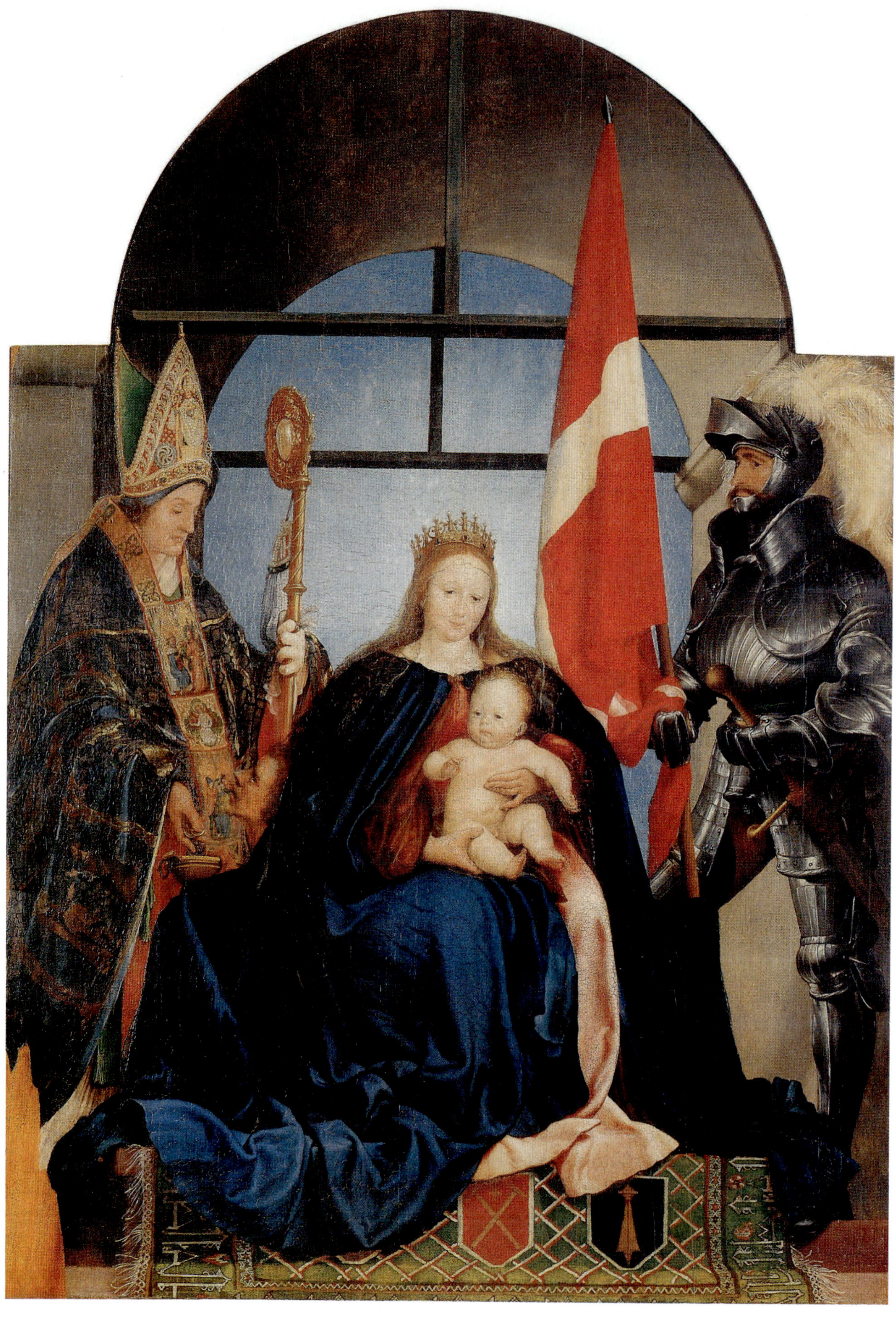

Left and right (detail): *The Solothurn Madonna*, 1520–22, lime wood, 143.5 x 104.9cm (56.5 x 41.3in), Kunstmuseum, Solothurn, Switzerland

This was Holbein's first known altarpiece of a traditional 'sacred conversation', a holy dialogue between the Virgin and Child and saints. It was possibly intended as a devotional work for a family chapel in the Church of St Martin in Basel, commissioned by Johannes Gerster (1466–1535), Basel's town secretary, and his wife Barbara Guldinknopf (c.1477–c.1542). The donors' escutcheons are woven into the carpet beneath the Madonna's feet. A beggar kneeling to the left, his head just appearing behind the Madonna's robes, is receiving alms from St Martin. The knight depicted at right is identified by the flag as a soldier of the ancient Theban legion, possibly the martyred St Ursus, beheaded AD303 by Romans for refusing to attack Christians. Holy relics, believed to be his bones, were discovered in Solothurn in 1473, not far from Basel, the location of this painting since 1864.

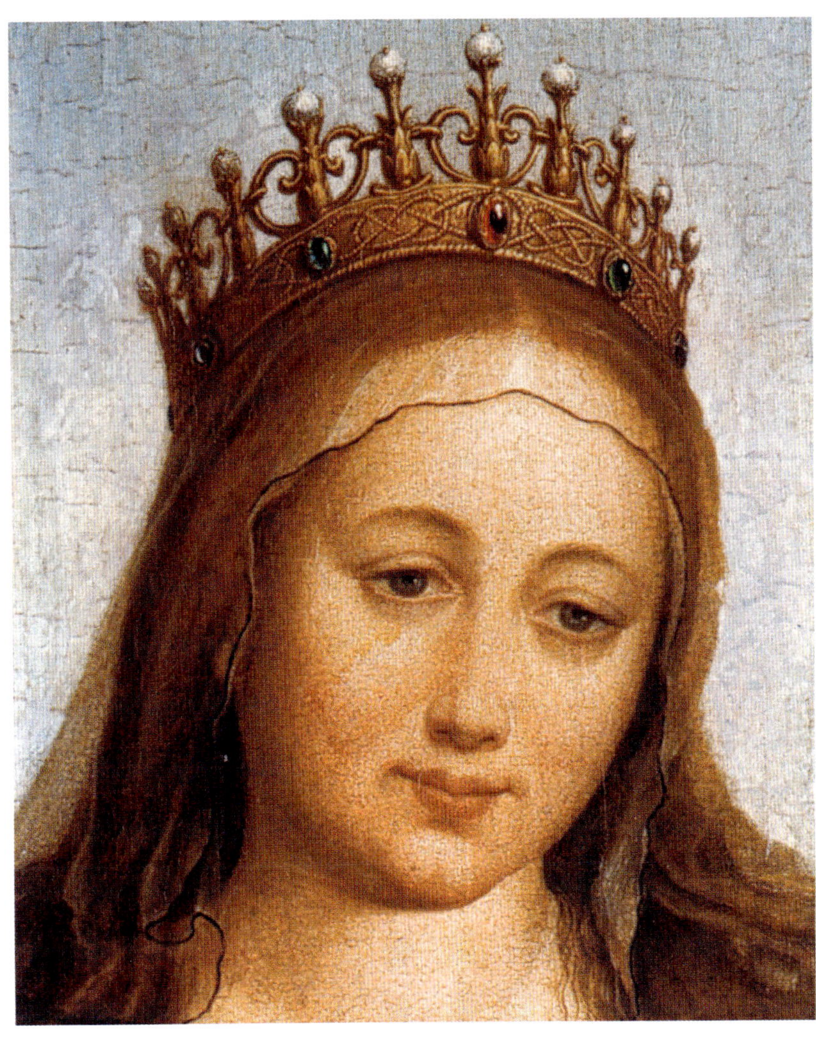

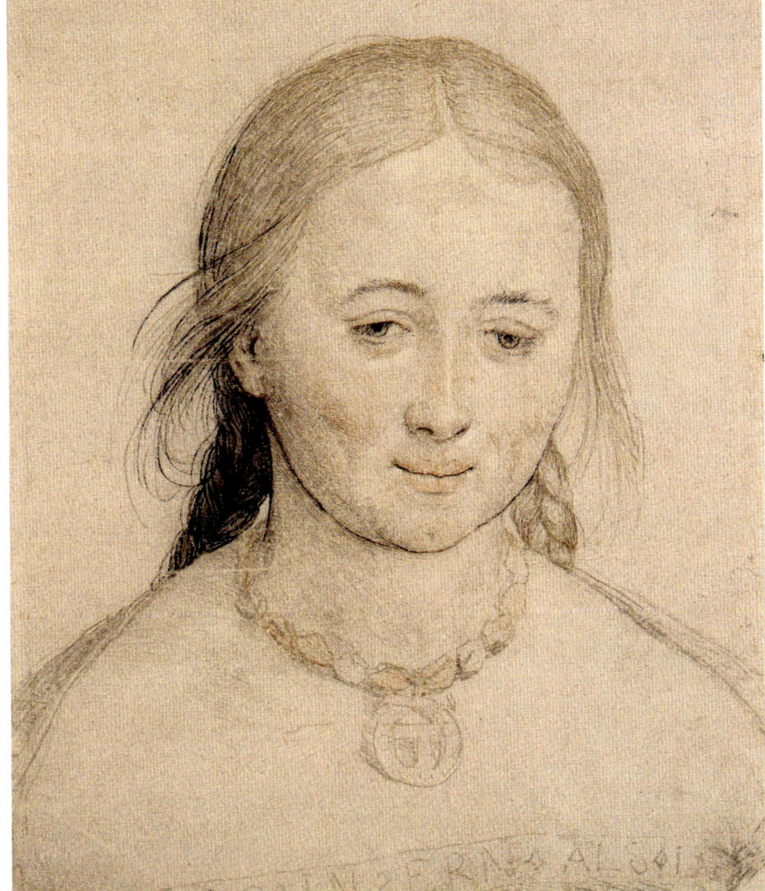

Left: *Portrait study of a young woman*, c.1520–22, silverpoint, pen and ink, white heightening and white and red chalk on pink-primed paper, 19.7 x 15.5cm (7.75 x 6.1in), Musée de Louvre, Paris, France

The small, highly detailed drawing in silverpoint of an unknown sitter is most likely a preliminary work for the altarpiece known as *The Solothurn Madonna* (shown above and opposite). The motto printed along the top of the woman's bodice reads 'Als in Ern', or 'All in honour'. Some historians suggest that this young woman may be Holbein's wife Elsbeth but no documents substantiate this.

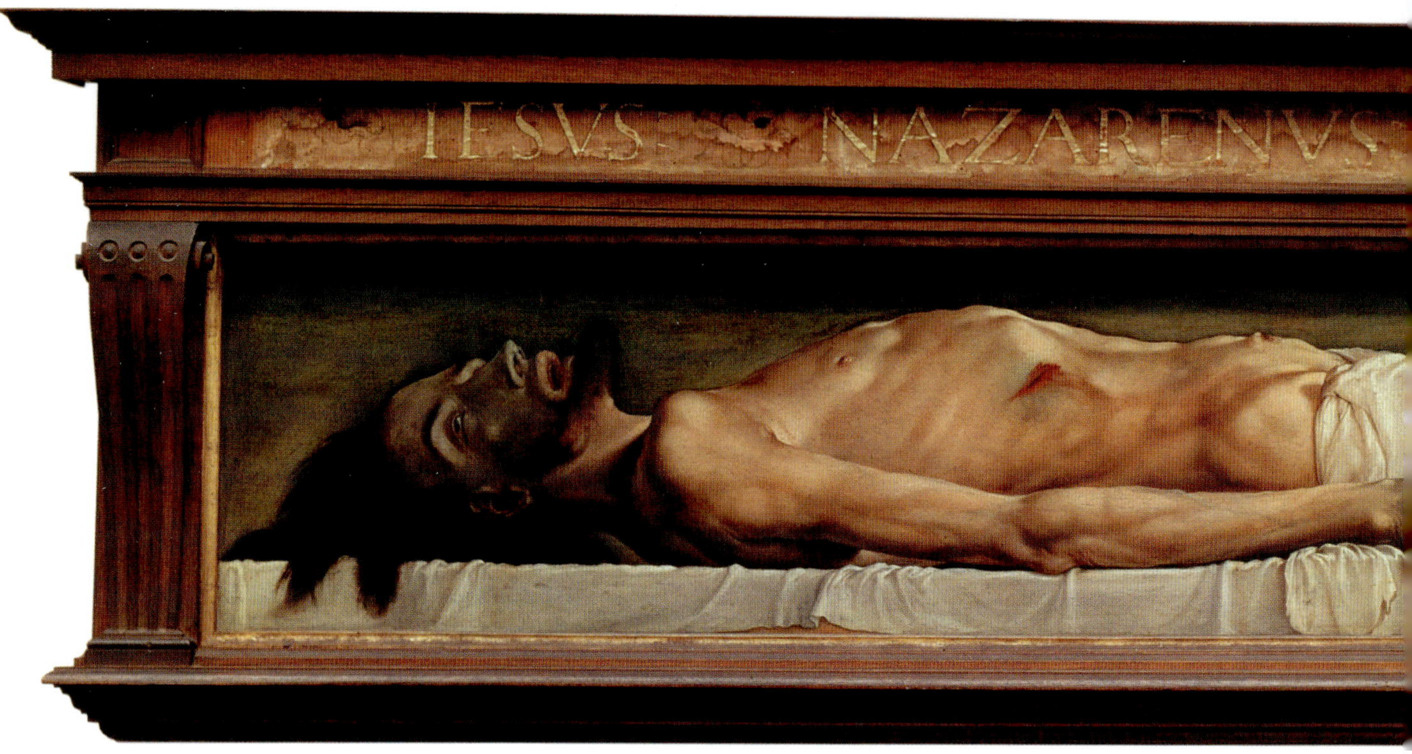

Dead Christ in the Tomb, 1521, oil and tempera on lime wood panel, 32.4 x 202.1cm (12.75 x 79.75in), Kunstmuseum, Basel, Switzerland

This remarkable painting, possibly intended as part of a predella panel for a chapel, depicts the near-skeletal dead body of Christ, placed in a stone sepulchre, very soon after his death by crucifixion. His face is tired, worn, his hands and feet bruised and punctured from the heavy nails driven through them. Holbein instils pathos, sadness and disbelief in his depiction of man's inhumanity to man.

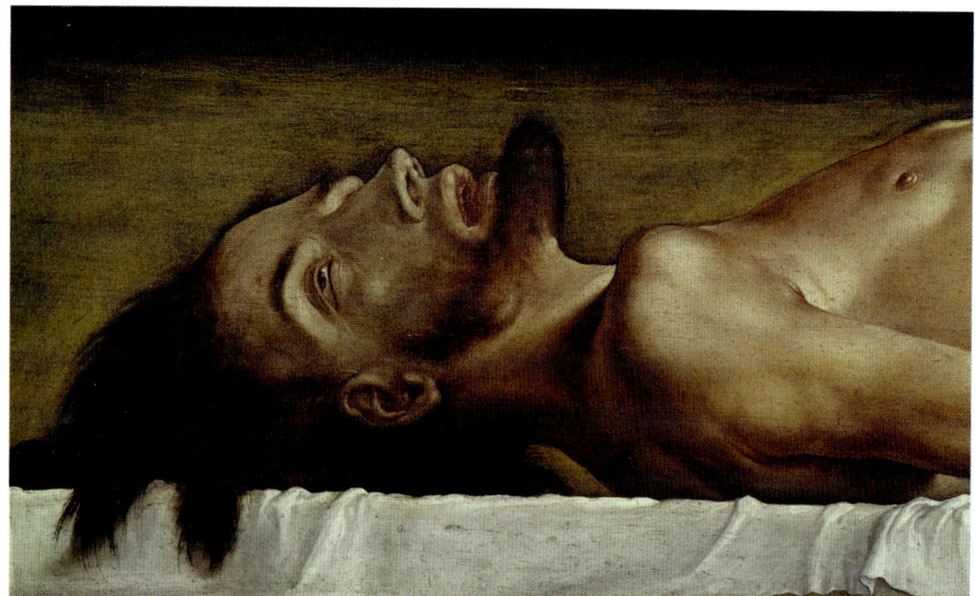

Detail of the head, *Dead Christ in the Tomb* (1521)

Holbein captures the brutality to the body, highlighted in its decomposition, its physical change from life to death. The Russian writer Dostoyevsky, viewing the painting, wrote 'This face in the picture was beaten all over, there were swollen, awful bloody and blue traces on it, the eyes were open, the pupils distorted, the white of the eyes shining with a kind of deadly, glassy light'.

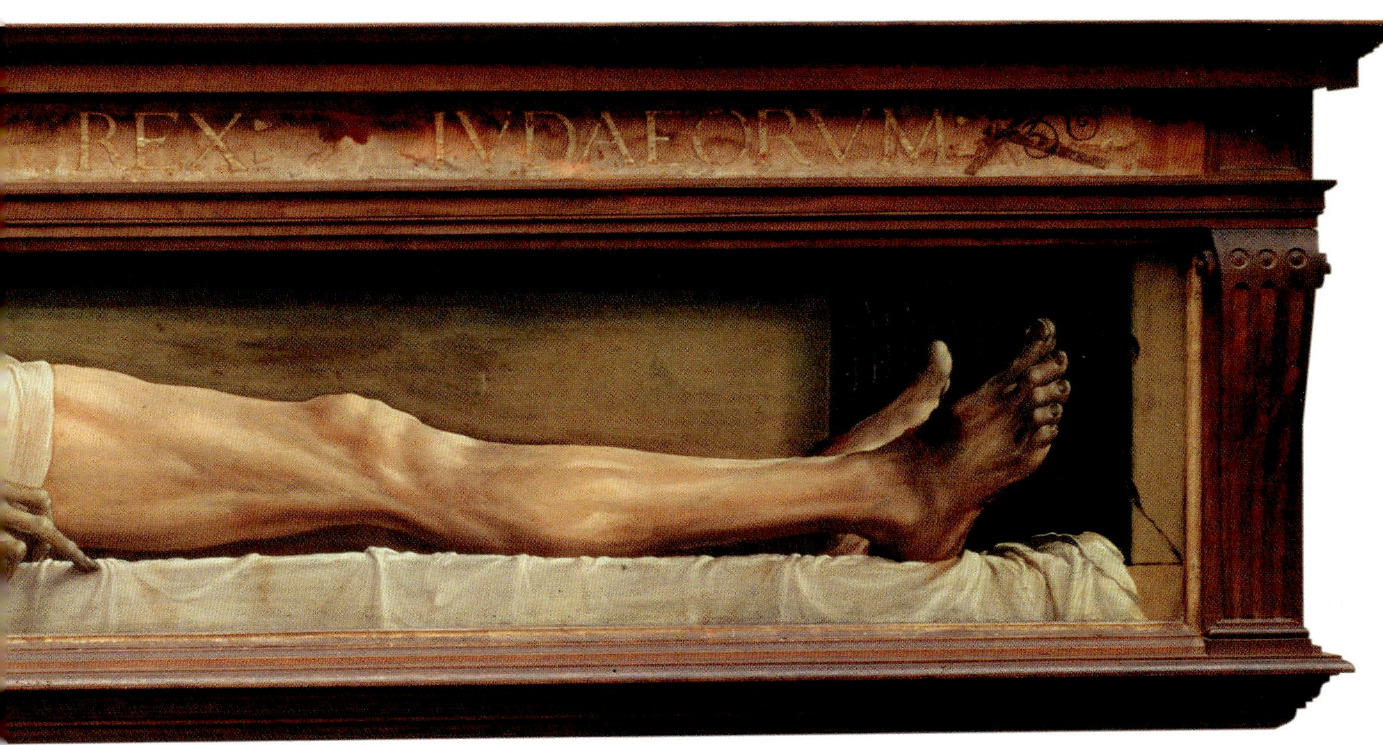

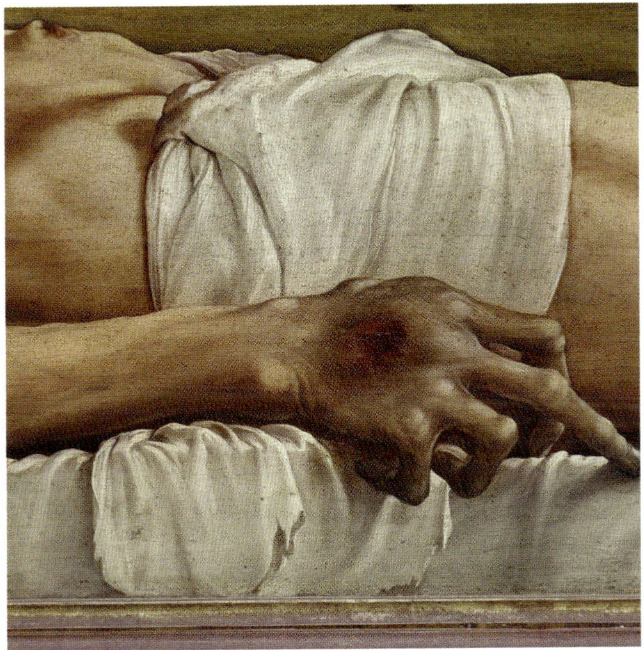

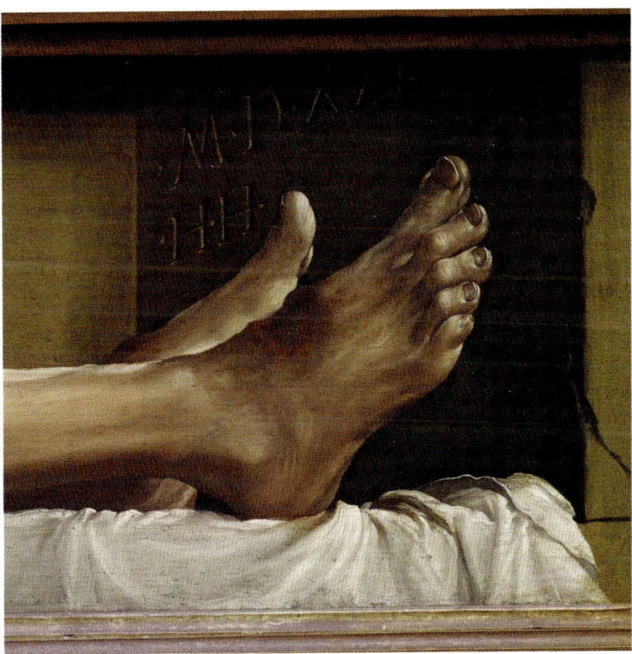

Detail of the hand, *Dead Christ in the Tomb* (1521)

Holbein accentuates the discoloured skin of Christ's hand, created by the puncturing through the bones to hammer in nails for crucifixion. The large hole created is visible. The painter draws attention to Christ's human frailty in his death by slow torture, executed for his faith. It is a recognition of his human suffering for mankind.

Detail of the feet and signature, *Dead Christ in the Tomb* (1521)

In his brutal depiction of the human body of Christ after death, Holbein focused on the large empty holes in his feet, created by the hammering-through of large nails. Holbein added his signature and dated the work. The painting was possibly meant for a private tomb, perhaps for Ambrosius Amerbach, a patron.

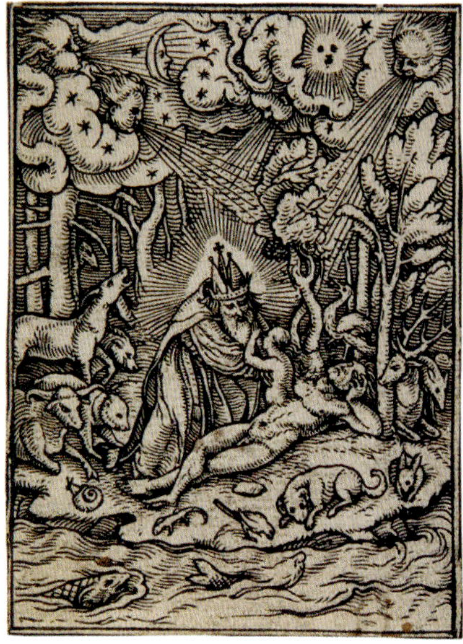

The Creation of Adam and Eve, the first in the series *The Dance of Death*, *c.*1523–26, woodcut, 6.4 x 4.8cm (2.5 x 1.9in)

Holbein created his series of woodcuts in *c.*1523–6, of which 41 were published in 1538, then 52 in 1545. The 'Dance of Death' begins with God's Creation of Earth, and the first humans. Eve is born, fully formed, from Adam's rib. In God's Garden of Eden, Adam and Eve live in paradise; there is no sense of death.

Death Goes Forth

After banging the drums to signify action, Death and his congregated accomplices begin their routine of rounding up those who will die that day.

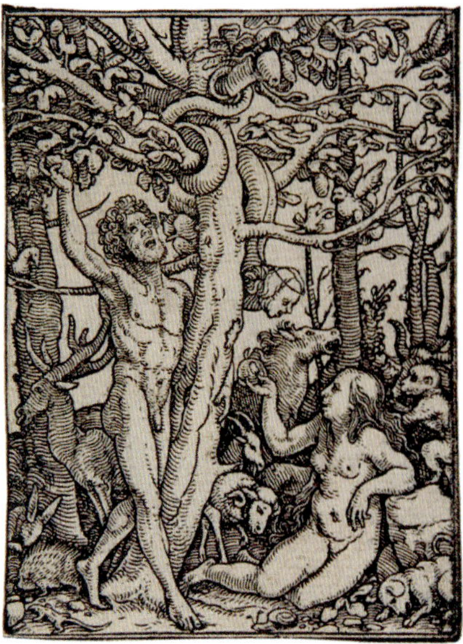

The Temptation and Fall of Adam and Eve
Holbein focuses on the Bible narrative in Genesis 2: 16–17: 'And the Lord God commanded him, "You may eat freely from every tree of the garden… but you must not eat from the tree of the knowledge of good and evil; for in the day that you eat of it, you will surely die."'

Death and the Pope

Holbein depicted the medieval Dance Macabre as a reformist satire. The Pope is in the act of crowning an Emperor, who kneels before him. Two Cardinals attend him. One is impersonated by Death, enjoying the materiality of the occasion, embracing the Pope with one arm while the other leans on a crutch.

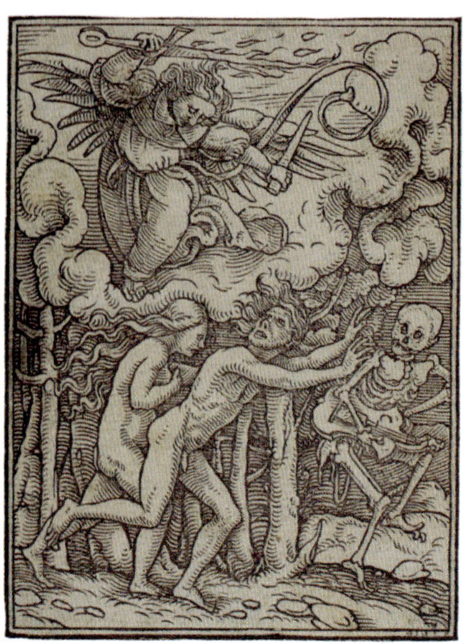

The Expulsion from Paradise
Holbein depicts Adam and Eve running through the lush garden of Eden, chased by St Michael, his sword in hand, swooping down on a vast heavenly cloud to chase them out of Eden. A skeletal Death, playing a stringed instrument, awaits the now-mortal pair.

Death and the King

The bearded king, wearing royal robes and hat, is seated at his dining table, attended by servants pouring wine and looking after him, failing to notice the hourglass of time amidst the joyful clutter. Death steps up to the table. Its eyes and the king's meet. The sands of time have run out.

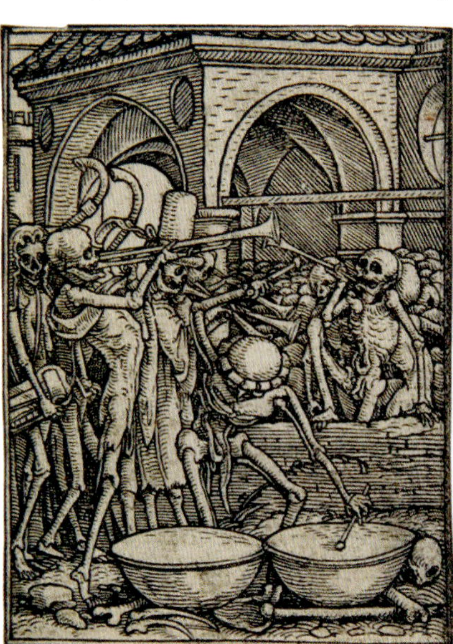

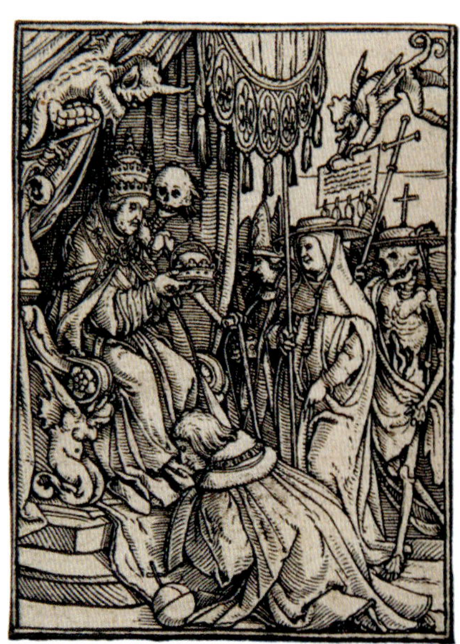

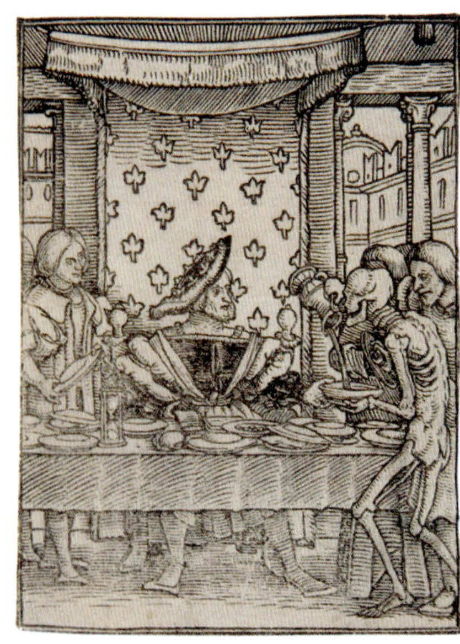

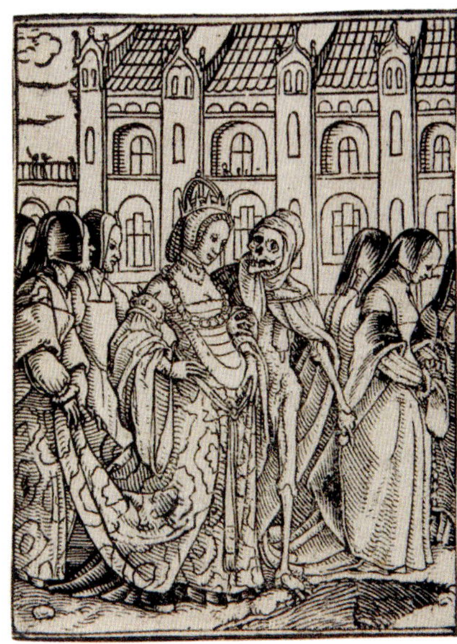

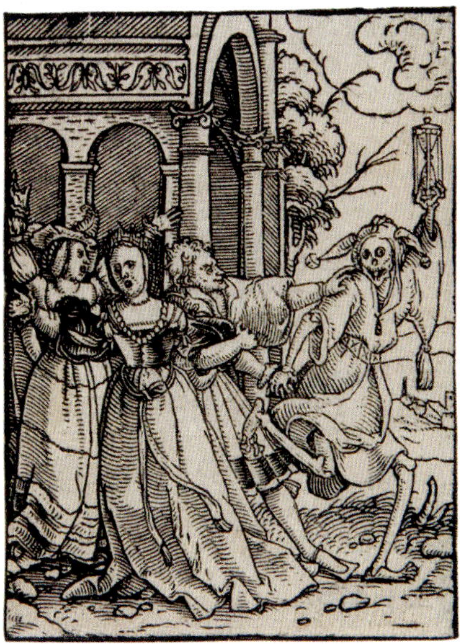

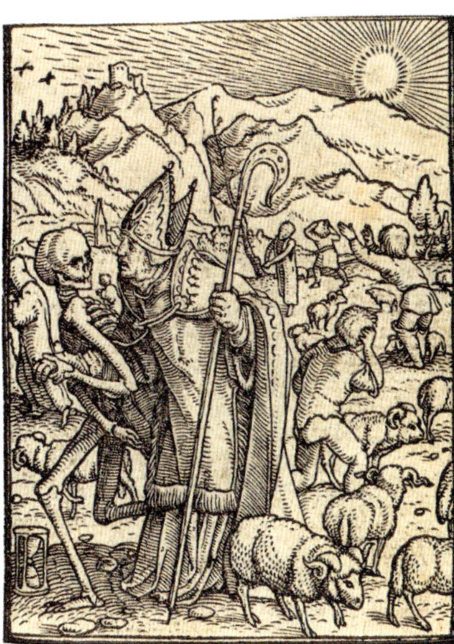

Death and the Empress

Clothed in a cloak and hood, skeletal Death intervenes in a royal procession. An empress surrounded by her royal court, her train held by ladies-in-waiting, has her grand, sumptuous life interrupted, as Death, the mortal equaliser, steps toward her, and looks into her face.

Death and the Abbot

In a hilly landscape under a tree, a skeletal figure of Death grabs the robes of an abbot, to steer him towards Death. The holy book that the monk holds up in his left hand will not help him. The hourglass of time, its sands running out, rests in the tree's branches above his head.

Death and the Queen

The Queen, aided by her attendants, tries to flee Death's grip, who is wearing a jester's cap. He holds up, for all to see, an ornamental hourglass in his left hand, symbolic of her remaining time alive. The skeletal Death grabs her hand, pulling her away.

Death and the Abbess

Death, his skeletal head wearing a wreath of fronds, drags the screaming Abbess from her convent, tugging at her vestments, her rosary beads still in her hands. Holbein captures a moment in time as a nun, standing in the doorway watching the scene, screams and throws her arms up in shock, but the sands of time are running out in the hourglass.

Death and the Bishop

Under a brilliant sun in a hilly landscape, people run and sheep scatter as a Bishop, holding the pectoral cross, dressed in episcopal vestments and mitre, is apprehended by the skeletal personification of Death.

Death and the Duchess

Holbein depicts the Duchess fully clothed, lying on her four-poster bed, her pet dog at her feet. Two skeletal figures of Death surprise her, tugging at the bedclothes to get her up, to accompany them. Within this small composition Holbein – the initial 'H' on an escutcheon on the bed – animates the scene, the duchess's surprise, and her comfortable surroundings being of no value in death.

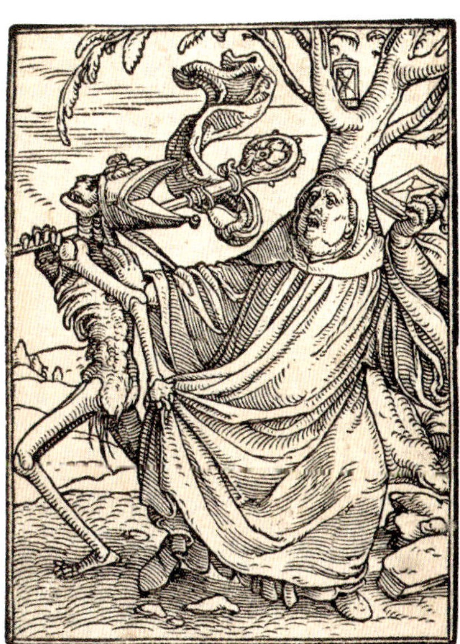

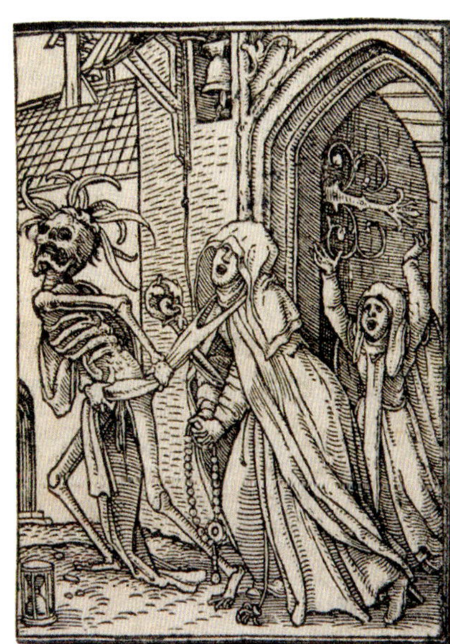

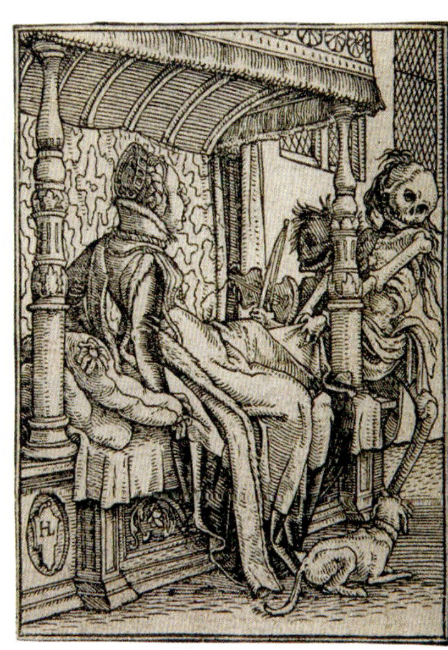

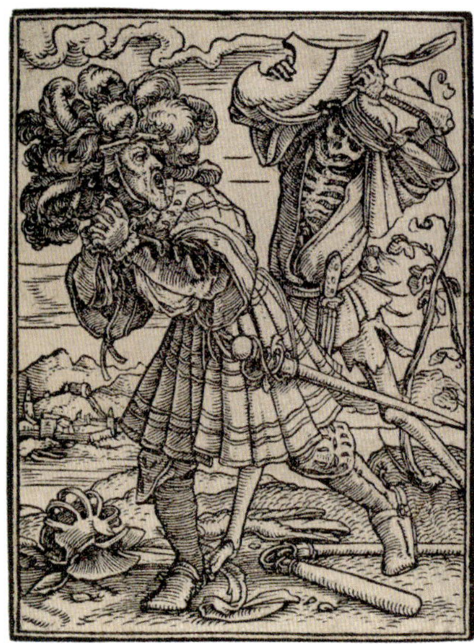

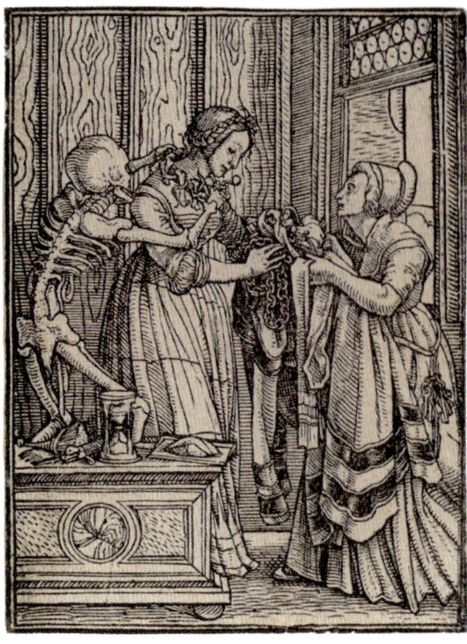

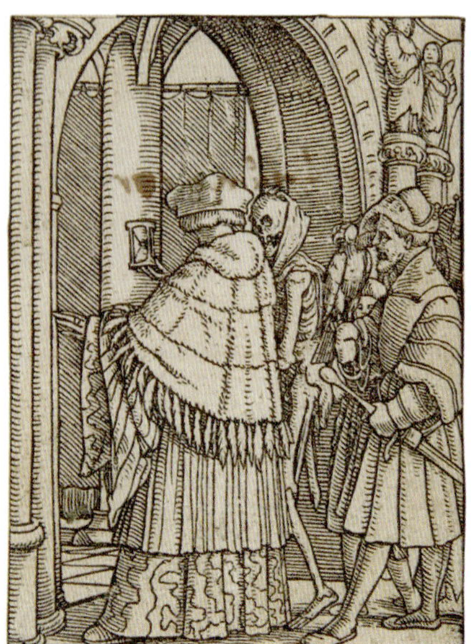

Death and the Count

A Count, wearing a richly feather-adorned helmet, is depicted in shock, fleeing Death, who gleefully seizes the Count's armour and claims his life. Holbein divided the pictures roughly into four social lifestyles: the clergy; the nobility and aristocracy; the judiciary, and others.

Death and the Countess

A Countess is helped to put on her finery by her maidservant, and by Death who adorns her before taking her life. The hourglass shows that her time on Earth has run out. The 'Dance of Death' images, also known as 'Pictures of Death', reveal the end of mortal life to be the leveller whatever a person's social rank.

Death and the Canon

Holbein's Dance of Death highlights that death claims all mortal lives. Here, with an entourage behind him, a Canon walks forward to enter a church. Death, smiling, walks beside him, waiting the destined moment to seize the Canon's life, accompanying the cleric on his final journey to Heaven or Hell.

Death and the Preacher

The Preacher leans over his pulpit, engaging with the congregation who, some standing, some seated, gather around to hear his words. Unawares, Death is standing behind the preacher, ready to take him, as the hourglass on the pulpit denotes that the preacher's time on Earth is at an end.

Death and the Judge

 A deal with money is being made between a judge and a man holding a staff, standing in the street to the left. Death stands between, waiting for the judge's time to run out.

Death and the Nun

A young nun on her knees is praying before an altar in her bedroom. She turns to look at the young man playing a lute who sits opposite, on her bed. Is it her lover? Whatever the reason for his presence, skeletal Death extinguishes the nun's altar candle, to summon her.

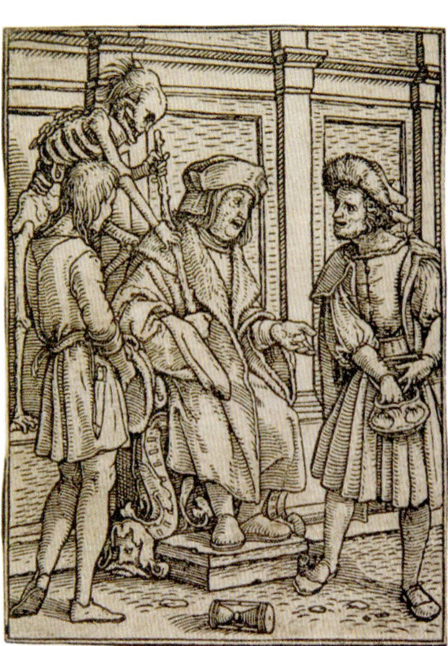

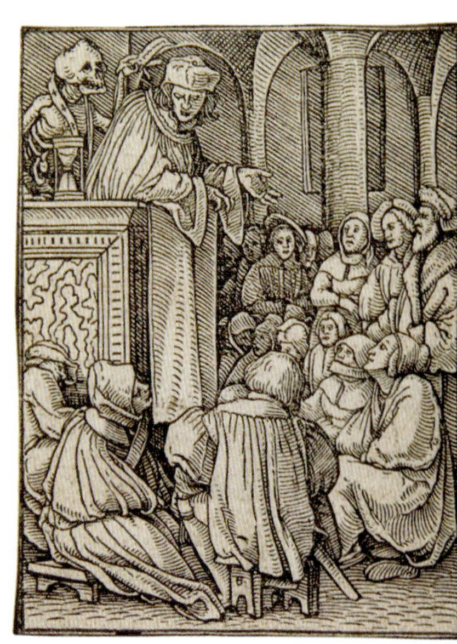

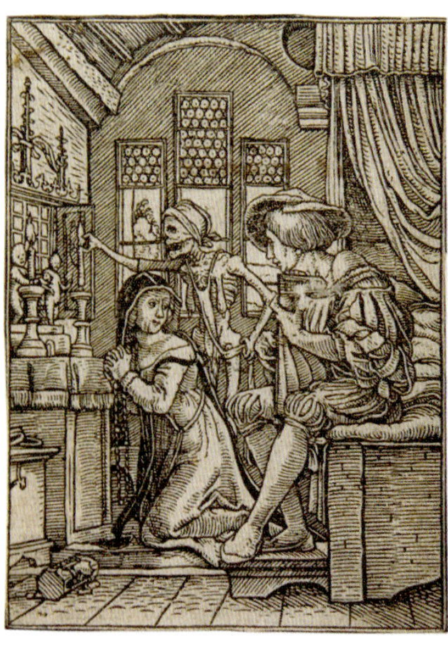

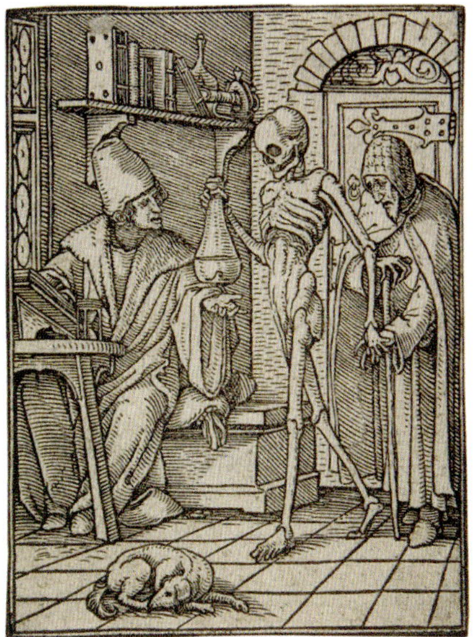

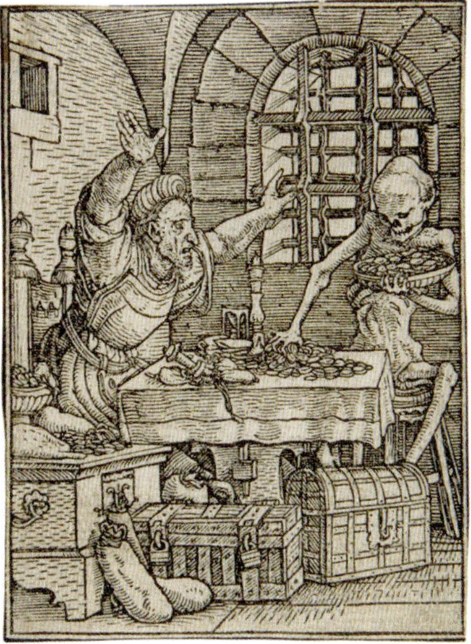

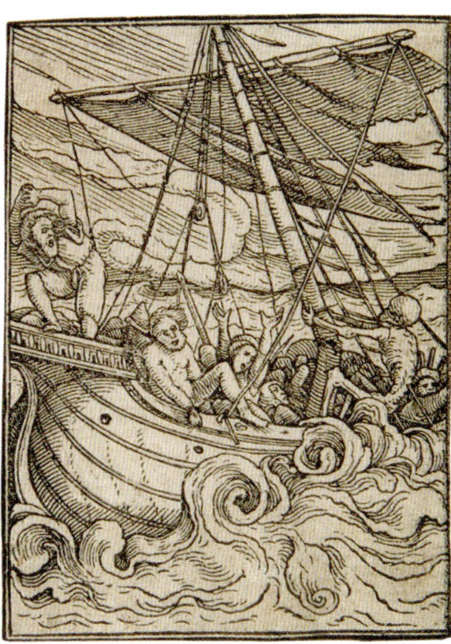

Death and the Physician

An old man is consulting the doctor in his surgery-study when a smiling skeletal Death intervenes, stepping between them, proffering a flask (a urinary sample from the old man?), before summoning the doctor to his mortal death, as the hourglass on his desk shows the sands of time running out.

Death and the Old Man

At left, an old man, his back stooped with age, takes the skeletal arm of Death, as a companion in his last moments alive, not noticing the open grave before him, in which he is about to fall. Death smiles kindly on the old man. In the background at left, on a low wall, an hourglass shows the sands of time running out.

Death and the Miser

Holbein depicts a wonderful scene, set in a chamber with heavy bars across a large arched window. Trunks of money are on the floor. Death starts to fill a bowl with the miser's money, who gesticulates for him to stop, but the hourglass shows that his life is at an end.

Death and the Old Woman

An old lady walking slowly, feeling the rough road surface with her stick, fails to see the animated skeletons alongside her. One marches ahead, playing a hammered dulcimer instrument. The other, its head crowned with a wreath, approaches.

Death and The Seaman

A boat with sails in tatters, ploughing through a stormy sea, is flooded and sinking, as Death pulls on its broken mast, sinking the boat, taking those on board beneath the waves to their death.

Death and the Peddler

Two skeletal figures stop a peddler who carries a large basket, laden with goods. One skeleton plays a long marine trumpet, a stringed instrument, to accompany him to death, or announce his demise. The other grabs his arm. The peddlar, armed with a sword and with a lion-dog as a companion, points toward the next town where he is heading, to no avail. The fearful look on his face registers that his time has come.

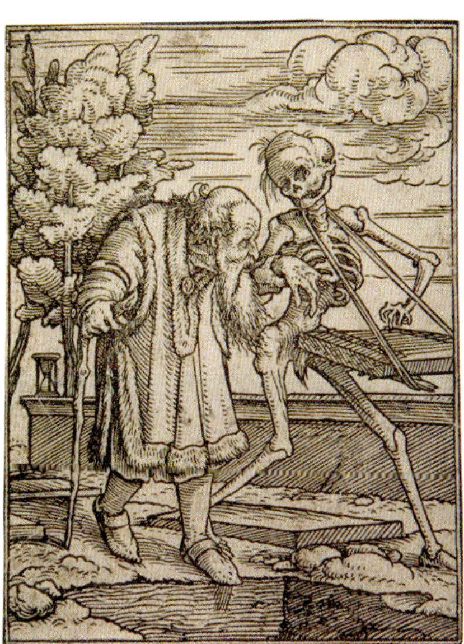

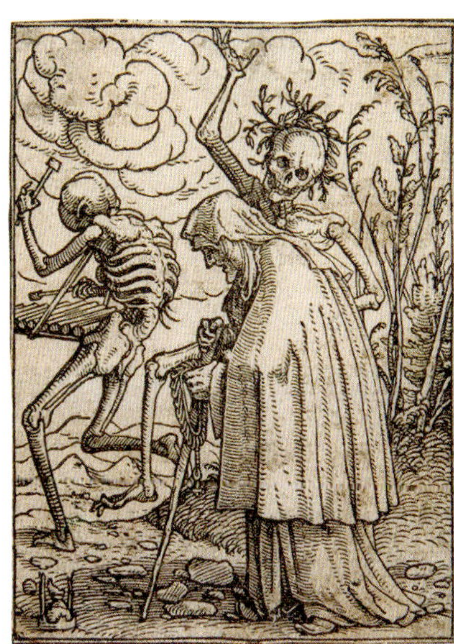

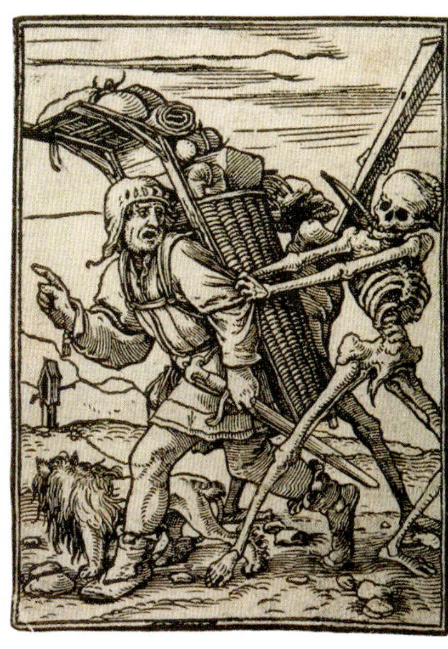

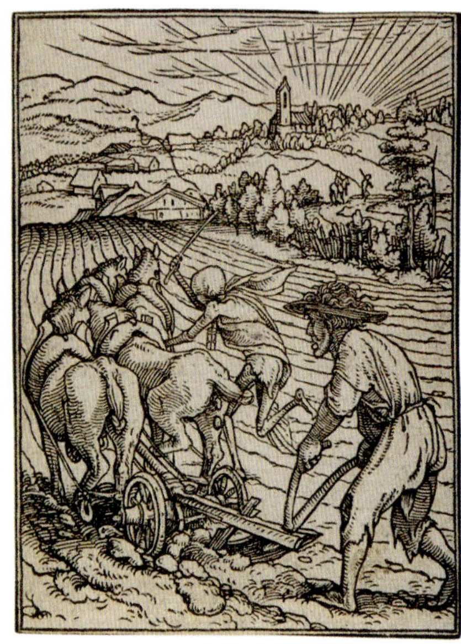

Death and the Ploughman

The ploughman, in frayed clothing, holds on to his plough behind his scraggy horses, ploughing the field. On the horizon, a hilltop village is bathed in a glorious sunset. Death appears and frightens the horses, one relieving itself with shock. Death whips them to go faster, toward the ploughmen's end.

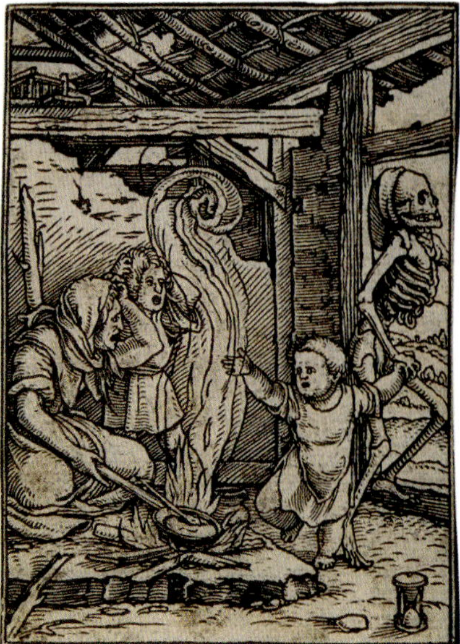

Death and the Child

A sad, deeply poignant depiction of a young child, led by the hand by Death out of its home, a tumbled-down shack, where its mother is cooking at an open fire, with smoke rising. The child turns quickly to wave to the mother who watches with another child in horror at the scene as her child is taken away.

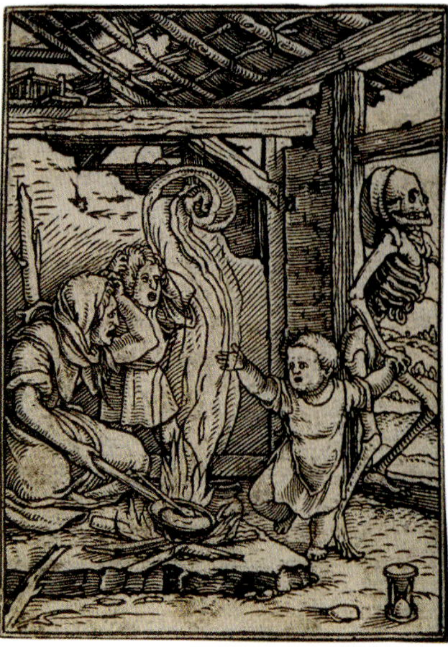

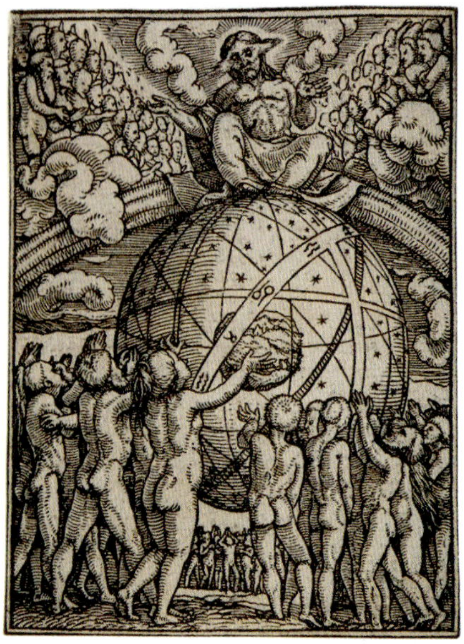

The Last Judgement

In the biblical account, at the second coming of Christ, resurrection of the dead will occur, and all humanity will be judged and separated to enter Heaven or Hell. The final scene in Holbein's series depicts the coming together of risen dead, looking up to God's son, Jesus Christ sitting on a celestial globe.

Study for the Child in the Dance of Death c.1523–26

Holbein captures the horrified expressions of a family as the youngest is led away by a jaunty Death. The poignant scene depicts the pain of losing a son or daughter, with the

mother's grief and disbelief etched on her face. The young child, unaware of the finality of what is happening, turns to her for help. The finished woodcut is shown above.

The Allegorical Escutcheon of Death

This was the last in the series of the 'Dance of Death' published in Lyon, 1538. Death's Coat of Arms reveals a smartly dressed man at left, and his bejewelled wife at right, standing either side of an escutcheon on which there is a smiling skeletal death-head.

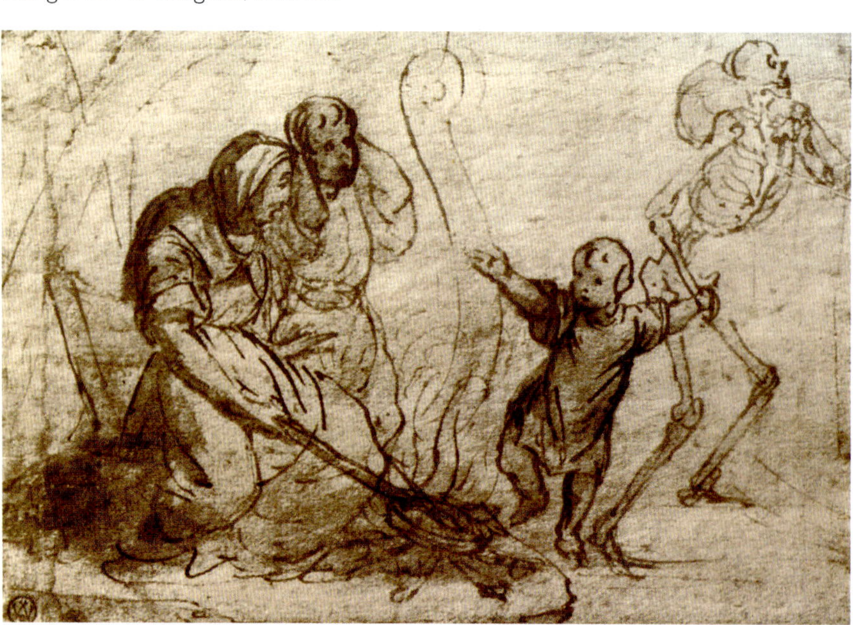

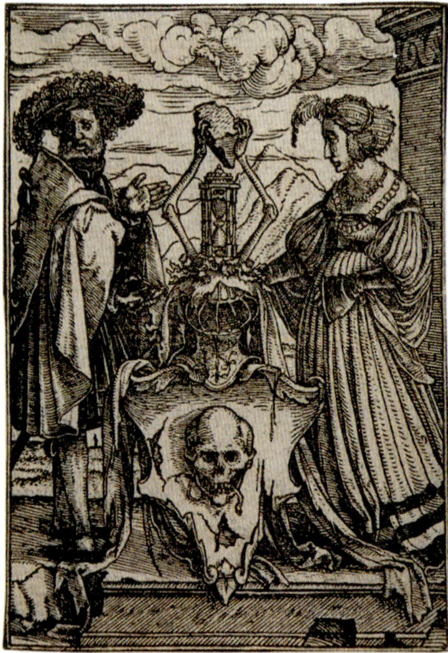

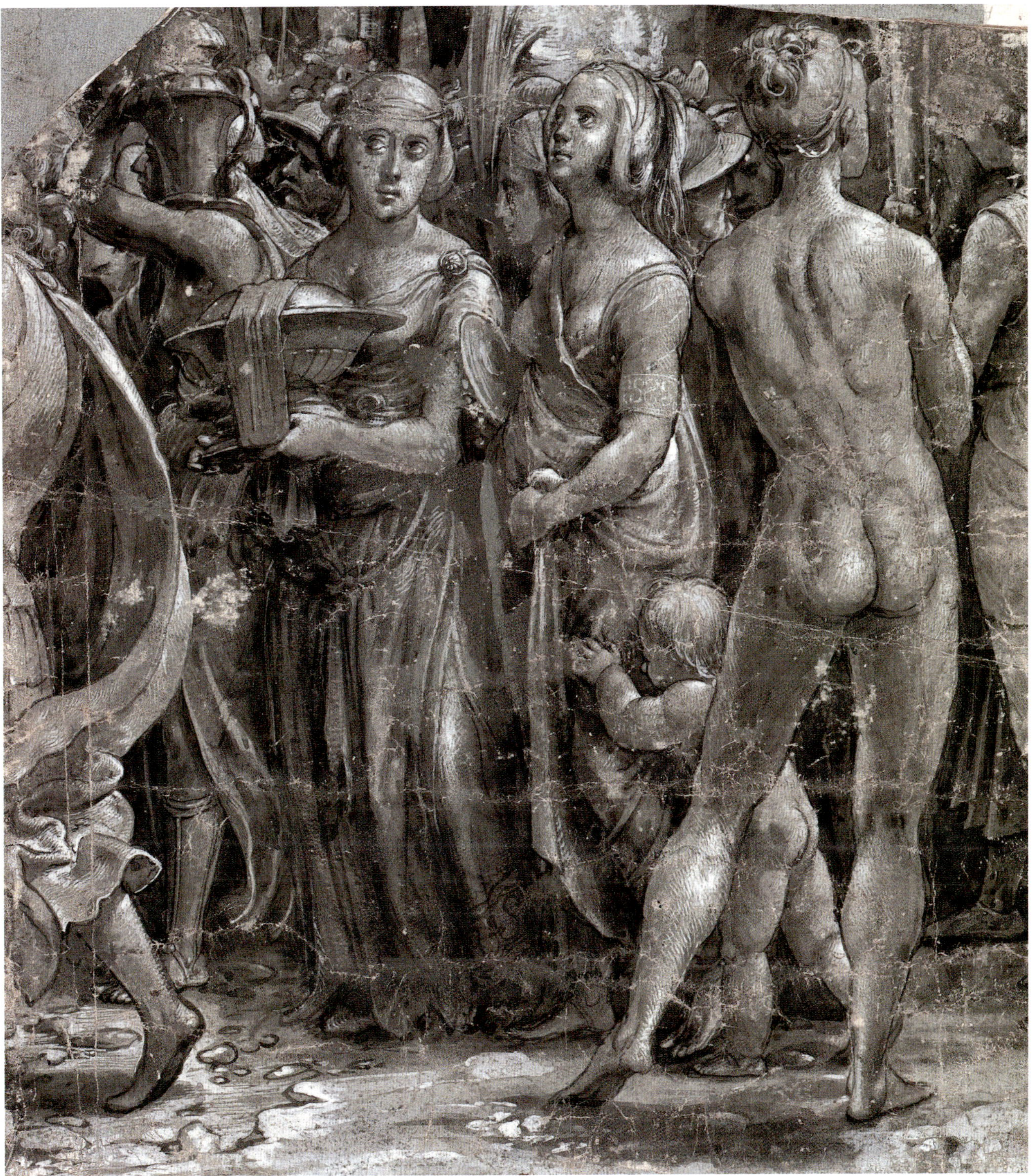

Triumphal Procession, c.1519–20, black ink, grey wash and white heightening, on dark olive-green prepared paper, 20.4 x 18.7cm (8 x 7.3in), Staatliche Graphische Sammlung, Munich, Germany

A fragment of a scene with classical figures. The drawing may be a preparatory work for one of Holbein's decorative commissions. Much later he would create two similar triumphal procession murals for the Hanse merchants in London: *The Triumph of Riches*, and *The Triumph of Poverty*, c.1532, for the Banqueting Hall of the Guildhall of the Steelyard (see pages 174–75).

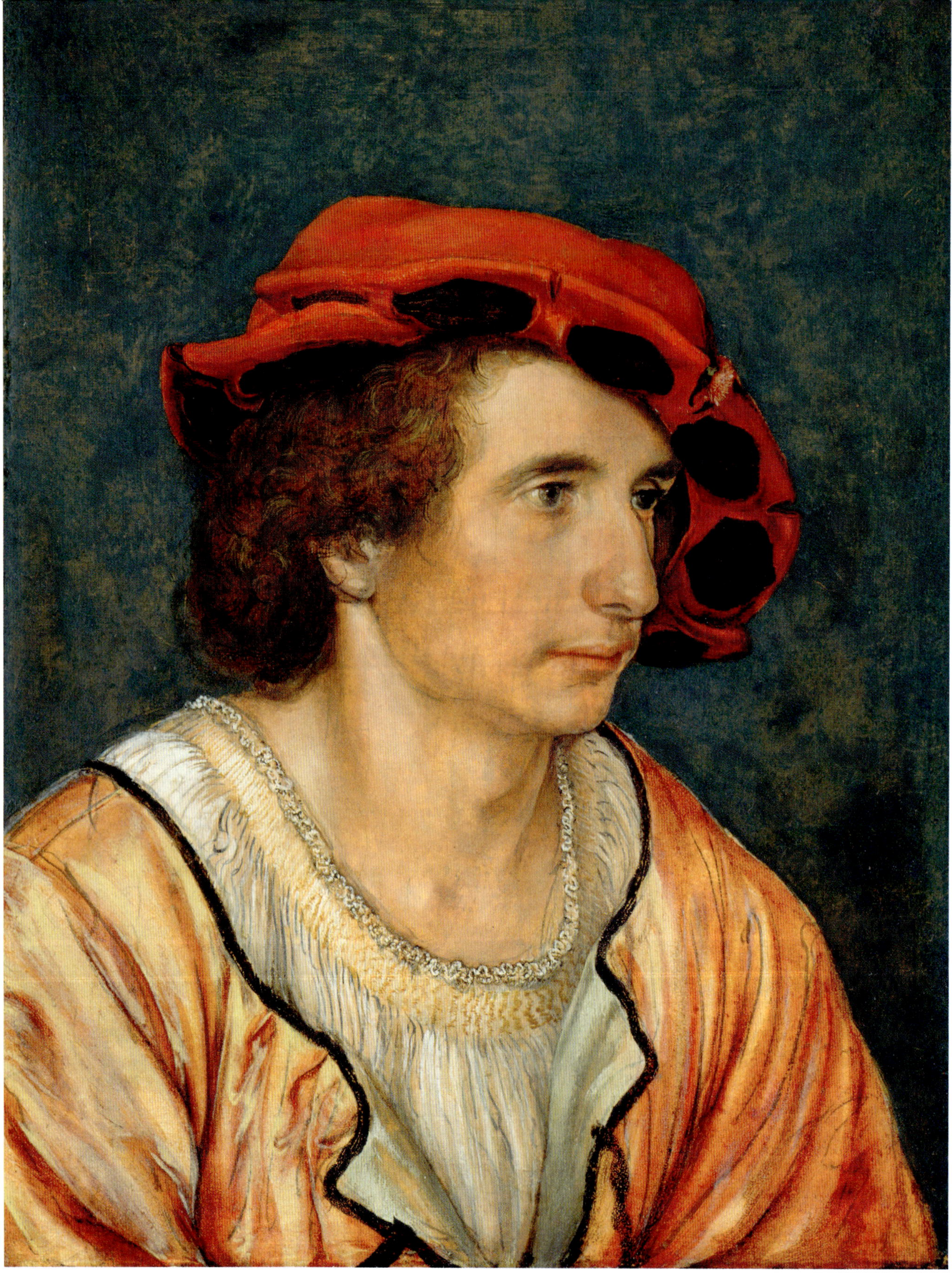

Portrait of a Young Man, c.1520–1530,
oil on panel, 22 x 17cm (8.7 x 6.7in),
National Gallery of Art, Washington
DC, USA

The artist creates the work in a
colour palette similar that used for the
portraits of Jakob and Dorothea Meyer
(page 111). A young man is depicted
in profile, in a half-length portrait. He
wears a fashionable red hat on top of
his auburn hair. The brim is interwoven
in a ribbon-style with contrasting fabric.
It has the brim pulled down to the left
side. A fine silk shirt is worn under a
satin-type overshirt, connoting status.
The painting is attributed to Holbein.

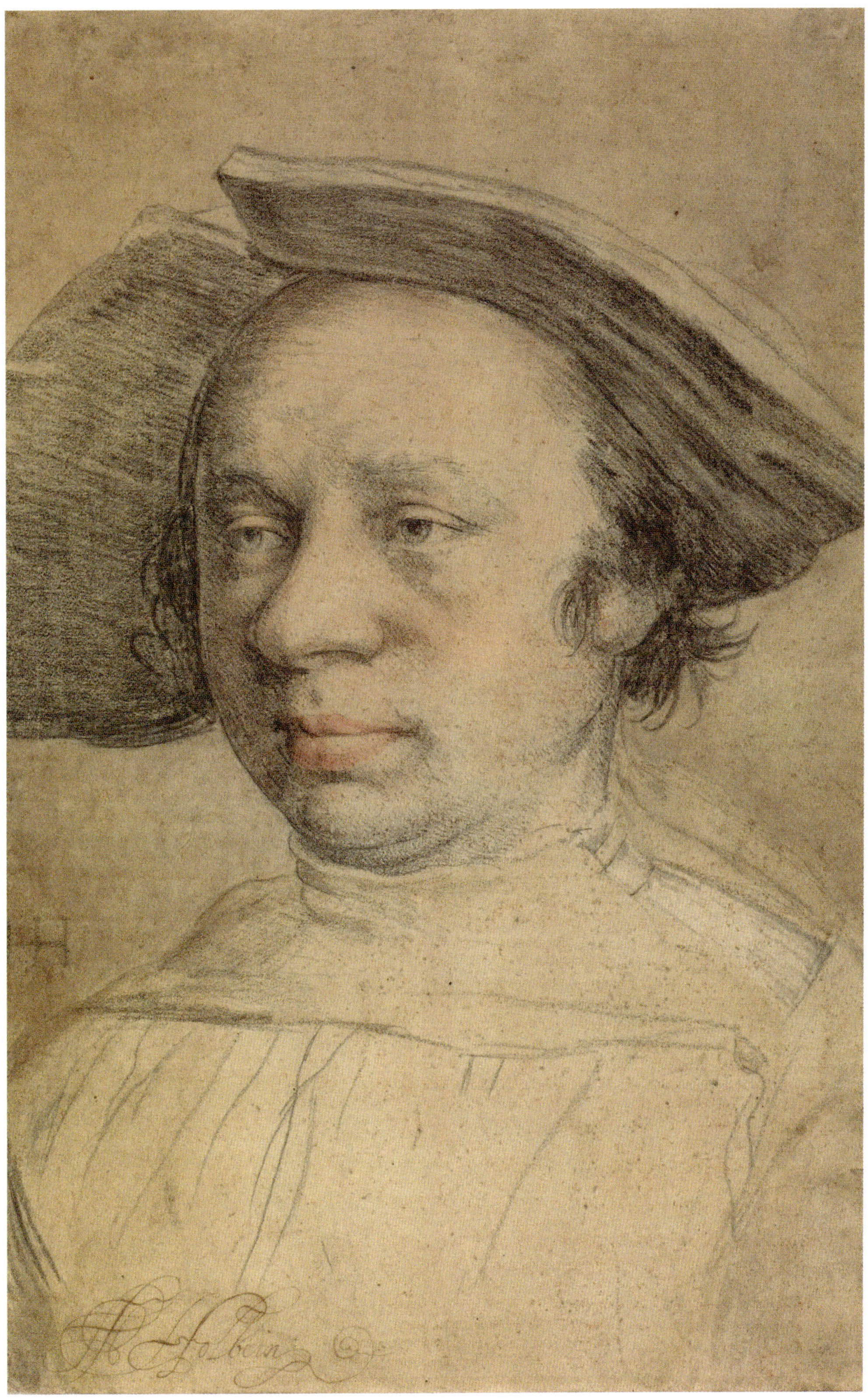

Portrait of a Man in a Broad-brimmed Hat,
*c.*1526, black chalk and wetted red chalk
with brown wash on laid paper, 30.3 ×
19.6cm (11.9 × 7.7in), National Gallery of
Art, Washington DC, USA

A bust-length drawing of a middle-aged
unknown man in three-quarter profile facing
to his right, wearing a broad-brim hat set back
on the head.

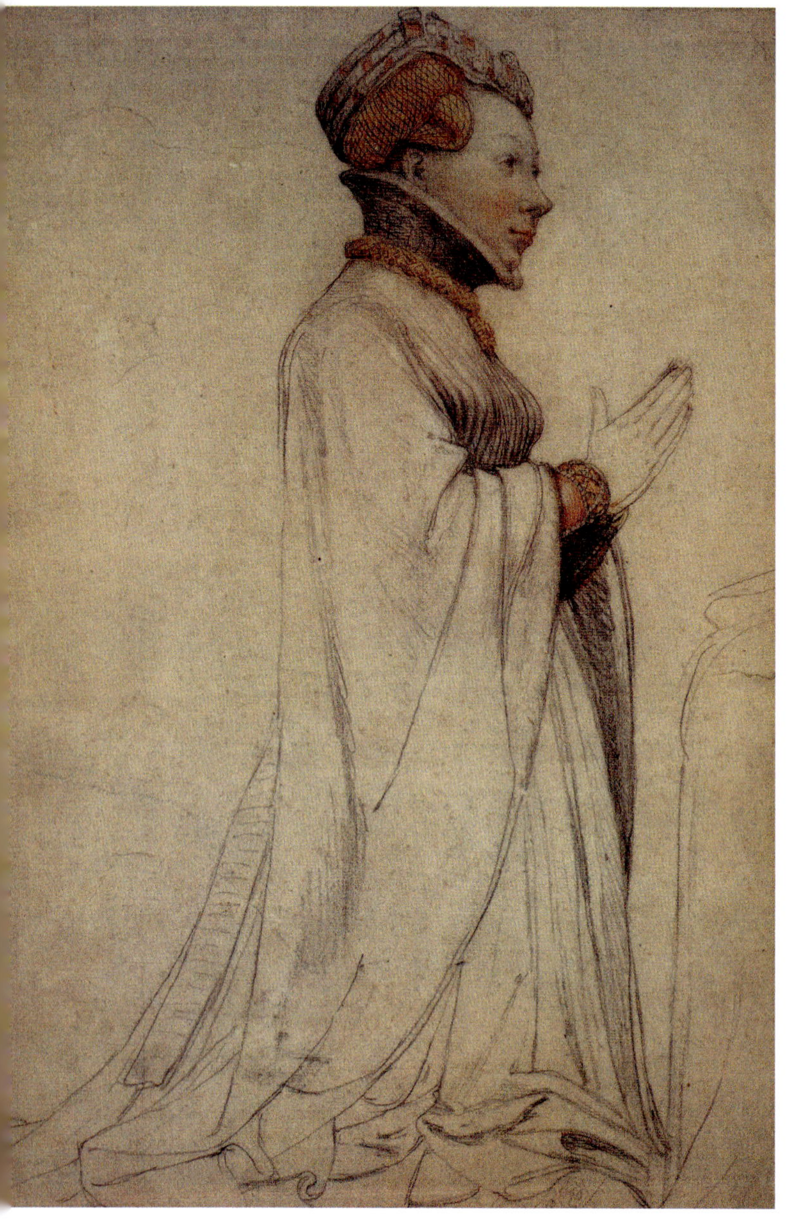

Left: *Jeanne de Boulogne, duchess of Berry,* 1523–24, black, yellow, and coloured chalk on paper, 39.6 x 27.5cm (15.5 x 10.8in), Kunstmuseum, Basel, Switzerland

A portrait drawing of Jeanne de Boulogne (1378–1424) duchess of Berry (from 1394), second wife of Jean de France, duke of Berry (see below). Holbein copied from life-size limestone polychromatic kneeling-portrait sculptures of the duke and duchess. These were created by the French sculptor Jean de Cambrai (c.1350–1438), in the duke's service from 1386–1416. The sculptures were placed in the burial chapel of the ducal palace in Bourges, which Holbein visited in 1523–24. Holbein used yellow chalk for the first time during his travels through France, and to great effect in these drawings.

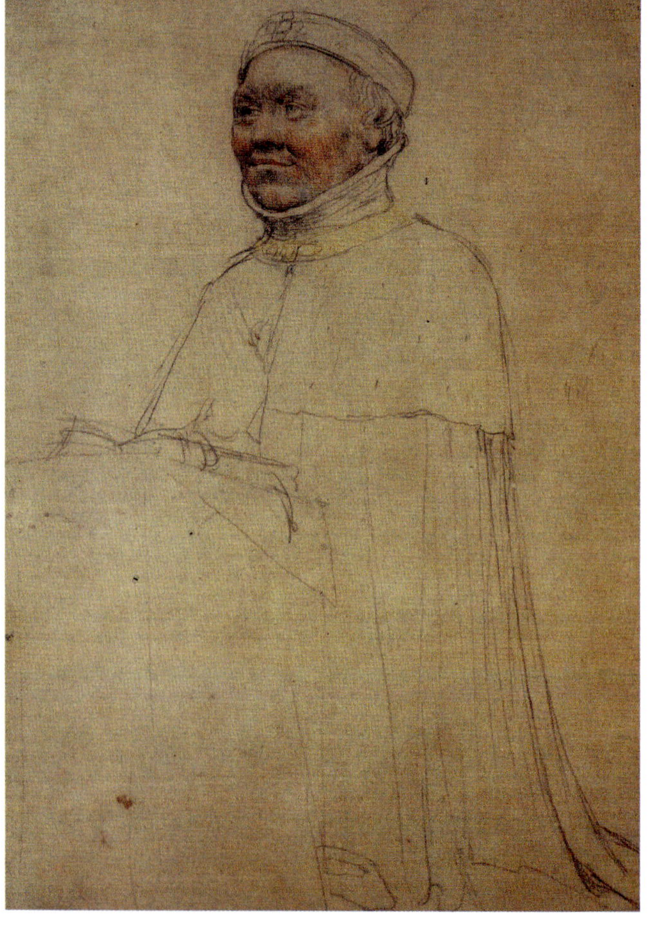

Right: *Jean de France, duke of Berry*, 1523, black, yellow and coloured chalk on paper, 39.6 x 27.5cm (15.5 x 10.8in), Kunstmusem, Basel, Switzerland

Holbein's companion portrait drawing depicts Jean de France (1340–1416), duke of Berry. The heads of the duke and duchess were badly damaged during the French Revolution. In 1913, Holbein's drawings allowed replica heads to be created that were true to the original sculptures. The paired sculptures are now in Bourges Cathedral.

Right: *Resting Lamb and Head of a Lamb*, c.1523, brush over black pen, watercolour and white heightening, 20.6 x 24.6cm (8.1 x 9.6in), Kunstmuseum, Basel, Switzerland

A small study of a lamb at rest. Its face and limbs, and texture of its thick wool, is finely depicted. At top left, a study of the head of a lamb, both possibly preparatory drawings for a religious work.

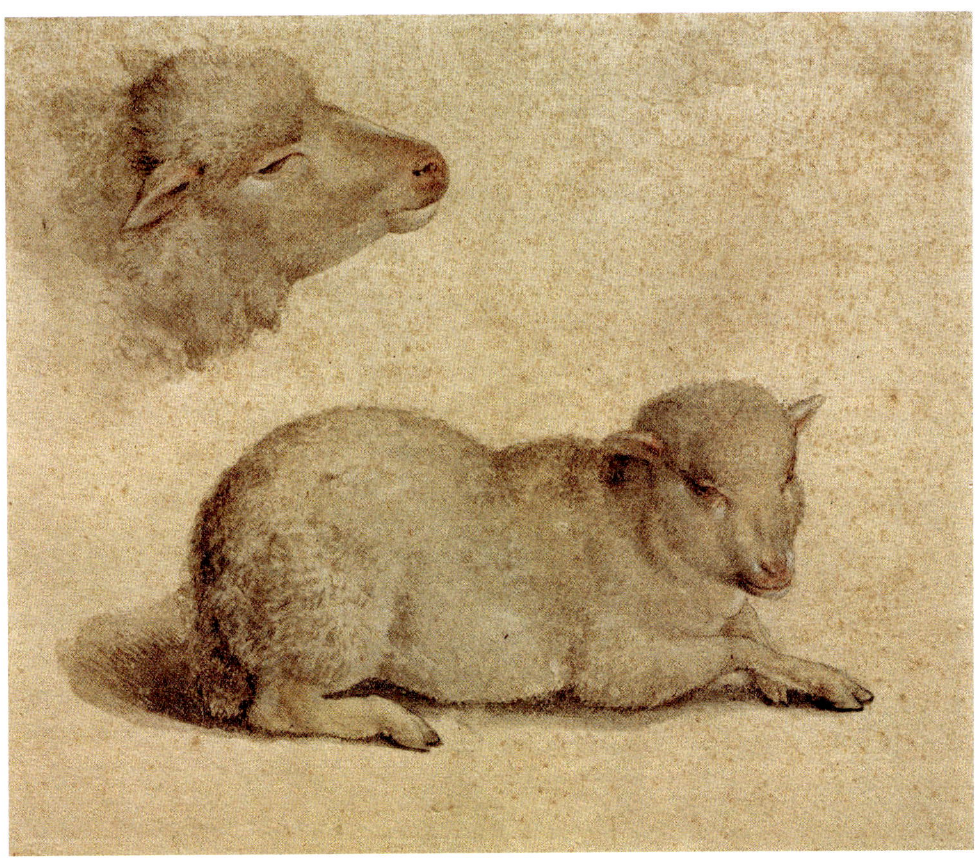

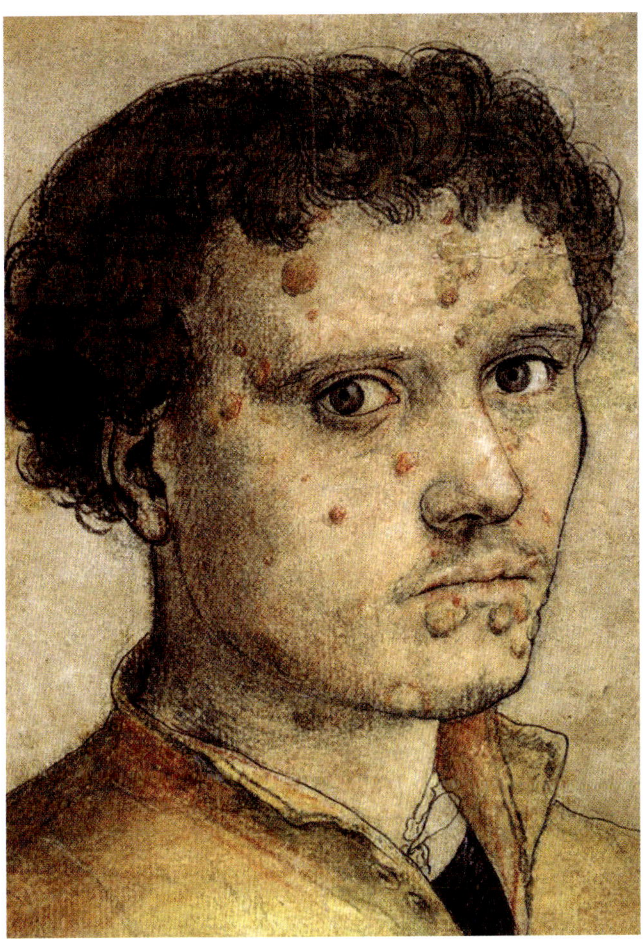

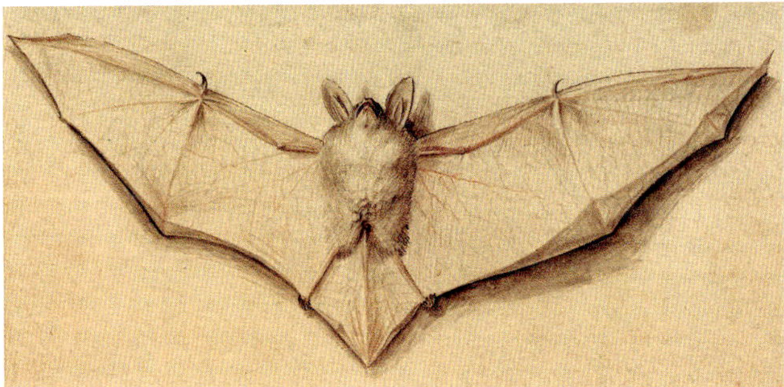

Above: *Bat with Spread Wings*, c.1523, black pen, grey and brown ink, washed with watercolour in reddish brown, 16.8 x 28.1cm (6.6 x 11in), Kunstmuseum, Basel, Switzerland

A realistic portrait of a bat with outspread wings. This drawing highlights Holbein's consummate skill in minute detail, from the bat's large ears to the claw-fingers and feet which hold on to the threadlike membrane of its vast wingspan.

Left: *Head of a Young Man*, 1523, black and grey ink and black, red, yellow, and white chalk, on cream antique laid paper, heavily restored, 20.5 x 15.2cm (8.07 x 5.98in), Fogg Art Museum, Harvard, Cambridge, MA, USA

A closely observed head and shoulders portrait of a young man who suffers from boils and warts, with pustules spread across his face and neck.

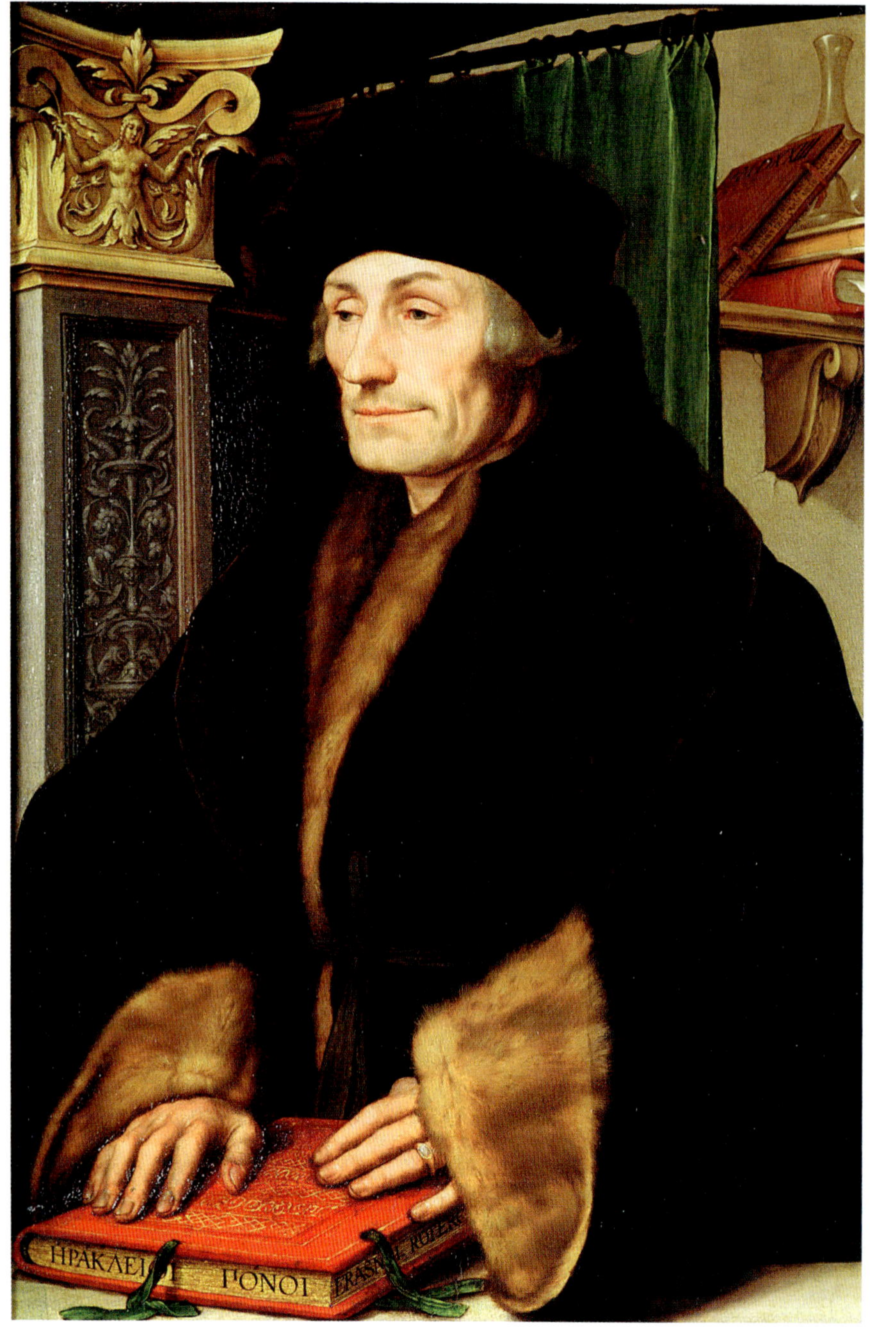

Above: *Portrait of Erasmus of Rotterdam*, 1523, oil and egg tempera on panel, 73.6 x 51.4cm (28.9 x 20.2in), National Gallery, London, UK

A profile, half-portrait, of Desiderius Erasmus in his study. One of two portraits sent to England, this went to Bishop William Warham, Erasmus's friend and patron. A popular composition in Holbein's portraits was to surround his sitter with material possessions that reflected his/her profession and accomplishments; one of the first and most successful is this portrait of Erasmus. The Latin couplet on the book visible on the back shelf, possibly written by the artist, or Erasmus, praises Holbein's artistic skill: 'I am Johannes (i.e. Hans) Holbein, whom it is easier to denigrate than to emulate.'

Above: Drawing studies of Erasmus' hands, *c.*1523, Musée de Louvre, Paris, France

A preparatory study of Erasmus's hands reveals Holbein's attention to detail.

Opposite: *Portrait of Desiderius Erasmus*, 1523, oil on panel, 42 x 32cm (16.5 x 12.5in), Musée de Louvre, Paris, France

One of the most well-known portraits of Desiderius Erasmus, Holbein depicts the scholar and humanist writing his commentary on Saint Mark's Gospel, in his text 'Paraphrases on the New Testament'. Erasmus is portrayed against a green background illustrated with small yellow and red flowers. (Another version of the painting in the Kunstmuseum, Basel, has a plain dark green background.) Holbein draws attention to the concentration on the scholar's face, shown in profile, with eyes cast down.

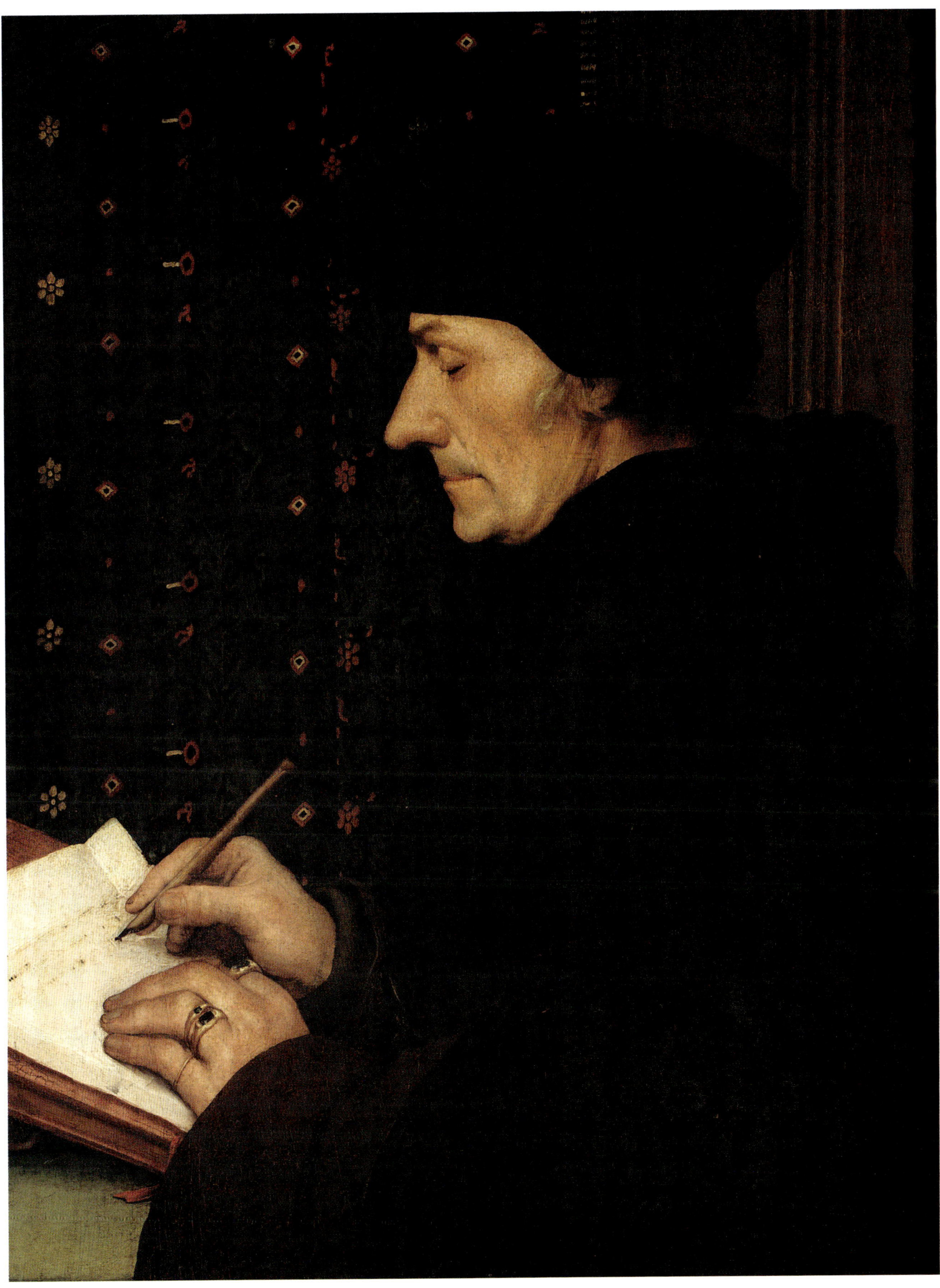

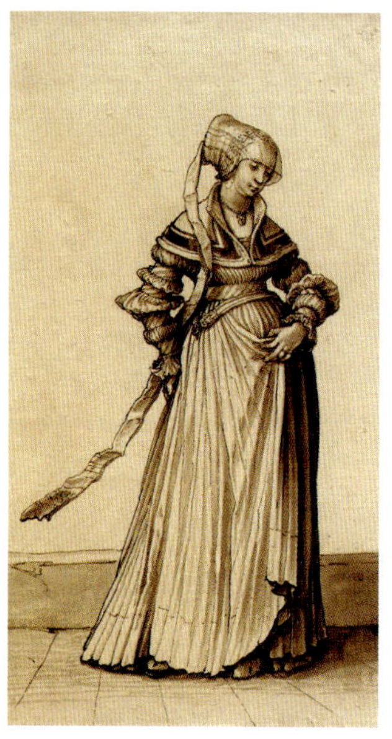 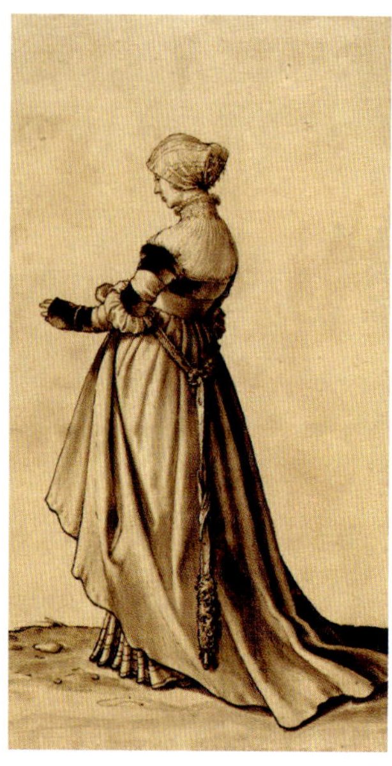 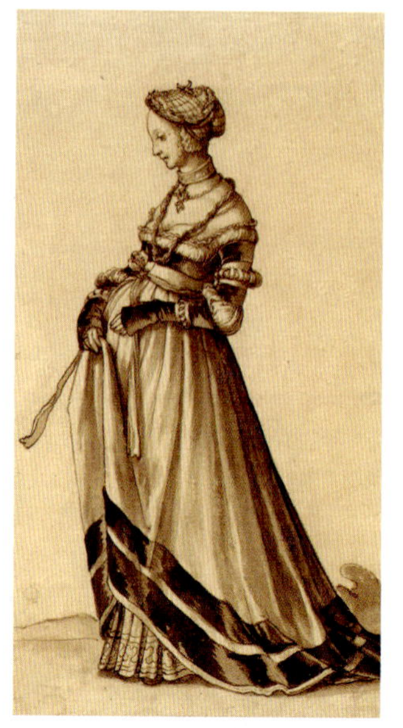

Left: *Women from Basel, three drawings, c.1523,* pen and some brush (black), and grey wash, each about 29.1 x 19.7cm (11.5 x 7.75in), Kunstmuseum, Basel, Switzerland

Holbein created a set of six figure drawings, thought to be paired: two prostitutes, two merchant-class women and two noblewomen, though it is difficult to decipher the differences. In these three illustrations, Holbein focuses on their deportment and fashionable clothing.

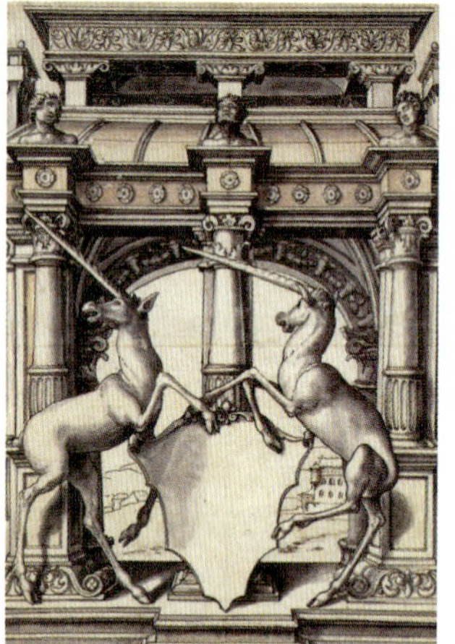

Left: *Etched design for a stained glass window,* 1523, pen and ink, and brush, 20.9 x 27.4cm (8.2 x 10.8in), Kunstmuseum, Basel

Holbein created numerous and intricate stained glass designs. Basel artists, together with craft designers, worked from drawn glass design to completed windows, installed in churches or private homes.

Right: *Archangel Michael Weighing Souls,* 1523, pen and ink, 38.8 x 22.8cm (15.2 x 8.9in), Kunstmuseum, Basel, Switzerland

A superb depiction of Archangel Michael, weighing souls for entry to Heaven. By the archangel's feet the devil looks up, possibly hoping for a few fallen souls to join him in the fiery furnace of Hell.

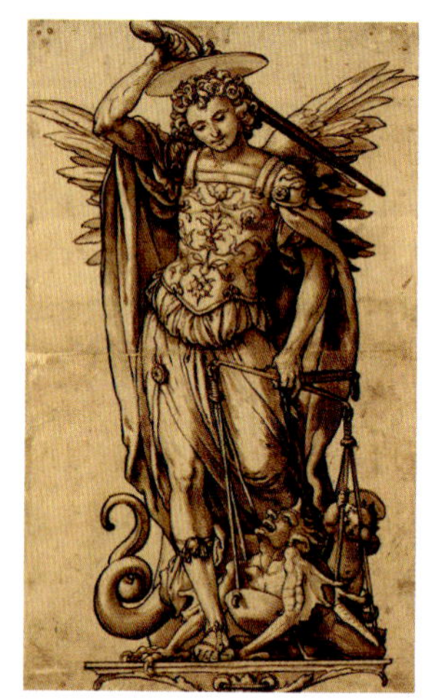

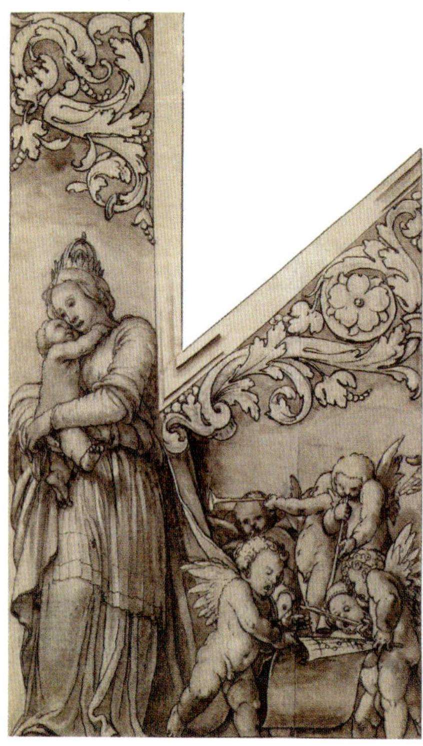 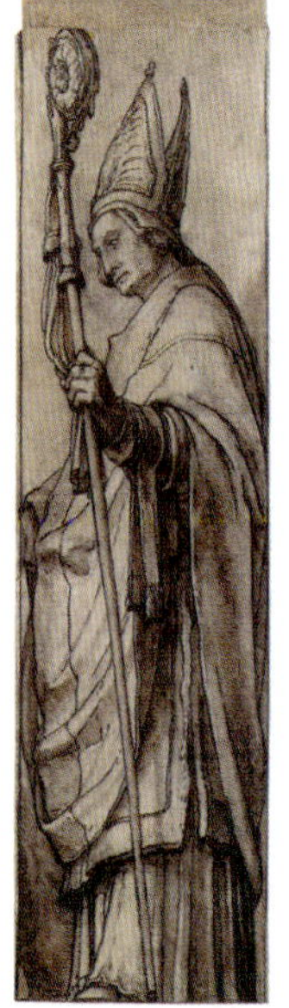

Below: *Studies for the organ wings of Basel Minster,* with detail of the Madonna, angels and St. Pantalus (shown left), *c.*1525–26, pen and ink and brush over chalk, brown and grey wash, Kunstmuseum, Basel, Switzerland

The organ shutters painted for Basel Cathedral depict Empress Kunigunde and Emperor Heinrich II on the left pair of wing pieces, and Madonna with child, angels playing music, and St. Pantalus on the right.

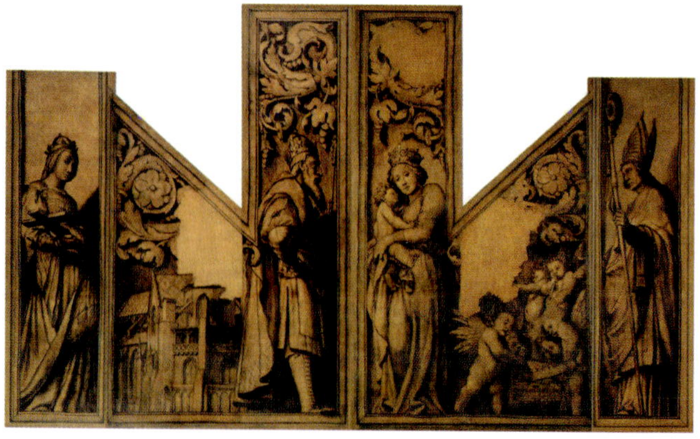

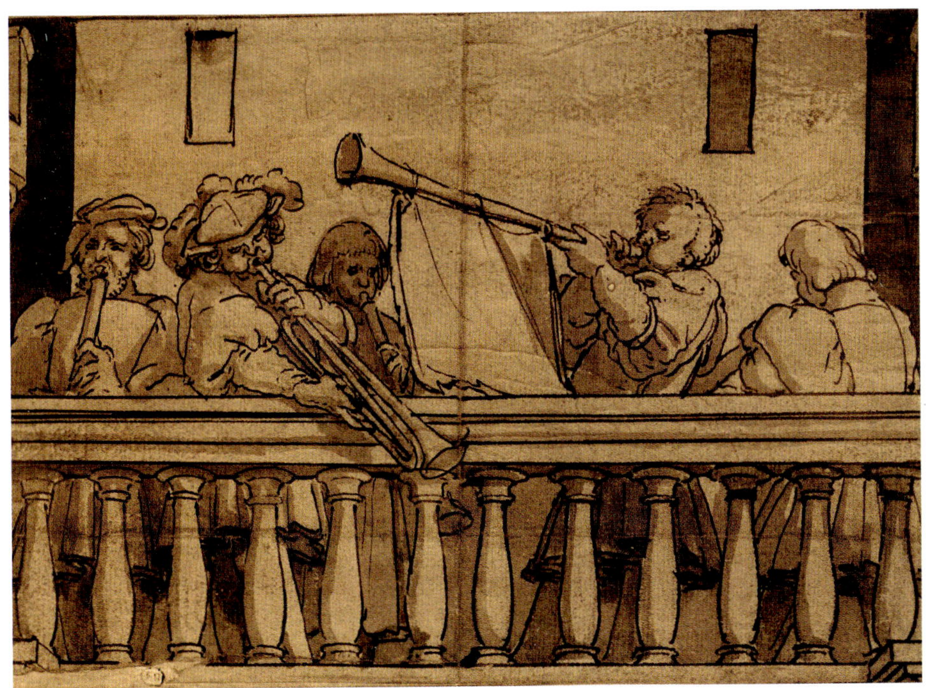

Left: *Minstrel's Gallery, c.1524–26*, pen and black ink with grey and black wash on paper, 13 x 18.1cm (5.1 x 7.1in), British Museum, London, UK

From a larger composition cut down in size, the drawing depicts five musicians – two playing shawms (double-reed woodwind instruments), two playing long trumpets, and one possibly playing a sackbut (a type of trombone from this era) – who perform their music from a balustraded balcony. Dating is due to similarities between the pen and wash style of this work and Holbein's *Study for the organ wings of Basel Minster c.1525–26*.

Right: *Battle Scene, c.1524*, pen and some brush (black), and grey wash, 28.6 x 44.1cm (11.2 x 17.36in), Kunstmuseum, Basel

Formerly the centrepiece of a larger composition, this is a dynamic depiction of a hard-fought battle. Later, on the reverse of a triumphal arch created in a dining hall at Greenwich Palace, Holbein depicted a similar battle scene, of the English defeating the French at the battle of Thérouanne, Pas-de-Calais, in the Hauts-de-France region of France but that was an aerial view, so this may be an unrelated, earlier creation from Basel.

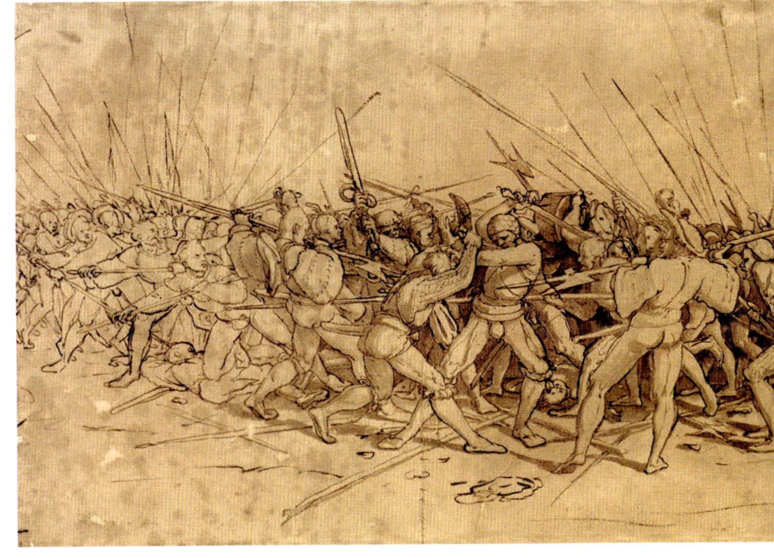

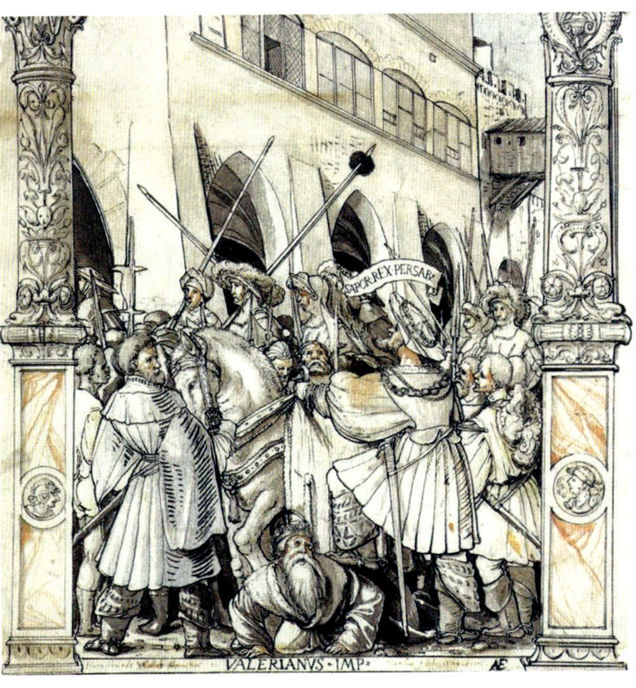

Left: *The Humiliation of Valerian by Shapur I, Edessa, AD259*, 1521, pen and some brush (black), and grey wash, 28.6 x 44.1cm (11.2 x 17.36in), Kunstmuseum, Basel, Switzerland

A significant commission for Holbein was the decoration of Basel's Great Council Chamber. As part of a series he depicted the capture of Valerian in a preparatory drawing. Valerian the Elder was taken captive by the Persian king Shapur I after the Battle of Edessa, becoming the only Roman emperor who was captured as a prisoner of war and causing wide-ranging instability across the empire.

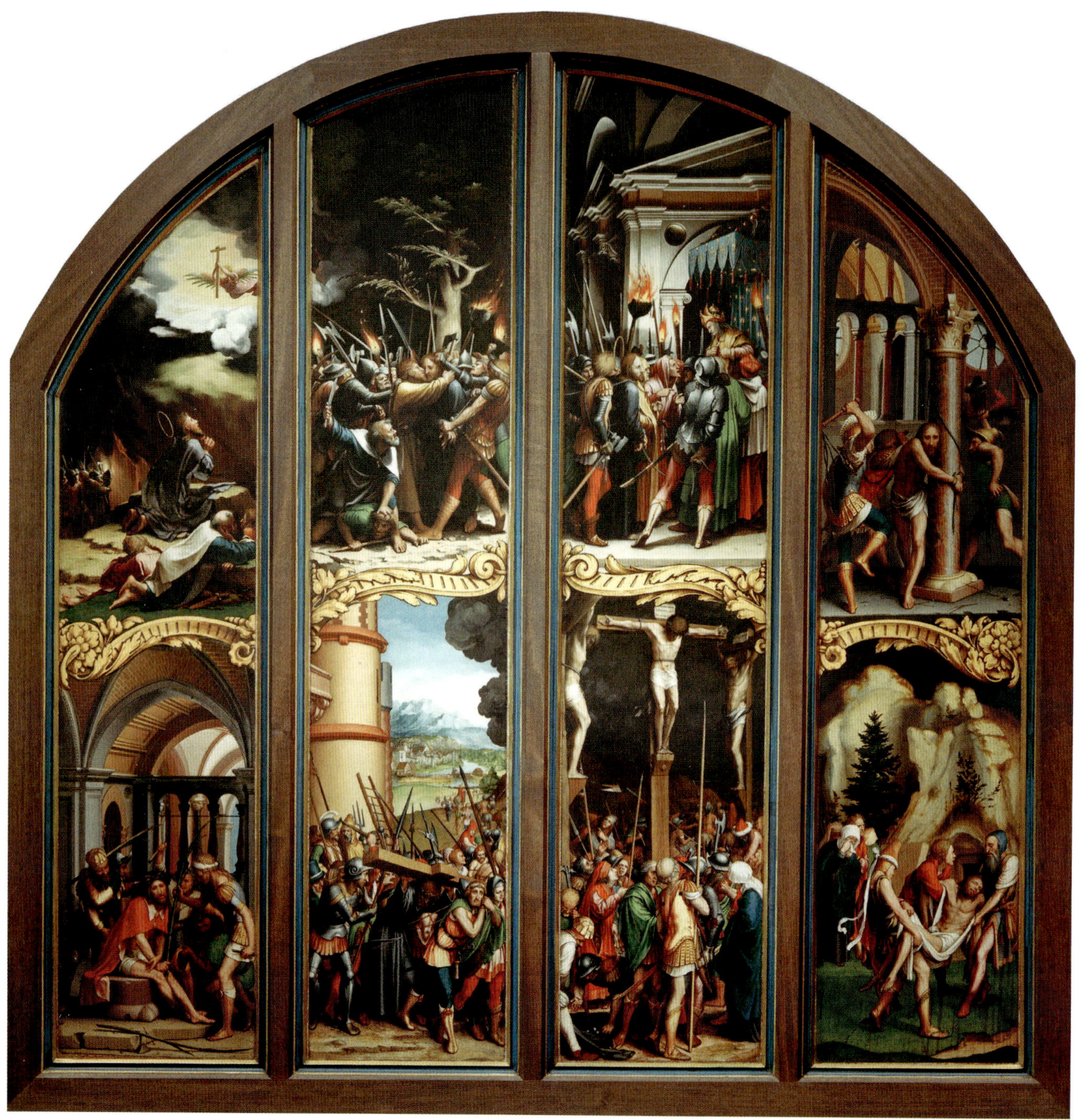

The Passion of Christ, c.1524, oil on lime wood panels, each 149.5 x 124cm.(58.85 x 48.2in), Kunstmuseum, Basel, Switzerland

Holbein's stupendous Passion altarpiece, with eight stacked sections depicting stages of the Passion of Christ, from Luke 22:1. Depicted top row, from left to right are the Mount of Olives; the Arrest in the Garden; Before Caiaphas; and the Scourging. On the bottom row, from left to right are the Crowning with Thorns; Christ Carrying the Cross; the Crucifixion; and the Entombment. Originally two wings of an altarpiece, probably designed to fit a niche in Basel's Minster church, the altarpiece was commissioned from Holbein by Maria Zscheckenbürlin.

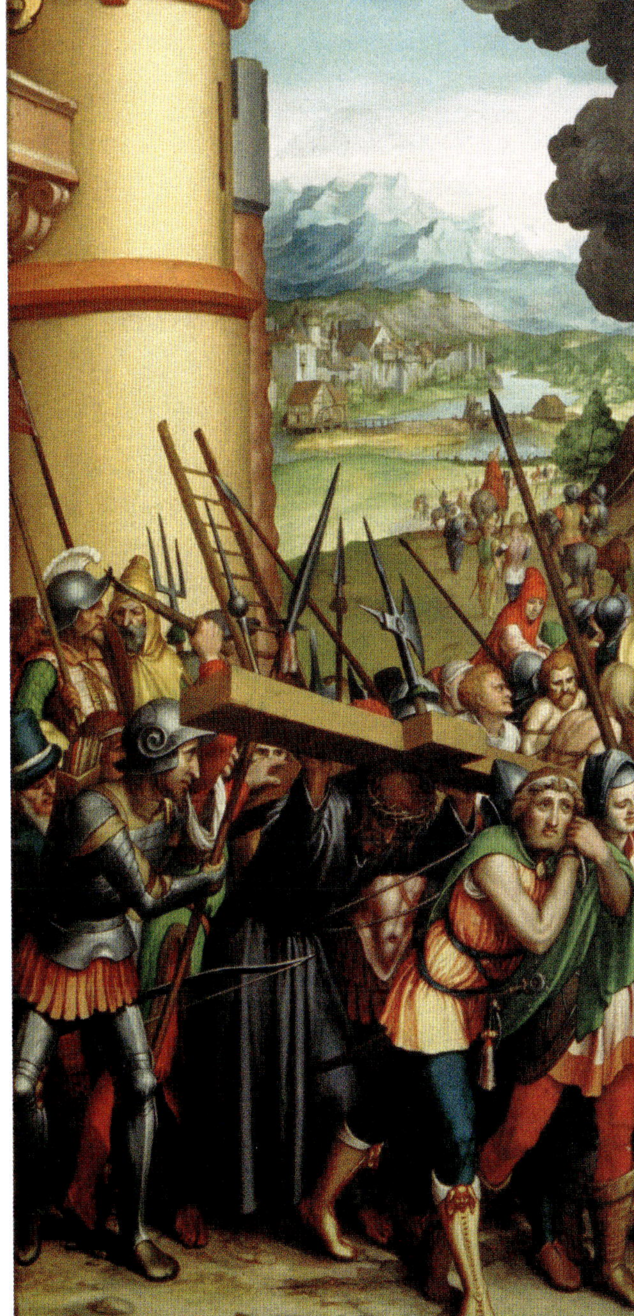

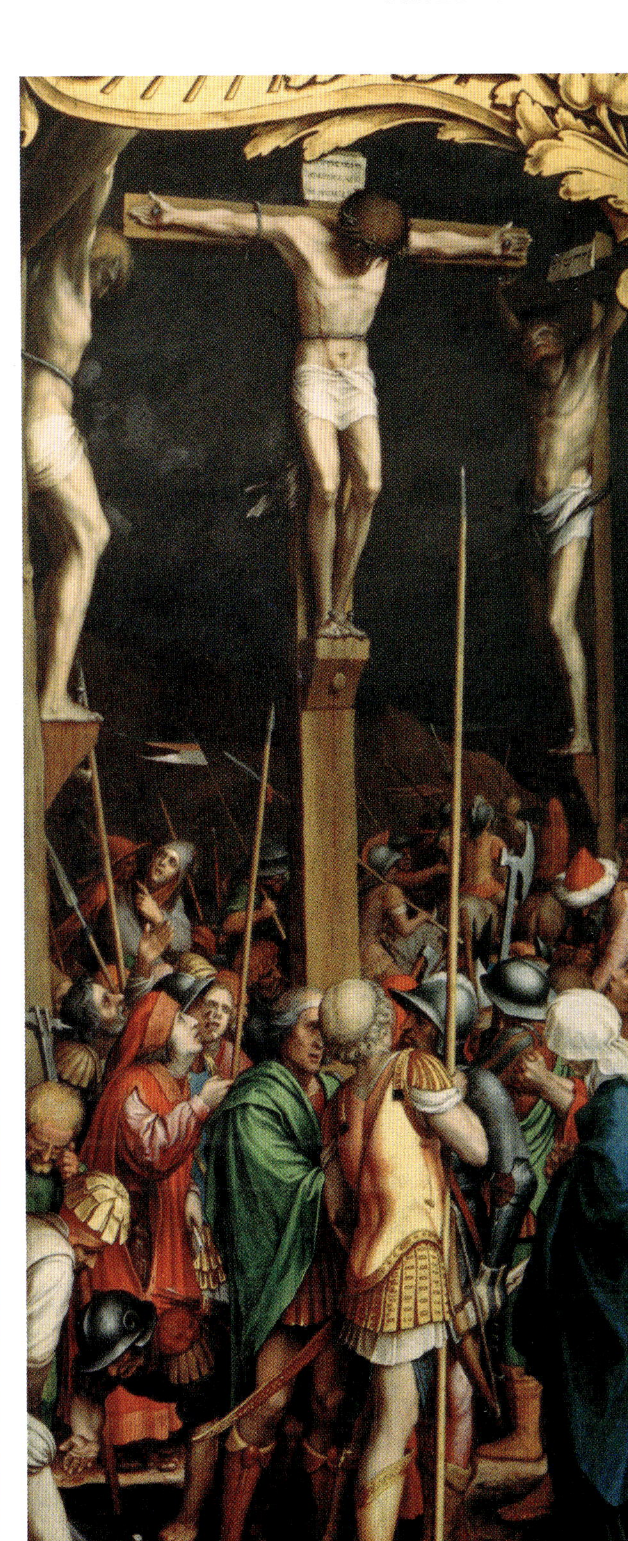

Details from two panels of *The Passion of Christ* altarpiece, c.1524

The two centre panels of the lower register of the altarpiece show Christ Carrying the Cross (left) and The Crucifixion (right). The scenes work as one continuous event. As Christ, tortured, suffers the burden of carrying a heavy Cross, the crowd that gathers and pushes forward on the road are the jostling mob that surround the three men crucified at Calvary. Holbein connotes the impending event in the darkening clouds, visible in the left panel, obliterating the skies in the right panel, as Christ is crucified.

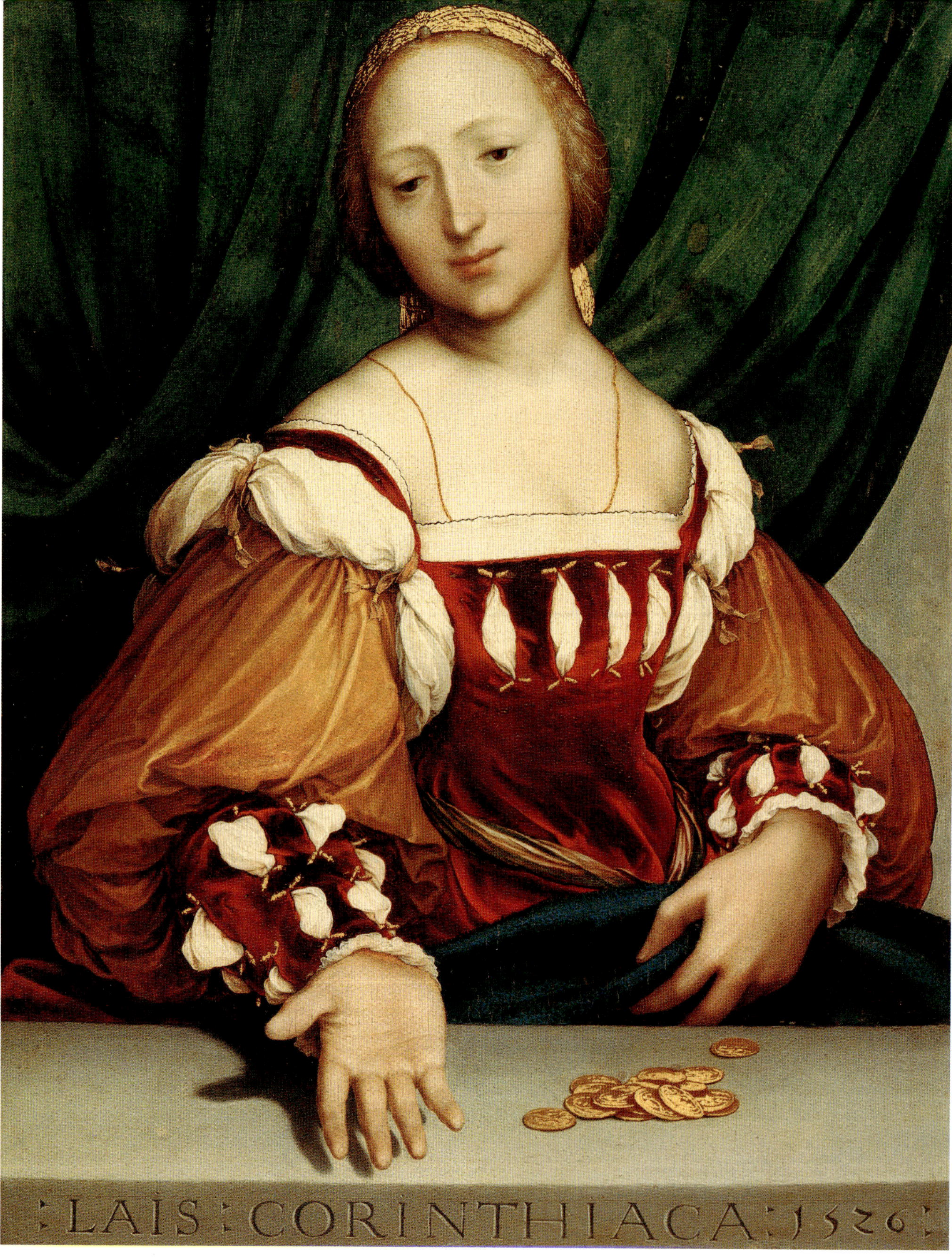

Laïs of Corinthiaca, 1526–28, oil on lime wood, 35.6 x 26.7 cm (14 x 10.5in), Kunstmuseum, Basel, Switzerland

The title refers to the ancient Greek figure of Laïs Corinthiaca (of Corinth, Greece), a famed hetaira, or courtesan. The painting is informed by Holbein's knowledge of Italian art of the period. The model for this work, and for *Venus and Cupid*, is thought to be Magdalena Offenburg. In the 1586 inventory of the Bonifacius Amerbach collection, two oil panels depicting Offenburg painted by Hans Holbein are mentioned. One is inscribed 'Lais Corinthiaca', the other included a child.

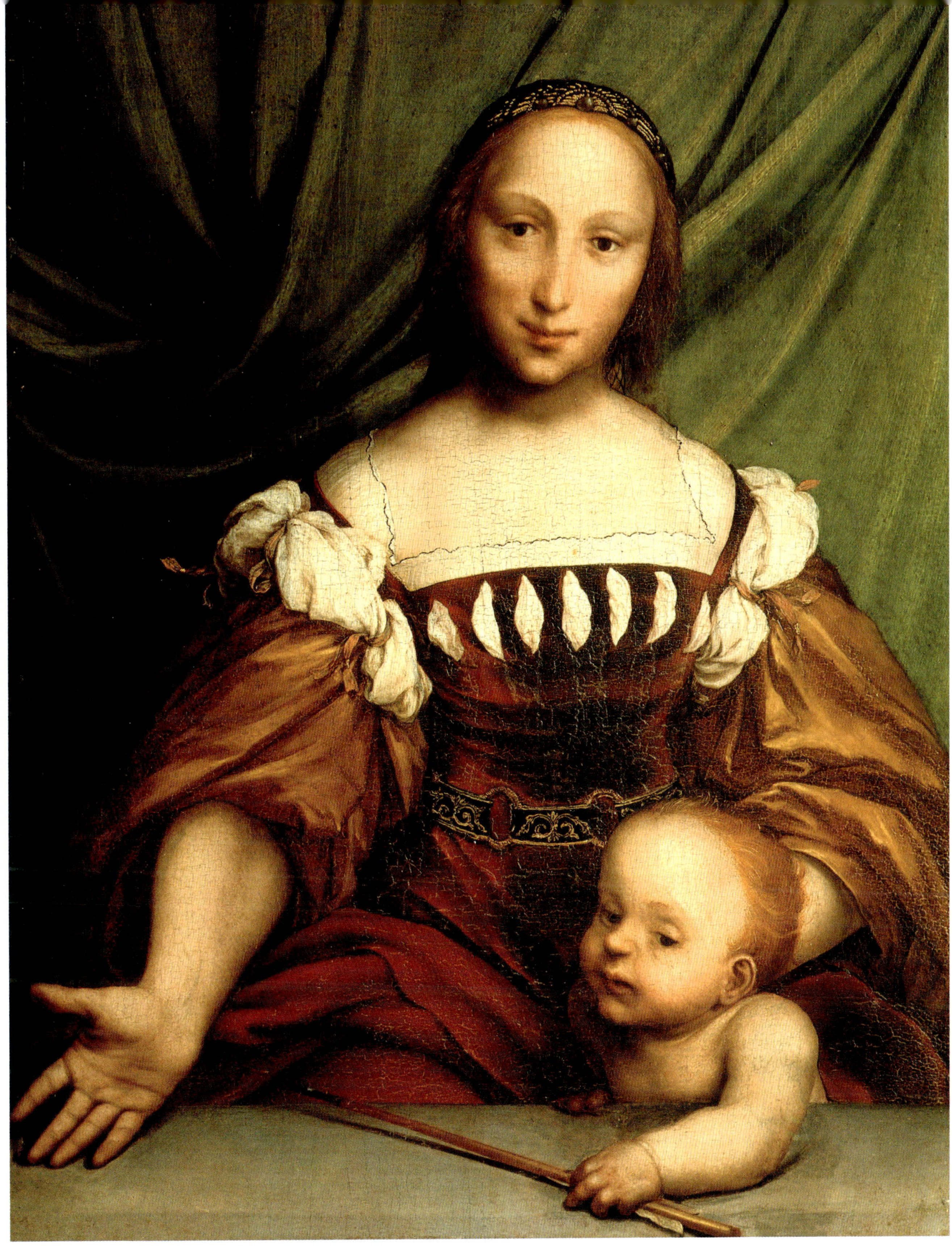

Venus and Cupid, 1526–28, workshop of Hans Holbein, oil on lime wood, 34.5 x 26cm (13.6 x 10.2in), Kunstmuseum, Basel, Switzerland

X-radiography has shown that *Venus and Cupid* was created by Holbein's workshop, probably from a Holbein drawing. The unknown artist, a highly-skilled workshop employee is called the 'Venus painter' by art historians. The mythological goddess Venus is with her infant son Cupid. He plays with an arrow, a symbol of his piercing love. The figures' placement beyond the parapet gives the illusion of space. Cupid has facial features similar to Holbein's daughter Katharina (born c.1526) portrayed in *Portrait of the Artist's Wife with the Two Elder Children* (see page 166).

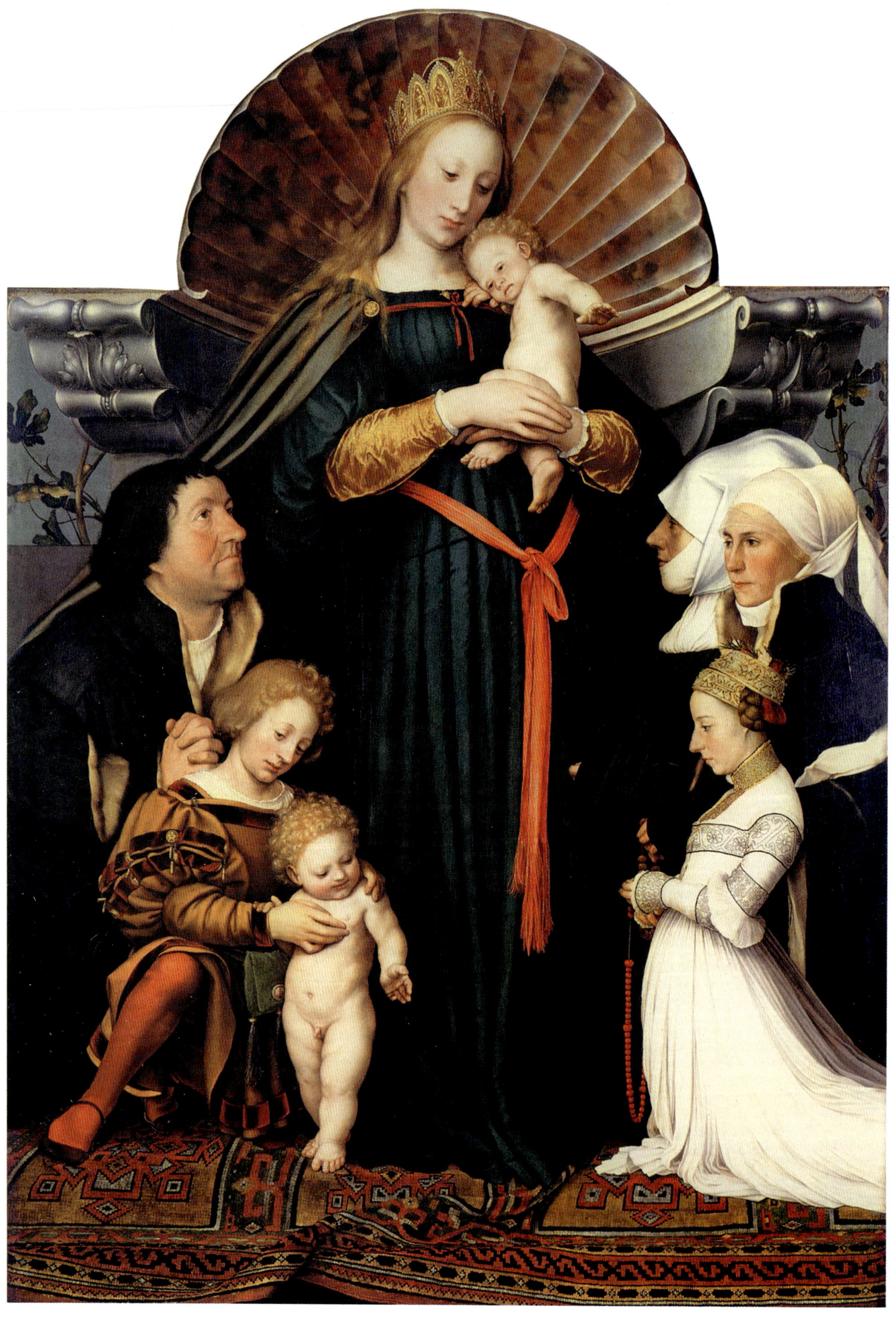

Left: *Darmstadt Madonna*, 1526–after 1528, oil on lime wood, 147 x 102cm (57.8 x 40.1in), Schlossmuseum, Darmstadt, Germany

Darmstadt Madonna, also known as the *Madonna of Jakob Meyer zum Hasen* after the painting's patron, was begun *c*.1526 and completed after 1528, the gap in dates relating to Holbein's absence in England. His mastery of spacial awareness is evident in the depiction of the Madonna standing in a scalloped-shell niche holding the Christ Child and looking down on the Meyer family members whom she protects. The Madonna is a 'Virgin of Pity' (Schutzmantebild) composition, which includes the donor and his family gathered around Mary and the infant Christ. Featuring patrons was not unusual for portraits at this time, even deceased members of the family, something which Holbein would use again in a dynastic portrait of King Henry VIII's family. The Madonna wears an Imperial crown on her head, an indication of unity between secular and religious life.

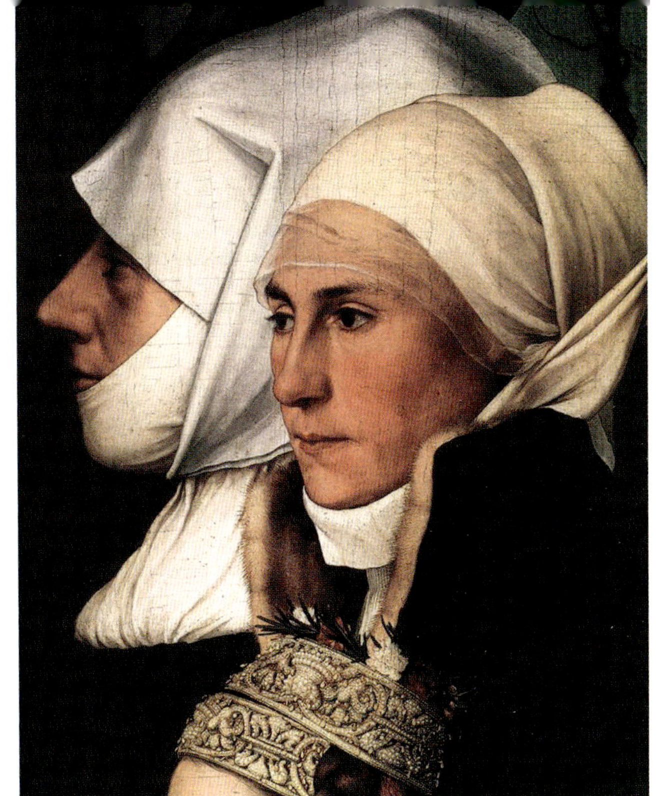

Above: Detail of Magdalena Baer and Dorothea Kannengiesser, *Darmstadt Madonna*, 1526–after 1528

In semi-profile is Dorothea Kannengiesser, Jakob Meyer's second wife. Behind her in profile and kneeling next to her is Magdalena Baer (d.1511), Meyer's deceased first wife. Holbein positions the family members very close to the Virgin, and life-size in proportion to her. He depicts Dorothea in a plain fur-lined coat, pulled up to her chin, which focuses interest on her face which is in profile, illuminated by an unseen light source.

Left: Detail of boy and infant, *Darmstadt Madonna*, 1526–after 1528

A boy with money bag at waist, supporting a naked infant, features on the Madonna's right, kneeling below Jakob Meyer. The older boy might be a deceased son of Meyer but the green money pouch he wears is an attribute of Christ's apostle James the Greater. The child he steadies may reference the older cousin of Christ, John the Baptist.

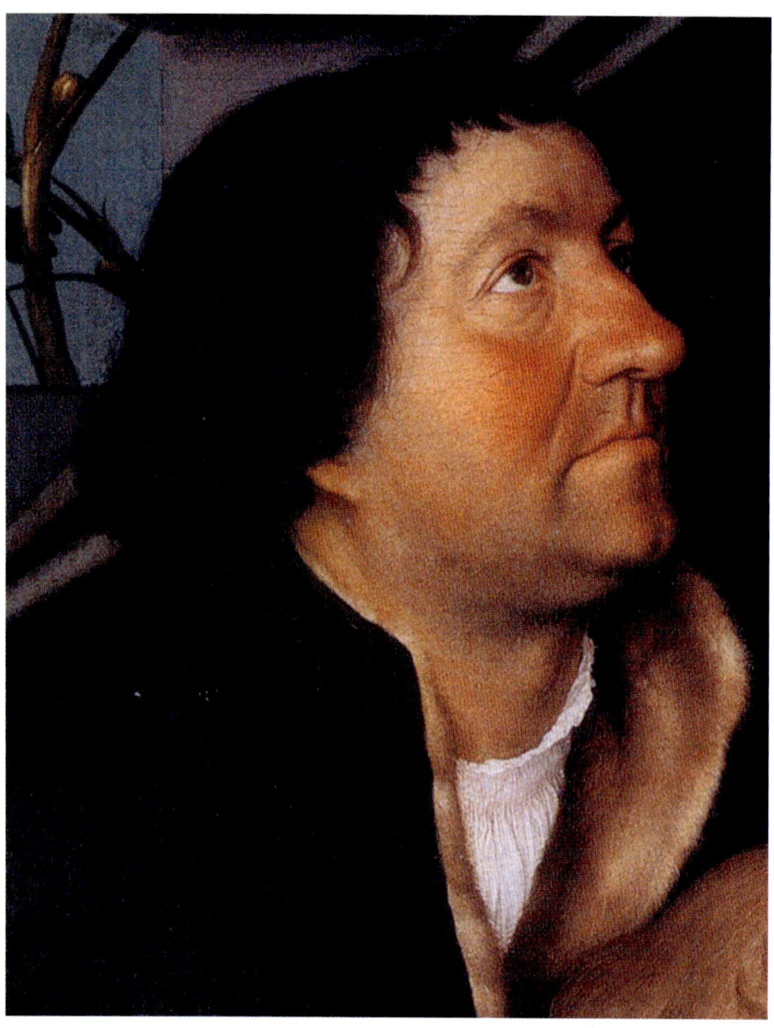

Detail of Jakob Meyer, *Darmstadt Madonna*, 1526–after 1528

By the time this portrait was painted Jakob Meyer zum Hasen, a money changer, military leader and the first non-patrician mayor of Basel, elected in 1516, had in 1521 lost his prestigious position as mayor due to accusations of financial fraud, which he denied.

Portrait study of Jakob Meyer zum Hasen, Mayor of Basel, 1525–29, black and coloured chalks on paper, 36 x 27.5cm (14 x 10.8in), Kunstmuseum, Basel, Switzerland

A preparatory drawing of Jakob Meyer zum Hasen, a study for the devotional painting known as *Darmstadt Madonna*, an altar painting for Meyer's private chapel. Begun before Holbein left Basel in 1526, the painting was not completed until after 1528.

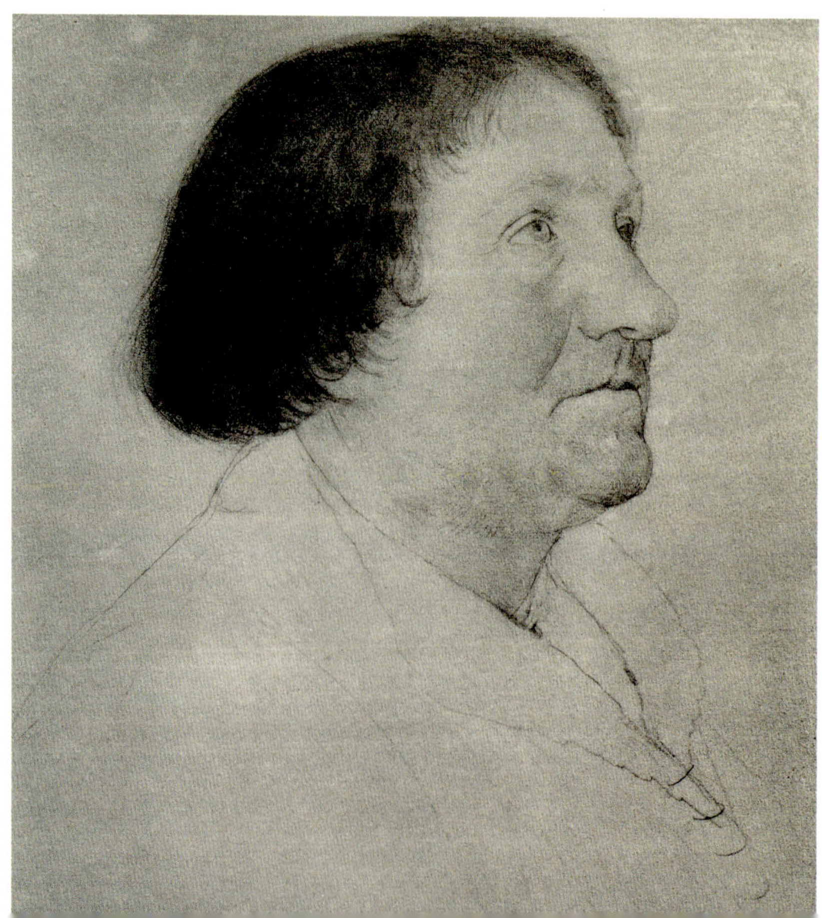

Portrait study of Anna Meyer, c.1526,
black and coloured chalks, 15.9 x
22.5cm (6.3 x 8.8in), Kunstmuseum,
Basel, Switzerland

Anna Meyer, younger daughter of
Dorothea and Jacob Meyer zum
Hasen, is depicted kneeling in the
Darmstadt Madonna painting (below).
For the preparatory drawing, she
looks quite different in details of
clothing and hairstyle, but the face and
expression are similar. Holbein used
black chalk with pale coloured chalks
to pick out skin tones and the yellow-
gold of her hair.

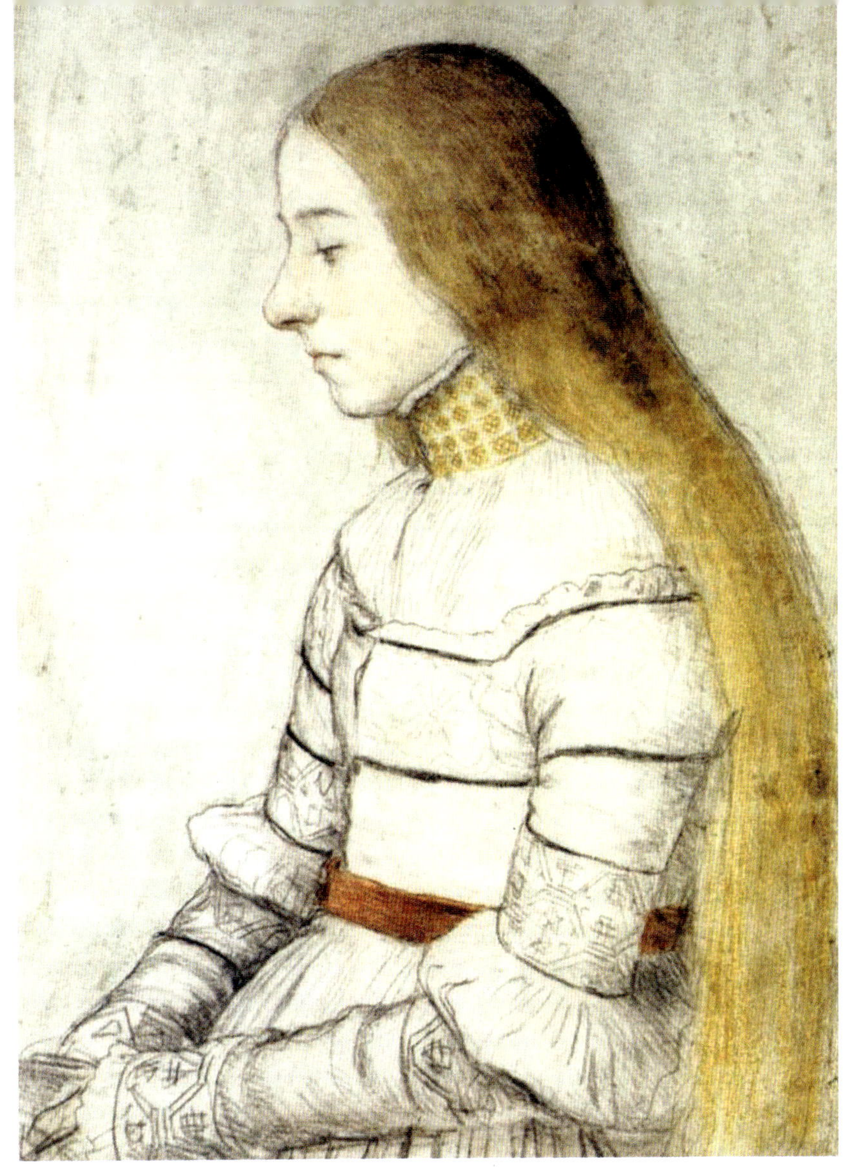

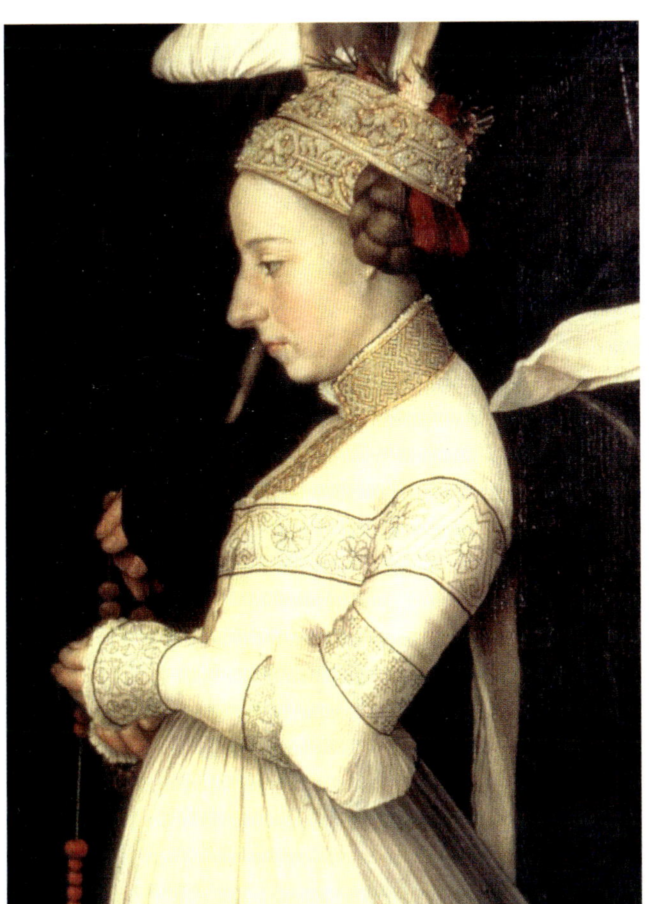

Detail of Anna Meyer,
Darmstadt Madonna, 1526–
after 1528

The Meyer's young daughter,
Anna, is shown kneeling in
profile, holding a flower. Here
she wears her hair coiled,
plaited and dressed in fine
material, quite different in
appearance to Holbein's
preparatory drawing.

Right: *Christ before the High Priests*, 1526–28, design for a stained glass window; pen and ink drawing, black and grey wash over chalk, 42.9 x 30.5cm (16.9 x 12.1in), Kunstmuseum, Basel, Switzerland (for all designs)

First of a series of ten designs for stained glass windows depicting the Passion of Christ. A Jewish high priest Caiaphas had, according to the Gospel of St Matthew 26: 57-67, organised a plot to kill Jesus Christ.

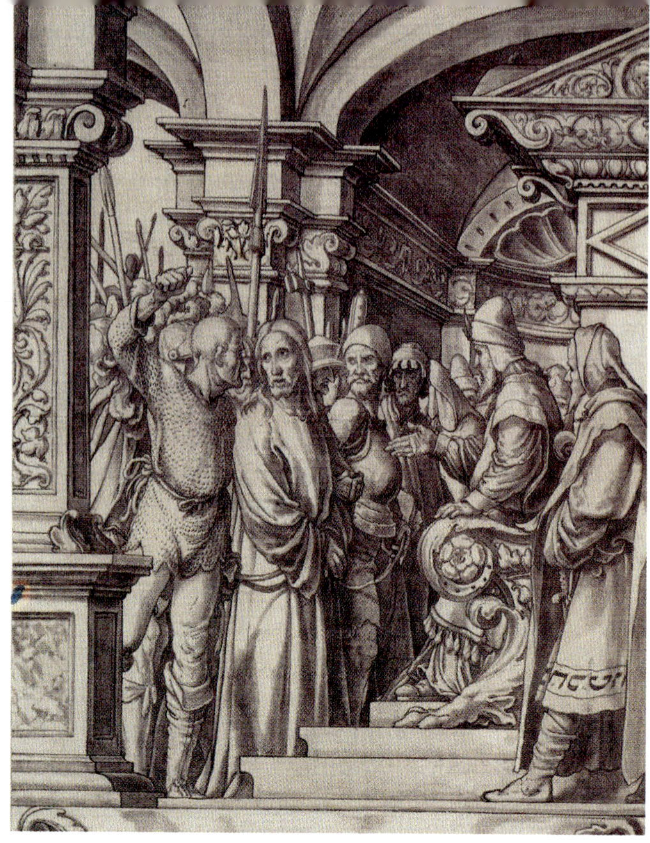

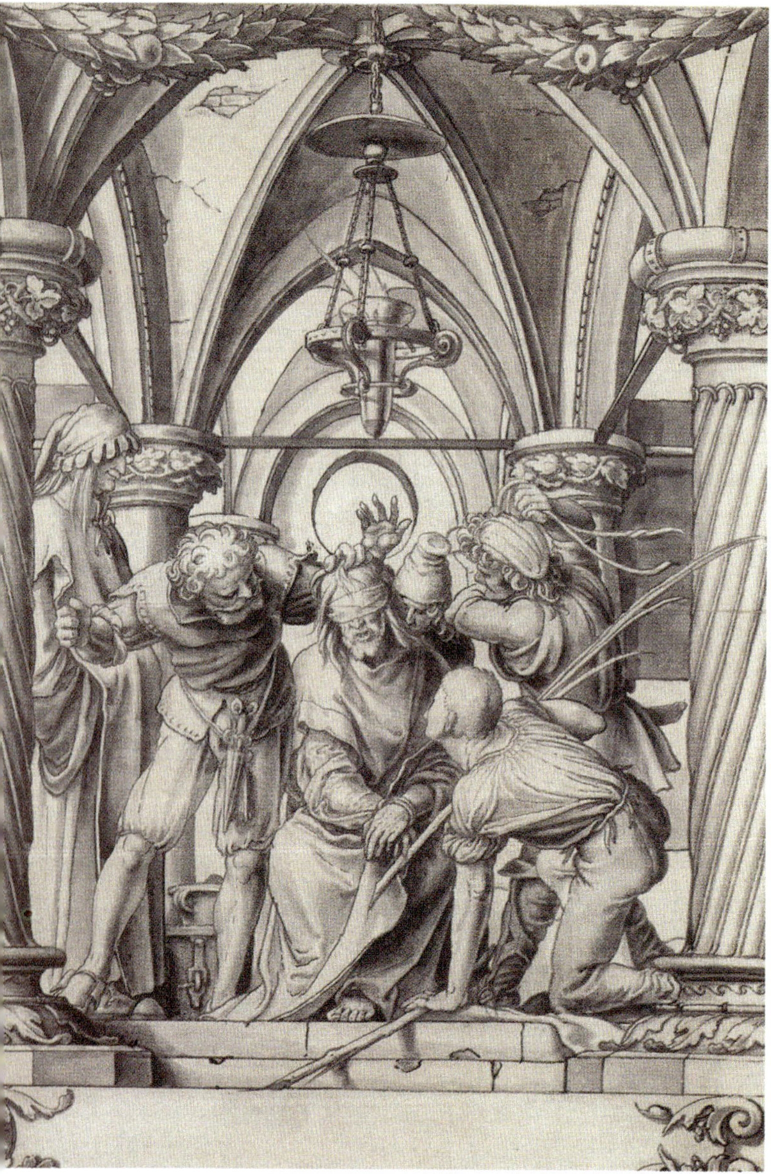

Left: *The Mocking of Christ*

Holbein depicts Christ being mocked by his torturers as 'King of the Jews'. During his Passion, Christ, as he had predicted, was cruelly mocked three times: first, following his trial; second, after Pontius Pilate's conviction of him; and third, at his crucifixion. All are retold in the gospels of Matthew 20:19, Mark 10: 34, and Luke 18:32.

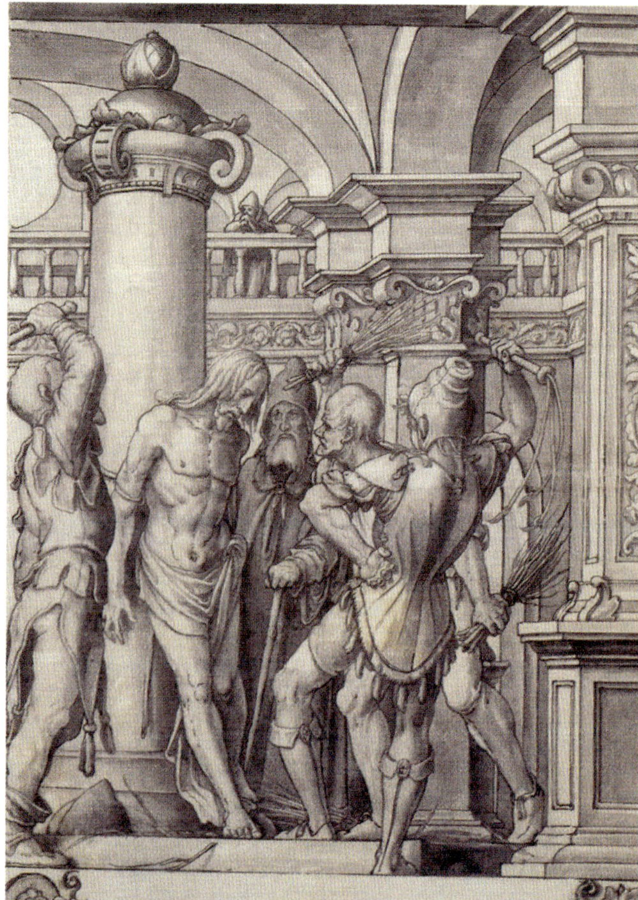

Right: *The Scourging of Christ*

Holbein accentuates the pressure that the torturers, shown in close proximity to Christ, add to his suffering, which he endures with head bowed.

Right: *Crowning Christ with Thorns*

In this depiction, one of the series of the Passion of Christ from betrayal to crucifixion, Holbein imagines an emaciated Christ, ribs showing, his head 'crowned' with thorns and bowed, as he is tortured by blows from the scourging of whips and sticks by his persecutors. The richly decorative architectural backdrop highlights Christ's weak position in this powerful enclave. It bears resemblance to Holbein's earlier depiction in *Christ as the Man of Sorrows with the Virgin Mary*, 1518–20 (see page 109).

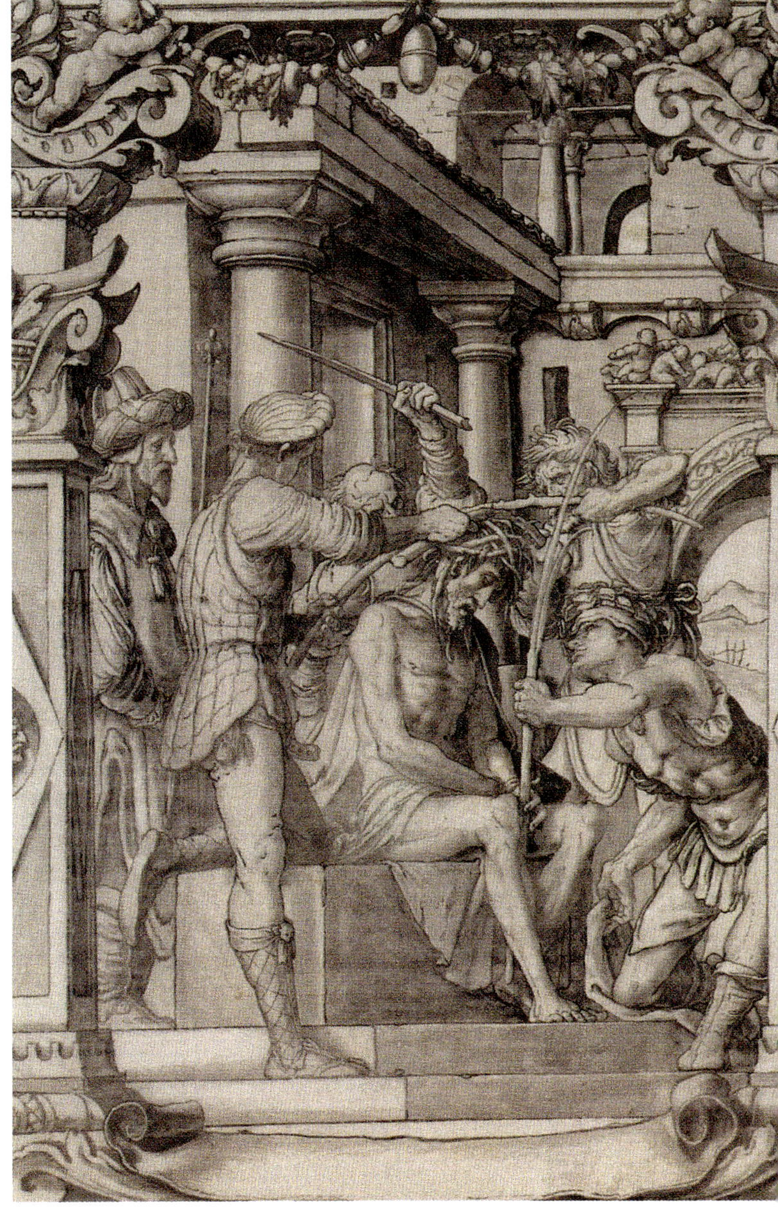

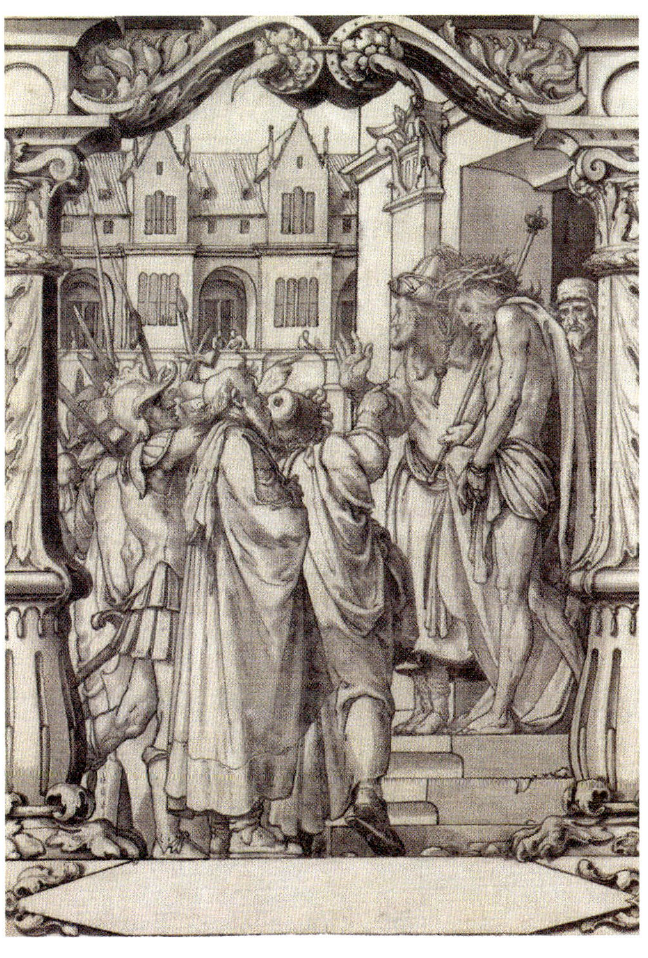

Left: '*Ecce Homo*'

The Latin words *Ecce Homo* 'Behold the Man' were uttered by Pontius Pilate according to the Gospel of St John 19:5, when he presented Christ, bound, scourged and tortured with a 'crown' of thorns, to an angry baying crowd in Jerusalem. The background shows the architecture of a German town.

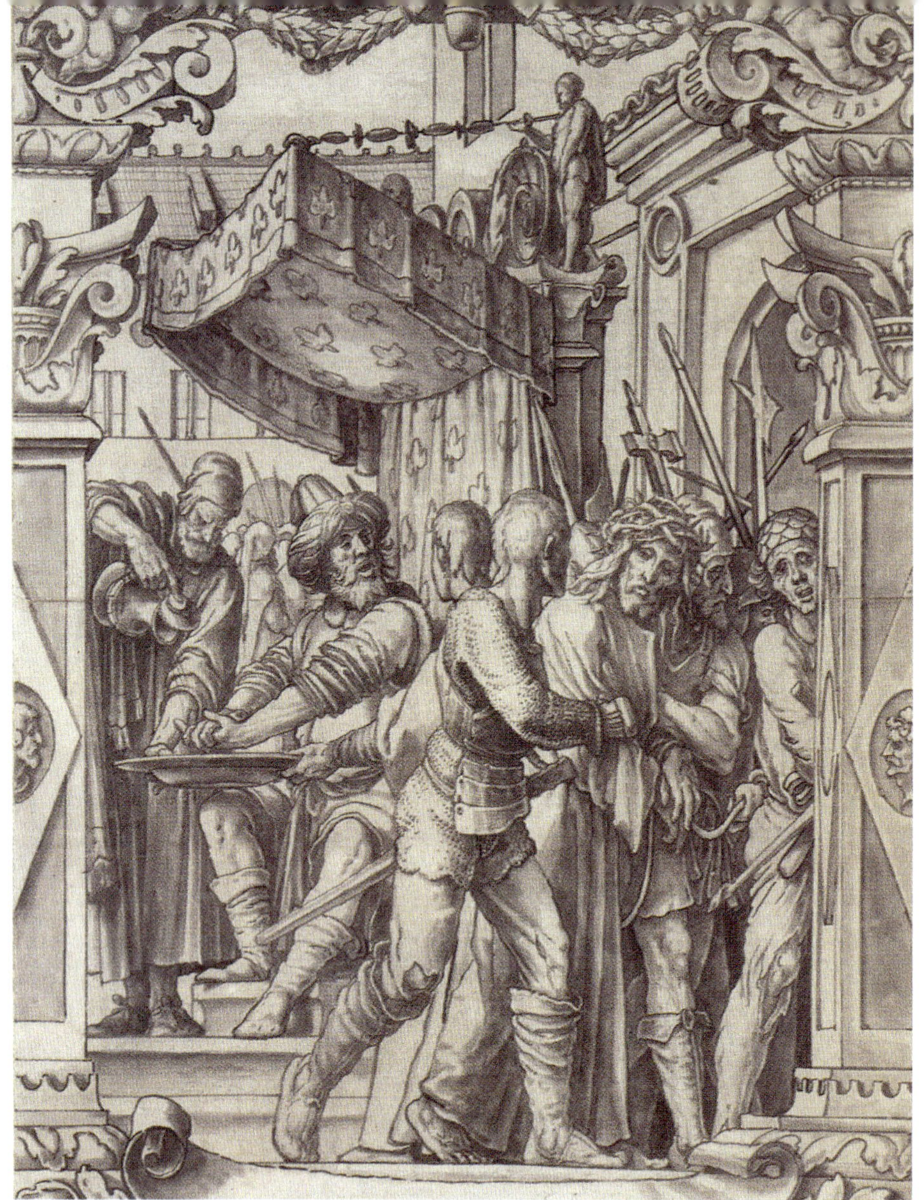

Left: *Handwashing of Pontius Pilate*

Pilate is depicted symbolically 'washing his hands' of the sentence served on Christ, after asking an angry mob of people to decide Christ's fate, written in the Gospel of St John 19: 6.

Right: *Christ carrying the Cross*

Holbein depicts the gruesome scene surrounding Christ, forced to carry the heavy burden of a wooden cross, on his way to Calvary, to crucifixion. Facial expressions denote anger, passivity, cruelty and submission in this interwoven narrative, a masterpiece.

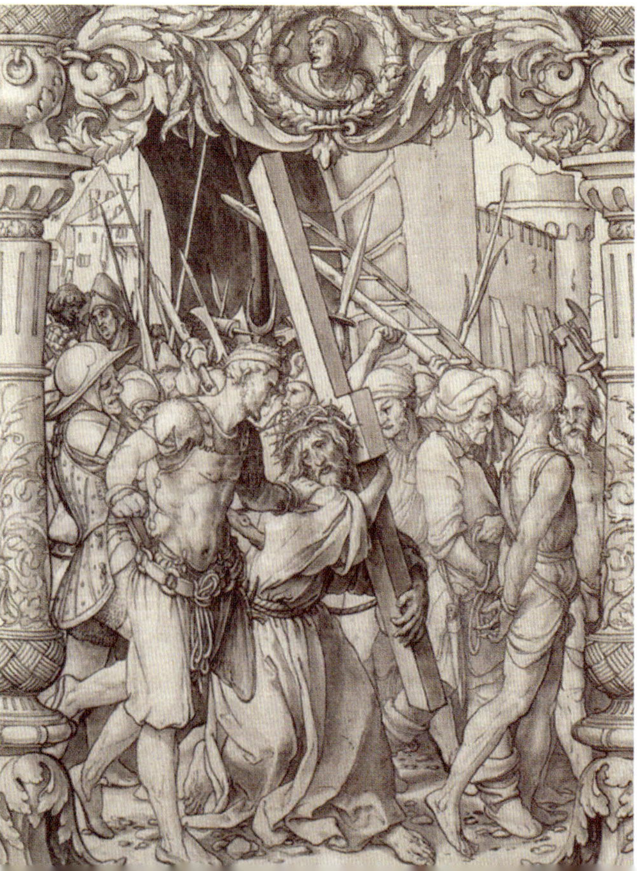

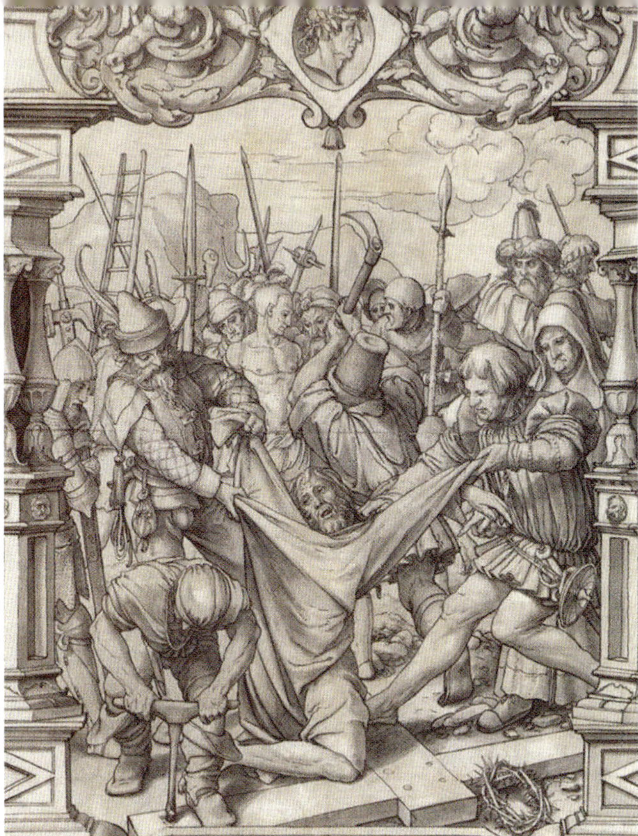

Right: *Nailing to the Cross*

Human chaos surrounds the nailing of Christ to the Cross. Holbein creates a grotesque scene of inhumanity. A man at right, dressed in a fur-edged coat and hat, resembling Erasmus of Rotterdam, a priest of Christ, observes the sacrificial cruelty, witnessed too by satyrs in the foreground.

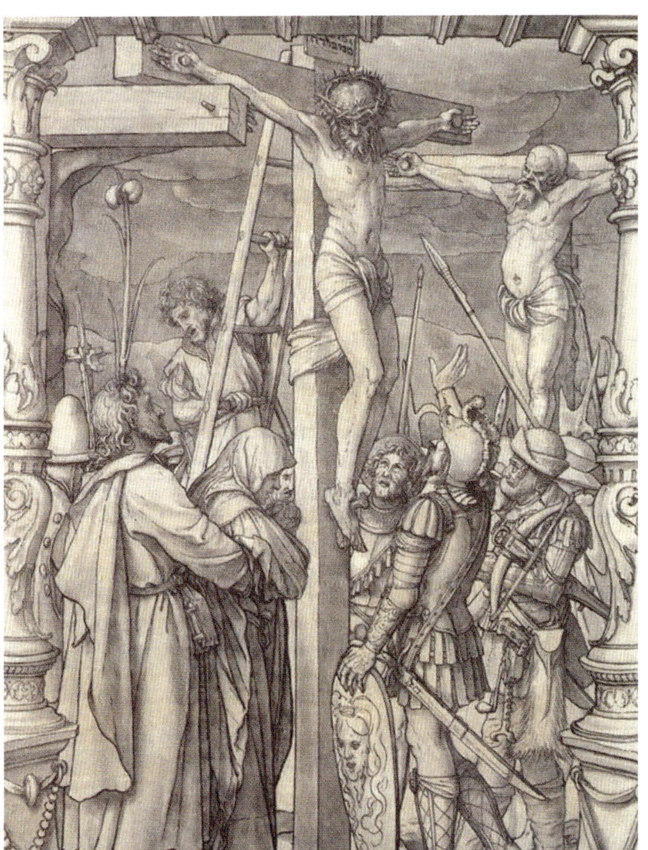

Left: *Disrobing of Christ*

Composed within an architectural setting, soldiers and attendants are shown cruelly ripping Christ's clothing from his body, before he is nailed to the cross. Holbein captures the sneering faces and brutal actions of Christ's persecutors.

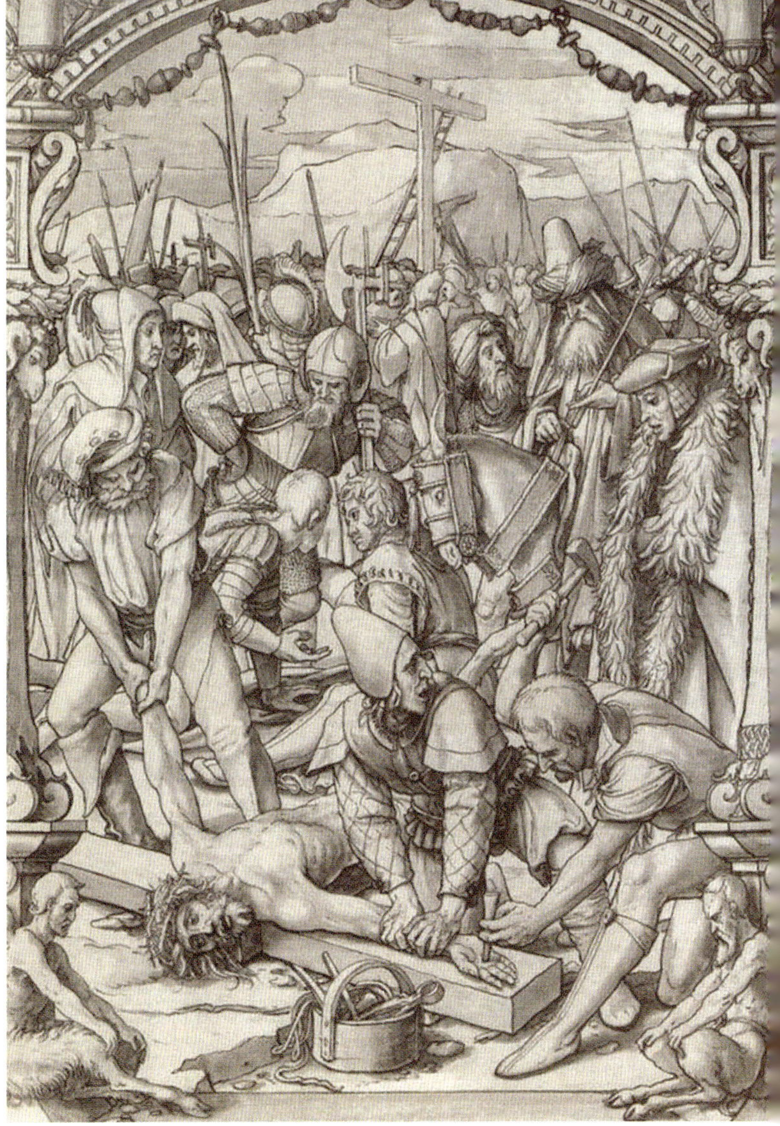

Left: *Christ Crucified*

In a Roman architectural setting with richly ornate columns, Christ, hoisted on the cross, is surrounded by a group that includes Roman soldiers, and his parents. Mary has her head bowed with hands clasped in prayer, and Joseph, holding her so that she does not collapse with grief, is looking up toward his son. Christ, wearing the 'crown of thorns', is crucified along with two thieves on either side of him. Holbein portrays a dramatic scene of intense cruelty.

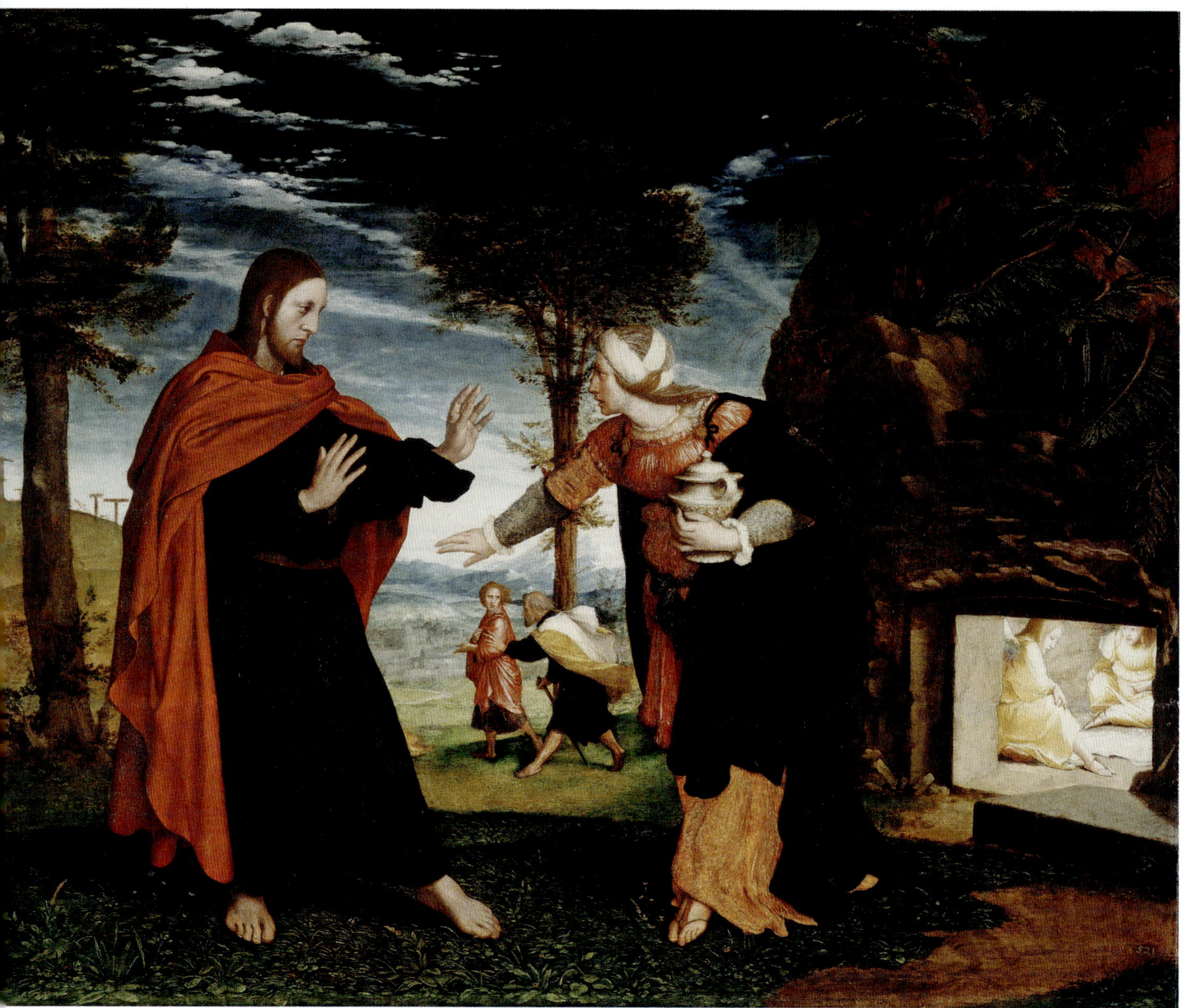

Noli me tangere or *Touch Me Not*, c.1524, oil on oak panel, 78.7 x 95.8cm (31 x 37.6in), Royal Collection Trust, UK

Holbein depicts the moment in the bible narrative, Gospel of St John 20:17, where Christ commands Mary Magdalene 'Touch me not; for I am not yet ascended to my Father'. Christ moves backwards to stop her touching him. Holbein captures the intimacy of the meeting, registering Christ's immediate concern, and Mary Magdalene's surprise. The tomb where Christ had lain after crucifixion is empty. Holbein depicts angels seated within the luminously lit sepulchre. He paints the figures of Christ and Mary Magdalene, and the figures of St Peter and St John in the middle distance, in clothing of dramatic complementary colours.

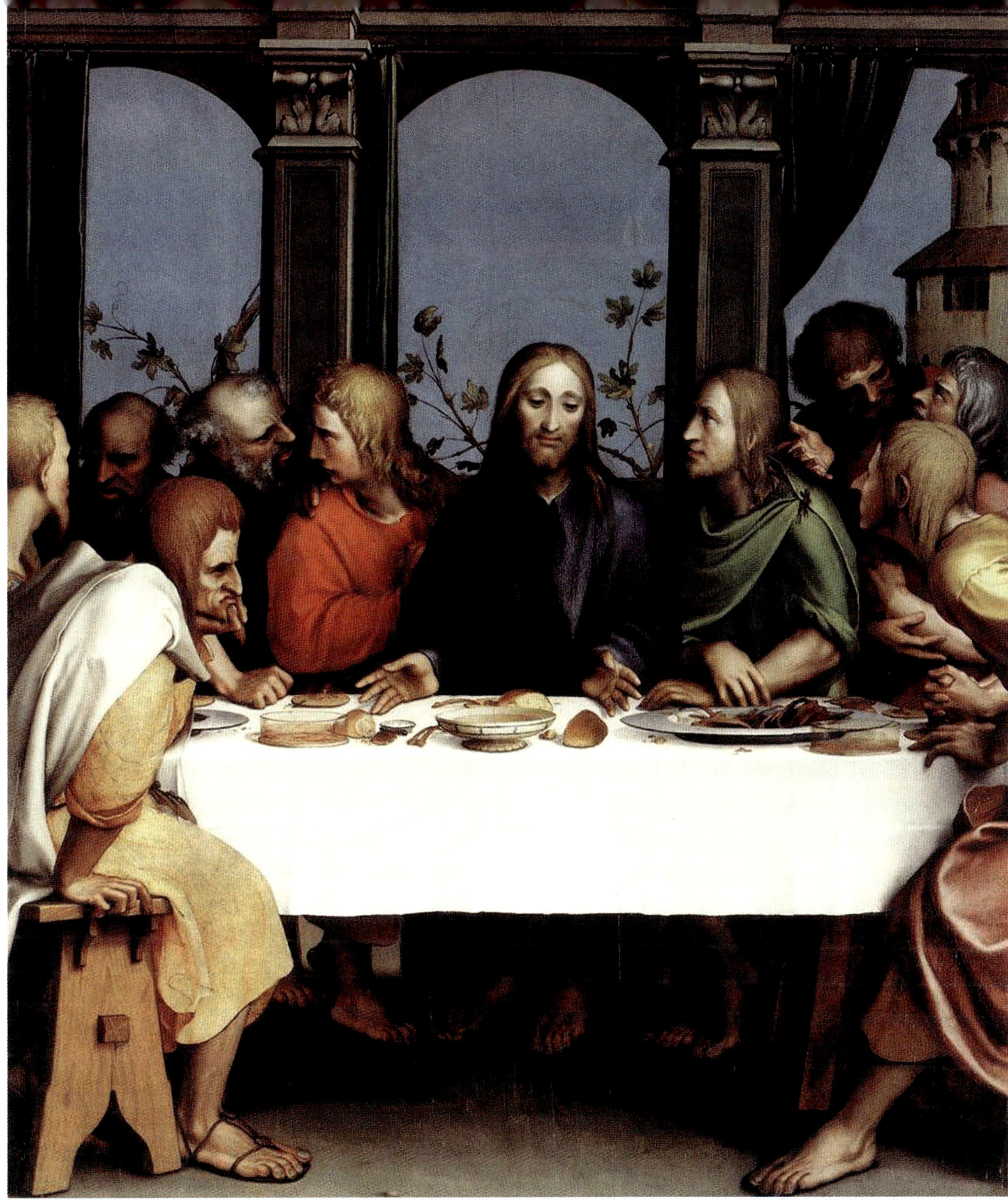

Last Supper, c.1527, oil and tempera on lime wood, 115.5 x 97.5cm (45.47 x 38.38in), Kunstmuseum, Basel, Switzerland

The painting's figurative structure resemblances Leonardo da Vinci's *Last Supper* c.1495–6, copies of which were in circulation. There are only nine apostles because it is a cut-down section of a larger triptych. The side panels were destroyed in February 1529 during iconoclast riots in Basel by Protestant reformers. The head of Christ was sawn out, possibly to preserve it. Many scholars consider the artist to be Holbein, as it is listed as such in the Amerbach inventory. However, the Kunstmuseum, Basel, where it resides, attribute it to the 'Venus painter', a highly skilled employee in Holbein's workshop, working with Holbein and completing the work when the artist left for England in 1526. Holbein's signature style of foliage backdrop links it to him and his workshop.

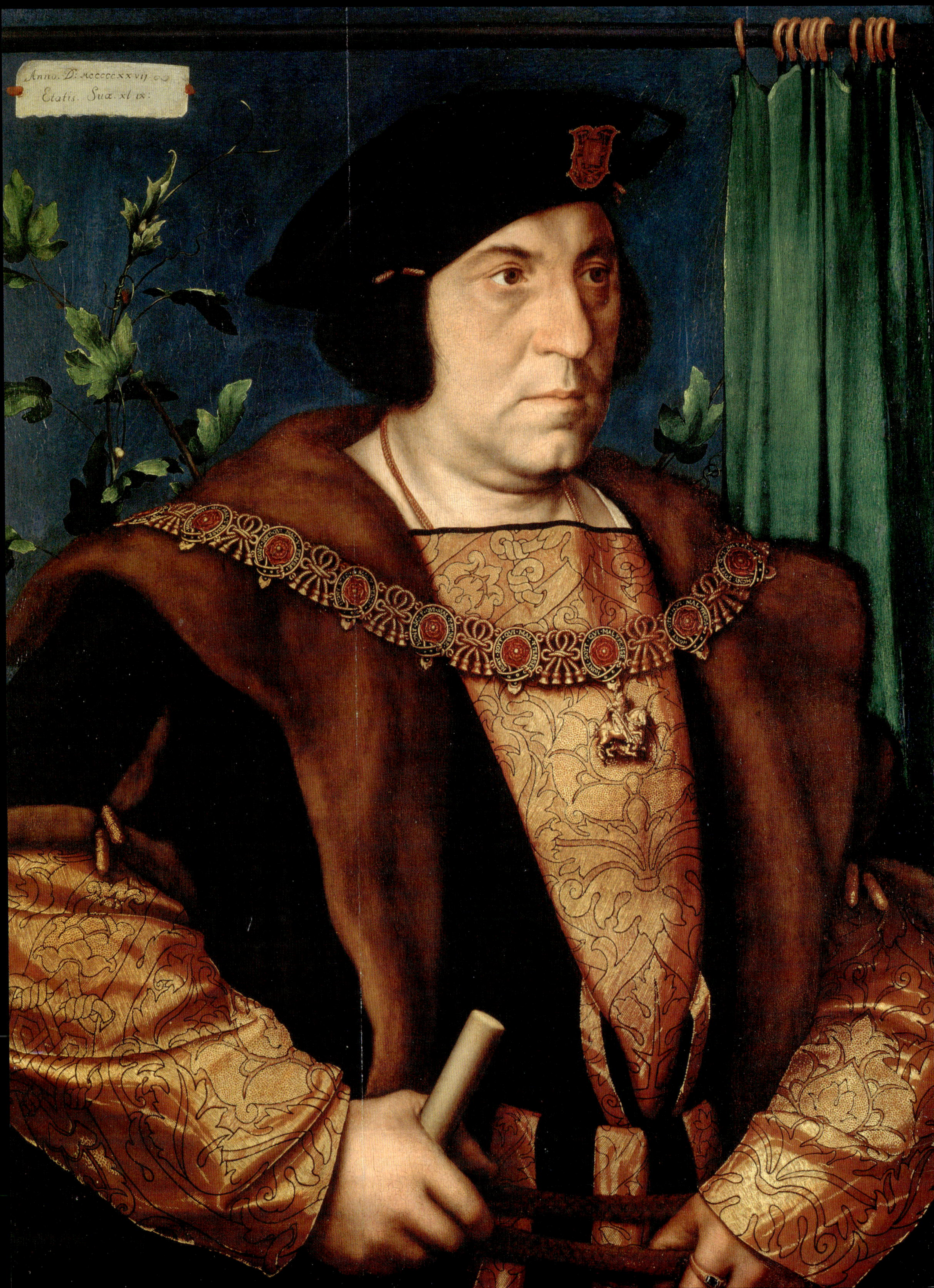

Anno. D: MCCCCCXXVIJ
Etatis. Suæ. xl ix:

LONDON
1526–1528

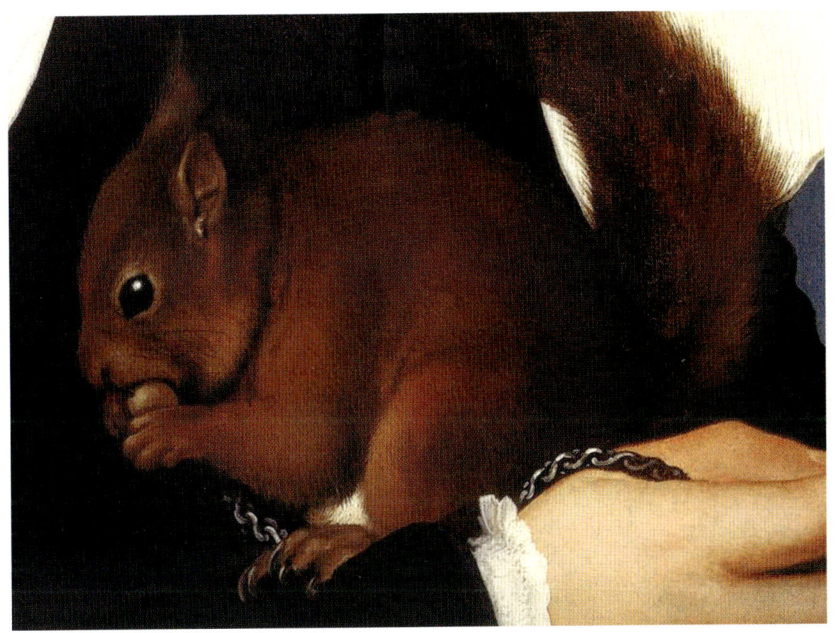

Hans Holbein the Younger travelled to England at the latter end of 1526, visiting Antwerp on his way from Basel to London. He carried a letter of introduction from Erasmus to Sir Thomas More, who would be Holbein's first client to sit for a portrait. Through More's connections, Sir Henry Guildford, in attendance on Henry VIII, employed Holbein to create theatrical scenery for festivities at Greenwich Palace. Word of the German artist's remarkable talent for portraiture spread, and commissions from nobility followed.

Above: Detail of a squirrel from Portrait of a Lady with a Squirrel and a Starling, *1526–28 (see page 164). The unnamed lady holds her pet squirrel on a chain. Eating a nut, it sits peacefully in her arms; the tip of its bushy tail brushes the bust of her dress, and its long chain threads though her hands. The small animal is superbly painted by Holbein.*

Left: Sir Henry Guildford (1489–1532) a close confidant of king Henry VIII, employed Hans Holbein for the Greenwich Revels of 1527 soon after his arrival in England. Guildford's inner circle eventually would lead Holbein to become painter to the king. Holbein depicts him wearing the emblems of the Order of the Garter, and carrying the white staff of the Comptroller of the Household. In the portrait background is Holbein's signature vine foliage. (See also page 160.)

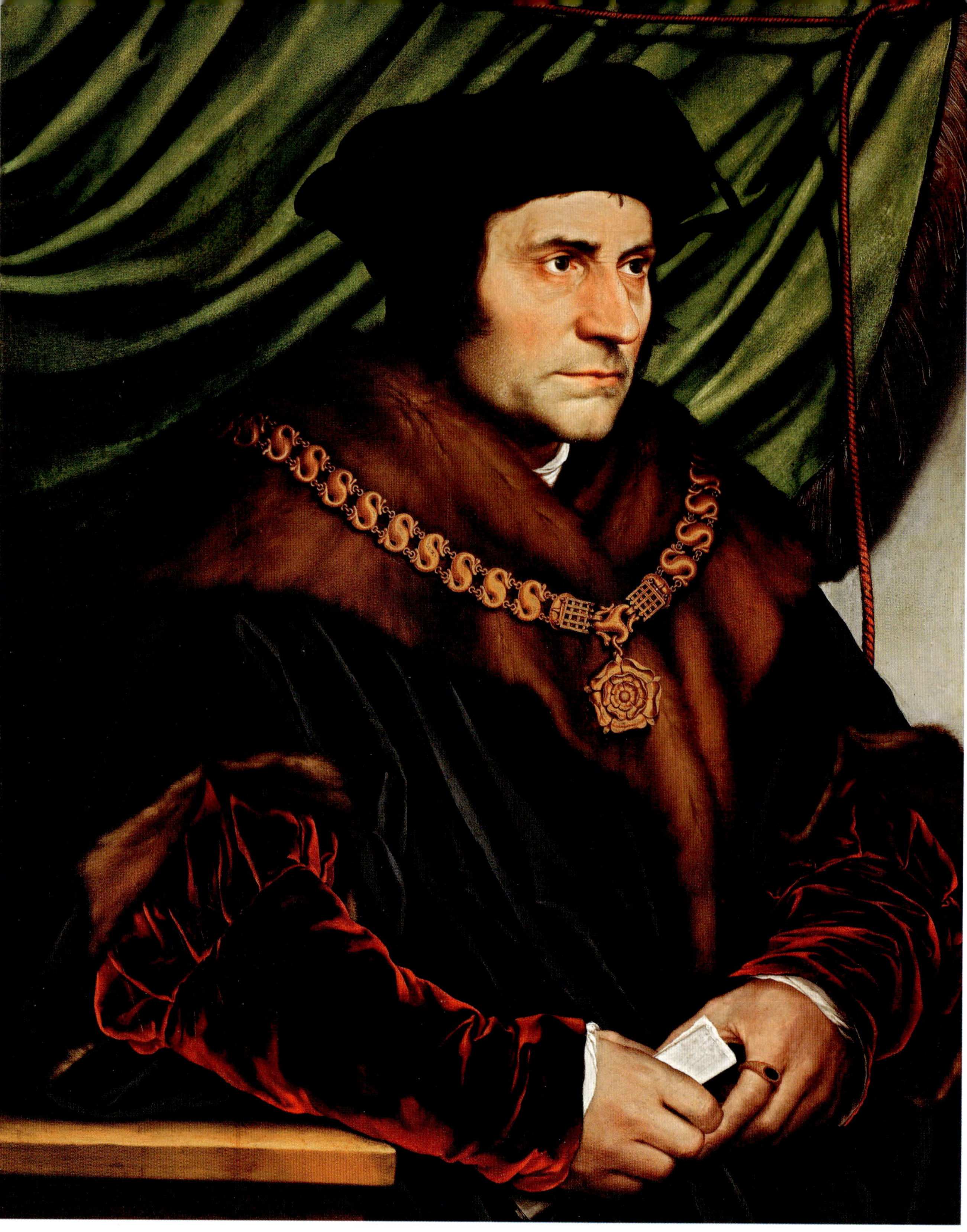

Portrait of Sir Thomas More,
1527, oil on oak panel, 74.9
x 60.3cm (29.6 x 23.75in),
Henry Clay Frick Bequest,
The Frick Collection, New
York, NY, USA

This portrait was painted
during the year following
Holbein's arrival in England
with a letter of introduction
from Erasmus to Sir Thomas
More, Privy Councillor to
King Henry VIII. Holbein
depicts not only denotations
of More's high status, from
the rich velvet of his clothing,
to the linked S-S *Souvent me
souvien* gold chain of service
to the king, translating as
'Think of me often', but
personal touches, such as
beard-stubble on his chin.

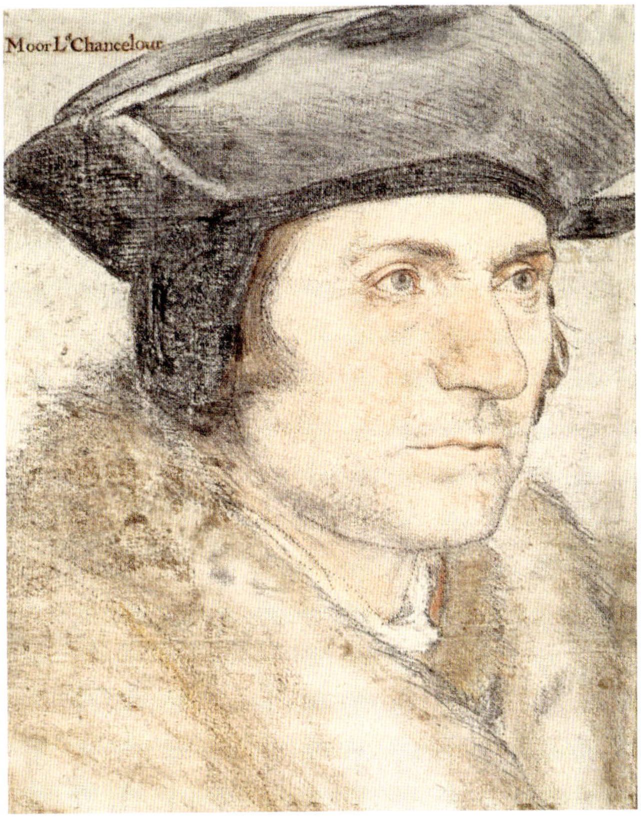

Right: *Portrait study of Sir Thomas More*, 1526–27, black and coloured chalk, ink on prepared paper, 40.2 x 30.1cm (15.8 x 11.8in), Royal Collection Trust, UK

Sir Thomas More (1478–1535) was an English lawyer, statesman, author, humanist and philosopher. He acted as a councillor to Henry VIII. This head and shoulders depiction, pricked out for transfer, is one of two preparatory drawings for the 1527 oil portrait.

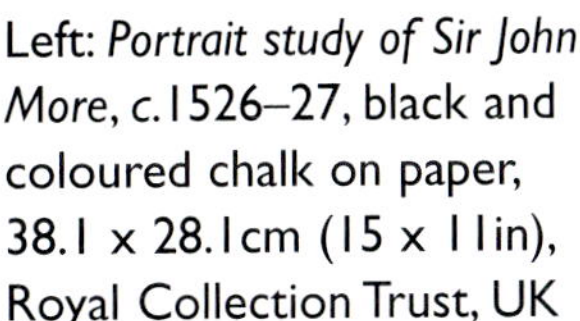

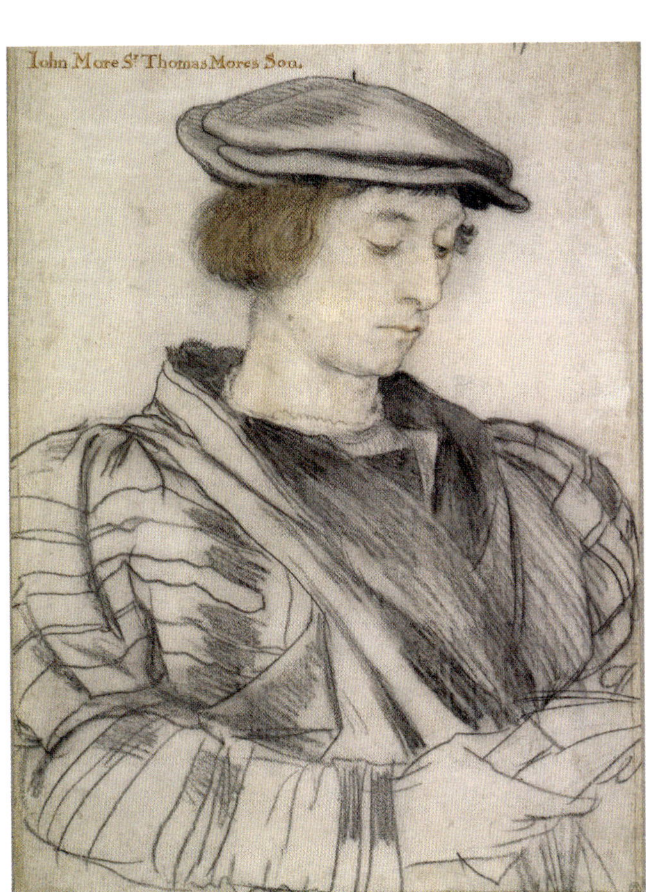

Left: *Portrait study of Sir John More*, c.1526–27, black and coloured chalk on paper, 38.1 x 28.1cm (15 x 11in), Royal Collection Trust, UK

This drawing of John More II, only son of Sir Thomas More, depicts the young man in repose, looking down, reading a book. He wears a flat hat. The vivid stripes of his costume are dramatically drawn. This is a preparatory study for Holbein's group portrait (see overleaf). John More's hat was removed in the painted work.

Right: *Portrait study of Sir John More*, c.1526–27, black and coloured chalk on paper, 35.1 x 27.3cm (13.8 x 10.7in), Royal Collection Trust, UK

A bust-length portrait study of Sir John More (c.1451–1530), the father of Sir Thomas More, and Henry VIII's Lord Chancellor. He wears a black hat and fur collar. This work is a preparatory study for the Thomas More family group. The inscription upper left was added in the 18th century.

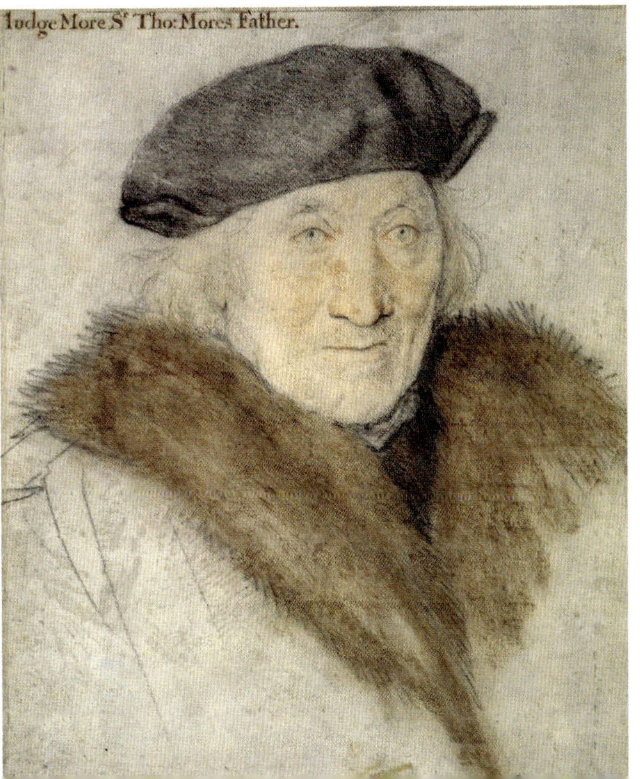

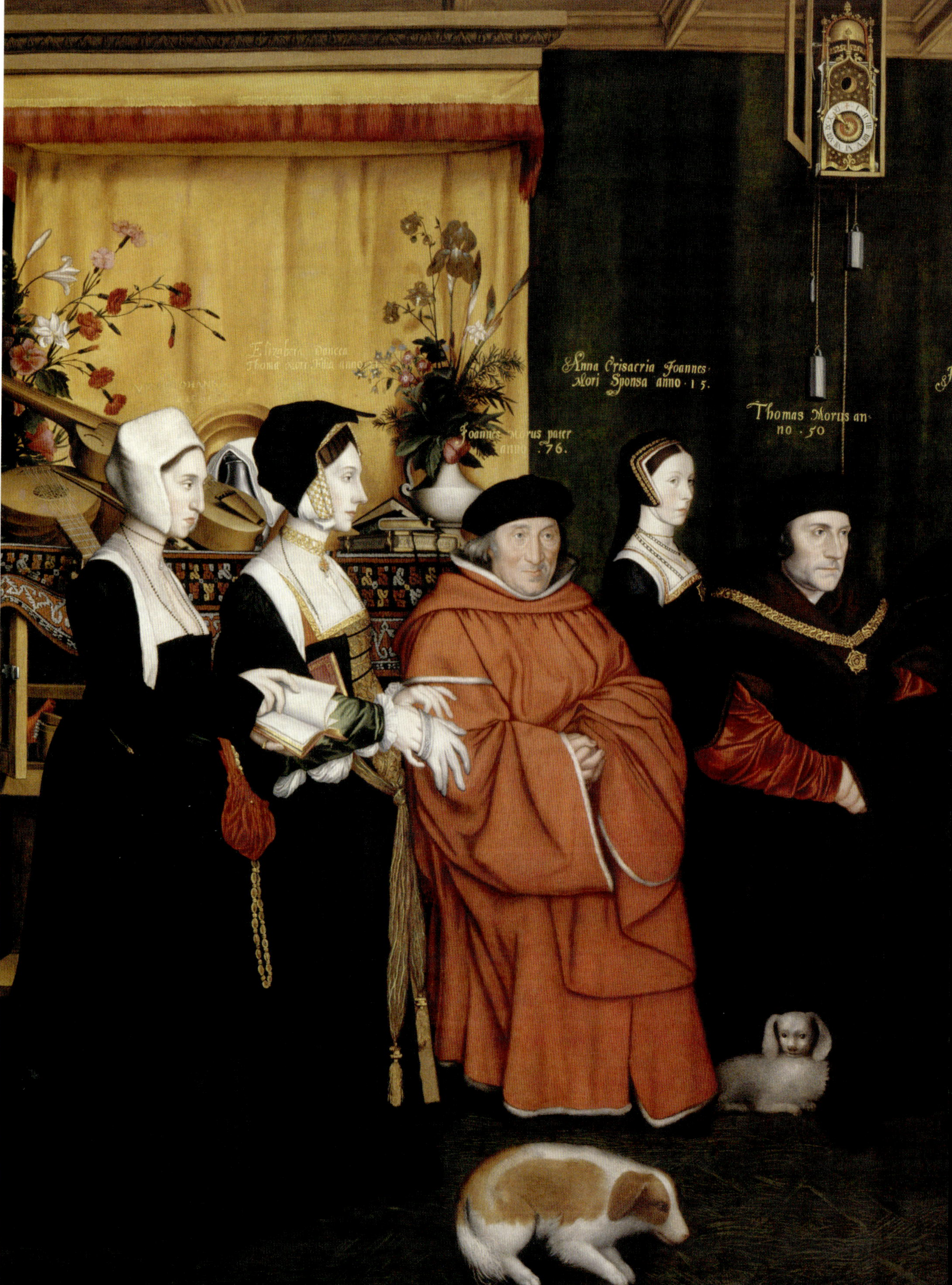

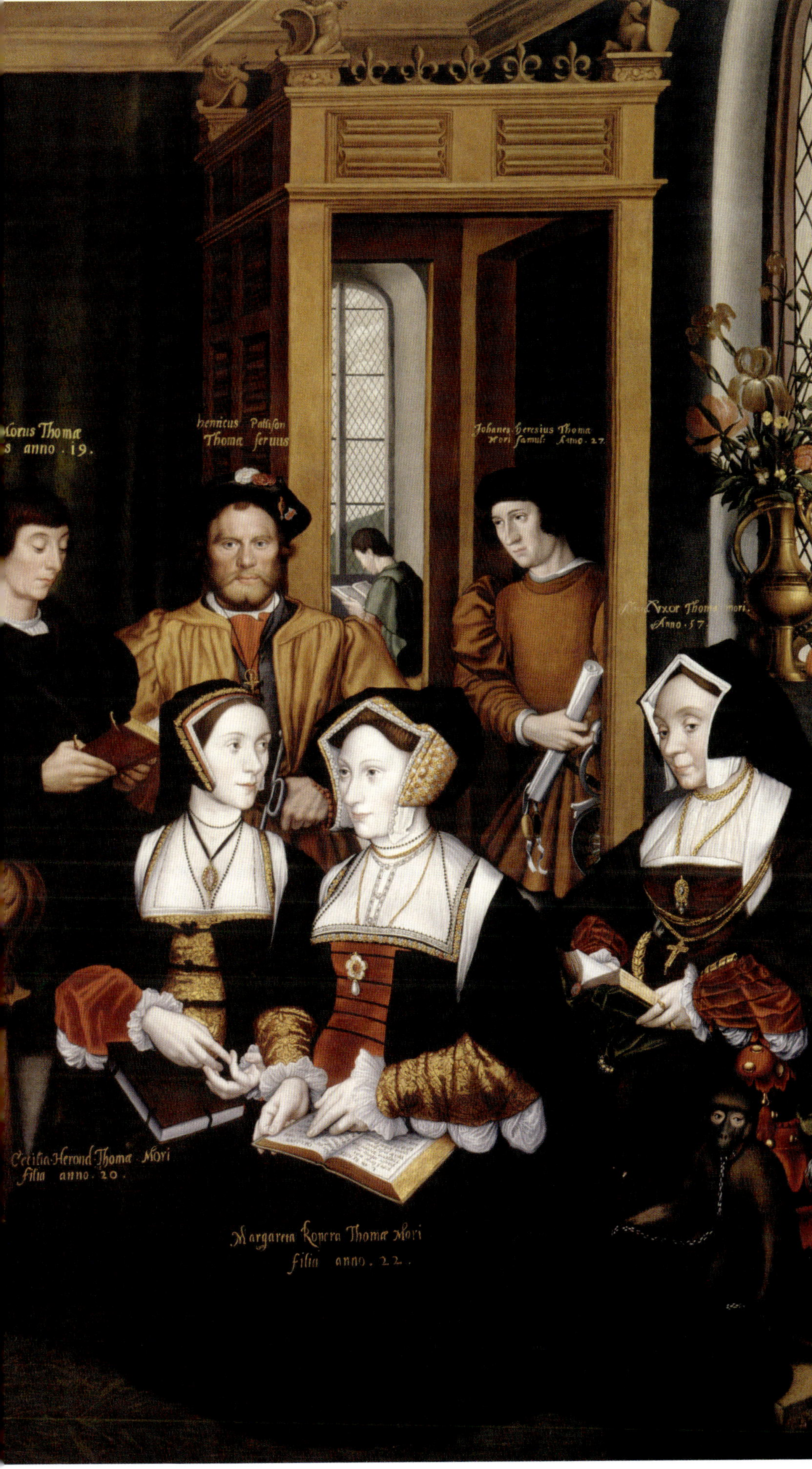

*Sir Thomas More and
his household, and his
descendants, c.1592, by
Rowland Lockey after a
1527 original by Holbein, oil
on canvas, 49.8 x 36.3cm
(19.6 x 14.3in), Nostell
Priory, National Trust, UK*

Rowland Lockey painted
this copy of an earlier work
by Holbein (destroyed by
fire in 1752). The portrait
of the family of Thomas
More has been described
as the first 'conversation
piece' in German art. The
painted work was copied
several times, by the same
artist Lockey among others,
though differences between
the copies and the original
sketch (see overleaf) suggest
that intervening versions may
also have existed. (See also
pages 51 and 97.)

The sitters are, from left to
right: Margaret Clement, née
Giggs, adopted daughter of
Thomas More and wife of
Dr John Clement; Elizabeth
Dauncey, née More, second
daughter of Sir Thomas
More and wife of Sir William
Dauncey; Sir John More,
Thomas More's father; Anne
Cresacre, fiancée of John
More II; Sir Thomas More;
John More II, More's son;
Henry Patenson or Patterson
(More's Fool, or Jester);
Cicely Heron, née More,
More's youngest daughter
and wife of Giles Heron; an
unknown man reading in a
back room; Margaret Roper,
née More, More's eldest
daughter and wife of William
Roper; John Norris, Thomas
More's secretary; and Lady
Alice, née Middleton, second
wife of Sir Thomas More. The
family pets are included.

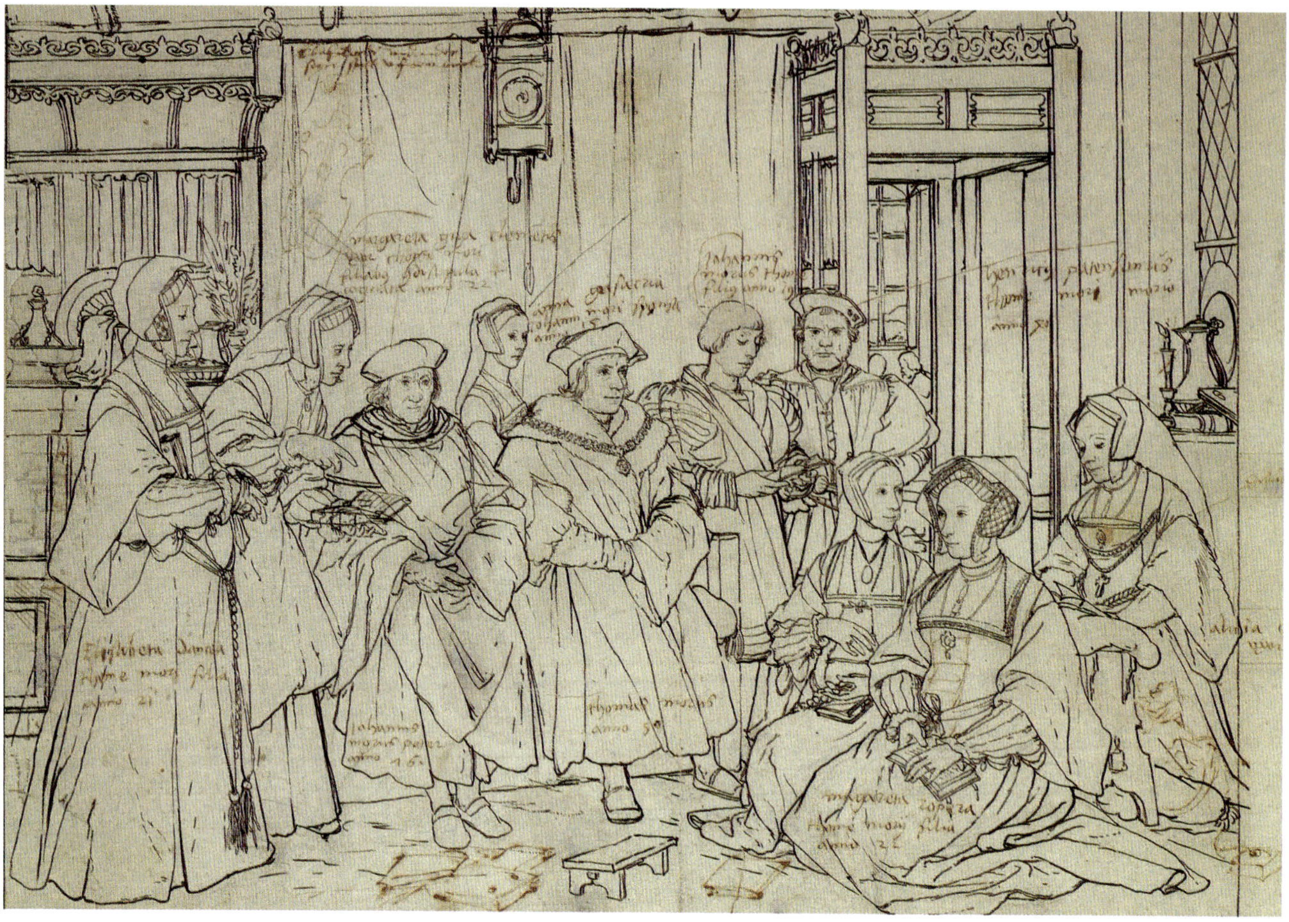

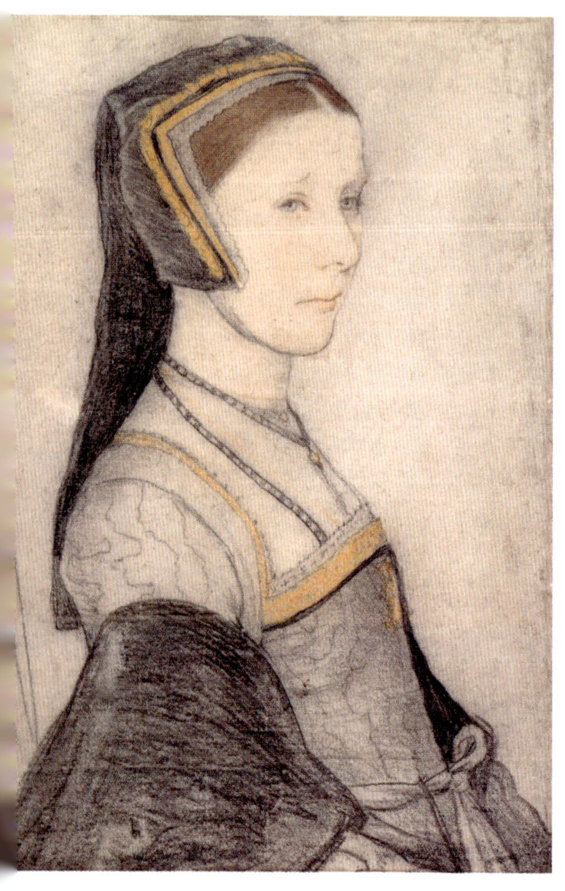

Above: *Study for the Family Portrait of Thomas More*, 1526–7, pen and brush in black on chalk, 38.9 x 52.4cm (15.2 x 20.6in), Kunstmuseum, Basel, Switzerland

This is a preparatory sketch for Holbein's portrait of the family of Thomas More, now lost. Some of the characters and positioning changed in the painting (or in Rowland Lockey's copy, see previous page). Nikolaus Kratzer, a friend of Holbein and More, and the tutor of More's children, added the names and ages of the sitters in Latin on to the sketch in brown ink. These are, left to right: Elizabeth Dauncey, daughter of Thomas More, age 21; Margaret Giggs, Thomas More's foster-daughter, age about 22; John More, father of Thomas More, age 76; Anne Cresacre, John More II's fiancée, age 15; Sir Thomas More, age 50; John More, Thomas's son, age 19; Henry Patenson, Thomas More's jester, age 50; Cicely Heron, Thomas More's daughter, age 20; Margaret Roper, Thomas More's daughter, age 22; and Alice More, age 57.

Left: *Portrait study of Anne Cresacre*, 1526–27, black and coloured chalk on paper, 37.2 x 26.6cm (14.6 x 10.5in), Royal Collection Trust, UK

A preparatory study for the More family group portrait. Anne Cresacre (1511–77) was the ward of Thomas More. He had taken her into his family after the death of her father. In 1527, she was betrothed to More's only son, John. They married in 1529. The half-length portrait faces three-quarters to her left. She wears a double-band headdress, a dress with a square décolletage, and is seated on a roughly sketched chair.

Right: *Portrait study of Elizabeth Dauncey*, c.1526–27, black and coloured chalk on paper, 37.1 x 26.2cm (1.6 x 10.3in), Royal Collection Trust, UK

A preparatory drawing of Elizabeth Dauncey (1506–1564), second daughter of Thomas More, for the More family group portrait. This drawing is one of seven fine surviving studies drawn by Holbein for his group portrait study of Thomas More's family. In the bust-level depiction, she is portrayed in profile, wearing a dress with a square décolletage, and a headdress. In 1525 she married William Dauncey, Knight of the Body, and Privy Councillor to King Henry VIII.

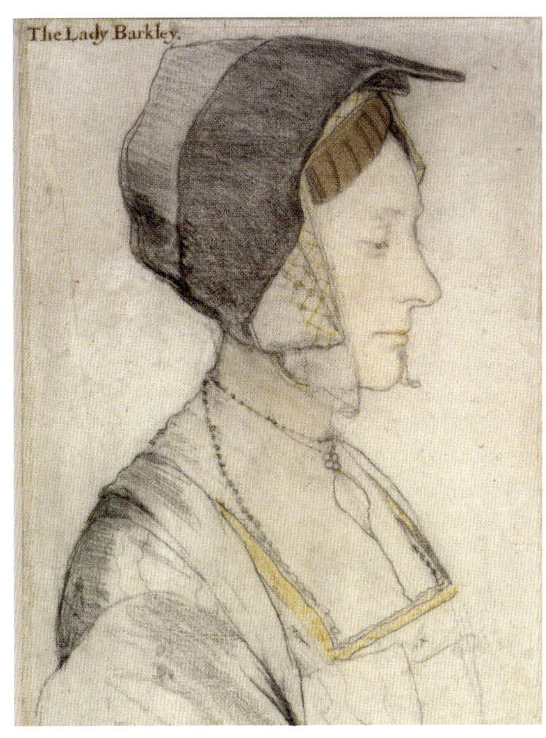

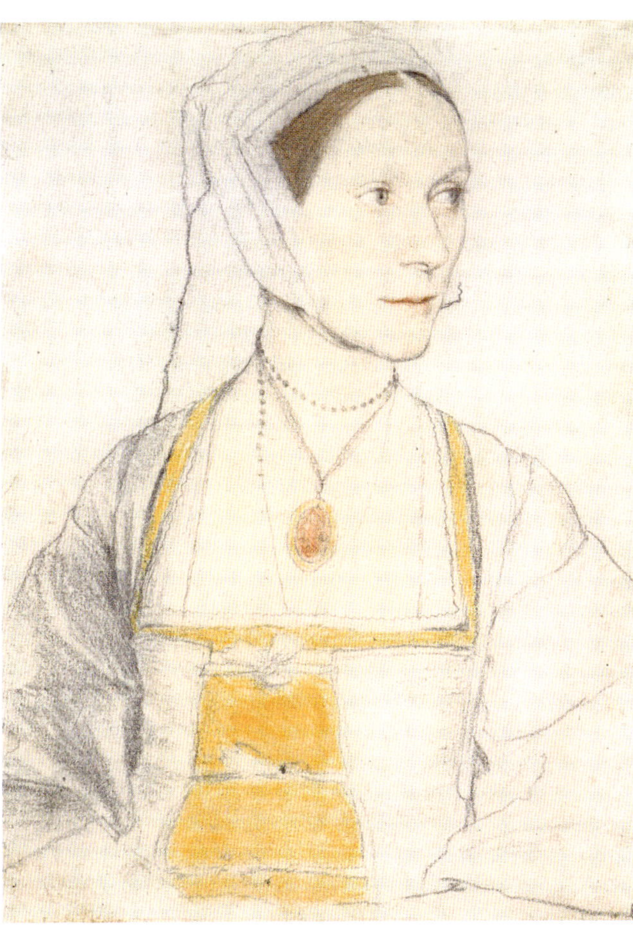

Left: *Portrait study of Cicely Heron*, c.1526–27, black and coloured chalk on paper, 37.8 x 28.1cm (14.8 x 11in), Royal Collection Trust, UK

A preparatory drawing of Cicely Heron (born 1507), third and youngest daughter of Sir Thomas More, created by Holbein for the group family portrait. Her dress has a square décolletage, worn with a pendant. The yellow kirtle visible through the sitter's loosened bodice infers her to be pregnant. Cicely (or Cecilia) was married to Giles Heron, hanged for treason in 1540.

Right: *Portrait study of Margaret Giggs*, c.1526–27, black and coloured chalk on paper, 38.5 x 27.3cm (15.1 x 1.7in), Royal Collection Trust, UK

Margaret Giggs (1508–70), foster-daughter of Sir Thomas More. In the family portrait study, Margaret is leaning towards Thomas More's father, Sir John More, as if showing him a passage in a book, and she wears a different headdress. In a copy of Holbein's lost painting by Rowland Lockey, however, she wears the same cap as in the present drawing. She was married to Dr John Clement.

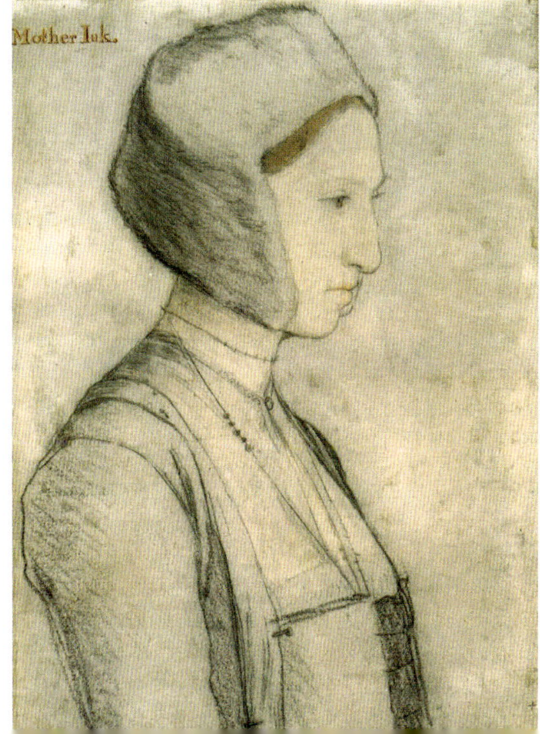

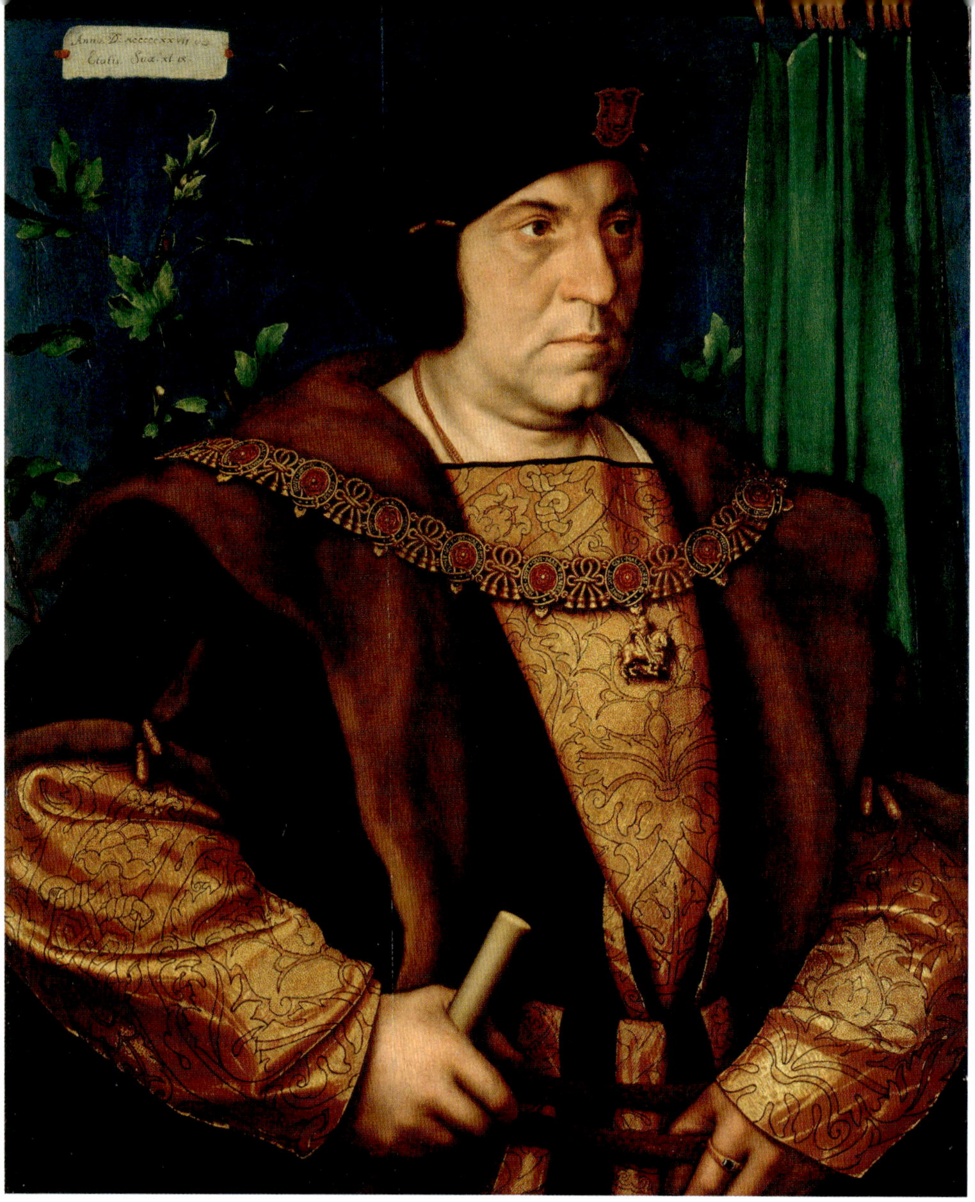

Portrait of Sir Henry Guildford,
1527, oil on panel, with
shell-gold paint and gold
leaf, 82.7 x 66.4cm (32.5 x
26.1in), Royal Collection
Trust, UK

Sir Henry Guildford (1489–
1532) is dressed in a cloth
of spun gold, reserved for
higher nobility. He wears
the emblem of the Order
of the Garter on his hat
and on a thick gold chain,
denoting the highest level
of knighthood. The white
staff of the Comptroller of
the Household is in his right
hand. Holbein connects the
two companion paintings
of Sir Henry and Lady
Guildford with a curtain
rail, which traverses the
backdrop of both works, and
his signature vine foliage.

Portrait study of Sir Henry Guildford, 1527, black and coloured chalks with pen and ink on paper, 38.8 x 29.8cm (15.2 x 11.7in), Royal Collection Trust, UK

Sir Henry Guildford and his second wife, Mary Wotton, were amongst the first people to commission Hans Holbein for portraits on his arrival in England. Preparatory sketch-drawings were created prior to painting. This drawing of Henry Guildford has been cut-down in size from its original. One can see Holbein's parallel line-markings on the work. The face is slightly plumper than in the finished painting.

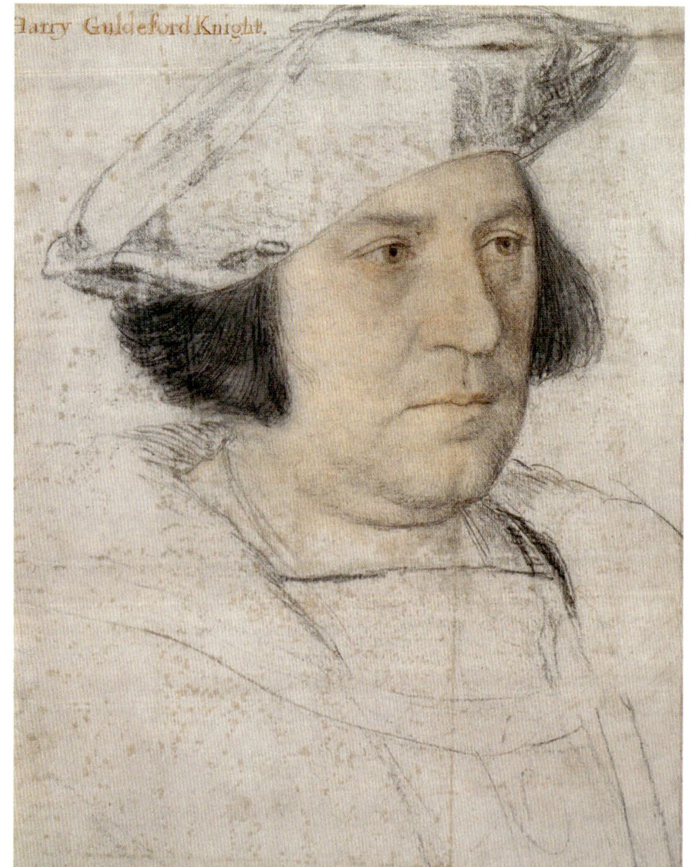

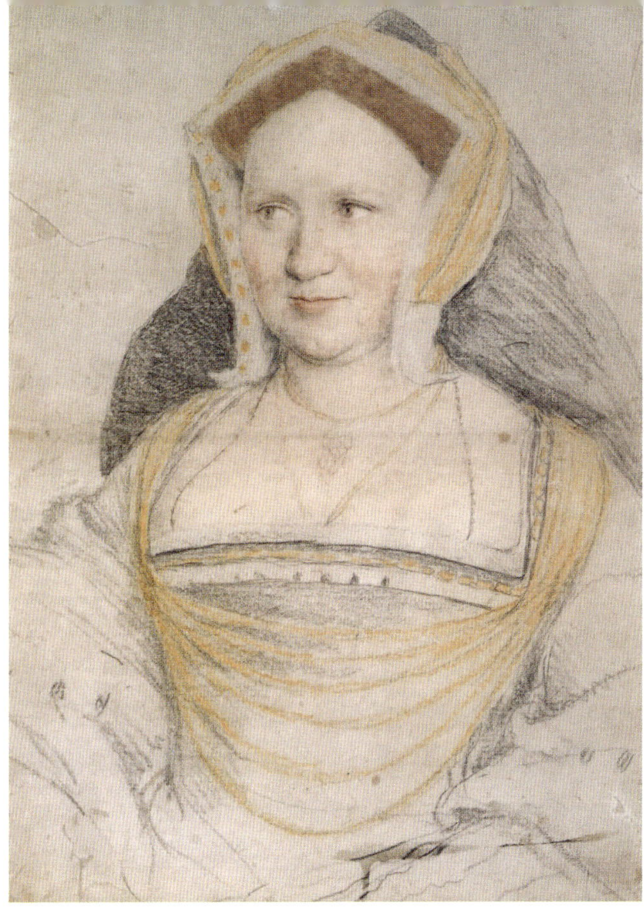

Portrait study of Mary Wotton, Lady Guildford, 1527, drawing, black and coloured chalks on paper, 55.2 x 38.5cm (21.7 x 15in), Kunstmuseum, Basel, Switzerland

The drawing of Lady Guildford differs from that of Holbein's finished painting. In the drawing Holbein captures Lady Guildford relaxed with a slight smile on her lips, reflected in her eyes that look toward her right, toward where the portrait of her husband would hang. The facial expression was changed to a sterner look staring out toward the viewer in the oil-on-panel work.

Portrait of Mary Wotton, Lady Guildford, 1527, oil on panel, 83 x 66.7cm (32.6 x 26.2in), Royal Collection Trust, UK

Mary Wotton married Henry Guildford in 1525. In three-quarter pose, the finished work was slightly altered from the preparatory drawing, possibly in line with the holy book that Lady Guildford holds. Her expression is solemn with a steadfast gaze toward the observer, achieved by Holbein's alteration of the angle of the eye-pupils and a downward turn to the corners of her mouth.

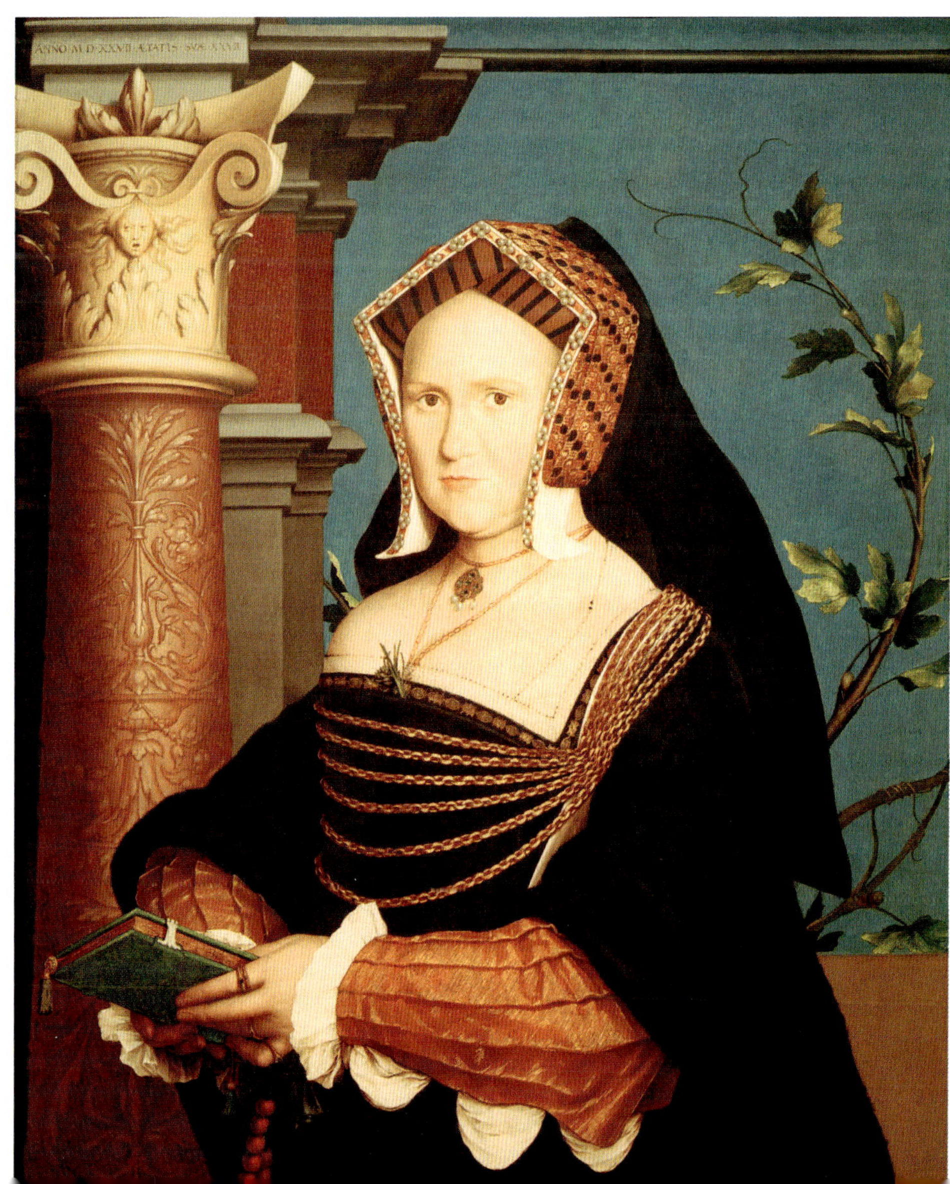

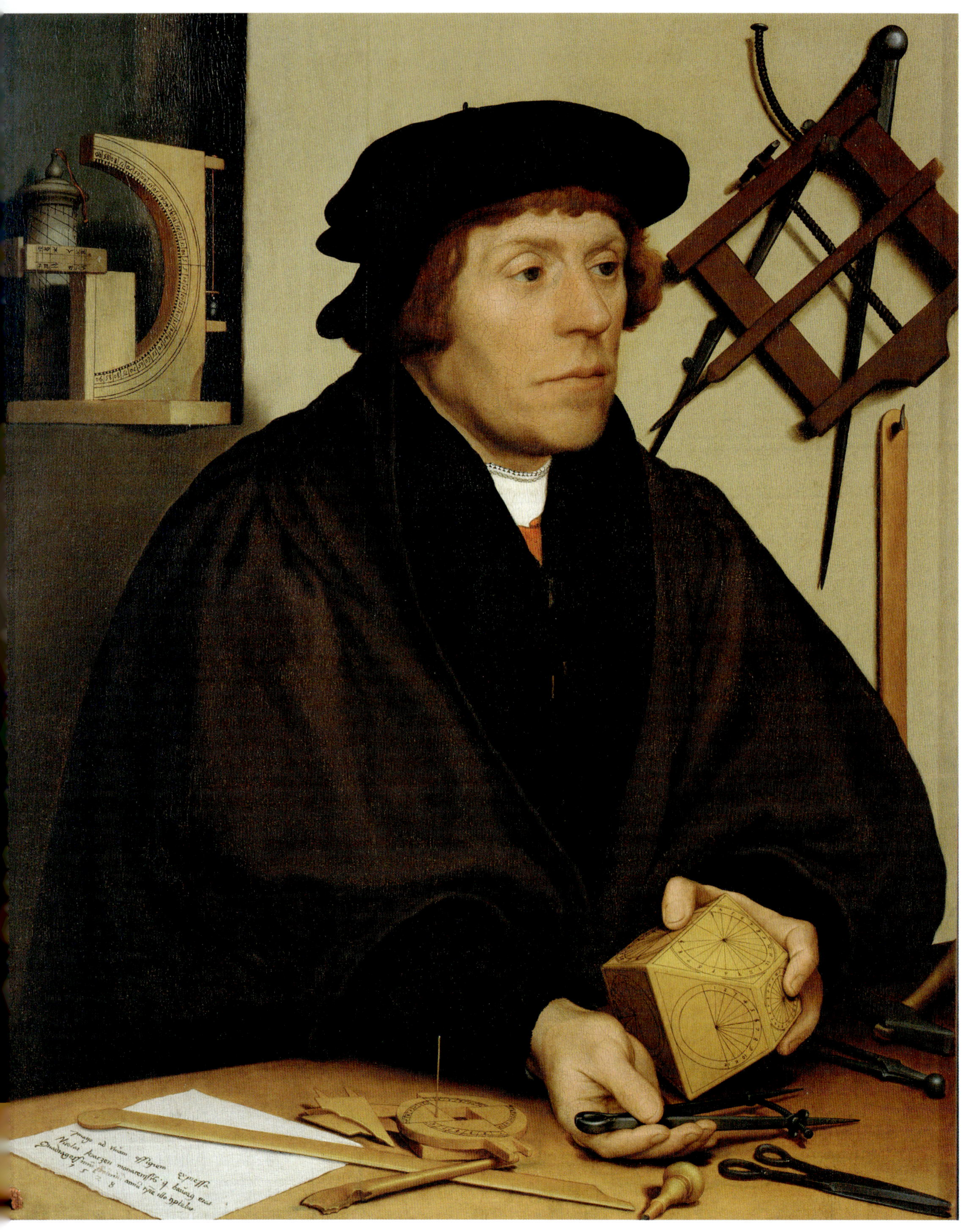

Opposite: *Portrait of Nikolaus Kratzer*, 1528, tempera on wood, 83 × 67cm (32.7 × 26.4in), Musée du Louvre, Paris, France

Mathematician, and Astronomer Royal to Henry VIII, Nikolaus Kratzer, tutor to the king's daughters, is portrayed holding a pair of dividers and an incomplete polyhedral dial. The gnomons for it are depicted on the table, alongside tools, including a pivoting rule, a ruling knife, scissors and burin. In Latin, a piece of paper on the table states: 'The portrait of Nicolaus Kratzer of Munich, a Bavarian, taken from life when he was completing his forty-first year'.

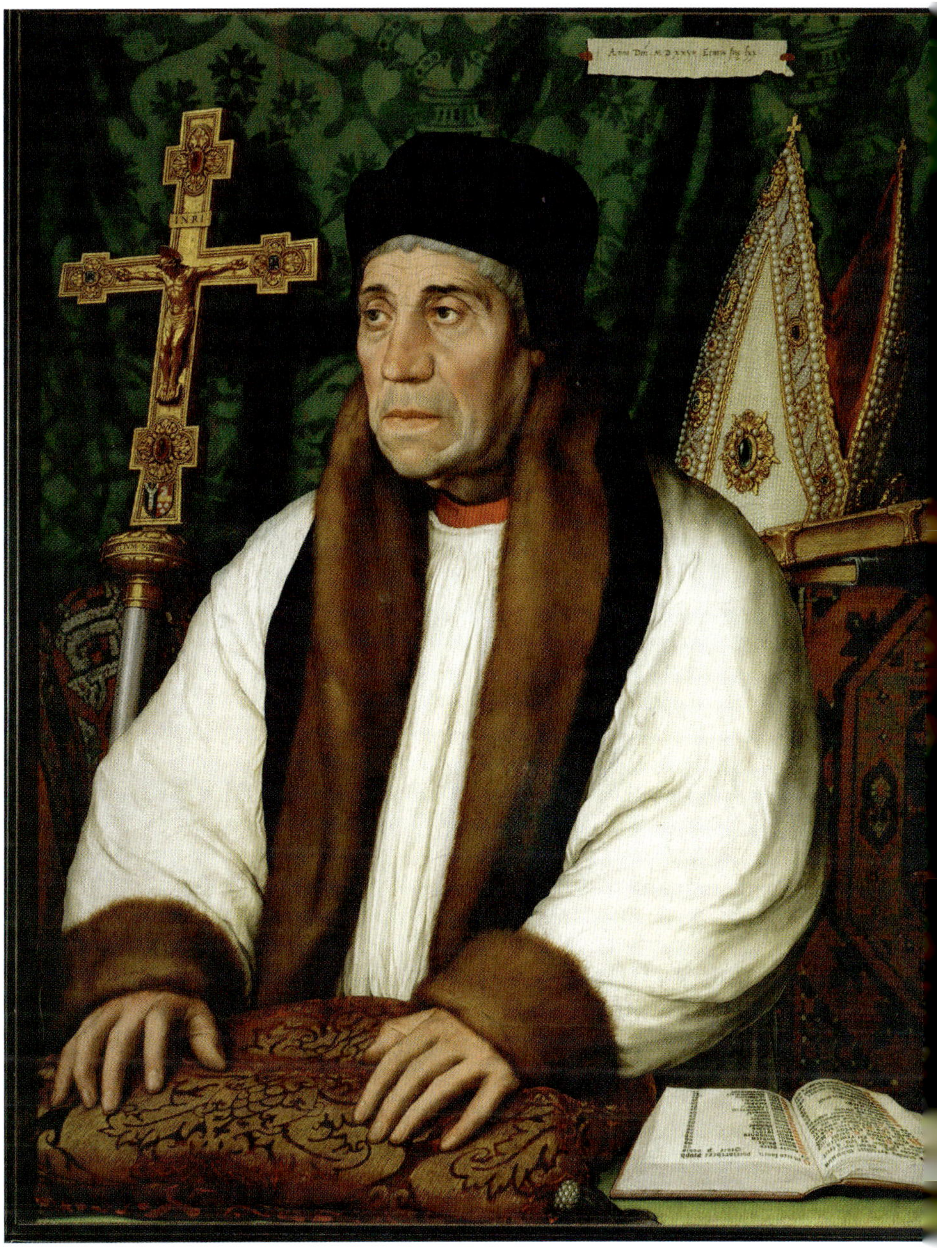

Right: *William Warham, Archbishop of Canterbury c.*1527, oil on wood, 82 × 66cm (32 × 26in), Musée du Louvre, Paris, France

Matthew Parker, a later Archbishop of Canterbury (1559–75), stated in *De Antiquitate Britannicae Ecclesiae* (1572) that William Warham sat for his portrait to Holbein, the earliest referral to this work. Warham had two identical portraits painted by Holbein. One was sent to his friend Erasmus. Of the two painted works, the Louvre is the primary edition.

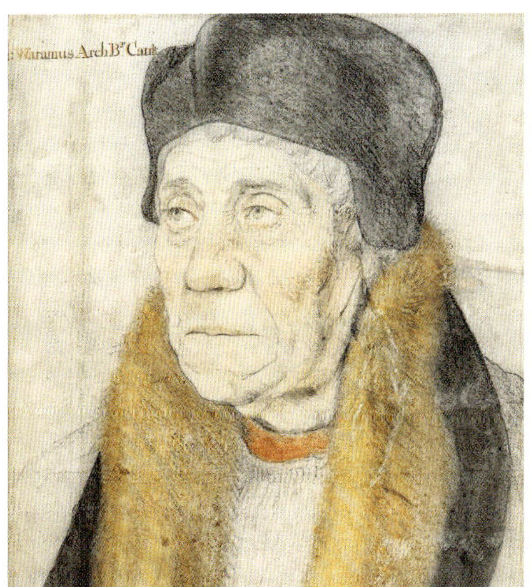

Left: *Study of William Warham,* 1527, chalk on paper, 40.7 × 30.9cm (16.1 × 12.1in), Royal Collection, UK

A preparatory drawing in chalk for the portrait of William Warham, Archbishop of Canterbury, painted by Holbein in 1527. Warham commissioned two identical portraits; one was to hang in the Archbishop's palace and the other was sent to Erasmus, in return for a portrait of him. Holbein's painting of Erasmus (painted in 1523, see page 134) is similar in composition to the one of Warham and they may have been hung together in Erasmus's home.

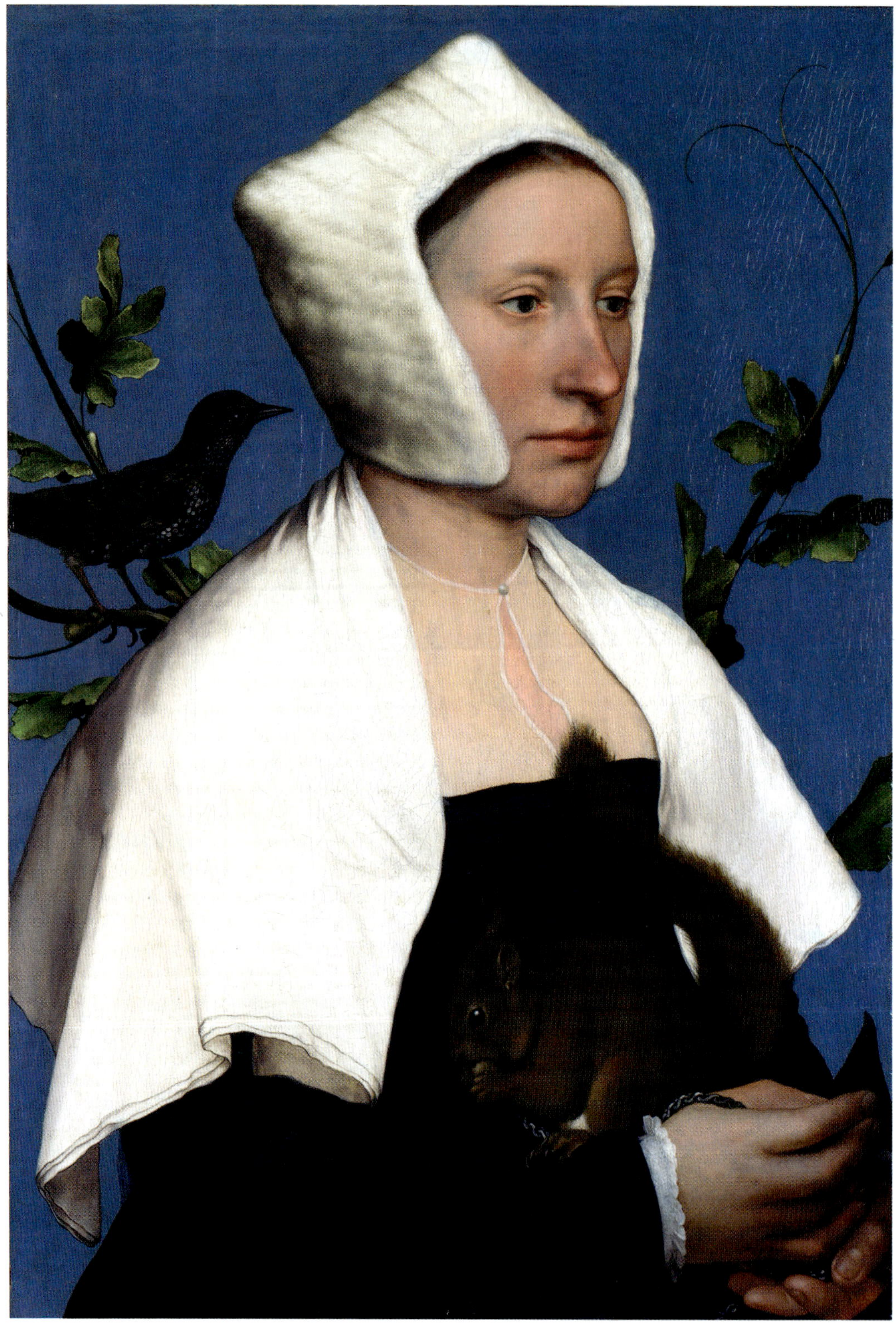

Portrait of a Lady with a Squirrel and a Starling, 1526–28, oil on oak, 56 x 38.8cm (22 x 15.2in), National Gallery, London, UK

This work might be a commemorative portrait of Anne Lovell, wife of Sir William Lovell (died 1551), to mark the birth of their son in early 1526. The Coat of Arms of the Lovell family, of East Harling, Norfolk, featured squirrels. There are no preparatory drawings of this portrait. The half-length oil-on-oak portrait depicts the lady in three-quarter profile facing to her left. The sitter's eyes capture a moment of thought, of contemplation, giving her young face a passive expression. She wears a fashionable headpiece, and holds a pet squirrel. On a branch behind her is an inquisitive starling. Holbein added the squirrel to the painting as the work progressed. It is not in underlayers of the painting.

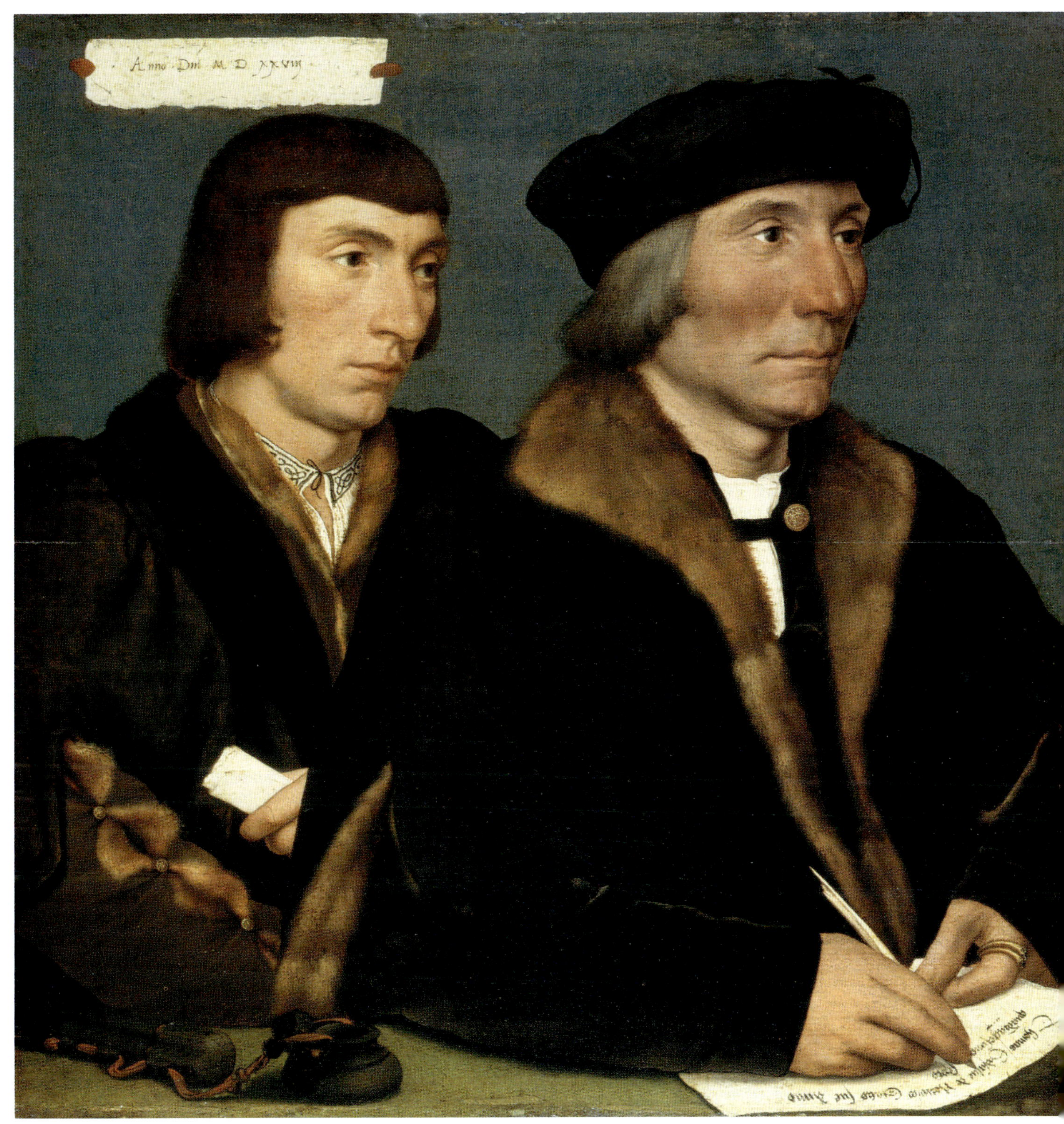

Double portrait of Thomas Godsalve and his son Sir John, 1528, oil on oak, 35 x 36cm (13.7 x 14.1in), Alte Meister, Gemaldergalerie, Dresden, Germany

Thomas Godsalve (1481–1542), a prosperous landowner and notary in Norfolk, was one of the first courtiers to commission a portrait from Holbein. In a half-length double portrait of father and son, Thomas and John respectively, Holbein portrays them seated together at a table, facing to their left, looking toward something or someone unseen. Thomas, with writing paper, holds a pen. John holds a paper in his left hand. Sir John was secretary to Thomas Cromwell.

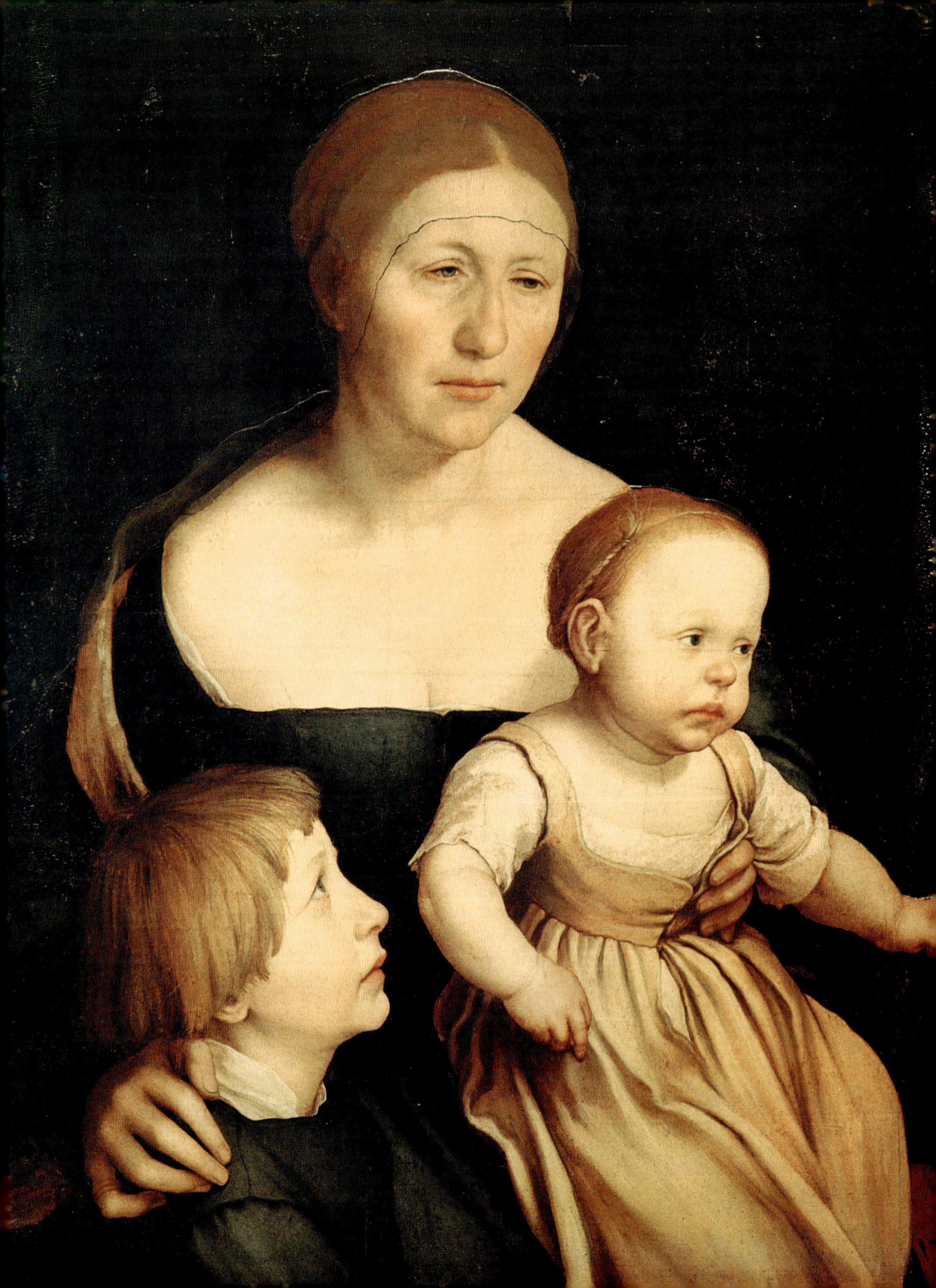

BASEL
1528–1532

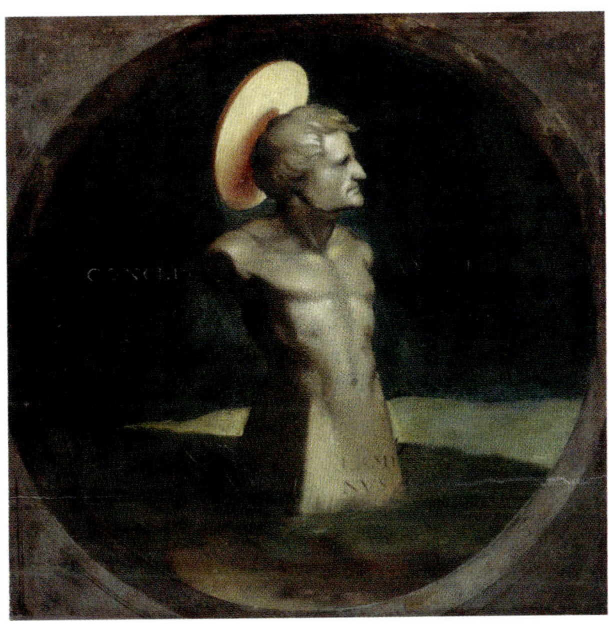

Holbein's necessary return to Basel in 1528, to retain his citizenship after a two-year leave of absence, brought him a welcome from the city's officials, who wanted him to stay permanently. It was a momentous four-year period in his private life: he gained commissions, purchased two houses, and Elsbeth gave birth to two further children. However, in Basel there was uneasiness after major iconoclast riots in February 1529, with artworks and books destroyed and burned. Protestantism became the official religion of the city that year, lessening art commissions. In 1532, Holbein returned to London.

Above: Terminus, the Device of Erasmus, c. 1532, oil on wood, 21.6 x 21.6cm (8.5 x 8.5in), Cleveland Museum of Art, Ohio, USA. Desiderius Erasmus, the Rotterdam-born humanist, theologian, and scholar of ancient Greek and Roman literature, infused his own writings with the moral arguments of ancient texts. Erasmus's interest in Terminus, the Roman god of boundaries, is utilised in Holbein's unusual portrait of the scholar on an ancient bust of Terminus. Erasmus appropriated Terminus's 'dictum concedo nulli' ('I concede to no one'), as his own creed.

Left: Portrait of the Artist's Wife with the Two Elder Children, 1528–29, mixed media on paper mounted on wood, 77 x 64cm (30 x 25in), Kunstmuseum, Basel. A family portrait of Holbein's wife Elsbeth, at around thirty-three years of age, and their two elder children Katharina, about two years of age, and Philipp, aged about six. Their portrayals are slightly smaller than life-size. It is thought that Holbein painted this work on his return to Basel from England in 1528, due to his younger children, Jakob, born 1529, and Küngold, born 1530, not present.

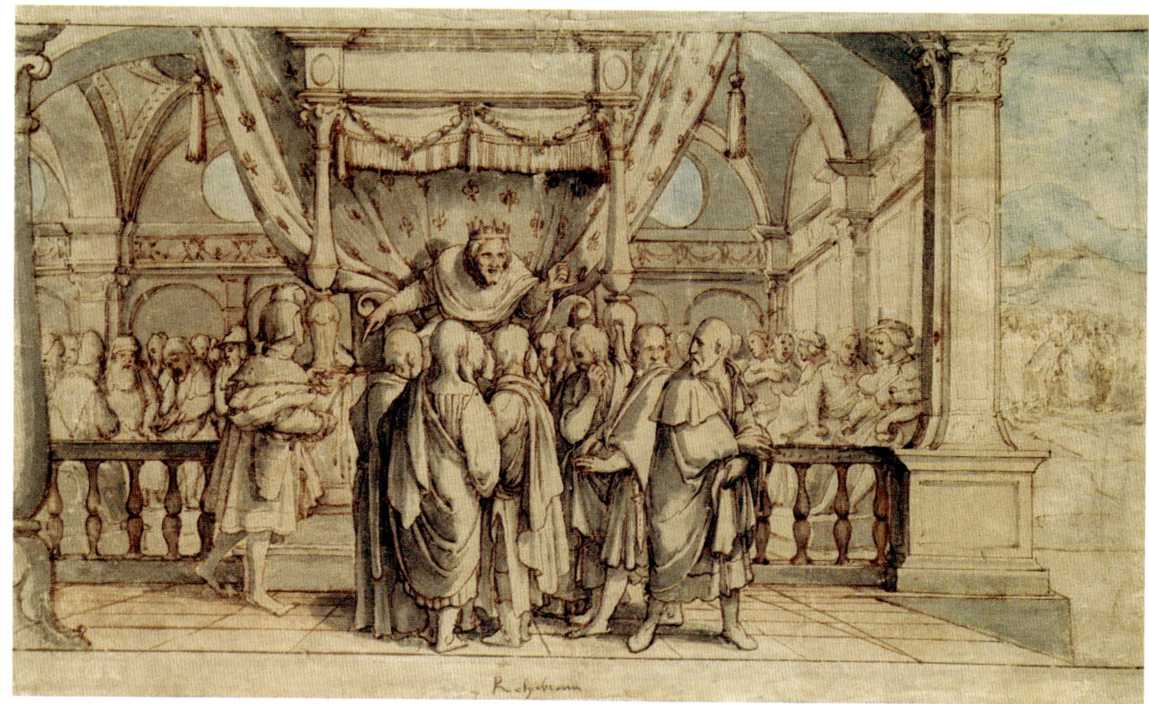

Rehoboam rejecting the advice of the elders, 1530, pen and ink, chalk and watercolour, 22.5 x 38.3cm (8.8 x 15.1in), Kunstmuseum, Basel, Switzerland

A preparatory drawing for the remaining wall painting for the Great Council Chamber, Basel, informed by biblical scripture, I Kings 12:8. 'But Rehoboam rejected the advice that the elders gave him and consulted the young men who had grown up with him.' Holbein returned to Basel as a celebrated painter. A commission from 1520–21 to create a series of mural paintings for the new Great Council Chamber had been successful but one wall remained blank. Holbein was commissioned to paint it, continuing the Old Testament history of the Kings of Israel.

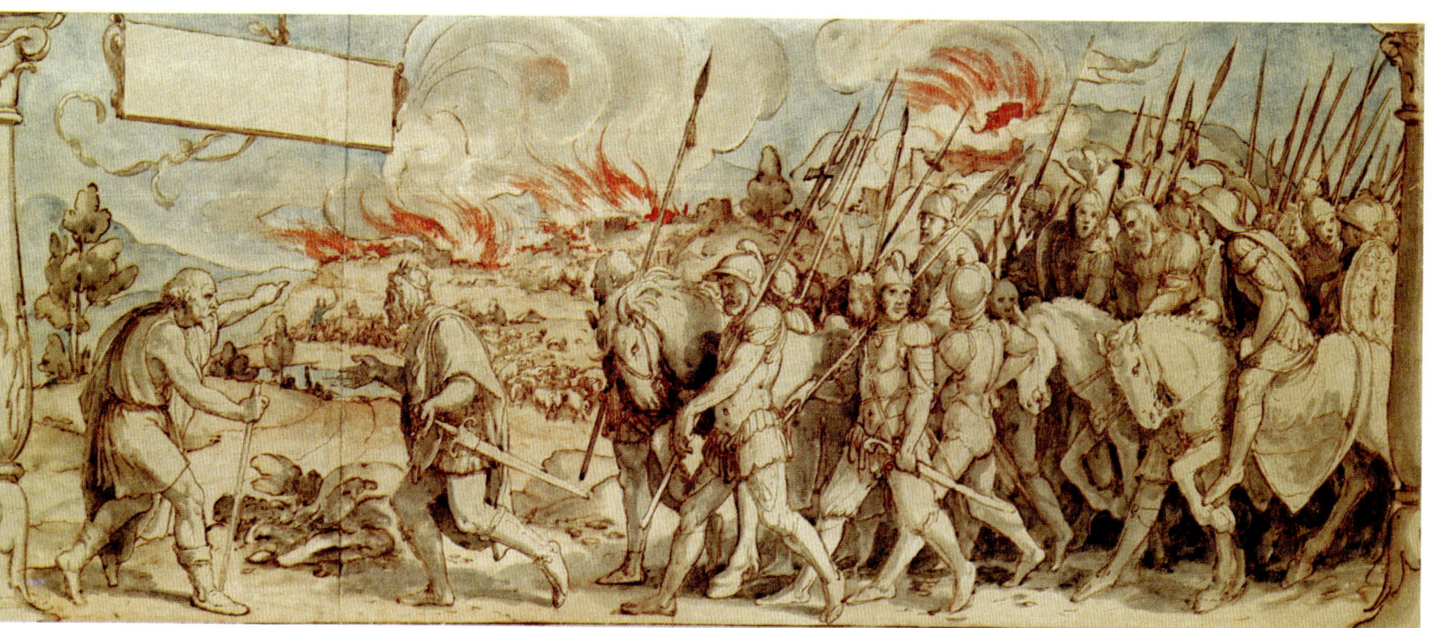

Flight from Saul, 1530, pen and ink, chalk and watercolour, 21 x 52.4cm (8.2 x 20.6in), Kunstmuseum, Basel, Switzerland

A preparatory drawing for the wall painting in the Great Council Chamber of Basel. The subject is the flight from Saul, described in the bible scriptures, Samuel 21 10–15. It begins 'That day David [King of Israel] fled from Saul and went to the Achish king Gath...'

Portrait of a man with a red hat, c.1530, black and coloured chalks, watercolour and pen and ink, 40.9 x 34.3cm (16.1 x 13.5in), Hanfstaengl Kollektion, Munich, Germany

A half-length portrait of an unknown man depicted in three-quarter profile. Holbein uses complementary colours of green for the background, and rich red for the man's hat, which accentuates the content of the composition, including the fashionable jacket the sitter wears, and his face, which is full of character.

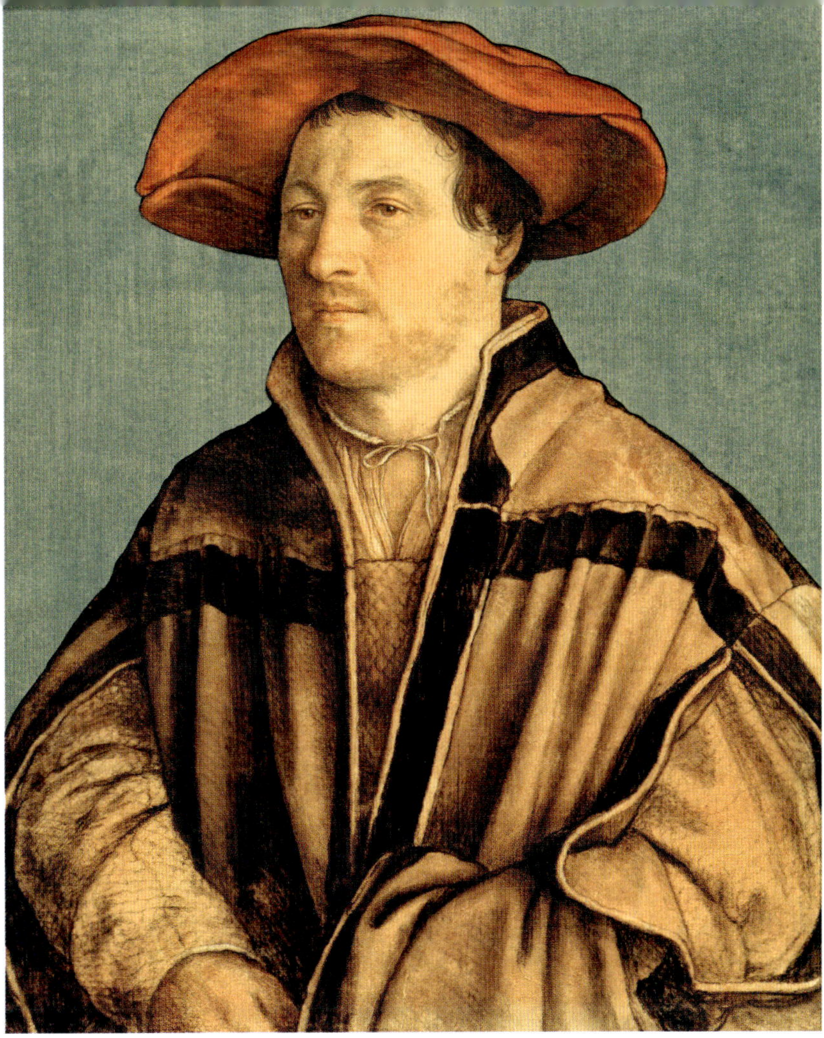

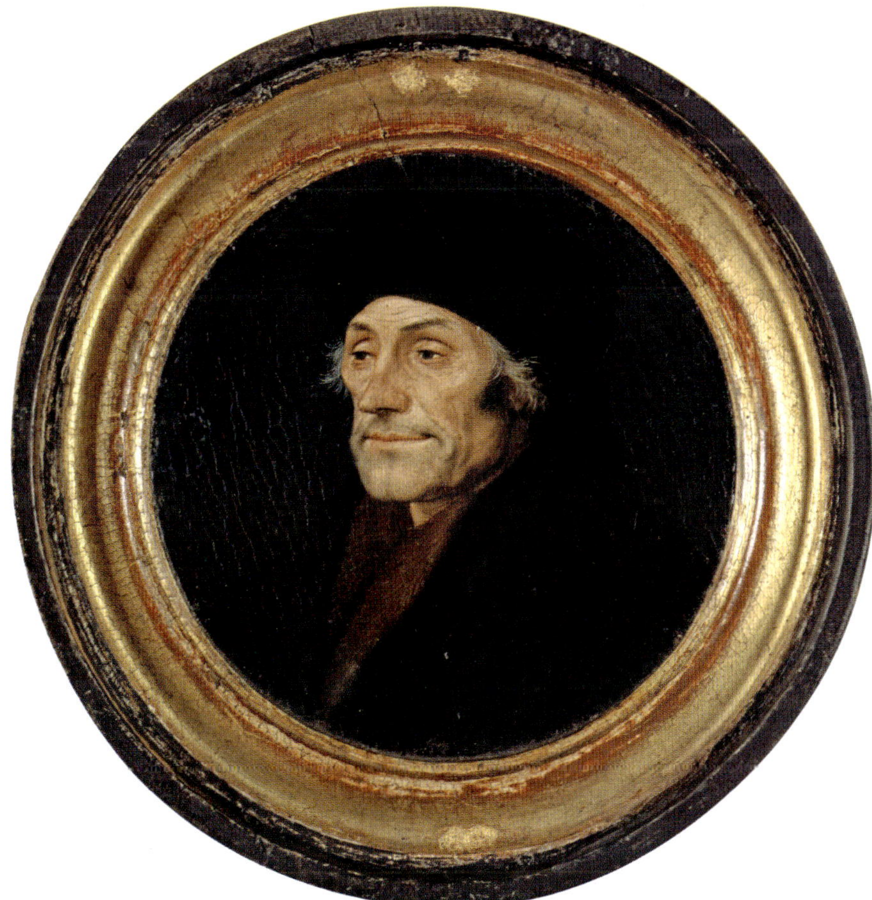

Roundel Portrait of Erasmus of Rotterdam, 1532, oil on lime wood, 14.2cm (5.59in) diameter (including the circular wood frame), Kunstmuseum, Basel, Switzerland

In 1532 Holbein, prior to his departure from Basel to England, created this small roundel portrait of Erasmus Desiderius, in three-quarter profile. It is probably based on the earlier 1523 half-length portrait of the humanist scholar (see page 134); Holbein must have still had the preparatory drawings of this painting. The commission might have come from the Basel publisher Hieronymus Froben (1501–63), the owner of the work, and eldest son of the publisher Johann Froben (died 1527). Hieronymus was Erasmus's godson. At the time of its creation, Erasmus had left Basel, due to iconoclast unrest in the city, and settled across the German border, about fifty miles away, in Freiburg.

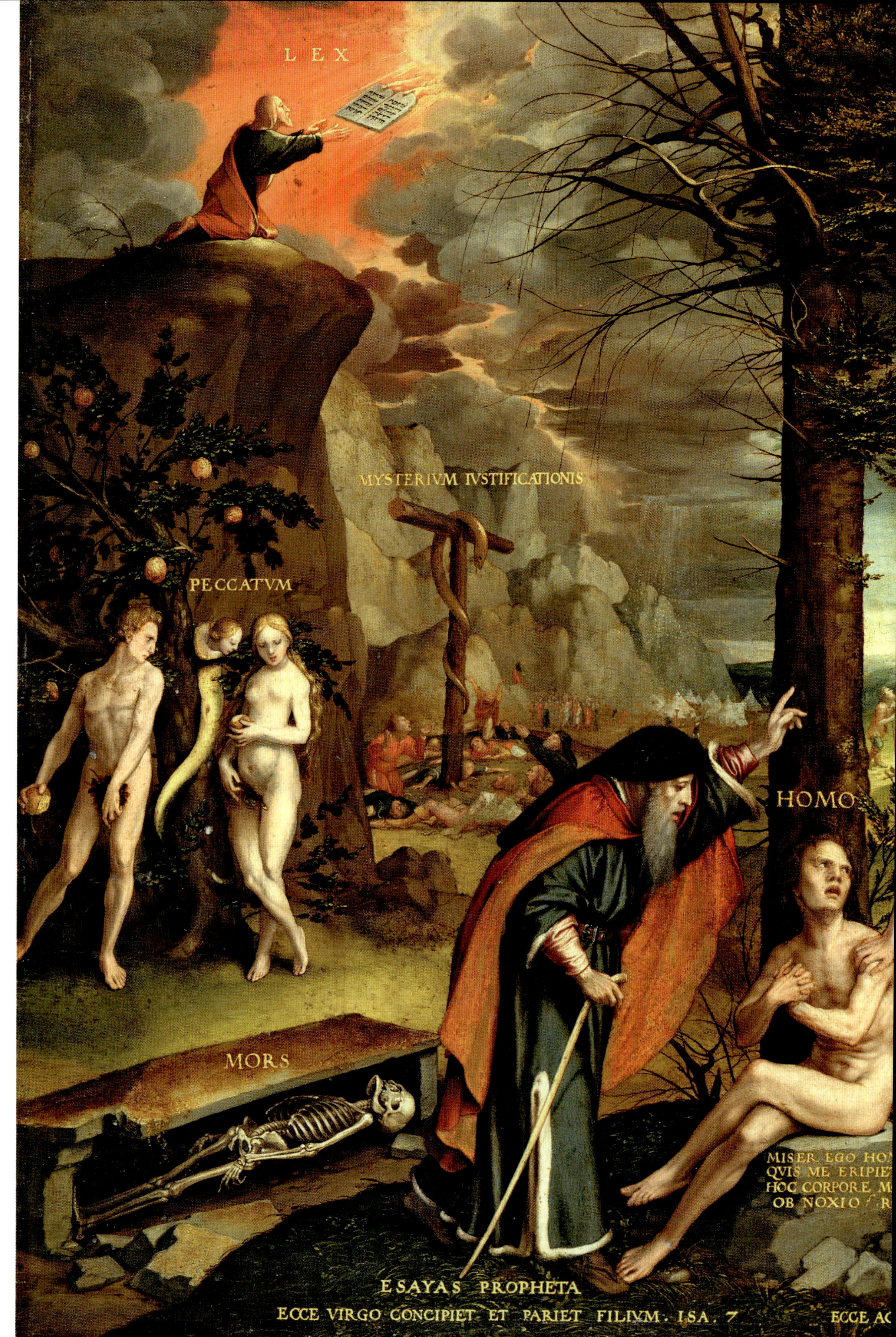

LEX
MYSTERIVM IVSTIFICATIONIS
PECCATVM
HOMO
MORS
MISER EGO HO
QVIS ME ERIPIET
HOC CORPORE M
OB NOXIO R
ESAYAS PROPHETA
ECCE VIRGO CONCIPIET ET PARIET FILIVM. ISA. 7
ECCE AG

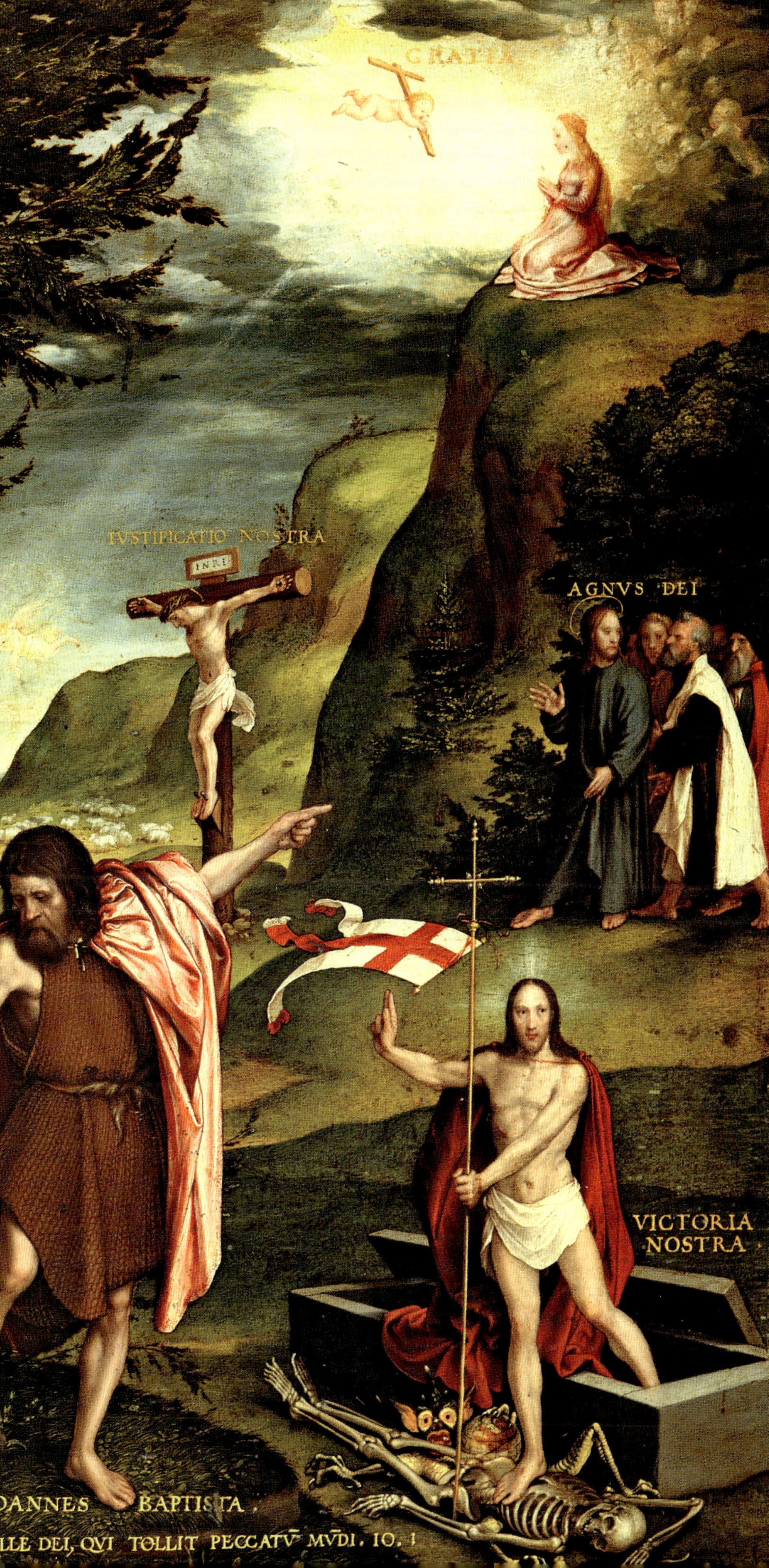

Allegory of the Old and New Testaments, early 1530s, oil on panel, 50 x 60.5cm (19.7 x 23.8in), Scottish National Gallery, Edinburgh, Scotland, UK

Holbein began this painting before he left Basel and it was completed in England by the early 1530s. The painting is divided into two halves by a large tree at its centre. The left side is devoted to the Old Testament beginning with Adam and Eve. The 'brazen serpent' is depicted draped around a cross (MYSTERIUM IUSTIFICATIONIS). The right side, from the New Testament, leads toward salvation. The Old Testament Law (LEX) is seen as intolerant, the New Testament Law (GRATIA) as forgiving. In the foreground Man (HOMO) is sitting at the base of the tree, between the Old Testament prophet Isaiah and New Testament St John the Baptist. The Baptist points toward Christ (AGNUS DEI), the 'Lamb of God'. Inscriptions guide the viewer through a visual sermon from the original sin of Adam and Eve (PECCATUM), leading to death (MORS), to Christ's crucifixion (IUSTIFICATIO NOSTRA), and Man's salvation (VICTORIA NOSTRA).

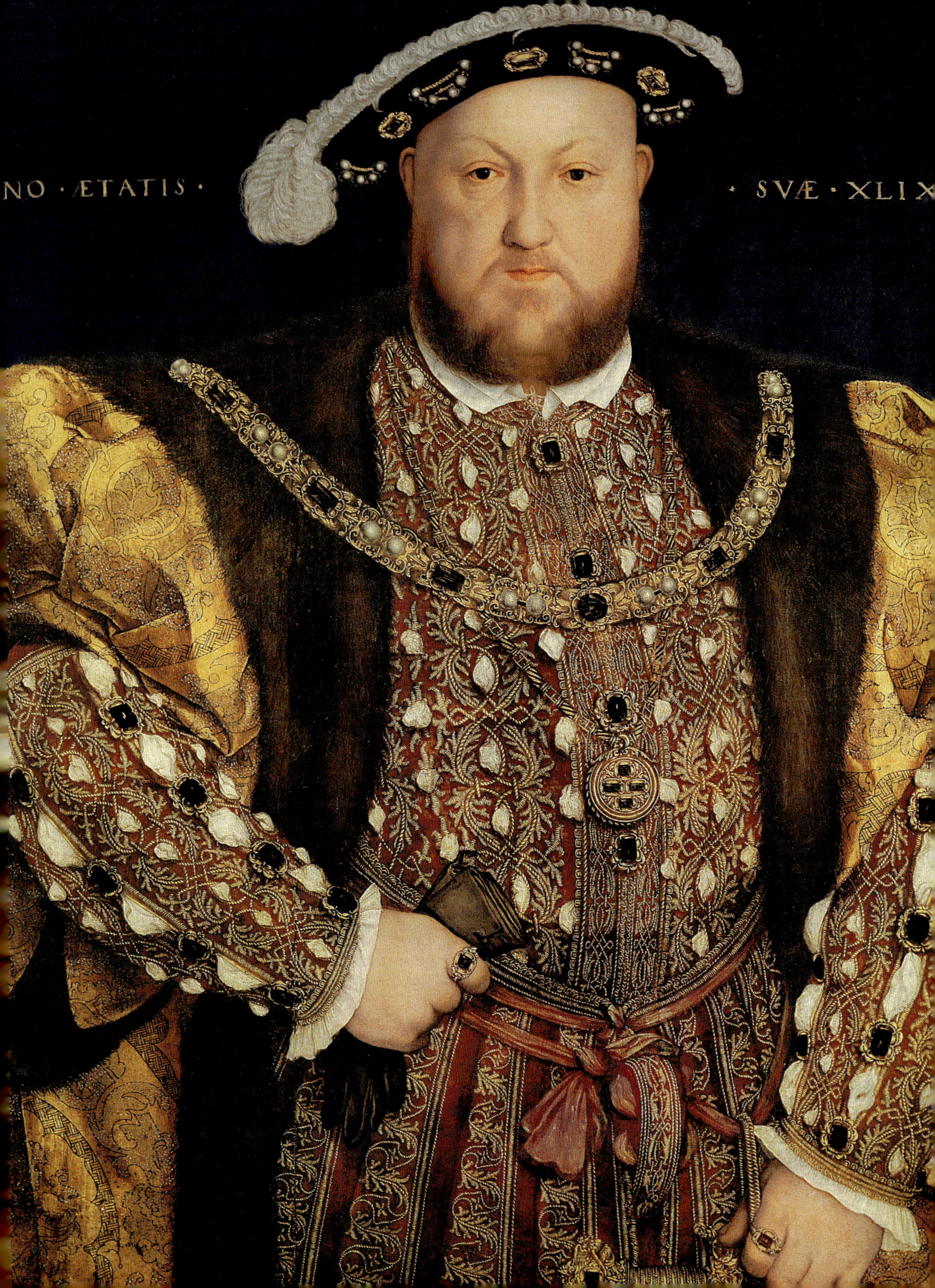
NO · ÆTATIS ·
· SVÆ · XLIX

LONDON
1532–1543

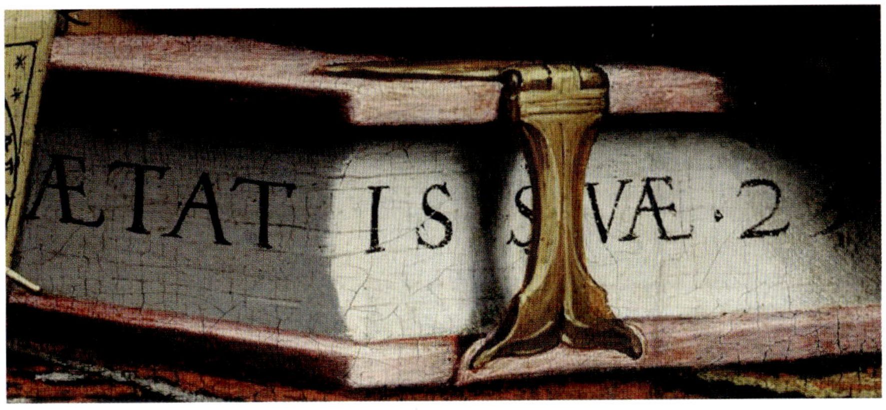

Holbein's second stay in England proved to be his finest period as a painter. Portrait commissions from the German Hanse merchants in London, and the nobility, and his spectacular life-size painting, *The Ambassadors*, 1533, led to commissions from the most important patron in England, King Henry VIII. For every sitter Holbein captured a moment in time, portraying intimacy, character, and realism in each work. It was inevitable that he would become the King's Painter in 1536. After a month-long return to Basel in autumn 1538, Holbein was back in London. He became a denizen of the city in 1541, which allowed him to establish a formal workshop. His untimely death in 1543 robbed Basel and London of a magnificently gifted portraitist: Hans Holbein, the German 'Apelles'.

Above: detail from The Ambassadors, *1533 (see pages 182–3). The name of George de Selve and his date of birth are painted on the closed pages of the book on which he rests his hand. The intricate details in this life-size double portrait would help seal Holbein's reputation.*

Left: Portrait of Henry VIII aged 49, 1540, oil on wood, 88.5 x 74.5cm (34.8 x 29.3in), Barberini Gallerie Nazionali Corsini, Rome, Italy. A majestic portrait of the King of England attributed to Hans Holbein. Lettering on the dark blue background informs that the king was forty-nine years old when this portrait was painted, on the occasion of his marriage to Anne of Cleves, his fourth marriage (and one that displeased him greatly). The king in a three-quarter length portrait directly faces the viewer. The fabrics and patterning of his clothing are sumptuously illustrated, giving great definition to the silk brocades and fur, and his ornate, magnificent jewels.

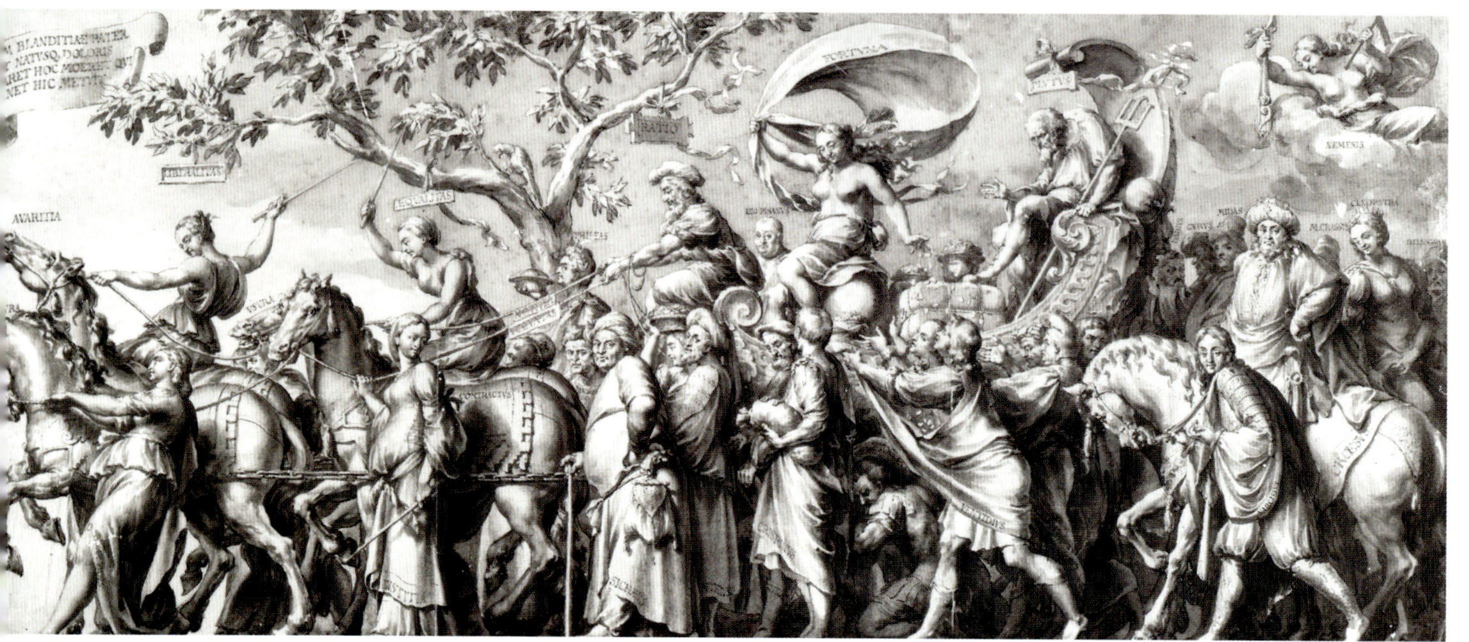

The Triumph of Riches, c.1650 after Holbein c.1532, oil on canvas, 244 x 616cm (96 x 242in), The Banqueting Hall of the Guildhall of the Steelyard, London, UK

Drawn in pen and ink and wash on paper c.1650, by the Dutch painter and printmaker Jan de Bisschop (1628–71) copied from Holbein the Younger's original work.

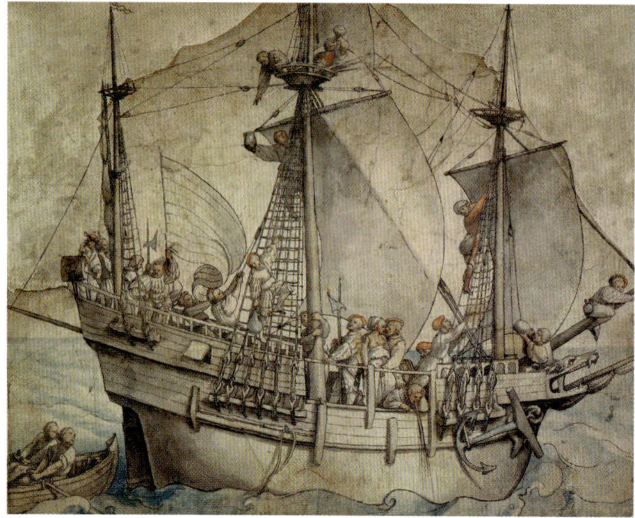

Ship with Revelling Sailors, Lansquenets and a Sutleress, c.1532–33, watercolour, pen and ink on paper, 40.5 x 50.9cm (15.9 x 20in), Städel Museum, Frankfurt am Main, Germany

In an unusual work for Holbein, a bawdy 'ship of fools' are all at sea. A bare-breasted woman, possibly the Sutleress, one who does dirty work, a prostitute, stands amongst an unruly ship's crew of sailors and lansquenets (German mercenaries), amongst scenes of drinking. At left a rowing boat nears the ship. The commission or idea for this work is unknown.

Below: *Movement Study of a Female Body* (or *Stone Thrower*), 1532–43, brush in grey and black, white raised, on red tinted paper, 20.3 x 12.2cm (8 x 4.8in), Kunstmuseum, Basel, Switzerland

The origin of this drawing and what it was intended for, is unknown. The date places it as a work created by Holbein in England, possibly a figure study for *The Triumph of Riches* c.1532, for the Hanseatic League in London.

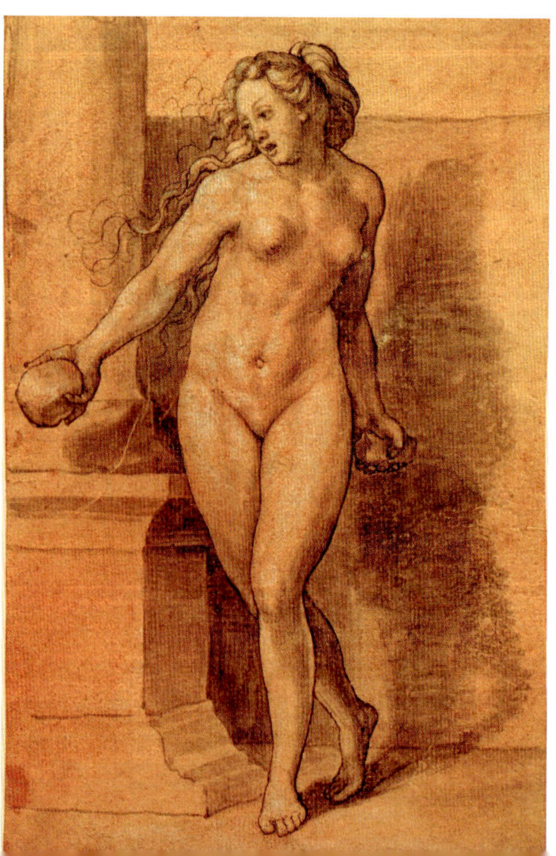

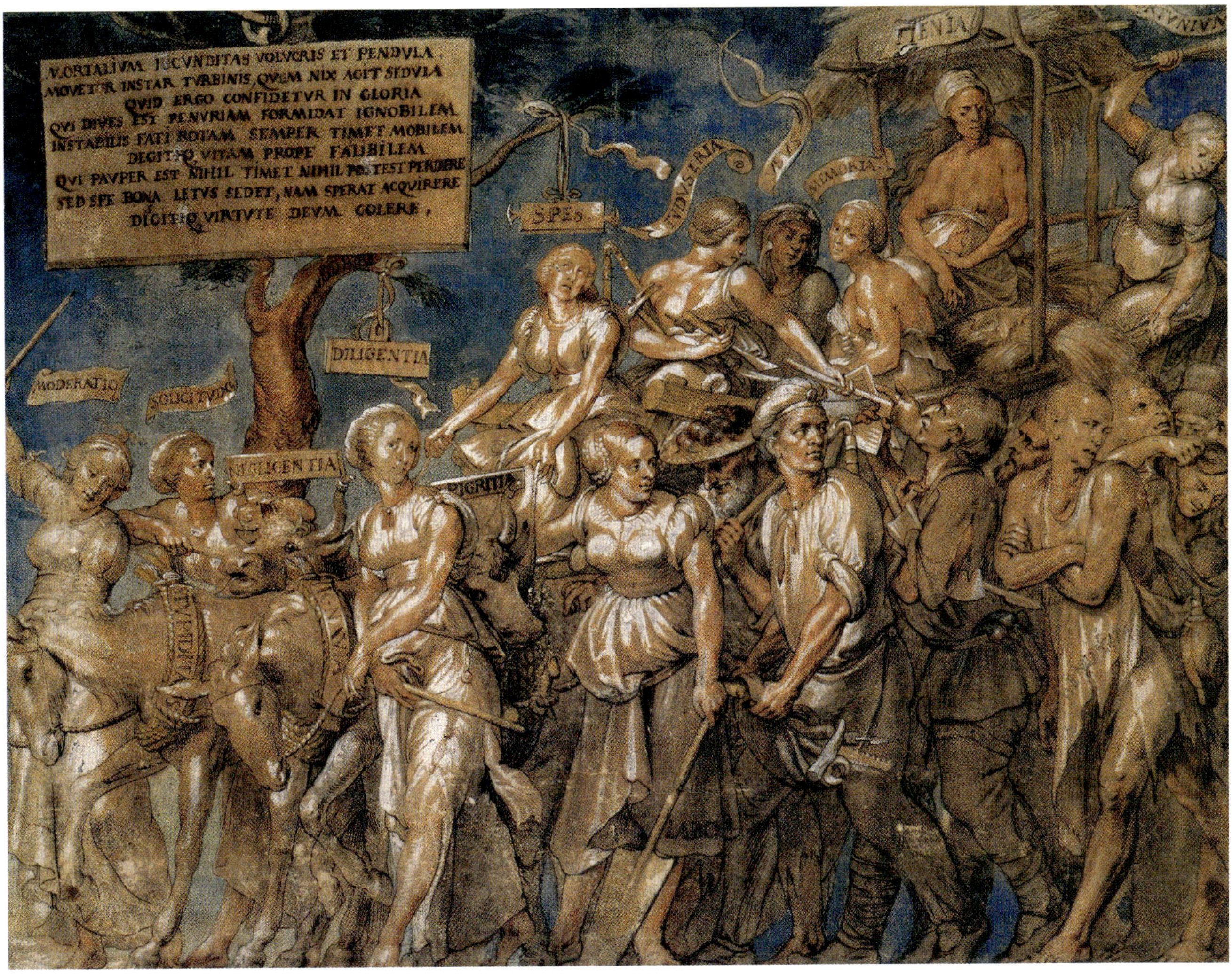

The Triumph of Poverty, c.1650 after c.1532, oil on canvas, 222 x 301cm (87.4 x 118.5in), The Banqueting Hall of the Guildhall of the Steelyard, London, UK

A commission for wall paintings for the prestigious Banqueting Hall of the Guildhall of the Steelyard led Holbein to create two allegorical works. These are known to us through copies by the Dutch artist Jan de Bisschop in pen, ink and wash on paper, after the original work of c.1532. A later fire in 1752 destroyed the original murals. The works highlight Holbein's diversity and skill in creating large murals.

Typus Cosmographicus Universalis (Map of the World), 1532, woodcut in black on cream laid paper, 25.4 x 19.1cm (10 x 7.5in), attributed to Hans Holbein the Younger, Art Institute of Chicago, USA

In Holbein's 'Map of the World' the globe is oval in shape with titled continents: Europe, Attica, Asia and America. Two angels turn the world with cranks attached to poles. Scenes from America (lower left), Arabia (lower right), Africa (upper left), and Asia (upper right) are placed in the space around the world. First published in *Simon Grynaeus, Novus Orbis regionum ac insularum veteribus incognitarum*, J. Herwagen, Basel, 1532.

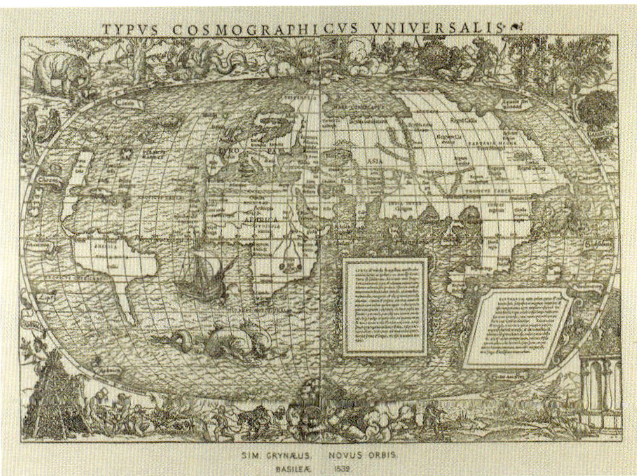

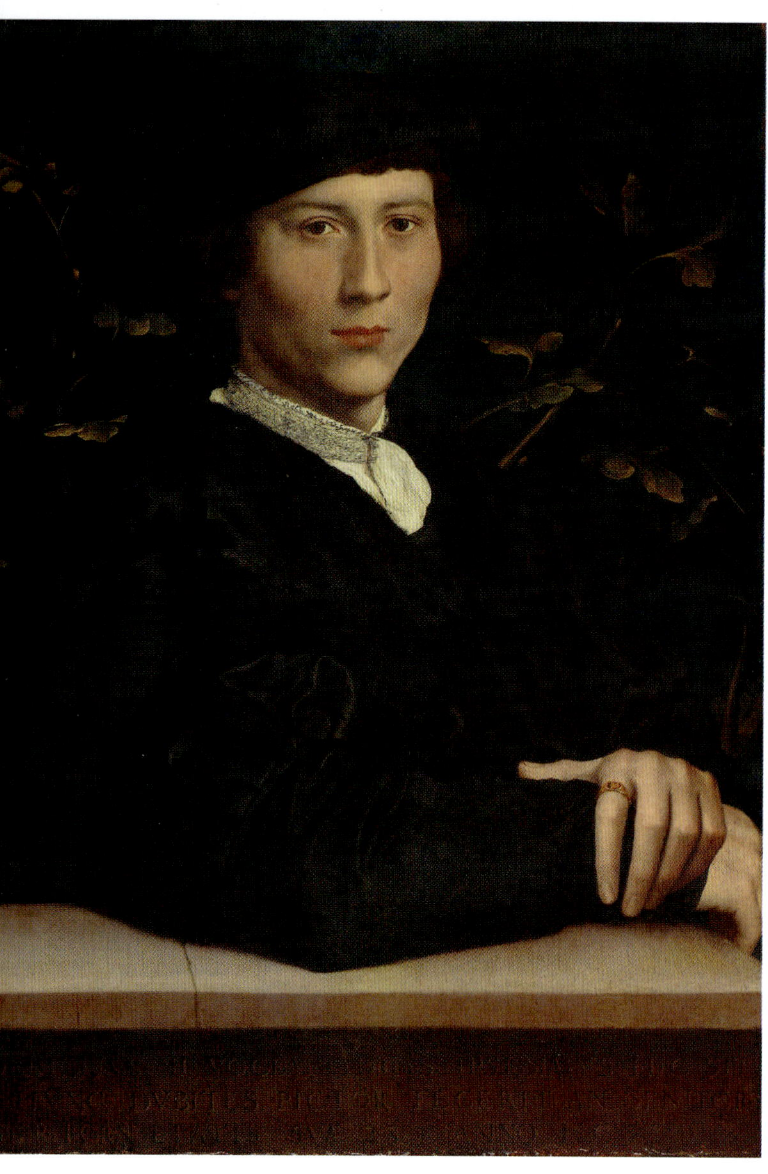

Derich Born, 1533, oil on panel, 60.3 x 45.1cm (23.7 x 17.75in), Royal Collection Trust, UK

The sitter Derich Born (*c.*1510–49), a Hanseatic merchant from Cologne, is shown in three-quarter profile to his left with his head turned directly toward the viewer. In the half-length portrait, Born rests his right arm on a stone parapet that juts out from the picture plane. Light from an unseen source illuminates the sharp, unlined features of his face. Born was twenty-three years of age at the time of the portrait commission. Holbein connotes the young merchant's wealth in the sumptuously rich fabrics of Born's elegant clothing, from the embroidered collar of his silk shirt to the satin doublet and black, fur-lined robe. The long inscription 'carved' below the stone parapet includes a reference to its lifelike realism. It reads: 'DERICHVS SI VOCEM ADDAS IPSISSIMVS HIC SIT/HVNC DVBITES PICTOR FECERIT AN GEINITOR/DER BORN ETATIS SVAE 23.ANNO 1533'. Translating as: 'If you added a voice, this would be Derich himself. You would be in doubt whether the painter or his father created him. Der Born aged 23, in the year 1533'.

Cyriacus Kale, 1533, oil on panel, 22.4 x 32cm (8.8 x 12.6in), Herzog Anton Ulrich-Museum Braunschweig, Germany

Cyriacus Kale, a Hanseatic merchant, although not listed as a member of the London branch, holds documents addressed to him at the Hanse Steelyard headquarters. In the half-length portrait Kale looks directly at the viewer. His merchant's mark – an arrow with crosses – can be seen on the top page of the papers he holds. Holbein inscribes the painting 'IN ALS GEDOLTIG/SIS ALTERS.32 / ANNO.1533' verifying Kale's family motto 'Patient in all things', the sitter's age of thirty-two, and the year the painting was created, 1533. Holbein used inscriptions, dates and merchants' marks to give context to the Hanse merchants' portraits, features not so evident in his portraits of English sitters.

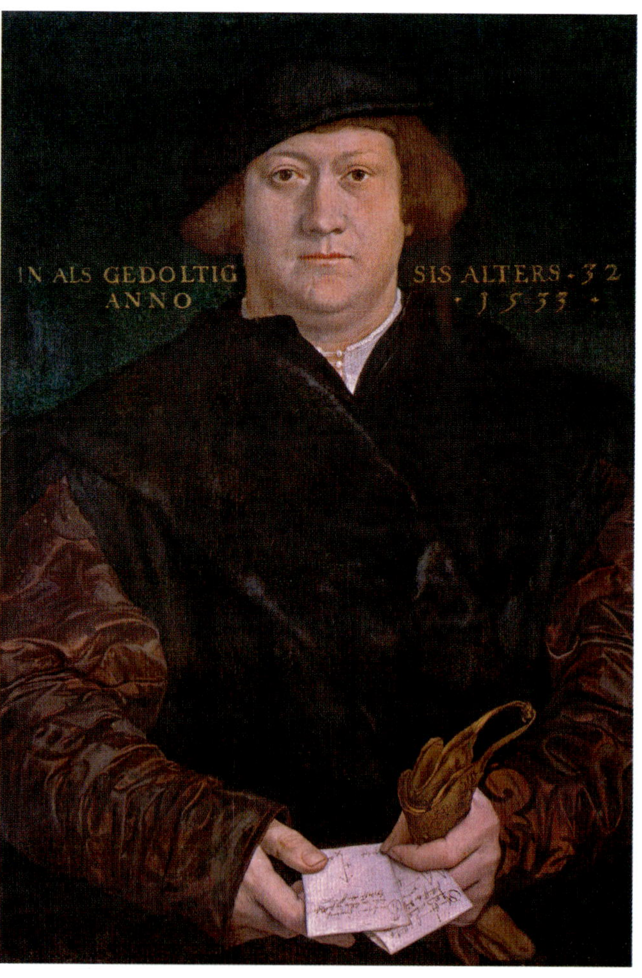

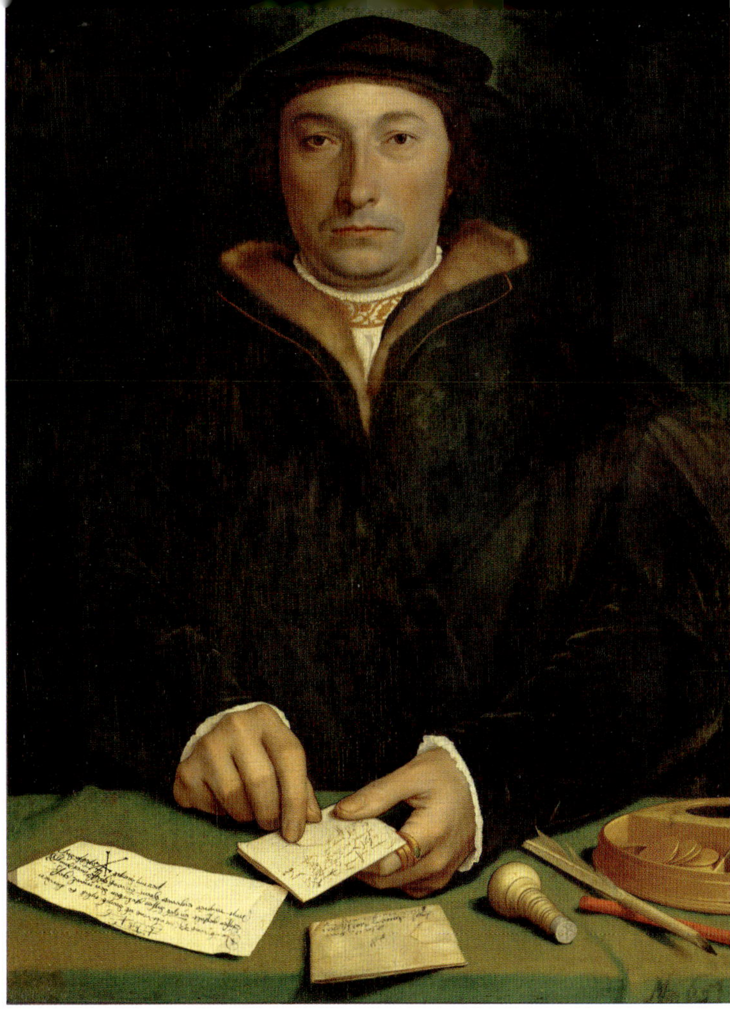

The Duisburg merchant Dirck Tybis, 1533, oil on oak, 47.7 x 34.8cm (18.7 x 13.7in), Kunsthistoriches Museum, Vienna, Austria

One of the 'Steelyard Merchants' portraits by Holbein of Dirck (or Deryck; Dirk) Tybis of Duisburg, is linked to those of Georg Gisze, Cyriacus Kale and Derick Berck, through iconographical details in each work, including letters and a trademark to show their status and success as merchants. This work includes a fascinating statement in the letters Tybis holds, which states that 'When I was 33 years old, I , Deryck (Dirck) Tybis at London, had this appearance and marked this portrait with my device in own hand, in the middle of March, 1533...'

A merchant of the German steelyard, 'Hans of Antwerp', c.1532–33, oil on panel, 63 x 48.4cm (24.8 x 19in), Royal Collection Trust, UK

Hans (or John) of Antwerp was a leading goldsmith in London, living in the city for about seventeen years before Holbein's arrival. From the address on the letter that the goldsmith holds, the portrait was painted at the Steelyard in London, on the banks of the Thames in the Dowgate Ward, a base for the Hanseatic German and Netherlandish merchants. The goldsmith was known also as 'Mr John of Anwarp', and a witness to Hans Holbein's Will, written on 7th October 1543 (see page 93). It was noted in the Will that Holbein owed him £6.00 sterling, which would be paid. The longevity of their relationship suggests a strong working friendship.

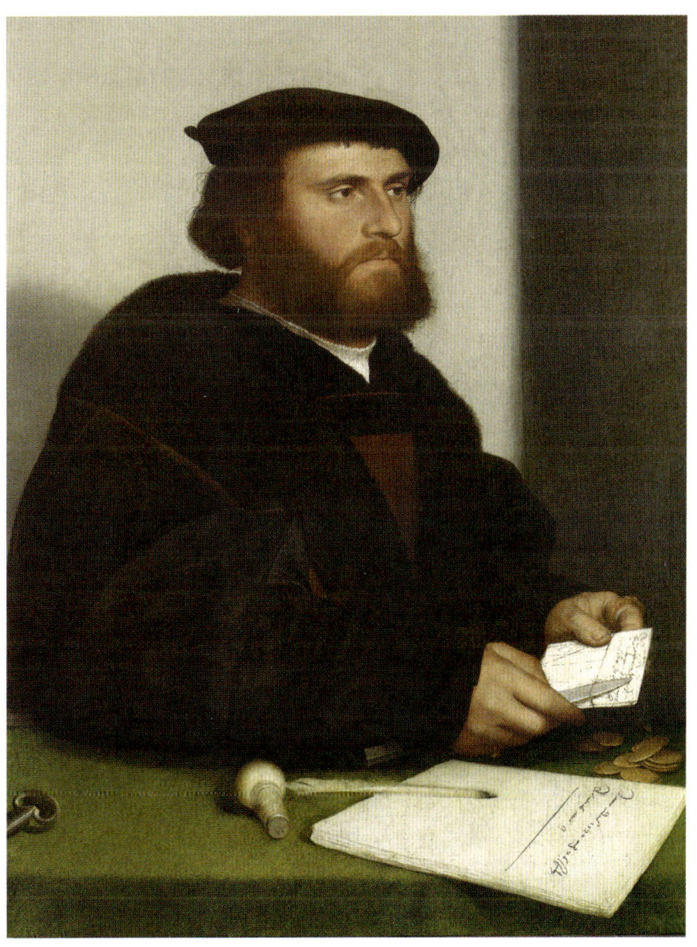

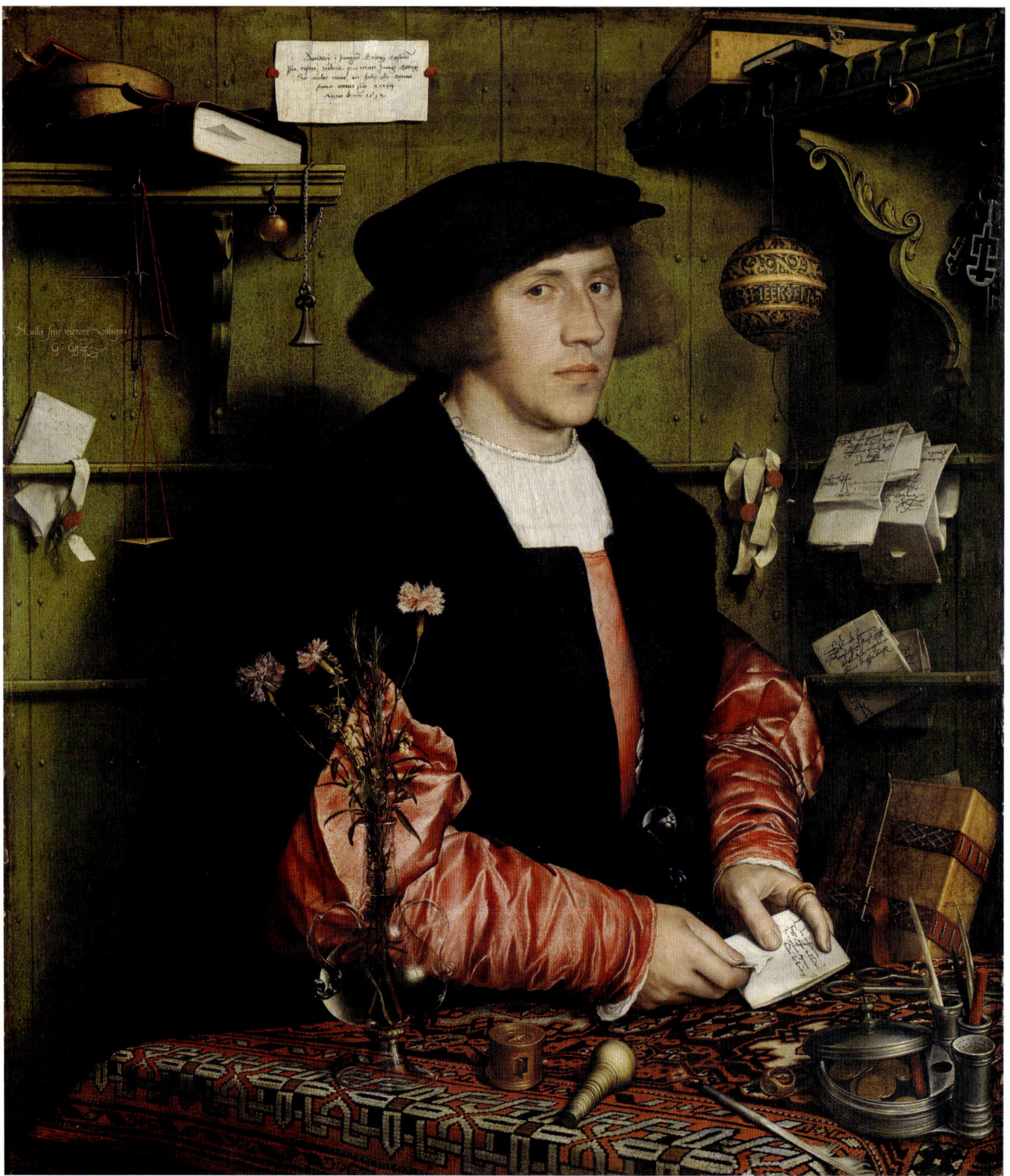

Portrait of the merchant Georg Gisze, 1532, oil on oak, 86.2 x 97.5cm (33.9 x 38.3in), Gemäldegalerie, Berlin, Germany

The portrait of George Gisze, the first, the largest and most detailed of the Hanseatic merchants' portraits produced by Holbein, is masterful in its realism. The superb likeness of Danzig-born merchant Georg Gisze (1497–1562) and meticulous rendition of his Steelyard office with its abundance of objects, from the oriental carpet covering the work table, to his motto 'No Joy without Sorrow' on the wall, was to encourage other merchants to commission the artist. Holbein placed emphasis on the trappings of Gisze's profession. Each subsequent portrait of Hanse merchants included their trademark, their age and date of the portrait. The London headquarters of the Hanseatic merchants was in the Steelyard, a complex of buildings near the banks of the Thames river.

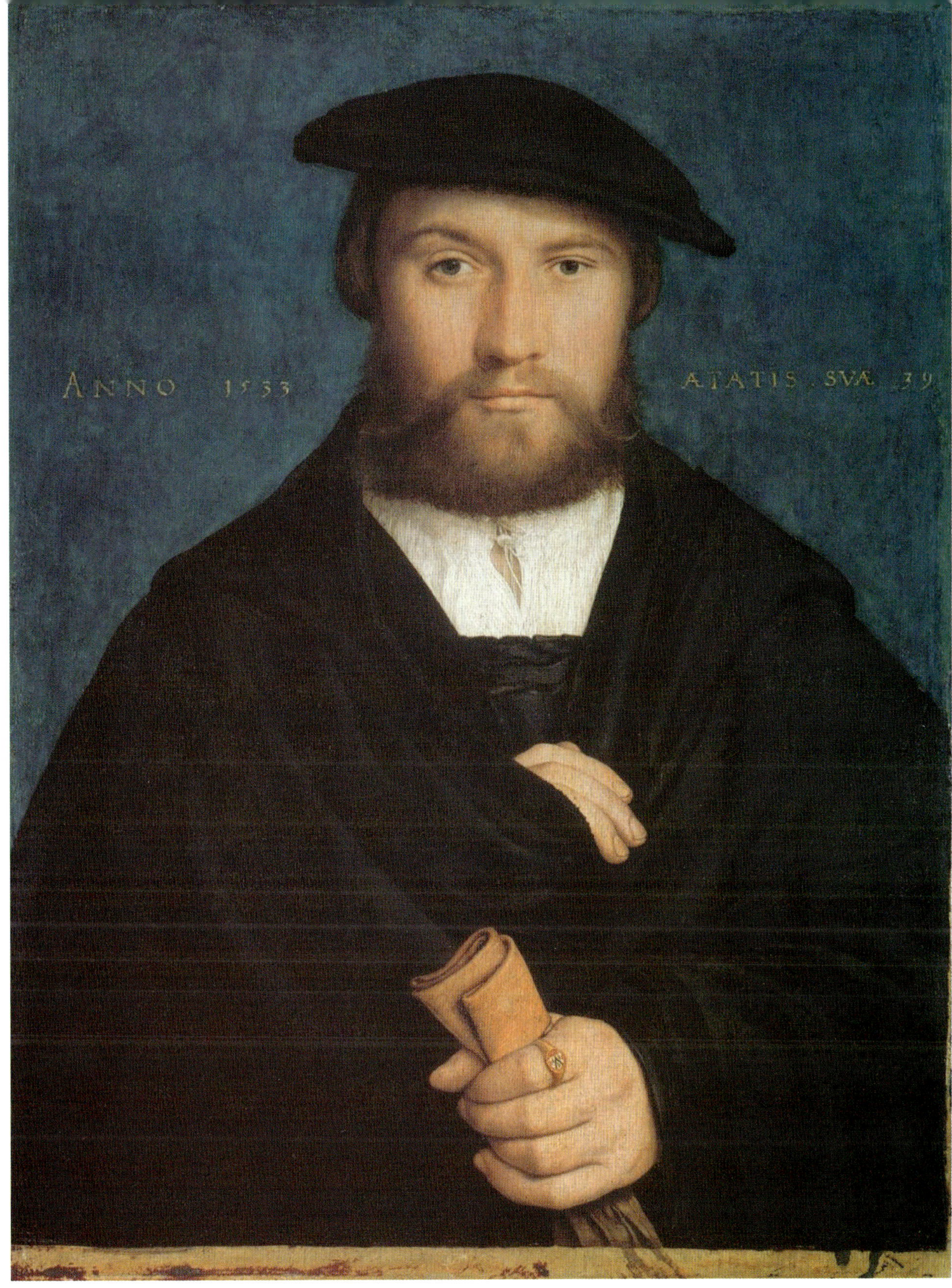

Portrait of the Hermann Hillebrandt von Wedigh, 1533, oil on oak, 21.1 x 27cm (8.3 x 10.7in), Gemäldegalerie, Berlin, Germany

A half-length frontal portrait of Hanse merchant Hermann Hillebrandt von Wedigh (born *c.*1494), possibly a relation of Hermann von Wedigh III, painted by Holbein in 1532 (overleaf). The rich, dark cloak, fully wrapped around von Wedigh's body, focuses attention on the brightly lit facial features and head of reddish hair with trimmed moustache and beard. He holds a pair of leather gloves in his left hand. On the forefinger is a signet ring incised with the von Wedigh coat of arms. Inscribed in Latin on the portrait's background is: 'ANNO 1533 AETATIS SUAE 39', the date of the portrait, and von Wedigh's age.

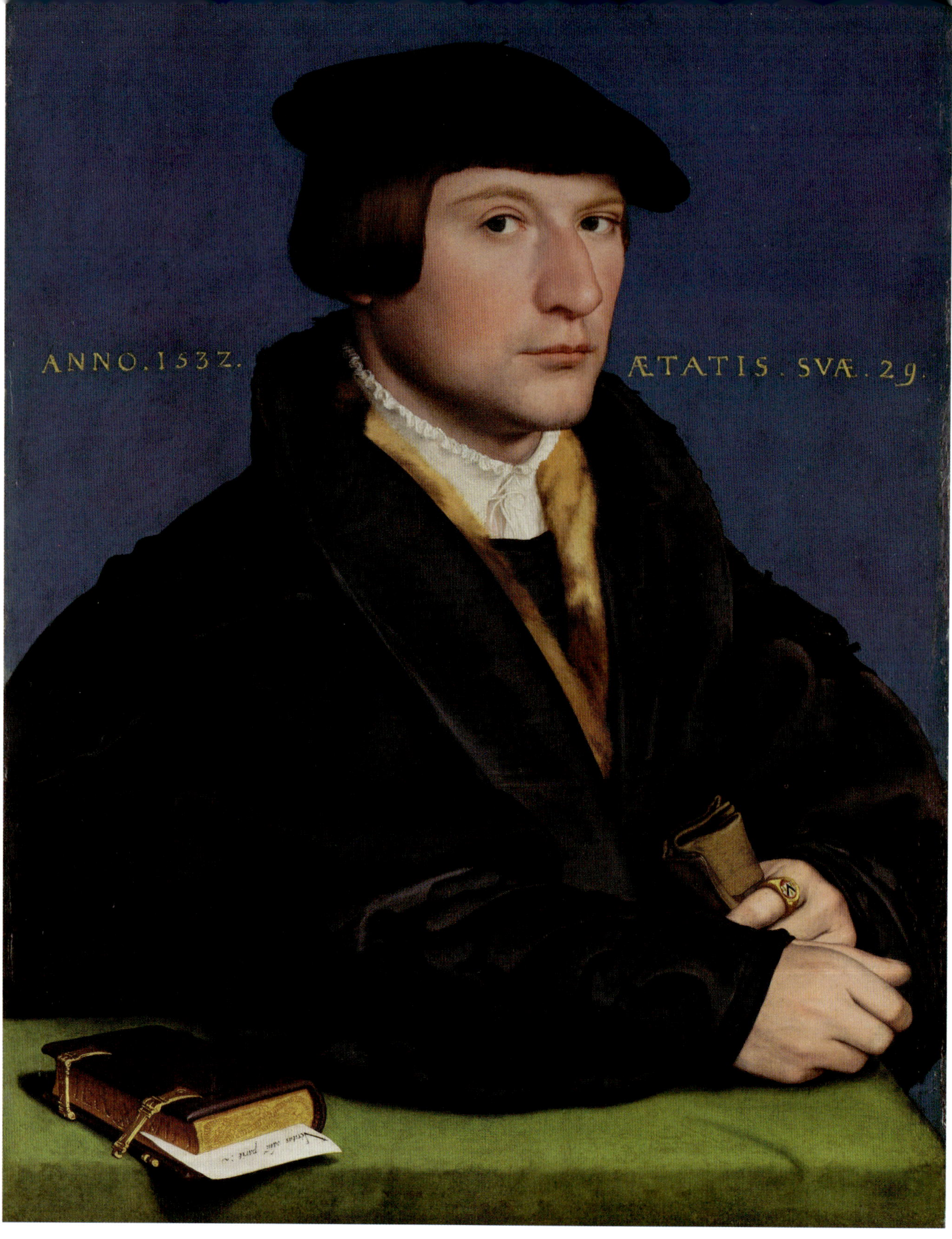

Portrait of Hermann von Wedigh III, 1532, oil and gold on oak, 42.2 x 32.4cm (16.5 x 12.75in), Metropolitan Museum of Art, New York, NY, USA

In his portrait Hermann von Wedigh III (died c.1560) a merchant of the Steelyard, sits in three-quarter profile, his right arm resting on a table covered in green cloth. His head turns to the viewer, as if caught in a moment in time. He wears a coat of black silk damask and a hat. On his forefinger is a signet ring incised with the von Wedigh of Cologne coat of arms. His book, jutting slightly over the edge of the table, is inscribed with the initials HH. Its clasp is undone. The paper, slid between its pages, has the words 'Veritas odiu[m] parit', 'Truth breeds hatred', a quote from the Roman writer Terence, and a motto used by the humanists. Inscribed in gold on the background is 'ANNO.1532. AETATIS. SVAE. 29.; HH.; HER WID.'; the date of the portrait, the sitter's age, twenty-nine, and his name.

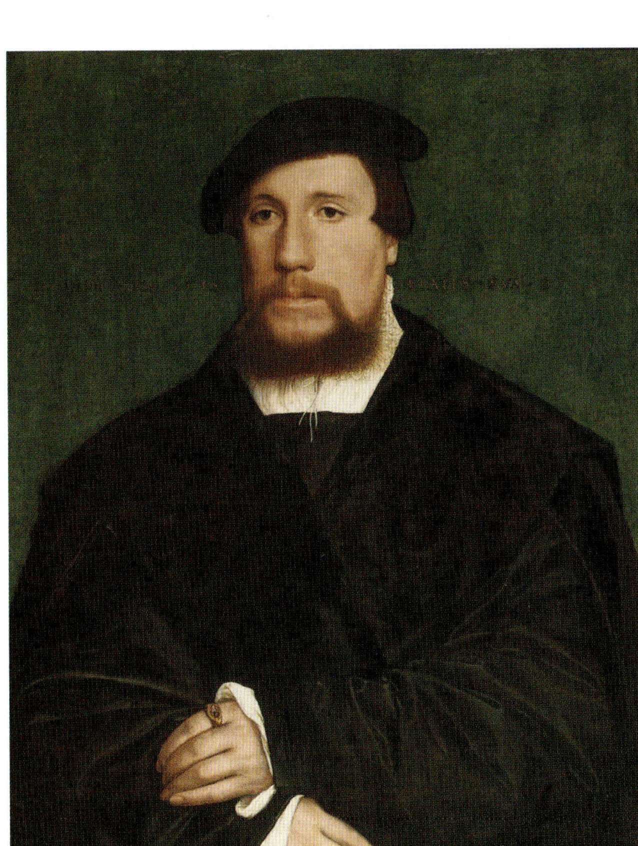

Portrait of a Hanseatic Merchant, 1538, oil on panel, 49.6 x 39cm (19.5 x 15.35in), Yale University Art Gallery, New Haven, USA

A Holbein portrait of an unidentified Hanseatic merchant who is depicted facing front with head and eyes turned toward his right. The inscription behind the sitter states that he is thirty-three years of age but does not give the year of the portrait's creation. Sir Thomas More, in capacity of lawyer, had connections to the Hanseatic merchants of the Steelyard in London, possibly introducing them personally to Holbein, although Holbein would have known of the Hanseatic League in Augsburg. In London, the artist moved freely within this group of fellow-Germans, and received many commissions from them.

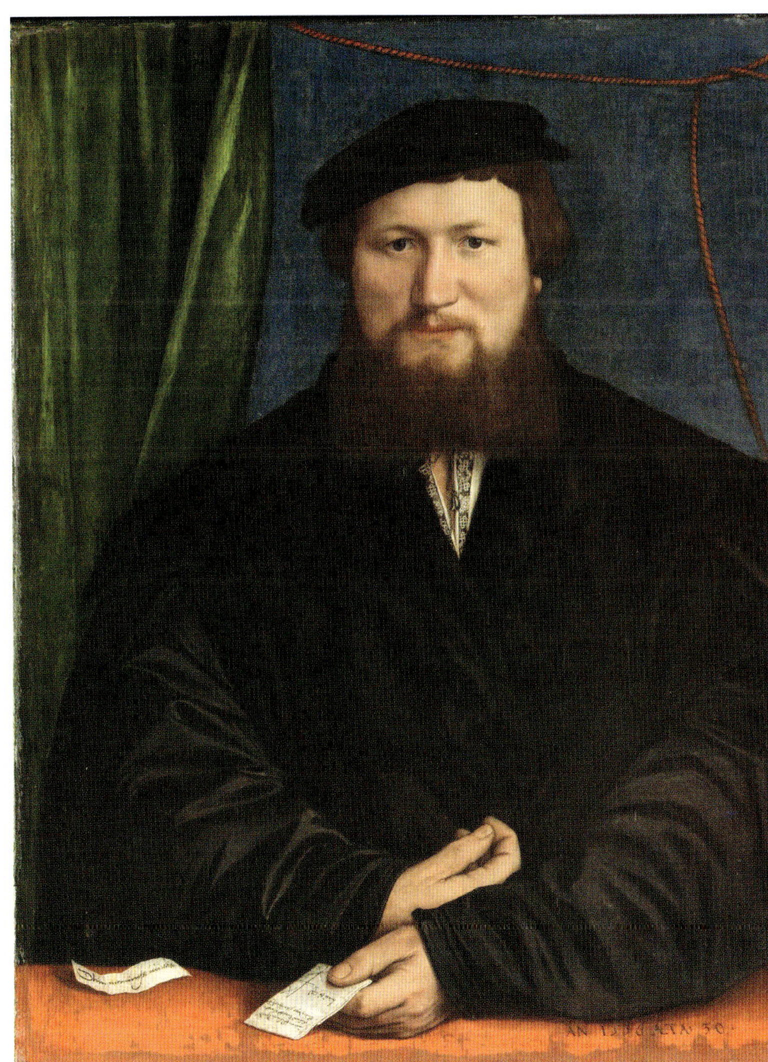

Derick Berck of Cologne, 1536, oil on canvas transferred from wood, 53 x 42.5cm (20 x 16.7in), Metropolitan Museum of Art, New York, NY, USA

Derick Berck, a successful merchant of the London Steelyard, is depicted wearing a near-black hat, and robe of silk, with his white embroidered shirt just visible. He leans on a table covered in red cloth, facing forward, looking directly at the viewer, in a half-length portrait. In the background a green silk curtain, pulled to one side with red strings, reveals a backdrop of blue. Holbein's portrait of Derick Berck follows earlier portraits, such as that of Dirck Tybis and Cyriacus Kale. The letter that Berck holds in his left hand shows his address and trademark 'Demn Ersame u(n)dfromen Derich berk i. London uit. Stalhoff', and his motto: 'Besad dz end, 'Consider the end'. A small strip of paper on the table states in Latin 'Olim meminisse juvabit', a quote from the Roman poet Virgil 'It will delight us to recall these things'.

The Ambassadors, 1533, oil on panel, 207 x 209.5cm (81.5 x 82.4in), National Gallery, London, UK

A life-size double portrait of two friends. At left, Jean de Dinteville, Sieur de Polisy, the French ambassador to the court of King Henry VIII. At right, the priest Georges de Selve, Bishop of Lavaur. The painting is a masterpiece, considered to be Holbein's greatest double portrait. A majestic, yet relaxed portrayal of two friends, residing in London and attendant at the court of Henry VIII, the choice of composition and detailed content illustrates wealth and status. The objects and books are intricately painted and symbolic, alluding to the sitters' celestial, literary, musical and spiritual interests (see also pages 64–65). The location of the room in which they stand, due to the loosely-hung, green silk damask behind them, is thought to be an outer chamber in Bridewell Palace, near Blackfriars, London, a royal residence of Henry VIII, which was lent to visiting ambassadors.

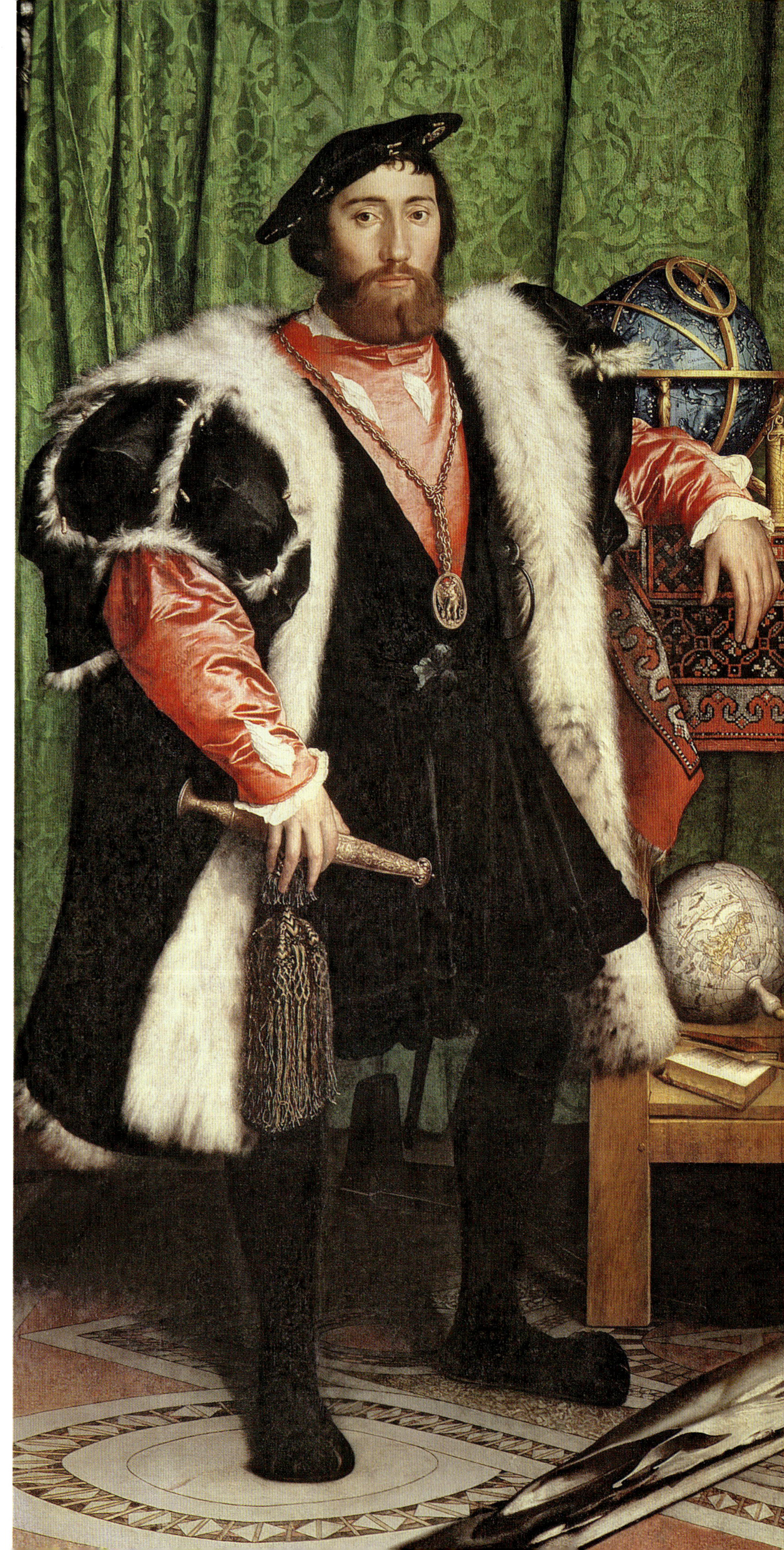

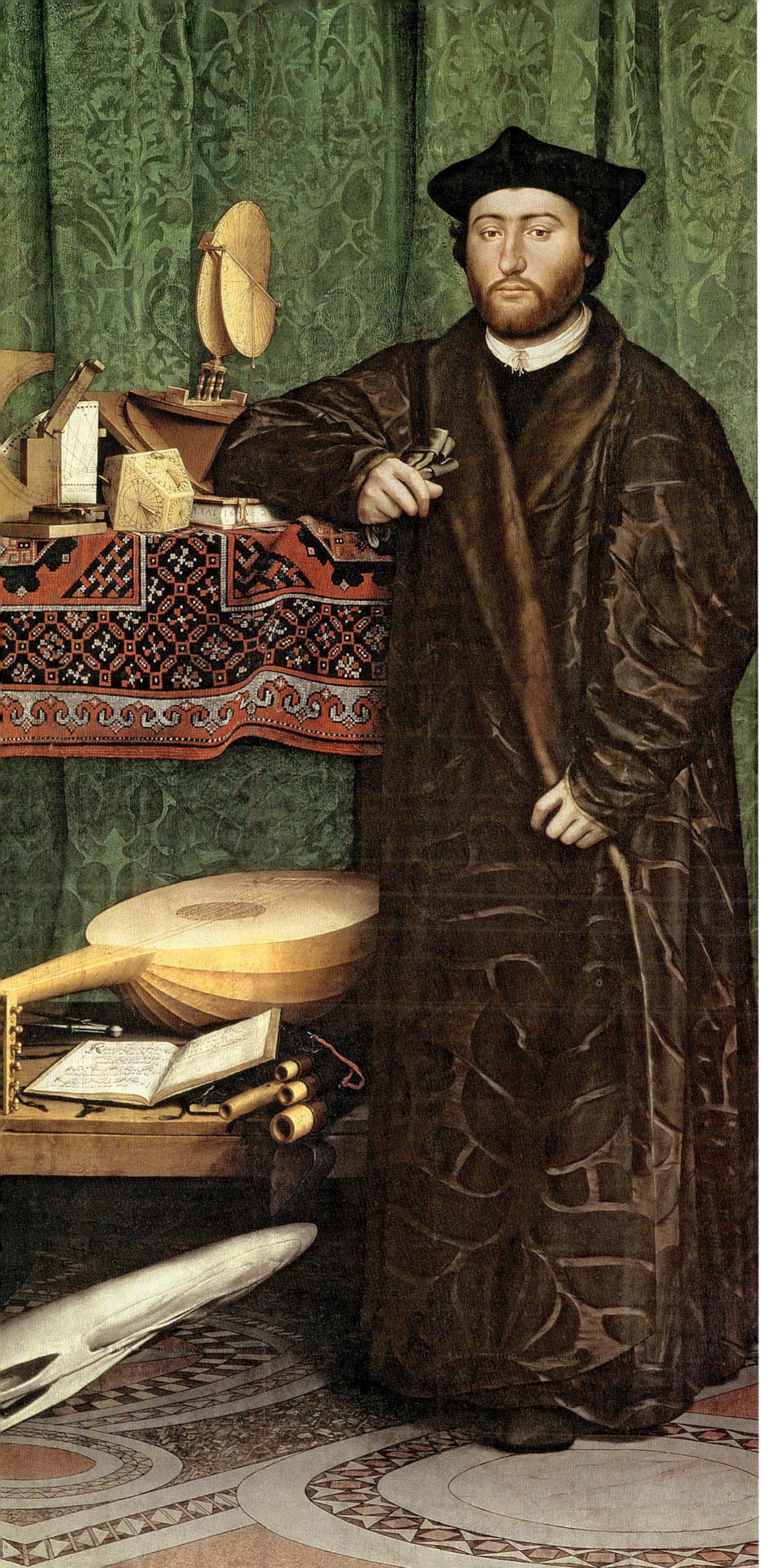

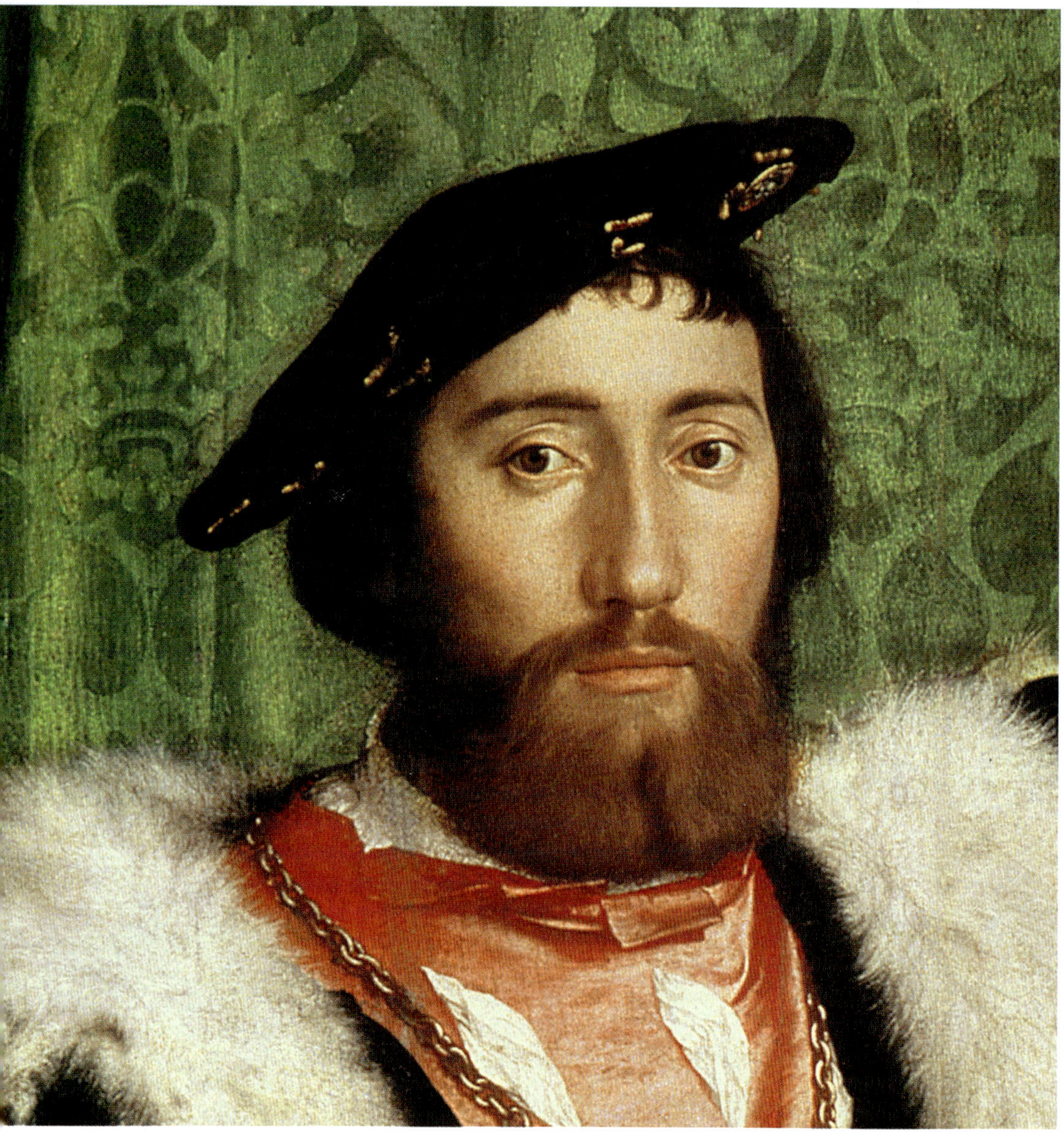

*Detail of Jean de Dinteville,
The Ambassadors, 1533*

Holbein paid meticulous
attention to his realistic
portrayal of Jean de
Dinteville. The character
of the young ambassador,
facing full-front, is denoted
in the clear eyes, and strong,
steady gaze toward the
viewer. De Dinteville, both
a highly-successful and
well-connected courtier
and diplomat at the French
court, was acting on behalf
of the king of France, Francis
I (1494–1547). Holbein
concentrated on each
detail of the fur-lined robe
and fine clothing that de
Dinteville wore. Around the
ambassador's neck is the
ceremonial collar, the French
Royal Order of St Michael.
His hat, or beret, is similar in
style but worn at a different
angle, to that of Duke Anton
'the Good' of Lorraine (see
page 248).

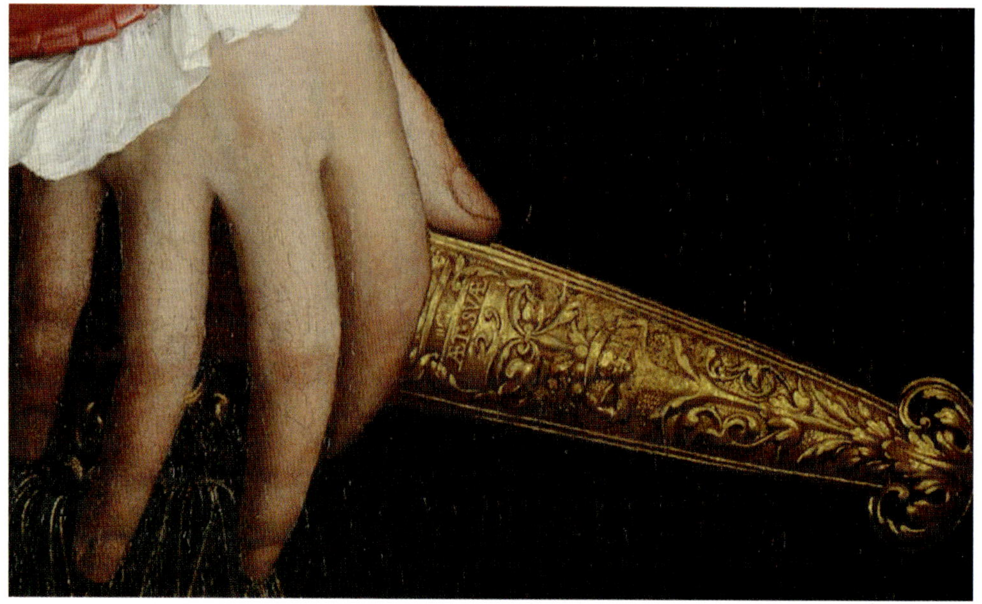

*Detail of dagger sheath, The
Ambassadors, 1533*

The Latin script on the
sheath says that the holder
(Jean de Dinteville) is
twenty-eight years old.

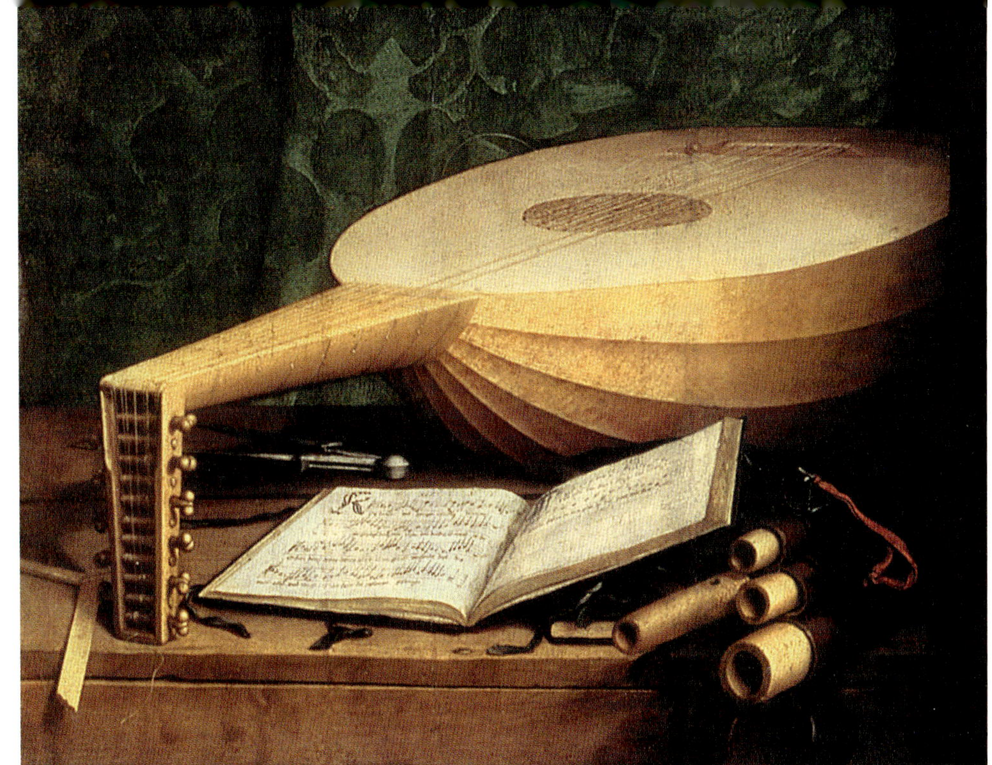

Detail of lute, *The Ambassadors*, 1533

The lute has its middle string broken, a symbol of discord. There is the possibility of harmony should it be mended. An open hymn book lies between the lute and a flute case. The tenor part depicted was the only book publication to include works recognised by both Catholic and Reformant faiths.

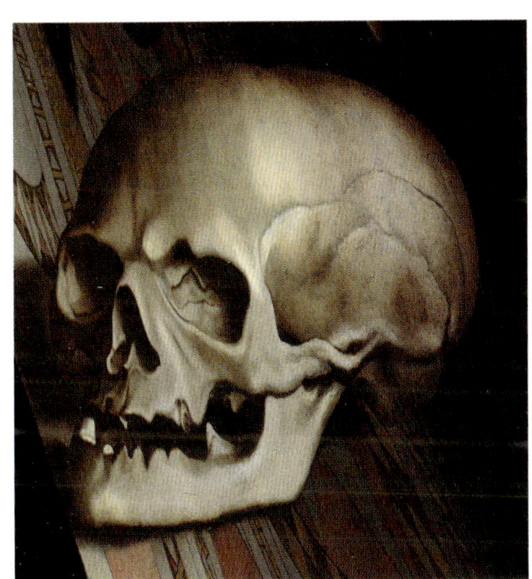

Detail of distorted skull, The Ambassadors, 1533

Holbein's anamorphic skull (below) is made whole when looked at it from a certain angle (left), which must have related to where it would hang in Jean de Dinteville's residence in Polisy, France.

The painted anamorphic skull connotes Holbein's knowledge of geometry which complements the interests of de Dinteville and de Selve. Its inclusion in *The Ambassadors* highlights Holbein's mastery of large-scale illusion.

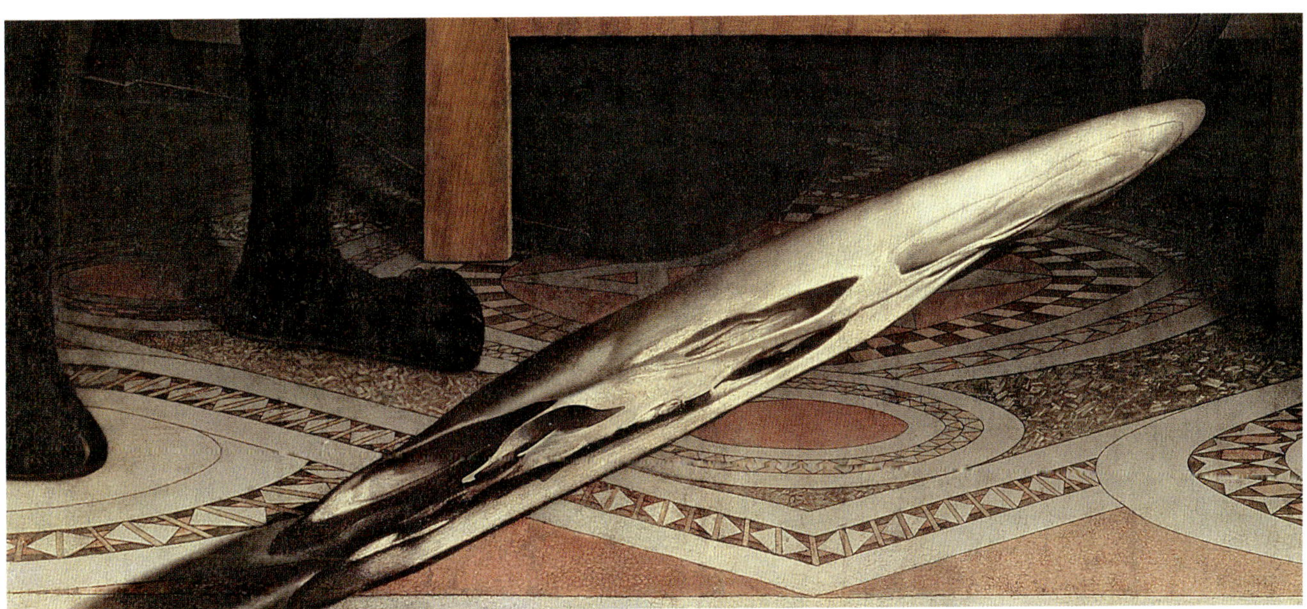

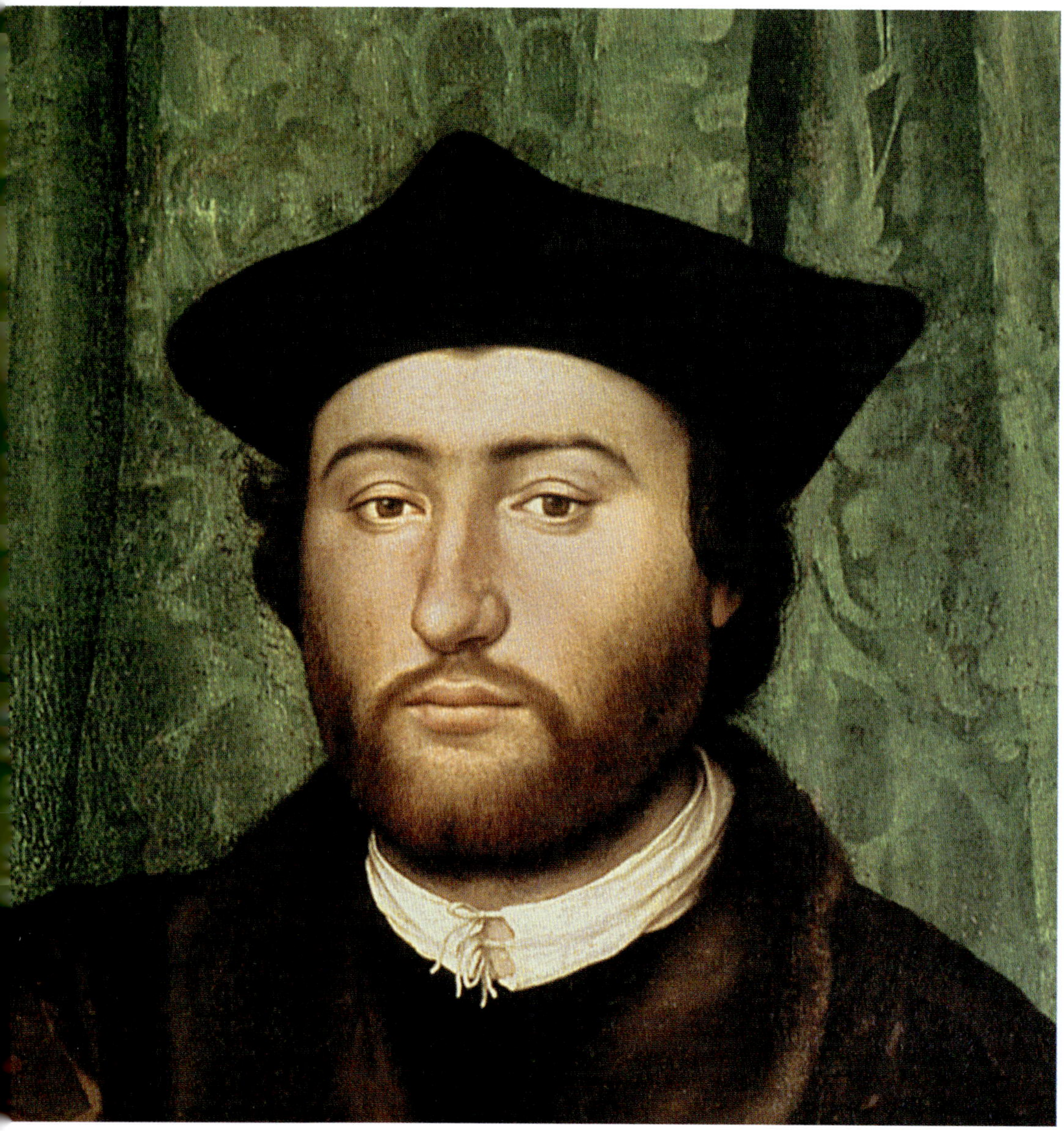

Detail of George de Selve, The Ambassadors, 1533

George de Selve (1508–41) was described in a document as an intimate friend of Jean de Dinteville and all his family. The life-size double portrait was for de Dinteville's private residence. It may represent a cherished relationship between the men, in life and death. De Selve is shown in more informal cleric's daywear compared to the grander clothes of de Dinteville.

Detail of half-hidden crucifix, The Ambassadors, 1533

At top left, near-hidden behind a partly-drawn green curtain, hangs a superbly painted silver crucifix, with the body of Christ just visible. A skull and a crucifix were often depicted together in religious art, for example *St Jerome,* 1521, by Lucas van Leyden (Ashmolean museum, Oxford, England). Its inclusion here links to the ground-level anamorphic skull, a symbol of man's mortality, and Christ's body on the crucifix, as a symbol of the resurrection that awaits all of the Christian faith, both Catholic and Protestant.

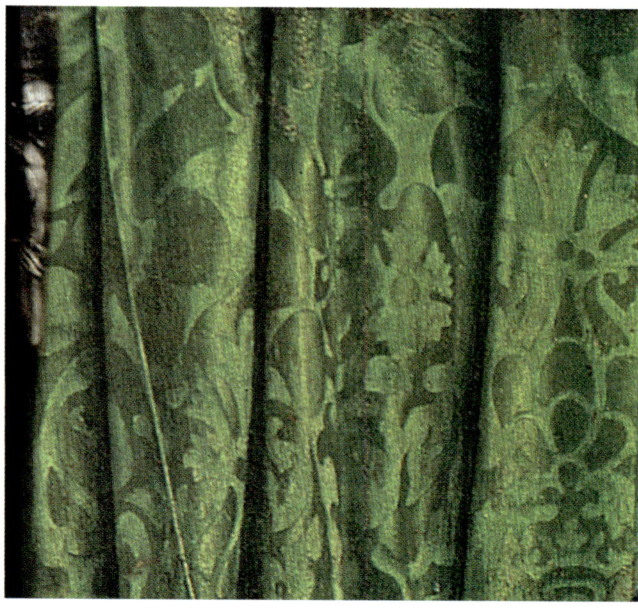

Detail of sundial, The Ambassadors, 1533

The complicated shape of the polyhedral sundial denotes the many ways in which it can be used to tell the time. The polyhedral in this painting may have been loaned by Nikolaus Kratzer, Astronomer Royal, maker of clocks and sundials for Henry VIII (see page 162).

Detail of scientific and astronomical instruments, The Ambassadors, 1533

A raised shelf of astronomical instruments alludes to the sitters' earthly and astrological interests. The collection of instruments was possibly borrowed from Holbein's friend, the astronomer Nikolaus Kratzer. Clues are embedded as to the date and time: April 11 at 9.30 or 10.30am.

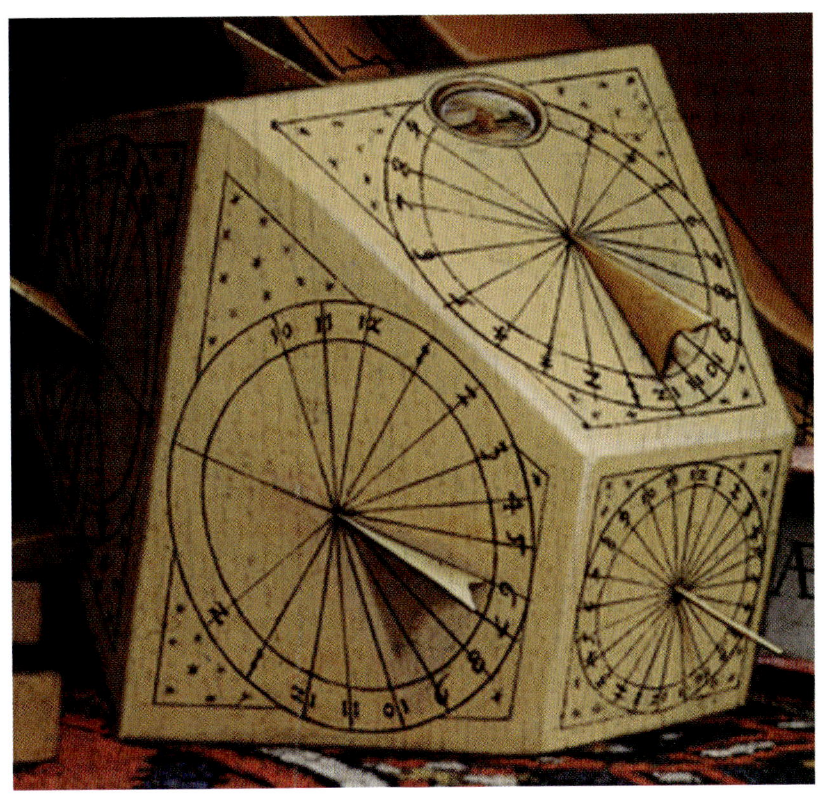

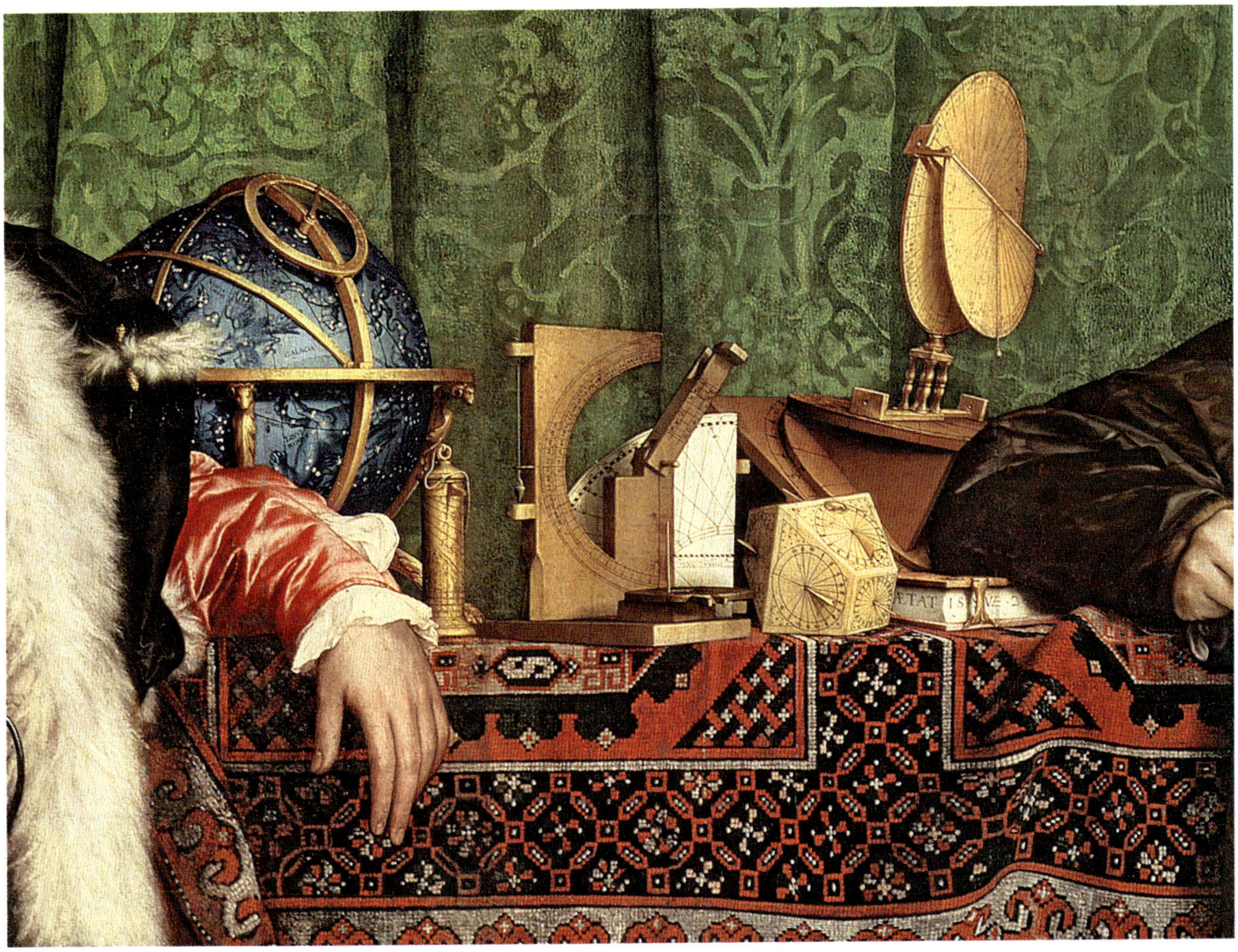

Detail of music book, The Ambassadors, 1533

The sheet music on display is the tenor part of the 2nd edition of Johann Walther's spiritual vocal *Geistliches Gesangbüch lein*, a Lutheran hymn book published in 1525. Its inclusion in this portrait highlights de Dinteville's and de Selve's – both humanists – interest in Lutheran debate.

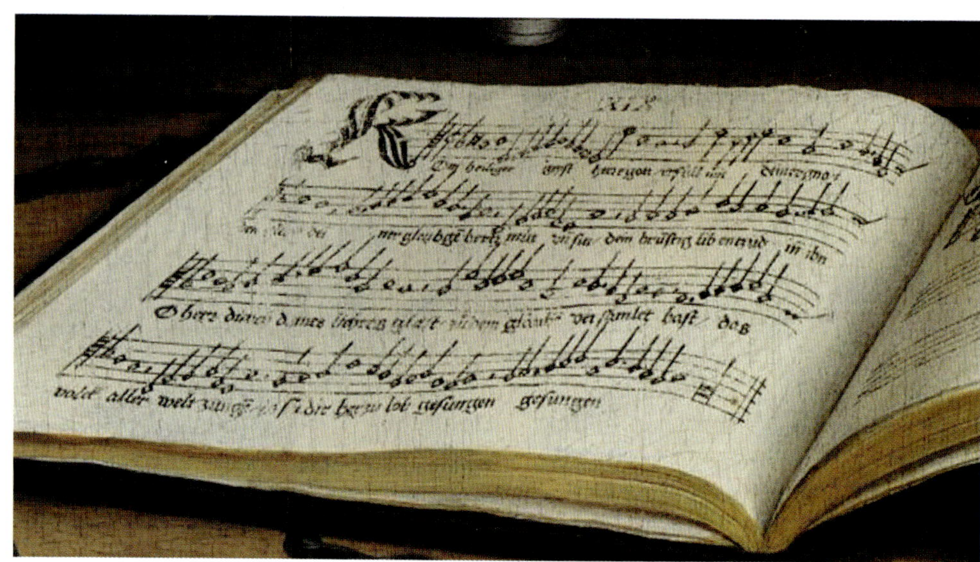

Detail of arithmetic book, The Ambassadors, 1533

The small red book on the lower shelf at left, close to de Dinteville, is held partially open with a set square. It is *Eyn Newe unnd wohlgegründte undenveysung aller Kauffmanss Rechnung*, by the German humanist and cosmologist Peter Apian (1495–1552), the text dated to 1527. The page heading of 'dividert' (divided) may connote in this painting the argument between Lutherans and Catholics.

Detail of terrestrial global map, The Ambassadors, 1533

The detail shown pinpoints Rome, Venice and Genoa in Italy, and de Dinteville's estate at Polisy, in the region of France. The map was personalised to include the French ambassador's château where the painting would be placed.

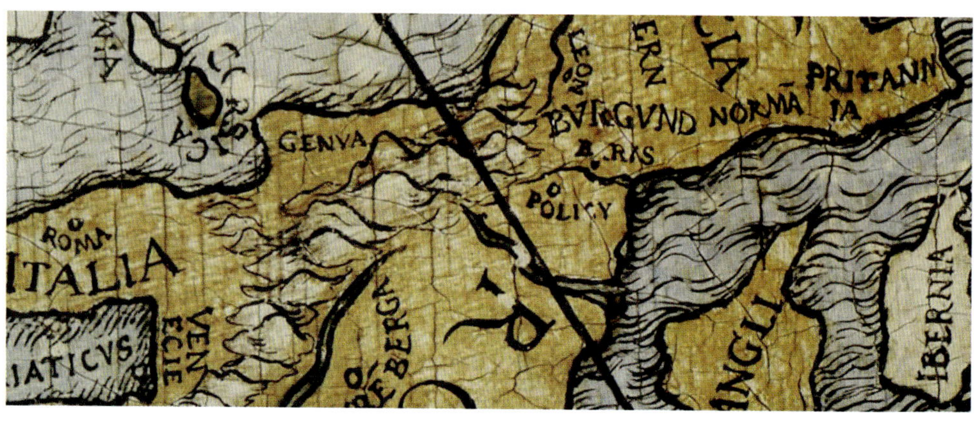

Detail of celestial globe,
The Ambassadors, 1533

The celestial globe on the upper shelf, at the level of de Dinteville's shoulder, accurately pinpoints the 1,022 stars of Ptolemy's star catalogue of the 2nd century. Claudius Ptolemy (AD100–170) was an Egyptian-born Roman, a mathematician, geographer, astronomer and astrologer.

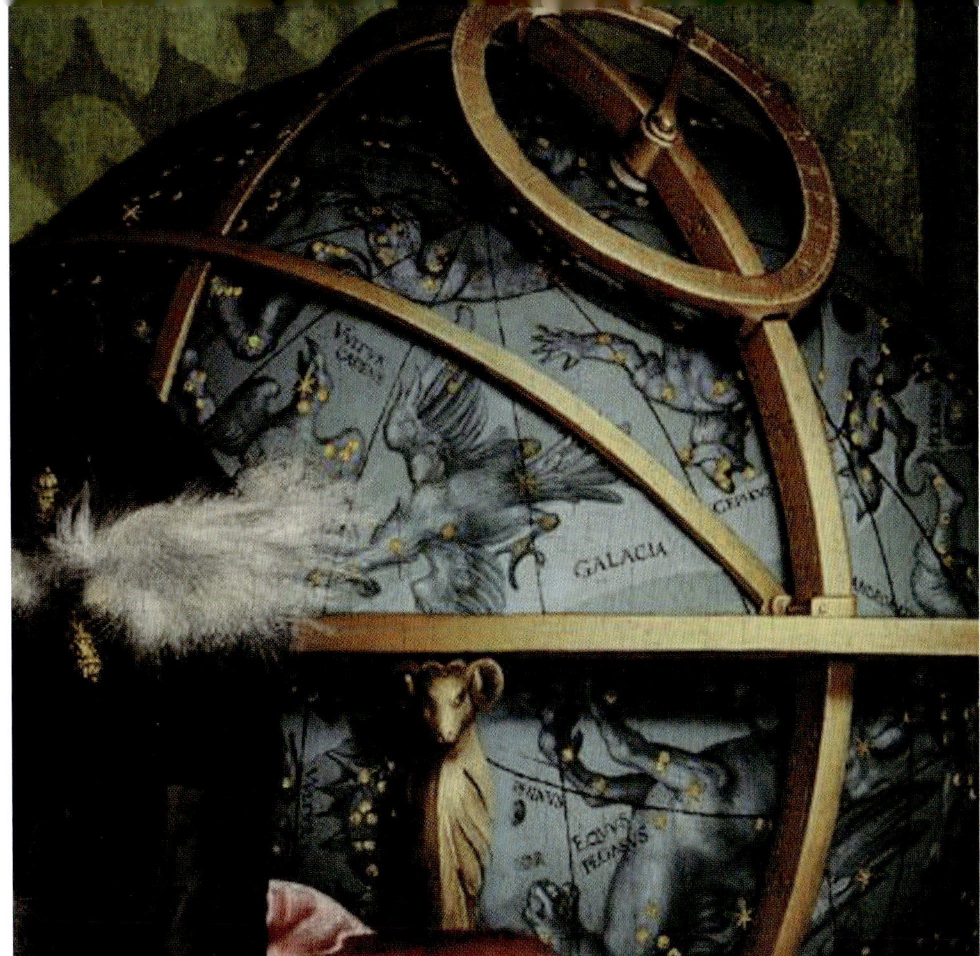

Detail of terrestrial globe, The Ambassadors, 1533

An interesting detail from the terrestrial cartographical global map showing parts of the northern and southern hemispheres, the seas and oceans, and land masses including Italy and 'Affrica' (Africa) amongst other locations.

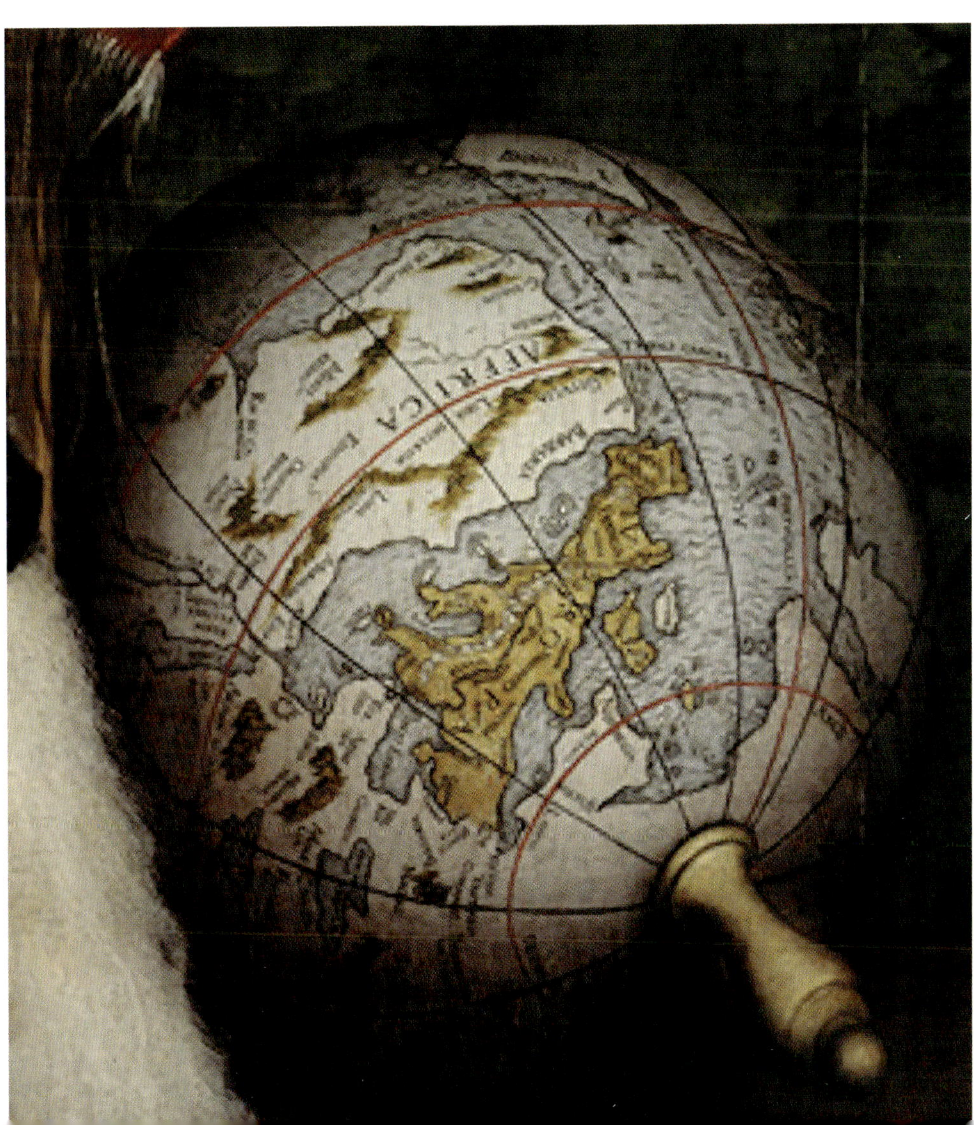

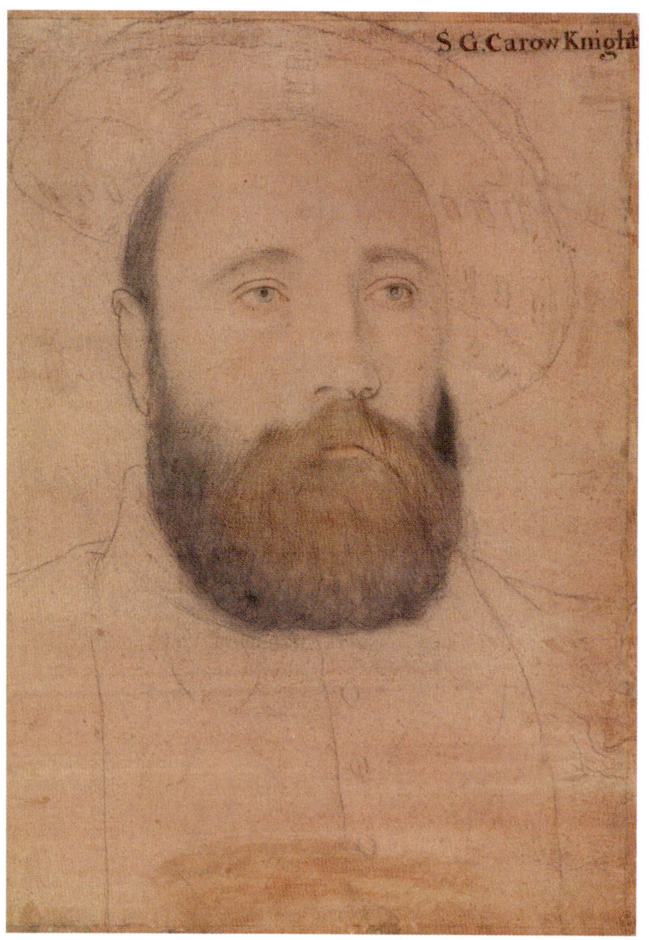

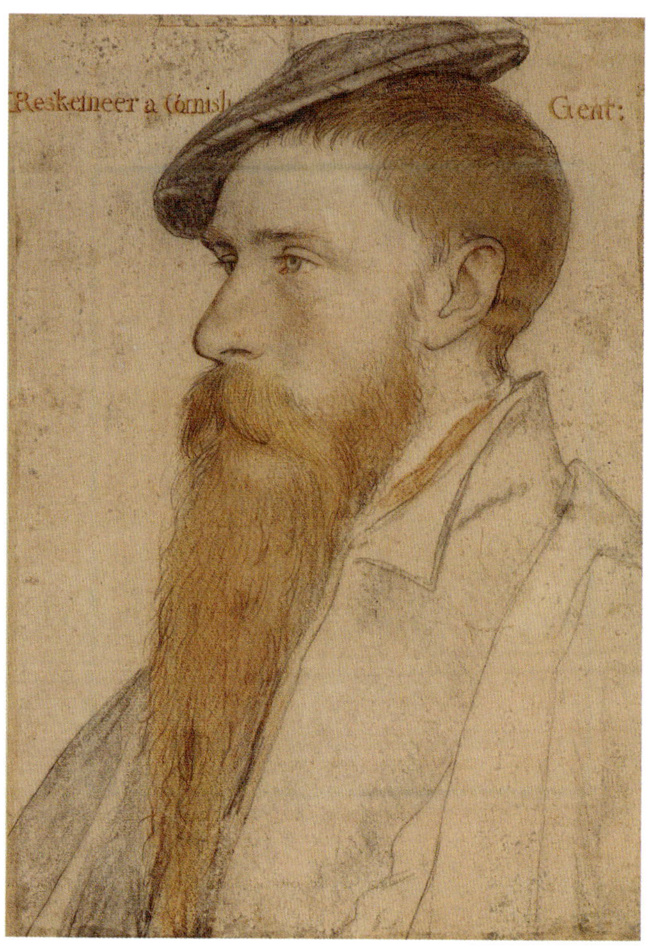

Drawing of Sir George Carew, c.1532–43, black and coloured chalks, and metalpoint on pale pink prepared paper, 31.6 x 23.3cm (12.4 x 9.1in), Weston Park Foundation, UK

A preparatory drawing of Sir George Carew. The bust-length portrait of Carew faces three-quarters to his left. Upper right, an 18th-century addition states 'S. G. Carow Knight'.

Drawing of William Reskimer c.1532–34, pen and ink, chalk and metalpoint on pink paper, 29 x 21cm (11.4 x 8.2in), Royal Collection Trust, UK

A preparatory drawing of William Reskimer, identified as 'Reskimer a Cornish Gent' on the later 18th-century inscription. The bust-length portrayal depicts him in profile. The pink paper, used by Holbein from his second visit to England, indicates the dating.

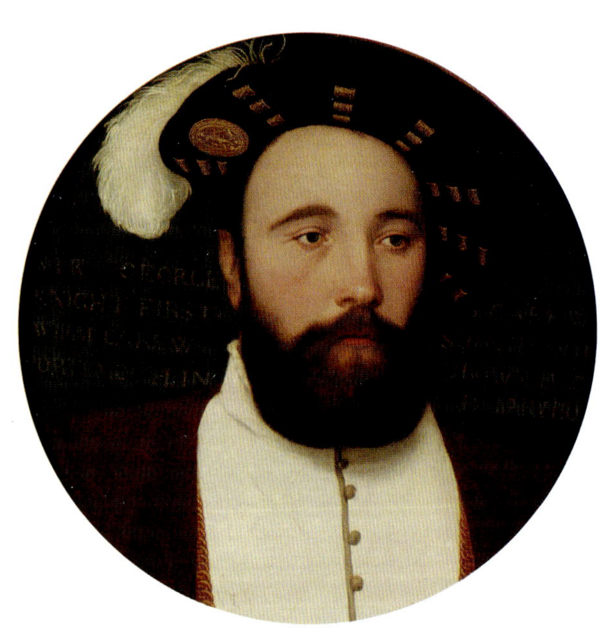

Sir George Carew, c.1540, gouache and gold, 24 x 24cm (9.4 x 9.4in), Royal Collection Trust, UK

A circular-shaped miniature portrait of Sir George Carew (c.1504–1545), Henry

the VIII's Vice Admiral of the Royal Fleet, and commander of the navy flagship the Mary Rose (in action from 1511–45, when it sank in the Solent between mainland England and the Isle of Wight).

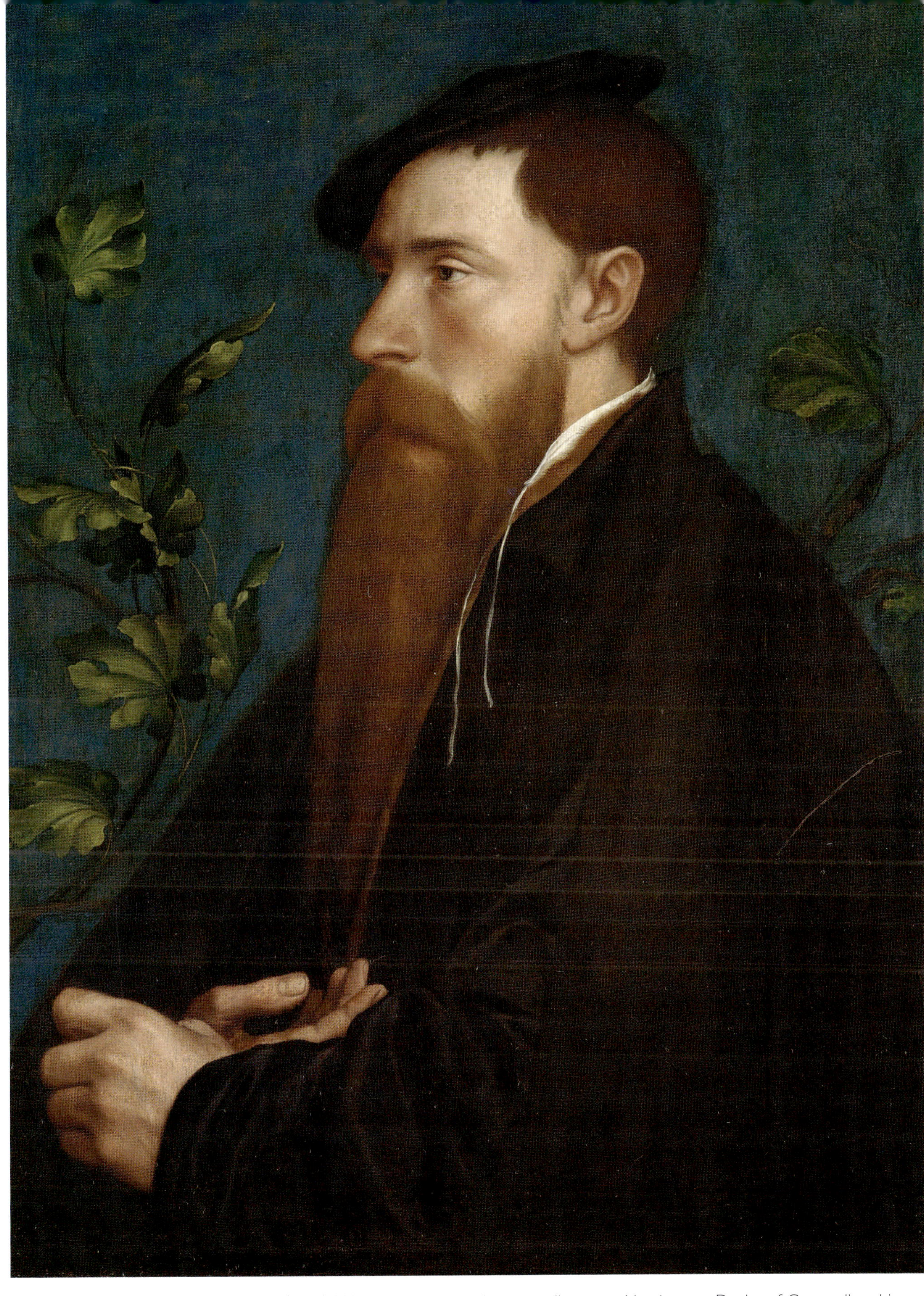

William Reskimer, c.1532–34, oil on panel, 46.4 x 33.7cm (18.2 x 13.2in), Royal Collection Trust, UK

The sitter is William Reskimer (d.1552), made Page of the Chamber to Henry VIII in 1526. At the time of this portrait he had been royally granted land in Warwickshire, perhaps a reason for the commission. By 1543 Reskimer was Keeper of the Ports of the Duchy of Cornwall and in 1546 a Gentleman Usher at court.

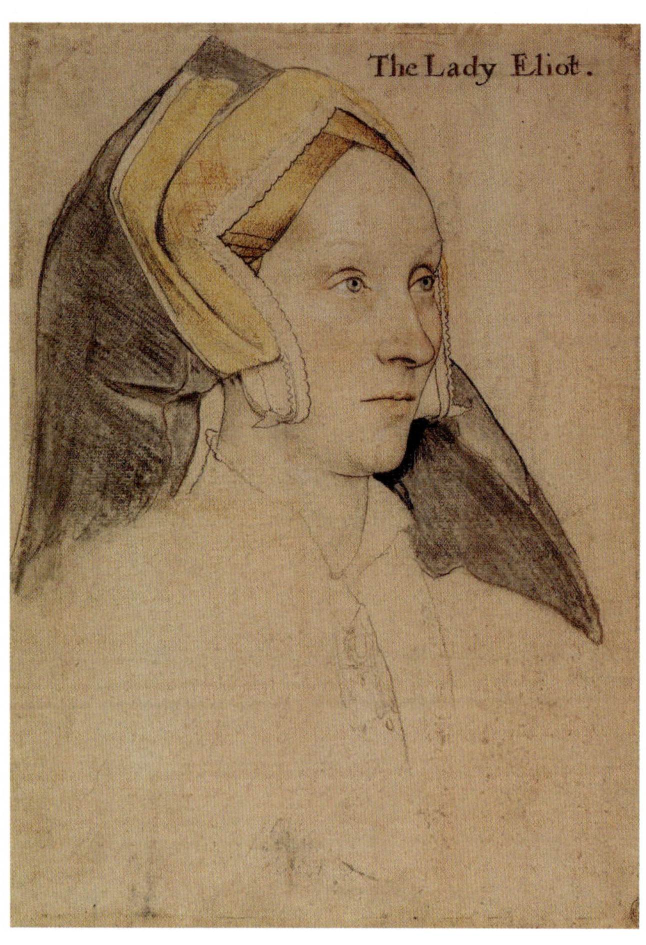

Drawing of Margaret, Lady Elyot, c.1532–34, black and coloured chalks, white bodycolour, and pen and ink on pale pink prepared paper 27.8 x 20.8cm (11 x 8.2in), Royal Collection Trust, UK

A pair of companion portrait-drawings, of The Lady Elyot, Margaret Abaragh (c.1500–1560), daughter of Sir Maurice à Barrow, and her husband Sir Thomas Elyot (see below), were presumably commissioned for oil paintings. The head and shoulders preliminary drawing, in black and coloured chalks, pen and ink, illustrates Lady Elyot facing to her left. Her facial features and the gable headdress she wears are accentuated in detail. At the age of twenty, Margaret married the author Thomas Elyot. Historic documents relate that Lady Elyot was an intellectual, interested in literature, which makes her marriage to a writer significant.

Drawing of Sir Thomas Elyot, c.1532–34, black and coloured chalks, white bodycolour, and pen and ink on pale pink prepared paper 27.8 x 20.8cm (11 x 8.2in), Royal Collection Trust, UK

A preparatory drawing of Sir Thomas Elyot (c.1490–1546), a companion to that of his wife Margaret, Lady Elyot (see above). Holbein concentrates on the detail of the writer Elyot's facial features with stubbled chin, and straight, cropped hair, worn under a hat. Both studies were presumably intended for oil paintings, which, if they were completed, have not survived. There is debate that the portraits, one or both, were intended as single works because Lady Elyot is shown facing left. For a companion portrait it was more usual for the lady to face right and her husband to face left.

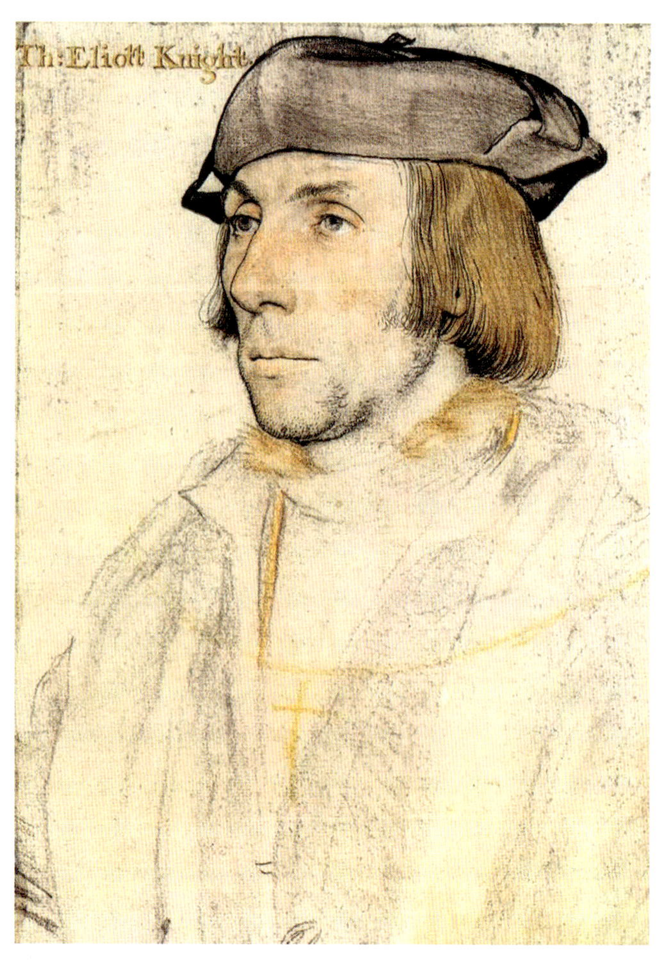

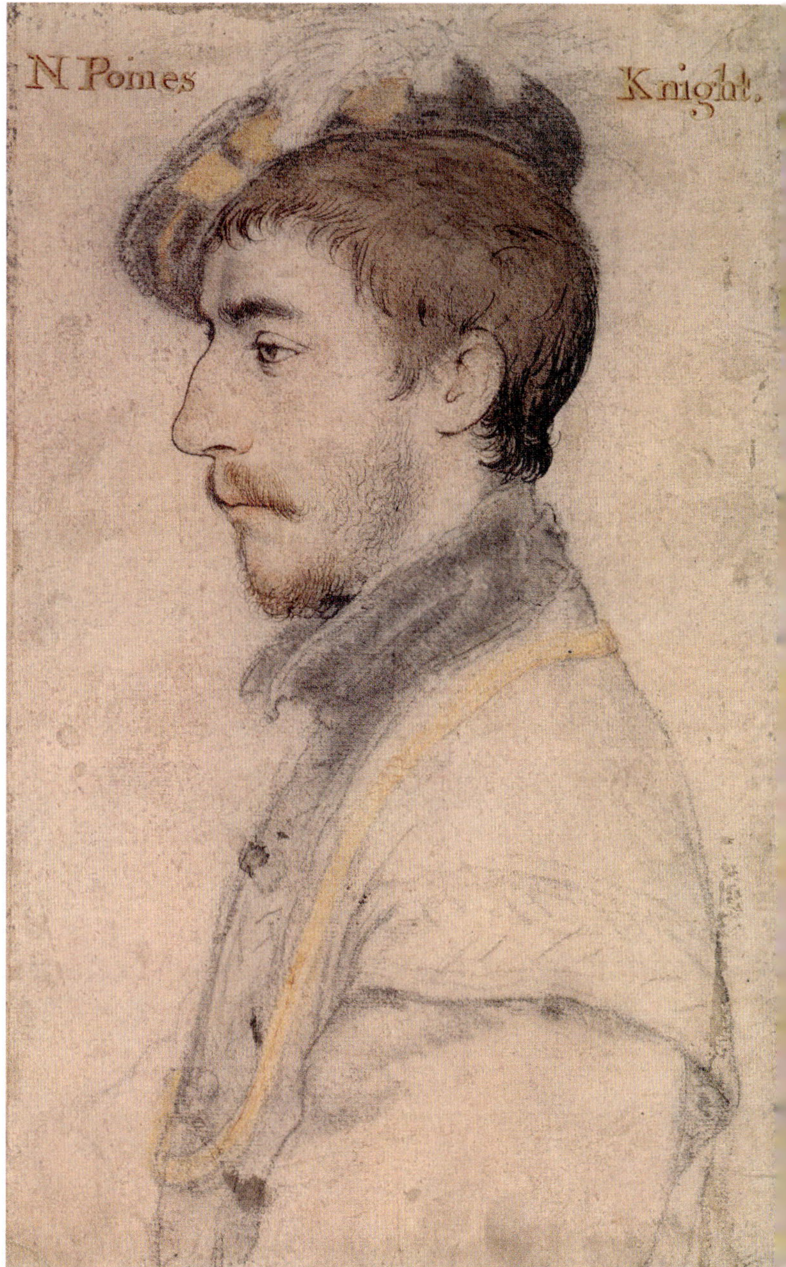

Drawing of Sir Nicholas Poyntz, *c.*1533–43, black and coloured chalks, and pen and ink on pale pink prepared paper, 28.4 x 18.3cm (11.1 x 7.2in), Royal Collection Trust, UK

Nicholas Poyntz (1510–57) was an English aristocrat and courtier of Henry VIII.

Holbein depicts him in this half-length portrait drawing, in profile facing toward the sitter's right. The features are well-defined. He wears his chain of knighthood. His highly-fashionable hat is adorned with badges and a fabulous feather. Sir Nicholas was a nephew of John Poyntz.

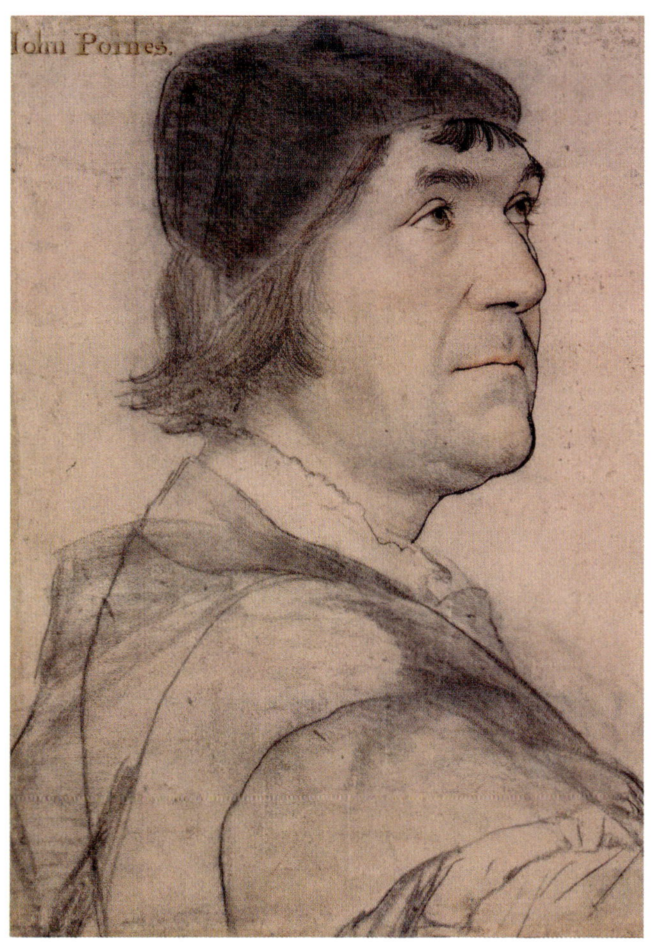

Drawing of John Poyntz, *c.*1532–33, black and coloured chalks, pen and ink, and brush and ink on pale pink prepared paper, 29.5 x 23.3cm (11.6 x 9.in), Royal Collection Trust, UK

A preparatory drawing of John Poyntz of Alderley, Gloucestershire (c.1485–1544), royal courtier, and Member of Parliament for Devizes. The bust-length portrait depicts Poyntz's body in profile with head facing three-quarters to the right. He wears a skull cap. The drawing was later inscribed in an 18th-century hand: 'Iohn Poines'.

Portrait study of Sir Nicholas Carew, c.1527–8, black and coloured chalks, 22.4 x 31.9cm (8.8 x 12.6in), Kunstmuseum, Basel, Switzerland

The preparatory sketch of Sir Nicholas Carew is highly finished, bearing a close likeness to the finished portrait. Holbein pays attention to Carew's defining facial features with a minimal outline of the armour he wears.

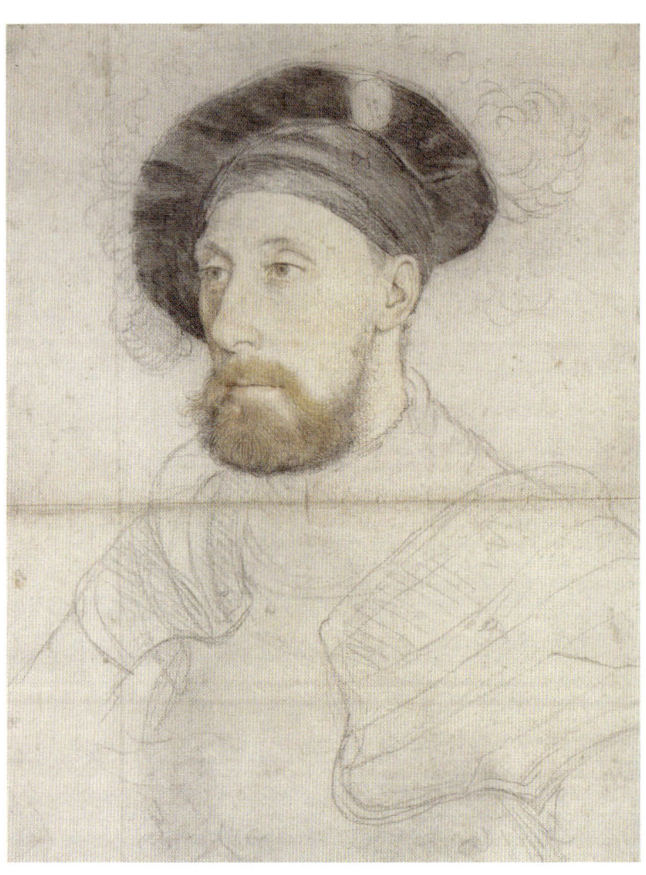

Sir Nicholas Carew, c.1532–3, Holbein workshop, tempera on panel, 92 x 76cm (36.2 x30in), Drumlanrig Castle, Dumfries and Galloway, Scotland, UK

Sir Nicholas Carew (c.1496–1539) was an English courtier and diplomat during the reign of King Henry VIII who was a friend of Henry in his youth and became Knight of the Garter in 1536, but was later executed for his alleged part in the Exeter Conspiracy. He is shown in armour, brown slashed trunks and a black cap, trimmed with a white plume and an octagonal gold badge (of a tree stem, raguly and a banderole inscribed 'sola') over a cloth of gold coif.

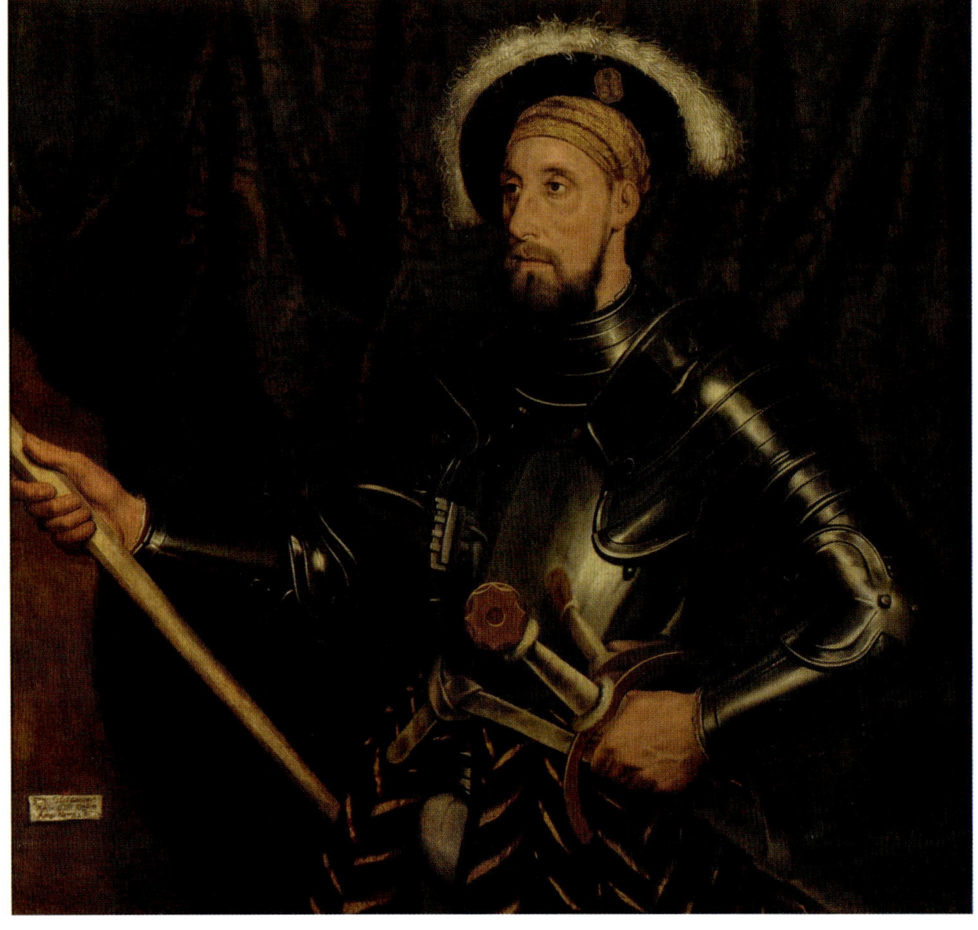

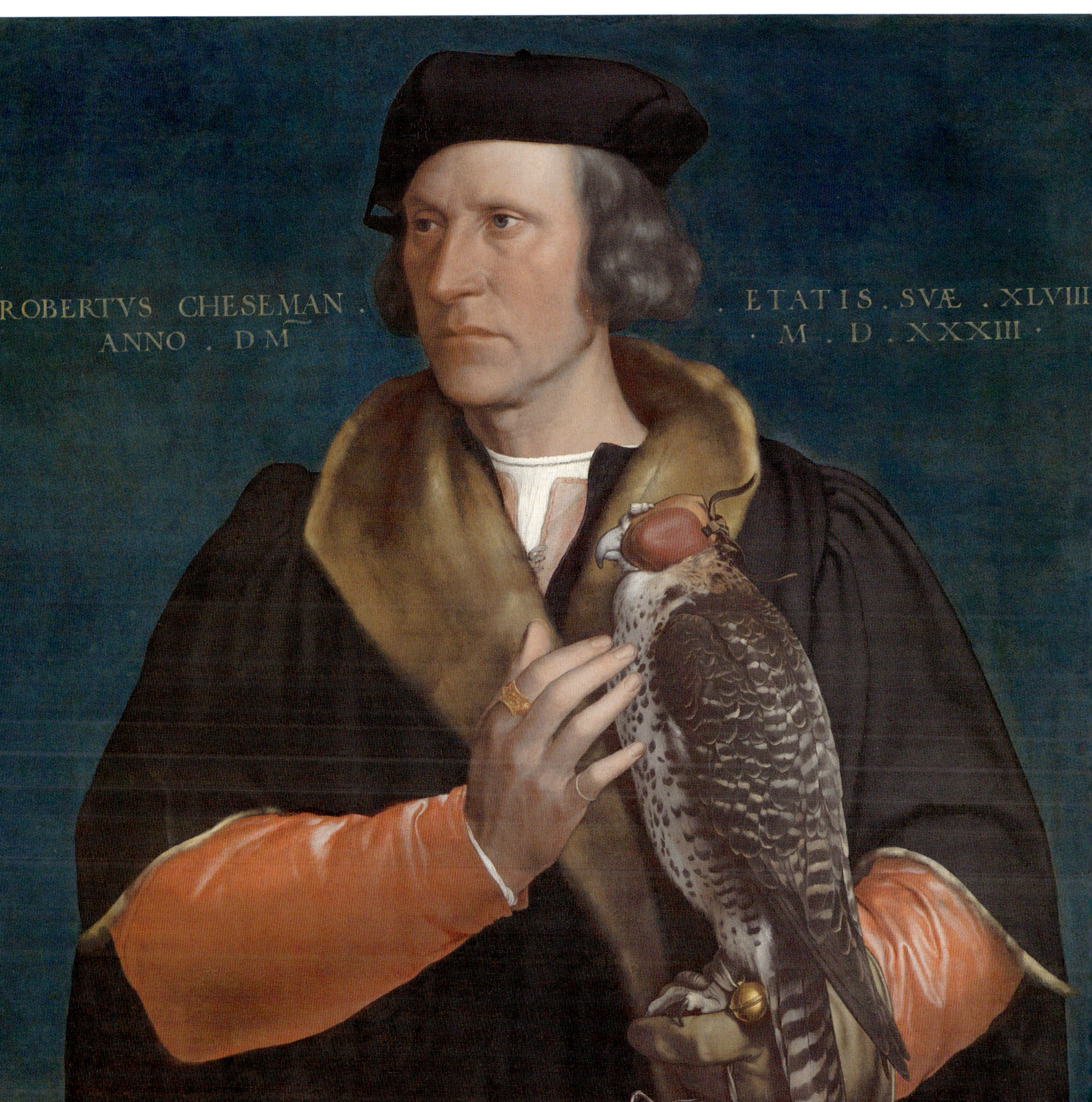

Portrait of Robert Cheseman holding a Falcon, 1533, oil on panel, 58.8 x 62.8cm (23.1 x 24.7in), Mauritshuis, The Hague, The Netherlands

The printed letters behind state 'Cheseman, aged 48, chief falconer to Henry VIII'. Cheseman is depicted with the tools of his profession, stroking the feathers of a hooded gyrfalcon, a breed of falcon that is the largest in the world, between 56–61cm (22–24in) tall. Holbein deftly flicks his wet paintbrush to create the falcon's stunning feathers. In the three-quarter length portrait, which allows for a full portrait of the bird he supports on his gloved hand, Robert Cheseman faces forward but turns his head to his right, looking to the distance.

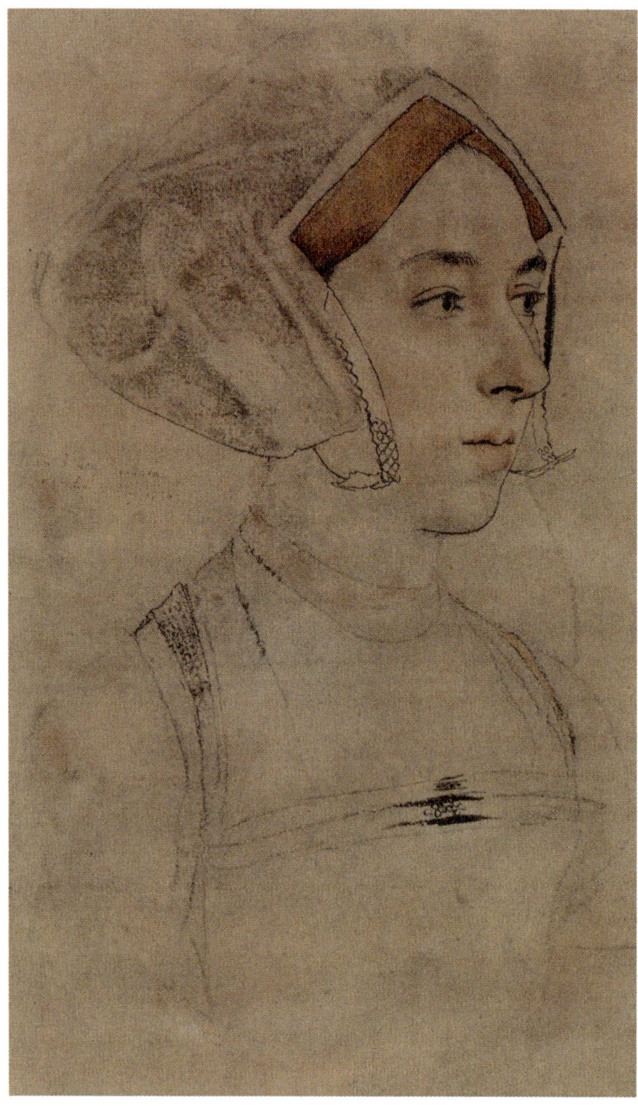

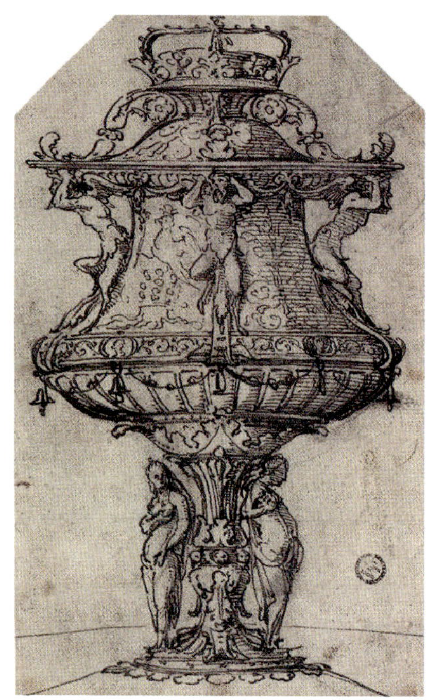

Above: *Design for a Table Fountain with Caryatides,* 1533–36, pen and black ink over chalk on paper, 25.1 x 16.4cm (9.9 x 6.5in), Kunstmuseum, Basel, Switzerland

This elaborate design for a table ornament with caryatides was possibly created for Queen Anne Boleyn. It places Holbein at the royal court between 1533 and 1536, in spite of royal household records for the period being lost. Holbein designed many precious objects, to be created by craftsmen.

Drawing of Anne Boleyn, c.1532–1533, black and coloured chalks on pink prepared paper, 31.5 x 23cm (12.4 x 9in), Royal Collection Trust, UK

A bust-length figure drawing thought to be of Anne Boleyn and attributed to Holbein, with hair under a gable hood, wearing a low gown and bodice, and necklace. Anne became a patron of Holbein but if he did paint finished oil portraits of her they have since been lost.

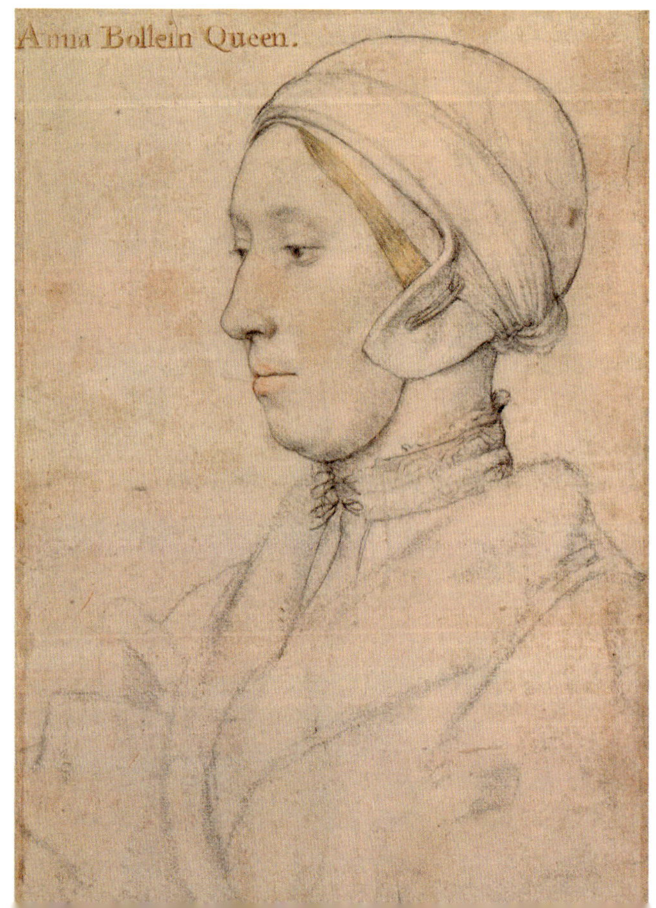

Drawing of lady, thought to be Anne Boleyn, c.1533–36, black and coloured chalks on pink prepared paper, 28.2 x 19.3cm (11.1 x 7.6in), Royal Collection Trust, UK

A chalk drawing by Holbein, inscribed at a later date 'Anna Bollein Queen'. Her face is shown in three-quarter profile, with hair hidden beneath a bonnet. It is thought this may show her clothes for the coronation.

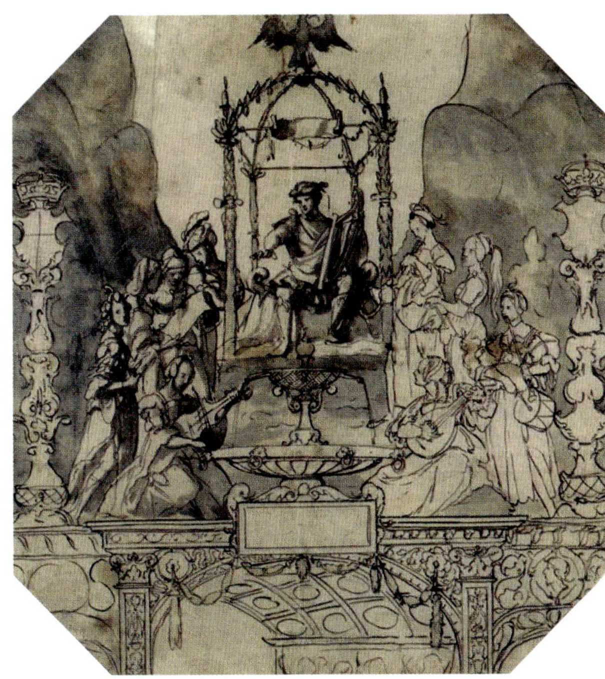

Apollo and the Muses on Mount Parnassus, 1533, pen and black ink over chalk on paper, 42 x 8cm (16.5 x 3.1in), Staatliche Museen, Berlin, Germany

Holbein was commissioned by Anne Boleyn to design displays for her coronation processions on the 31st May and 1st June 1533. One tableau was erected in Gracechurch Street and was a representation of Apollo.

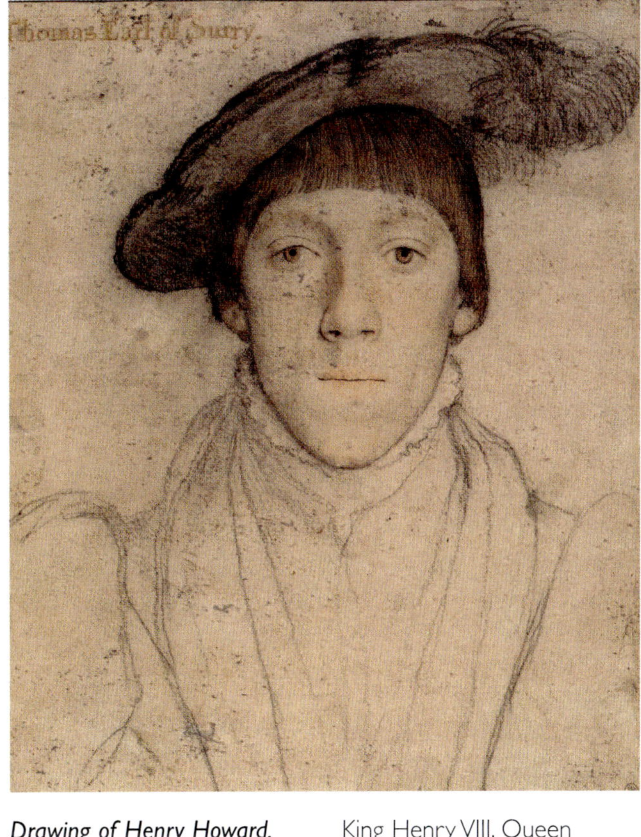

Drawing of Henry Howard, Earl of Surrey, c.1532–1533, black and coloured chalks, pen and ink and watercolour drawing on pink prepared paper, 25.1 x 20.5cm (9.9 x 8in), Royal Collection Trust, UK

Henry Howard (1517–47), Earl of Surrey, was first cousin to two wives of King Henry VIII, Queen Anne Boleyn and Queen Katherine Howard. Holbein depicted the earl twice: as a boy and a young man (see page 242). Henry Howard, a politician and poet. was one of the founders of English Renaissance Poetry. He died at an early age in suspicious circumstances.

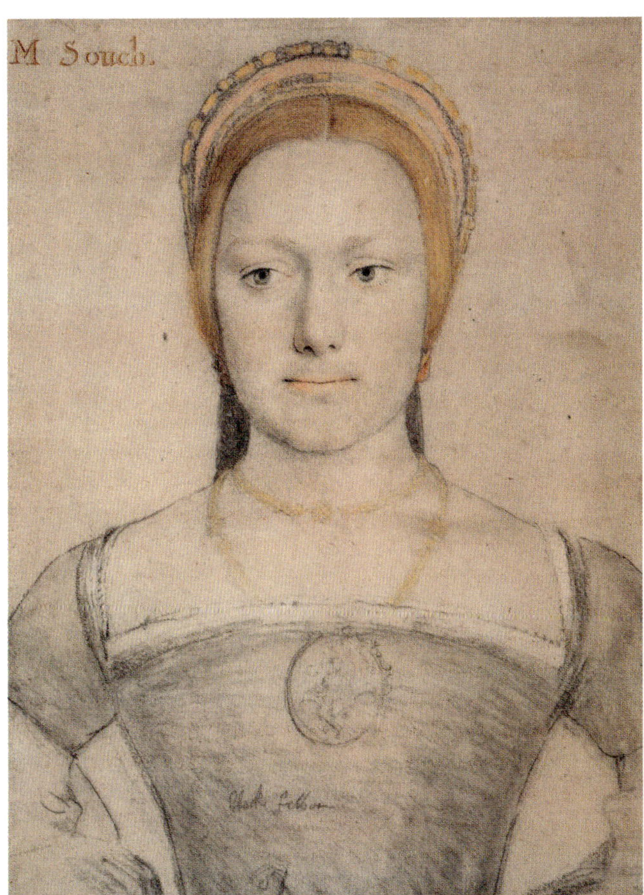

Drawing of Mary Zouch (attr.), c.1532, black and coloured chalks, and pen and ink on pale pink prepared paper, 29.6 x 21.2cm (10.4 x 7.8in), Royal Collection Trust, UK

A highly descriptive drawing, possibly of Mary Zouch, Lady in Waiting to Queen Jane Seymour, or Anne Zouche, née Gainsford, Lady in Waiting to Queen Anne Boleyn. The bust-length portrait depicts a young woman facing forward, her eyes glancing down to her right. She wears a large medallion and a necklace and holds a flower. Holbein noted the ornament on her headdress, and the bodice fabric as 'black felbet' (black velvet).

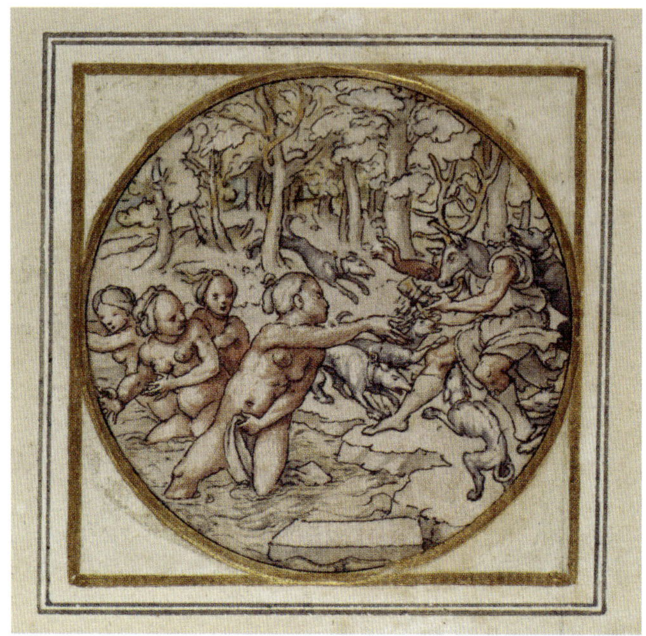

Diana and Actaeon, c.1532–4, pen and ink on paper, 5.1 x 5.1cm (2 x 2in), Collection of the Duke of Devonshire, Chatsworth House, UK (all)

In a series of designs for pendants or hat badges, Holbein, informed by the Greek myth of Diana and Actaeon, here depicts Diana the huntress, Roman goddess of the moon transforming Actaeon, a famous Theban hero, into a stag, to have him hunted down and killed by her hounds after he caught sight of her bathing.

Allegory of Time, c.1532–43, pen and ink on paper, 5.5 x 5.5cm (2.1 x 2.1in)

In this design, Holbein depicts a man asleep under a tree, while nearby an infant pulls on a rope to release the bell of a large timepiece, to waken him. A banner reads in Italian 'aspetto la hora', loosely translated as 'look at the hour', or 'I await the hour'.

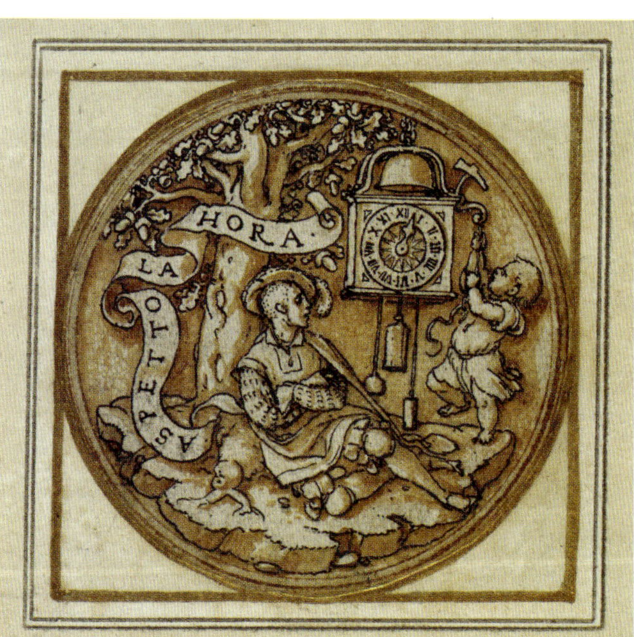

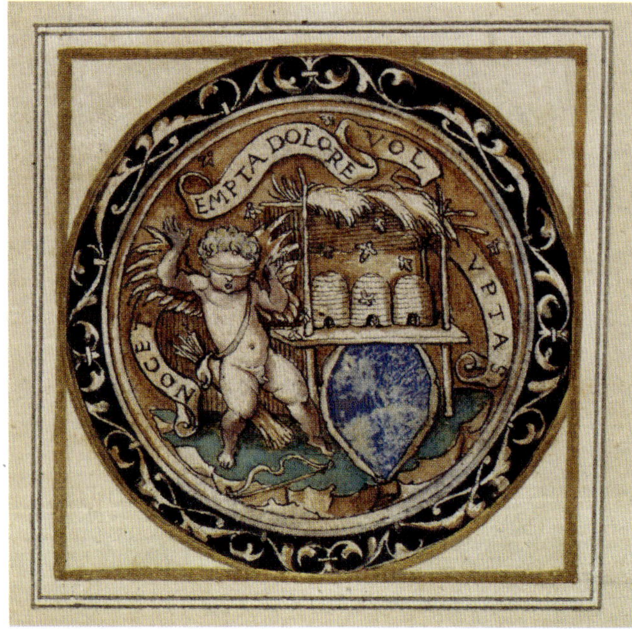

Cupid Stung by Bees, c.1522–43, pen and ink on paper, 5.6 x 5.6cm (2.2 x 2.2in)

'Cupid stung by Bees' was a design for a pendant or hat badge. It depicts blindfolded Cupid wandering too close to the bees hives and being stung. An inscription written in Latin, a quotation from Horace, reads 'nocet empta dolore voluptas', translated as 'pleasure bought by pain is injurious'.

Hagar and Ishmael, c.1532–43, pen and ink on paper, 5.4 x 5.4cm (2.1 x 2.1in)

This design is informed by the bible text Genesis 16:3, depicting Hagar – the handmaiden of Sarah, barren wife of Abraham – who has been chosen by Sarah to have Abraham's child. Sarah mistreats Hagar, who runs away to give birth to her son Ishmael. God, through an angel, depicted here, tells her to return to Abraham and Sarah with her newborn son.

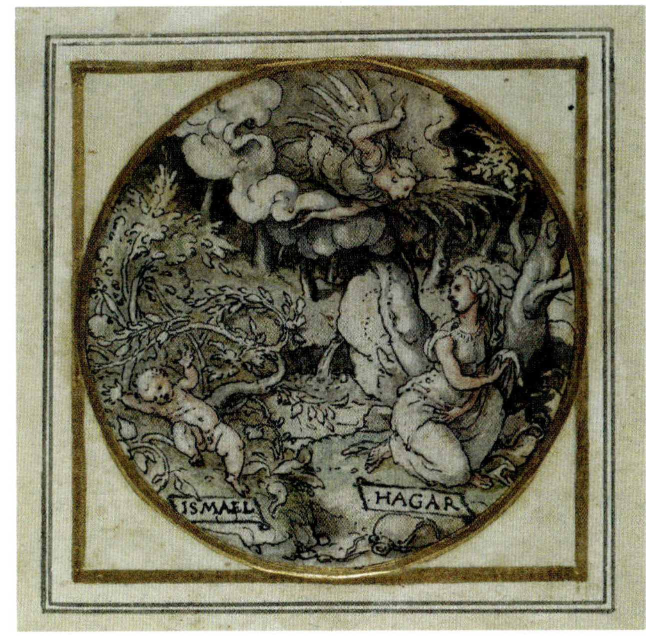

The Fall of Icarus c.1532–43, pen and ink on paper, 5.1 x 5.1cm (2 x 2in)

In this design Holbein, informed by the tale of Icarus from Greek mythology, divides the composition in two parts. The upper half depicts Icarus in his horse-driven chariot riding across the sky above the clouds, ignoring his father's advice not to get too close to the sun or the wax in his wings would melt. The lower half depicts Icarus falling to Earth, to drown in the sea, when his wax wings melt.

The Last Judgement, c.1532–43, pen and ink on paper, 4.4 x 4.7cm (1.7 x 1.7in)

Holbein depicts here the familiar narrative of the Last Judgement when earthly mortals discover if their life has been lived well enough to rise to Heaven, or to be sent to Hell.

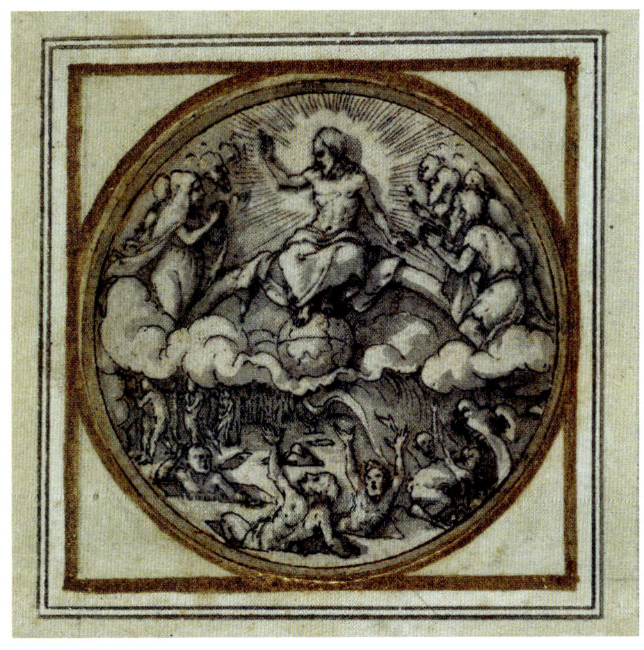

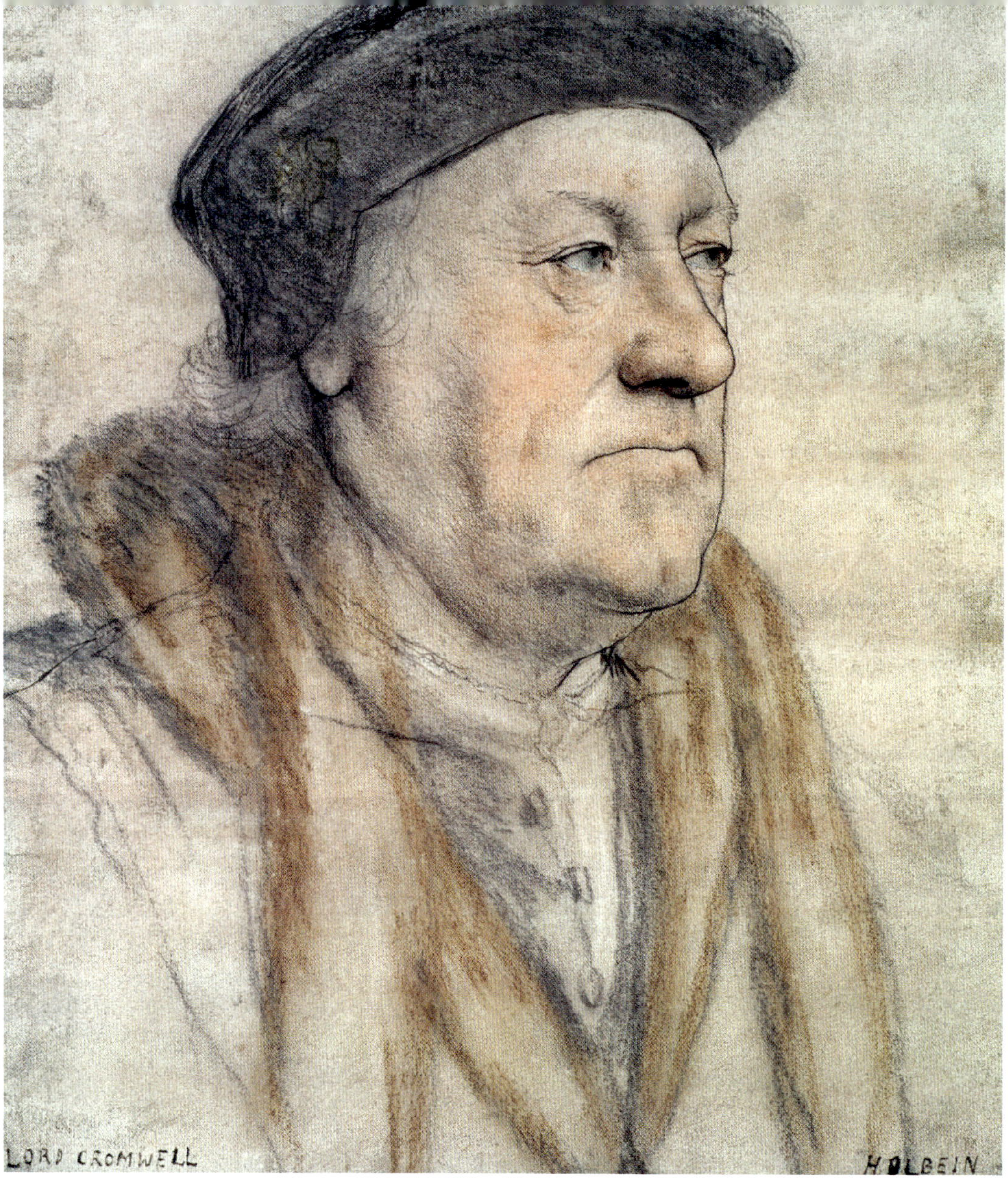

Above: *George Nevill, 3rd Baron Bergavenny, c.1532–35*, pen and ink, chalk, wash and bodycolour on paper, 27.3 x 24.1cm (10.7 x 9.4in), Collection of the Earl of Pembroke, Wilton House, Wiltshire, UK

A highly-finished bust-length drawing in half- to three-quarter profile, highlighting his ruddy complexion and piercing blue-green eyes, directed at someone to his left. The fur of his robe is detailed. The nobleman 3rd Baron Bergavenny KG, PC, George Nevill (c.1469–1535), held the office of Lord Warden of the Cinque Ports. (Later, the work was erroneously labelled Lord Cromwell.)

Right: *John Fisher, Bishop of Rochester, c.1532–34*, black and coloured chalks, wash, pen, brush and ink on paper, 38 x 23cm (15 x 9in), Royal Collection Trust, UK

Holbein depicts John Fisher (1469–1535) in a preparatory drawing for a portrait. Fisher was appointed Bishop of Rochester in 1504. He was a friend of Erasmus and probably learned of Holbein through him. The Bishop was a supporter of Queen Katherine of Aragon during her divorce from Henry VIII. Fisher was made a Cardinal in 1535, the year of his execution for treason.

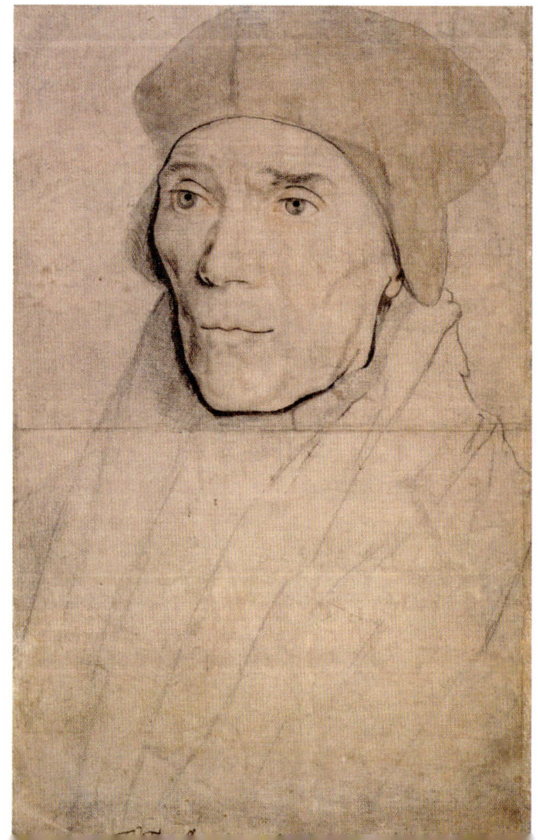

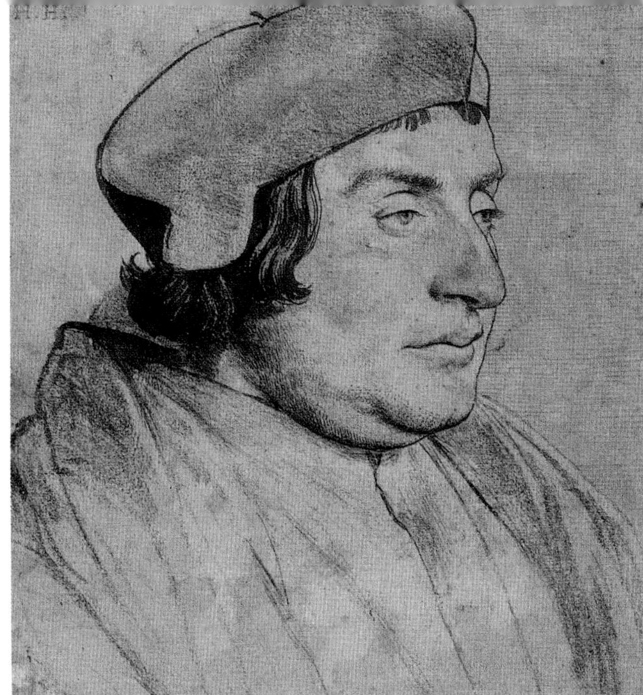

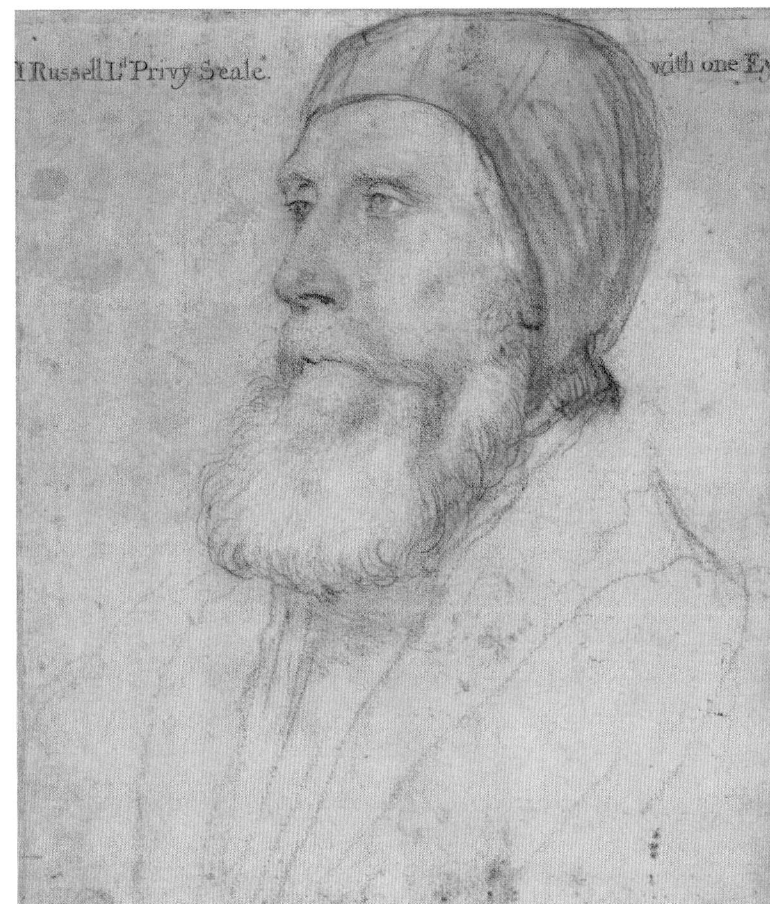

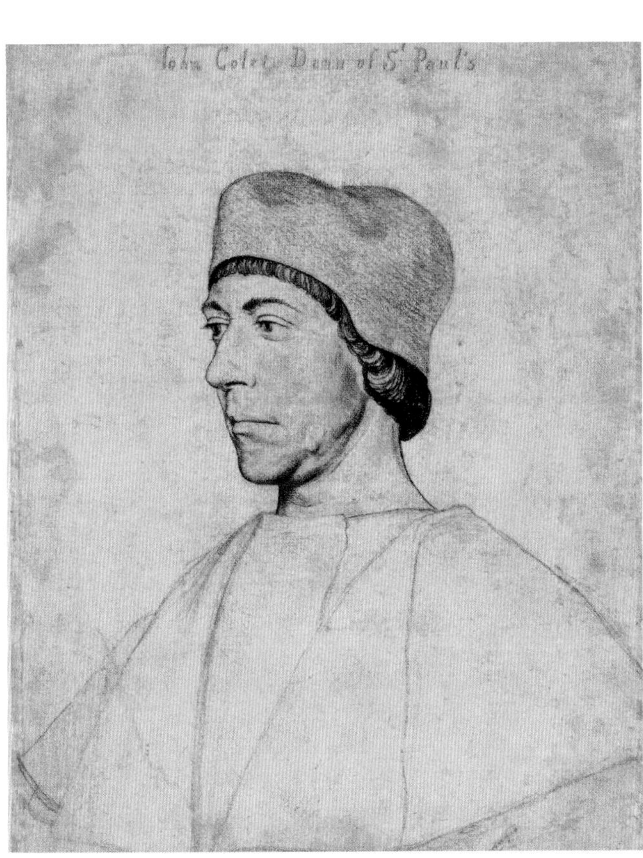

Left: *Portrait of a Man* (aka *Portrait of a Scholar or Cleric*), c.1532–35, black and red chalk, pen and brush and black ink on pink prepared paper, 21 x 18.4cm (8.6 x 7.2in), The John Paul Getty Museum, Los Angeles, USA

A head and shoulders profile portrait of a man, possibly a scholar or a cleric, identified from the blocked felt cap and hooded robe worn by clerics in this period. Historians suggest it may be Stephen Gardiner (1483–1555), Bishop of Winchester (from 1531), a scholar and a cleric, and one of the wealthiest bishops in England, and confidant of Henry VIII. It is inscribed HH and a pricked initial H.

Above: *John Colet*, c.1535, black and coloured chalks, pen and ink, brush and ink, metalpoint on pale pink prepared paper, 26.8 x 20.5cm (10.5 x 8in), Royal Collection Trust, UK

Holbein created this bust-length portrait drawing of John Colet (1467–1519) Dean of St. Paul's Cathedral, not from life but from a bust of Colet created by Pietro Torrigiano, a Florentine sculptor, and contemporary of Michelangelo. Colet was a scholar, humanist and friend of Erasmus. He faces three-quarters to his right, in semi-profile.

Above: *John Russell, 1st Earl of Bedford*, c.1532–43, black and coloured chalks, and white bodycolour on pale pink prepared paper, 34.9 x 29.2cm (13.7 x 11.5in), Royal Collection Trust, UK

The bust-length portrait of Dorset-born John Russell depicts him in semi-profile, facing to his right, and wearing a skull cap. Russell was knighted in 1513, and present with Henry VIII at the Field of Cloth of Gold meeting in France in 1520. The later-added 18th-century annotation says: 'Russell Ld Privy Seale... with one Eye.' He had lost his right eye during a military campaign in 1522.

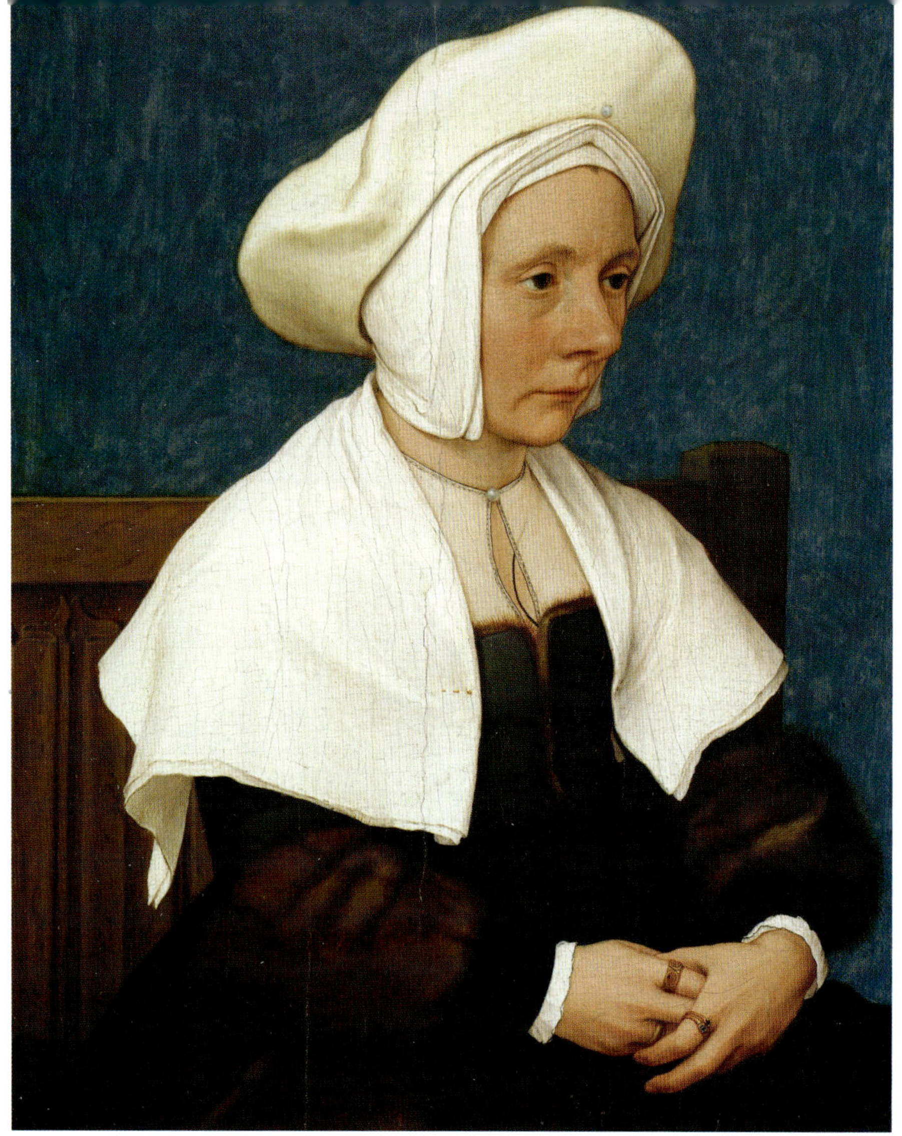

Portrait of a Woman in a White Coif, c.1532–34, oil and tempera on oak, 23.4 x18.8cm (9.2 x 7.4in), Detroit Institute of Arts, Detroit, Michigan, USA

The identity of the sitter is unknown. The clothing she wears places it during Holbein's second stay in London from 1532. In this small, exquisite portrait, possibly of the wife of a noble or a courtier, the lady wears a chemise with fur-trimmed bodice and a shawl around her shoulders. On her head is a large white bonnet worn over a close-fitting coif – a cap that covers the top, sides and back of the head – which dates to this period.

Portrait of a Man in a Red Cap, 1532–35, oil and gold on parchment, laid down on linden, 12.7cm (5in), diameter, Metropolitan Museum of Art, New York, NY, USA

The young sitter can be identified as a court official, for he wears the livery of Henry VIII, with the initials H[enricus] R[ex], embroidered in black on his red coat. Royal Wardrobe records describe it as a coat of broad cloth, coloured red, lined with black cotton, and embroidered with the letters H and R.

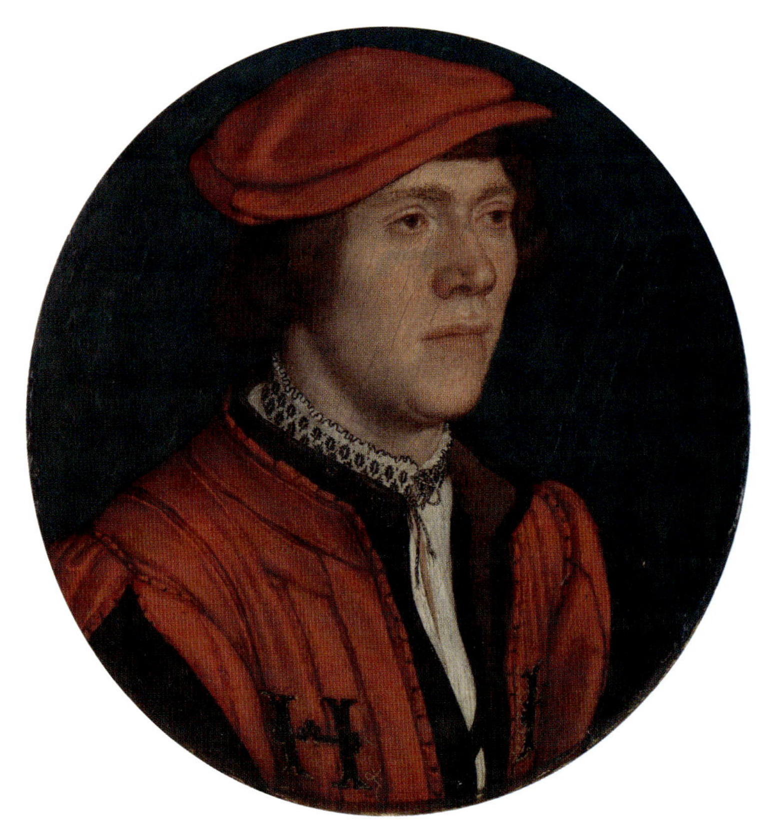

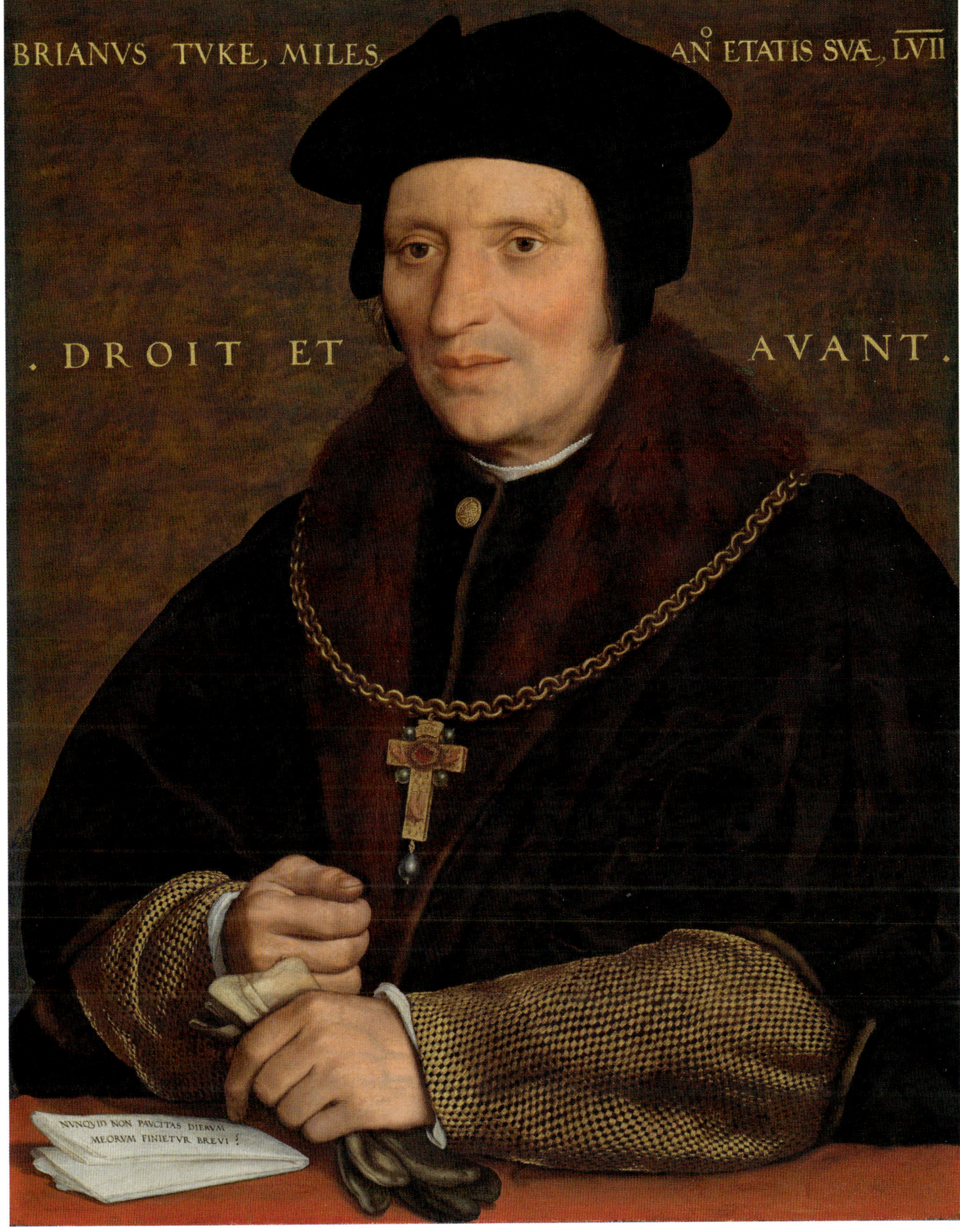

Sir Bryan Tuke, c.1532–34, oil on panel, 49.1 x 38.5cm (19.3 x 15.1in), National Gallery of Art, Washington DC, USA

Holbein portrays Sir Bryan Tuke, Master of the King's Posts, court administrator, supervising dispatches, at fifty-seven years of age. At the time of this portrait he had received the prestigious role of Treasurer of the Royal Household. In the superb half-length portrait Sir Brian sits at a table in three-quarter profile facing toward his right, looking ahead. Under his left hand is a piece of paper – a popular inclusion in Holbein portraits denoting realism – on it is written: 'Are my days not few?' from the Book of Job 10:20. There is some debate about the dating of the work; it possibly was started in 1527/8 and completed later.

Drawing of Thomas Wriothesley, 1st Earl of Southampton, c.1535, black and coloured pencil, pastels, pen and black ink, white highlights on pink prepared paper, 24.2 x 19.2cm (9.5 x 7.5in), Musée du Louvre, Paris, France

The chalk drawing may have been a preparatory work for a larger painting in oils – now lost – of Thomas Wriothesley, 1st Earl of Southampton, and for a miniature work (below).

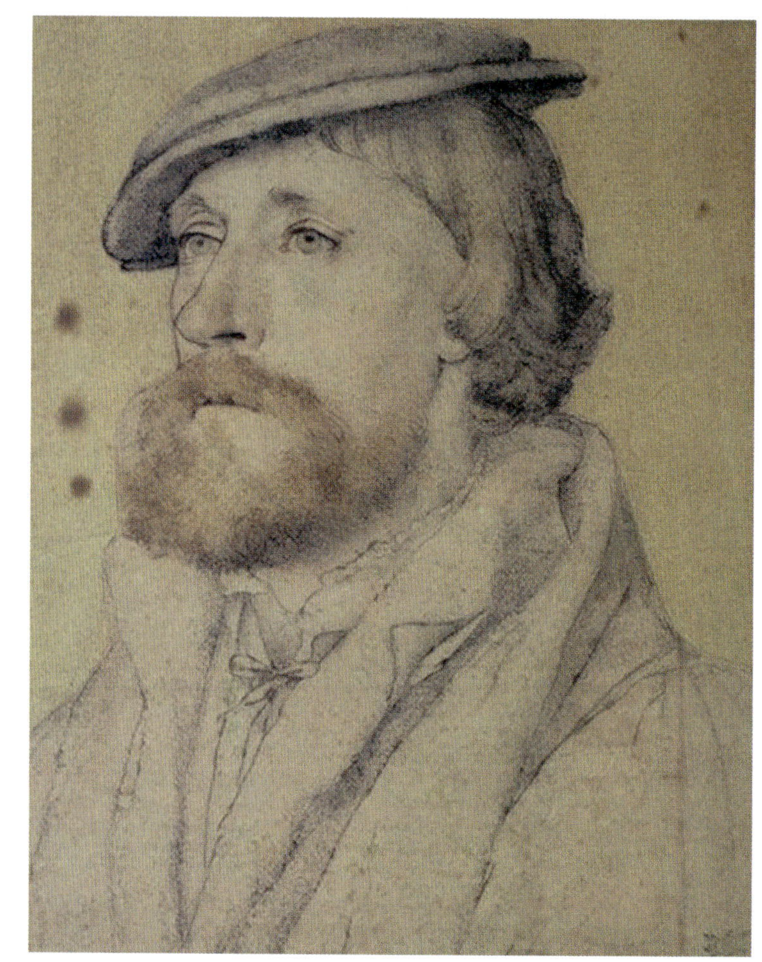

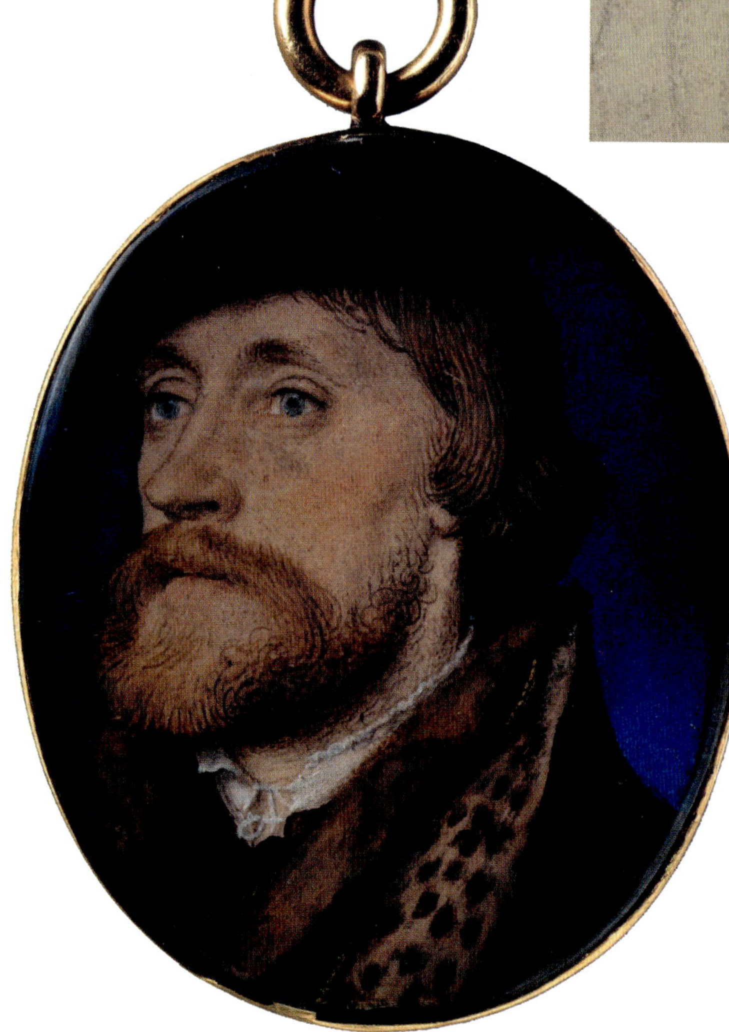

Thomas Wriothesley, 1st Earl of Southampton, c.1535, vellum laid down on card, 2.8 x 2.5 cm (1.1 x 0.89 in) diameter, Metropolitan Museum of Art, New York, NY, USA

Thomas Wriothesley (1505–50) was 1st Earl of Southampton, and secretary to King Henry VIII. In 1538 Wriothesley was sent as an ambassador to the Netherlands to meet Christina of Denmark, Duchess of Milan, to discuss marriage to the king. This miniature is said to be based on a chalk drawing by Holbein of Wriothesley, now in the Musée du Louvre, Paris. It is irregular in shape and probably cut down to fit the oval frame. Holbein's miniatures were usually circular.

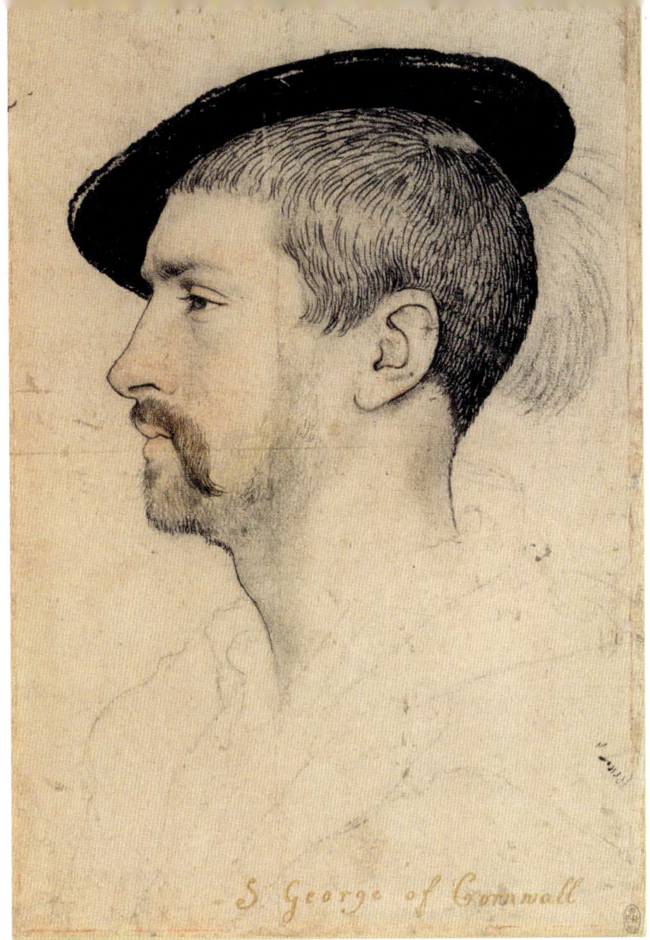

Drawing of Simon George, 1535, black and coloured chalks, pen and ink, brush and ink, and metalpoint on pale pink prepared paper, 27.9 x 19.1cm (10.9 x 7.5in), Royal Collection Trust, UK

The preparatory portrait drawing is of the head and shoulders of Simon George, shown in profile to the left (the sitter's right). He wears a cap with a large feather. Comparing the drawing to the finished painting (below). George has a moustache and short, stubble-beard and close-cut or shaved hair. In the painted portrait his full beard and moustache adjoin, and he holds a carnation in his hand, a traditional symbol of pure love in courtship and marriage.

*Portrait of Simon George of Cornwall, c.*1535–40, oil on oak, 32.4cm (12.7in) diameter, Stadeleches Kunstinstitut, Frankfurt am Main, Germany

This portrait was identified from the preparatory drawing in the British Royal Collection, which portrays a young man without full beard and inscription of Simon George on it. He is known to have married Thomasina Lanyon, and this may be linked to their courtship, through the inclusion of a red carnation, and the figure of Leda depicted on the George beret badge. The ancient god Jupiter courted Leda in the form of a swan. The original roundel has been cut down.

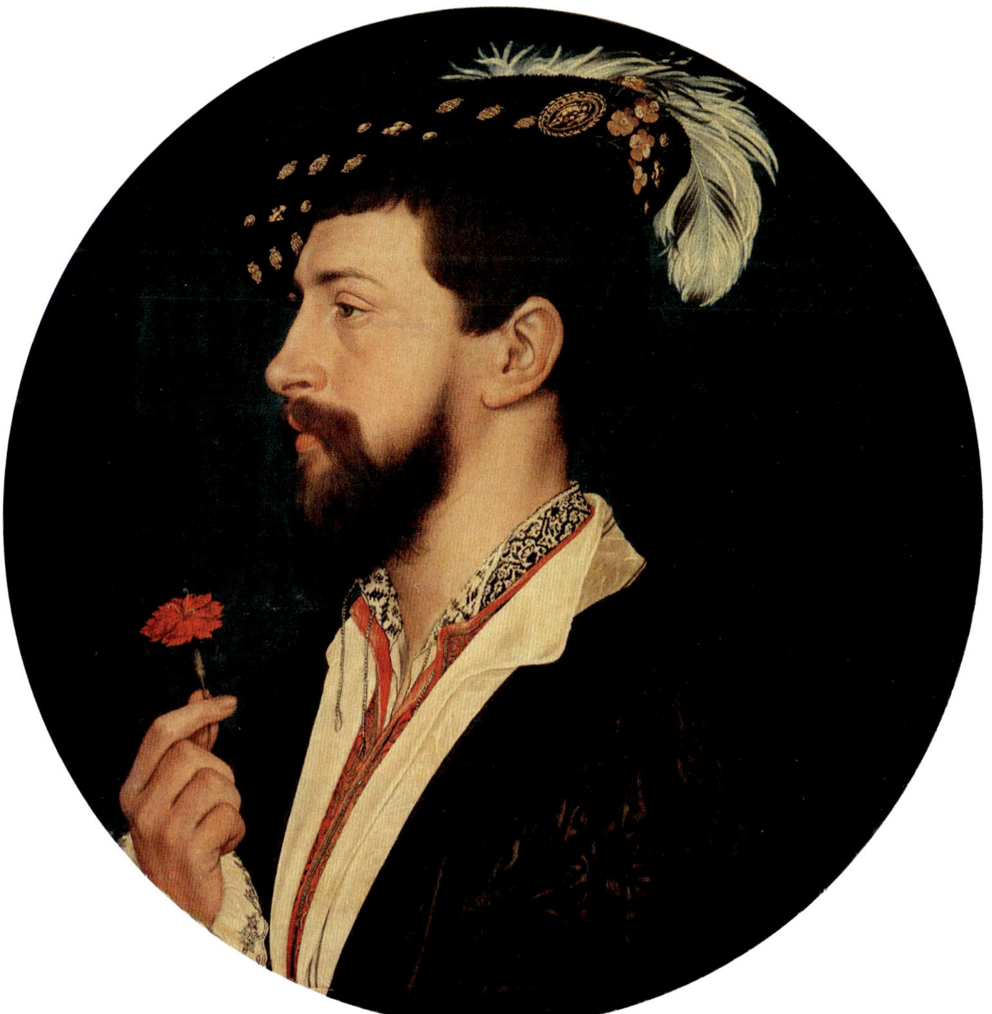

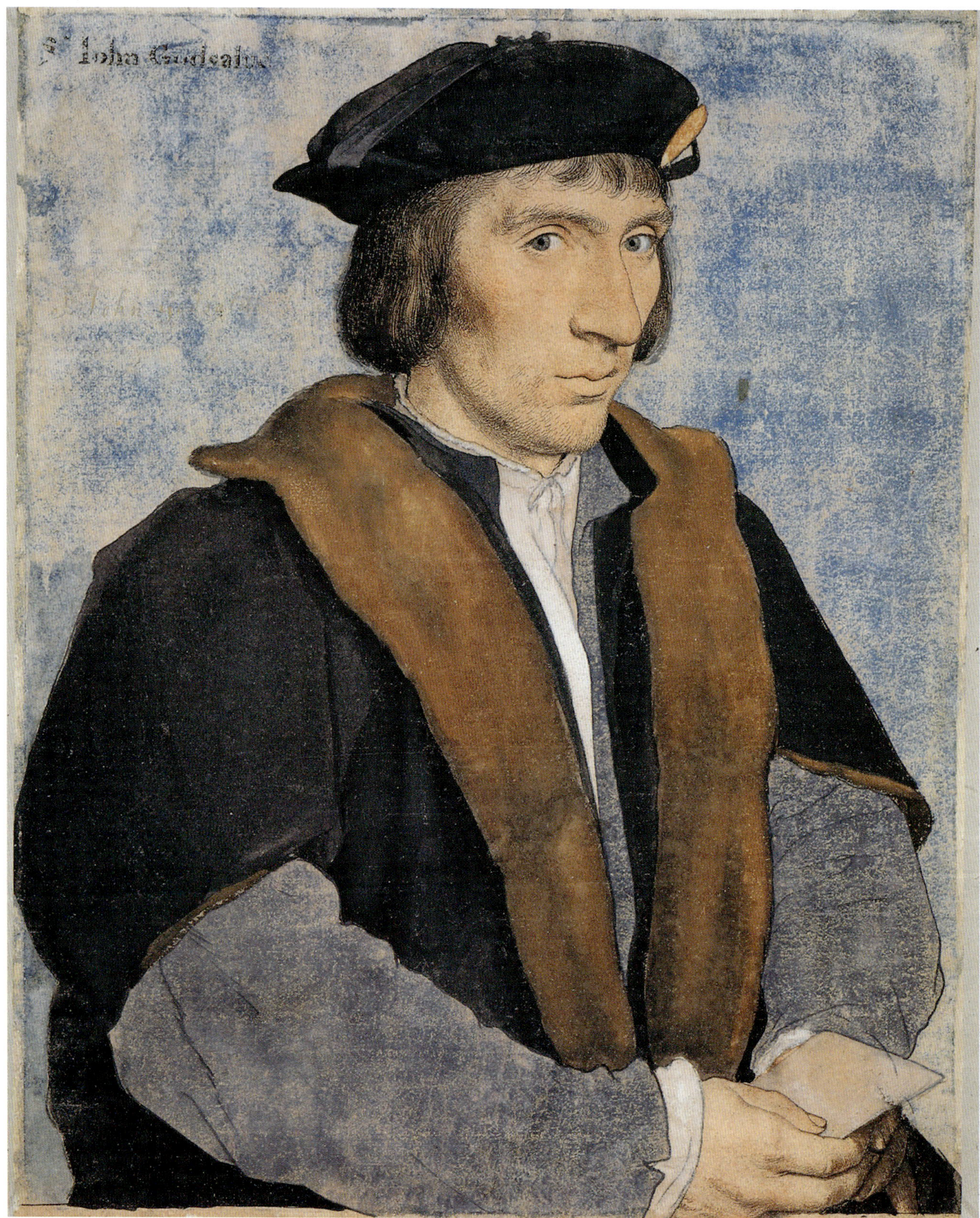

Sir John Godsalve, c.1532–34, black and red chalks, pen and ink, brush and ink, bodycolour, white heightening, on pale pink prepared paper, 36.2 x 29.2cm (14.2 x 11.5in), Royal Collection Trust, UK

A portrait drawing of Sir John Godsalve (c.1505–1556), first portrayed by Holbein in 1528 in a double portrait with his father (see page 165). A half-length portrait facing three-quarters to the right. Godsalve wears a fur collar, black gown and blue sleeves. He holds a letter. Inscribed in an 18th-century hand upper left is: 'Sr John Godsalue'.

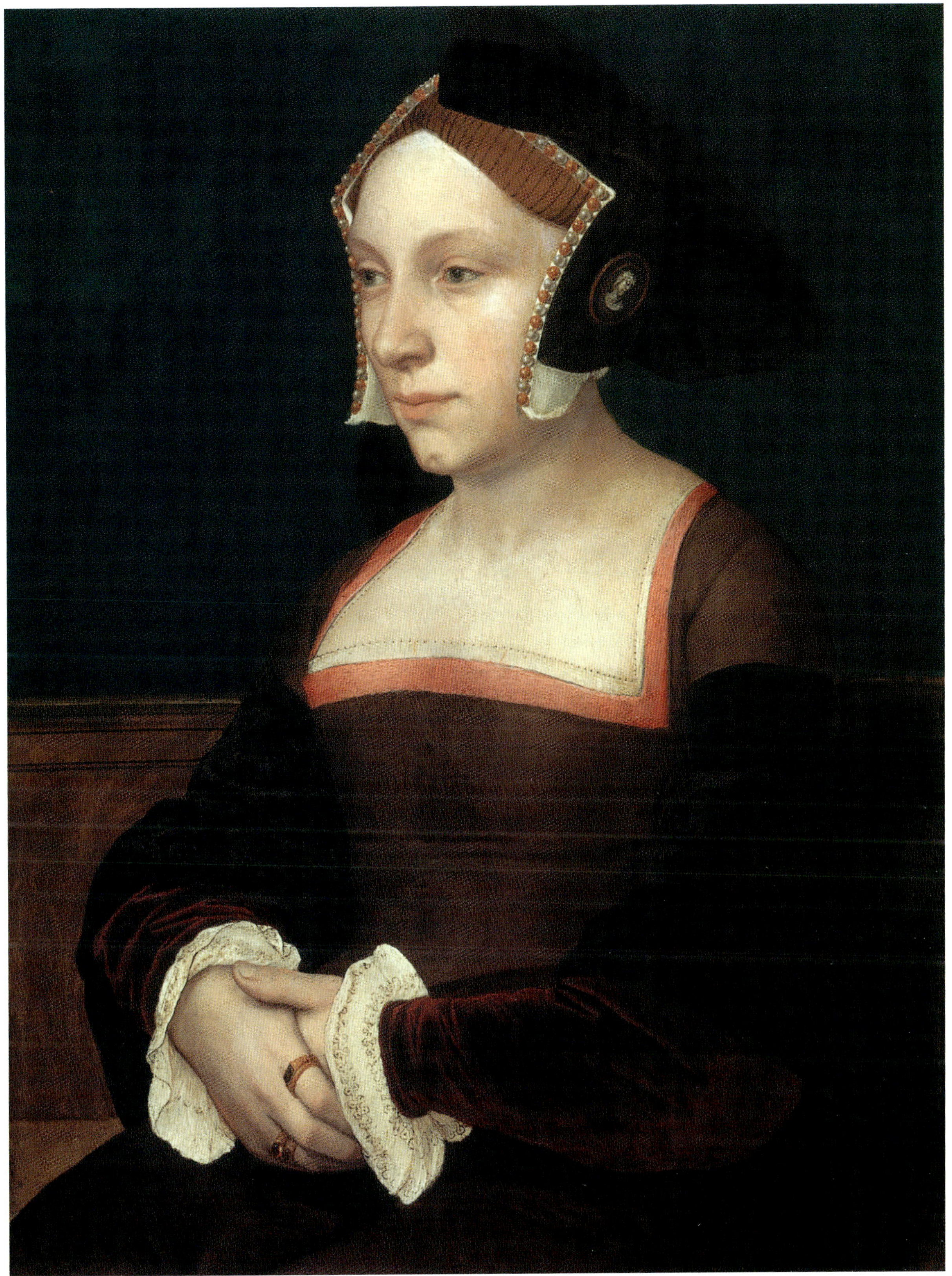

Portrait of Elizabeth Widmerpole, c.1536, tempera on oak, 32.5 x 25cm (12.7 x 9.8in), Oskar Reinhart Collection, Winterthur, Switzerland

Elizabeth Widmerpole married courtier Sir John Godsalve, son of Thomas Godsalve, before 1531. She was his second wife and together they had two sons, William and Thomas (d.1587). On his return to London, Holbein was commissioned to create this portrait painting of her.

Right: *Drawing of Elizabeth, Lady Vaux*, c.1536, black and coloured chalks, white bodycolour, wash, pen and ink, brush and ink, and metalpoint on pale pink prepared paper, 28.1 x 21.5cm (11 x 8.3in), Royal Collection Trust, UK

The Holbein painting created from this preparatory drawing is known only through copies. It was possibly planned as a companion portrait of Lady Vaux's husband, Thomas Vaux. Elizabeth (born 1509) was the daughter of Sir Thomas Cheney, an Esquire of the Body at the court.

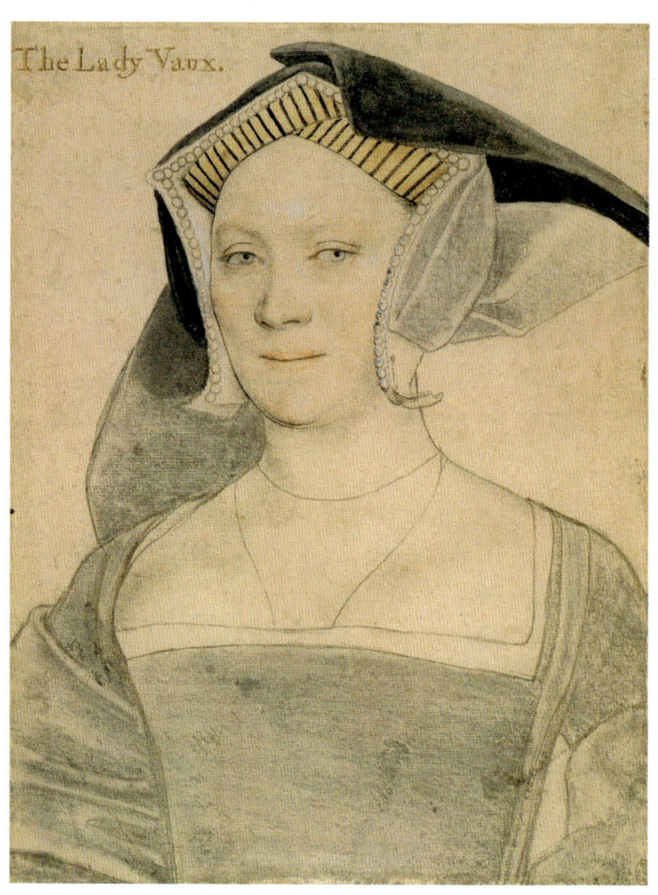

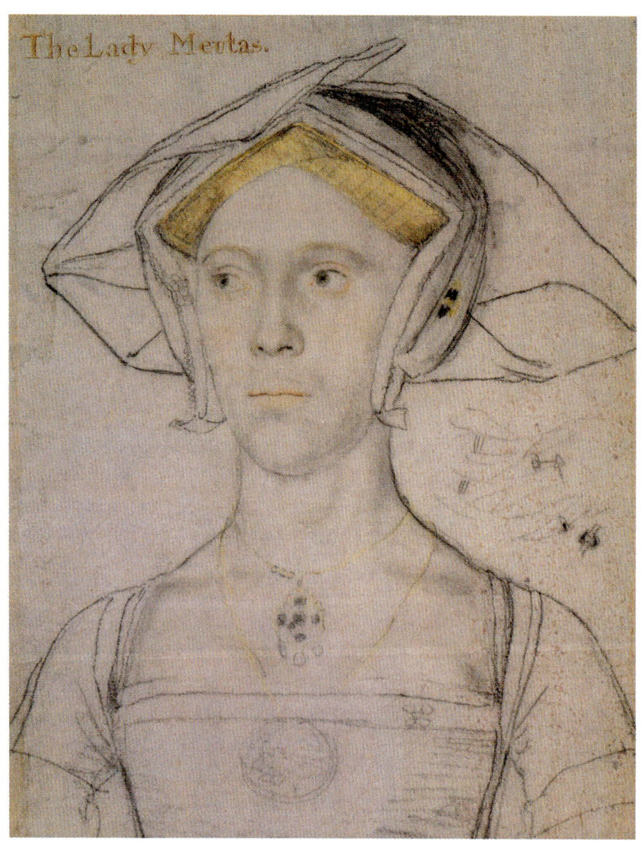

Above: *Drawing of Joan, Lady Meutas*, c.1536–43, black and coloured chalks on pale pink prepared paper, 28.1 x 21.0cm (11 x 8.2in), Royal Collection Trust, UK

Joan Ashley, Lady Meutas (died 1577), Lady of the Privy Chamber to Queen Jane Seymour, and wife of the courtier Sir Peter Meutas (1517–51), is depicted in a portrait drawing, a possible preparatory study for a painting. She wears a headdress, a necklace and a medallion; very fashionable jewellery.

Below: *Study of Lady Ratclif*, c.1530s, black and coloured chalks, pen and ink, 30.1 x 20.3cm (11.9 x 8in), Royal Collection Trust, UK

A preparatory drawing inscribed 'The Lady Ratclif', this is possibly a portrayal of Sir Robert Ratcliffe's third wife, Mary.

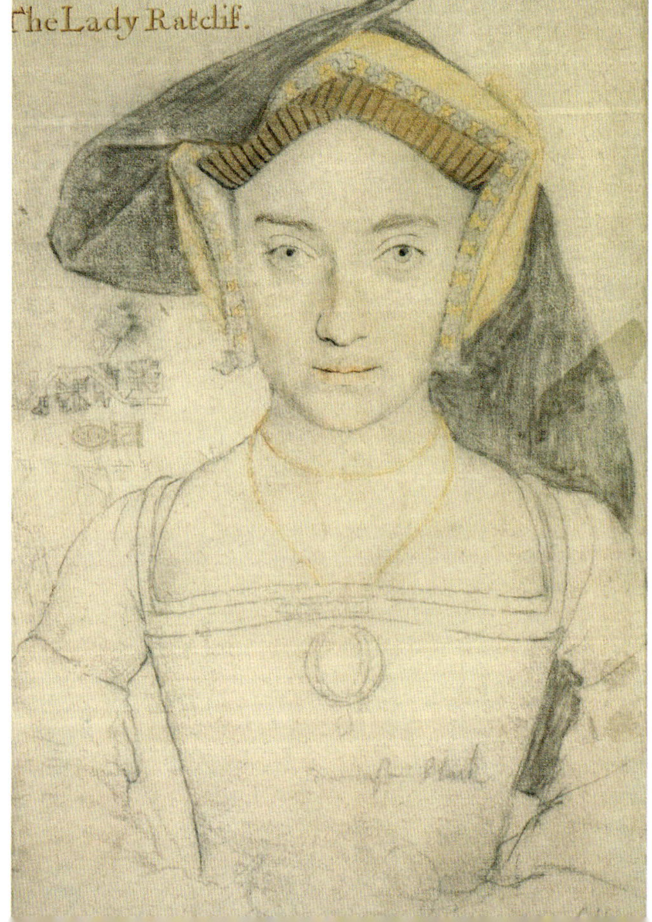

*Elizabeth, Lady Rich, c.*1540, workshop of Holbein, oil and gold on oak, 44.5 x 34cm (17.5 x 13.4in), Metropolitan Museum of Art, New York, NY, USA

Holbein created a detailed drawing study (see below) of Lady Rich (Elizabeth Jenks, d.1558) for this painting. Jenks was the daughter of William Jenks (or Gynkes) a London spice merchant. She married Richard Rich, solicitor general at the court of Henry VIII, in 1535, and bore at least twelve children. The reason that this painting was carried out by Holbein's assistants – most likely under his supervision – is not known. The underdrawing may have been executed by Holbein. In 1548 Richard Rich became 1st Baron Rich, and Lord Chancellor to the new king, Edward VI.

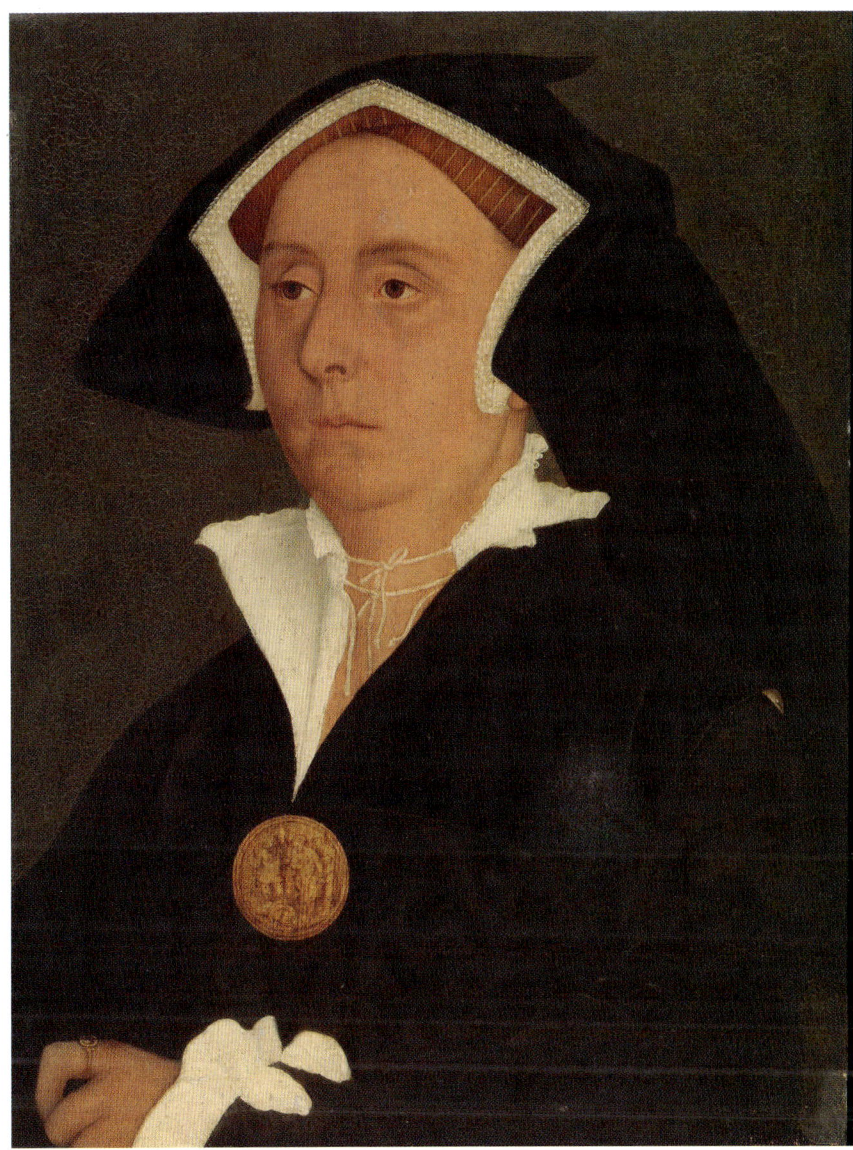

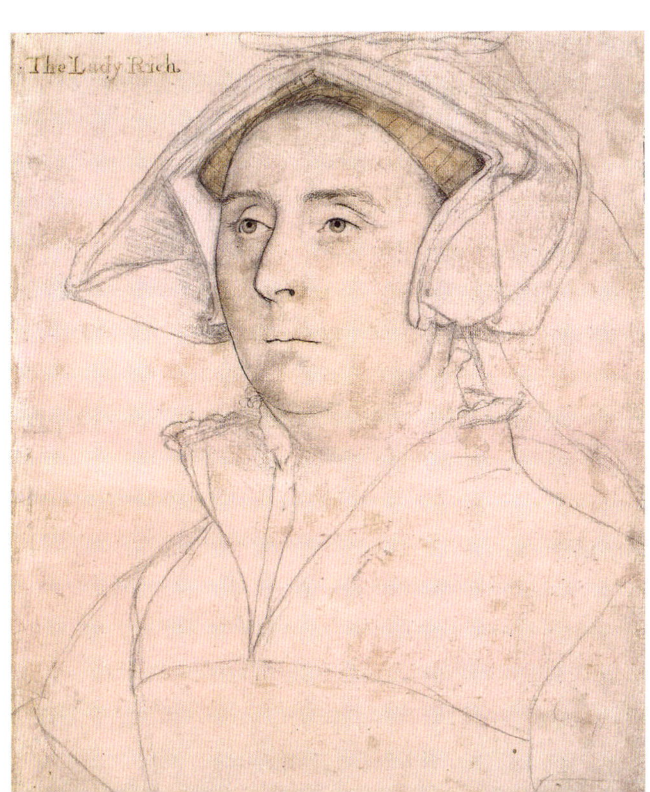

*Drawing of Elizabeth, Lady Rich, c.*1540–43, black and coloured chalks, pen and Indian ink, metalpoint, on pale pink prepared paper, 37.9 x 30.3cm (15 x 12in), Royal Collection Trust, UK

Holbein portrayed Elizabeth, Lady Rich, in three-quarter profile facing to her right, in this bust-length work. His left-handed hatching is visible on the left in her headdress. It is possibly a companion work to a lost portrait of her husband, Richard, 1st Baron Rich. The drawing was later inscribed in the 18th century, at top left: 'The Lady Rich'. Two oil-on-panel portraits were made by Holbein's workshop from this preparatory sketch. One is now in the Metropolitan Museum of Art in New York (above) and one is in the Museum Georg Schaefer, Shweinfurt, Germany.

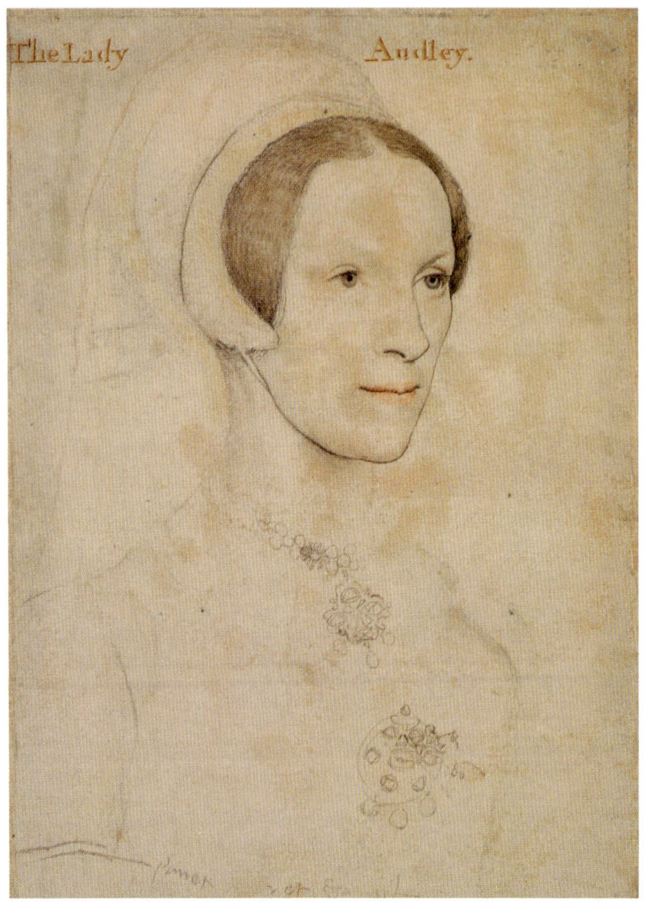

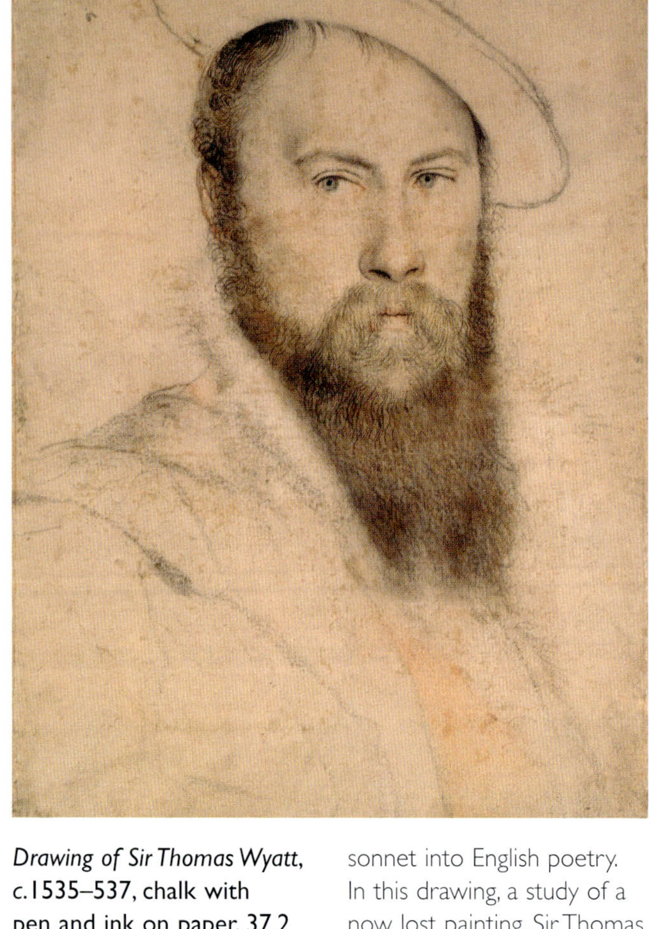

Drawing of Lady Audley, c.1538, black and coloured chalks, pen and ink, and metalpoint on pale pink prepared paper, 29.3 x 20.8cm (11.41 x 8.1in), Royal Collection Trust, UK

A bust-length portrait of Elizabeth, Lady Audley (d.1564), née Grey, facing three quarters to the sitter's left. The composition relates to the miniature portrait; Holbein included detailed depictions of her jewellery.

Drawing of Sir Thomas Wyatt, c.1535–537, chalk with pen and ink on paper, 37.2 x 26.9cm (14.6 x 10.5in), Royal Collection Trust, UK

Sir Thomas Wyatt (1503–42), knighted in 1537 – which may have instigated the portrait – was a lyrical poet credited with introducing the sonnet into English poetry. In this drawing, a study of a now lost painting, Sir Thomas wears a hat and a fur coat in a bust-length portrait, facing three-quarters to the right. He was temporarily arrested in 1536 after rumour of an affair with Anne Boleyn. His son was painted by Holbein in 1541 (see page 238).

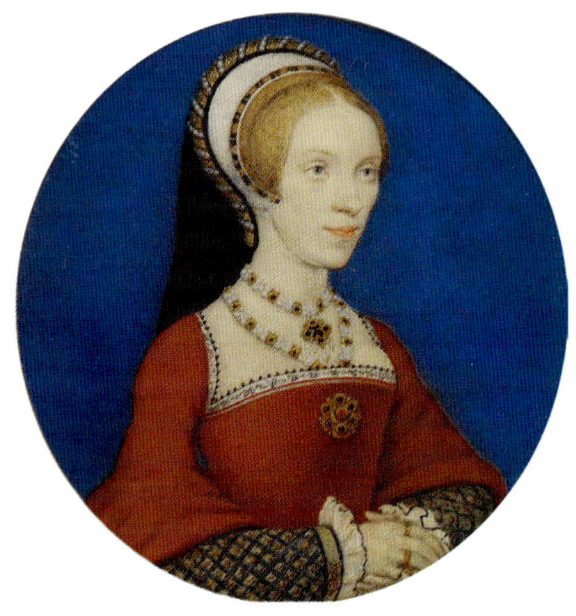

Elizabeth, Lady Audley, c.1538, watercolour on vellum laid on playing card, 37.3 x 38.4cm (14.7 x 15.1in) Royal Collection Trust, UK

Identified by the later 16th-century inscription on the matching preparatory drawing as 'Lady Audley', the sitter of this miniature is now generally accepted as Elizabeth Grey (d.1564), daughter of the second Marquess of Dorset. The miniature may have been commissioned in celebration of her marriage, in 1538, to Thomas, Lord Audley of Walden (d.1544), Lord Chancellor.

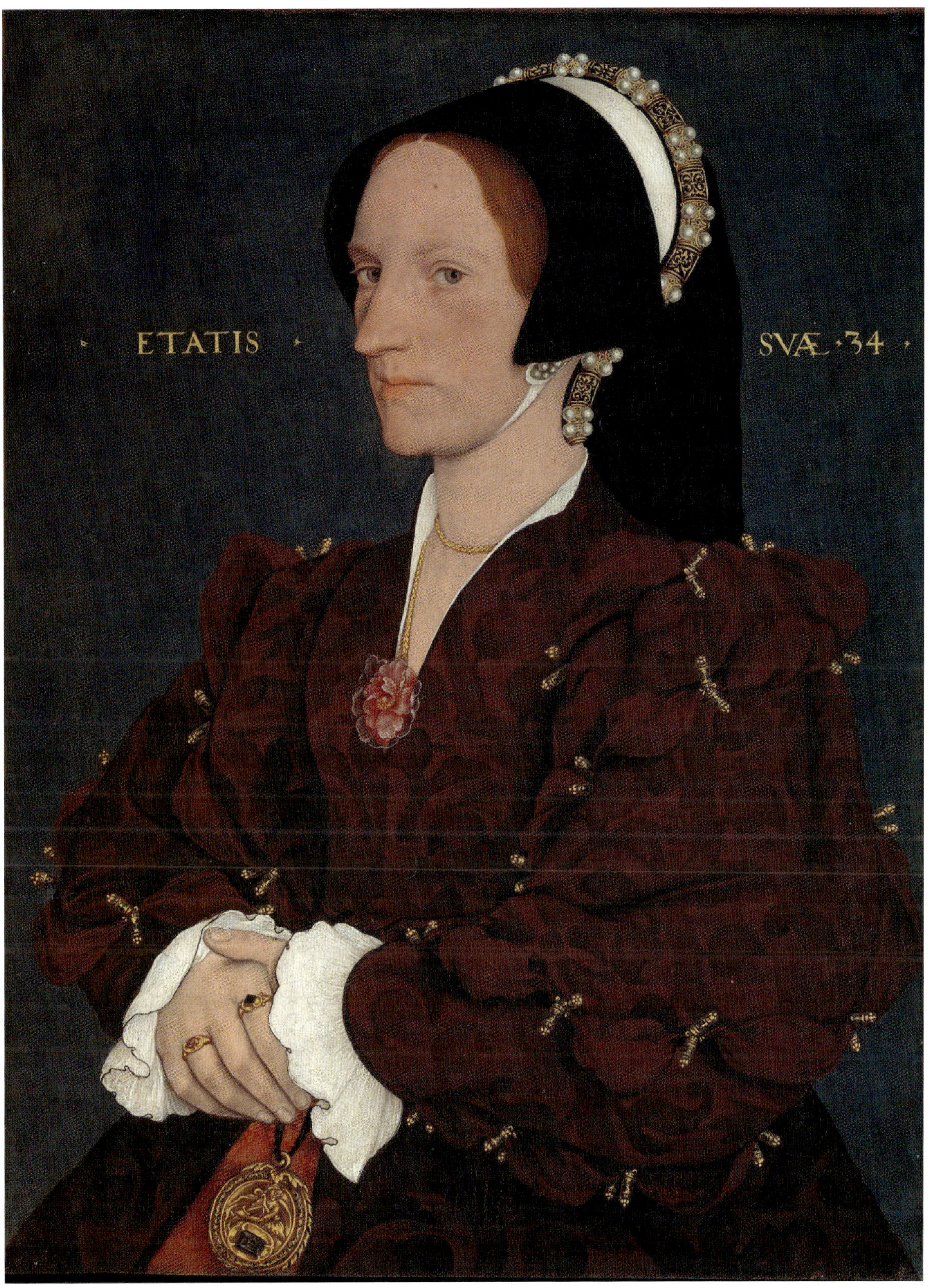

Portrait of Margaret Wyatt, Lady Lee, c.1540, oil and gold on oak, 44.1 x 34cm (17.3 x 13.3in), Metropolitan Museum of Art, New York, NY, USA

By the workshop of Hans Holbein the Younger, possibly with his input, or perhaps copied from a preparatory drawing by Holbein, this is a portrait of Margaret Wyatt, Lady Lee, daughter of Sir Henry Wyatt (the brother of Sir Thomas Wyatt), and husband of Sir Anthony Lee. The lettering in the background states that she is aged thirty-four. She is fashionably dressed, as a lady of the royal court. Her father served as treasurer to the king's chamber.

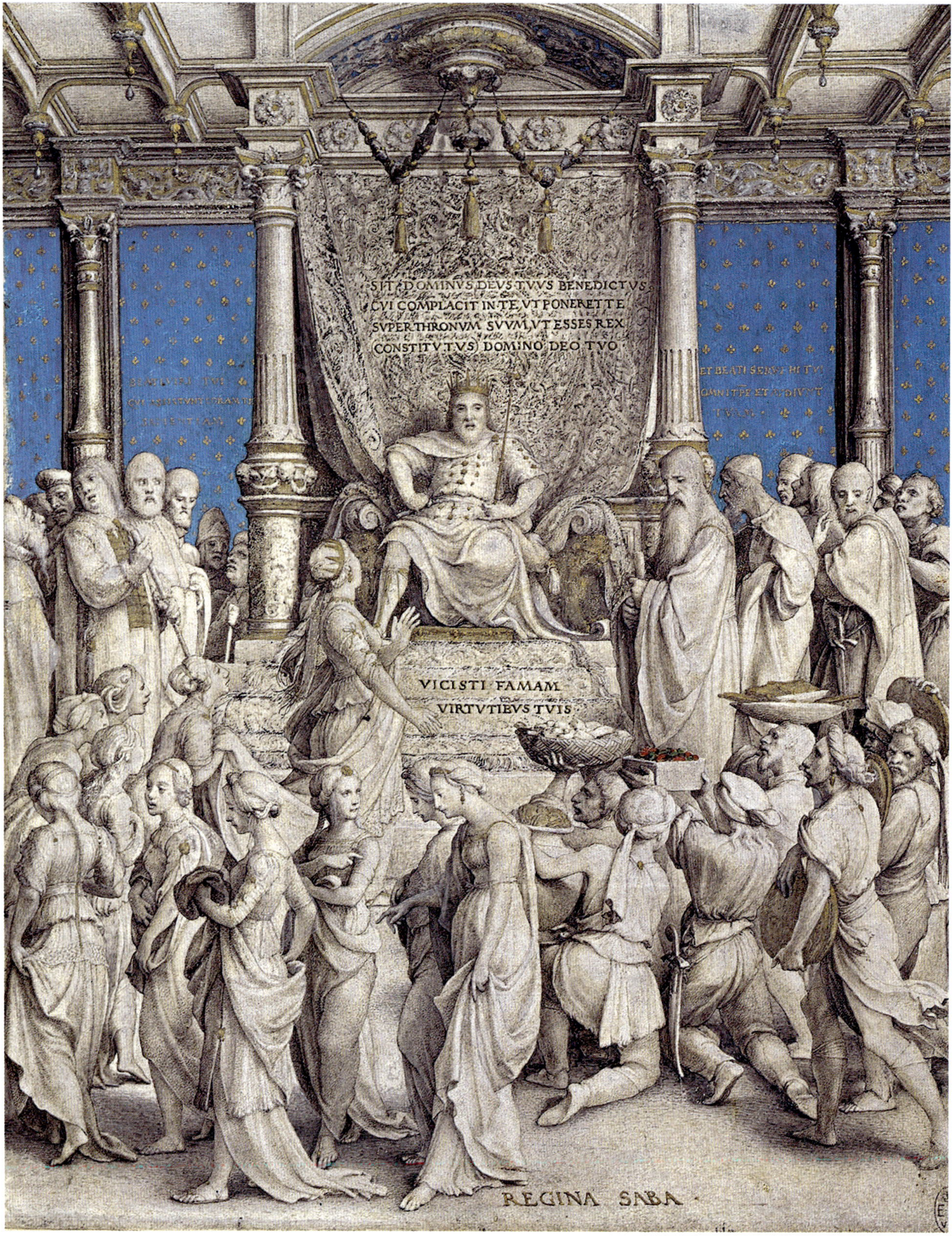

Solomon and the Queen of Sheba, c.1534, brown and grey wash, blue, red and green bodycolour, white heightening, gold, and pen and black ink over metalpoint on vellum, 22.9 x 18.3cm (9 x 7.2in), Royal Collection Trust, UK

A painting of significance as it is dated to soon after the Act of Supremacy when Henry VIII became Head of the Church of England in May 1533. In the composition Henry VIII is personified by King Solomon, on his throne. The Queen of Sheba, standing on the steps, a personification of the Church, turns to address the king.

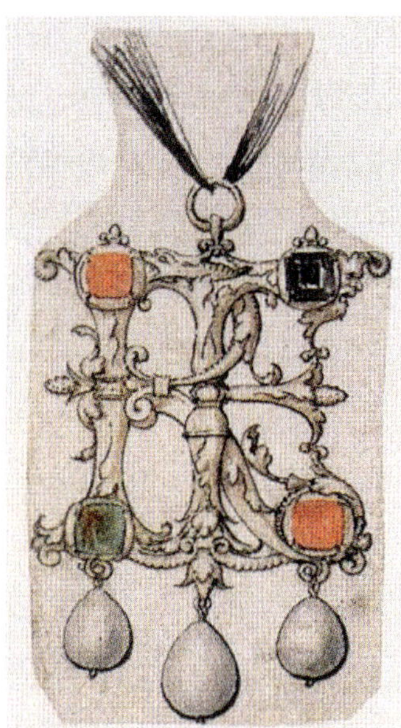

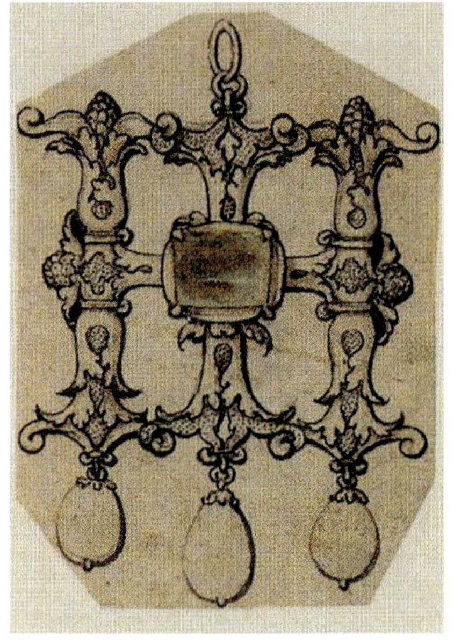

Below: *Design for Jane Seymour gold cup*, c.1533–37, pen and Indian ink with light washes of grey and pink, heightened in gold, 37.5 x 15.5cm (14.8 x 6.1in), Ashmolean Museum, Oxford, UK

Later recorded as a treasure in the collection, this intricately designed, bejewelled gold cup and cover, commissioned by Jane Seymour, is known today only through Holbein's design drawing. The initials of Henry VIII and Jane Seymour are intertwined on the cup.

Two designs for Pendant Jewelled Initials, c.1534–38, ink and watercolour on paper, 8.4 x 4.1cm (3.3 x 1.6in), British Museum, London, England, UK

Two designs for intricate jewelled pendants including initials. At left the pendant design incorporates a monogram, precious stones, and three suspended pearls. At right, a similar design with a large jewel at centre and three pearls suspended.

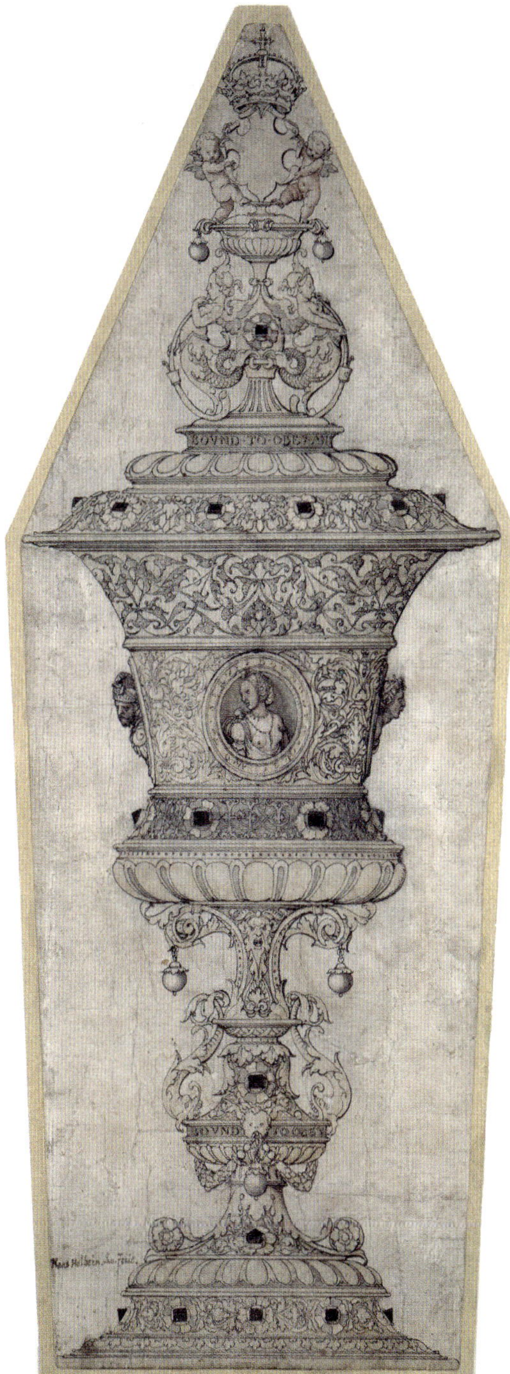

Designs for Sword Hilts, c.1534–38, pen and ink over chalk drawing on paper, with feather additions in brown, 20.1 x 15.1cm (7.9 x 5.9in), Kunstmuseum, Basel, Switzerland

One of several designs created by Holbein the Younger for ornamental daggers, swords and sword hilts, as worn by many of the sitters he portrayed, including Jean de Dinteville, and King Henry VIII.

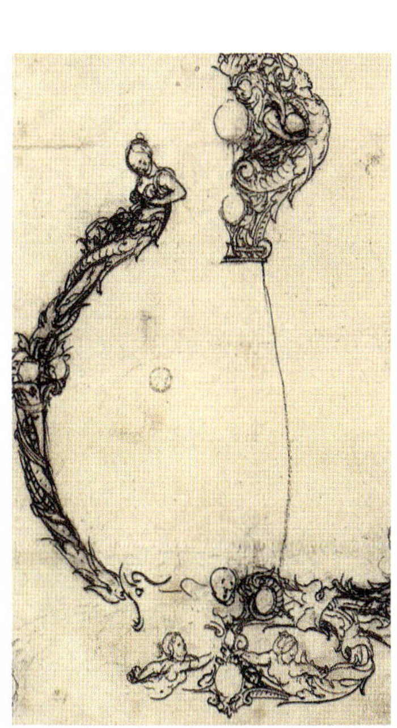

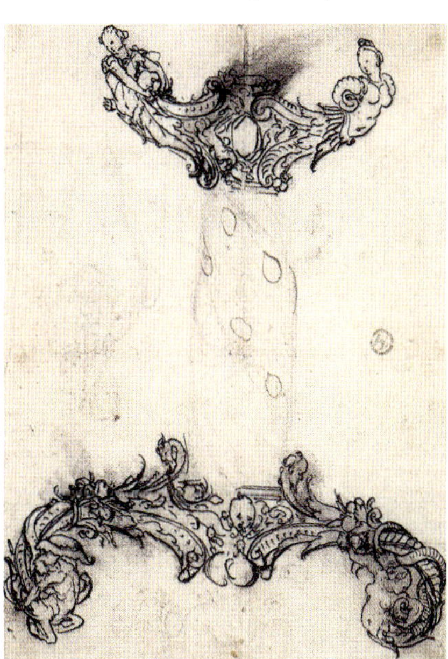

Study of Mary, Duchess of Richmond and Somerset, c.1532–33, black and coloured chalks, brush and ink, on pale pink prepared paper, 26.6 x 19.9cm (10.4 x 7.8in), Royal Collection Trust, UK

Holbein portrays Mary, Duchess of Richmond and Somerset (c.1519–55) facing front with eyes turned downward. The head-and-shoulders depiction gives detail of her face and feathered hat. Holbein made a colour and texture inscription: 'samet rot' (red velvet) and 'schwarz felbet' (black velvet). The duchess was married to Henry Fitzroy, the illegitimate son of King Henry VIII, appointed the royal title Duke of Richmond and Somerset.

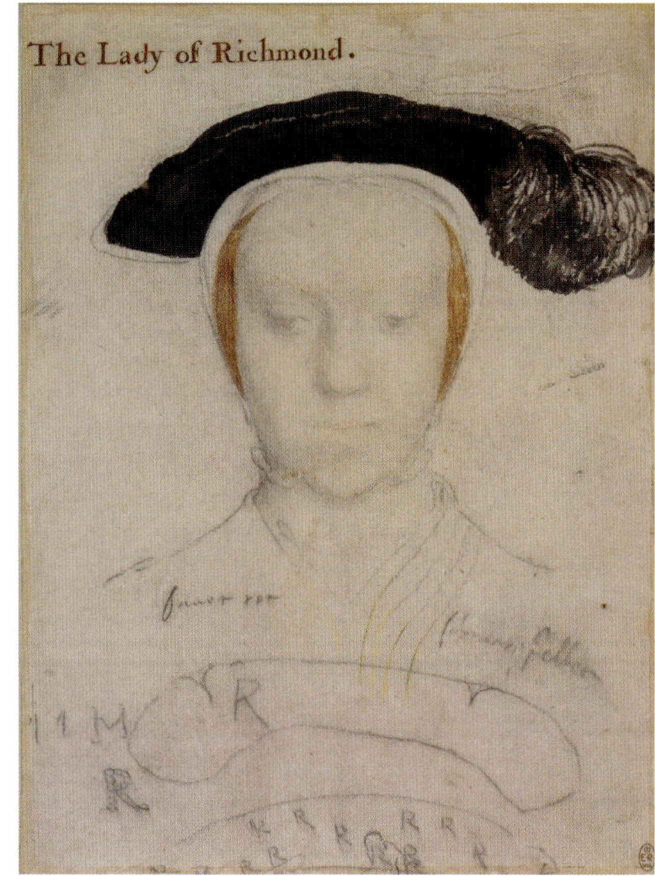

Study of an unidentified woman, c.1532–43, black and coloured chalks, white bodycolour, pen with black and brown ink on pale pink prepared paper, trimmed to outlines and pasted onto another sheet, 27.1 x 16.9cm (10.6 x 6.6in), Royal Collection Trust, UK

Annotated by Holbein, in reference to colours and textures for the proposed painting: 'samat' (velvet) and 'damast' (damask). The young lady in the preparatory study faces forward, her eyes directed at the viewer. Holbein gives finished detail of her facial features, hair and jewellery, but her clothing is in outline only. The identity of the sitter is unknown.

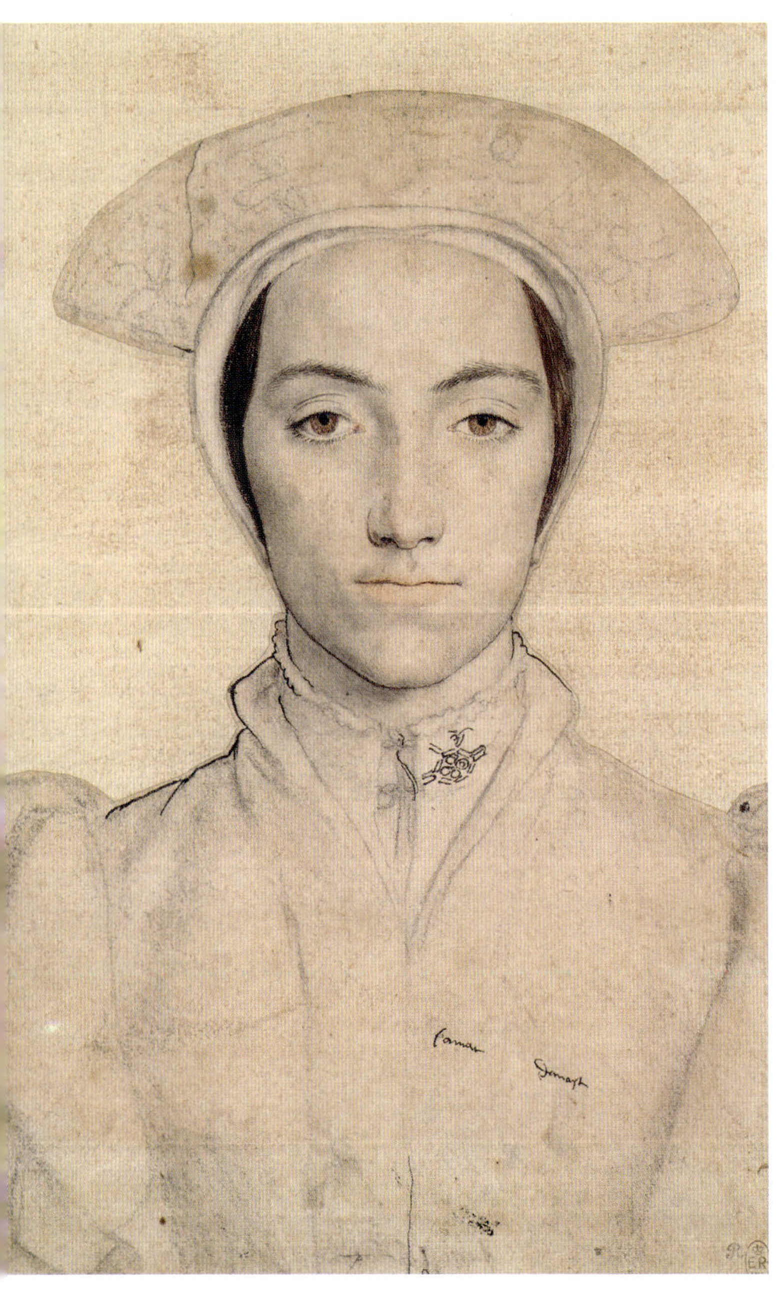

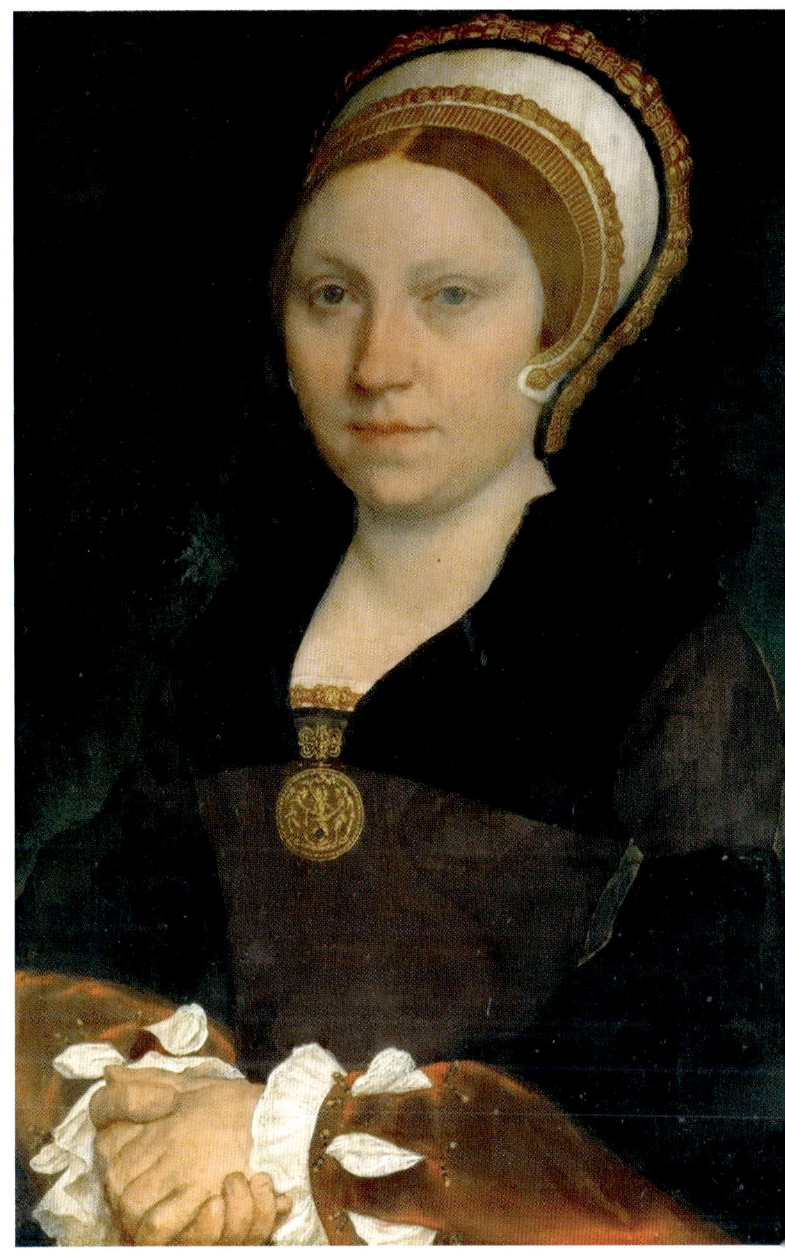

Portrait of an English Lady, c.1540-43, oil on panel, 22 x 18cm (8.6 x 7in), Kunsthistorisches Museum, Vienna, Austria

A portrait of an unknown lady, dated to the last years of Holbein's life. The refined clothing and half-length composition suggests a lady of the royal court, a wife of a noble or courtier. There are similarities in the style of headdress with *Portrait of a Lady,* 1535–40 (see page 221) and *Portrait of a Young Woman, possibly Katherine Howard, c.1540–1542* (see page 243).

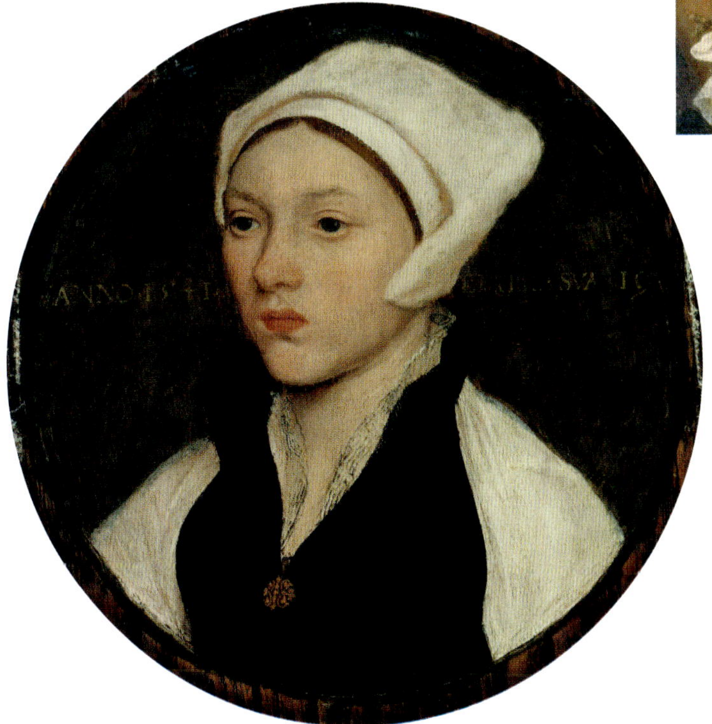

Portrait of a Young Woman with a White Coif, 1541, oil and tempera on panel, 11.11cm (4.37in) diameter, Los Angeles County Museum of Art, USA

Holbein created many portraits of women, including ladies of the royal court and the wives of royal courtiers, of which this may be one. The clothing is similar in style and fashion to *Portrait of Jane Pemberton* (see page 84).

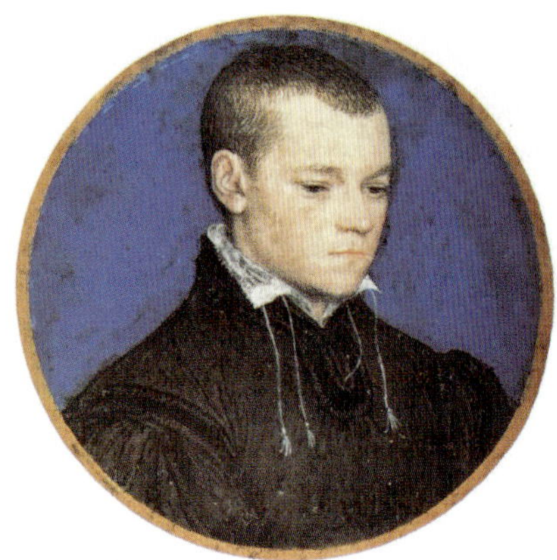

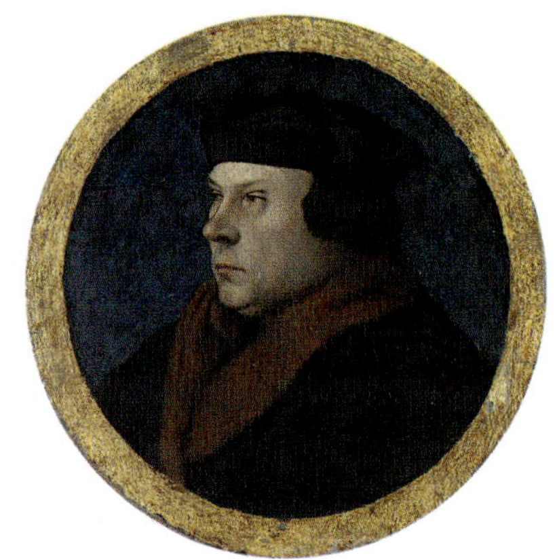

Portrait of a Young Man, or Gregory Cromwell, c.1535–40, watercolour on vellum, 3.8cm (1.4in) diameter, House of Orange-Nassau Historic Collections Trust, The Netherlands

This portrait miniature is now thought to depict Gregory Cromwell (c.1520–1551), the only son of Thomas Cromwell. He was later the 1st Baron Cromwell.

Portrait of Thomas Cromwell, Earl of Essex, 1532–33, watercolour and bodycolour on vellum playing card, 4.4cm (1.7in) diameter, National Portrait Gallery, London, UK

Attributed to Hans Holbein the Younger, a miniature roundel portrait of Sir Thomas Cromwell. This work may be associated with the oil on oak portrait in the Frick Collection (opposite).

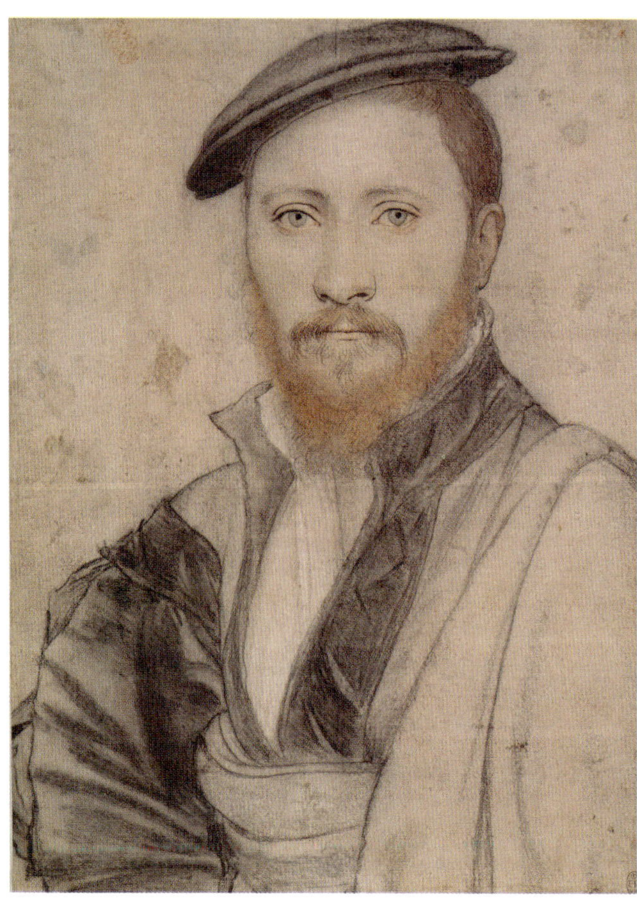

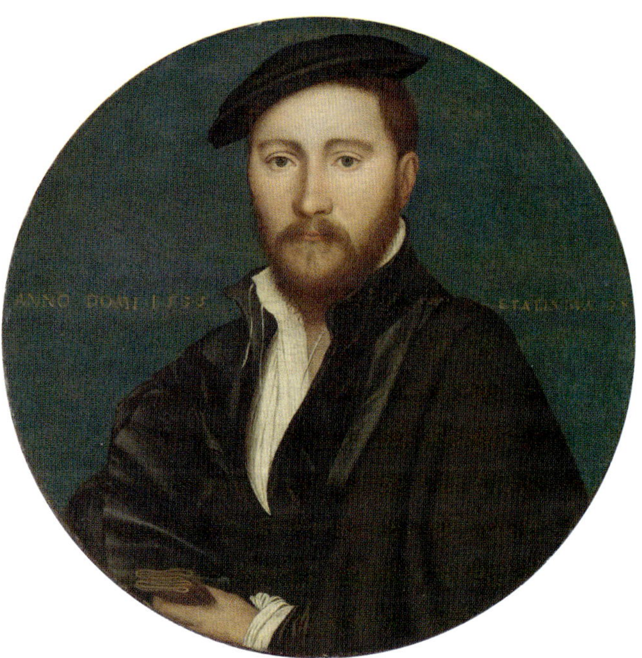

Portrait of a Man, 1535, black and coloured chalks, white bodycolour, pen and ink, and metalpoint on pale pink prepared paper, 29.8 x 22.2cm (11.7 x 8.7in), Royal Collection Trust, UK

The bust-length preparatory drawing is thought to be of Sir Ralph Sadler (1507–87), Privy Councillor, and Secretary of State to Henry VIII.

Portrait of a Man aged Twenty-eight, perhaps Sir Ralph Sadler 1535, oil and gold on oak, 30.5cm (12in) diameter, Metropolitan Museum of Art, New York, NY, USA

A roundel portrait painted by the workshop of Hans Holbein under his supervision, and closely following his drawing (left). The sitter faces forward, with body turned in three-quarter profile, with eyes that directly connect to the viewer. He has auburn hair, moustache and trimmed beard, and fashionable hat and clothing. Sadler lived in Cromwell's household as a boy, and had grown up and been educated with Gregory Cromwell. Thomas Cromwell later became godfather to Sadler's first two sons.

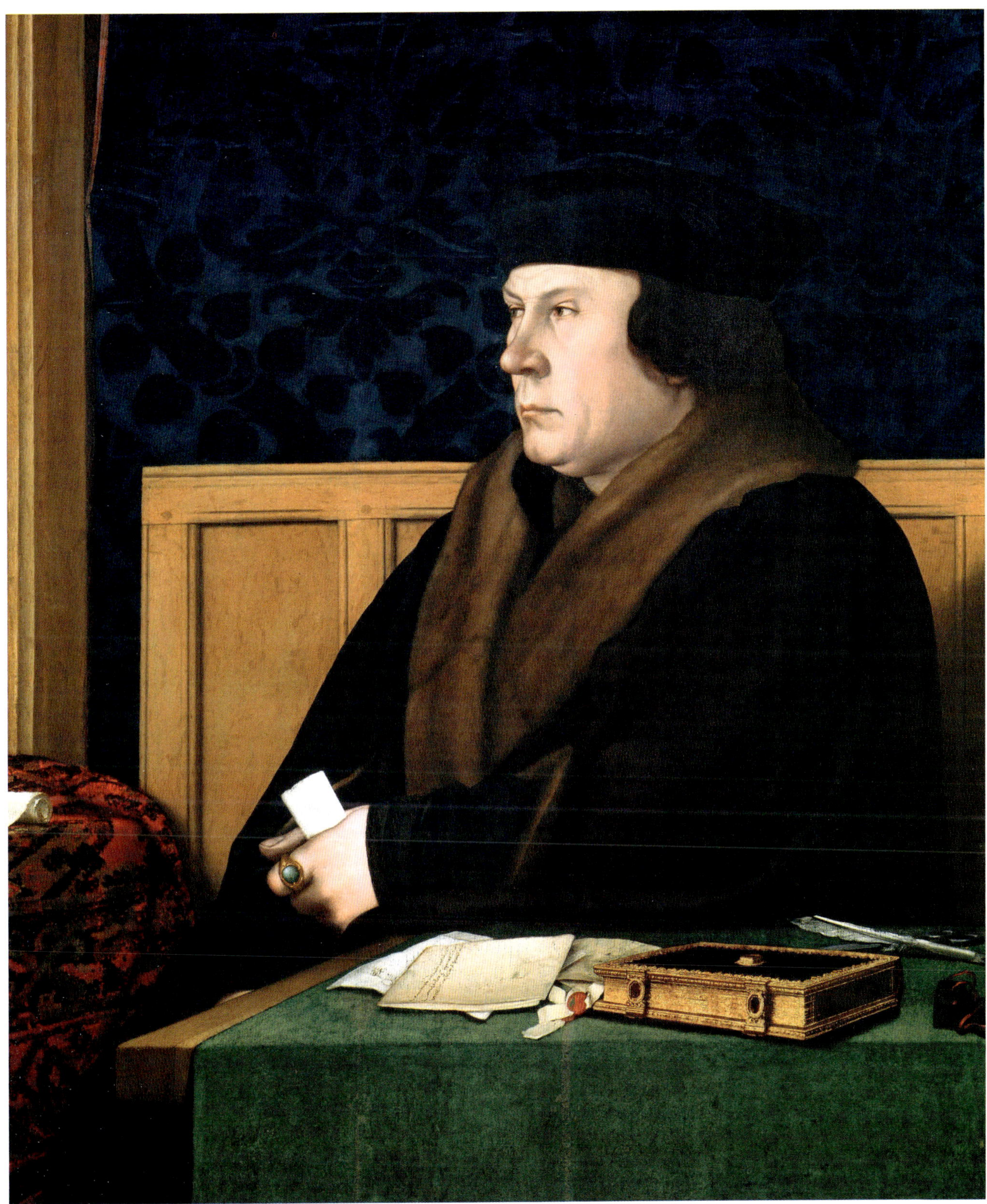

Thomas Cromwell, 1532–33, oil on oak panel, 78.4 x 64.5cm (30.8 x 25.3in), Frick Collection, New York, NY, USA

In the year this painting was commissioned Thomas Cromwell's Submission of the English Clergy was ratified by a convocation of English clergy, thereby severing Papal relations with Pope Clement VII, who threatened to excommunicate the king. Cromwell's paper gives control to Henry VIII and his Church of England. In the same year a small miniature of Cromwell by Holbein is made (see opposite, top).

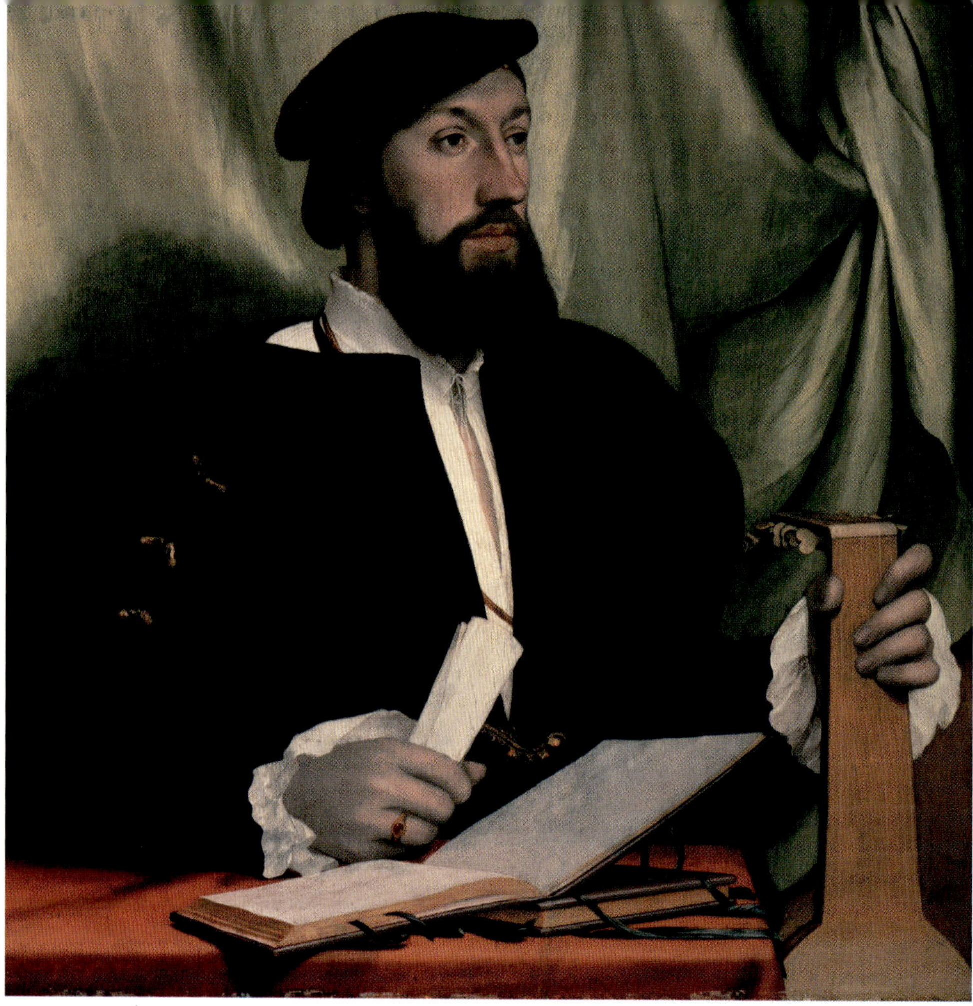

Unknown gentleman with music books and lute, c.1534, oil on panel, Staatliche Museen, Berlin, Germany

Attributed to Hans Holbein the Younger, this work is similar in its composition to the artist's portraits of the Hanse London Steelyard merchants. The theatrical curtain is reminiscent of *Laïs of Corinthiaca* (see page 140); the music book and the lute – content which would have been agreed on by the unknown sitter – are similar to objects in *The Ambassadors*, 1533 (see page 182). The gentleman's clothing infers affluent status. The style of the portrait dates to Holbein's second stay in England, from 1532.

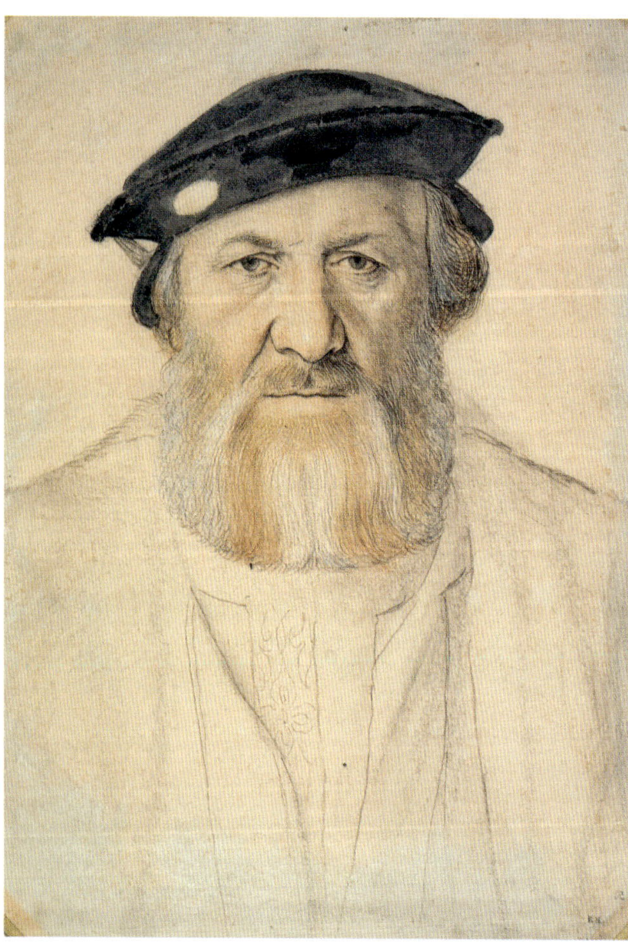

Portrait study of Charles de Solier, Sieur de Morette, 1534–35, black and coloured chalks, accented in white, pastels, ink wash, on pink prepared paper, 33 x 25cm (13 x 9.8in), Kunstmuseum, Basel, Switzerland

This remarkably realistic drawing of Charles de Solier, a preparatory study for the oil painting (opposite), highlights Holbein's meticulous sketching methods. He concentrated on the hat with badges, the strong, facial features with deep-set eyes, high cheekbones, and the auburn and silver hairs of the heavy beard, using different coloured chalks, pen and ink and wash. De Solier's clothing was recorded with a simple outline.

Opposite: *Charles de Solier, Sieur de Morette,* 1534–35, oil on panel, 92.5 x 7.55cm (36.41 x 29.72in), Gemäldegalerie, Dresden, Germany

The Piedmontese-born French diplomat Charles de Solier (1480–1552) serving at the court of Francis I of France, was French ambassador at the court of King Henry VIII from 1534, taking over from Jean de Dinteville. This magnificent life-size, three-quarter length, full-front portrait is in the style of artist Jean Clouet's portrait of Francis I (see page 81), and Holbein's later portrayals of Henry VIII.

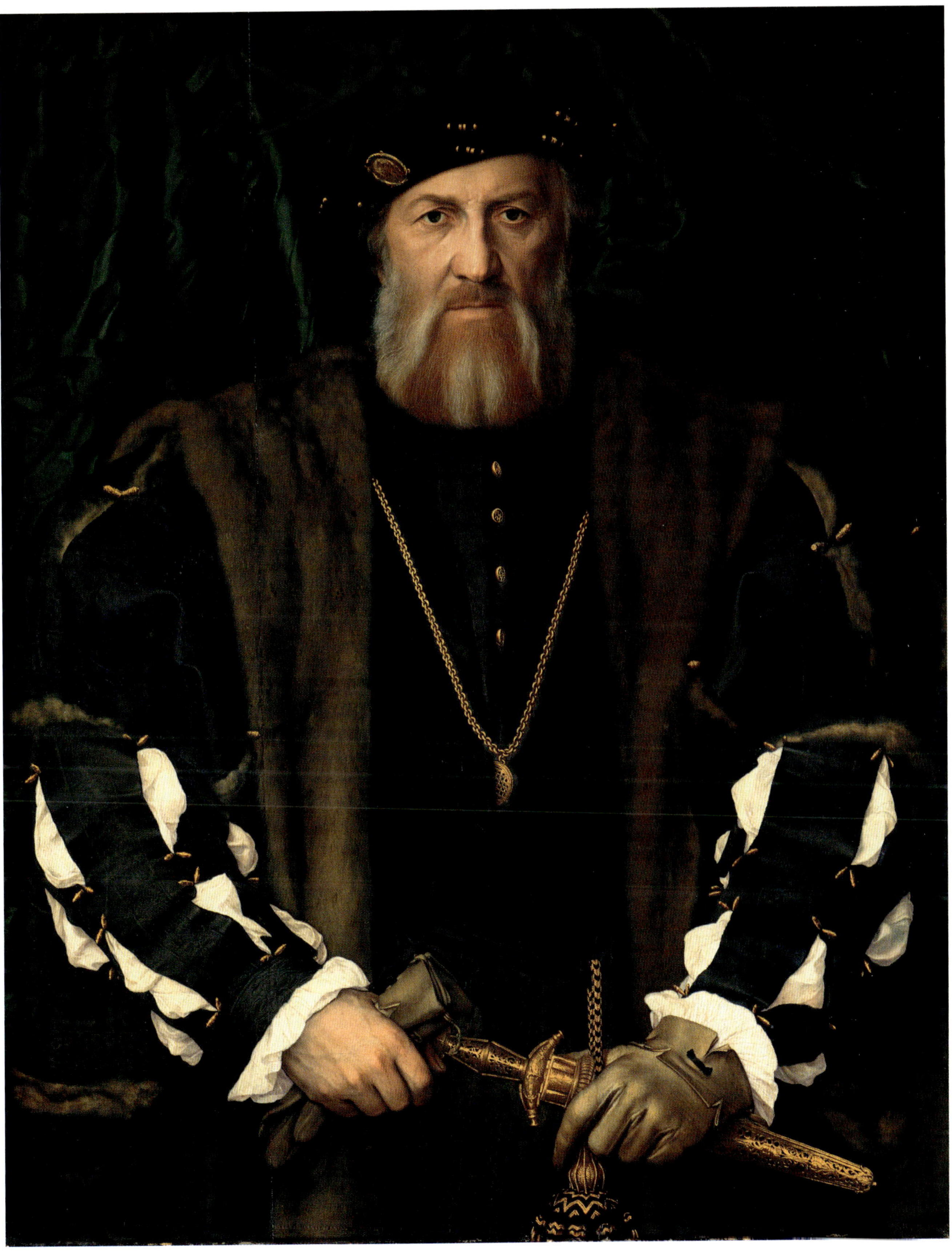

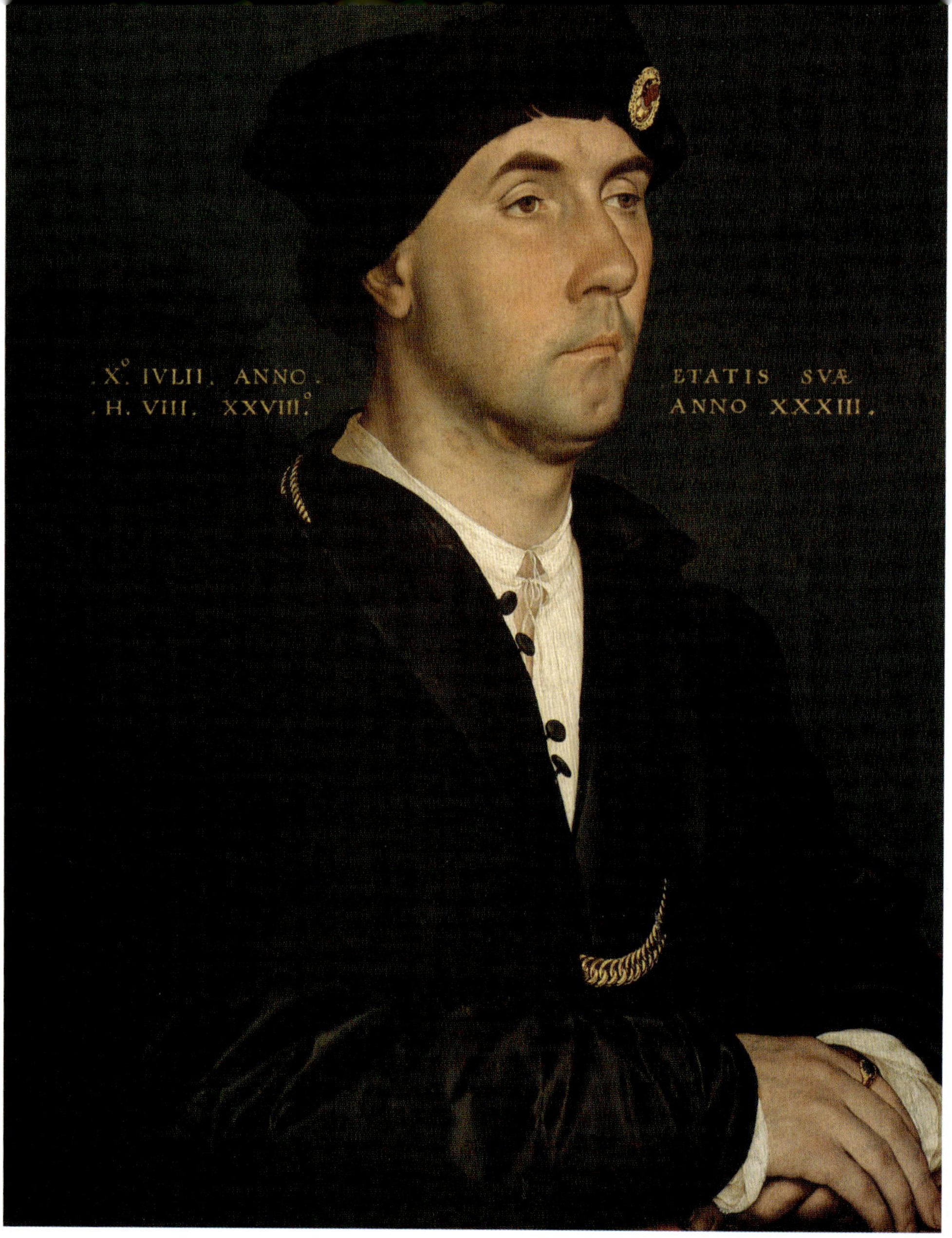

Sir Richard Southwell, 1535–36, resin-tempera on oak, 47.5 x 38cm (18.7 x 14.9in), Gallerie degli Uffizi, Florence, Italy

Sir Richard Southwell (1503/4–64), a prosperous country squire, was Privy Councillor to King Henry VIII. He was noted at times to be 'haughty and indecisive' and arrogant, which Holbein superbly captures in the glacial facial expression of the sitter. Southwell was known to side with those who would accelerate his position and drop associates, such as Henry Howard, Earl of Surrey, and Sir Thomas More, when they were ostracised by the king. Holbein captures Southwell's notable physical features, including the scars on his forehead and neck, the yellowish-brown colour of his eyes, and oily skin.

The painting is inscribed: X.IVLII. ANNO./.H.VIII.ETATIS SVAE/ANNO XXXIII, the relevance of the dates not known.

Drawing of Sir Richard Southwell, 1535–6, chalk with pen and ink and metalpoint on paper, 36.6 x 27.7cm (14.4 x 10.9in), Royal Collection Trust, UK

A preparatory study for a painting of Richard Southwell, aged thirty-three, the year he was appointed Receiver of Augmentations. Holbein made notes on the drawing, observing that Southwell had scars on his neck, and 'the eyes a little yellowish' ('Die augen ein wenig gelbatt'). A Norfolk landowner, Sir Richard Southwell was a Member of Parliament and a Justice of the Peace.

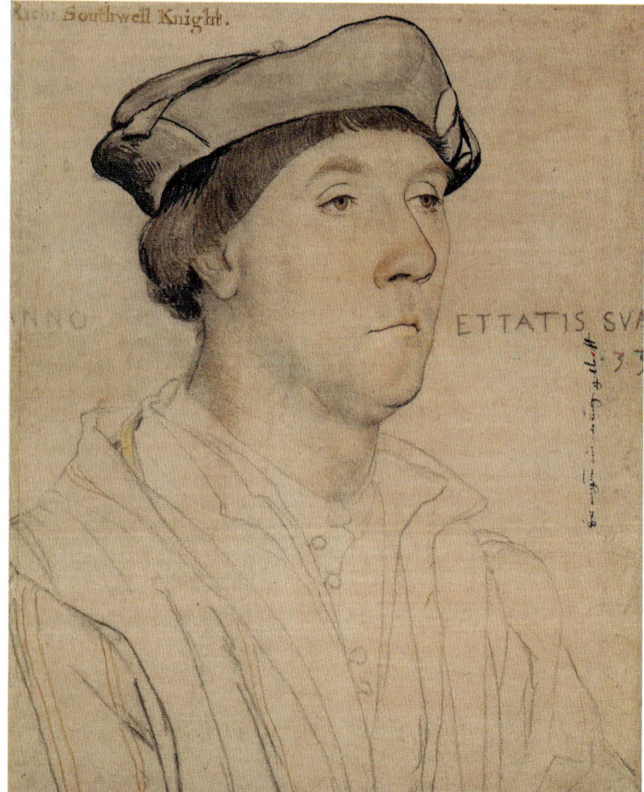

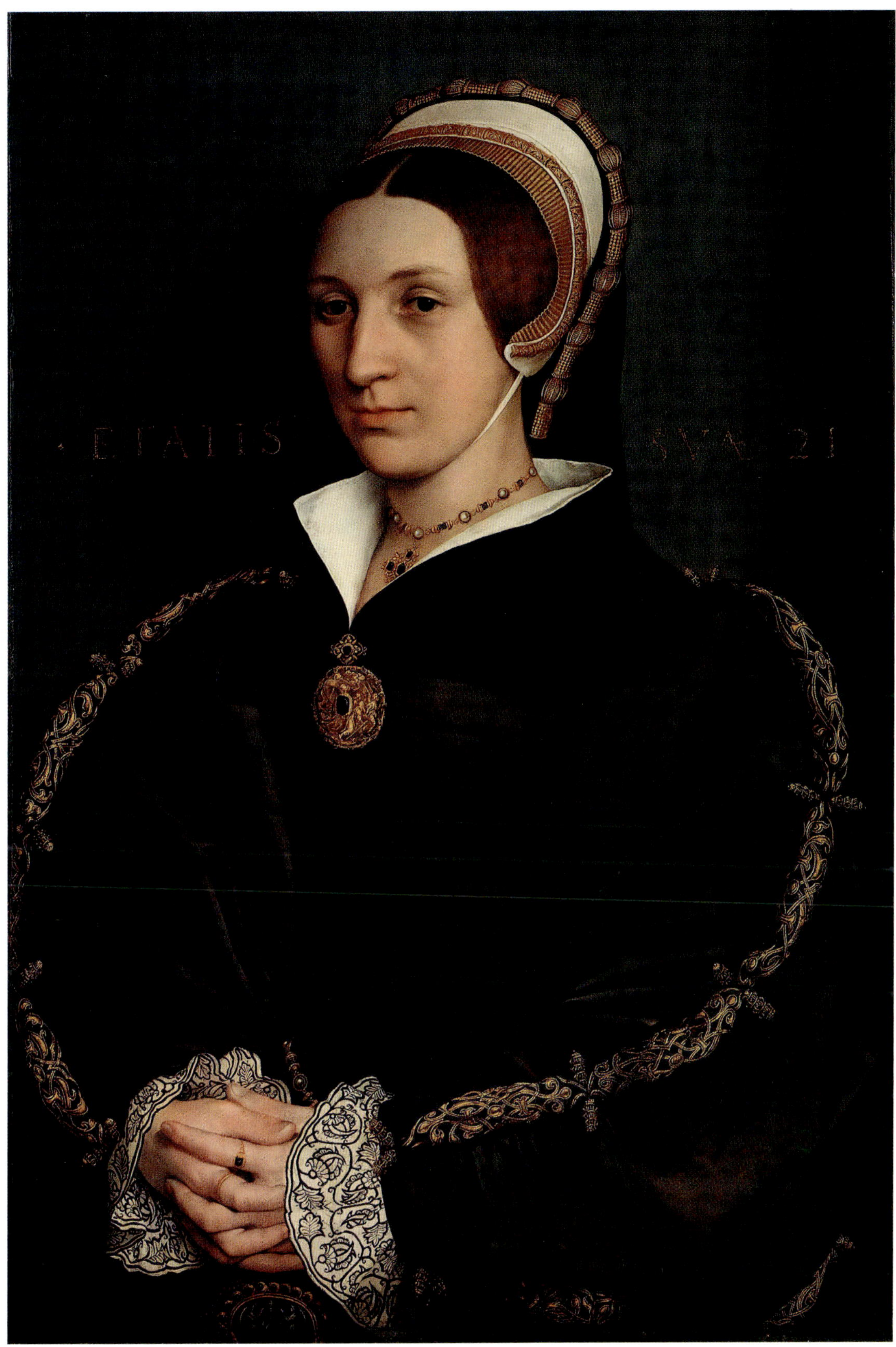

Portrait of a Lady, c.1535—40, oil on wood, 72.1 x 49.5cm (28.4 x 19in), Toledo Museum of Art, Ohio, USA

The sitter's identity is not given, though her age, twenty-one, is inscribed in gold on the painting. The painting belonged to the Cromwells for centuries, so she was probably a member of that prominent family. It has been suggested that she may be Elizabeth Seymour, daughter-in-law of Henry's powerful government minister Thomas Cromwell and sister of Henry's third wife, Jane Seymour.

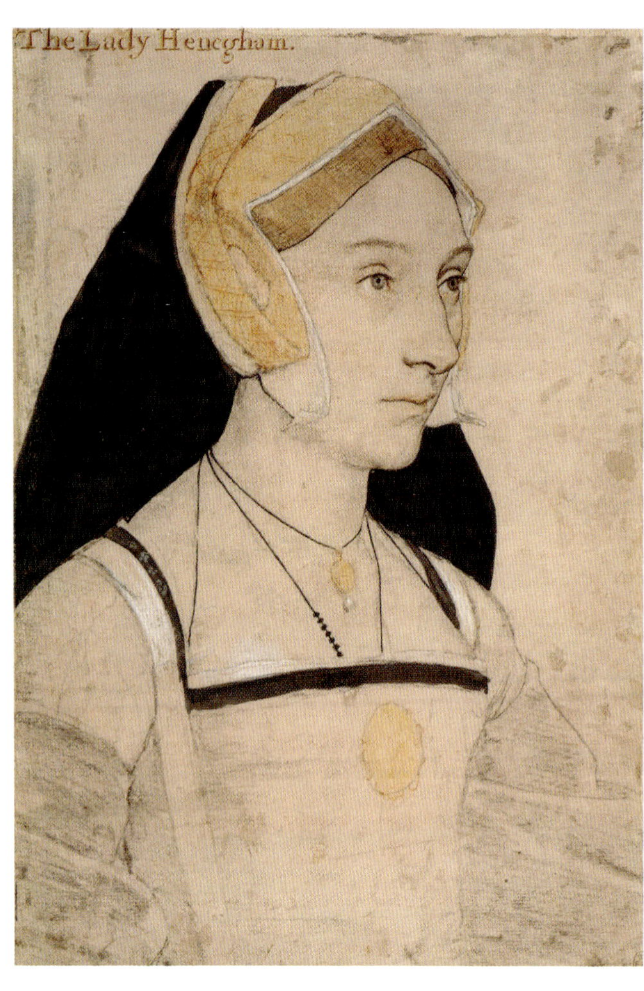

Study of Mary, Lady Heveningham, c.1532–43, black and coloured chalks, white bodycolour, pen and ink, and brush and ink on pale pink prepared paper, 30.3 x 21.1cm (11.9 x 8.3in), Royal Collection Trust, UK

A preparatory bust-length portrait drawing in three-quarters profile to the left, of Mary Shelton, daughter of Sir John Shelton, and wife of Sir Anthony Heveningham. She wears a fashionable headdress, medallion, pendant and necklace. There is no known painted portrait from this work. A cousin of Anne Boleyn, she attended the queen at court. Mary Shelton was a noted poet.

Study of William Parr, 1st Marquess of Northampton, c.1538–40, black and coloured chalks, white bodycolour, pen and ink, and brush and ink on pale pink prepared paper, 31.7 x 21.2cm (12.4 x 8.3in), Royal Collection Trust, UK

This bust-length drawing of William Parr (1513–71), in three-quarter profile to the sitter's right, wears a fur-edge robe, a medallion, and a hat ornamented with badges. The drawing stands out for the many notes and sketches made on it by Holbein – references to the sitter's attire, and jewelled accessories: 'wis felbet' (white velvet), 'burpor felbet' (purple velvet), 'wis satin' (white satin), 'w' (for weiss, white) five times, 'Gl' (gold) twice, 'gros' (size) and 'MORS' (death). William Parr, made Marquess of Northampton in 1546, was in the service of Henry Fitzroy, the illegitimate son of Henry VIII, and was the brother of the king's sixth wife Katherine Parr.

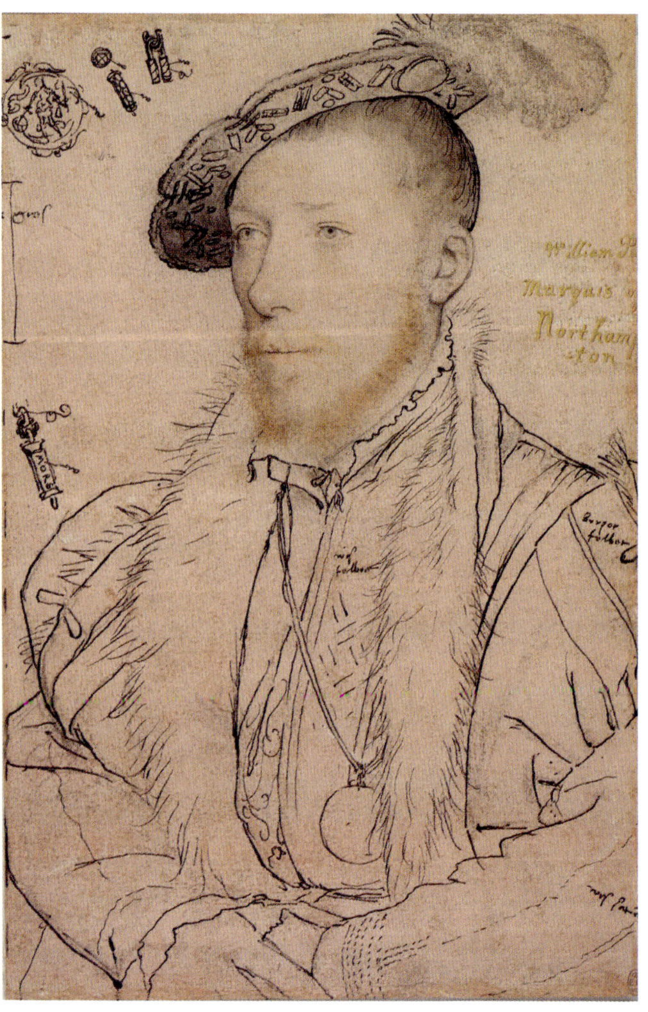

Study of Nicholas Bourbon, 1535, black and coloured chalks, and pen and ink on pale pink prepared paper, 30.8 x 25.9cm (12.1 x 10.1in), Royal Collection Trust, UK

Nicholas Bourbon (c.1503–49/50) was a French scholar and poet. He arrived in England in 1535, becoming part of the inner circle of King Henry VIII's court. Holbein depicts him as a scholar, in the process of writing. It was Bourbon who referred to Holbein as the 'Apelles' of painting, a complimentary reference to the revered ancient Greek painter.

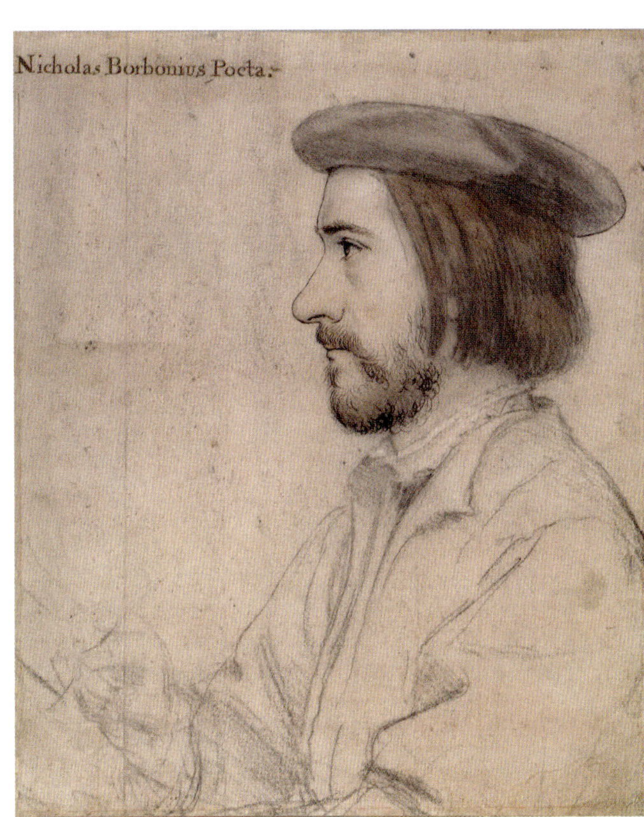

Below: *Study of Sir William Sharington*, c.1540, black and coloured chalks, pen and ink, and metalpoint, on pale pink prepared paper, 15.4 x 23.3cm (6.1 x 9.2 in), Royal Collection Trust, UK

Sir William Sharington, or Sherington, MP (c.1495–1553), of Cranworth, Norfolk. By 1539 he was Page of the King's Robes, subsequently promoted to Groom of the King's Robes, Page of the Privy Chamber, and Groom of the Chamber. In 1544 he joined the household of Queen Katherine Parr. Later he was made Vice-Treasurer of the Mint, and Sheriff of Wiltshire.

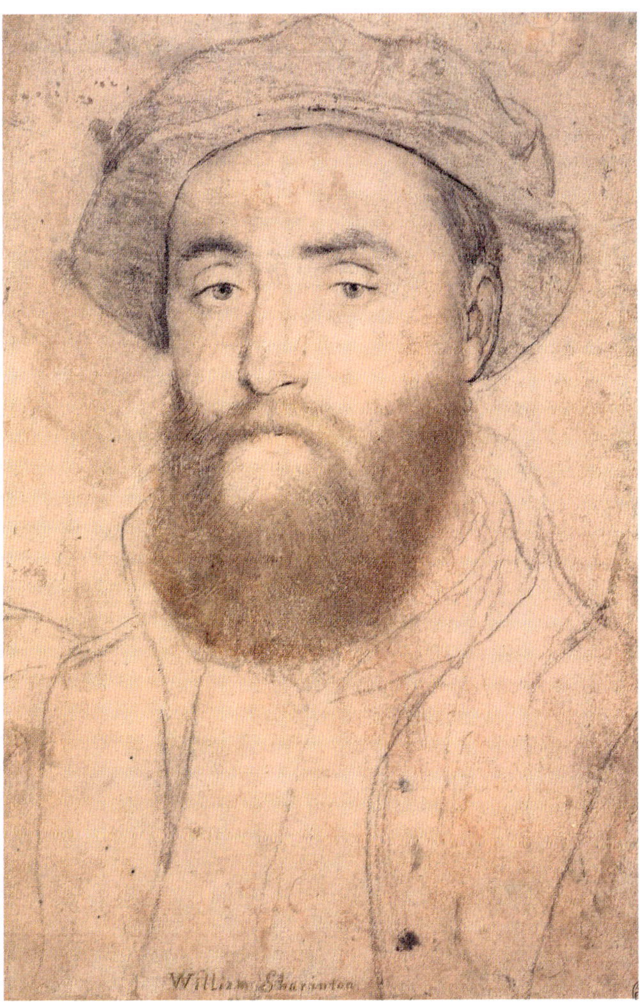

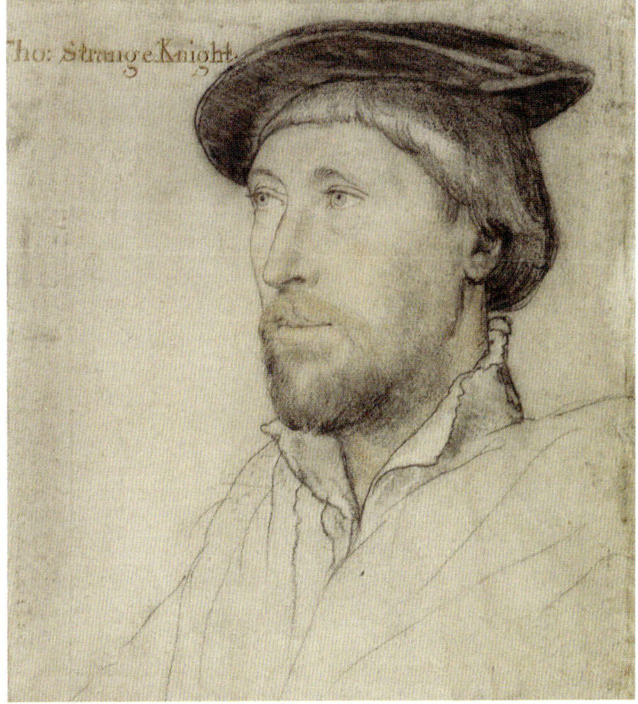

Above: *Study of Sir Thomas Lestrange*, c.1536, black and coloured chalks, pen and ink, and metalpoint, on prepared paper, 24.3 x 21.0cm (9.5 x 8.2in), Royal Collection Trust, UK

A bust-length drawing of Sir Thomas Lestrange (c.1490–1545), facing three-quarters to his right. Several paintings were created from this study of Lestrange, who was Squire of the Body to King Henry VIII, an important role.

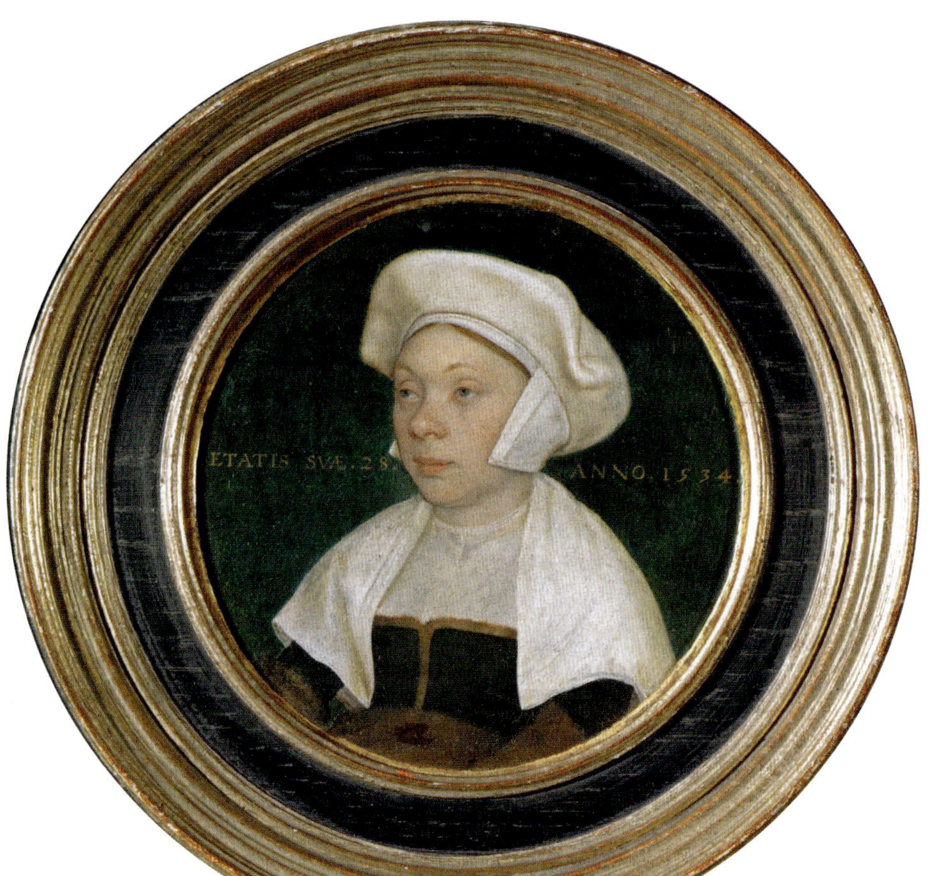

Wife of Courtier of Henry VIII, 1534, oil on lime wood, 11.8cm (4.6in) diameter, Kunsthistoriches Museums, Vienna, Austria

A companion miniature portrait of the wife of a courtier at the court of Henry VIII (see below). She wears a white headdress and chemise, similar in style to *Woman in a White Coif* (see page 202). The identity of the sitter is unknown. For both husband and wife to be portrayed by Holbein indicates a special position at court, or a special friendship with Holbein.

Courtier of Henry VIII, 1534, oil on lime wood, 11.8cm (4.6in) diameter, Kunsthistoriches Museums, Vienna, Austria

A miniature portrait of a court official and personal servant, possibly a groom, to King Henry VIII. It is inscribed 'AETATIS SVAE 30. ANNO 1534', the age of the sitter and date painted. The portrait is a companion piece to a miniature of the courtier's wife (see above). The sitter wears one of the king's liveries with the initials H R for H[enricus] R[ex], embroidered in black on his red coat; a similar court livery as worn in *Portrait of a Man in a Red Cap* (see page 202).

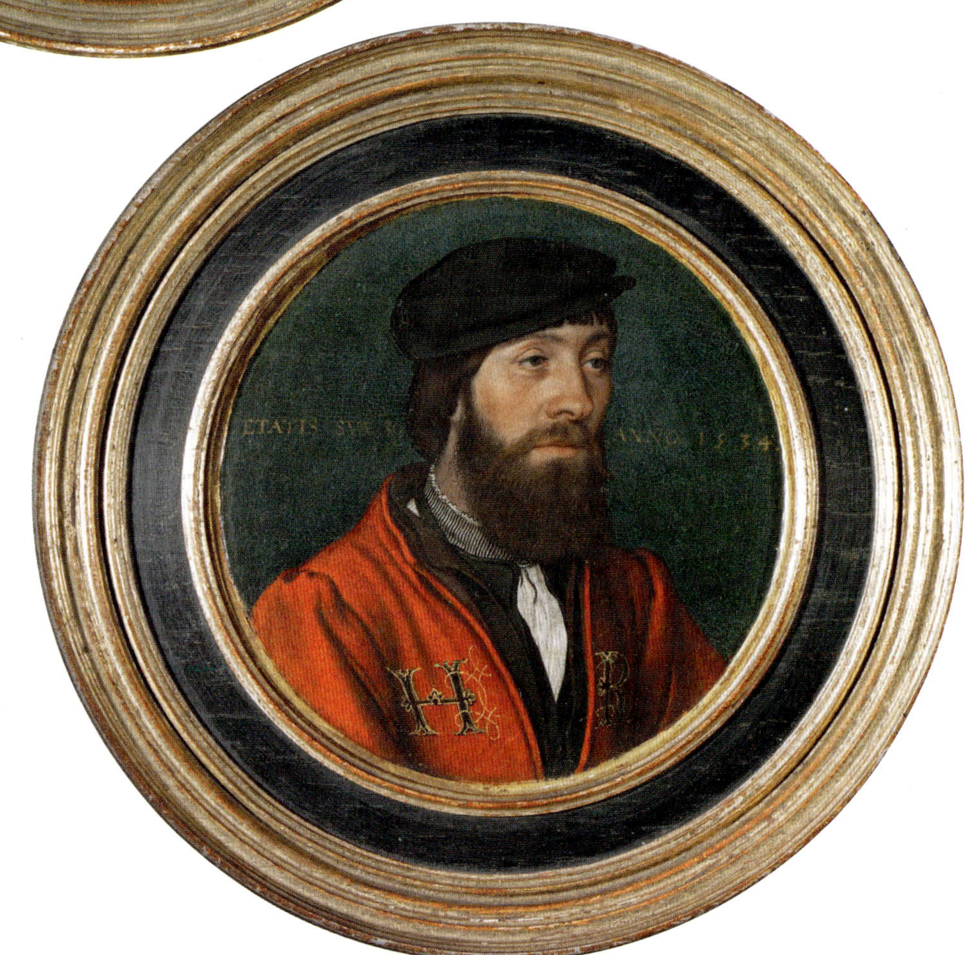

Portrait of William Roper, 1535–36, vellum laid on card, 4.5cm (1.7in) diameter, Metropolitan Museum of Art, New York, NY, USA

William Roper (b.1493/4), a lawyer and Member of Parliament, was a successful landowner in Kent. His marriage in 1521 to Margaret More, eldest daughter of Sir Thomas More, allowed him to become a close member of the family. In 1557 he wrote a sympathetic account of life in the More household, *Lyfe of Sir Thomas Moore*.

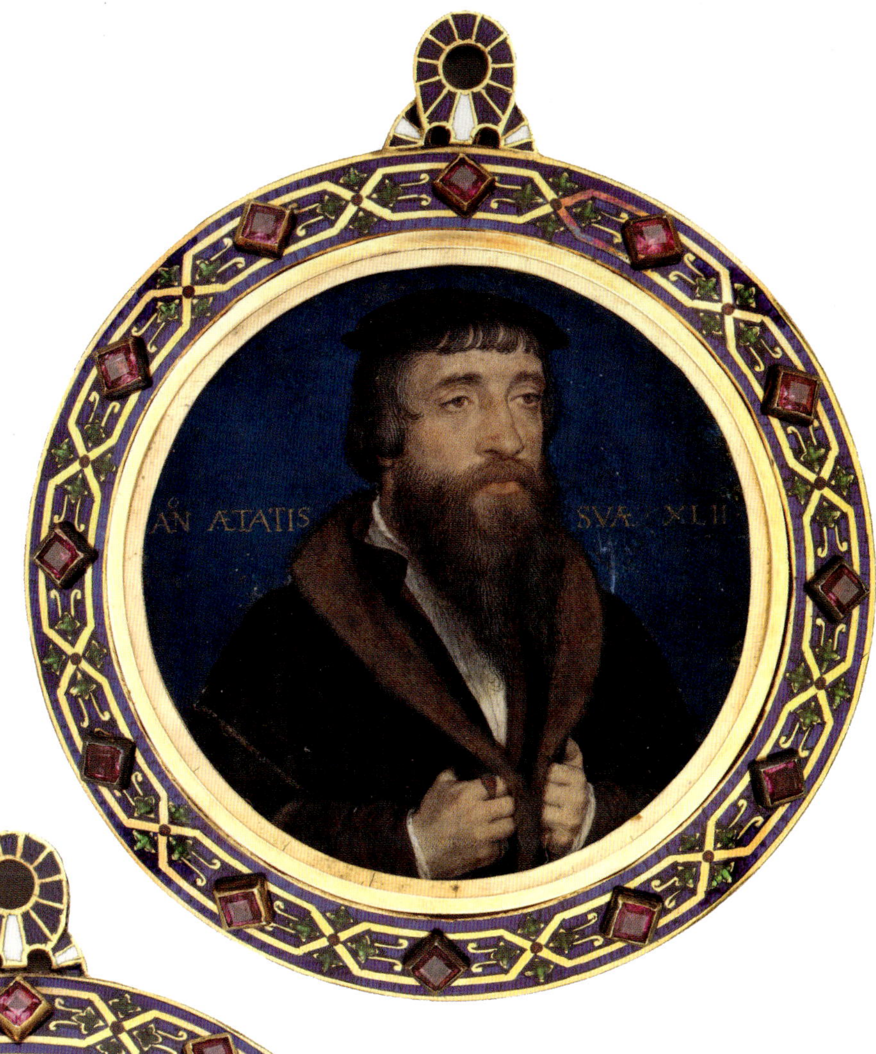

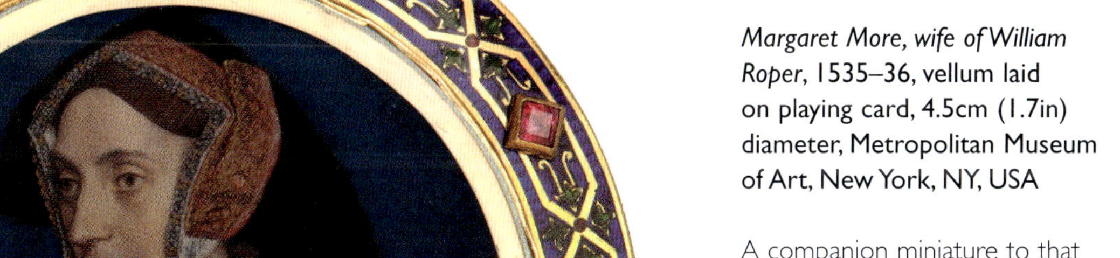

Margaret More, wife of William Roper, 1535–36, vellum laid on playing card, 4.5cm (1.7in) diameter, Metropolitan Museum of Art, New York, NY, USA

A companion miniature to that of her husband, this portrait of Margaret Roper (1505–44) née More, eldest daughter of Sir Thomas More, is thought to have been painted shortly after her father's execution. She married William Roper in 1521.

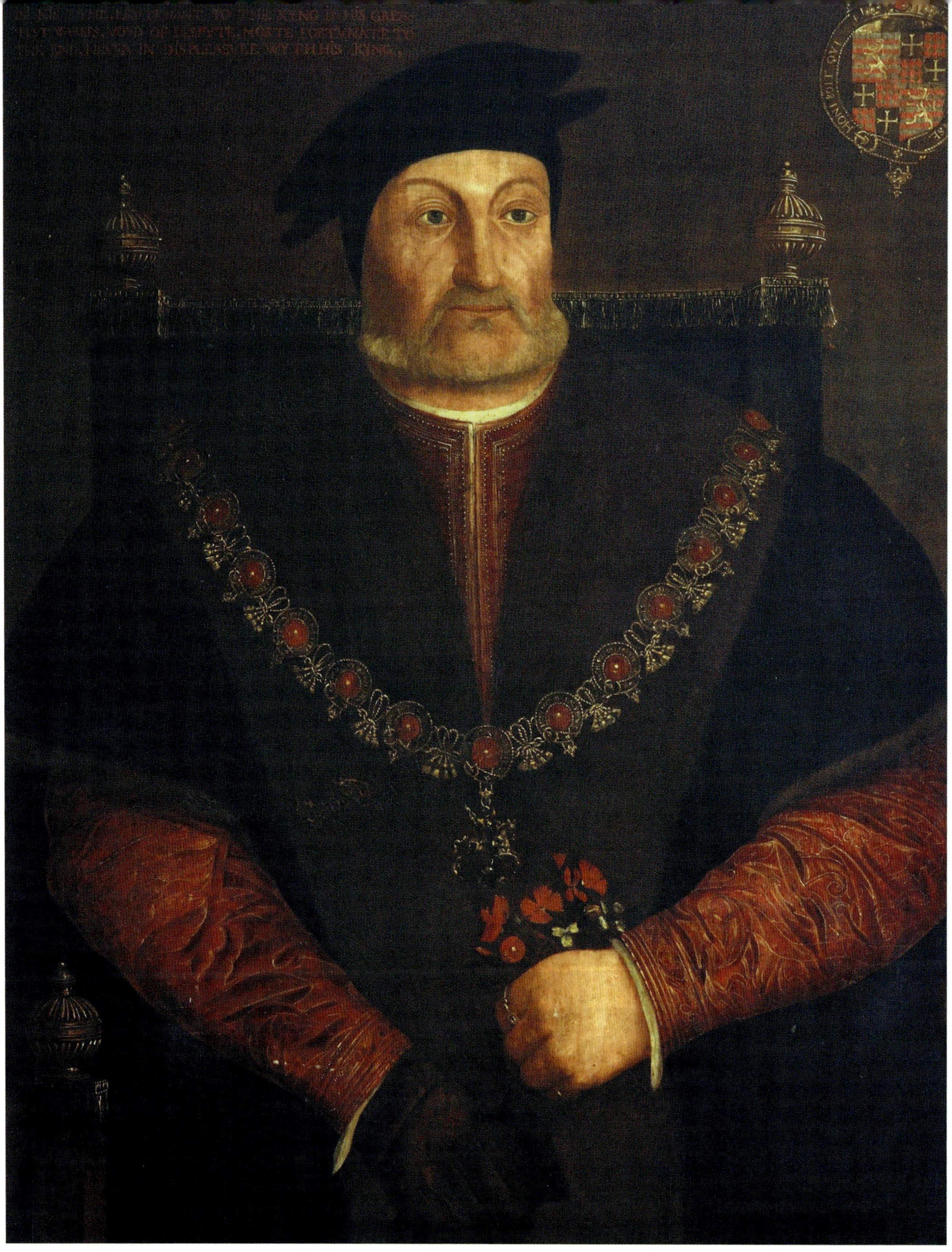

Charles Brandon, 1st Duke of Suffolk (1484–1545), after an original by Hans Holbein the Younger, artist unknown, tempera on wood, 90 x 72cm (35.4 x 28.3in), National Trust, The Vyne, Hampshire, UK

Charles Brandon, 1st Duke of Suffolk, stood out for his brilliance on the jousting field, and in 1512 was made Master of the Horse by Henry VIII, and in 1514, Duke of Suffolk. He had a reputation as being irresistible to women with wives to prove it, including Mary Tudor, the king's half-sister, marrying her without royal permission, in mid-February 1515, just over a month after the death of Mary's husband, the French king Louis XII. Holbein depicted him as regal and handsome, in a three-quarter length portrait.

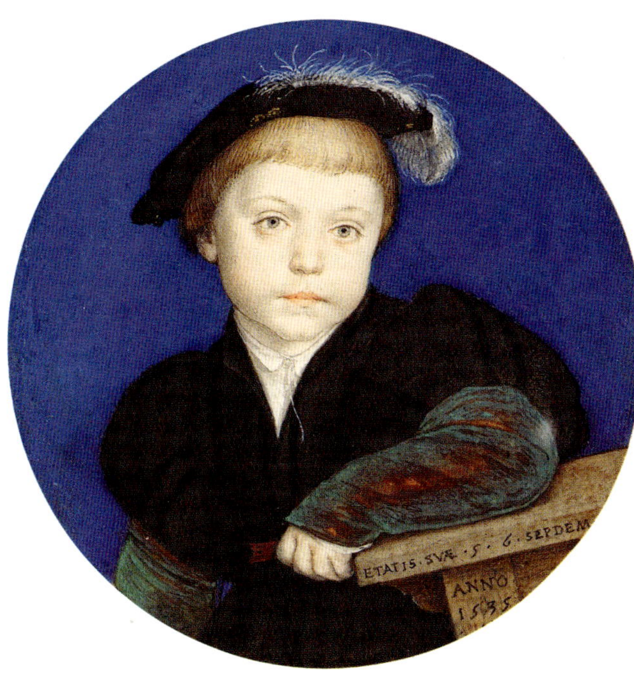

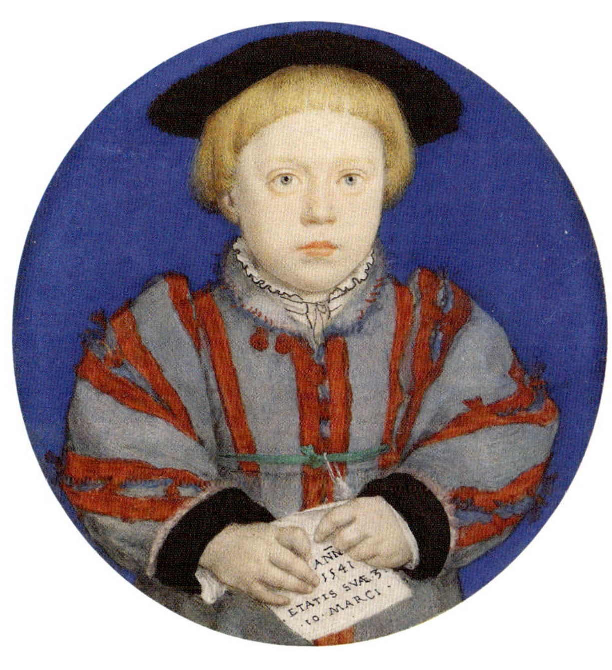

Drawing of Katherine, Duchess of Suffolk, c.1532–43, black and coloured chalks, pen and ink, and brush and ink on pale pink prepared paper, 28.9 x 20.9cm (11.3 x 8.2in), Royal Collection Trust, UK

Katherine Willoughby Brandon (1519–80), Duchess of Suffolk, was Charles Brandon's fourth wife, and mother of Charles and Henry Brandon. In Holbein's bust-length depiction, she faces three-quarters to her right. Her clothing is sparingly illustrated; most noticeable is an embroidered collar, and a medallion and necklace. Holbein added a note: 'rot' (red) and 'damast' (damask). A later 18th-century hand has written 'Dutchefs of Suffolk'.

Henry Brandon (1535–51), c.1541, watercolour on vellum laid on playing card, 5.6cm (2.2in) diameter, Royal Collection Trust, UK

A companion miniature portrait to that of Charles Brandon, Henry Brandon's younger brother (below), both rare portraits of children by Holbein, except for his own children, and the children of Henry VIII. This is one of around twenty miniature portraits created by the artist. His gift for capturing likeness in miniature is superb.

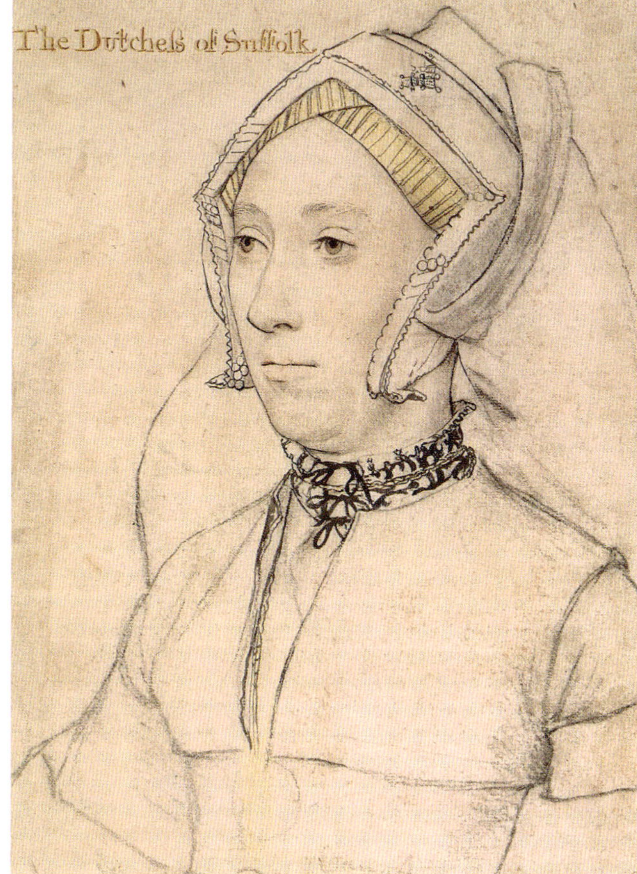

Charles Brandon (1537/8–51), c.1541, watercolour on vellum laid on playing card, 5.6cm (2.2in) diameter, Royal Collection Trust, UK

This is a portrait miniature companion to Henry Brandon, both sons of Charles Brandon, 1st Duke of Suffolk and his fourth wife Katherine Willoughby. The first duke's marriage in 1515 to Princess Mary, younger sister of Henry VIII, promoted his status at court. Henry and Charles Brandon were educated with Edward VI. Both Brandon boys died within the same hour in 1551, of sweating sickness.

Right: *Portrait study of Jane Seymour*, 1536

Comparing the study of Jane Seymour with the finished oil painting (opposite) highlights how close the finished work was to Holbein's preliminary drawing. He pays attention to her facial features, her pensive mouth, her clear eyes, and to the elaborate headwear. Other details, such as her hands, and the dress and jewellery, are precisely drawn but with less detail.

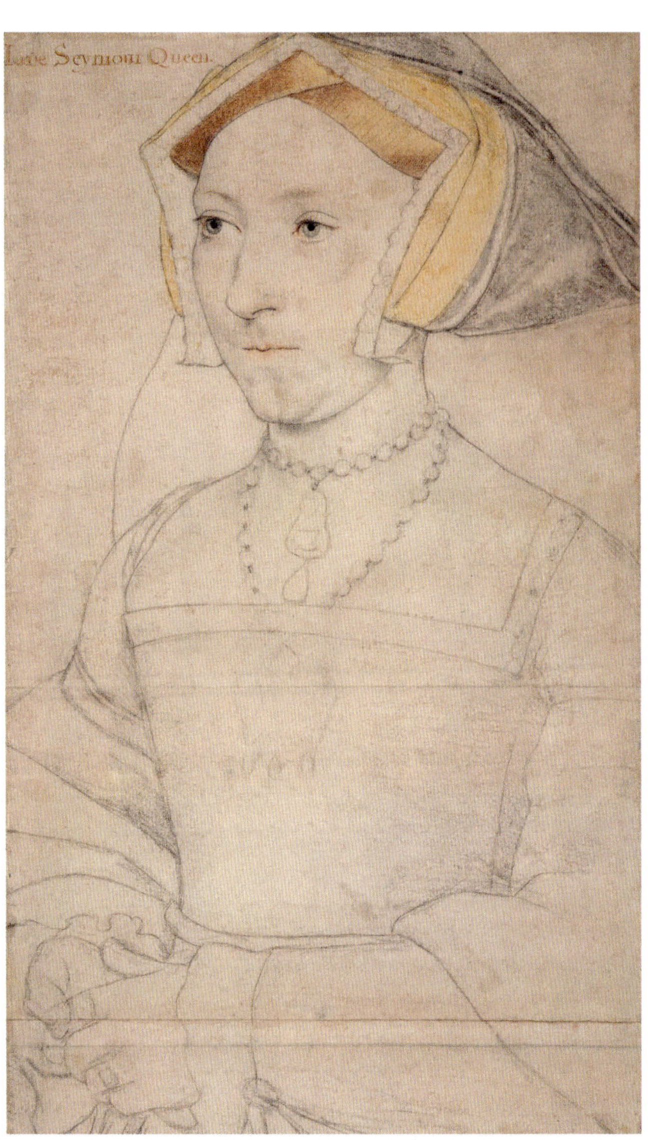

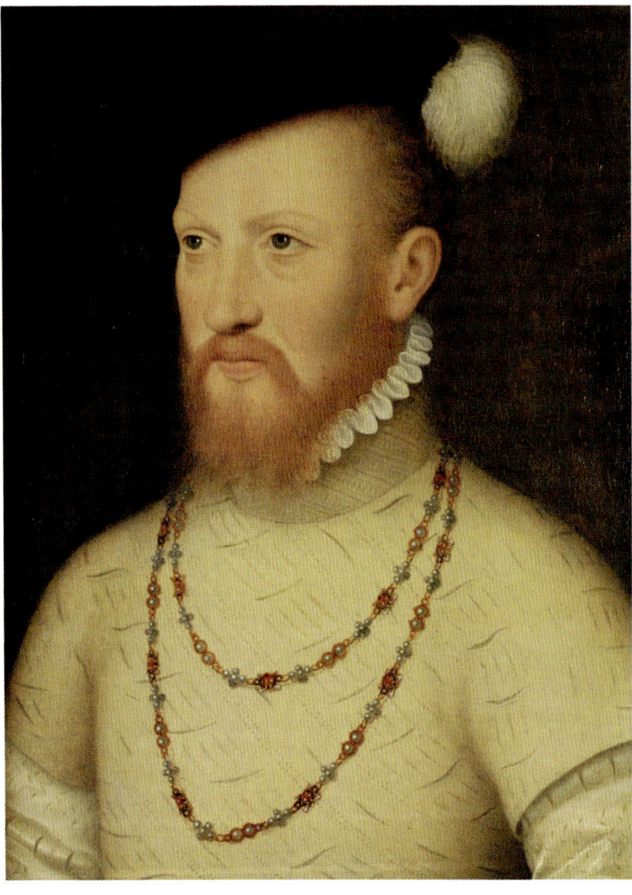

Above: *Sir Edward Seymour,* oil on panel, 31 x 23cm (12.2 x 9in), Weston Park Foundation, UK

Sir Edward Seymour (c.1506–52), later Duke of Somerset, was brother of Jane Seymour, uncle of Edward VI and Lord Protector after Henry VIII's death. He was executed in 1552.

Right: *Detail of hands and sleeves, Jane Seymour,* 1536

'Blackwork' or 'Spanish blackwork', is a form of embroidery using black thread. It was fashionable in England from the time of Katherine of Aragon, Spanish wife and first queen of Henry VIII, who is credited with its introduction. Traditionally blackwork is stitched in silk thread on white or off-white linen with metallic thread often used for accent Here, Jane Seymour wears clothing with beautiful blackwork.

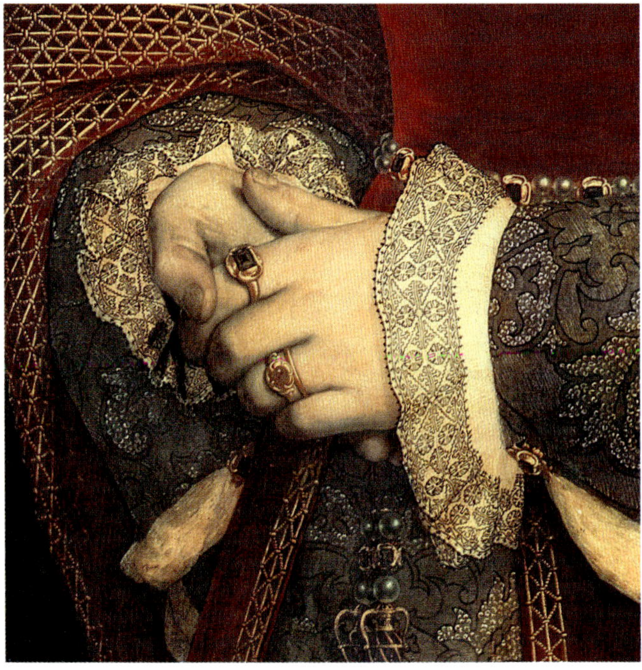

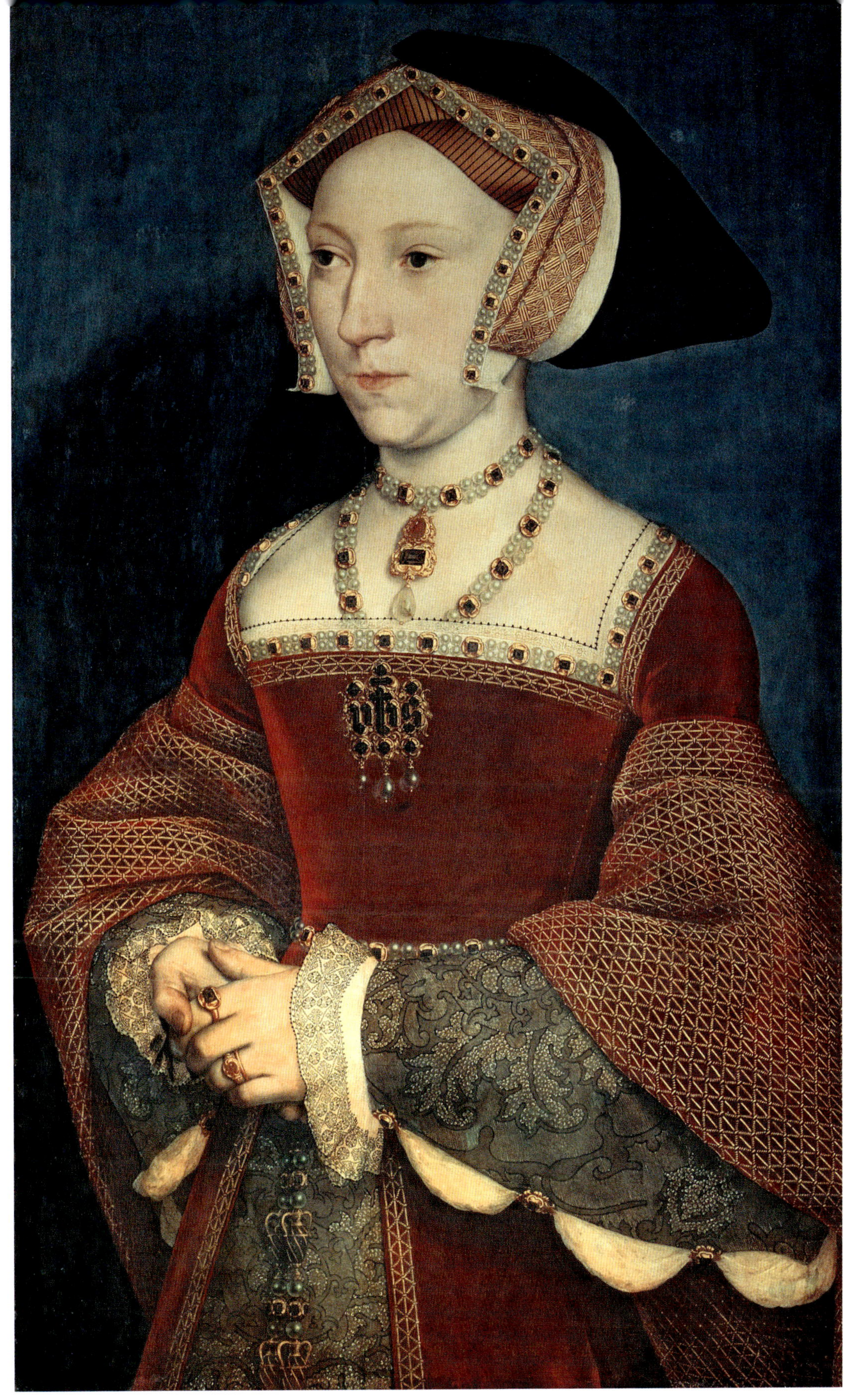

Jane Seymour, 1536–37, oil on panel, 65.4 x 40.7cm (25.7 x 16in), Kunsthistorisches Museum, Vienna, Austria

Jane Seymour (1508/9–37) was Queen Consort of England; third wife of Henry VIII and mother of Edward VI. Holbein depicts Queen Jane in three-quarter profile looking ahead to her right. On a smalt-blue background, the artist draws attention to her fabulous jewels, from the necklace to the ringed fingers of her hands, all set against the warm, rich red of her bodice-shaped velvet dress with blackwork underdress and sleeves. Holbein used silverleaf to prepare the underdress and sleeves.

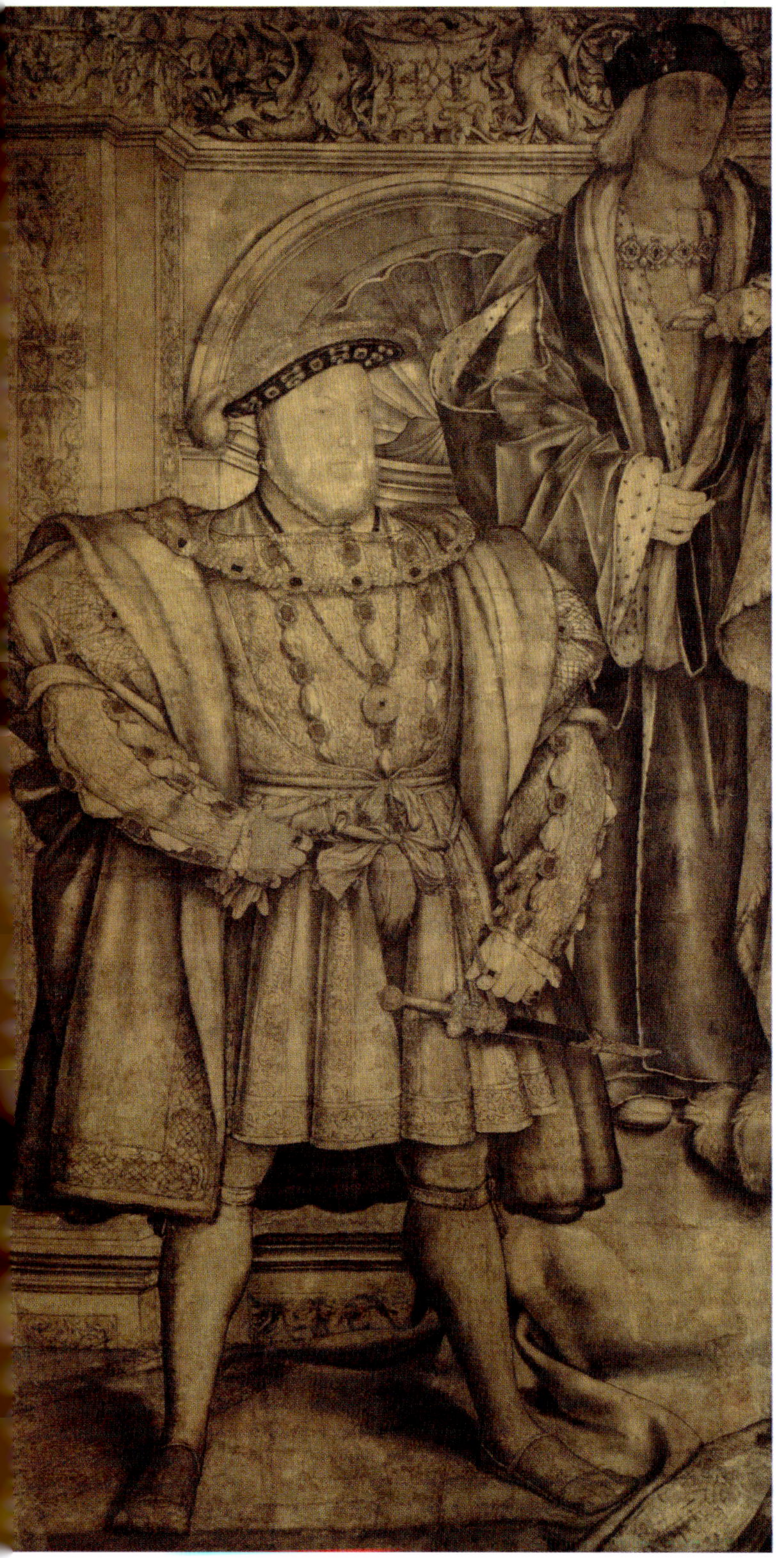

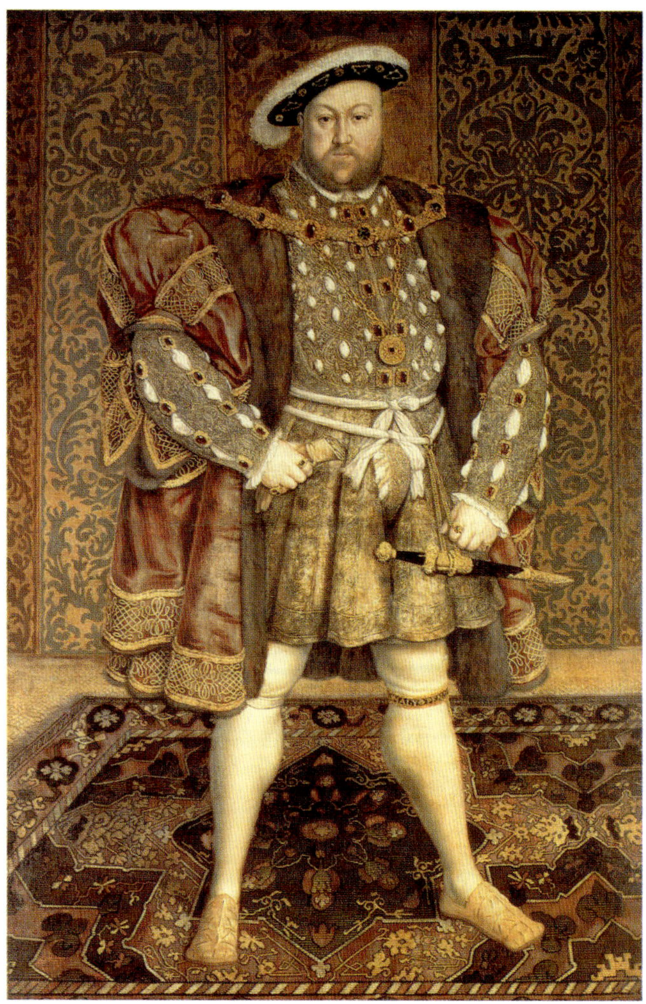

Above: *Portrait of Henry VIII, c.*1537, oil on canvas, workshop of Hans Holbein, Belvoir Castle, Leicestershire, UK

Opposite: *Portrait of Henry VIII,* 1537–47, workshop of Hans Holbein, oil on canvas, 239 x 134.5cm (94 x 53in), Walker Art Gallery, Liverpool, UK

The painting is a near-contemporary copy of Holbein's Whitehall mural of the Tudor dynasty, now isolating Henry VIII from the other royal figures. Many nobles would order copies of paintings of the king; these would be carried out under the artist's supervision, and created from the original drawings, or larger cartoons, by Holbein's highly-qualified assistant painters.

Another copy based on the original wall painting by Holbein, generally considered to be one of the most accurate copies. It was commissioned by Edward Seymour, brother of the late Queen Jane, shortly after the original painting was created.

Above: *Henry VIII,* fragment of a preparatory cartoon, 1536–37, ink and watercolour on paper, National Portrait Gallery, London, UK

This is the only extant work by Holbein's hand of his dynastic Privy Chamber wall mural (see page 78). It depicts Henry with his late father Henry VII behind.

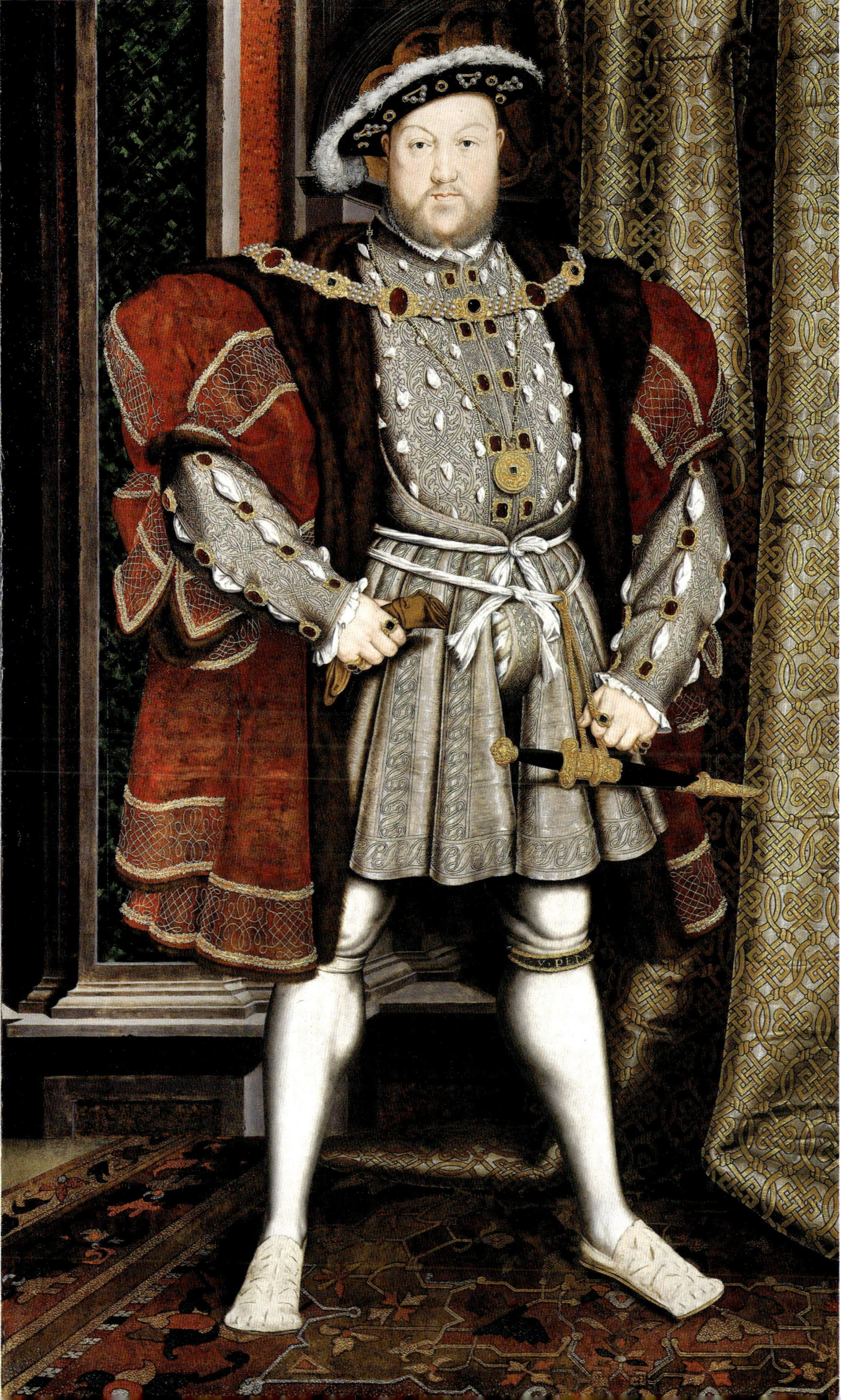

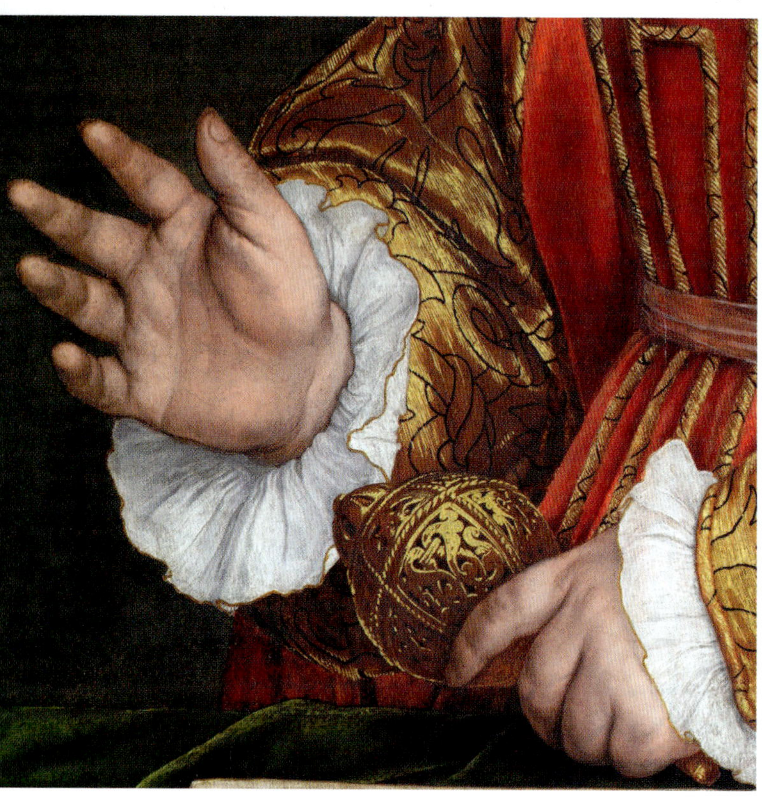

Detail of hands and sceptre rattle, Edward VI, as Prince of Wales, 1538–39

The young prince leans on a parapet, a traditional representation for royal portraits. He holds a tiny rattle 'sceptre' in his left hand, a symbol of the role determined for him as future king. His right hand is raised in the gesture of blessing, mirroring his father as king of England.

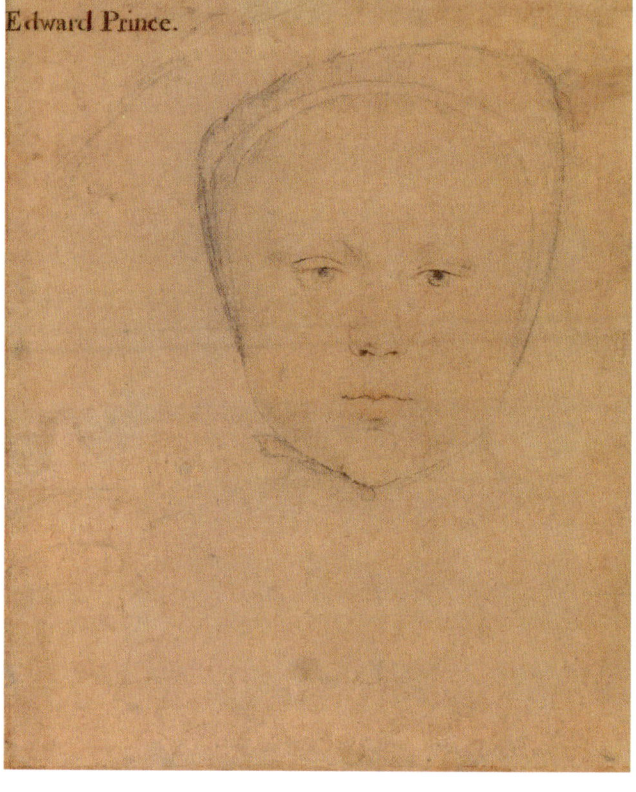

Above: *Portrait study of Edward VI, as Prince of Wales,* 1538, black and coloured chalks, and pen and ink on pale pink prepared paper, 26.4 x 22.4cm (10.4 x 8.8in), Royal Collection Trust, UK

A preparatory unfinished drawing is smaller in size than the finished painting in oils, confirming that Holbein did not use it to transfer an outline to the oak panel. The drawing captures a gentle gaze, clear-set eyes, and expressive concentration.

Left: *Portrait study of Edward, Prince of Wales, c.1540–43,* black and coloured chalks, and pen and ink on pale pink prepared paper, 27.3 x 22.7cm (10.7 x 8.8in), Royal Collection Trust, UK

A later portrait study of Edward, Prince of Wales as a young boy. It is possibly a preparatory drawing for an oil painting. In this head-and-shoulder study, Holbein depicts the child facing front, wearing a cap. It was later inscribed (not by Holbein) 'Edward Prince of Wales'.

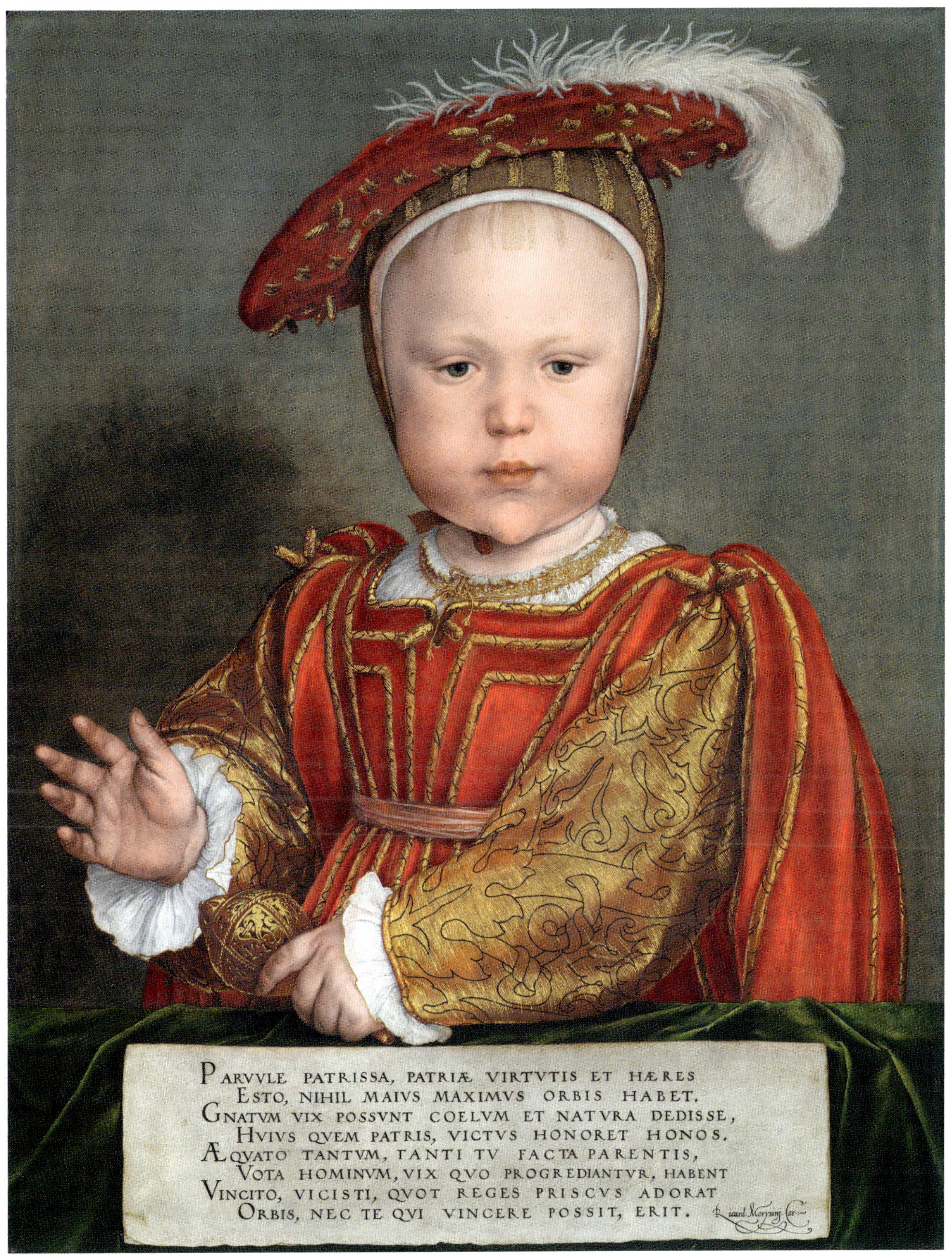

Edward VI, as Prince of Wales, 1538–39, oil on oak, 56.8 x 44cm (22⅜ x 17⁵⁄₁₆in), National Gallery of Art, Washington DC, USA

Edward, Prince of Wales (1537–53), the much-loved son and legitimate heir of Henry VIII and Queen Jane Seymour, was born on 12th October 1537. As a New Year's gift to the king in 1539, Holbein painted a portrait of the infant prince. The acclamatory inscription in Latin below the portrait, composed by the poet Richard Morison, urges the little prince to endeavour to surpass his father.

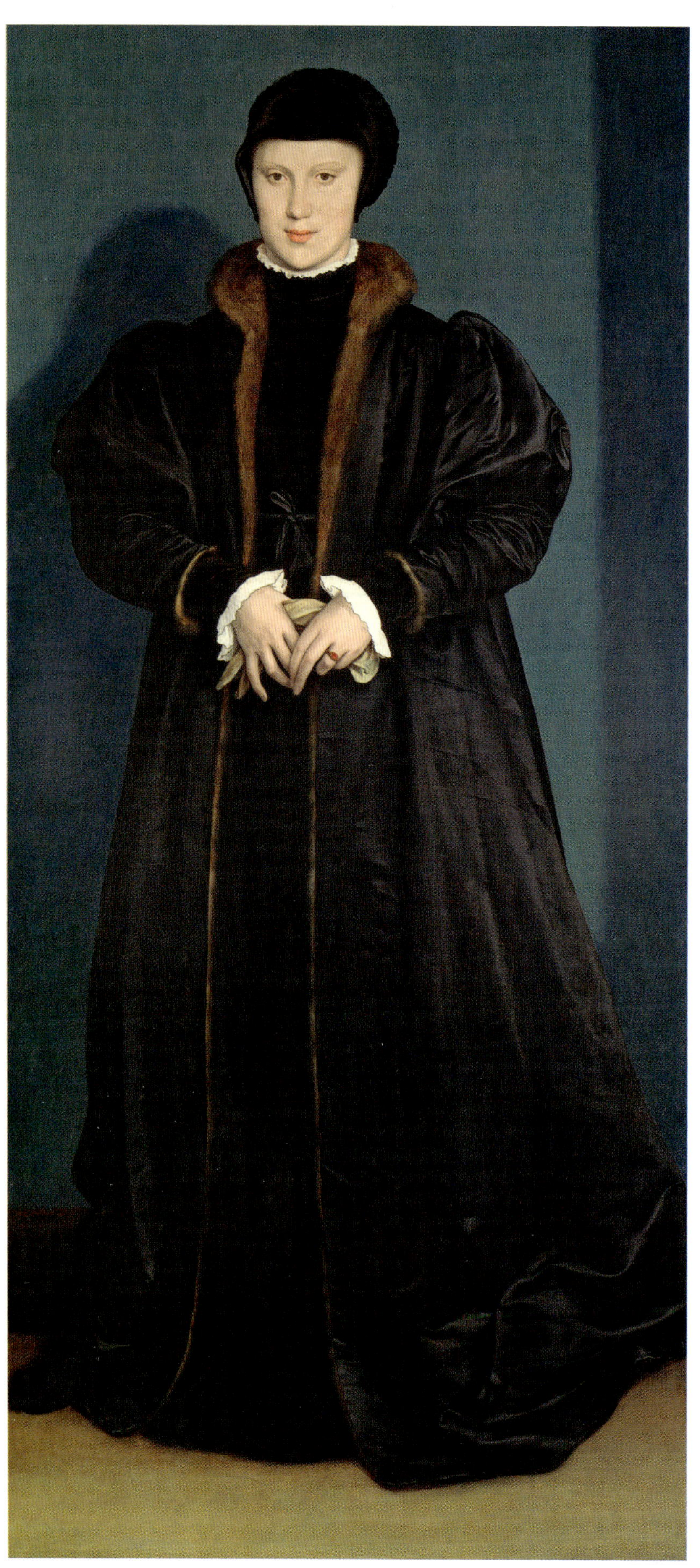

Left: *Christina of Denmark*, 1538, oil on panel, 179.1 x 82.6cm (70.5 x 32.5in), National Gallery, London, UK

Hans Holbein, as court painter to Henry VIII, met 16-year-old Christina of Denmark, Duchess of Milan, in Brussels, on 12th March, 1538. It is said that the sitting lasted only a few hours, from 1–4pm. The series of preliminary drawings Holbein made led to the creation of one of his finest portraits; it has the illusion of her actual presence, but is one that the duchess never saw. She turned down the king's marriage proposal (see pages 86–87) although the king kept her portrait until his death in 1547. The full-length portrayal of Christina captures her finesse and striking beauty; contemporary reports referred to her as 'Very pure, fair of colour she is not, but a mervelous good brownishe face she hathe, with fair red lippes, and ruddy chekes.'

Opposite: *Portrait of Anne of Cleves*, 1539, oil on parchment, mounted on canvas, 65 x 48cm (25.6 x 18.9in), Musée du Louvre, Paris, France

A magnificent three-quarter length portrait of Anne of Cleves, commissioned from Henry VIII, to discover what his future bride (number four) looked like. Holbein painted an interesting woman. The king liked the portrait but on meeting Anne of Cleves, felt he had been duped, calling her a 'fat Flanders mare'. Henry VIII was angry, and Holbein lost prestigious commissions following the king's displeasure. Anne was not crowned Queen Consort as the marriage was annulled.

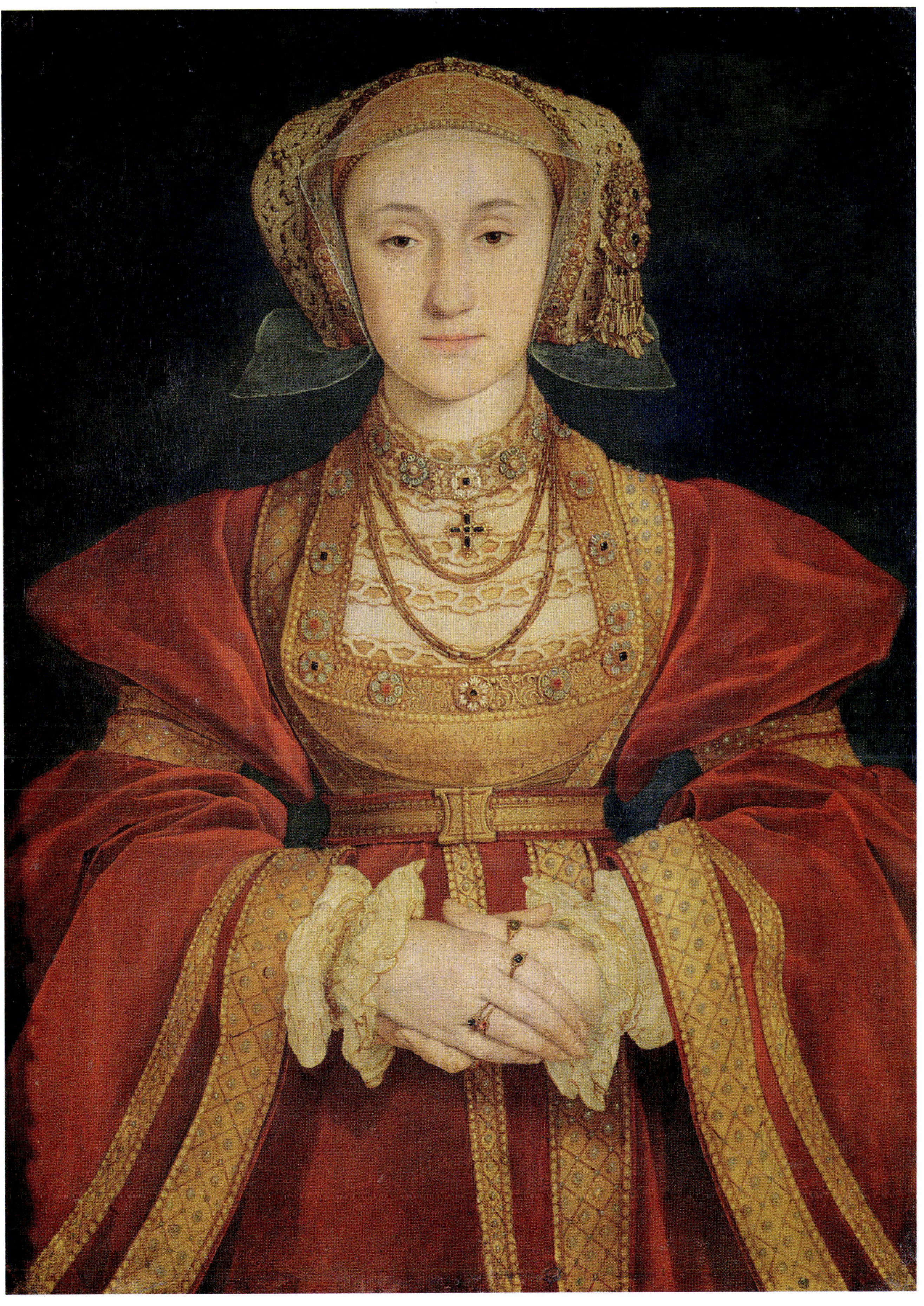

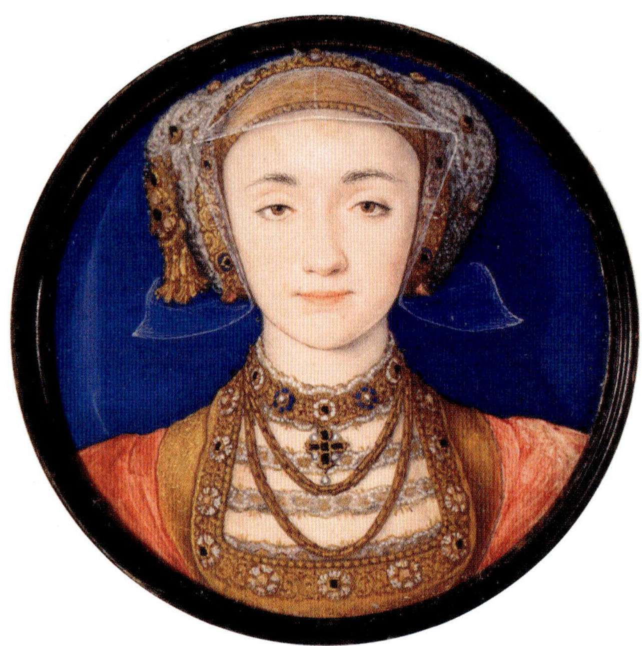

Anne of Cleves, 1539, watercolour on vellum, stuck to a playing card (a court card), 44.5cm (17.5in) diameter, Victoria & Albert Museum, London, UK

A miniature of Anne, the fourth wife of King Henry VIII, who was described by contemporary accounts as both pretty, and as plain. The king did not like her. Holbein focused on facial character and clothing, to create a charismatic depiction. It was his undoing, as his portraits of Anne, in the king's opinion, did not match the lady in person.

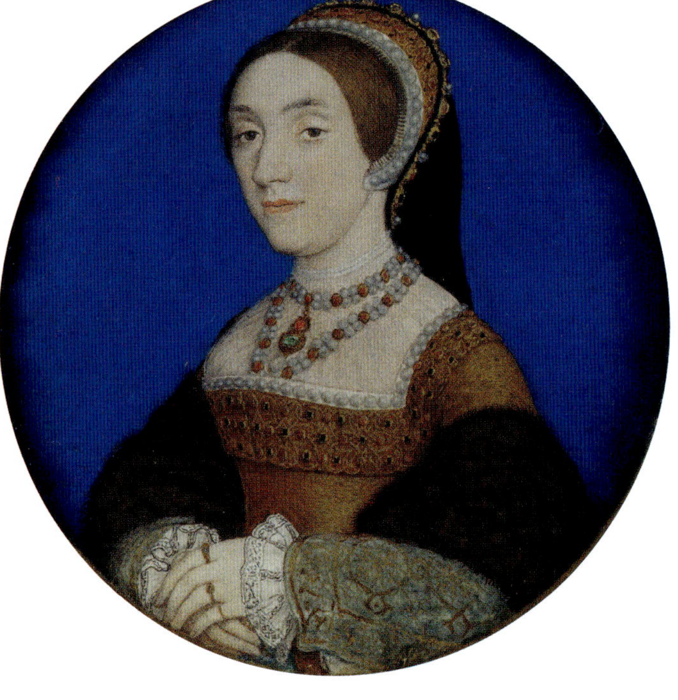

Portrait of a Lady, perhaps Katherine Howard, *c.*1540, watercolour on vellum on playing card (four of diamonds), 6.3cm (2.9in) diameter, Royal Collection Trust, UK

Possibly a portrait miniature of king Henry VIII's fifth wife, Katherine Howard, beheaded after accusations of adultery. The identification of the sitter as Queen Katherine rests on the jewels she wears: a jewelled band closely worn around her neck, possibly a gift from Henry VIII on their marriage in 1540; and a ruby, emerald and pearl necklace, previously worn by the king's third wife Queen Jane Seymour.

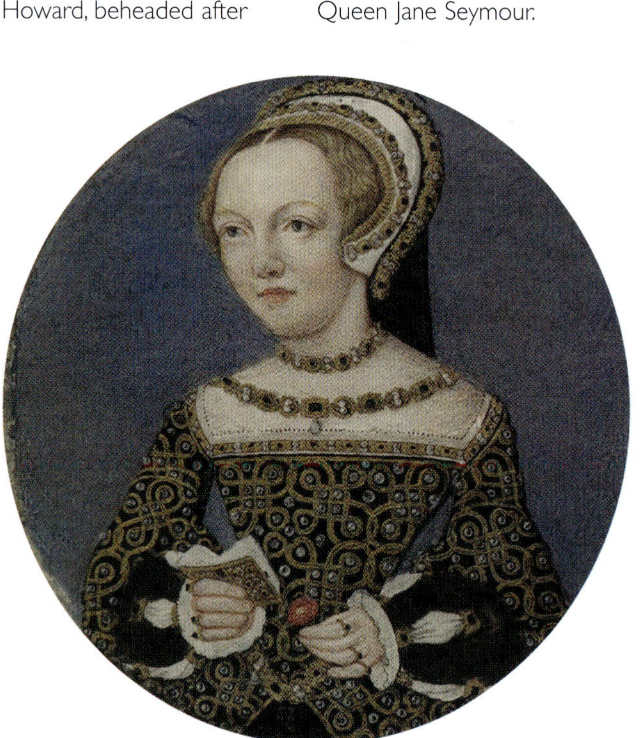

Lady Mary Howard, *c.*1533 (after Holbein the Younger), watercolour on parchment, Nationalmuseum, Stockholm, Sweden

Wearing a fashionable dress with slashed sleeves, this is a portrait of Lady Mary Howard (1519–1557), the daughter of the 3rd Duke of Norfolk, married to Henry VIII's illegitimate son Henry Fitzroy, Duke of Richmond and Somerset in 1533, aged fourteen or fifteen. She was first cousin to Anne Boleyn and Katherine Howard, and second cousin to Jane Seymour.

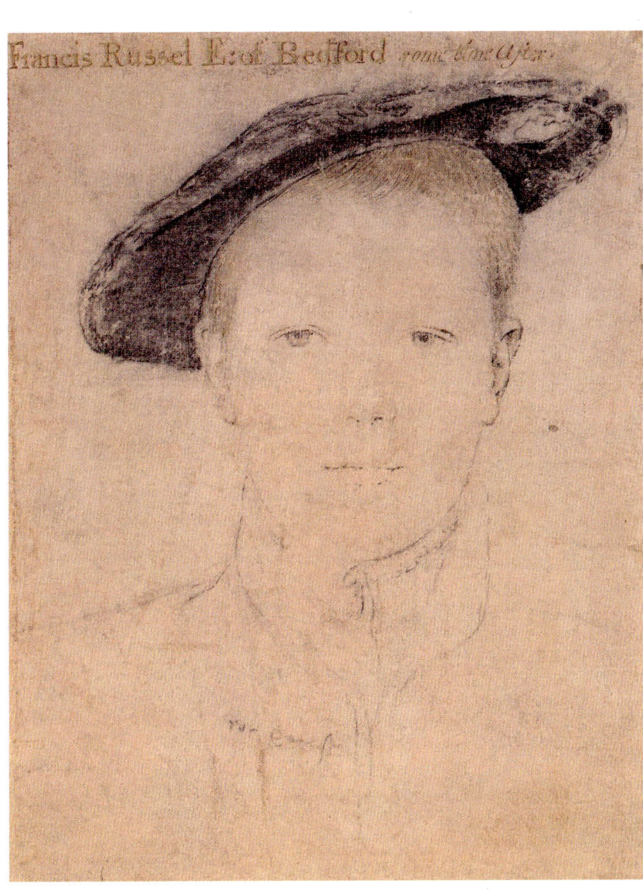

Portrait drawing of Lord Francis Russell, c.1540, black and coloured chalks, and pen and ink on pale pink prepared paper, 23.9 x 17.9cm (9.4 x 7in), Royal Collection Trust, UK

A preparatory head and shoulders portrait drawing of a young boy, facing forward. It is the teenage Lord Francis Russell (1527–85), 2nd Earl of Bedford, son of John Russell, 1st Earl of Bedford. Holbein depicts him in a hat with badges, and makes the note 'rot Damask' (red damask). The painting for which this would be a preliminary drawing is not known. Soon after Russell sat for this work, he served under his father in the French campaign of 1544. In 1547 he was elected as a Member of Parliament.

A *Boy with a Marmoset (also known as Edward VI, Prince of Wales)*, 1542, watercolour, 39.6 x 30.7cm (15.5 x 12in), Kunstmuseum, Basel, Switzerland

A young boy holds his pet, a marmoset. Holbein illustrates the marmoset's distinctive facial features and striped tail. Once considered to be a portrait of Henry's son, due to the composition and affluent clothing, it is now thought to depict another young noble of similar age. He wears opulent velvets and silks, with a flat, bejewelled hat.

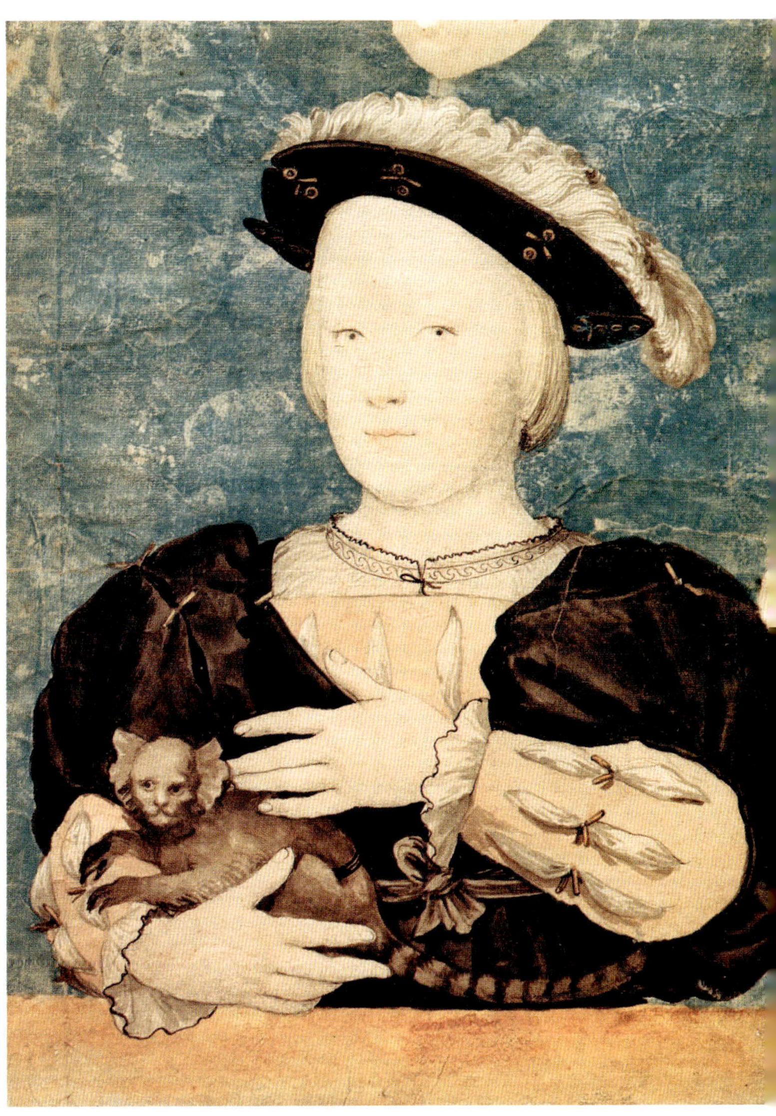

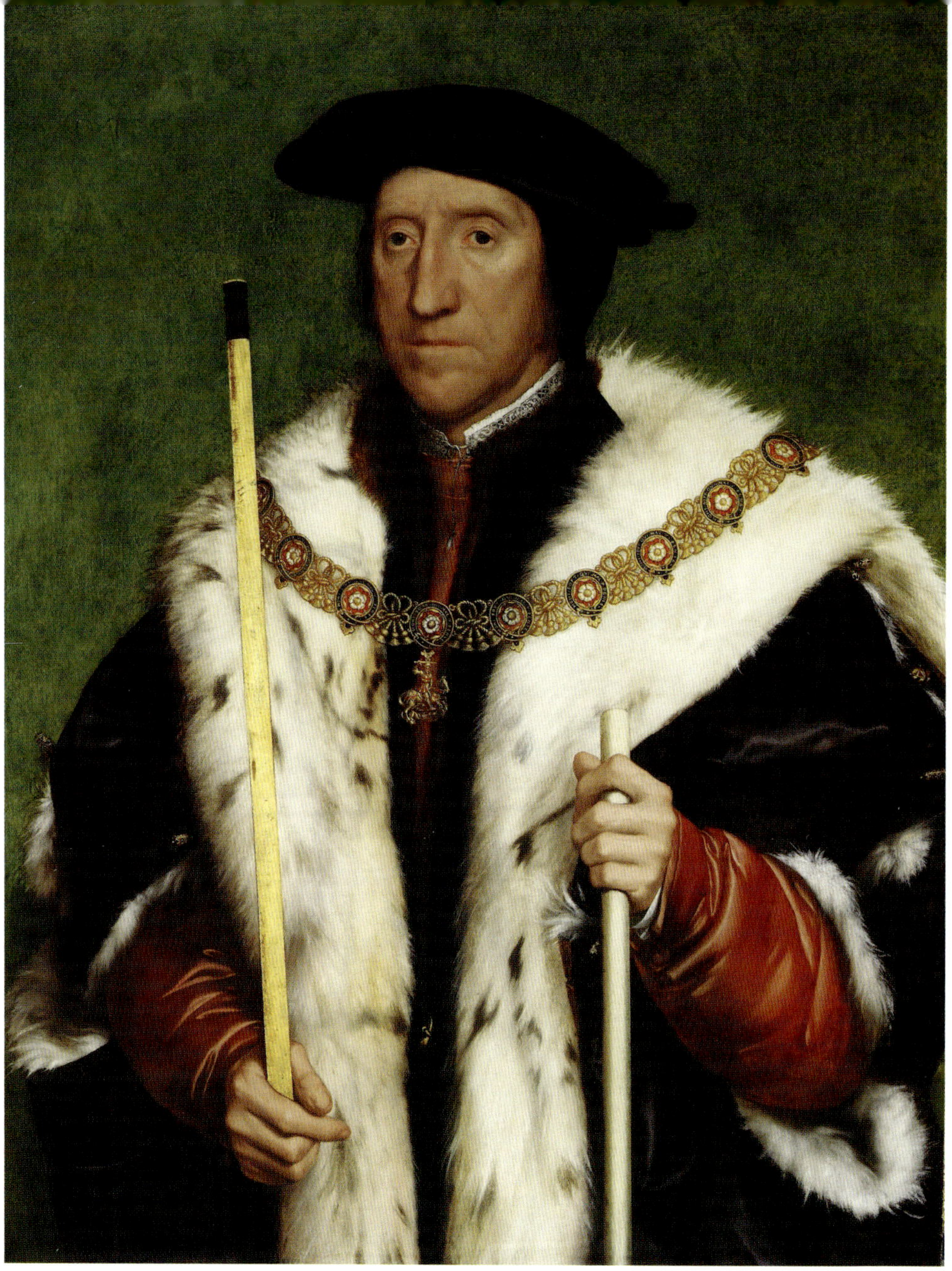

Thomas Howard, 3rd Duke of Norfolk, c.1539, oil on oak panel with gold leaf, 80.1 x 61.4cm (31.5 x 24.1in), Royal Collection Trust, UK

Described as 'small and spare in person' by a Venetian ambassador, Holbein adds grace and stature to Thomas Howard, 3rd Duke of Norfolk's portrayal, in a three-quarter length portrait, a rare format for Holbein, reserved for nobility. The duke wears the royal Order of the Garter, gifted by King Henry VIII in 1510. Howard holds the emblems of his prestigious roles: in his right hand the gold baton of Earl Marshall, and in the left hand, the white staff of Lord High Treasurer. Holbein superbly creates not only the illusion of the sumptuous fabrics and cloak of lynx fur worn by the duke, but the serious expressiveness in Howard's eyes.

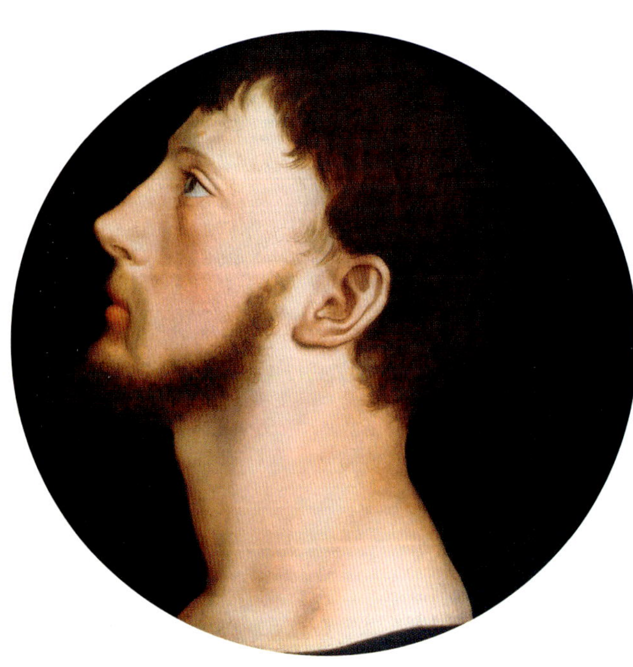

Thomas Wyatt the Younger c.1541–42, oil on circular panel, 32cm (12.6in) diameter, Private Collection

Sir Thomas Wyatt the Younger (1521–1554) was the son of the English poet and ambassador Sir Thomas Wyatt (1503–42). This portrait may have been commissioned by him. A young man at the time of Holbein's death in 1543, Wyatt the Younger's head, facing toward his right, is depicted in profile, looking up toward an unseen light source. From 1543–c.49 he served in the army, mainly in France as a worthy, distinguished officer. A rebellious leader during the reign of Mary I of England, he was beheaded in 1554.

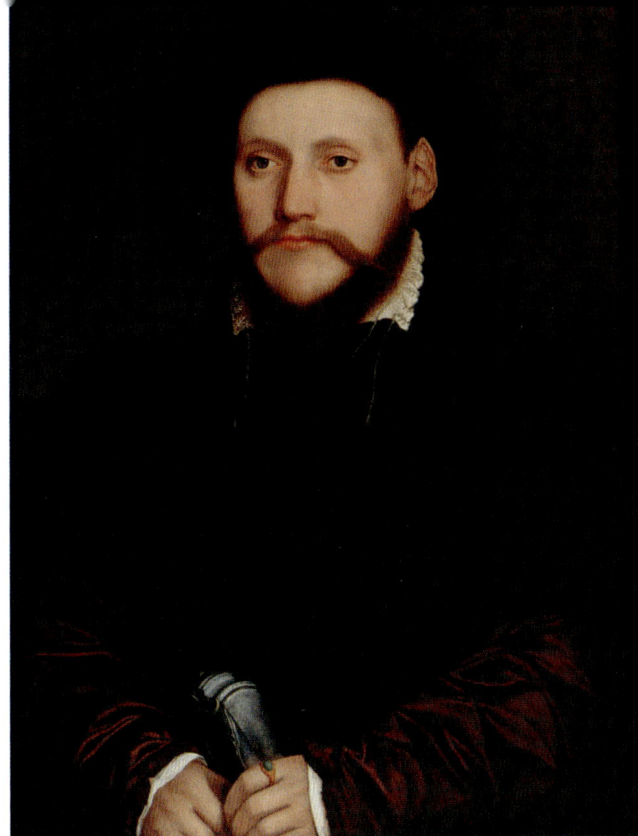

Portrait of an Unknown Man, c.1540–43, oil on tempera on oak panel, Audley End, Essex, England

Dating to the latter years of Holbein's career, the half-length portrait of an unknown young man, possibly a courtier, depicts him facing front, his eyes directed toward his right. An unseen light source highlights his pale, clear skin and auburn hair, with finely trimmed moustache and beard. He is dressed in a furlined black coat with superbly embroidered high-neck shirt just visible. X-radiography has revealed that the gloves were added to the original composition, and the placement of the sitter's hands changed.

Portrait of a Man holding a letter and gloves, c.1540, tempera on wood, 32.2 x 25.4cm (12.6 x 10in), Kunstmuseum, Basel, Switzerland

Holbein scholars are divided on this work, to be attributed, or not, to the artist. The sitter is possibly English or Scots. Depicted in three-quarter profile looking ahead toward his right, he has a full beard with moustache. The fine black robe and hat he wears, denote that he may be a wealthy merchant. He holds leather gloves, with a letter folded around them. It has two lines of writing on it, barely legible. The last line might refer to the surname 'Primrose', Members of a Primrose (Prymrose) family had resided in Trunch, Norfolk, England since the medieval era, but he is not confirmed to be a relative.

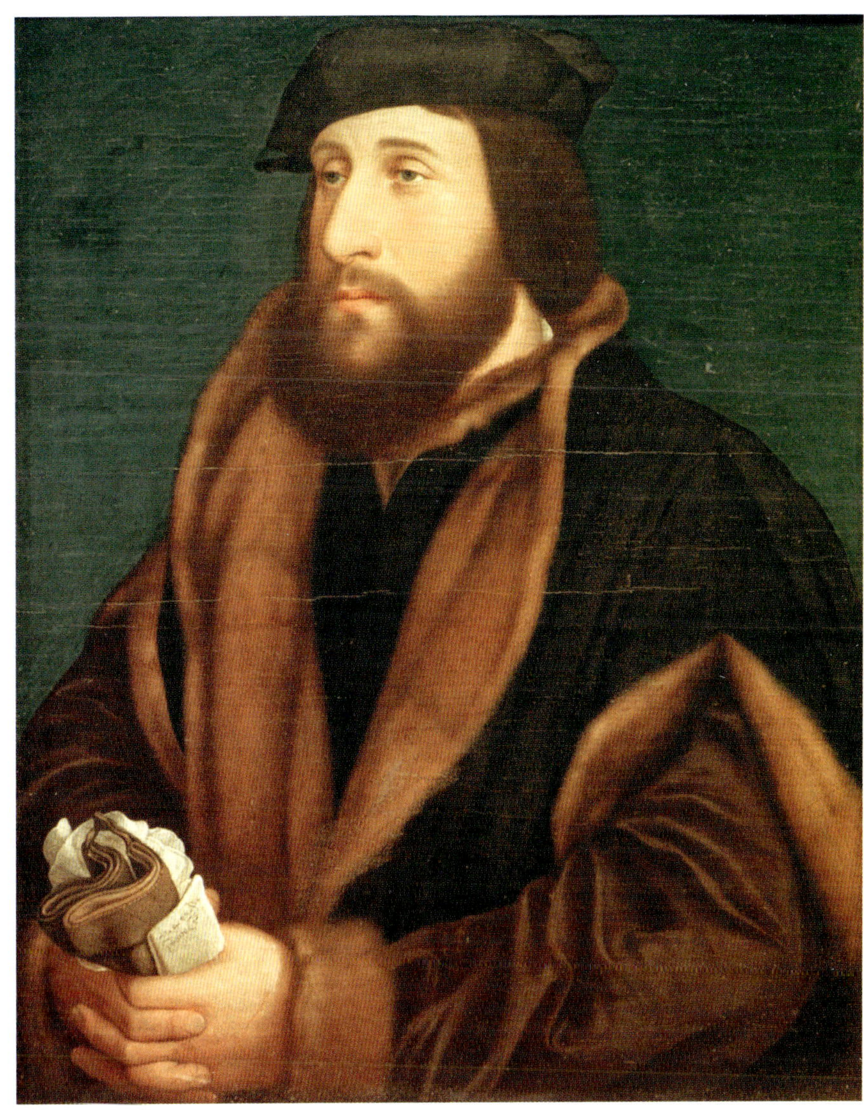

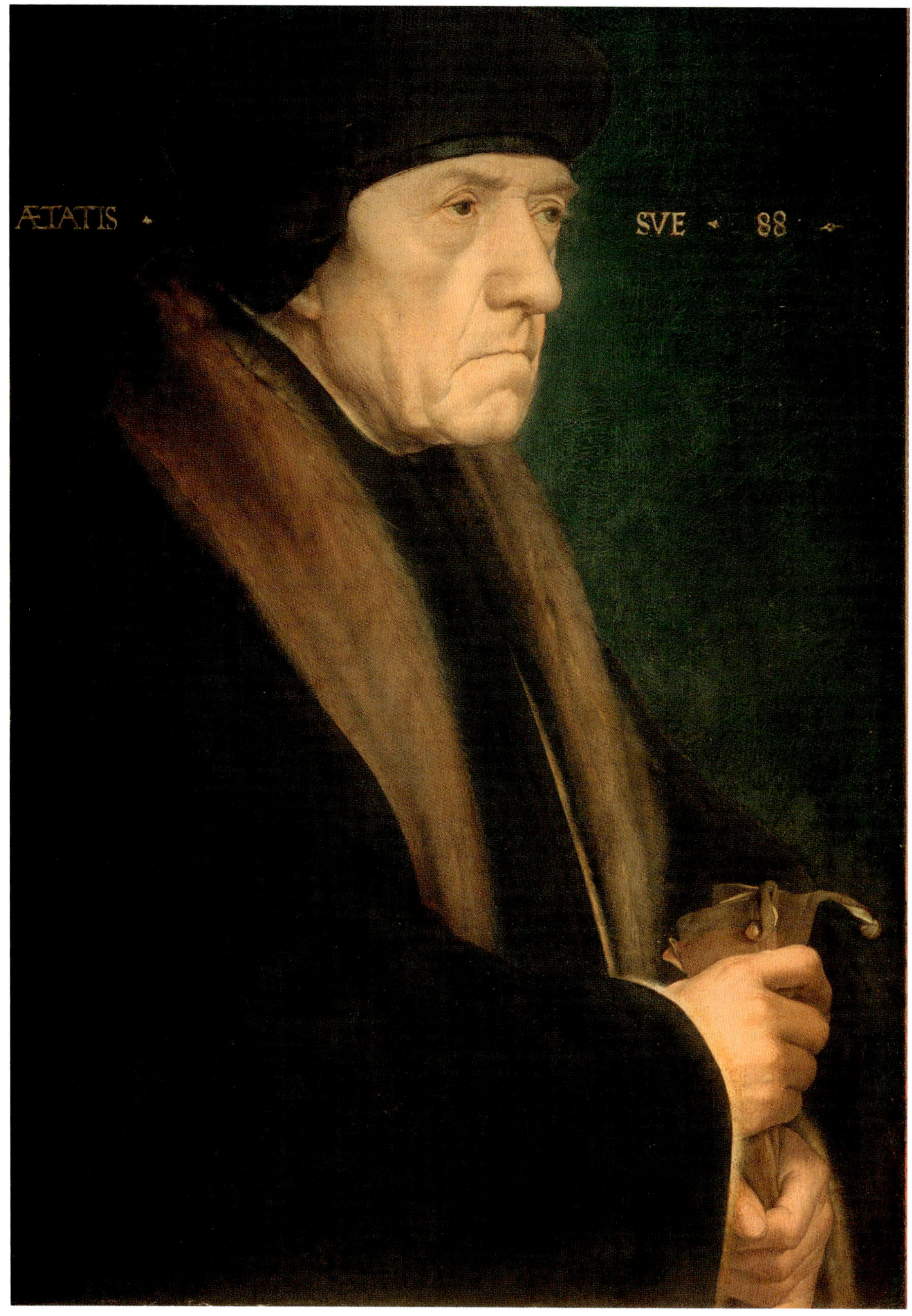

Dr John Chambers, c.1541– 43, resin tempera on oak wood, 58 x 39.7cm (22.8 x 15.6in), Kunsthistoriches Museum, Vienna, Austria

On a dark green background the half-length near-profile portrait of Dr John Chambers, physician to King Henry VIII, shows him standing. He wears a large hat that covers his hair, and a dark coat with light fur collar. In his hands he holds his gloves.

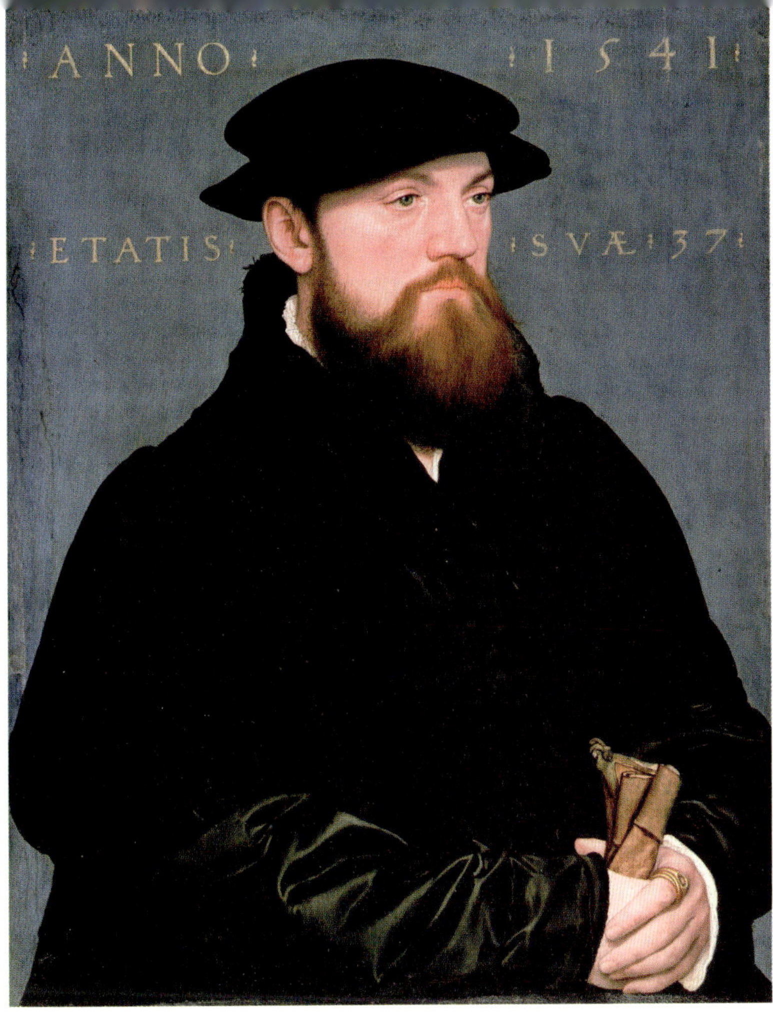

De Vos van Steenwijk, 1541, oil on panel, 47.5 x 37.3cm (18.7 x 14.6in), Staatliche Museen, Berlin, Germany

The sitter wears a gold ring on his index finger with a coat of arms of the Dutch de Vos van Steenwijk family. It is possibly a portrait of Roelof de Vos van Steenwijk (c.1504–64) He firmly holds a money bag in his hands. Facing toward his left suggests that this was a companion portrait to one of Roelof's wife, Christine Seidel, whom he married between 1537–43.

Portrait of a Merchant, 1541, oil on oak wood, 46.5 x 34.8cm (18.3 x 13.7in), Kunsthistoriches Museum, Vienna, Austria

In three-quarter profile, his head facing directly toward the viewer, the merchant is seated on a bench, his lower arms resting on a table covered with a verdant green cloth. Presumed to be a portrait of a Hanseatic merchant Hans von Muffel from Nuremberg, Holbein depicts him placing the fingers of one hand inside a book, to hold a place. The action gives the composition a lifelike moment in time.

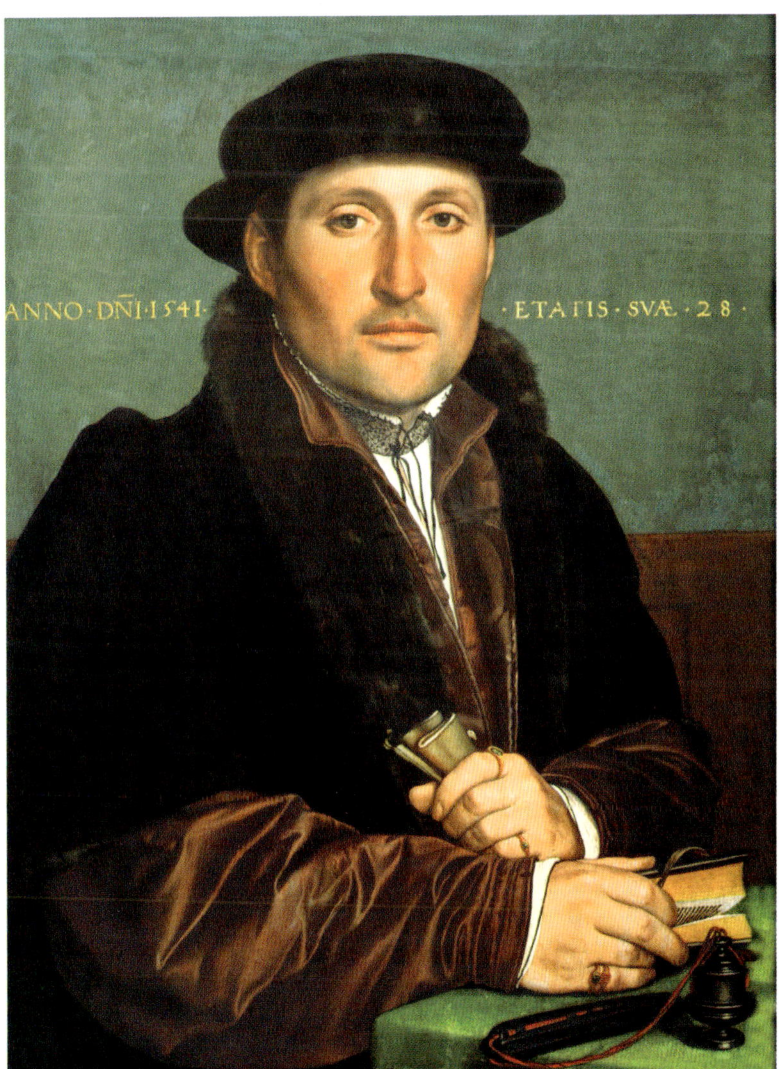

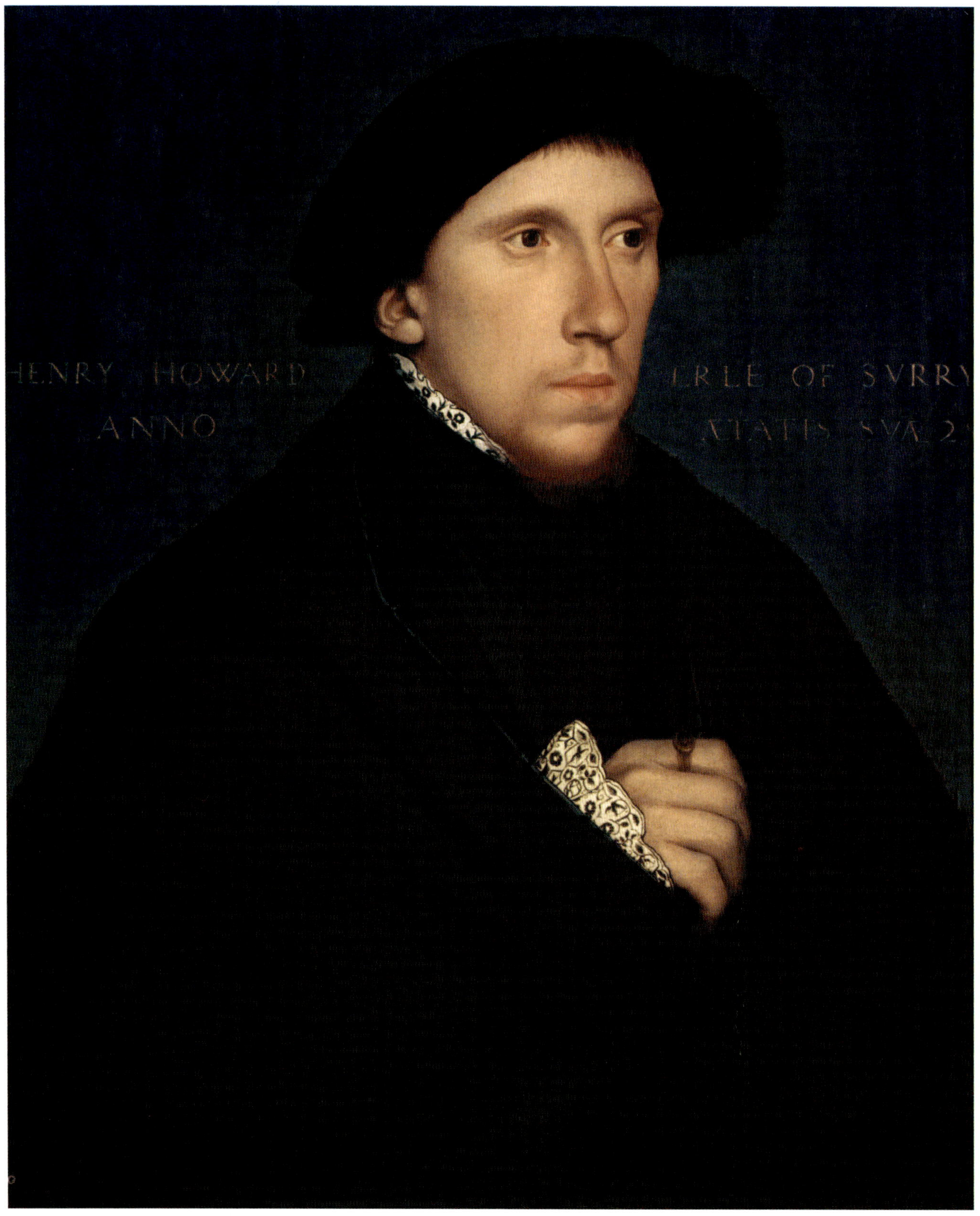

Henry Howard, Earl of Surrey, 1542, oil and tempera on oak wood, 55.5 x 44.5cm (21.8 x 17.5in), Museo de Arte, Sao Paolo, Brazil

A later portrait of Henry Howard (c.1517–47), Holbein's earlier work was a study in coloured chalks (see page 197). The Earl was an English poet. Holbein depicts him close-up, in a half-length composition, in three-quarter profile, looking toward his left. Against a mid-blue background, the Earl's dark brown fur hat and robe serve to focus attention on his youthful face, pale skin, wispy beard and moustache of auburn hair, and the ring he wears on the index finger of his right hand.

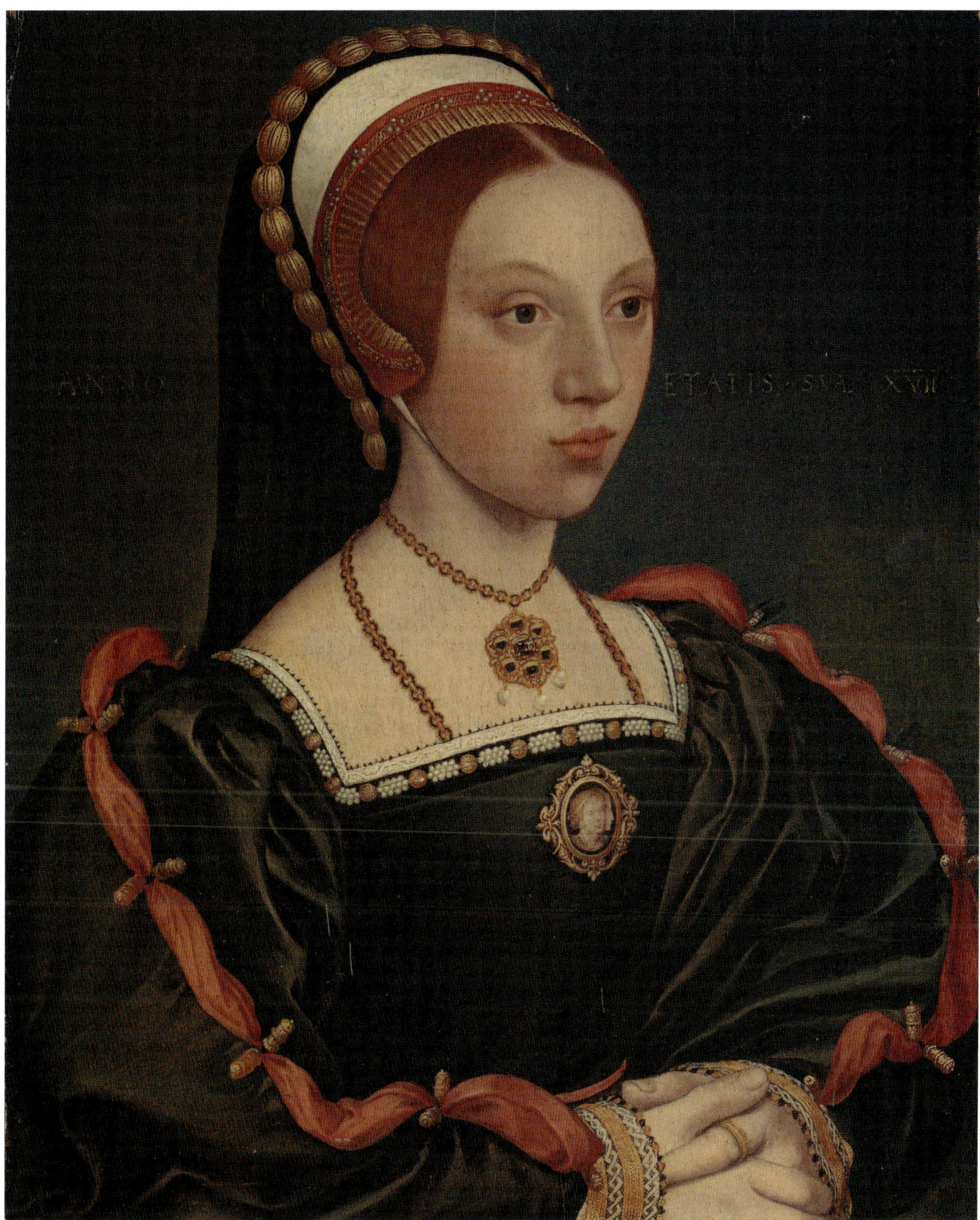

Portrait of a Young Woman, possibly Katherine Howard, c.1540–1542, workshop of Hans Holbein the Younger, oil and gold on oak wood, 28.3 x 23.2cm (11.1 x 9.1in),

Metropolitan Museum of Art, New York, NY, USA

The portrait attributed to Holbein's workshop, working under his agreement, is

possibly Henry VIII's fifth wife, Katherine Howard (1523–42), recognised from the clothing she wears. The Latin inscription across the centre reads 'ANNO ETATIS·SVÆ

XVII', referring to 'age seventeen', which would date the portrait to c.1540, the year she married the king.

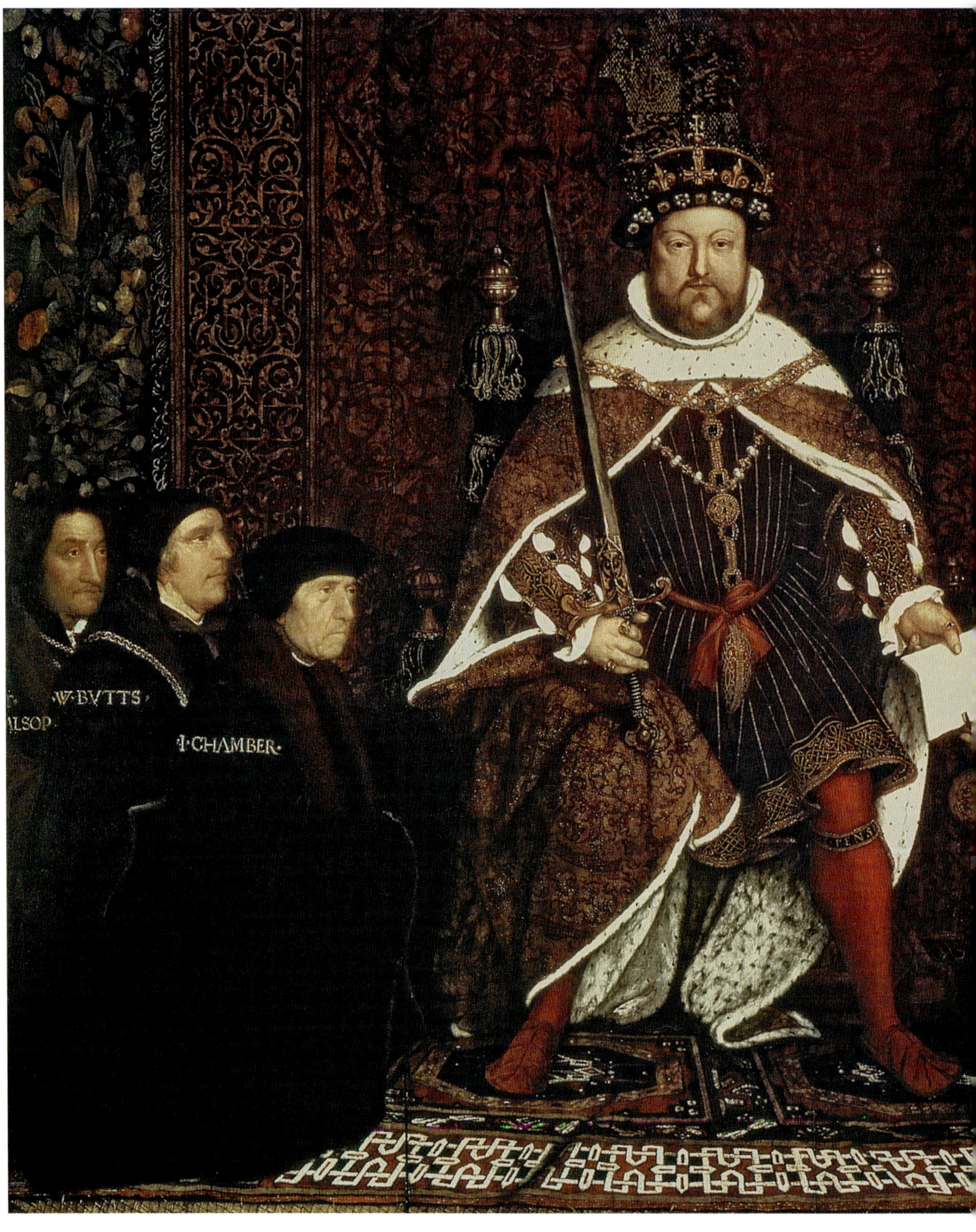

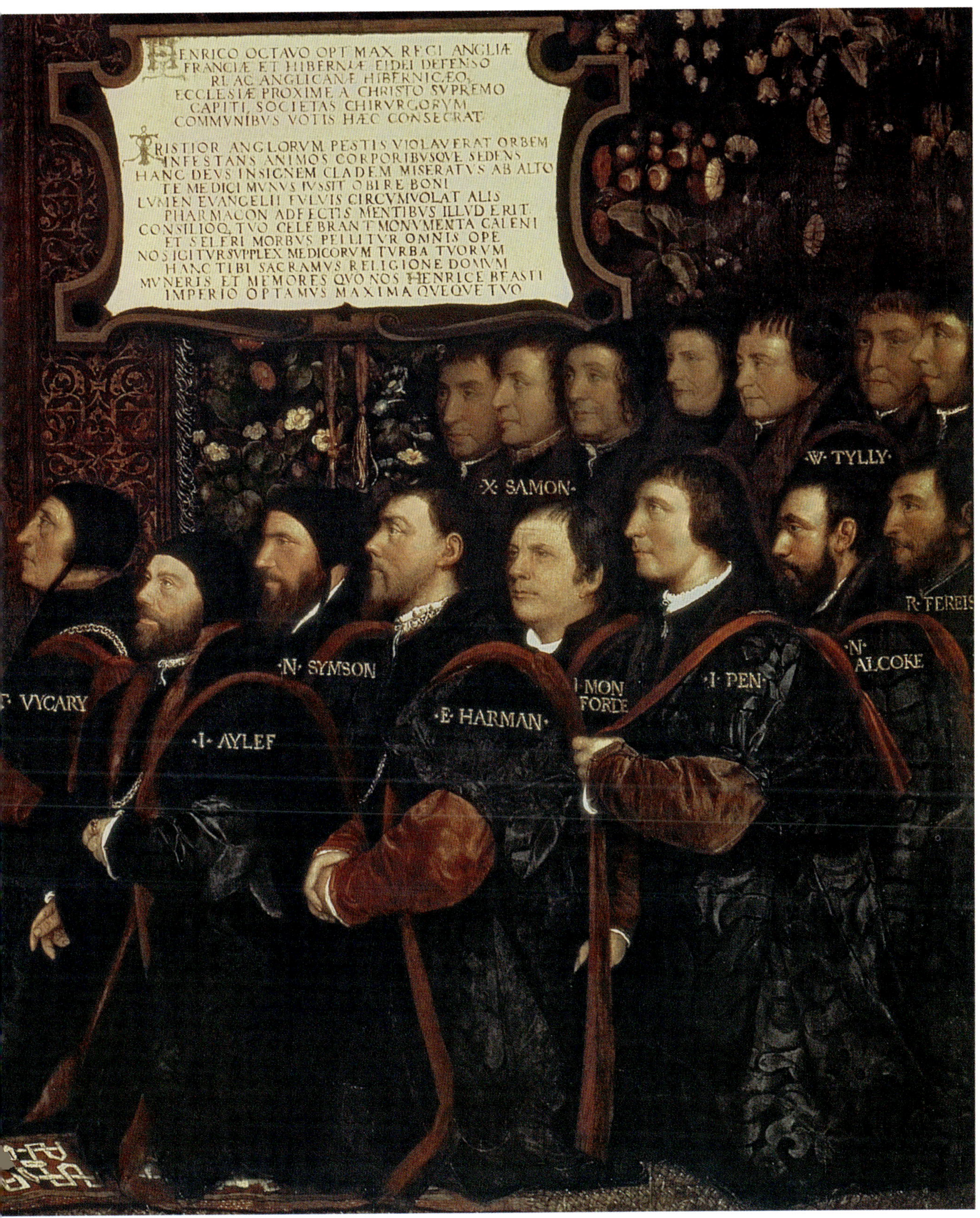

Henry VIII and the Barber-Surgeons, 1541, oil on panel, 180.3 x 312.4cm (70.9 x 123in), Barber-Surgeons' Hall, London, England, UK

The work of Hans Holbein the Younger and his workshop. The painting depicts the monarch, Henry VIII handing over a charter to Thomas Vicary, an English physician, surgeon and anatomist, to commemorate the joining of the Barbers and Surgeons Guilds. Another copy of the painting shows an ornate window as backdrop to the scene (see page 90).

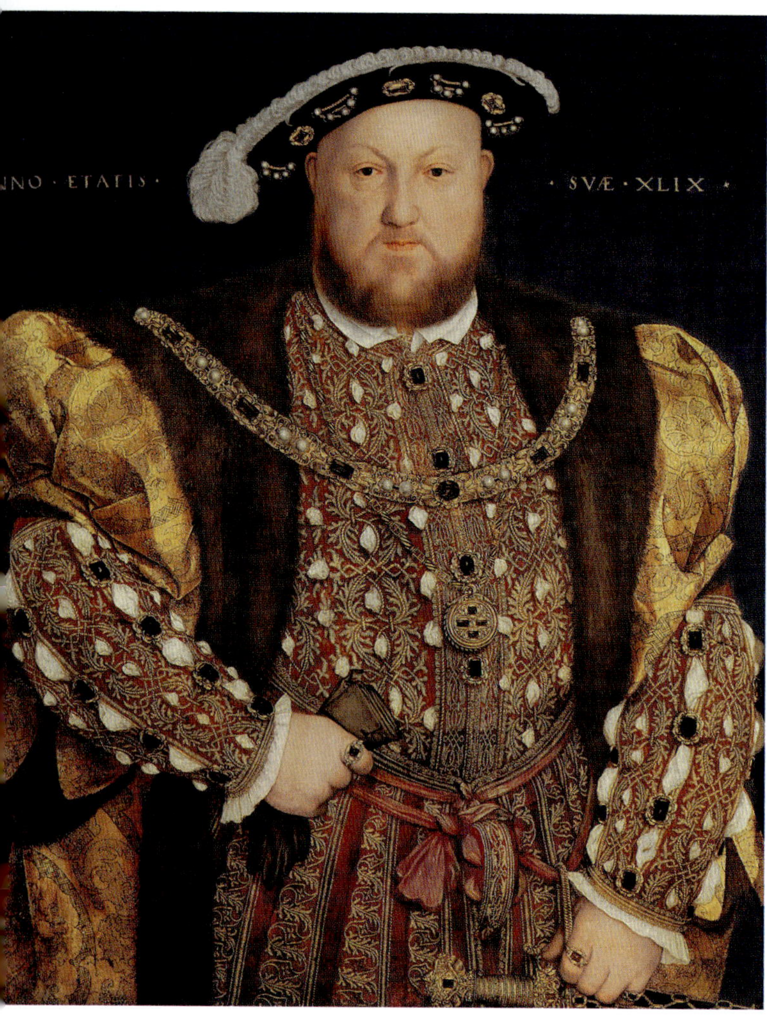

Left: *Portrait of Henry VIII aged 49,* 1540, oil on wood, 88.5 x 74.5cm (34.8 x 29.3in), Barberini Gallerie Nazionali Corsini, Rome, Italy

There is debate as to whether this was by Holbein's hand or from his workshop, but not about the impressiveness of this portrait of Henry VIII. The preparatory sketch below is thought to connect to this portrait, among others. The inscription states that the king was forty-nine years old, which would date it to his marriage to Anne of Cleves. It is a magnificently ornate image (see also page 172).

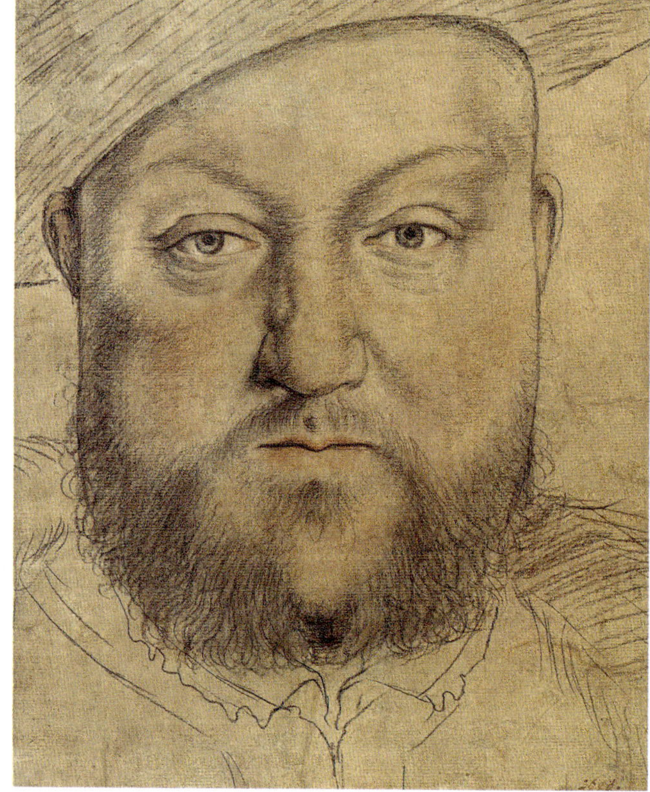

Right: *Portrait study of King Henry VIII,* c.1540, black and coloured chalks, 33.4 x 42cm (13.1 x 16.5in), Staatliche Graphische Sammlung, Munich, Germany

Most probably the preparatory drawing for the 1540 portrait above.

Here, on pink prepared paper, Holbein closely scrutinises the face of the king. He notes the steady gaze, defined high-arched eyebrows, small, neat mouth, the lines and bags under his eyes, and the king's wispy light beard with thin moustache.

Opposite: *Portrait of Henry VIII,* 1542, workshop of Hans Holbein the Younger, oil with gold and silver on oak panel, 93 x 68cm (36.6 x 26.75in), Castle Howard, North Yorkshire, England

One of a few contemporary copies of Holbein's last portrait of Henry VIII. Depicted standing, in three-quarter length, the king looks heavy in build. He holds a staff in his left hand, which historians say that he needed to aid his walking at this time, and a pair of leather gloves in the right hand. The richly embroidered red velvet surcoat he wears is sewn with silver thread and worn over a doublet made from cloth of gold. Holbein captures the steady, unnerving gaze of the king through pale green-grey eyes, and the facial characteristic of lightly-coloured wispy beard. The king's pale face contrasts with the richly ornamented costume he wears. The staff is inscribed 'H' and the date '1542'. Another copy of note was in the Warwick Castle collection, in which Henry is depicted in a blue-green, silver and gold coat.

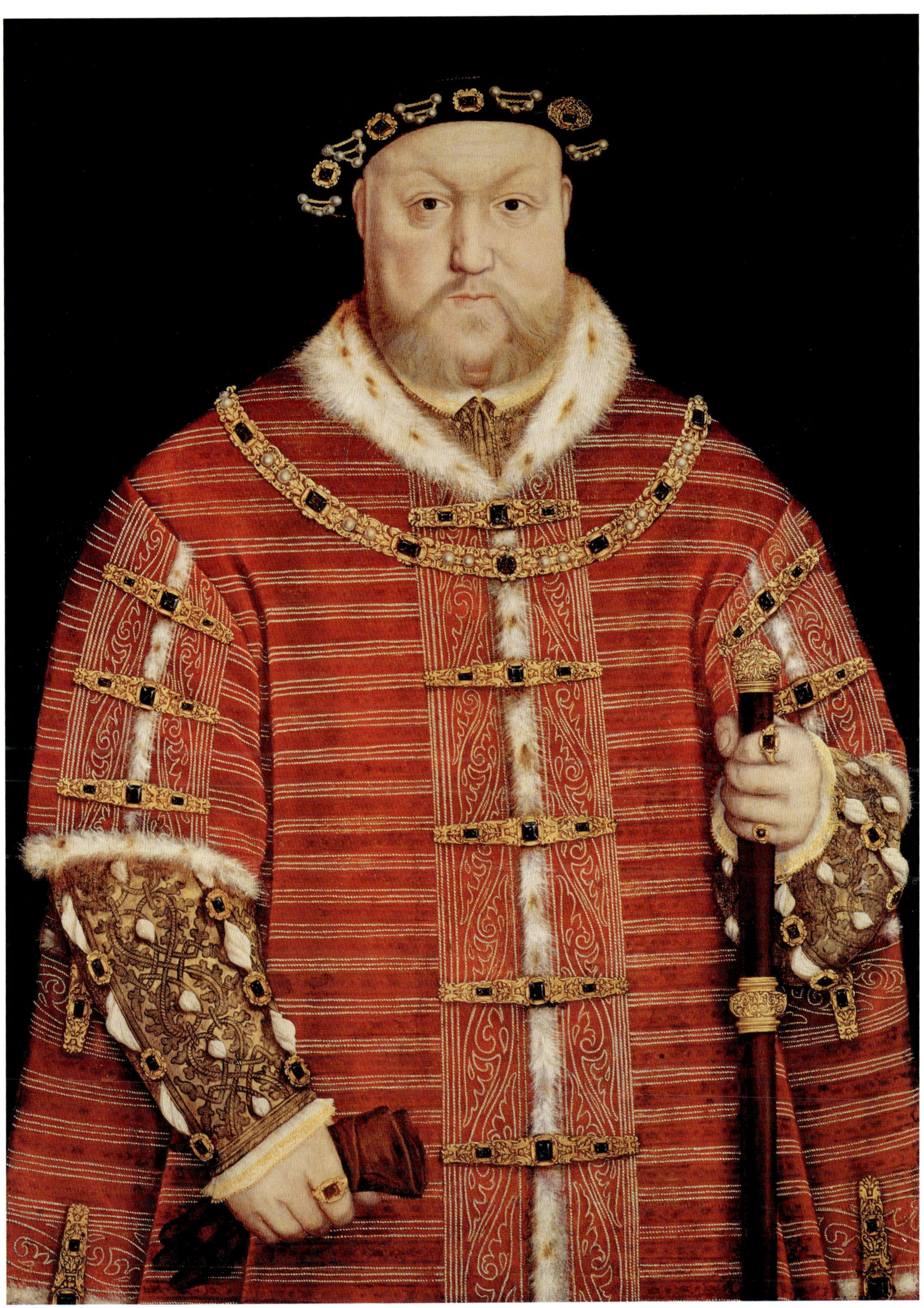

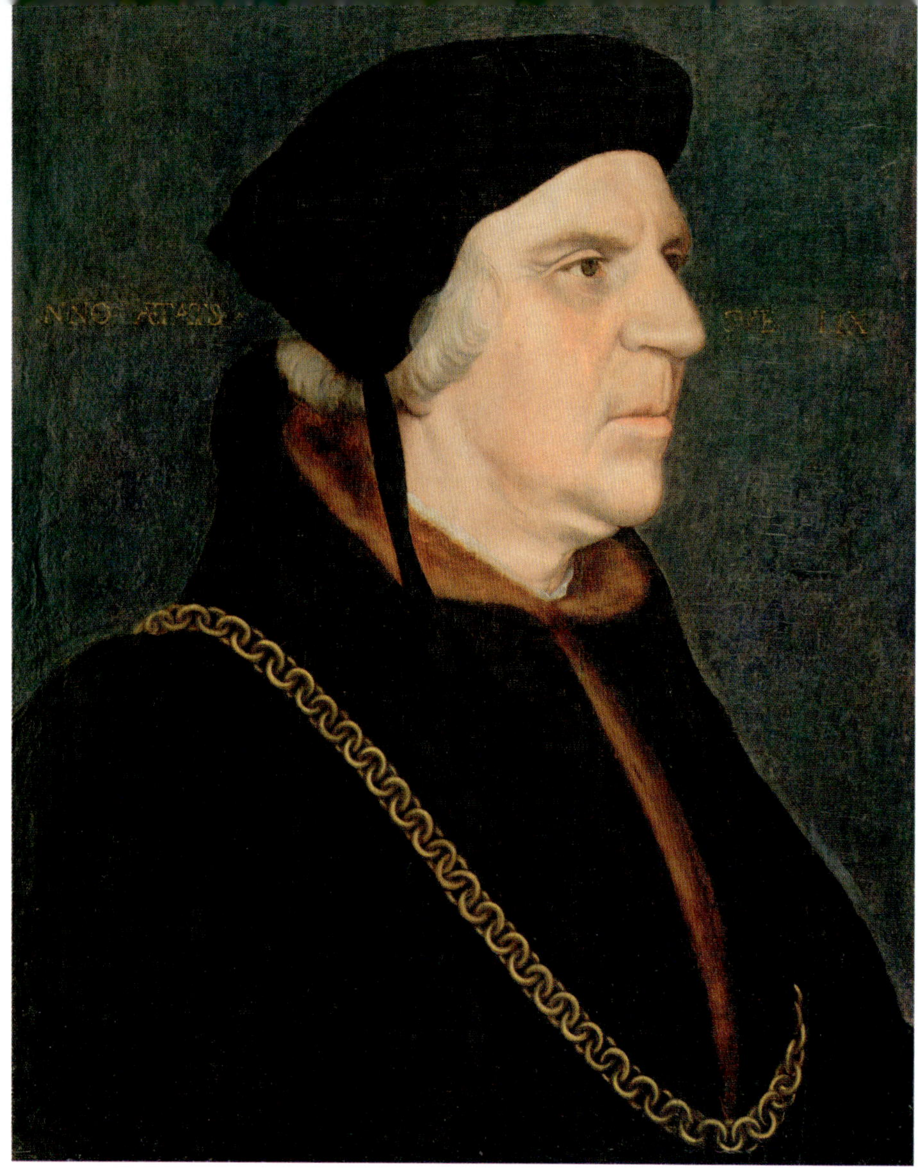

Sir William Butts, M.D., c.1543, oil on panel, 47.2 x 36.9cm (18.5 x 14.5in), Isabella Stewart Gardner Museum, Boston, MA, USA

In near-profile, the half-length portrait set on a sage green background of Sir William Butts (1486–1545) was created as a companion portrait to that of his wife Lady Margaret Butts. He was a member of the court of Henry VIII, and personal physician to the king. He appears in the large group portrait *Henry VIII and the Barber-Surgeons*, 1541–43, standing on the King's right side (see pages 244–45).

Duke Anton 'the Good' of Lorraine, 1543, oil on panel, 52.4 x 37.8cm (20.6 x 14.8in), Gemaldergalerie der Staatlichen Museen, Berlin, Germany

The French duke, Anton 'the Good' of Lorraine (1489–1544), was the father of Anna of Lorraine, whom Holbein was instructed by Henry VIII to draw and paint in 1538, as a prospective fourth bride for the king. Some Holbein scholars consider that the duke's portrait may date from that time, and finished at a later date, in the year leading to Holbein's death. X-radiography reveals that the shape of the original clothing, and placement of the duke's left arm, was changed. Lettering in gold on the pale blue backdrop states that the duke was fifty four years of age at the time this portrait was completed, a year before his death. It is a half-length portrait in three-quarter profile. The duke looks toward his left, which suggests the portrait was intended as a companion to one of his wife. His facial features and lengthy beard are meticulously detailed. He wears a hat embellished with gold pins, a rich black mantle and a doublet with satin sleeves. His hands are concealed within a muff.

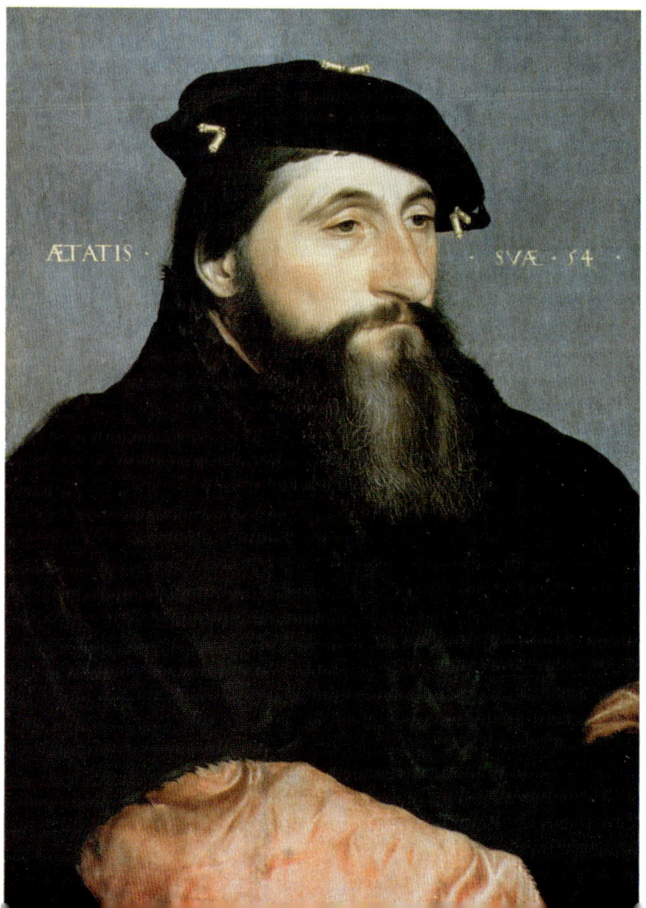

Margaret, Lady Butts, c.1543,
oil on panel, 47.2 x 36.9cm
(18.5 x 14.5in), Isabella
Stewart Gardner Museum,
Boston, MA, USA

Margaret Bacon, Lady Butts
(c.1485–1545) served as lady
in waiting to King Henry's
daughter Princess Mary and
moved in the court circle of
Queen Katherine Parr. She
was the wife of Sir William
Butts, and the daughter of
John Bacon.

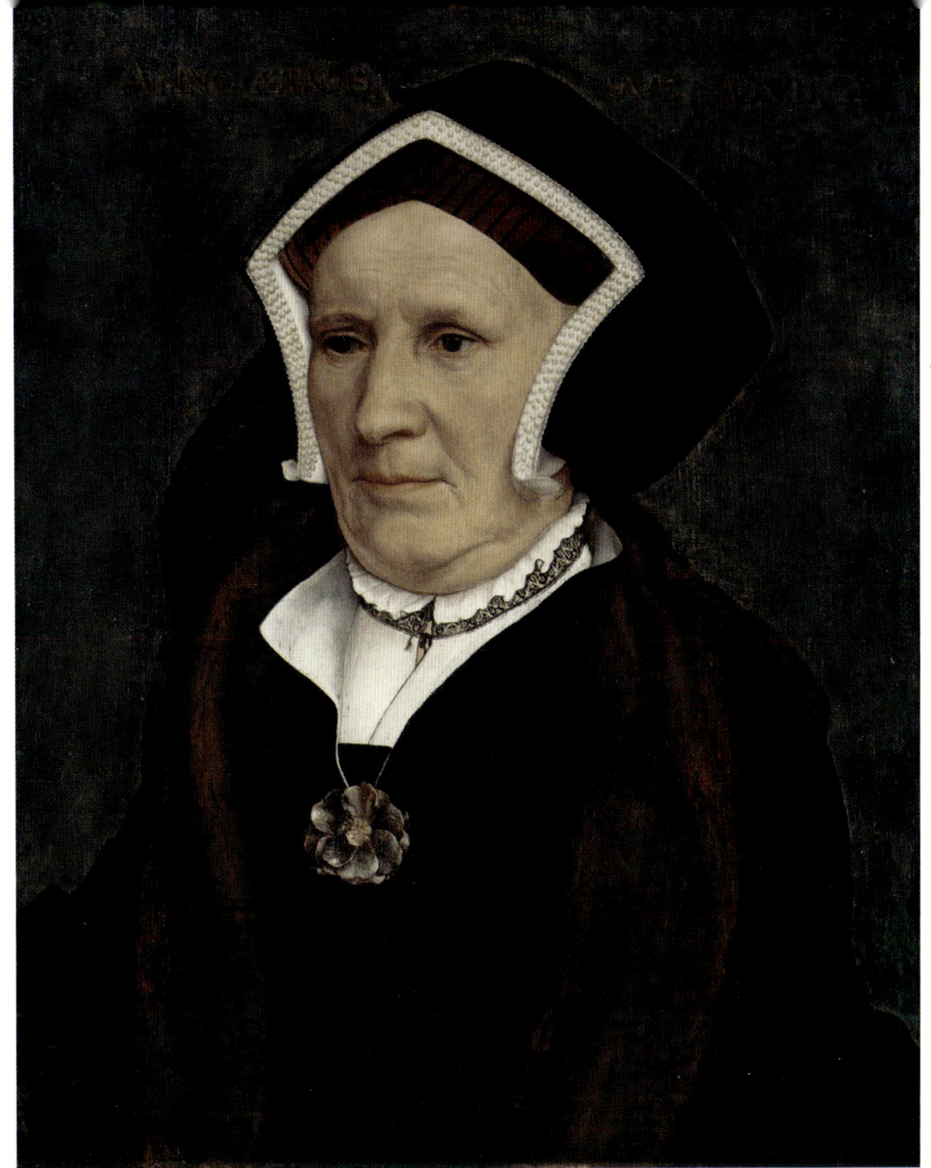

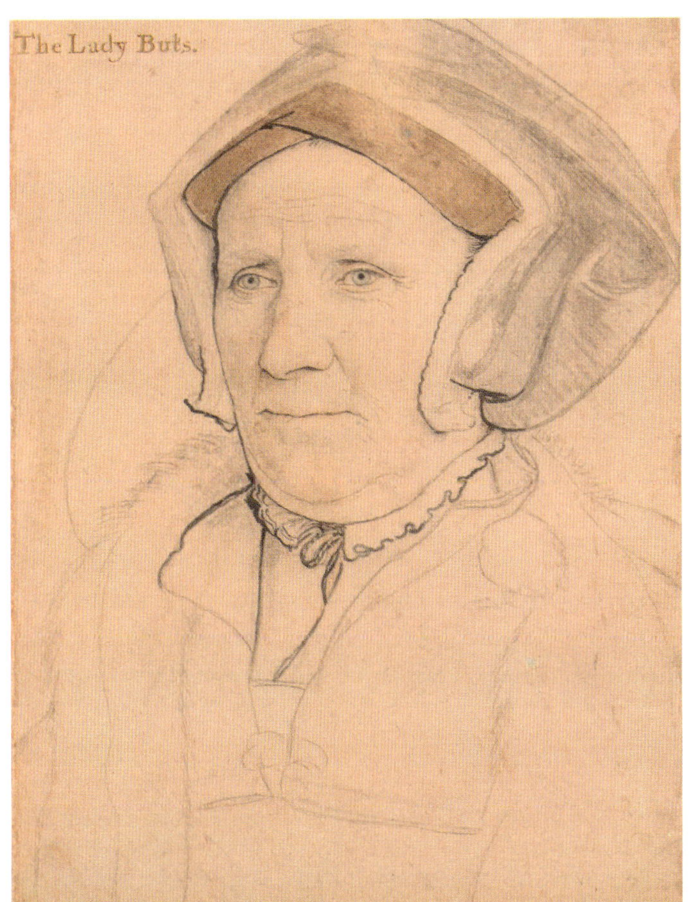

Portrait study of Margaret,
Lady Butts, c.1541–43, black
and coloured chalks, pen
and ink, brush and ink,
and metalpoint on pale
pink prepared paper, 37.7
x 27.2cm (14.8 x 10.7in),
Royal Collection, UK

A preparatory drawing
of Margaret, Lady Butts
(c.1485–1545) bust-length
in three-quarter profile,
wearing a gabled headdress
and fur collar.

One of Holbein's last commissions, the design for a magnificent clock comprises an hour-glass (a clocksalt), a sundial and a compass. The clock was to be presented by Sir Anthony Denny to Henry VIII on New Year's Day 1544. Two of the notes on the sketch are in the hand of Holbein's friend the royal astronomer Nikolaus Kratzer, who assisted in the technical design of the piece. The presentation was made, unfortunately, after Holbein's death.

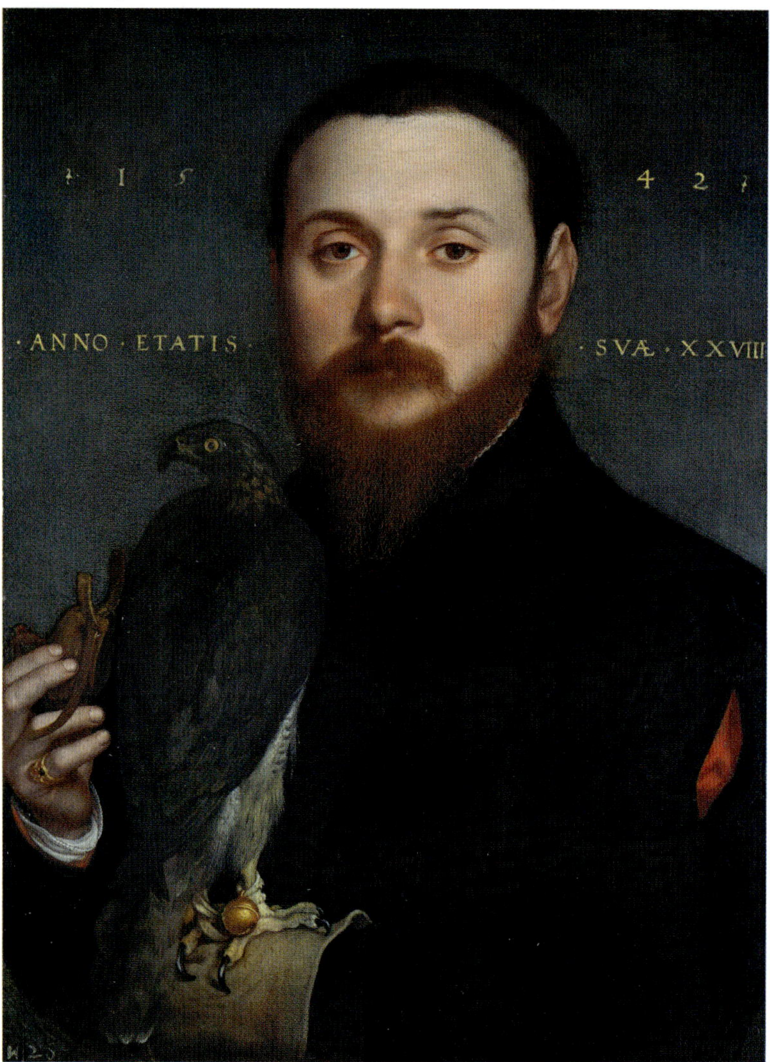

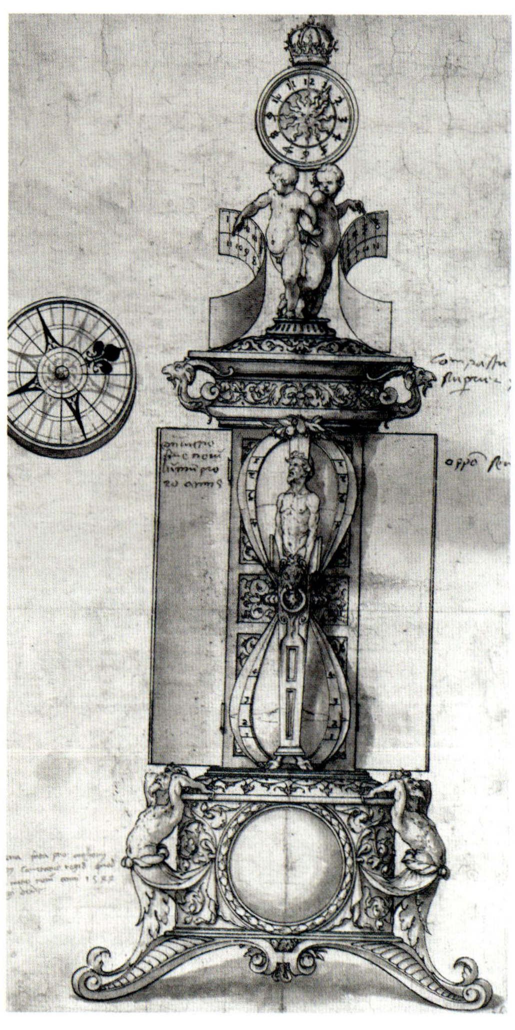

Portrait of a Nobleman with a Hawk, 1542, oil on panel, 24.6 x 18.8cm (9.6 x 7.4in), Mauritshuis, The Hague, The Netherlands

Painted in the year before Holbein's death, this portrait connotes wealth and breeding in the noble's distinguished features, fine clothing, and elite hobby of falconry, also called hawking. There is a facial similarity with the *Portrait of an Unknown Man*, 1540–43 (see page 239), and possibly related. The painting background is inscribed 'ANNO. ETATIS. SVÆ.XXVIII', the date of the painting, 1542, and the age of the sitter, twenty-eight years. One of Holbein's first portraits of a nobleman with a hawk was a small margin illustration titled 'Aristocrat with a Hawk', in Oswald Myconius's copy of the *Praise of Folly*, by Desiderius Erasmus (see pages 22–23).

Opposite: *Self-Portrait*, 1542–43, black and colour chalk pastels on pink paper, 23 x 18cm (9 x 7in), Galleria degli Uffizi, Florence, Italy

A rare Holbein self-portrait possibly created 1542–43, just before his sudden death in London. The small portrait is a close-up head and shoulders, the body in three-quarter profile facing Holbein's right, with the artist's head, and green eyes, directed toward the viewer. Holbein has a rounded face, neat, cropped beard and small moustache. His name, that he is a citizen of Basel, and his age, are inscribed on it, 'IONNES HOLPENIVS BASILEENSIS / SVI IPSIVS EFFIGIATOR Æ: XLV'.

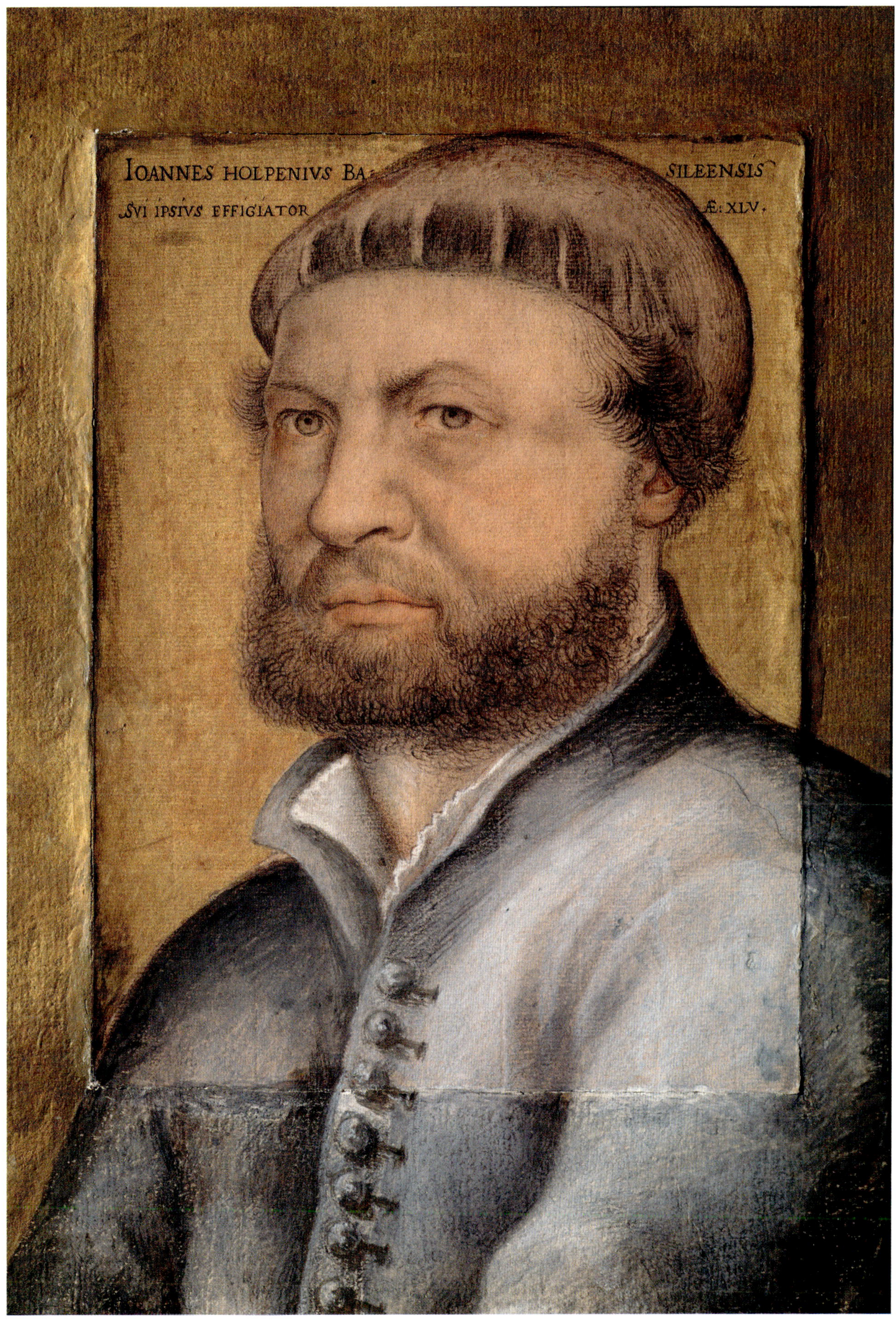
IOANNES HOLPENIVS BA·   SILEENSIS
SVI IPSIVS EFFIGIATOR   Æ: XLV·

BIBLIOGRAPHY

Bätschmann, Oskar & Griener, Pascal. *Hans Holbein*, Reaktion Books, London 1997 (Revised and expanded edition, 2014)

Beerbühl, Margrit Schulte. *The Forgotten Majority: German Merchants in London, Naturalization, and Global Trade, 1660–1815*. Translation by Cynthia Klohr. New York: Berghahn Books, New York, 2014

Betteridge, Thomas & Lipscomb, Suzannah. *Henry VIII and the Court: Art, Politics and Performance*, Ashgate Publishing, England, 2013

Buck, Stephanie & Sander, Jochen. *Hans Holbein the Younger: Painter at the Court of Henry VIII*, Thames & Hudson, London, 2003

Button, Victoria. *The portrait drawings of Hans Holbein the Younger: function and use explored through materials and techniques*, PHD thesis, Royal College of Art, London.

Campbell, Thomas P. *Henry VIII and the Art of Majesty: Tapestries at the Tudor Court*, Paul Mellon Centre for Studies in British Art, London, and Yale University Press, New Haven and London, 2007

Cooper, Tarnya. *Citizen Portrait: Portrait Painting and the Urban Elite of Tudor and Jacobean England and Wales* (The Paul Mellon Centre for Studies in British Art), Yale University Press, 2012

Dackerman, Susan. (Ed) *Prints and the Pursuit of Knowledge in Early Modern Europe*, Harvard Art Museums, Yale University Press, 2011

Foister, Susan. *Holbein in England*, Tate Publishing, London, 2006

Foister, Susan. *Holbein and England*, Yale University Press, New Haven & London, 2004

Foister, Susan. Ashok, Roy. & Wyld, Martin. *The Ambassadors*, National Gallery Publications (Making and Meaning series), London, 1997

Häberlein, Mark. *The Fuggers of Augsburg: pursuing wealth and honor in Renaissance Germany*, University of Virginia Press, Charlottesville, USA, 2012

Hervey, Mary F.S. *Holbein's Ambassadors: The Picture and the Men*, George Bells & Sons, London, 1901

Holbein, John. *Dance of Death*, Hamilton, Adams & Co., London; Thomas D. Morrison, Glasgow, 1887

Jones, Susan Frances. *Van Eyck to Gossaert: Towards a Northern Renaissance*, National Gallery Company, London / Yale University Press, 2011

Koerner, Joseph Leo. *The Moment of Self-Portraiture in German Renaissance Art*, The University of Chicago Press, Chicago, and London, 1993

Langdon, Helen. *Holbein*, Phaidon Press, London, 1976

Laurie, A.P. *The Painter's Methods and Materials*, Dover Publications Inc., New York, USA

Michael, Erika. *Hans Holbein the Younger: A Guide to Research*, Garland Publishing, Inc., New York, and London, 1997

More, Thomas. *Utopia* (1515), Penguin Books, 2012 (translated and edited by Domini Baker-Smith)

Nash, Susie. *Northern Renaissance Art*, Oxford University Press, Oxford, 2004

Phillips, Margaret Mann. *Erasmus and the Northern Renaissance*, The Boydell Press, Rowman & Littlefield, 1981.

Rublack, Ulinka, *Hans Holbein: The Dance of Death*, Penguin Classics, London, 2016

Smith, Jeffrey Chipps. *The Northern Renaissance* Phaidon Press, 2004

Strong, Roy. *Holbein and Henry VIII*, Routledge & Kegan Paul, 1967

Thurley, Simon. *The Royal Palaces of Tudor England*, Yale University Press, New Haven and London, 1993

Thurley, Simon. *Houses of Power: The Places that shaped the Tudor World* Bantam Press, London, 2017

Van Mander, Karel. *Schilder-Boeck* (1603)

Wedd, Kitt. Peltz, Lucy. & Ross, Cathy. *Artists' London: Holbein to Hirst*, Merrell Publishers, London

Wolf, Norbert. *Hans Holbein the Younger: The German Raphael*, Taschen publishing, 2017

CATALOGUES & REFERENCE

Hans Holbein the Younger The Basel Years 1515–532, with contributions by Christian Müller, Stephan Kemperdick ... [et al.]. Prestel, Munich, Berlin, London, New York, 2006

The Northern Renaissance: Dürer to Holbein edited by Kate Heard & Lucy Whittaker, Royal Collection Publications, London 2011

Artists of the Tudor Court: The Portrait Miniature Rediscovered, 1520–1620 (exh. cat. by Roy Strong, London, V&A, 1983), pp. 34–43

'Venice: May 1527', *Calendar of State Papers Relating to English Affairs in the Archives of Venice, Volume 4: 1527–1533* (1871), pp. 56–66.

Daniel Lysons, 'Greenwich', in *The Environs of London: Volume 4, Counties of Herts, Essex and Kent* (London, 1796), pp. 426–493. British History Online http://www.british-history.ac.uk/london-environs/vol4/426-493

Foister, Susan. Wyld, Martin and Ashok, Roy. 'A Lady with a Squirrel and a Starling', *National Gallery Technical Bulletin*, 1994, Vol.15 pp.6–19

Gier, Helmut, & Schwarz, Reinhard (Eds.) *Reformation und Reichsstadt: Luther in Augsburg*, (exhibition catalogue), Verlag Dr. Wißner, Augsburg, 1996

Starkey, David & Doran, Susan. *Man and Monarch: Henry VIII*, (exhibition catalogue), The British Library, London 2009

Renaissance and Reformation: German Art in the Age of Dürer and Cranach, Staatliche Museen Zu Berlin, and Staatliche Kunstsammlungen Dresden, Germany, 2016

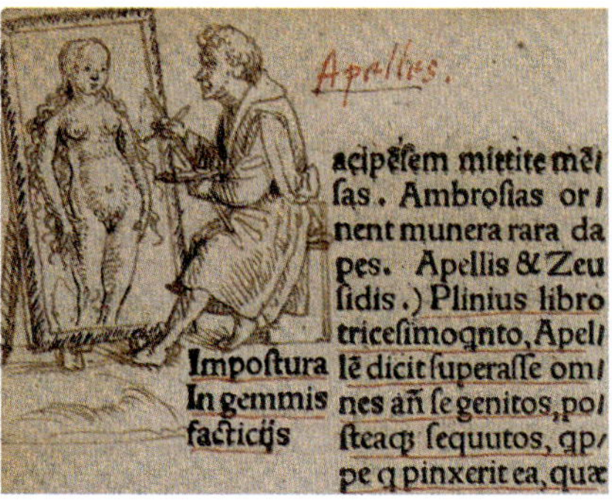

INDEX

Portraits by Hans Holbein the Younger are indexed under the title name except when they are indexed under 'portraits' ('identified subjects' and 'unidentified subjects'). Entries for 'Holbein' refer to Hans Holbein the Younger. Other artist's works are indexed under the artist's name. Italics indicate pictures.

A

Act of Supremacy, 1534 51, 72, 74, 212
Adam and Eve 34–5, *34*, 107
Adoration of the Magi, The 19, 118
Allegorical Escutcheon of Death, 128
Allegory of the Old and New Testament 59, *59*, 170–1
Allegory of Time 198
Amalia of Cleves 88–9
Ambassadors, The 64–5, *65*, 66–7, 99, 182–9
detail *64*, *173*, *184–9*
Amerbach, Ambrosius 123
Amerbach, Basilius 25, 36, 47, 114
Amerbach, Bonifacius 32–3, *33*, 36, 40, 41, *117*, 140
Amerbach, Johannes 30, 32, 43
Amman, Jost 91, *91*
Anne of Cleves (Queen) 72, 84, 88–9, *88*, *89*, 235, 236
Antwerp, Belgium 49, 63
Apelles 6, 42, 43, 56, 68, 73, 74, 223
Apollo and the Muses on Mount Parnassus 70, 197
Archangel Michael Weighing Souls 136
Artist's Wife with the Two Elder Children, The 46–7, *46*, 59, *166*
see also Holbein, Elsbeth Binzenstock (wife)
Asper, Hans 47, 59
Audley, Elizabeth, Lady *210*
Augsburg, Bavaria 13, 14–15, *14*, *15*, 23
Cathedral altarpiece 17, *17*
Holbein family in 16, 18–9, 20, 21
Martin Luther's visit to 29

B

Baer, Magdalena 45, *142*, *143*
Baldung, Hans 42
barbers 91
Barber-Surgeons' Picture, The 90–1, *90*, 244–5
Baschenis, Simone, *Danse Macabre 38*
Basel, Switzerland 20, 22–3, *22*, 24–5, 42, 96
see also Darmstadt Madonna
citizenship of 48, 59
designs for Cathedral stained glass 43, *108*, *136*

Erasmus's visit to 40–1
Great Council Chamber murals 43, 58–9, 98, 119
Flight from Saul 168
Humiliation of Valerian by Shapur I, Edessa, The 43, 98, *137*
King Rehoboam 119
Manius Curius Dentatus rejects the gifts of the Samnites 119
Rehoboam rejecting advice of the elders 58, *168*
printing industry in 30
Zum Tanz House 33, *33*, 115
Bat with Spread Wings 133
Battle Scene 137
Bedford, John Russell, 1st Earl of *201*, 237
Bellini, Giovanni 56
Mary Magdalene 56, *57*
Benninck, Simon 94
Benson, Ambrosius, *Portrait of Jean de Dinteville 66*
Berck, Derick *181*
Bergavenny, George Nevill, 3rd Baron *200*
Berry, Jean de France, Duke of 44, *132*
Berry, Jeanne de Boulogne, Duchess of 44, 98, *132*
Bild, Beatus 42, *42*
Binzenstock, Elsbeth see Holbein, Elsbeth Binzenstock (wife)
Birth of Christ 118
Bisschop, Jan de, *Triumph of Riches; Triumph of Poverty, The 174*, *175*
Blount, Elizabeth 83
Boleyn, Anne (Queen) 54, 68, 70–1, *70*, 74, 76, 77, 196
Holbein's drawings of 71, *71*, *196*
Boleyn, Sir Thomas 70–1
Born, Derich *176*
Bosch, Hieronymus, *The Seven Deadly Sins and the Four Last Things* 39, *39*
Bourbon, Nicholas 68, *69*, 74, 223
Boy with a Marmoset, A 83, 237
Brandon, see Suffolk, Duke of
Breu, Jörg, *Augsburger Monatsbilder 14*
Bruyn the Elder, Bartholomaeus, *Portrait of Anne of Cleves 89*
Burgkmair, Thomas (grandfather) 6
Burgkmair the Elder, Hans (uncle) 20, 26
Double Portrait of Hans and Barbara Schellenberger 26, *26*
Burnet, Gilbert 89
Butts, Margaret, Lady *249*
Butts, Sir William 91, *248*

C

Carew, Sir George *190*
Carew, Sir Nicholas *194*

Chambers, Dr John 91, *240*
Chapuys, Eustace 76
Charles V, Holy Roman Emperor 15, 48, 86
Charles VII, King of France 81, *81*
Cheseman, Robert 100–1, *195*
Christ as the Man of Sorrows with the Virgin Mary 26, *109*
Christ before the High Priests 146
Christ carrying the Cross 148
Christ Crucified 149
Christian II, King of Denmark 86, 87
Christina of Denmark 86–7, *86*, *87*, 204, 234
Christus, Petrus, *Goldsmith in his Shop, The* 13, *13*
Cleve, Joos van
Portrait of Francis I 67
Portrait of Henry VIII, king of England 74, *80*
Cleves, Anne of see Anne of Cleves (Queen)
Cleves, John III, Duke of 88
Clocksalt 250
Clouet, Jean 84, 85
Portrait of Francis I 81, *81*, 218
Portrait of Jean de Dinteville, Sieur de Polisy 67
Colet, John *201*
Cornwall, Henry, Duke of 83
Coxcie, Michiel van, *Portrait of Christina of Denmark 87*
Cranach the Elder, Lucas 28–9, 31, 42
Allegory of the Law and the Gospel, 59, *59*
Creation, The 28
Martin Luther's Sermon 29
Portrait of Martin Luther 29
Creation of Adam and Eve, The 124
Cresacre, Anne 156–7, 158, *158*
Crewe, John 95
Cromwell, Gregory 216, *216*
Cromwell, Thomas 55, 72, *72*, 77, 85, *85*, 89, 216, *217*
Crowning Christ with Thorns 147
Cupid Stung by Bees 198

D

da Vinci, Leonardo 44, 45, 56–7, 81, 96–7
Lady with an Ermine 56–7, *56*
Madonna of the Rocks 45, 47, *47*
Portrait of a Musician 57
Portrait of Isabella d'Este, Duchess of Mantua 45, *45*
Dance of Death (series) 11, 23, 34, 38–9, *39*, 124–8
Alphabet 93, *112*
Danckerts, Hendrick, *Whitehall Palace* 68
Darmstadt Madonna 35, 44–5, *44*, *142–5*

Dauncey, Elizabeth 156–7, 158, 159
Dauncey, William 156–7, 159
David, Jacob 59
Dead Christ in the Tomb 25, 36–7, *36*, 99, *122–3*
Deer Hunting 105
Denny, Sir Anthony 96, *250*
Desiderius Erasmus see Erasmus of Rotterdam
Diana and Actaeon 198
Dinteville, Jean de 64–5, *65*, 66–7, *182–3*, 184, 188–9
Dinteville family, *Moses and Aaron before Pharaoh: An Allegory of the Dinteville Family* (unknown artist) 67, *67*
Disrobing of Christ 149
Döring, Christian 28
Dorothea of Denmark, Princess 87
Dostoyevsky, Fyodor 37, 122
Dürer, Albrecht 26, 42, 56, 96
Self-portrait aged twenty-eight 13, 56

E

'Ecce Homo' 147
Edward VI, King 76, 82–3, 94–5, 237
Edward, Prince of Wales (drawing) 232
Edward, Prince of Wales (Scrots) 94, *95*
Edward VI, as a Child 82, *82*, 232, 233
Edward VI, Duke of Cornwall (unknown artist) 82
Edward VI, King of England (Scrots) 83
Edward VI as Prince of Wales (unknown artist) 83
Elizabeth I, Queen 74, 84, 94–5
Elizabeth of York 78, *78*, 79
Elyot, Margaret, Lady *192*
Elyot, Sir Thomas *192*
Erasmus in his Study 104
Erasmus of Rotterdam 40–1
friends of 33, 36, 43, 55, 68
Thomas More 48, 49, 50, 51, 94
Praise of Folly 20, 23, *23*, 34, 40, *40*, 41, *104–5*, 250, 252
Statue of Erasmus, Rotterdam 41
Terminus, the Device of Erasmus *113*, 167
portraits of
Desiderius Erasmus) 41, *135*
Erasmus of Rotterdam 10, *134*
Erasmus of Rotterdam (Massys) 40
Praise of Folly drawing 41
Roundel of Erasmus of Rotterdam 169

Essex, Thomas Cromwell, Earl of see
    Cromwell, Thomas
Etzlaub, Erhard, *Roadmap of central
    Europe* 12
Expulsion from Paradise, The 124
Eyck, Hubert van 18
Eyck, Jan van 12, 18, 27
    Arnolfini Portrait, The 13

F
Fall of Icarus, The 199
Family of Henry VIII, The (unknown
    artist) 94–5
Family of Sir Thomas More see *Sir
    Thomas More and his household,
    and his descendants*
Field of Cloth of Gold, The (unknown
    artist) 53
Fisher, John, Bishop of Rochester
    200
Flagellation, The 25, 25
Flight from Saul 168
Folly in the Pulpit 104
Folly Steps Down From the Pulpit
    105
Fontebasso, Francesco, *Apelles
    painting Campaspe, the mistress of
    Alexander the Great* 43
Fouquet, Jean, *Charles VII, King of
    France* (detail) 81, 81
France 48, 59
Francis I, King of France 48, 53, 66,
    67, 81, 81, 84
Froben, Hieronymus 169
Froben, Johannes 30, 31, 43, 43,
    113, 114, 116
Fugger, Jakob 14, 15, 15

G
Galle, Philip
    Beatus Bild 42
    *Color Olivi (The Inside of a Painter's
        Studio)* 24
Gardiner, Stephen 201
George, Simon 69, 69, 205
Germany 12, 13, 30, 42
    see also Augsburg, Bavaria;
        Wittenberg, Germany
Gerster, Johannes 121
Giggs, Margaret 156–7, 158, 159
Gillis, Pieter 49, 50, 51
Gisze, Georg 8, 62, 63, 178
Godsalve, Sir John 55, 55, 73, 165,
    206, 207
Godsalve, Thomas 55, 55, 165, 207
Gossaert, Jan 63
    *Children of Christian II, King of
        Denmark* 87
    Portrait of a Merchant 63, 63
Greenwich Palace 53, 54, 96, 137
Grey, Lady Jane 85
Grünewald, Mathias 21
    The Crucifixion (detail) 37
Guildford, Sir Henry 52, 52, 96,
    152, 153, 160
Guildford, Mary Wotton, Lady 52,
    52, 161
Guldinknopf, Barbara 121

Gutenberg, Johannes 30, 30
Gutenberg press 30, 30, 31

H
Hagar and Ishmael 199
Handwashing of Pontius Pilate 148
Hans of Antwerp 177
Hanseatic League, The 62–3, 70, 85,
    174, 176–81, 218, 241
Harris, Virgil M. 93
Head of a Female Saint 34, 106
Head of a Male Saint 34, 107
Henry VII, King 78–9, 78, 79, 230
Henry VIII, King
    Act of Supremacy and
        reformation 51, 72, 74, 212
    control of the plague 92
    creates Holbein as 'the King's
        painter' 74–5
    marriages and children 71, 72,
        76, 83, 84, 86, 88–9
        see also Anne of Cleves;
        Boleyn, Anne; Edward VI; Howard,
        Katherine; Katherine of Aragon;
        Seymour, Jane
    Holbein's portraits of 6, 75
        Barber-Surgeons' Picture, The
            90–1, 90, 244–5
        Henry VIII 230, 231
        Henry VIII aged 49 (1540) 80,
            81, 172, 246
        Henry VIII, King of England
            60, 74, 74
        Whitehall mural (copy) 75,
            78–9, 78, 79, 99, 99, 230
    portraits of (by other artists)
        80–1, 89
        Family of Henry VIII, The
            (unknown artist) 45, 94–5
        Henry VIII (English School) 75
        Henry VIII (Metsys) 80, 81
        Henry VIII, king of England
            (Cleve) 74, 80
        Henry VIII sees Anne of Cleves
            (engraving) 89
        King Henry VIII (c.1534–44)
            (Horenbout) 85
        King Henry VIII (unknown
            artist) 49
        King Henry VIII of England
            (c.1525-6) (Horenbout) 54,
            55
Herbst, Hans 22, 24–5, 59
    Flagellation, The 25
    Last Supper 25, 151
Herbster, Johannes 24, 25
Heron, Cicely 156–7, 158, 159
Heron, Giles 159
Hertenstein, Benedikt von 32, 32,
    102
Hertenstein, Jakob von 32, 103
Hertenstein house, Lucerne 32
Heveningham, Mary, Lady 222
Heveningham, Sir Anthony 222
Hever Castle, Kent 71
Hilliard, Nicholas 84
Hoby, Sir Philip 86, 86
Holbein, Ambrosius (brother)

see also Erasmus of Rotterdam,
    Praise of Folly
    early life and family 6–7, 7, 19,
        18, 20–1
    as journeyman, for Hans Herbst
        24–5
    moves to Basel 22–3
    works
        Portrait of a Young Man 21, 21,
            27
        Portrait of Johannes Herbster
            24
        Portrait of Jörg Schweiger 21,
            22
        *School Teacher Explaining the
            Meaning of a Letter to
            Illiterate Workers* 23
        View of Utopia, The 31
Holbein, Anna née Mair
    (grandmother) 16
Holbein, Barbara née Burgkmair
    (mother) 6
Holbein, Elsbeth Binzenstock (wife)
    46–7, 46, 59, 96, 166
Holbein, Jakob (son) 47, 59
Holbein, Katharina (daughter) 46,
    47, 140, 166
Holbein, Küngold (son) 47
Holbein, Michael (grandfather) 16
Holbein, Philipp (son) 46, 47, 59,
    166
Holbein, Sigismund (uncle) 7, 16,
    18, 20, 21
    Four Heads (study) 21
    *Martyrdom of the Apostle
        Bartholomew, The* 21
Holbein the Elder, Hans (father) 6,
    16–17, 21, 22
    artistic style 13, 17, 19
    Augsburg workshop 18–19
    Hertenstein house 32
    works by
        *Ambrosius Holbein and Hans
            Holbein the Younger* 6, 18, 19
        Basilica of San Paolo triptych
            6, 7, 17, 18, 19
        Crown of Thorns, The 25
        Death of the Virgin 17
        Fountain of Life, The (detail) 19,
            20
        Martyrdom of St. Sebastian 18,
            19
        Portrait of a Man 16
        Portrait of a Woman 16
        Self-portrait 16
        Virgin and Child 35
Holbein the Younger, Hans 6–7, 7,
    19, 61, 96
    artistic style 13, 19, 44, 98–9
        decorative facades 33, 33, 115
        jewellery 70, 198–9, 213
        organ wings 136
        ornaments 196, 213, 250
        portraiture 19, 26–7, 49, 84–5,
            98–9
        see also portraits
    stained glass window designs
        24, 108, 136, 146–9

Basel workshop 42
    created 'the King's painter' 74–5
    death 92–3
    early life and family 18, 22–3,
        24–5
    marriage and children 46–7
        *Artist's Wife with the Two Elder
            Children, The* 46–7, 46, 166
    religious views 34
    residence in London 62
    self-portraits 7, 93, 93, 251
    sources on life of 96–7
    timeline of life events 6
    will 92–3
Holbein's Coat of Arms 114
Hollar, Wenceslaus 74
Holy Family, The 109
Horenbout, Lucas 54, 84, 85, 94
    Hans Holbein the Younger 61
    *Portrait Miniature of Queen Jane
        Seymour* 76
    *Portrait Miniature of Queen
        Katherine of Aragon* 85
    *Portrait of Katherine of Aragon,
        holding a Monkey* 54, 54
    Portrait of King Henry VIII (c.1534–
        44) 85
    *Portrait of King Henry VIII of
        England* (c.1525–6) 54, 55
Howard, Henry 197, 242
Howard, Katherine (Queen) 89,
    236, 243
Howard, Lady Elizabeth 70
Howard, Lady Mary 236
    see also Richmond and Somerset,
        Mary Fitzroy, Duchess of (Lady
        Mary Howard)
humanism 28, 52
*Humiliation of Valerian by Shapur I,
    Edessa 259 AD, The* 43, 98, 137
Hutton, John 87

I
iconoclast riots 7, 34, 41, 151
Iconoclasts, The (anonymous artist)
    12
indulgences 28, 113

J
Jenks, William 209
John of Antwerp 93
John of Denmark, Prince 87

K
Kale, Cyriacus 176
Kannengiesser, Dorothea 26, 26, 45,
    111, 142, 143
Katherine of Aragon (Queen) 51,
    54, 61, 76, 83, 200, 228
    Horenbout portraits of 54, 85
King Rehoboam 119
    see also Basel, Switzerland, Great
        Council Chamber murals
Kratzer, Nikolaus 51, 64, 68, 96–7,
    158, 187, 250
    Holbein portrait of 64, 162

L

Laïs of Corinthiaca 42, 42, 140, 218
Last Judgement, The (Dance of Death series) 11, 128
Last Judgement, The (pendant design) 199
Last Supper 25, 151
Lee, Margaret Wyatt, Lady 211
Leemput, Remigius van 78
Lestrange, Sir Thomas
limning 84
Lochner, Stefan, *The Presentation of Christ in the Temple* 44, 45
Lockey, Rowland, *Portrait of Sir Thomas More and his family* 51, 51, 97, 97, 156–7
London, England 48, 49, 49, 59, 63, 68, 92, 92
see also Hanseatic League, The
Greenwich Palace 53, 54, 96, 137
Mayden Lane 62
Whitehall, Palace of 68, 68, 74, 75, 79, 79, 94
London Company of Painters-Stainers 53
Lorraine, Anton 'the Good', Duke of 248
Lotter the Elder, Melchior 28
Louis XII, King of France 45, 84, 85
Lovell, Anne 57, 57, 164
see also portraits (unidentified subjects), *Lady with a Squirrel and a Starling, A*
Lovell, William 164
Luther, Martin 28–9, 30, 31, 37, 41, 61
Lützelburger, Hans 23, 39

M

Madonna of the Burgermeister Meyer see Darmstadt Madonna
Mander, Karel van 79, 84, 91, 93, 96, 96, 97, 98
Manius Curius Dentatus rejects the gifts of the Samnites 119
Mantegna, Andrea, Lamentation of Christ 36
Map of the World (*Typus Cosmographicus Universalis*) 175
Margaret of Austria, Archduchess 70–1
Mars and Venus Caught in Bed by Vulcan 105
Mary I, Queen 84, 94–5
Masaccio, Tommaso, *Expulsion of Adam and Eve from Eden* 34, 35
Massys, Quinten 49, 50
Portrait of Erasmus of Rotterdam 40, 50
Portrait of Pieter Gillis 50, 51
Mathematical Scholar, A 105
Maximilian I, German Emperor 26
Mayden Lane, London 62
Maynaert, Harry 93
memento mori 64, 65, 31
Memling, Hans 12, 13, 18, 27
Diptych of Maarten van

Nieuwenhove, and Madonna and Child 27
merchants see Hanseatic League
Metsys, Cornelis, *Portrait of Henry VIII* 80, 81
Metsys, Quinten see Massys, Quinten
Meutas, Joan, Lady 208
Meutas, Sir Peter 208
Meyer, Anna 45, 45, 98, 98, 145
Meyer Family Coat of Arms 111
Meyer Madonna, The see Darmstadt Madonna
Meyer zum Hasen, Jakob 26, 26, 44, 45, 110, 111, 142, 144
Minstrel's Gallery 137
Mocking of Christ, The 146
More, Alice 97, 158
More, Margaret see Roper, Margaret née More
More, Sir John 155, 158
More, Sir Thomas 40, 49, 50–1, 50, 154, 155, 220
friendship with Erasmus 48, 49, 50, 51, 94
Sir Thomas More and his household, and his descendants 51, 97, 97, 156–7, 158, 159
Utopia 20, 31, 48, 113
Moria see Erasmus, *Praise of Folly*
Morison, Sir Richard 82
Moses and Aaron before Pharaoh: An Allegory of the Dinteville Family (unknown artist) 67, 67
Movement Study of a Female Body 174
Muffel, Hans von 241
Mule Sings to the Accompaniment of a Harp, A 104
Myconius, Oswald 20, 23, 104, 250
Signboard for a schoolmaster 23, 23, 103

N

Nailing to the Cross 149
narrative realism 12
naturalism 12, 13
Netherlands 12, 18, 48, 99
Nieuwenhove, Maarten van 27
Noli me tangere 25, 150
Norfolk, Thomas Howard, 3rd Duke of 238
Northampton, William Parr, 1st Marquess 222
northern renaissance 12–13, 27, 63, 81

O

Oberried Altar, 118
Obynger, Obryche (Ulrich Obinger) 93
Offenburg, Magdalena 42, 42, 140

P

Painters' Guild 18, 22, 24
Parker, Matthew 163
'Passion of Christ' series 25, 138, 139, 146–9

Flagellation, The 25, 25
Last Supper 25, 151
Patenson, Henry 156–7, 158
Peace Accord, 1527 52, 53
Pemberton, Jane 84, 85
Perréal, Jean 44, 45
Portrait Miniature of King Louis XII of France 84, 85
Pictures of Death see Dance of Death (series)
plague 12, 76, 92, 92

portraits (identified subjects)
Ambassadors, The 64–5, 65, 66–7, 99, 182–3
detail 64, 173, 184–9
Amerbach, Bonifacius 32–3, 33, 117
Anne of Cleves (Queen) 84, 88–9, 88, 89, 235, 236
Artist's Wife with the Two Elder Children, The 46–7, 46, 59, 166
Audley, Elizabeth, Lady 210
Bedford, John Russell, 1st Earl of (drawing) 201
Berck, Derick 181
Bergavenny, George Nevill, 3rd Baron (drawing) 200
Berry, Jean de France, Duke of 44, 132
Berry, Jeanne de Boulogne, Duchess of 44, 98, 132
Boleyn, Anne (Queen) (drawing) 70, 71, 196
Born, Derich 176
Bourbon, Nicholas (drawing) 68, 69, 223
Butts, Margaret, Lady 249
Butts, Sir William 248
Carew, Sir George 190
Carew, Sir Nicholas 194
Chambers, Dr John 240
Cheseman, Robert 100–1, 195
Christina of Denmark 86–7, 86, 87, 204, 234
Colet, John (drawing) 201
Cromwell, Thomas 72, 72, 85, 216, 217
Edward VI, King 82, 82, 232, 233
Elyot, Margaret, Lady (drawing) 192
Elyot, Sir Thomas (drawing) 192
Erasmus 10, 40–1, 40, 41, 134, 135, 169
Fisher, John, Bishop of Rochester (drawing) 200
Froben, Johannes 43, 116
George, Simon 69, 69, 205
Gisze, Georg 8, 62, 63, 178
Godsalve, Sir John 73, 206
Godsalve, Sir John (diptych) 55, 165
Godsalve, Thomas (diptych) 55, 165
Guildford, Sir Henry 52, 52, 96, 152, 160
Guildford, Mary Wotton, Lady 52, 52, 161
Henry VIII, King 6, 75, 231

Barber-Surgeons' Picture, The (copy) 90–1, 90, 244–5
Henry VIII 230
Henry VIII aged 49 (1540) 80, 81, 172, 246
Henry VIII, King of England (c.1536–7) 60, 74, 74
Whitehall mural (copy) 75, 78–9, 78, 79, 99, 99, 230
Hertenstein, Benedikt von 32, 102
Heveningham, Mary, Lady (drawing) 222
Hoby, Sir Philip (drawing) 86
Howard, Mary, Lady 236
Kale, Cyriacus 176
Kannengiesser, Dorothea 26, 26, 45, 110, 111, 142, 143
Kratzer, Nikolaus 64, 64, 162
Lee, Margaret Wyatt, Lady 211
Lorraine, Anton 'the Good', Duke of 248
Meutas, Joan, Lady (drawing) 208
Meyer, Anna 45, 45, 98, 98, 145
Meyer zum Hasen, Jakob (diptych) 26, 26, 44, 45, 110, 111, 144
More, Margaret 225
More, Sir Thomas 50, 50, 154, 155
see also *Sir Thomas More and his household, and his descendants*
Norfolk, Thomas Howard, 3rd Duke of 238
Northampton, William Parr, 1st Marquess (drawing) 222
Pemberton, Jane 84, 85
Poyntz, John (drawing) 193
Poyntz, Sir Nicholas (drawing) 193
Ratclif, Lady (drawing) 208
Reskimer, William 68–9, 69, 190, 191
Rich, Lady Elizabeth 73, 73, 209
Richmond and Somerset, Mary, Duchess of (drawing) 214
Roper, William 225
Russell, Lord Francis 237
self-portraits 7, 93, 93, 99, 251
Seymour, Jane (Queen) 75, 76, 77, 78, 94–5, 228, 229
Seymour, Sir Edward 76, 228
Sharington, Sir William (drawing) 223
Solier, Charles de 69, 69, 218, 219
Southampton, Thomas Wriothesley, 1st Earl of 204
Southwell, Sir Richard 73, 73, 220
Suffolk, Charles Brandon, 1st Duke of 226
Suffolk, Charles Brandon, 3rd Duke of 227
Suffolk, Henry Brandon, 2nd Duke of 227

Suffolk, Katherine, Duchess of (drawing) *227*
Surrey, Henry Howard, Earl of *197, 242*
Tuke, Sir Bryan *203*
Tybis, Dirck *177*
Vaux, Elizabeth, Lady *208*
Warham, William 55, *55*, 98, *98, 163*
Wedigh III, Hermann von *180*
Wedigh, Hermann Hillebrandt von *179*
Widmerpole, Elizabeth 73, *73, 207*
Wyatt, Sir Thomas (drawing) *210*
Wyatt the Younger, Thomas *238*
Zouch, Mary *197*

portraits (unidentified subjects)
Boy with a Marmoset, A (also known as *Edward VI, Prince of Wales*) 83, *237*
Courtier of Henry VIII, A 73, *73, 224*
De Vos Van Steenwijk 241
English Lady, An 215
Hanseatic Merchant, A 181
Head of a Female Saint 34, *106*
Head of a Male Saint 34, *107*
Head of a Young Man 133
Lady with a Squirrel and a Starling, A 56–7, *57*, 99, *99, 153, 164*
Lady, A 221
Lady, A (Anne Boleyn?) (drawing) *196*
Lady, A (Katherine Howard ?) *236*
Man (*A Scholar or Cleric*) (drawing) *201*
Man aged Twenty-eight (Sir Ralph Sadler?) *216*
Man holding a letter and gloves, A 239
Man in a Broad-brimmed Hat, A 131
Man in a Red Cap, A 202
Man with a Red Hat, A 169
Merchant, A 241
Merchant of the German Steelyard, A 177
Nobleman with a Hawk, A 250
Unidentified woman, An (drawing) *214*
Unknown gentleman with music books and lute 218
Unknown Man, An 239
Wife of Courtier of Henry VIII 73, *73, 224*
Woman in a White Coif, A 202
Young Man, A 130
Young Man, A (Gregory Cromwell?) *216*
Young Woman with a White Coif, A 215
Young Woman, A (drawing) *121*
Young Woman, A (Katherine Howard?) *243*

R
Ratclif, Lady *208*
Ratcliffe, Sir Robert *208*
reformation 7, 28–9, 34, 36, 59
Rehoboam rejecting the advice of the Elders 58, 168
see also Basel, Switzerland, Great Council Chamber murals
religious commissions 34–5
see also *Dance of Death* (series); *Darmstadt Madonna; Dead Christ in the Tomb*
Renaissance see northern renaissance
Reskimer, William 68–9, *69*, 190, *191*
Resting Lamb and Head of a Lamb 133
Reynolds, Sir Joshua, *Master Crewe as Henry VIII* 95
Rhenanus, Beatus (Bild) 42, *42*
Rich, Lady Elizabeth 73, *209*
Richmond and Somerset, Henry Fitzroy, Duke of 83, 214, 222, 236
Richmond and Somerset, Mary Fitzroy, Duchess of (Lady Mary Howard) *214*
Rippingall, Richard 53
Roper, Margaret née More 156–7, *158, 225*
Roper, William *225*
Rubens, Peter Paul, *Portrait of Sir Thomas More* 50
Russell, Lord Francis *237*

S
Sacrament (lost) 25
Sadler, Sir Ralph *216*
Sanzio, Raphael 56
The Deposition 37
Satire of Barber-Surgeons (unknown artist) 91
Schedel, Hartmann, *Liber Chronicarum* (Nuremberg Chronicle) 39
Schilder-Boeck 96–7, 98
Schmid, Thomas 20, 24
Scholar Treads on a Basket of Eggs, A 104
Schwarz, Matthäus 15, *15*
Schweiger, Jörg 22, *22*

Scourging of Christ, The 146
Scrots, Guillaume 94
Edward VI, King of England 83
Portrait of Edward, Prince of Wales 95
Selling of Indulgences 113
Selve, George de 64–5, *65*, 66–7, *173, 182–3, 186, 188*
Sertorius and the Example of Horses 104
Seymour, Elizabeth *221*
Seymour, Jane (Queen) 74, 75, 76–7, *76*, 83, 213
Whitehall mural 75, 78–9, *78, 79, 99, 99, 230*
Holbein's portraits of *77, 78*, 94–5, *228, 229*
Seymour, Sir Edward 76, *228*, 230
Sharington, Sir William *223*
Shepherd, Thomas Hosmer 91
Ship with Revelling Sailors, Lansquenets and a Sutleress 174
Sidney, Mary Dudley, Lady *85*
Signboard for a Schoolmaster 23, *23, 103*
Sir Thomas More and his household, and his descendants 51, 97, *97, 156–7, 158, 159*
Small, Nicholas 85
Snetcher, Anthony 93
Snoeck, Jan Jacobsz 63
Solier, Charles de 69, *69, 218, 219*
Solimar, Thomas 68
Solomon and the Queen of Sheba 212
Solothurn Madonna, The 35, *35, 120, 121*
Somers, Will 94–5
Somerset, Mary Fitzroy, Duchess of (Lady Mary Howard) *214, 236*
Southampton, Thomas Wriothesley, 1st Earl of *204*
Southwell, Sir Richard 72, *73, 220*
Steenwijk, De Vos Van *241*
Steelyard 62, *63*
Stone Thrower 174
Suffolk, Charles Brandon, 1st Duke of *226*
Suffolk, Charles Brandon, 3rd Duke of *227*
Suffolk, Henry Brandon, 2nd Duke of *227*
Suffolk, Katherine, Duchess of *227*
surgeons 91
Surrey, Henry Howard, Earl of *197*, 220, *242*

T
Teerlinc, Levina 84, 94–5
Portrait miniature of Mary Dudley, Lady Sidney 85
Portrait miniature possibly depicting Elizabeth I 95
Portrait of a Lady, possibly Lady Jane Grey 85
Temptation and Fall of Adam and Eve, The 124

Terminus, the Device of Erasmus 167
Theologian Reads, A 105
Torrigiano, Pietro 201
Touch Me Not 25, *150*
trade guilds 23
Painters' Guild 18, 22, 24
Triumph of Poverty, The (copy) 129, 175
Triumph of Riches, The (copy) 129, *174*
Triumphal Procession 129
Tuke, Sir Bryan *203*
Two Skulls in a Window Niche 114
Two Women Dedicating Candles 105
Tybis, Dirck *177*
Typus Cosmographicus Universalis (Map of the World) *175*

U
Utopia, see Thomas More

V
van Eyck, Jan see Eyck, Jan van
van Sandrart, Joachim 68
Vaux, Elizabeth, Lady *208*
Vaux, Thomas *208*
Venus and Cupid (unknown artist) 42, 140, *141*
Vicary, Thomas 90, *245*
Vinci, Leonardo da see da Vinci, Leonardo

W
Warham, William 54–5, *55*, 98, *98, 134, 163*
Wedigh, Hermann Hillebrandt von *179*
Wedigh III, Hermann von *180*
Weyden, Rogier van der 12, 18
Whitehall, Palace of 68, *68*, 74, 75, 79, *79*, 94
Whitehall mural 75, 78–9, *78, 79, 99, 99, 230*
Widmerpole, Elizabeth 73, *73, 207*
see also Godsalve, Sir John
Wittenberg, Germany 28–9
Wolf Hall, Wiltshire 76, 77
Wolgemut, Michael, *Dance of Death* 38, 39
Women from Basel, drawings 136
woodcutting 17, 23, 31, 39
Worshipful Company of Barber-Surgeons, the 90–1, *90, 91, 244–5*
Wotton, Nicholas 88
Wrythoke, Robert 53, 96
Wyatt, Margaret (Lady Lee) *211*
Wyatt, Sir Thomas 96, *210, 211*
Wyatt the Younger, Thomas *238*
Wyngaerde, Anthonis van den, *Greenwich Palace 53*

Z
Zscheckenbürlin, Maria, *138*
Zouch, Mary *197*
Zum Tanz House, Basel 33, *33, 115*

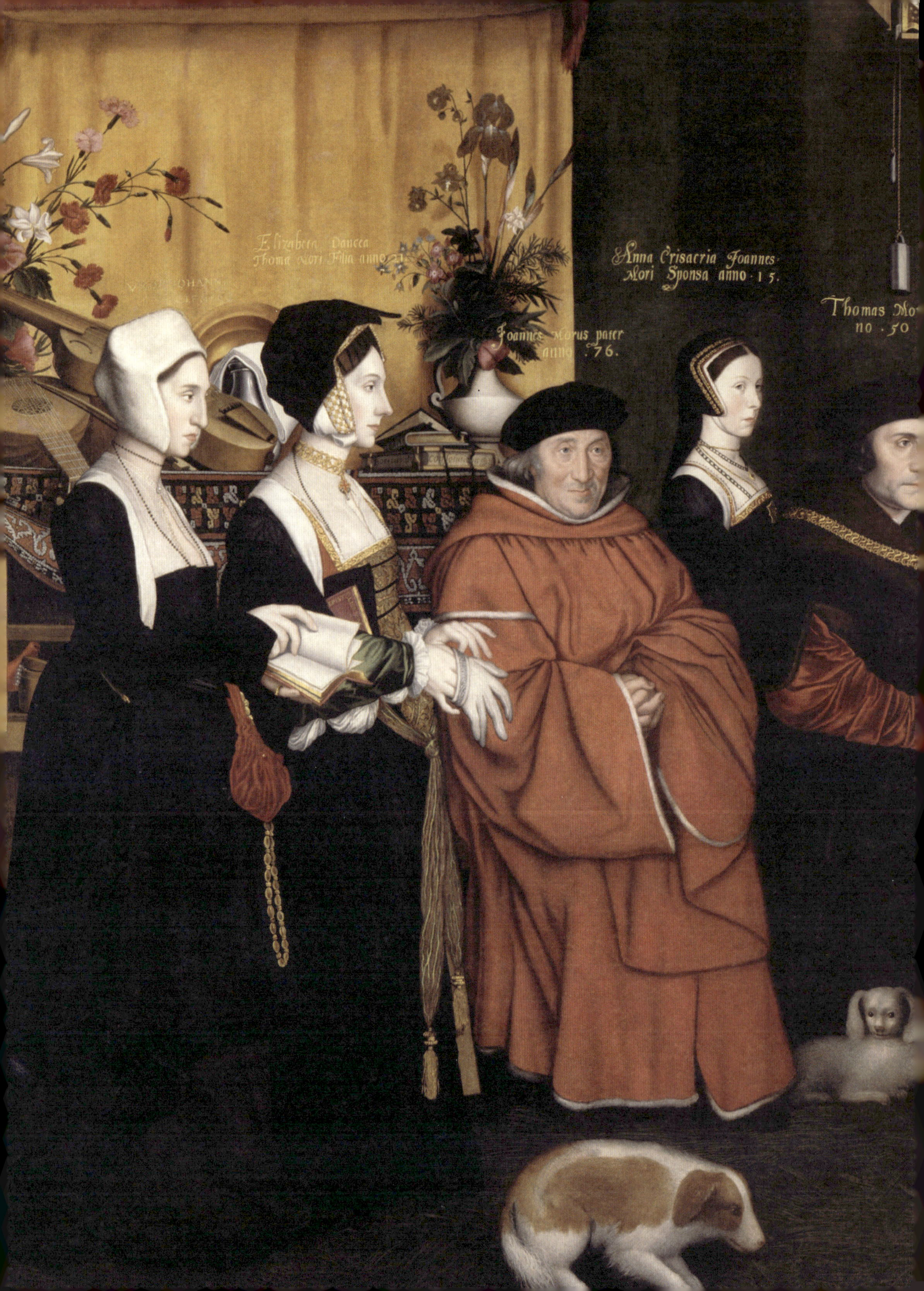
Elizabeta Dancea
Thomæ Mori Filia anno 21
Anna Crisacria Joannes
Mori Syonsa anno · 15.
Joannes Morus pater
anno · 76
Thomas Mo
no · 50